Special Education at the Century's End

*Evolution of
Theory and Practice
Since 1970*

Edited by

Thomas Hehir
Thomas Latus

Reprint Series No. 23
Harvard Educational Review

Library of Congress Catalog Card Number 92-070561

ISBN 0-916690-25-3

Harvard Educational Review
Gutman Library Suite 349
6 Appian Way
Cambridge, MA 02138

Contents

106450

Introduction

In the past two decades, special education has emerged as a major component of education within the United States. Currently, one out of nine public school students is officially classified as "handicapped" and receives special educational services; the annual cost of these services exceeds $20 billion (OSERS, 1990).[1] Since the inception of mandated special education in the 1970s, many have applauded its movement toward greater educational equity, which has given new respect and hope to children who once were denied full educational opportunity. Yet the burgeoning special educational enterprise has also come under increased criticism from practitioners, researchers, and policymakers. In recent years, these critics have spoken out loudly in response to certain practices and trends, including the separation of students with disabilities from the mainstream, the escalating costs of special education, the overrepresentation of minorities in some special programs, the perceived inefficacy of many special services, and the rift between regular and special education. During the past twenty years, the *Harvard Educational Review* has published a number of articles on the emerging field of special education. In this book, we have compiled thirteen articles, which together trace the development of contemporary special education from a period of anticipation and promise to the current era of controversy and uncertainty.

Part One, "The Promise of Special Education," includes four articles written in the early to mid-1970s, a time when rights of children (including those with disabilities) to educational equity were being established in the courts and legislatures. A chief concern of these five authors was the right of children to due process protection in the identification and placement of students with disabilities. Of particular concern was the misclassification and placement of children from minority groups into special education classrooms. One of David Kirp's central concerns in his 1974 article, "Student Classification, Public Policy, and the Courts," is the stigmatization and potential educational damage experienced by children who are inappropriately labelled as disabled and consequently segregated in special education. Kirp

---

[1] Office of Special Education and Rehabilitative Services, *Twelfth Annual Report to Congress on the Implementation of the Education of the Handicapped Act* (Washington, DC: U.S. Department of Education, 1990).

applies the constitutional principles of due process and equal protection to placement in special education. Due process protection eventually became the legal basis for federal and state special education regulations.

In "Engendering Change in Special Education Practices," Milton Budoff (1975) uses the making of Massachusetts' special education statute — Chapter 766, passed in 1972 — to illustrate how a coalition of parent groups, child advocates, and educational reformers successfully codified the principles and rights that Kirp and others had articulated. Chapter 766 was the first state law to require a comprehensive individualized evaluation and placement system, frequent reevaluations, strong parental involvement, and a powerful due process system. The law also required maximal integration of students with special needs with nondisabled peers. All these aspects of Chapter 766 were later incorporated in the federal special education statute, the Educational for All Handicapped Children Act (EHA), passed in 1975.[2]

Like Budoff, Carl Milofsky ("Why Special Education Isn't Special," 1974) and Richard Weatherley and Michael Lipsky ("Street-Level Bureaucrats and Institutional Innovation: Implementing Special Education Reform," 1977) recognize the need for far-reaching structural changes in schools in order to fulfill the promise of special education; the new legislation of the 1970s alone was not sufficient to produce the hoped-for changes. Through their study of Chapter 766's implementation, Weatherley and Lipsky established the concept of "street-level bureaucracy" by demonstrating that school personnel used a variety of strategies to cope with the competing demands of special education regulations, given limited resources and historical modes of operation. This discretionary use by on-line staff distorted the actual implementation of the law. The mandate for sweeping educational change far exceeded the teachers' and administrators' readiness for change, as well as the resources available to them.

These 1970s articles together produce a hopeful picture of reformed special education as opening new possibilities, not only for children with disabilities but for public schools in general. It is important to observe, however, that all these authors strike a cautionary note, pointing out that more fundamental school reforms were needed if the issues of equity and fairness were to be fully addressed.

Part Two, "The Reassessment of Special Education," consists of three key articles written in the late 1980s that assess the impact and effectiveness of special education reform initiated in the previous decade. In "The Education for All Handicapped Children Act: Schools as Agents of Social Reform,"

---

[2] The Education for All Handicapped Children Act is often referred to by its statute number, Public Law 94-142 (PL 94-142). In 1990, this act was superceded by a modified statute, the Individuals with Disabilities Education Act (IDEA). In this book, we use EHA to refer to the federal special education law — in all its versions — since 1975.

Judith Singer and John Butler (1987) argue that, overall, the current state of special education realizes many of the hopes of the 1970s: students with special needs are appropriately identified, due process procedures usually function well, and special services tend to be highly regarded by parents and school personnel. In their analysis, EHA represents a model of how liberal legislation can successfully promote genuine, positive social change.

In "Beyond Special Education: Toward a Quality System for All Students," Alan Gartner and Dorothy Lipsky (1987), though recognizing that special education has been successful in reaching students who before the 1970s tended not to be educated, argue that the main thrust of special education has had a negative impact on public education. They claim that in the 1980s there was an increase in the segregation of children with disabilities, contrary to the mainstreaming intent of EHA. In essence, they believe that special education has become a separate and unequal school system that has created new forms of stigmatization and inequality.

In "The Special Education Paradox: Equity as the Way to Excellence," Thomas Skrtic (1991) looks back on special education in the 1980s and contends that special education is forcing schools to recognize the pathology of current school organization and practices. He believes that the current tension between special and regular education — which Gartner and Lipsky see as destructive — can be constructive if it leads to a new school order that emphasizes "adhocracy": that is, flexible, situational problem-solving rather than bureaucracy generated by regulatory reform models that stress rigid "professionalization" of education. Special education legislation has demonstrated the limitations of exclusive reliance on imposed reforms and the need for a more decentralized, less rule-oriented approach to educating children, both those with disabilities and "regular" students. Skrtic demonstrates a potential link between the broader school reform movement, which emphasizes decentralized school-based governance, and special education reform.

Part Three, "From Theory into Practice," contains six articles written in the late 1970s and 1980s that take a close-up look at special education. These pieces describe in rich detail students who have been labelled "learning disabled," "emotionally disturbed," "autistic," "hearing impaired," "dyslexic," and "language disabled." These descriptions provide a concrete context for the abstract category of "handicap." A common concern of the authors in Part Three is the ways in which society and schools limit the growth of students with disabilities by emphasizing deficits rather than competencies. In "The Deaf as a Linguistic Minority: Educational Considerations," Timothy Reagan (1985), for example, examines the ways in which schools reflect society's view that nonoral communication is inferior to spoken language, thus automatically relegating all deaf students to a second-class status, no matter how developed their nonverbal communication skills might be. In "Screening, Early Intervention, and Remediation: Obscuring Children's Potential," Anne Martin (1988), looking at her own kindergarten class, describes how pull-out special education programs — which focus time and attention on student weaknesses — often inhibit the development of children's strengths by separating them from full participation in classroom activities. Peter Johnston, in "Understanding Reading Disability: A Case Study Approach" (1985), examines in depth the reading strategies of three adults. His analysis reveals that these individuals' actual approaches to reading are much more complex and active than those portrayed in standard descriptions of dyslexia. By describing "handicapped" individuals in detail, the authors in Part Three potently demonstrate the destructiveness of special educational labels and the stereotypes that accompany them.

These articles also illustrate the liberating educational progress that can occur when educators reject labels, stereotypes, and assumed limitations. In "Communication Unbound: Autism and Praxis," Douglas Biklen (1990) tells the story of an educational pioneer in Australia who refused to accept restrictive views of autism and discovered ground-breaking new pathways for communication. These new methods not only radically increased autistic children's learning but also threw into question commonly held understandings of autism. In "Tipping the Balance," Joseph Cambone (1990) describes how a teacher of young children with severe emotional and behavioral problems constantly struggled to free her thinking and her teaching from defeatist perspectives that focused on her students' limitations. Through continual attention to each "student-as-he-is" and unflagging belief in her children's potential to progress, this teacher and her class were able to make substantial gains.

The authors in Part Three, however, do not support the belief that moving beyond the limitations of labels is simply a matter of will on the part of special education teachers and students. As Gerald Coles ("The Learning-Disabilities Test Battery: Empirical and Social Issues," 1978), Biklen, and Martin point out, a culture of special education has arisen that has borrowed from the medical world its concern for pathology, diagnosis, and scientifically based prescription. This medicalization of special education reinforces the labelling process, making it ever more difficult for participants — teachers, administrators, parents, and students — to reject a deficit-biased view of learners. Moreover, echoing the concerns of the authors in Part Two, the authors in this final section also allude to the ways in which current school organizations separate out students who do not fit into routine classrooms, dichotomize faculties into "regular" and "special" educators, and interfere with the development of classroom communities—practices that inhibit growth for all students.

Taken together, the articles collected in this book represent a slice of opinion and practice in special education during the 1970s and 1980s, as the field developed into a major institution. From these writings, we can clearly see that there is no "final word" on what special education is, can be, or should be. Although there is consensus that the last twenty years have brought many educational advantages to students with disabilities, there is also consensus that special education is far from an ideal enterprise. Yet exactly what the nature of special education's problems might be and how to remediate them are topics of heated controversy. Do we need more of special education as we know it? Should the current system be reformed—that is, streamlined or reorganized? Or is the best solution to abolish special education altogether, while radically restructuring the entire public school system?

As we read these articles and consider our own experiences as special educators, we see that major challenges lie ahead in the 1990s and the early twenty-first century for those who wish to re-create public education within the United States as a more equitable and excellent enterprise. Chief among these concerns is how to keep the best in what we have now — the national commitment to providing all students a free, appropriate education, no matter what their special needs might be — while ridding the schools of long-standing, dehumanizing problems, such as stigmatization, reinforcement of stereotypes, limitation of individual potential, dissolution of community. If nothing else, these articles attest to the enduring resolve of many within the educational domain to meet these challenges.

THOMAS HEHIR
Chicago Public Schools

THOMAS LATUS
Bay Cove Elementary School
Boston, Massachusetts

Part 1:

The Promise of
Special Education

Student Classification, Public Policy, and the Courts

DAVID L. KIRP

In this article, David Kirp examines school sorting and exclusionary practices based on academic performance or potential, including the placement of students into special education classrooms, and applies the constitutional principles of equal protection and due process to these actions. Kirp cites research available in 1974, which established that a disproportionate number of minority students were placed in special education and that the efficacy of these programs was questionable. He further asserts that such placements often carry with them potential stigma and lack of opportunity. Given the gravity of the decision to place a child in special education, the author asserts that placement raises a plausible constitutional claim of denial of equal education opportunity. Citing additional research that demonstrated that existing procedures frequently misdiagnosed students, he further raises a due process challenge to the legitimacy of special education classifications. Kirp argues that decisions to place students in special education should be subjected to due process review. His recommendation was followed up by policymakers, who incorporated due process protection into PL 94-142 — the Education for All Handicapped Children Act — in 1975. Kirp's article and others in this book, particularly the article by Alan Gartner and Dorothy Lipsky, are noteworthy in pointing out that, contrary to what lawmakers may have intended, the disproportionate placement of minority students and the segregation of students with disabilities persisted ten years after the implementation of the law. Kirp continues to write extensively in education, including a more recent analysis of the implementation of PL 94-142 in School Days Rule Days *(1986), in which he reflects on due process implementation.*

Public schools regularly sort students in a variety of ways.[1] They test them when they first arrive at school and at regular intervals thereafter in order

A substantially longer and more amply footnoted version of this article, "Schools as Sorters: The Constitutional and Policy Implications of Student Classification," was published in the *University of Pennsylvania Law Review, 121* (1973), 705–797. It is reprinted in edited form with the permission of the *Pennsylvania Law Review.*

Harvard Educational Review Vol. 44 No. 1 February 1974

to identify aptitude or the capacity to learn.[2] From primary school until graduation, most[3] schools group (or track) students on the basis of estimated intellectual ability, both within classrooms and in separate classes.[4]

In primary school grouping, the pace of instruction, but typically not its content, is varied. Grouping decisions may be made for each school subject, or a given group may stay intact for the entire curriculum. During the school year, students' grades, taken together with IQ and achievement tests, determine whether children are advanced to the next grade and into which group they are assigned.

In secondary school, placements in educational tracks reflect both interest and ability. There, for the first time in their educational careers, students may be offered choices. In practice, however, prior achievement usually determines program placement: grammar school success means college track or academic high school assignment, while mediocre grade school performance frequently leads to placement in a noncollege preparatory program. Counselors, not students, frequently make these decisions by matching school offerings to their own estimates of each student's ability and potential.[5] That classification determines both the nature of the secondary school education — Shakespeare, shorthand, or machine shop — and the gross choices — college or work — available after graduation.

Students whom the school cannot classify in this manner are treated as "special" or "exceptional." Such students by no means resemble one another. They may have intellectual, physical, or emotional handicaps; they may not speak English as their native language; they may simply be hungry or unhappy with their particular school situation. The number and variety of differentiating characteristics is large; overlapping among the characteristics (multiple differentnesses) further complicates the pattern. Yet the school, in part because its resources are scarce, cannot tailor individual programs to satisfy individual needs. Instead, it develops classifications that attempt to reconcile the variations among exceptional children with the limitations of school resources. Most school districts offer several special programs, differentiating both among levels of retardation (educable, trainable, profound) and between retardation and such other school handicaps as learning disabilities and emotional disturbance. Students unamenable to such special help — either because the school concludes that they are ineducable, that is, unable to profit from any presently provided educational program, or because they make life difficult for teachers and classmates — may be excluded from school.

This article examines three of the seemingly infinite range of school classifications: exclusion from publicly supported schooling, placement in special education programs,[6] and ability grouping.[7] Several factors distinguish these from other school classifications. First, they are each of relatively long duration: exclusion is almost invariably a one-way ticket out of school; movement between special and regular programs or between slow and advanced ability groups is infrequent.[8] Second, their consequences are both significant and difficult to reverse: the child barred from school as "ineducable" becomes more difficult to educate because of his or her exclusion; the student assigned to a slow track, or a special education class, cannot easily return to the schooling mainstream. Third, the questionable bases for these sorting decisions suggest that the possibility of misclassification, and consequent serious injury to the child, is significant. Fourth, these placement decisions (unlike within-class grouping decisions, for instance) are highly visible. Typically, they are made not by classroom teachers but by school or district administrators. Fifth, each of these classifications carries the potential of stigmatizing students. In sum, exclusion, special class assignment, and track placement are of greater moment to the student than, for example, a failing grade on a particular exercise. They are also more obvious candidates for judicial review.

School Classification and School Needs

While, as one testing manual contends, "the original [classification] was when God . . . looked at everything he made and saw that it was *very good*," only during the past sixty years have public schools devoted considerable effort to classifying and sorting students.[9] The prototypal common school, energetically promoted by Horace Mann and Henry Barnard, was designed to provide a shared educational experience for all who could afford to stay in school for an extended period of time. Through most of the nineteenth century, a uniform curriculum was characteristic of schools that, at least in theory, respected neither class nor caste.

The arrival of hundreds of thousands of immigrants from eastern and southern Europe in the late nineteenth century obliged school officials to provide instruction for children who spoke no English and had little, if any, previous schooling. To professional educators it made little sense to place these students in regular classes; they needed assistance of a kind that common schools had not previously been asked to provide. Urban school systems created "opportunity classes," special programs designed to overcome the students' initial difficulties and to prepare them for regular schoolwork.

Other societal factors served to promote the need for differentiation among students.[10] As the insistence that schools be businesslike and efficient was increasingly heard, U.S. educators began to adopt the modern business corporation's complex organizational structure and with it a complex division of labor analogous to classification. Further, the increasingly industrial U.S. economy seemed to demand a differentiation of skills that a common school education simply could not provide. As Boston's superintendent of schools argued in 1908: "Until very recently [the schools] have offered equal opportunity for all to receive *one kind* of education, but what will make them democratic is to provide opportunity for all to receive such education as will fit them *equally well* for their particular life work."[11] Varied curricula were developed for students of varying ability.

The advent of standardized aptitude testing early in the twentieth century provided a useful means of identifying and placing students. Intelligence tests were increasingly used by U.S. educators because they accorded with the educators' demand for categorization and efficiency. Tests offered scientific justification for the differentiated curriculum, enabling it to function with apparent rationality.[12] By World War I, the use of classification was common practice among U.S. educators. Today, federal and state support has increased the attractiveness to school districts of specialized programs — notably industrial and agricultural trade courses. Differentiated special education programs, also given impetus by state and federal legislation, have expanded with the same speed (if not the same universality) since the 1920s.

Current ability grouping, special education assignment, and exclusion of ineducable children have significant and similar school purposes. They provide mechanisms for differentiating among students, offer rewards and sanctions for school performance, ease the tasks of teachers and administrators by restricting somewhat the range of ability among students in a given classroom, and purportedly improve student achievement.

Interestingly, the first two purposes, sorting and reward-punishment, are seldom mentioned by school officials. The sorting function is self-evident: classification permits the parceling out of students among different educational programs.[13] That certain of these classifications reward and others punish is apparent from investigations of the effects of grouping on students' self perception.[14] The reward-punishment facet of classification represents one aspect of the schools' stress on intellectual competition, with praise given only for performance that the teacher defines as successful.[15]

It is more commonly asserted that classification eases the tasks of teachers and administrators, and affords educational opportunities tailored to students' needs. These purposes — one emphasizing benefits to teachers and administrators, the other emphasizing benefits to students — permit school officials to view classification as an unmixed blessing. There is little recognition that classification may have decidedly limited educational benefits for schoolchildren or that certain sorting practices may even do educational injury.[16] It is the belief that classification helps everyone, and not its questionable empirical foundation, that is significant here. It partially explains the popularity that grouping enjoys among teachers: only 18.4 percent of teachers surveyed by the National Education Association preferred to teach nongrouped classes.[17] It also underscores the problems that reformers who are unhappy with present classification practices are likely to encounter in seeking to restructure them.

School sorting practices also have their critics. The fashionable educational innovations of the past twenty years — nongraded classes, team teaching, open classrooms — all represent efforts to modify school classifications by introducing elements of flexibility, and to diversify the school program while making any particular classification of more limited duration and significance.

Educational research poses a quite different kind of challenge to present classification in practice. It increasingly has undermined one of the essential premises of sorting: that it benefits students. The research concerning the educational effects of ability grouping and special education reveals that classification, as it is typically employed, does not promote individualized student learning, permit more effective teaching to groups of students of relatively similar ability, or, indeed, accomplish any of the things it is ostensibly meant to do. Rather, the findings indicate that classification effectively separates students along racial and social-class lines, and that such segregation may well cause educational injury to minority groups. They also suggest that adverse classifications stigmatize students, reducing both their self-image and their worth in the eyes of others.[18]

Even those who accept the basic premises of school sorting have reason to question whether schools can adequately do the job. Two recent reappraisals of students assigned to classes for the retarded reveal notable errors. A study done by the Washington, DC, school system found that two-thirds of the students placed in special classes in fact belonged in the regular program.[19] Retests of 378 educable mentally retarded students from thirty-six school districts in the Philadelphia area revealed that "[t]he diagnosis for 25 percent of the youngsters found in classes for the retarded may be considered erroneous. An additional 43 percent [may be questioned]."[20] The authors of the study were troubled by these results. "One cannot help but be concerned about the consequences of subjecting these children to the 'retarded' curriculum. . . . The stigma of bearing the label 'retarded' is bad enough, but to bear the label when placement is questionable or outright erroneous is an intolerable situation."[21]

Classification on the basis of intellectual ability has also been attacked by those who assert that such distinctions are based on judgments of inherited rather than acquired intelligence, and are therefore undemocratic. Fifty years ago, Walter Lippmann criticized intelligence testing on precisely those grounds, predicting that the use of such tests "could not but lead to an intellectual caste system in which the task of education had given way to the doctrine of predestination and infant damnation."[22] Milton Schwebel, discussing the practice of grouping students, makes a similar charge:

> The most direct evidence of a school system's stand on ability is the way it educates the mass of its children. . . . Only the school system which regards the genetic factor as paramount, and the environment as . . . insignificant [would] rightly subdivide its population in accordance with native ability [as] revealed by achievement tests and would proffer a curriculum suitable to the talents of each group. The decision whether it is wise to group children by ability depends upon one's view of the origin of intelligence.[23]

The claim that ability grouping treats intelligence as determined by heredity and not environment is political dynamite.[24] It encourages Blacks to view grouping as the pedagogical equivalent of genocide and radical Whites to regard it as "not the means of democratization and liberation, but of [class] oppression."[25] This hostility to ability grouping has been translated into varied forms of political pressure. Black psychologists and community groups have demanded, with some success, that intelligence testing be abandoned. Others have urged the abolition of all classifications in which racial minorities are overrepresented relative to their proportion of the school population. Some of these efforts minimize the real differences among children that, whatever their source, do require varied educational programs; their equation of classification and the doctrine of inherited intelligence oversimplifies a complex problem. But whatever the objective merits of such attacks, they have had significant political impact.

These varied criticisms of classification are not couched in legal terms. Yet, as the balance of this article suggests, they do give rise to questions concerning constitutional rights. In that sense, classification is both descriptive of public educational practice and useful as a tool for constitutional analysis.

School Classification and the Courts

Since the 1954 Supreme Court opinion in *Brown v. Board of Education,* courts have increasingly scrutinized decisions once made solely by school administrators and boards of education.[26] Most prominently, racial policies and practices of states and school districts and methods of allocating financial resources among school districts have been subjected to extensive legal analysis and challenge. Such challenges have addressed school policy on the grand scale. They focus on the state, the metropolitan area, or the school district as the entity whose conduct is to be reviewed. That approach implies a model of educational reform that presumes, first, that racial and fiscal inequities ought to be undone (a proposition with which there can be little quarrel), and second, that the most effective means of undoing them is to focus on the largest governmental unit that can be haled into court.

For some issues, the grand scale approach is demonstrably correct. For example, the problem of interdistrict resource inequality can be addressed most cogently only at the state or national level. But in those matters that directly and tangibly affect the quality of children's schooling experiences, the equation of largest with best makes little sense. The school, not the state or even the school district, has primary impact. It is at the school or classroom level that many of the critical decisions about teacher assignment, classroom composition, and curriculum are made.

There are obvious and understandable reasons underlying judicial reluctance to intrude in such matters as student grouping ostensibly based on ability, or student assignment to special programs designed for children with particular disabilities. The minuteness of many within-school (and within-class) decisions makes it difficult to conceive of them as posing legally manageable problems. Such decisions are complex, interrelated, and numerous. For that reason, a court that undertook to review them might well find itself acting as schoolmaster in an uncomfortably literal sense. The necessarily limited capacity for judicial review of within-school policy questions does not, however, foreclose all judicial inquiry. Properly framed, certain aspects of the school classification process can be addressed in intelligible and manageable fashion by courts.[27]

Courts have begun to limit the schools' discretion in the ways they sort students and the categories into which they sort them. Judge J. Skelly Wright's decision in *Hobson v. Hansen,* which abolished tracking in the District of Columbia, is the most famous, but not the only case addressing the constitutional propriety of school classification practices.[28] Exclusion of children from school, whether because of asserted ineducability,[29] alien status,[30] or pregnancy,[31] has been overturned by a number of courts; the manner in which students are assigned to classes for the mildly retarded has been reviewed to determine the rationality of the classification procedures employed;[32] and courts have rejected attempts of formerly *de jure* segregated school districts to employ ability grouping, finding such efforts inconsistent with the obligation to desegregate.[33]

What general constitutional standards underlie these discrete cases? One approach considers the educational harm attributable to exclusion and to assignment to either special education programs or slow-ability groups. The assorted ill effects of these classifications render plausible the claim that they deny students an equal educational opportunity. The deprivation represents a real disadvantage, which is given additional significance by virtue of the psychic injury that it occasions.[34]

A second constitutional approach focuses on the fact that minority children are assigned to slow-learners' groups and special education classes in numbers far exceeding their proportion of the school population, and are thus denied classroom contact with White and middle-class schoolmates. The existence of such racial isolation, coupled with evidence of the racially specific injury it produces, should be sufficient to require a demonstration that these classifications are in fact based on adequate nonracial grounds, and that their educational benefits outweigh the racially specific harm of within-school isolation.[35]

The equal educational opportunity and racial analyses both rely on the equal protection clause in challenging the legitimacy of at least some school classifications. A third approach focuses not on the legitimacy of the classifications themselves, but on the procedure by which the school determines how a particular student or class of students should be treated. This due process approach is triggered by two related factors: a significant school-imposed change in educational status and the stigma that invariably attaches to students placed in these programs.

These three legal strategies, assessed in succeeding sections of this article, are at least plausible. Each draws on previous court decisions that have sought to define with particularity the meaning of the equal protection of the laws and due process guarantees of the Fourteenth Amendment. Yet legal plausibility does not necessarily or automatically yield educationally sound results. This caveat assumes particular importance when courts begin to raise questions about matters as central to the educational enterprise as school classification determinations. In these, as in other issues of educational policy, decisions based on the constitution can have a salutary effect. They can determine the bounds of constitutionally permissible school action, reveal arbitrary conduct, and impose some measure of fairness on school procedure. But the courts can neither revamp the educational system nor improve the quality of those who administer that system.

Equal Educational Opportunity

The Supreme Court declared in *Brown v. Board of Education* that the opportunity for education, where the state has undertaken to provide it, "is a right which must be made available to all on equal terms."[36] While the inequality against which *Brown* inveighed was racial, nonracial educational inequities have been struck down by the lower courts. Those decisions note the constitutional importance of education and view with sympathy the claims of children — a voteless, relatively powerless minority. Is the child's interest in an equal education sufficiently diminished by placement in a slow track or special class, or by exclusion from school, to warrant constitutional scrutiny?

School sorting practices, unlike explicitly racial classifications, cannot be condemned as inherently harmful. Some classification is clearly necessary if schools are to cope with the bewildering variety of talent and interest that characterizes children. Whether particular classifications are harmful, and hence equality-depriving, is essentially an empirical question. Thus, in a lawsuit attacking school sorting practices, demonstration of injury may well be as important as constitutional theory. Adverse school classification may result in two kinds of injury: educational ineffectiveness and stigmatization of students.

Efficacy

What does the evidence concerning the educational efficacy of school sorting demonstrate? Little research has been carried out on the effects of school exclusion, with good reason: excluded children are difficult to locate.[37] Further, the educational effects of exclusion are likely to be inseparable from the impact of other social adversities, making it difficult to isolate the cause of harm. Yet the few studies that do consider the effect of exclusion (or the impact of school shut-downs) on children predictably conclude that the lack of schooling does retard achievement.[38]

While abundant research has been undertaken with respect to internal school classifications,[39] that research is flawed by a host of methodological difficulties: some studies are too abbreviated and thus do not take into account the possibility that children behave differently because they are part of an exciting (or at least novel) experiment; experimental groups, assigned to particular classifications, are not adequately matched with control groups, so that performance variation may be explained by initial student differences; measures of change and growth vary from study to study; responses to questionnaires prove inadequate to reckon with the subtleties of sorting; and, most important, the definition of what constitutes ability grouping or a program for the educable mentally retarded varies from study to study. Despite these problems, the consistency of research findings (particularly among those studies most carefully executed) is impressive. The research indicates that most student classifications have marginal and sometimes adverse impact on both student achievement and psychological development.

The research concerning the efficacy of special education programs is best treated as two sets of data. Studies of programs for children with profound problems — for example, autistic children or those whose IQ is below 25 — reveal that careful intervention can secure substantial benefits.[40] Of course, the measure of benefit differs for these children: the ability to tie one's own shoes or to talk is a major success. But the benefits are real and for the most part unquestioned.

Research concerning classes for children with etiologically more ambiguous handicaps — the educable mentally retarded, mildly emotionally disturbed, and perceptually handicapped — reaches quite different conclusions. Those programs do not tangibly benefit their students, whose equally handicapped counterparts placed in regular school classes perform at least as well and without apparent detriment to their normal classmates.

> It is indeed paradoxical that mentally handicapped children having teachers especially trained, having more money (per capita) spent on their education, and being enrolled in classes with fewer children and a program designed to provide for their unique needs, should be accomplishing the objectives of their education at the same or at a lower level than similar mentally handicapped children who have not had these advantages and have been forced to remain in the regular grades.[41]

The methodological difficulties, noted earlier, suggest one reason for treating these findings with some caution. Where, for example, special education is a euphemism for a day-sitting room staffed by an unqualified teacher, as is too often the case, any benefits it yielded would be remarkable. Yet the philosophy of isolated special-class treatment also makes the failure of such ventures understandable. These programs typically adopt a passive-acceptant approach, reflecting the assumption that

> the retarded individual is essentially unmodifiable and, therefore, that his performance level as manifested at a given stage of development is considered as a powerful prediction of his future adaptation. . . . Strategies aiming at helping him to adapt . . . will consist of molding the requirements and activities of his environment to suit his level of functioning, rather than making the necessary efforts to raise his level of functioning in a significant way. *This, of course, is doomed to perpetuate his low level of performance.*[42] (emphasis added)

Thus, even if children perform admirably in the special class, they inevitably fall further behind their counterparts in the regular program. Only an active-modificational approach — which rejects the educational isolation and early labeling of retarded children — is likely to reverse this pattern.[43]

In sum, the research conclusion about special education programs is consistent, if modest: programs for the severely handicapped do benefit those children, while classes for the mildly retarded and mildly emotionally disturbed do not serve those children better than regular class placement. Nor, it should be pointed out, do those classes markedly impair academic performance. If the empirical findings are correct, special education assignment has little effect on student achievement.

Studies of ability grouping generally reach a similar conclusion: differentiation on the basis of ability does not improve student achievement. It improves the performance of the brightest only slightly (and only for some academic subjects), while slightly impairing the school performance of average and slow students.[44] William Borg, whose tracking study is perhaps the most careful yet undertaken, found that

> neither ability grouping with acceleration nor random grouping with enrichment is superior for all ability levels of elementary school pupils. In general, the relative achievement advantages of the two grouping systems were slight, but tended to favor ability grouping for superior pupils and random grouping for slow pupils.[45]

The National Education Association, surveying the tracking literature, concludes: "Despite its increasing popularity, there is a notable lack of empirical evidence to support the use of ability grouping as an instructional arrangement in the public schools."[46]

The premises of ability grouping are in many respects similar to those of special education programs. Both assume the relative immutability of learning capacity; both structure educational offerings to match what is presumed to be the maximum capacity of the child. While students do change tracks, the amount of such movement appears relatively small — prediction of student ability becomes its proof as well. James Coleman has made a similar point:

> The idea inherent in the new [ability-grouped] secondary school curriculum appears to have been to take as given the diverse occupational paths into which adolescents will go after secondary school, and to say (implicitly): there is greater equality of educational opportunity for a boy who is not going to attend college if he has a specially designed curriculum than if he must take a curriculum designed for college entrance.
>
>   There is only one difficulty with this definition: it takes as a *given* what should be problematic — that a given boy is going into a given post-secondary occupational or educational path.[47]

These studies define the effects of school sorting in terms of test-measured achievement. A quite different approach considers the effect of sorting on subtler measures of attitude and outlook, examining the possibility that certain classifications function to stigmatize students.

Stigmatization

Stigma, which Erving Goffman calls "an undesired differentness," is a fact of social life.[48] In U.S. society, no class is officially branded outcast; indeed, the concept of equality that theoretically governs democratic social relations refuses to recognize any class-based traits. Nonetheless, for segments of the society, labels as varied as "blind," "Negro," "homosexual," or "convict" convey broadly accepted social stigmas.

  A stigma is not inherently value-laden: the stigmatizing attribute is neither creditable nor discreditable per se. Its value lies in how people perceive it — that is, its socially accepted meaning. Stigma is thus properly defined in relational terms.

13

Stigmatization, whether formal or informal, facilitates interaction with certain types of individuals by prescribing appropriate social strategies for managing encounters with them. Society pities the blind, shuns the criminal, disdains the homosexual, all without reference to the personal qualities that complicate the labeling process. Individual differences are subsumed under the common, negatively perceived attributes.

Even in an egalitarian society, some stigmas are legitimately imposed through official action. The convicted murderer is labeled and punished for a deed that society feels deserving of punishment. His or her stigma is justified as a form of social control. This process, which might be termed just or permissible social stigmatization, is so basic to society that it typically passes unnoticed. Yet there are other more subtle stigmas, equally real and debilitating, that are officially imposed by the state. Many laws classify: they divide the world into classes of people, only some of whom are eligible for or benefit from particular treatment. And many classifications can be said to stigmatize: zoning laws perpetuate a "wrong side of the tracks"; licensing laws separate the qualified from the charlatan. The agency that creates these classifications may well not intend this result. It is more likely to be interested in providing humane treatment or in securing administrative ease. Involuntary confinement in mental hospitals and even the incarceration of criminals, for example, are asserted to be rehabilitative. Yet in understanding stigma, motive matters less than consequences. The relevant inquiry is whether individuals are effectively branded in a manner that they and those with whom they come into contact regard as undesirable.

Many of the classifications that schools impose on students are stigmatizing. However well-motivated or complex the decision leading to a particular classification, the classification lends itself to simplified labels. The slow learner or special student becomes a "dummy." The student excluded from the school system is an outcast, "told . . . that he is unfit to be where society has determined all acceptable citizens of his age should be."[49]

For many children, adverse school classification is particularly painful because it is novel. It represents the first formal revelation of differences between them and other children. The school's inclination to cope with a particular learning or social problem by isolating those who share that problem reinforces children's sense of stigma. Children perceive all too well what the school's label means. Jane Mercer observes that those assigned to special education classes "were ashamed to be seen entering the MR room because they were often teased by other children about being MR . . . [and] dreaded receiving mail that might bear compromising identification."[50]

Differences among children clearly exist, and it would be educational folly to ignore them: to treat everyone in exactly the same fashion benefits no one. Yet the consequence of the school's classification remains an awesome fact with which the child must cope. Its psychological ramifications extend beyond the child: they reach his family, and others with whom the child has contact. The child assigned to a special education class or a slow-learners' group discovers that his society is totally altered. His differentness is what matters most to the school.

The stigma is further exacerbated by the school's curriculum. The curriculum offered to the slow or special child is less demanding than that provided for normal children. Even if children assigned to the special class do creditable work, they fall further behind the school norm. The initial assignment becomes a self-fulfilling prophecy: children's belief in their inferiority is reinforced by the knowledge that they are increasingly unable to return to the regular school program.[51] Because classmates and teachers make fewer demands on such children (for by definition less can be expected of the handicapped than the normal), they come to accept others' assessments of their potential. As one student in a slow track said: "All the kids here are victims. They've finally believed it."[52]

The effects of school-imposed stigmas do not cease when the child leaves school, for schools are society's most active labelers. Slow-track assignment makes college entrance nearly impossible and may discourage employers from offering jobs; assignment to a special education program forecloses vocational options. While many children labeled retarded by the school do come to lead normal lives, the stigma persists.[53] For the children who cannot escape their past — as by moving from the South to the North to seek employment, leaving all school records except a diploma behind them — the retarded label may stick for life.

Constitutional Standards

The fact that certain school classifications — exclusion, special education, and slow track placement — do not benefit and may well injure students readily evokes the policy conclusion that such sorting is educationally dubious practice. Yet bad policy is not necessarily, or even usually, unconstitutional policy.[54] If the transition could be effortlessly made, courts would in fact function as super-legislatures. If, however, the interests at stake are closely linked to constitutionally guaranteed rights, or if the class of assertedly injured persons is demonstrably vulnerable to abuse by the majority, then the claim that particular policies operate unequitably becomes more susceptible to judicial analysis. In a challenge to school sorting, the possible bases for such judicial treatment are, first, inequitable deprivation of education — an important, if not a "fundamental" interest[55] — and second, the status of children, a class of individuals who deserve the protection of the courts in securing their rights.

15

San Antonio Unified School District v. Rodriguez[56] casts considerable doubt on the vitality of constitutional arguments premised on the importance of education. In that case, a closely divided Supreme Court concluded that wealth-based disparities in the financing of public education did not offend the equal protection clause of the Constitution. The Supreme Court affirmed its "historic dedication to public education," yet could find no constitutional warrant for distinguishing educational inequities from inequities in the provision of any other publicly supported good or service.[57] Having identified no special status for education explicit or implicit in the Constitution, the Court proceeded to apply the traditional equal protection test — to determine whether the goals implicit in the state financing schemes were rational, and whether the means adopted by the state reasonably furthered the state's legislative goal.

The *Rodriguez* analysis is profoundly troubling. Even if education is not of fundamental moment, it clearly bears upon the exercise of constitutionally guaranteed rights. For that reason, in reviewing assertions of inequity, the Court should be able to distinguish education from regulation of economic interests, where the lenient standard of rationality historically has been applied. Indeed, in a host of cases — particularly involving state legislation that assertedly diminished the individual's right to privacy — the Court has, under the guise of rationality, applied a more stringent standard of judicial review. That approach does not, as the majority opinion suggests, require the Court "to create substantive constitutional rights in the name of guaranteeing equal protection of the laws,"[58] or "mark an extraordinary departure from principled adjudication under the Equal Protection Clause of the Fourteenth Amendment."[59] Instead, as Justice Marshall's dissent notes, it calls for a determination of "the extent to which constitutionally guaranteed rights are dependent on interests not mentioned in the Constitution,"[60] requiring the Court to consider "[w]hat legitimate state interest does the classification promote? What fundamental personal rights might the classification endanger?"[61]

In rejecting the claim that education is of fundamental constitutional significance, *Rodriguez* appears to foreclose all challenges to inequities in the provision of education — or, at least, inequities that are neither racial in nature nor represent complete denial of schooling. Yet the analytic formula that the Court adopts is unsatisfactory, at least in part because it *is* a formula. It seems more constitutionally appropriate (if less result-oriented) to review each assertedly adverse educational classification in order to determine whether it suitably furthers an appropriate governmental interest. This approach would "close the wide gap between the strict scrutiny of the new equal protection and the minimal scrutiny of the old not by abandoning the strict but by raising the level of the minimal from virtual abdication to genuine judicial inquiry."[62]

If such an approach were to be adopted by a court considering the constitutionality of school sorting practices, the possibility of successful challenge would be strong. The very factors that link education to rights guaranteed by the Constitution — political participation, the capacity to frame and express individual points of view — seem to be directly affected by school classification. This cause-and-effect relationship between the impact of the injury and the nature of the right is most readily established with respect to school exclusion. Since exclusion represents a total deprivation of schooling, all of education's benefits are necessarily denied the excluded child. Special education or slow-learner assignment presumably also affects subsequent opportunities for political participation and intellectual growth, although the link is not so easily fashioned.

That the rights of children are affected by school classification may also be of constitutional significance. There is reason for the courts to treat with special judicial solicitude the constitutional claims of children, requiring a degree of inquiry greater than a determination of mere rationality but less demanding than insistence upon compelling justification for inequalities.

The status of children is unique in the legal system. Because of their age, children cannot pursue their interests through political avenues. Nor can they directly seek redress through the courts; they must be represented by an adult, typically a parent, whom the law presumes will act on their behalf. Their lives are managed and directed to an extent that adults would find intolerable. Educational decisions are routinely made by the state: in almost all states, children are compelled to attend school for at least nine years. This initial compulsion serves as a basis for the imposition of further constraints.

Most remarkable has been the ease with which the state has been able to justify its imposition of values on those occasions when its interests and those of children collide. For example, the Supreme Court has held that the distribution of religious literature, fit activity for adults, impairs the health and welfare of children,[63] books suitable for adult consumption cannot be sold to children, whose moral growth might be stunted.[64] In each case, the Court has viewed children's interests in liberty as conflicting with the state's general concern for the well-being of children; in resolving that conflict, children have lost. It is instructive that the Supreme Court only four years ago declared explicitly for the first time that children "are 'persons' under our Constitution."[65] Their rights as persons have been minimal.[66]

Courts have recently begun to recognize the civil rights of children independent of the rights of their parents. *Tinker v. Des Moines Independent Community School District*, which asserted the First Amendment rights of children, is of course the leading case.[67] *Weber v. Aetna Casualty & Surety Co.* reveals judicial concern for the rights of one class of children — those born out of wedlock.[68] In at least two other kinds of cases, lower courts also have explicitly recognized children's personal rights. The Supreme Court of Pennsylvania, in a case involving the right of a Jehovah's Witness to refuse medical treatment for her sixteen-year-old child where the child's life was not in imminent danger, remanded for a hearing to ascertain the wishes of the child.[69] In *Chandler v. South Bend Community School Corp.*, a federal district court upheld the independent interests of children in education.[70] The district court, which struck down a school policy of suspending students and withholding their report cards unless their parents either paid a textbook fee or established their indigency, declared: "The student fee collection procedure . . . conditions [children's] *personal* right to an education upon the vagaries of their parents' conduct, an intolerable practice."[71]

The claim that adverse and harmful student classifications deny equal protection recognizes another interest of children: a concern for educational choice, for securing the maximum liberty possible within the constraints of a compulsory student system. Children are both too unformed and too precious to be treated arbitrarily by the state. This claim of worth, and the family's interest in securing the child's individuality, has received passing judicial recognition.[72] It underlies the Court's observation in *Tinker* that children may not be viewed as "closed-circuit recipients of only that which the State chooses to communicate."[73] This proposition logically applies with ever greater force to school instruction than to political activities that happen to transpire in the schoolhouse. The presumed equality of all children provides strong basis for contesting actions that threaten that equality by restricting the child's potential for growth.

Applying the Constitutional Standard

Not all school classifications assume equal importance in the life of a child. Exclusion, ability grouping, and assignment to special education have been singled out as the three most consequential sortings, and thus are most likely to warrant judicial inquiry. The important distinctions among these classifications suggest that the application of a constitutional standard should differ for each.

School exclusion, the most extreme classification, is the simplest to confront in legal terms. Exclusion represents the complete denial of a service. Even if education plays only a marginal role in shaping opportunities, denial of education is not a trivial matter: without instruction, children are unlikely to reinvent physics or reading. In addition, exclusion based on a judgment of ineducability is likely to cause irreversible harm to both the child's achievement and psyche. Thus, even without a showing of actual injury, courts can hold that exclusion from school is unconstitutional as a denial of equal protection. Several courts appear to have adopted this theory;[74] most prominently, in *Mills v. Board of Education*, the district court ordered that the

Washington, DC, school system readmit all excluded children "regardless of the degree of the child's mental, physical or emotional disability or impairment."[75]

All that excluded children can constitutionally demand is access to some form of publicly supported education and special assistance to permit them to overcome the school-imposed handicap. To insist on more, to require as a matter of constitutional law that the school system make an educationally "correct" placement, calls on the court to treat complex judgments of educational needs in constitutional terms, a position that courts will be justifiably reluctant to adopt. As one federal district court noted, in a somewhat different context, "[T]here are no discoverable and manageable standards by which the court can determine when the Constitution is satisfied and when it is violated."[76] Yet the two district courts that have confronted the issue of exclusion based on asserted ineducability have, in defining a remedy, spoken in terms of individual needs and appropriate placement, leaving those matters in the hands of a court-appointed master or school officials.[77] That remedial approach assures that the educational opportunity that is in fact offered is not meaningless and unusable; it tailors the remedy to fit the constitutionally cognizable harm.

Challenges to within-school classifications pose more difficult constitutional problems. They demand that a court weigh the different benefits and costs associated with varied educational approaches, a task usually — and quite properly — left to educators. The difficulty is compounded because the balancing process is riddled with ambiguity. If, for example, few students return from special to regular classes, does the explanation lie with the structure of the educational offering or the capacities of the child? As the court of appeals' decision in *Hobson* notes: "In some cases statistics are ineluctably ambiguous in their import — the fact that only a small percentage of pupils are reassigned [from slow to faster programs] may indicate either general adequacy of initial assignments or inadequacy of review."[78] How does a court confronted with two equally plausible but ambiguous hypotheses, which existing evidence can neither affirm nor reject, resolve the issue?

One easy but unsatisfactory solution to such dilemmas is to treat all within-school sorting decisions similarly, as matters of educational discretion beyond the ambit of judicial review. That approach ignores distinctions between the benefits and harms associated with special education placement on the one hand, and track assignment on the other; these are differences of degree, to be sure, but differences upon which constitutional distinctions can logically rest.

Special education placement is clearly more onerous than tracking. Even the euphemism "special" conveys a judgment of abnormality, which all the well-intentioned efforts to label both the handicapped and the gifted as exceptional children cannot undo. Students with mild disabilities are isolated from their normal peers. They are not routinely considered as candidates for readmission into the mainstream of the educational program. Furthermore, such programs typically present only scaled-down educational offerings, presuming that children placed in them can never hope to be more than marginal members of the society. And often that presumption becomes fact.

These demonstrable harms — stigmatization, diluted educational offerings, and reduced life chances — suggest that special education placement for the mildly handicapped denies those individuals equal educational opportunity. For that reason, in a suit challenging special-class placement, it seems appropriate to shift the burden of proof from parents and children to school officials. Once evidence of harm has been introduced, school officials should be required to show that the special education program accomplishes what it is supposed to do: that it sufficiently benefits students to justify the inevitable stigma that attaches to such placement. If benefit cannot be demonstrated, either for particular students or for all those placed in classes for the mildly retarded or handicapped, it makes constitutional (and pedagogical) sense to reassign those students to regular classes, providing them with supplementary instruction to help recapture lost educational ground. The standard seems both manageable and just. Defining justification in terms of efficacy imposes a burden aptly suited to the problem. It also encourages more frequent evaluation of each student's progress, thus assuring that special classes are not transformed into a "penitentiary where one could be held indefinitely for no convicted offense."[79] The demonstrated ineffectiveness of special education programs for the mildly handicapped indicates that few will survive if obliged to prove their mettle.

A successful challenge to placement in inefficacious programs for the educable mentally retarded or mildly emotionally disturbed has a relatively modest and accomplishable goal: the effective integration of those students into the general life of the school. A challenge to tracking, on the other hand, goes to the heart of the educational enterprise. Tracking decisions — unlike special education assignments — reach all students and are not premised on marked differences in the potential of children. For that reason, a general objection of tracking readily converts into an attack on any educational practice that rewards some students while punishing others. If none of the sorting that schools engage in appears to benefit students, why not discard it? Such a question frames the point too broadly, confusing what educators might do with what courts can legitimately do in order to secure equal protection of the laws. Although phrasing a question as one of educational policy does not render the courts impotent to act, the very facts that render research concerning the efficacy of tracking so unsatisfying — tracking's near-universality, its links with other school differentiations, its varied connotations — counsel for judicial restraint rather than potentially disruptive action.

A challenge to tracking on grounds that it impairs equality of educational opportunity may well be a disguised demand that schools eliminate disparities between student outcomes. The difficulty with that demand is simply that it cannot be accomplished through any educationally sound and administratively feasible remedy presently available. Since individuals' capabilities clearly differ, it would be a cruel hoax, a "deceit of equality," to premise a challenge to tracking on the argument that tracking caused school failure, implicitly promising that the educational differences would vanish if tracking were done away with.[80] The example of Washington, DC, is instructive here. The holding in *Hobson v. Hansen,* that tracking as practiced in the District of Columbia must "simply be abolished," has had little if any impact.[81] School officials — relying on the court of appeals decision in *Hobson,* which limited the applicability of the district court order to the existing tracking system while permitting "full scope for . . . ability groupings" — simply changed the label and retained the full panoply of student differentiation.[82]

IQ Tests: The Facilitators of Classification

The fact that tracking should not be judicially abolished unless harm can be empirically demonstrated does not imply that all issues linked with ability grouping should be skirted by the courts. Even if the assumptions underlying tracking prove correct — or, more likely, unverifiable — the mechanisms of sorting may be defective. The resulting risk of mistreating students necessitates a careful examination of sorting devices such as tests, grades, or teacher recommendations.

School systems employ a host of factors in determining how to sort students. Past performance in school, student willingness to adapt to the particular classroom regime laid down by the teacher, or parental intervention — all play some part in determining whether a given student is assigned to a regular or slow class for the coming year.

Yet schools do use more objective measures of ability: IQ tests carry great weight in determining the child's educational future. In many school systems, IQ tests form the primary basis for sorting decisions. Students who score between 55 and 75 are assigned to classes for the educable mentally retarded; students who score between 75 and 90 are placed in slow-learners groups; and so on.[83]

These tests are at least nominally objective: they purport to measure factors other than such admittedly irrelevant ones as teacher prejudice and social class. They are also decent predictors of subsequent school success, better than school grades, teacher recommendations, or parental pressure. IQ tests do measure with considerable accuracy the adaptability of a given student to the school's expectations.[84]

IQ tests and the uses to which they are put have been sharply criticized on varying grounds. Their questions are ambiguous, a trap for those who rightly recognize that more than one answer may be correct. They treat intelligence (or, more accurately, school intelligence) in aggregate terms, failing to recognize that a given student is likely to be competent at some things but not at others, and that combining those strengths and weaknesses into a single score inaccurately describes and oversimplifies the notion of intelligence. They fail to measure "adaptive behavior," the capacity to survive in society. The tests also do not indicate *why* a given student did poorly in a particular subject, and thus provide no basis for educational intervention to improve performance.[85] Finally, these tests define intelligence in static, not dynamic terms: they fail to account for the "uneven growth patterns of individual children."[86]

Those who design IQ tests rightly argue that many of these criticisms are properly directed not at the tests but at those who use them. IQ tests need not be employed in punitive, prophecy-confirming ways; test results can be of some use in developing appropriate educational strategies. Yet too often the tests are misused: a single score becomes the basis for student assignment to a particular track from which there is no escape until the next test is administered. The school's apparent incapacity to test students accurately makes test administration appear even more dubious.[87]

The criticisms of testing acquire particular force when minority children are disproportionately assigned to slower learner groups and educable mentally retarded classes on the basis of IQ test results. Tests are condemned as culturally biased, confirming White middle-class status rather than measuring intellectual potential. The deficiencies of such tests were the basis on which Judge Wright overturned the Washington, DC, tracking system. The court viewed the tests as "a most important consideration in making track assignments,"[88] concluding that "standardized aptitude tests . . . produce inaccurate and misleading test scores when given to lower class and Negro students,"[89] and that the school system had not advanced any more culturally neutral sorting alternatives.

For the advocate bent on undoing school classifications, an attack on testing holds considerable appeal. If it can be shown that IQ tests do not measure intelligence, the argument for sorting based primarily on the results of such tests collapses, and the basis for differential treatment becomes simply irrational. The difficulty with that approach rests in its failure to distinguish careful from careless test use. Tests can indicate something about a student's capacity to perform. They do not reveal, but merely remind, that non-middle-class and minority children fare badly in schools as they presently are organized.

When they are abused, testing processes are properly amenable to judicial scrutiny. The practice of administering tests in English to students whose native language is Spanish and using the results as a measure of ability is simply indefensible; the scores of those students are, at best, only a proxy for acculturation into the dominant culture. Further, when test scores serve as the primary basis for student assignment, their use becomes more suspect.

The importance that is attached to a single test is also constitutionally significant. Achievement tests, which purport to measure subject matter competence and not ability, are appropriately employed to group children in a particular subject for a limited time. But the use of tests to track students for a period of years — prohibiting either cross-tracking (which recognizes the varied abilities of any given student) or limiting egress from slow tracks — should raise considerable judicial suspicion.

Flexibility, test reliance, and the use of tests to identify particular learning difficulties all represent matters of careful and complex judgment. For a court to insist on them requires the elaboration of distinctions between appropriate and dangerous testing practices, avoiding the easier but inappropriate judicial alternatives of either abolishing IQ testing or treating testing questions as unmanageable. As long as some sorting is to be permitted (and sorting is likely to persist no matter what courts or school administrators might require), judgments about ability will necessarily be difficult to defend with precision. Nevertheless, since classification decisions greatly affect a student's educational career, schools should bear the legal burden of demonstrating that the IQ tests upon which many of these decisions are premised can reliably predict school performance for different types of students.

Racial Overrepresentation

Few schools sort students explicitly on the basis of race. Classification in large systems is routinely handled by school officials who know nothing about a given student except his or her academic record. When counselors discuss appropriate track placement with their students, their recommendations are premised on estimates of student ability and school needs. The grounds on which school personnel defend sorting reveal no apparent racial motivation.

Yet school sorting does in fact have racially specific consequences. It tends to concentrate minority children in less advanced school programs. While racial disproportionality does not characterize programs for students with readily identifiable handicaps (for example, classes for the trainable mentally retarded or the blind), the proportion of minority students in lower tracks and special education programs is typically two or three times greater than their proportion of the school-age population. Racial disproportionality also appears to have a particularly damaging impact on the attitudes and verbal achievement of minority students. The limited available evidence suggests that overrepresentation in these less advanced programs may be particularly harmful in minority students.[90] Although few studies have examined the racially specific harm of sorting, one reanalysis of *Equality of Educational Opportunity* did attempt to assess the impact of within-school segregation on the verbal achievement of Black students. It concluded that while *school* integration does not benefit Blacks, *classroom* integration does. "[C]lassroom desegregation has an apparent beneficial effect on Negro student verbal achievement no matter what the racial enrollment of the school."[91] The United States Civil Rights Commission's reexamination of the Coleman data noted a subtler (and difficult to document) effect of within-school segregation: Black students in nominally integrated schools, "accorded separate treatment, with others of their race, . . . felt inferior and stigmatized."[92] Such within-school segregation was perceived as having been based upon personal and pejorative judgments of ability.

The constitutional implications of these racially specific consequences of school sorting are not self-evident. Racial classifications typically run afoul of the Constitution if they result either from explicit legislative mandate[93] (as in the school desegregation cases) or from the discriminatory application of an apparently neutral legislative scheme.[94] The latter can be seen in the efforts of formerly dual school systems to couple desegregation with the adoption of an ability grouping scheme. In those instances, the motivation for initiating tracking is quite probably racial. The fact that segregated schools have typically provided Black students with fewer school resources than their White classmates suggests that such discrimination would be likely to recur in an ability grouped school. Since grouping inhibits school desegregation, it violates those districts' obligation to desegregate "at once."[95]

In most school systems, however, the overrepresentation of minority students in lower tracks stems neither from statutory command nor from discriminatory practice. It is, rather, an unintended consequence of a policy whose premises are meritocratic, not racial; the disproportionality is inadvertent.[96] Such unintended disproportionalities have not been recognized by the courts as necessarily stating a valid cause of action under the equal protection clause. In *Jefferson v. Hackney,* the Supreme Court was confronted with the contention that Texas' welfare policy was constitutionally suspect because it provided a less adequate subsidy for the Aid for Dependent Children (AFDC) program, whose beneficiaries were primarily Black, than for welfare programs whose recipients were primarily White. The contention was dismissed as a "naked statistical argument."[97]

In many instances, such curt treatment of claims premised solely on disproportionate racial impact seems proper. Except for those rare governmental actions that treat all persons uniformly, every statute classifies on some basis. And in all save the statistically freakish instance, an inadvertent consequence of that classification may be racial: for example, government-subsidized research on the causes of sickle cell anemia is of primary concern to Blacks; in a residentially segregated city, some municipal bus routes will attract more Black passengers while others carry mostly Whites. Surely such effects do not call for the compelling state justification demanded where racial discrimination can be proved.

Yet in considering the racial consequences of school sorting, the *Jefferson* standard is inappropriate for several reasons. Regardless of the presence or absence of racial motivation, the disproportionate impact of school sorting links race with education. Courts have long recognized the harm done by state-mandated school segregation. What differentiates school sorting from the run of desegregation cases is not the fact of harm — indeed, the evidence that within-school desegregation is educationally damaging is, if anything, stronger than the inherent or empirically demonstrated harm upon which *Brown* rests — but the nature of the state's responsibility in the two cases. Yet judicial inquiry involves more than blame-attaching; it also attends to the fact of harm.

The expansive view of state responsibility for school segregation adopted by several northern federal courts may be premised on just such considerations. Those courts have looked at the racial consequences of ostensibly neutral policies — school boundary-setting, construction, teacher assignment, and the like — and have been willing to infer state action from a finding of racially isolating effect. They suggest that a school district may be held to answer for the foreseeable consequences of its actions (and even its failure to act). What makes these decisions defensible is not the legal legerdemain that converts inaction into action, color blindness into culpability, but the fact that segregation, whatever its source, may inflict real and perceived injury.

The educational harm caused by disproportionate placement of minority students in the least advanced of educational programs is in part racially specific. That proportionately more Blacks than Whites populate the lower tracks and special education classes has more than statistical significance. If the reanalyses of the *Equality of Educational Opportunity* data are to be credited, such assignments affect Blacks more harshly than they do Whites; the injury has racial connotations. That fact distinguishes school sorting from such governmental actions as the Texas welfare policy affirmed in *Jefferson*, which, while hurting more Blacks than Whites, hurts the individual Black no more than her or his White counterpart.

The argument that minorities deserve special judicial solicitude because of their vulnerability to majoritarian abuse, so frequently advanced in cases involving racial discrimination, assumes particular force in the context of school classifications.[98] Track assignment (unlike, for example, welfare roll-trimming) is not a general, public decision around which the far-from-voiceless Black political leadership can coalesce. It is, in form if not in fact, not a political issue at all, but an individual judgment of intellectual worth that the Black parent feels particularly powerless to challenge.

These factors — that racially disproportionate sorting does plausible educational harm and affects a vulnerable minority — suggest that judicial attention is appropriate. Once significant racial disproportionality has been shown, a school district should be obliged to demonstrate that its classifications serve substantial independent educational purposes.

Taken together, however, these factors do not stress discrimination against minority students, but rather speak to the deprivation attributable to racial overrepresentation. This focus on deprivation, not discrimination, has several noteworthy implications. It shifts the analysis from blame-fixing to problem-solving, and thus is less concerned with the causes of injury than with the fact of injury. It limits the utility of the *prima facie* case approach, which fastens on evidence of disproportionate racial impact (with respect to the provision of municipal services, for example) as presumptively demonstrating racial discrimination, substituting an inquiry into the consequences of a school policy that isolates minority students in particular school programs. And it implies that providing identical schooling experiences for minority and White children might be constitutionally appropriate only if such evenhandedness promises to overcome the deprivation upon which the judicial inquiry is premised. The deprivation analysis is, in short, necessarily more fully attentive than traditional approaches to the problem posed by racial overrepresentation in a given school program.

Allegations of disproportionate racial impact in education and employment, couched in deprivation terms, have prompted several courts to shift the burden of demonstrating the efficacy of the classifying device to those responsible for implementing it. However, the analyses set forth in these cases are of limited utility because the courts, while tacitly accepting the deprivation theory for the purpose of shifting the burden of proof, continue to stress discrimination and the traditional equal protection analysis when determining what showing that burden requires.

To Judge J. Skelly Wright, for example, "the fact that those who are being consigned to the lower tracks are the poor and the Negroes" was a "precipitating cause" of the *Hobson v. Hansen* inquiry into the workings of the Washington, DC, track system.[99] Although the District of Columbia had initiated tracking shortly after it was ordered to dismantle its dual school system, *Hobson* did not treat the grouping scheme as racially motivated. Yet lack of evil motive did not exonerate the school system. As the court declared, "The arbitrary quality of thoughtlessness can be as disastrous and unfair to private rights and the public interest as the perversity of a willful scheme."[100] That Black children were most likely to be placed in the slowest programs revealed to the court "unmistakable signs of invidious discrimination" that demanded explanation.[101]

While racial overrepresentation provides adequate grounds for judicial scrutiny of school policy, the particular burden imposed in *Hobson* seems inappropriate.

> Since by definition the basis of the track system is to classify students according to their ability to learn, the only explanation defendants can legitimately give for the pattern of classification found in the District schools is that it does reflect students' abilities. If the discriminations being made are founded on anything other than that, then the whole premise of tracking collapses and with it any justification for relegating certain students to curricula designed for those of limited abilities.[102]

The critical word here is "ability." If the court is referring to the present level of proficiency, then reliance on IQ tests to classify students might well be rational. *Hobson*, however, equates ability with "innate capacity to learn," and correctly concludes that IQ tests do not reveal such inherited traits.[103] But few school officials would ever claim to base sorting decisions on grounds of innate capacity. The premise of tracking (and classification generally) is that, whatever the source of the differences, students with particular and varied learning styles and abilities require the special assistance that only a differentiated curriculum can offer. That premise does not countenance discrimination, except in the nonpejorative (and nonlegal) use of that word. Whether or not classification does serve those varied needs, or indeed has any educational consequences, is the crucial question for one concerned with school-caused deprivation. But the *Hobson* court's analytic misstep — equating ability with innate characteristics and stressing discrimination rather than deprivation — prevented it from confronting the question. The abolition of tracking remedy that followed from the court's analysis may have been unresponsive to the problem at hand.

Analytic difficulties also plagued *Larry P. v. Riles,* a suit challenging San Francisco's special education assignment policy as racially biased.[104] In that case, the district court asked only that school personnel provide a rational defense of their classification procedure. But the judicial inquiry was far more exacting than that typically associated with the requirement of mere rationality. The court dismissed the evidence that intelligence tests were but one of several bases on which placement decisions were made, and asserted that they were the primary criteria for placement in classes for the educable mentally retarded.

More significantly, the court rejected school officials' remarkably candid statement that "the tests, although racially biased, are rationally related to the purpose for which they are used because they are the best means of classification currently available."[105] While "the best . . . available" seems readily equatable with rational practice, the court reframed the issue, in effect penalizing the school authorities for their candor. "[T]he absence of any rational means of identifying children in need of such treatment can hardly render acceptable an otherwise concededly irrational means, such as the IQ test as it is presently administered to Black students."[106]

Contrary to the court's implication, however, the fact that other bases for grouping students — such as achievement tests, teacher recommendations, and psychological evaluations — exist does not automatically render the measures employed in San Francisco constitutionally irrational. None of these alternatives is self-evidently preferable to intelligence testing. The standard of review adopted in *Larry P.,* then, is both different from and more demanding than the courts' focus on rational school behavior indicates. The decision, in fact, calls for a demonstration that the classifying device used has real benefits — that it can predict student performance in school — that justify its continued use. Applying this standard to the racially disproportionate classifications themselves, the burden appropriately placed on the school is to show that its classifications actually serve a substantial educational purpose — that they provide real benefits for the affected students.

A challenge to classification that is based on racially specific consequences poses many of the same judicial dilemmas — notably, problems of proof and remedy — that a nonracial challenge to tracking might create. School officials will have a difficult time establishing that placement in a slow track or special class for the mildly retarded or disturbed does in fact make good its promise of improving school performance. Existing evidence simply does not support the proposition. Thus, the benefit that the present system provides is more candidly described in terms of teachers' and school bureaucrats' needs. While these needs must be kept in mind if a court decision is to be implemented, one can readily imagine educationally promising reforms that would produce neither new crises in the classroom nor administrative chaos.

But what can be done to remedy the deprivation? The seeming intractability of what economists term the "education production function" — the manipulation of school resources in a manner that affects student performance — differentiates education from most state-supported activities. Where discrimination in the provision of municipal services or representation on jury rolls has been proved, the problem in effect defines its own remedy: equalize services, assure minority representation on juries. But no such straightforward relationship between problem and resolution exists for school sorting. it is easier to identify the problem than the remedy. That fact argues against the adoption of a remedial approach that limits the school systems' options by seizing upon a single solution as necessarily appropriate. A racial quota system for school classifications or court-ordered abolition of sorting are equally misguided remedies, albeit for different reasons.

In *Larry P.*, plaintiffs proposed that "the percentage of black students in EMR classes could exceed the percentage of black students in the school district as a whole by no more than fifteen percent."[107] Such an approach is undesirable, for although it criticizes the racial implications, it embraces and sustains existing classifications whose pedagogical benefits are at best dubious. To the arbitrariness of existing sorting practice it adds another level of arbitrariness, responding not to real educational differences but to statistical nicety.

To require wholesale randomization of classes seems equally unwise. In a given sixth-grade class, the most advanced student may be reading at a ninth-grade level, the slowest at a third-grade pace; a uniform curriculum could not hope to confront such variation. It is tempting, but incorrect, to jump from the assertion that existing classifications mislabel and miseducate students to the remedy of doing away with all efforts to identify and intelligently address differences among students.

Judicial insistence on a modification of existing classifications, which seeks both to reduce racial overrepresentation in less advanced groups and to secure greater flexibility in grouping, represents a far better approach. That standard leaves the school district free to adopt a variety of grouping alternatives taking account of varied student needs, while not locking students into a tracked strait jacket. Given the existing uncertainty concerning the causes and cures of this particular deprivation, the command of reconsideration and flexibility has considerable virtue.

In rethinking and reconstructing its classification system, the school district should focus on three variables, linking remedial efforts in all three areas to develop a more rational and constitutionally justifiable system. First, gross extremes of racial separation should be reduced. Outside of the classroom, in those aspects of school life that are more social than academic (for example, assemblies, athletic events, lunch periods), efforts should be made to promote social mixing.

The second variable is the need for flexibility in the tracking scheme itself. Classification decisions should be based on criteria broader than the usual standardized tests; adaptive behavior, for example, should be taken into account. Placement of students should be reviewed frequently to allow greater mobility. Cross-track integration in those areas that the tests do not measure — music, art, physical education — will increase this flexibility. In the higher grades, testing and tracking by subject, rather than by general ability, will render the structure more rational, while increasing the possibilities of in-class mixing. Larger school systems might consider adopting stratified heterogeneous grouping, which reduces ability disparities within any given classroom, or team teaching with flexible grouping.

Assuming that some classes will remain predominantly segregated, attention should be focused on relieving educational deprivation within the minority-dominated tracks. The most obvious step would be to increase the per student allocation of educational resources in the lower tracks. But the educational benefits of such action remain unclear. Alleviation of racially (or culturally) specific deprivation may require something beyond more resources — the need may be for different reasons. Culturally sensitive pedagogical techniques, analogous to the creation of Spanish-language classes for Mexican Americans, may be employed. The use of pedagogical methods geared to the differences in minority learning patterns and cultural background, if combined with efforts to increase integration and create a more flexible system, should satisfy the valid educational purposes test.

Modification is a vague remedial standard until given substance by a school district plan. It would not necessarily eliminate all instances of racial disproportionality; indeed, it would not be designed to do so. While a modification approach encourages a school system to adopt a sorting scheme that fixes less pronounced labels on students, it does not pretend to remove all stigma. Yet modification of school classifications, if undertaken with an eye to integrating minorities into the life of the school, might well benefit both the school and the minority student on whom the preponderant burden of adverse classification presently falls, thus responding to the problems associated with racial overrepresentation.

Due Process

A third constitutional approach to the inequities caused by classification relies upon the due process clause of the Fourteenth Amendment, which declares that "no state shall . . . deprive any person of life, liberty, or property, without due process of law." That language, while commanding the government to act fairly, does not define what fairness means in particular situations. As the Supreme Court has observed:

> "Due process" is an elusive concept. Its exact boundaries are undefinable, and its content varies according to specific factual contexts. . . . Whether the Constitution requires that a particular right obtain in a specific proceeding depends upon a complexity of factors. The nature of the alleged right involved, the nature of the proceeding, and the possible burden on that proceeding, are all considerations which must be taken into account.[108]

That some procedural safeguards are attached to the provision of public education is by now well-settled law. While much of the case law concerns student discipline, several recent decisions have required that students be afforded procedural protection prior to such basic changes in their status as assignment to slow-learner groups, special education programs, or school exclusion. The appropriateness of applying such safeguards is premised on factors discussed earlier in this article: the educational effect of these decisions, the possibility of arbitrary decisionmaking, and the stigma that these adverse classifications convey.

That certain decisions previously left to the discretion of the school are subject to review and challenge should matter considerably to children and their families. Proceduralization makes the school's decision appear more fair — if only because the bases of the decision are shared and not secret — and minimizes the possibility that school discretion will be abused.[109] And proceduralization increases the likelihood of educationally sound decisions, since the exercise of review may force school officials to reexamine regularly both the premises and conclusions of sorting.

In this setting, the real significance of due process lies not in the recognition that school sorting is too consequential to be undertaken arbitrarily, but in the scope of procedural protection that the courts conclude is appropriate. The mere existence of a hearing says nothing about the rules governing the inquiry, or the likelihood that a particular showing will yield a given outcome; and it is the latter issues that frame the real points of contention.[110] To praise due process without providing either context or content for the concept risks elevating principled means above just ends.

In determining precisely what due process should mean in this context, courts are obliged to balance the needs and interests of several concerned parties. This balancing exercise is a familiar one, and distinguishes the request for procedural protection from the more novel claim that courts review such substantive educational issues as the efficacy of particular school placements. "[H]owever little courts may know about education . . . they do know about factfinding, decision-making, fairness, and procedure."[111] For that reason, the development of procedural safeguards that promote fair classification is an easier task for the judiciary to contemplate than is the development of substantive educational rights doctrines.

Interest Balancing

In school sorting disputes, the contending parties include the child, the family, and the school. The interest of each differs, and each has to be taken into account. The importance of education to the child's future well-being has often been recognized by courts. The panegyric to education in *Brown v. Board of Education* has been so often repeated by so many interested parties in support of such varied arguments that its force has been blunted, the language rendered a cliché. But this cliché, like so many others, is rooted in an important truth. Educational performance and educational status do affect life success, even if the nature of the relationship differs from the model that *Brown* had in mind. The child also has an interest in avoiding the unjust imposition of stigma and (to phrase the point in more familiar language) in liberty. School-imposed stigmas bedevil children because children are compelled to submit to them, to surrender at least a decade of their lives to the state. That infringement of liberty itself raises constitutional issues.[112] It also distinguishes school-imposed classifications from those created by governmental agencies whose control over the citizenry is in some sense voluntary.

The child's parents also have a stake in the issue, but their concerns should be distinguished from those of the child. Even if both share the same perception of the school's decision, its consequences will affect them differently. This point assumes particular importance when the school, by assigning a child to a special class or excluding him or her as ineducable, has in effect identified that child as less than normal. That determination may spawn a host of parental reactions: parents may, for example, hire outside experts to supplement the school's program, or they may embrace the school's decision. Parents may be unwilling to endorse the educational program that is objectively best for the child if the recommended course of action appears to compound parental problems. For those reasons, the distinctions between parents' and children's interests must be kept in mind when framing procedures for reviewing adverse school classification.

The school's interests are equally legitimate, and very different. The school has to concern itself with the aggregate welfare of all children as well as the individual welfare of any given child. It will resist any arrangement, such as the provision of a particular program not previously offered, that demands additional expenditures: the cost of that program, if not subsidized by state categorical assistance, will be borne by the district. And those added costs will require either additional tax dollars or trimming other parts of the budget. The education of an autistic child, for example, costs at least $10,000 — twenty times what most school districts annually spend for the average student. Yet the $10,000 investment could possibly enable the autistic person to break through the psychological barriers that cut him or her off from the world. To choose between those two interests poses problems of exquisite difficulty, unanswerable by recourse to such judicial formulas as "the [school district's] interest in educating the excluded children clearly must outweigh its interest in preserving its financial resources."[113]

There exist other, more subtle costs to the school: teacher resentment at being obliged to defend a judgment, or unwillingness on the part of school personnel to make any recommendations concerning special treatment for a particular child because of the procedural regime invoked by such decisions. Many of these arguments are recited whenever a student challenges a disciplinary decision of the school in the school board meeting room or the courtroom. In those circumstances, courts have generally concluded that serious infringements on a child's liberty cannot be imposed unless adequate procedural protection is provided.[114] The application of such safeguards to adverse school classifications poses an ostensibly different problem. It questions a judgment couched in education and not disciplinary terms, a decision central to the school's claim of pedagogical competence. For that reason, school officials are likely to resist terming such classifications as stigmatizing. They will also object to the creation of any process that distinguishes the interest of the school from that of the child, claiming that school classifications further both interests.

In reviewing school decisions more obviously punitive in nature than classifications, courts have not been unsympathetic to these assertions. But the distinction between educational and punitive decisions — which has its analog in the claim that juvenile criminal proceedings are intended to help and not punish youngsters, and therefore should be unfettered by procedures — makes little sense in either setting. However the school chooses to describe the enterprise, its consequences vary for the parties at interest; what is best for one may not be suitable for the others. And for the student, the effect of punitive and educational decisions is similar if not identical: exclusion, whether premised on incorrigibility or ineducability, results in absolute educational deprivation; suspension or special-class assignment both diminish educational opportunities and stigmatize the affected student.

The school may choose to ease teachers' burdens by separating children into groups according to tested measures of ability. If the school cannot afford the educational services that a severely retarded child requires, it may attempt to relinquish its obligation to educate the child by labeling him or her ineducable. Teachers who cannot cope with an "acting-out" child may propose assignment to a less advanced track or a special education program as a means of tempering behavior. Confronted with the school's statement that a child is ineducable or less educable than others, the child is at the very least entitled to an advocate who can distinguish his or her needs from those of the school and a forum in which to press this contention.

Requirements of Due Process

Characterizing the interests of children, parents, and school officials is essential to comprehending the nature of the potential dispute. It does not, however, define with precision the scope of procedural protection. The mechanical transplanting of procedural protections developed in the school discipline context to issues of school classification ignores differences between the two problems.

In the routine discipline case, the decisive issue is the truthfulness of the accusation: did X threaten the teacher with a knife? The hearing effectively concludes when this determination is made. The facts concerning the wisdom of a school classification are not so readily established. Is Y an educable mentally retarded child? On what basis is that judgment made? What alternative explanations can be suggested for this behavior? The appropriate remedy may also be more difficult to develop. If X did indeed brandish a knife, he or she will be punished by being suspended from school; the only determination that must be made is the duration of the suspension. But the fact of retardation does not warrant punishment. It requires careful and intelligent educational intervention that demonstrates some promise of benefiting the child. The range of plausible alternatives includes institutionalization, assignment to a special program, or placement in a regular class coupled with the provision of additional assistance.

Where the justness of diminished educational status is at issue, two critical questions require resolution: the accuracy of the school's classification and the appropriateness of the proposed treatment. The first query (whether the particular assignment is consistent with general guidelines for a given treatment) calls both for clarity and administrative regularity, obliging school personnel to specify the bases upon which they sort children. The second question (whether the particular assignment is likely to benefit the child) demands justification, joining substantive standards with procedural nicety.

It makes sense to place this burden of justification with school officials. Since it is they, not parents or children, who control the information on which a given decision is based, they can most readily answer these questions. School officials also determine the policies that the teachers and counselors carry out. The burden appropriately borne by the school is not satisfied by mere explications of policy. The potential stigma and educational inefficacy of certain treatments — assignment to special classes and exclusion — suggests that placement in a regular school program, supplemented with special help, should be viewed as the norm, inapplicable only when the school can demonstrate that another alternative offers substantially greater promise. As the *Mills* court notes: "Placement in a regular public school class with appropriate ancillary services is preferable to placement in a special public school class."[115] Either is to be preferred to institutional care.

Before reclassification or assignment to a special program becomes a fact, the school should inform the family and the child affected, should explain the proposed action and indicate what alternatives might be available. If such a process actually functioned, the need to secure the more formal protections of due process might well disappear. There is, however, little evidence from past school behavior to justify hope that such wise and preventive measures will be adopted voluntarily. Schools do not encourage parental involvement in any sorting decision. Even where state law requires parental consent before a child is assigned to a special education class, that requirement is often either ignored or satisfied by coercing parental acquiescence. Parents are informed that a particular placement is the only option available and occasionally threatened with criminal sanctions if they reject it. Misunderstanding or intimidation become even more common when parents speak little or no English and school officials speak only English. Schools are unwilling to discuss sorting decisions with parents for many of the same reasons that they object to formal procedural review: such discussions take time, they require that educational decisions be rendered in a language comprehensible to laymen, and they necessarily invite challenges over matters that the school treats as its prerogative.

Effective review of a classification decision requires access to the school's records and the opportunity to have the school's determination reviewed by an impartial outside authority. Unless parents can examine test scores, psychological interview write-ups, teacher recommendations, and the like, the school's design is not only unchallengeable, it is incomprehensible. And unless the parents can obtain the services of a disinterested professional, they may well lack the competence to understand the basis of the school's action. This need for expertise distinguishes classification from discipline cases. The significance and complexity of these adverse classifications, as well as the possibility of professional misjudgment, suggest that parents should be entitled to expert assistance, a right that should not depend on their capacity to pay for the expertise.[116]

If the need for expert help is greater in classification cases than in discipline disputes, the need for legal counsel may be less. A great deal of energy has been expended in deciding whether a child confronted with the possibility of punitive school action is entitled to legal assistance or, to make the point differently, whether lawyers should be barred from such proceedings because they might convert orderly discussions into miniature courtrooms. This energy seems misspent. Although children are likely to need the assistance of someone familiar with their particular problems and willing to represent their interests, that person can be a lawyer or almost any other outsider. While the lawyer may be a particularly useful advocate because of his familiarity with hearing procedures and awareness of the need to negotiate, he is by no means the only person who can effectively discharge the duties of an advocate.

For advocates to function effectively, they must be permitted to question those whose judgments are being reviewed. Such examination may well be both novel and frightening to school teachers and school psychologists. For that reason, there is real need for care and respect in probing and for avoidance of tactics suitable for courtroom confrontations that might increase discomfiture and tension. Such care is also likely to encourage candid conversation, and thus to illuminate the bases for the school's decision.

Several alternatives are conceivable. The school board could act as a reviewing agency. The limited expertise and already substantial agenda of that body, however, make that option unappealing. The school board could create an ad hoc group to make recommendations to the board; such a group might well develop the expertise that review of these decisions and judgments among competing alternatives require. An expert not otherwise connected to the school system might be appointed to consider classification matters. Yet another opinion, possibly linked with one of these three, would leave ultimate review in the hands of a higher education agency (a representative of the county or state department of education, for example) whose ostensible detachment from the school's recommendation would suggest fairness. None of these alternatives is constitutionally required. What is required is a tribunal sufficiently divorced from the initial decision to be capable of unbiased and informed judgment.

For children who have been excluded from school or improperly assigned to the wrong track for a considerable period of time, due process review comes rather late. If the arguments developed here carry any weight, such exclusion or misplacement was legally wrongful because students were not provided with procedural protection. More pertinently, injury has been done: children have been denied some or all of the benefits of an education to which they were entitled. Especially for handicapped or severely retarded children, who can be helped more quickly and more effectively early in life, the injuries are real indeed. For that reason, these children should be entitled to educational assistance equivalent to that which the school has denied them. Equivalency is, to be sure, a difficult concept to implement, since it requires a determination of what education the child has *not* had. In the clearest case — exclusion — requiring the school to make up the amount of schooling lost, measured simply in terms of school days, commends itself primarily because of its ease of application. One federal court, applying just such a standard, ordered periods of remedial work during the school day, after-school tutorial classes, guidance and psychological services, and summer make-up programs to remedy the wrongful exclusion.[117]

The Impact of Procedures

The procedural approach to sorting issues converts matters of substance into matters of form, leaving the critical placement determinations in the hands of assertedly neutral educators. The minimal judicial involvement implicit in the approach has considerable appeal to courts reluctant to make what appear to be educational policy decisions. Yet the ultimate impact of proceduralization on both the school and the student remains a subject for speculation. While hearings may force schools to adopt uniform decision criteria, that very fact may leave the school less willing to make (plausibly better) decisions tailored to specific cases. The possibility that a school might retaliate against a child intrepid enough to demand review of a sorting judgment, in subtle ways that a court could never hope to confront, represents a quite different cost of review. Further, neither the child nor his parents are likely to perceive themselves well-served if a formal hearing reveals that an adverse school classification has in fact been justly imposed. Such a finding denies both child and parent the opportunity to feel wronged, to view the school's action as a misrepresentation of the child's true potential. Process protects against the arbitrary imposition of unjust stigmas; it also reinforces the impact of stigmas found to be properly imposed.

The introduction of procedural niceties into the life of the school may also have unintended but important beneficial consequences. The school required to review each adverse classification may, in the face of that considerable burden, choose to reconsider the process of sorting. It may conclude that children are better served by labels that are less conclusory, and carry with them less pervasive consequences, than those presently in use. In this sense, the claims for procedural and substantive justice share identical aspirations.

One ardently hopes that this aspiration will become reality. Yet even if this hope is misplaced, even if schools continue to develop ever more intricate classifying schemes to sort the students they serve, the application of procedural standards makes public what has hitherto been hidden, and provides a means of contesting particular decisions. That represents at least a step in the right direction.

Conclusion

This article suggests that present classification practices raise three quite different kinds of constitutional questions. First, the exclusion of "ineducable" children and the assignment of other students to inefficacious special education programs may well embody a denial of equal protection. Second, the overrepresentation of minority students in slow-learner groups and classes for the mildly handicapped appear to have racially specific harmful effects; unless school officials can demonstrate that the educational benefits somehow outweigh the harm, some modification of present patterns appears constitutionally required. Third, it is constitutionally appropriate to protect students against the possibility of misclassification by affording them (and their parents) the right to a due process review of placement recommendations.

Educators may well fear that these legal arguments, if accepted by the courts, will require substantially uniform treatment of all, thus drastically limiting their capacity to confront the real and bewildering variations in children's needs and abilities. Yet, as the discussions of the scope of appropriate remedies indicate, such an outcome is neither desirable nor likely. If, for example, classes for the mildly handicapped have little pedagogical justification and also stigmatize students, they should be discontinued. But it does not follow that the tailoring of short-term, goal-specific programs for different kinds of students will routinely arouse judicial suspicion. The differential vulnerability of minority students to adverse classification poses both an educational and a political dilemma that can intelligently be addressed through increasingly flexible program offerings. Such rigid remedies as the establishment of a racial quota system seem singularly inappropriate, for they neither respond to the underlying problem nor offer a workable solution to it. Due process hearings, if handled with sensitivity to the real interests of both the school and the child, encourage better individual placements as well as reconsideration of the school's assumptions concerning which classification decisions are useful and necessary. Adherence to procedural regularity does not convert the school into a courtroom.

The ultimate test of the impact of judicial intervention in this realm will occur in the schools themselves. Court cases challenging one or another aspect of classification explicitly call into question the schools' perception of this mission. They threaten time-honored patterns of institutional behavior and demand nothing less than that what Seymour Sarason terms "the culture of the school" undergo convulsive change.[118] For that reason, reform will not come quickly or easily, whatever the courts ultimately say about these issues.

Yet to state that change will be difficult to accomplish does not imply that currently prevailing school practices will forever persist. Educators have changed their minds and altered their cultures before; they are likely to do so again. And judicial intervention to secure one or another of the constitutional principles discussed in this article may well serve to encourage such changes of mind by insisting upon changes in behavior. In short, the hope that significant school reform will follow judicial decisions is just that — a hope. But every notable constitutional claim embodies the similar expectation that a declaration of rights will lead people to change their lives, to act consistently with what has been held to be just behavior. In the school setting, the hope seems at least plausible, and justifies judicial efforts to protect schoolchildren against the too often ill-considered, arbitrary, and hurtful distinctions made by their elders.

Notes

1. This description of typical classification practice is based on survey data reported in Warren Findley and Miriam Bryan, *Ability Grouping* (Athens: University of Georgia Press, 1971), and in Christopher Jencks, Marshall Smith, Henry Acland, Mary Jo Bane, David Cohen, Herbert Gintis, Barbara Heyns, and Stephan Michelson, *Inequality: A Reassessment of the Effect of Family and Schooling in America* (New York: Basic Books, 1972), p. 250.

2. Test terminology is tricky. Some tests purport to measure aptitude — capacity to learn — while others test achievement — material mastered. In fact, "all tests measure *both* aptitude and achievement . . . [S]uccess on IQ tests, aptitude tests and achievement tests [reveal] varieties of intelligent behavior." Jencks et al., *Inequality*, pp. 54–57. By school convention, IQ tests are individually administered while aptitude tests are group tests; individual testing is commonly employed only for special class placement.

3. See Findley and Bryan, *Ability Grouping*, pp. 2–18. A 1958–1959 survey undertaken by the National Educational Association Research Division reported that among school districts with more than 2,500 pupils, 77.5 percent grouped by ability in the primary grades and 90.5 percent utilized ability grouping in secondary schools. A similar pattern was reported seven years later. Research Division, National Education Association, *Ability Grouping* (Washington, DC: NEA Publication, 1968), pp. 12, 15–17.

4. For a careful study of the rationale and effects of within-class grouping in one ghetto school, see Ray Rist, "Student Social Class and Teacher Expectations: The Self-Fulfilling Prophecy in Ghetto Education," *Harvard Educational Review, 40* (1970), 411–450.

5. Aaron Cicourel and John Kitsuse, *The Educational Decision-Makers* (New York: Bobbs-Merrill, 1963), describe the counselor as serving the school's and not the child's needs.

6. Special education refers to classes for students with particular and acute learning disabilities. The disability may be defined in terms of test scores, physical impediments (for example, classes for the blind, deaf and dumb, or perceptually handicapped), or psychological disturbances (such as classes for the emotionally disturbed). Special education classes are a relatively recent and increasingly common phenomenon. A recent national estimate of enrollment in special education concludes that 2,106,100 children (35 percent of those who need such help) are enrolled in some special program. Retarded children are somewhat better served than other children in need of special education — based on a prevalence estimate of 2.3 percent, close to one-half of retarded children are in special classes. Romaine Mackie, *Special Education in the United States: Statistics, 1948–1966* (New York: Teachers College Press, 1969), p. 39.

7. Ability grouping, or tracking, refers to the differential classification of students, ostensibly on the basis of aptitude, for instruction in the regular academic program. See Findley and Bryan, Ability Grouping, p. 4; NEA Research Division, Ability Grouping, p. 6.

8. See James Gallagher, "The Special Education: Contract for Mildly Handicapped Children," *Exceptional Children, 38* (1972), 527–529; "[D]ata collected informally by the Office of Education suggested that special education was *de facto*, a permanent placement. In a number of large city school systems far less than 10 percent of the children placed in special education classes are ever returned to regular education." *Report of the New York State Commission on the Quality, Cost and Financing of Elementary and Secondary Education*, 9B.2 (1972), pp. 9.22–9.39, offers one explanation for this phenomenon: children in special education classes are infrequently reevaluated. In New York City, during the school years 1969–1970, 1,603 retarded children had not been evaluated in over three years; 2,028 retarded children had not been evaluated in over five years. See also Jane Mercer, "Sociocultural Factors in the Education of Black and

Chicano Children," Paper presented at the 10th Annual Conference on Civil and Human Rights of Educators and Students, National Education Association, Washington, DC, February 1972; Jane Mercer, "Sociological Perspectives on Mild Mental Retardation," in *Social-Cultural Aspects of Mental Retardation,* ed. Carl Haywood (New York: Appleton-Century-Crofts, 1970), p. 287.

9. William Mehrens and Irwin Lehmann, *Standardized Tests in Education* (New York: Holt, Rinehart & Winston, 1969), p. 3.

10. For a fuller exposition, see Raymond Callahan, *Education and the Cult of Efficiency* (Chicago: University of Chicago Press, 1952).

11. Stratton D. Brooks, "Twenty-Eighth Annual Report of the Superintendent of Public Schools," in *Documents of the School Committee* (Boston: Boston City School Committee, 1908), p. 53.

12. See, e.g., Elwood Cubberly, "Foreword to Lewis Terman," in Lewis Terman, *The Measurement of Intelligence: An Explanation of and a Complete Guide for the Use of the Stanford Revision and Extension of the Binet-Simon Intelligence Scale* (Boston: Houghton Mifflin, 1916).

13. Certain critics charge that sorting is indeed all that schools do; see Florence Howe and Paul Lauter, "How the School System Is Rigged for Failure," *New York Review of Books, 14,* June 18, 1970, p. 14, or indeed all that they have ever done, Annie Stein, "Strategies for Failure," *Harvard Educational Review, 41* (1971), 158–204. See also Colin Greer, *The Great School Legend: A Revisionist Interpretation of American Public Education* (New York: Basic Books, 1972).

14. See Joan Lunn and Elsa Ferri, *Streaming in the Primary School* (New York: Fernhill House, 1970); W. Borg, *Ability Grouping in the Public Schools,* 2d ed. (Madison, WI: Dembar Educational Research Services, 1966); Maxine Mann, "What Does Ability Grouping Do to the Self-Concept?" *Childhood Education, 36* (1960), 357–360.

15. See Jules Henry, *Culture Against Man* (New York: Random House, 1963), pp. 283–322.

16. A recent study asked school officials why they favored ability grouping. The most common set of answers referred to the needs of teachers and administrators: "improves [teacher] attention to individual [student] needs," "facilitates curriculum planning," and "[makes] instruction easier." The second most frequently mentioned rationales refer to student benefits: "permits students to progress at their own learning rate," and "allows the student to compete on a more equitable basis." Findley and Bryan, *Ability Grouping,* p. 15.

17. Research Division, National Education Association, "Teachers' Opinion Poll: Ability Grouping," *NEA Journal, 57* (1968), 53.

18. Reginald Jones, "Labels and Stigma in Special Education," *Exceptional Children, 38* (1972), 561.

19. Hobson v. Hansen, 269 F. Supp. 401 (D.D.C. 1967).

20. Mortimer Garrison, Jr., and Donald Hammill, "Who Are the Retarded?" *Exceptional Children, 38* (1971), 13–18.

21. Garrison and Hammill, "Who Are the Retarded?" p. 20. One difficulty with the Garrison and Hammill study is that they, unlike the school districts they studied, used five different measures to determine retardation.

22. Walter Lippmann, "The Abuse of Tests," *New Republic, 32* (1922), 297–298.

23. Milton Schwebel, *Who Can Be Educated?* (New York: Grove Press, 1968), pp. 75–76.

24. See, e.g., Arthur Jensen, "How Much Can We Boost IQ and Scholastic Achievement?" *Harvard Educational Review, 39* (1969), 1–123.

25. Howe and Lauter, "How the School System Is Rigged," p. 14.

26. Brown v. Board of Education, 347 U.S. 483 (1954).

27. This article considers only the constitutional dimension of the classification issue. For a discussion of non-constitutional case law, see Stephen Goldstein, "The Scope and

Sources of School Board Authority to Regulate Student Conduct and Status: A Non-constitutional Analysis," *University of Pennsylvania Law Review, 117* (1969), 373. See also Elgin v. Silver, 15 Misc. 2d 864, 182 N.Y.S. 2d 669 (Sup. Ct. 1958); Board of Education v. State ex. rel. Goldman, 47 Ohio App. 417, 191 N.E. 914 (1934).

28. Hobson v. Hansen, 269 F. Supp. 401, 513 (D.D.C. 1967).

29. For example, Mills v. Board of Education, 348 F. Supp. 866 (D.D.C. 1972) (exclusion of children labeled as behavioral problems, mentally retarded, emotionally disturbed or hyperactive); Pennsylvania Association for Retarded Children v. Pennsylvania, 343 F. Supp. 279 (E.D. Pa. 1972) (consent decree enjoining exclusion of mentally retarded children).

30. Hosier v. Evans, 314 F. Supp. 316 (D.V.T. 1970).

31. For example, Ordway v. Hargraves, 323 F. Supp. 1155 (D. Mass. 1971).

32. See, e.g., Stewart v. Phillips, Civil No. 70–1199–F (D. Mass., February 8, 1971); reprinted in Harvard University Center for Law and Education, *Classification Materials* (Cambridge, MA: Author, 1972), p. 234 (denying defendants' motion for summary judgment); Diana v. California State Board of Educ., Civil No. 70–37 RFP (N.D. Cal. 1970) [reprinted in *Classification Materials,* p. 292] (consent decree); Spangler v. Pasadena City Board of Education, 311 F. Supp. 501, 504, 510–20 (C.D. Cal. 1970) (fact-finding in regard to grouping practices).

33. For example, Lemon v. Bossier Parish School Board, 444 F.2d 1400 (5th Circ. 1971).

34. See Frank Michelman, "The Supreme Court, 1968 Term-Foreword: On Protecting the Poor Through the Fourteenth Amendment," *Harvard Law Review, 83* (1969), 7.

35. See Frank Goodman, "De Facto School Segregation: A Constitutional and Empirical Analysis," *California Law Review, 60* (1972), 275.

36. Brown v. Board of Education, 347 U.S. 483, 493 (1954).

37. *Wall Street Journal,* March 22, 1972, p. 1, col. 1. Estimates of the number of excluded children range widely. See Task Force on Children Out of School, *The Way We Go To School: The Exclusion of Children in Boston* (Boston, MA: Beacon Press, 1971), p. 3, and 118 Cong. Rec. H1257 (daily ed. February 17, 1972; remarks of Congressman Vanik).

38. See *New York Times,* February 15, 1970, p. 1, col. 1 (children tested after year in which schools were closed for two months due to teachers' strike showed two months' loss in reading achievement); Robert Green and Louis Hofmann, "A Case Study of the Effects of Educational Deprivation on Southern Rural Negro Children," *Journal of Negro Education, 34* (1965), 327–341. The children studied by Green and Hofmann had attended school in Prince Edward County, Virginia, which closed its schools to avoid desegregation. Since the effects of school exclusion and the segregation controversy — either of which might have had adverse educational consequences — are inextricably linked, it is difficult to separate the impact of each adversity on achievement.

39. See, e.g., Borg, *Ability Grouping.*

40. See, e.g., Samuel Kirk, "Research in Education," in *Mental Retardation: A Review of Research,* ed. Harvey Stevens and Rick Heber (Chicago: University of Chicago Press, 1964).

41. G. Orville Johnson, "Special Education for the Mentally Handicapped — A Paradox," *Exceptional Children, 20* (1962), 62–66.

42. Reuvin Feuerstein, "A Dynamic Approach to the Causation, Prevention, and Alleviation of Retarded Performance," in *Social-Cultural Aspects of Mental Retardation,* ed. Carl Haywood (New York: Appleton-Century-Crofts, 1970), pp. 341–343.

43. Feuerstein, "A Dynamic Approach," p. 345; see also Aubrey Yates, *Behavior Therapy* (New York: John Wiley and Sons, 1970), p. 324.

44. See, e.g., Findley and Bryan, *Ability Grouping,* pp. 23–31.

45. Borg, *Ability Grouping,* p. 30.

46. NEA Research Division, *Ability Grouping,* p. 44.

47. James Coleman, "The Concept of Equality of Educational Opportunity," *Harvard Educational Review, 38* (1968), 7–23.

48. Erving Goffman, *Stigma: Notes on the Management of Spoiled Identity* (Englewood Cliffs, NJ: Prentice-Hall, 1963).

49. William Buss, "Procedural Due Process for School Discipline: Probing the Constitutional Outline," *University of Pennsylvania Law Review, 119* (1971), 545–577.

50. Mercer, "Sociocultural Factors."

51. Gallagher, "The Special Education."

52. "Putting the Child in Its Place," Unpublished paper, Harvard Center for Law and Education, 1972, p. 41.

53. See Robert Edgerton, *The Clock of Competence: Stigma in the Lives of the Mentally Retarded* (Berkeley: University of California Press, 1967).

54. Under the traditional equal protection doctrine, courts uphold legislatively imposed classifications which "bear some rational relationship to a legitimate state end." McDonald v. Board of Election Commissioners, 394 U.S. 802, 809 (1969); see "Developments in the Law — Equal Protection," *Harvard Law Review, 82* (1969), 1976–1987. This standard results in near-total deference to legislative discretion. The constitutional safeguard is offended only if the classification rests on grounds wholly irrelevant to the achievement of the state's objective. State legislatures are presumed to have acted within their constitutional power despite the fact that, in practice, their laws result in some inequality. A statutory discrimination will not be set aside if any state of acts reasonably may be conceived to justify it. McGowan v. Maryland, 366 U.S. 420, 425–426 (1961).

55. San Antonio Independent School District v. Rodriguez, 93 S. Ct. 1278 (1973). Where courts have identified an interest as fundamental they have required the state to show: a) that its interest in classifying is "compelling"; and b) that the means chosen to effectuate that interest are less onerous than available alternatives. See "Developments in the Law — Equal Protection." The result of applying such a test is predictable; the complainant invariably wins. See, e.g., Shapiro v. Thompson, 394 U.S. 618, 634 (1969); Loving v. Virginia, 388 U.S. 1, 9 (1967).

56. San Antonio v. Rodriguez, 93 S. Ct. 1278 (1973).

57. San Antonio v. Rodriguez, at 1295.

58. San Antonio v. Rodriguez, at 1297.

59. San Antonio v. Rodriguez, at 1310 (Stewart, J., concurring).

60. San Antonio v. Rodriguez, at 1332 (Marshall, J., dissenting).

61. Weber v. Aetna Casualty & Surety Co., 406 U.S. 164, 173 (1972).

62. Gerald Gunther, "The Supreme Court, 1971 Term-Foreword: In Search of Evolving Doctrine on a Changing Court: A Model for a Newer Equal Protection," *Harvard Law Review, 86* (1972), 24.

63. Prince v. Massachusetts, 321 U.S. 158 (1944).

64. Ginsberg v. New York, 390 U.S. 629 (1968).

65. Tinker v. Des Moines Independent Community School District, 393 U.S. 503, 511 (1969).

66. Even In re Gault, 397 U.S. 1 (1967), typically eulogized as protecting children from the excesses of juvenile justice, affords the child only a watered-down version of constitutional procedural protection. Earlier cases dealing with what could have been viewed as the rights of children were instead decided on the basis of the rights of parents or teachers. See, e.g., Pierce v. Society of Sisters, 268 U.S. 510 (1925); Meyer v. Nebraska, 262 U.S. 390 (1923). Even West Virginia State Board of Education v. Barnette, 319 U.S. 624 (1943), which came closest to recognizing an independent right in the child, also involved prosecution of the parents.

67. Tinker v. Des Moines, 393 U.S. 503 (1969).

68. Weber v. Aetna, 406 U.S. 164 (1972).

69. In re Green, 448 Pa. 338, 292 A.2d 387 (1972).

70. Chandler v. South Bend Community School Corp., Civil No. 71–S–51 (N.D. Ind., October 22, 1971).

71. Chandler v. South Bend, at 5.

72. See, e.g., Pierce v. Society of Sisters, 268 U.S. 510 (1925); Meyer v. Nebraska, 262 U.S. 390 (1923).

73. Tinker v. Des Moines Independent Community School District, 393 U.S. 503, 511 (1969).

74. See, e.g., San Antonio Independent School District v. Rodriguez, 93 S. Ct. 1278, 1298–99 (1973) (dictum) (denial of educational service); Shapiro v. Thompson, 394 U.S. 618, 633 (1969) (dictum) (exclusion of indigents); Ordway v. Hargreaves, 323 F. Supp. 1155 (D. Mass. 1971) (exclusion of pregnant students); Hosier v. Evans, 314 F. Supp. 316 (D.V.1, 1970) (exclusion of aliens).

75. Mills v. Board of Education, 348 F. Supp. 866, 878 (D.D.C. 1972); *accord,* Wolf v. Legislature, Civil No. 182, 646 (Utah District Court, January 8, 1969) [reprinted in *Classification Materials,* p. 171]; see Harrison v. Michigan, 350 F. Supp. 846 (E.D. Michigan 1972) (dictum).

76. McInnis v. Shapiro, 293 F. Supp. 327, 335 (N.D. Ill. 1968), aff'd mem. sub. nom. McInnis v. Ogilvie, 394 U.S. 322 (1969). See also Burruss v. Wilkerson, 319 F. Supp. 572 (W.D. Va. 1969), aff'd mem., 397 U.S. 44 (1970).

77. Mills v. Board of Education, 348 F. Supp. 866 (D.D.C. 1972); Pennsylvania Association for Retarded Children v. Pennsylvania, 343 F. Supp. 279 (E.D. Pa. 1972) (consent order).

78. Smuck v. Hobson, 408 F.2d 175, 187 (D.C. Circ. 1969).

79. Ragsdale v. Overholser, 281 F.2d 943, 950 (D.C. Cir. 1960) (concurring opinion).

80. Michael Young, *The Rise of the Meritocracy* (New York: Penguin Books, 1961), p. 49.

81. Hobson v. Hansen, 269 F. Supp. 401 (D.D.C. 1967).

82. Smuck v. Hobson, 408 F.2d 175, 189 (D.C. Cir. 1969) (en banc).

83. The following table, taken from Alfred Baumeister, *Mental Retardation: Appraisal, Education, and Rehabilitation* (Chicago: Aldine, 1967), p. 10, describes a system of classifying retardedness according to scores on two generally accepted IQ tests:

	I.Q. Range	
Level of Retardation	*Stanford-Binet Test*	*Wechsler Test*
Borderline	68–83	70–84
Mild	52–67	55–69
Moderate	36–51	40–54
Severe	20–35	25–39
Profound	below 20	below 25

84. See Anne Anastasi, "Some Implications of Cultural Factors for Test Construction," in *Testing Problems in Perspective,* ed. Anne Anastasi (Washington, DC: American Council on Education, 1966), pp. 453–456. The predictive validity of aptitude tests is far from perfect. "[T]he correlation between elementary school test scores and eventual educational attainment [years of schooling completed] seems to have hovered just under 0.60 for some decades." Jencks et al., *Inequality,* p. 144.

85. See, e.g., Banesh Hoffman, *The Tyranny of Testing* (New York: Crowell-Collier Press, 1962); Gerald Lesser, Gordon Fifer, and Donald Clark, "Mental Abilities of Children from Different Social Class and Cultural Groups," *Monographs of the Society for Research in Child Development, 30,* Serial No. 102 (1965).

86. Jane Franseth and Rose Koury, *Survey of Research on Grouping as Related to Pupil Learning,* (Washington, DC: U.S. Office of Education, 1966), p. 36.

87. In Hobson, school psychologists examined 1272 students assigned to the special education or basic track; almost two-thirds of them had been improperly classified by the school system. Smuck v. Hobson, 408 F. 2d 173, 187 (D.C. Cir. 1969) (en banc).

88. Hobson v. Hansen, 269 F. Supp. 401, 475 (D.D.C. 1967).

89. Hobson v. Hansen, 269 F. Supp. at 514.

90. The special education and ability-grouping research discussed in the context of equal opportunity arguments was carried out either in White or racially unspecified communities, and thus is of limited relevance. Since *Equality of Educational Opportunity* (Washington, DC: U.S. Office of Education, 1966) provides student performance information for only one point in time, it is difficult to mine that richest of education data sources for evidence of the consequences of reassigning students from one group to another, e.g., Marshall Smith, "Equality of Educational Opportunity: The Basic Findings Reconsidered," in *On Equality of Educational Opportunity,* ed. Frederick Mosteller and Daniel Moynihan (New York: Random House, 1972), pp. 69, 239, 313–315. (The report does not tell scholars and policymakers "what will happen if they change the status quo.")

91. James McPartland, "The Relative Influence of School and Classroom Desegregation on the Academic Achievement of Ninth Grade Negro Students," *Journal of Social Issues,* 25 (1969), 102. Tracking decisions also appear to have more significant effects for Blacks than Whites. While half of all White children assigned to a college track actually enter college, only a third of Whites in noncollege tracks continue their education beyond high school. For Blacks, the likelihood of college attendance is diminished even further by assignment to a noncollege track. Jencks et al., *Inequality,* pp. 156–158.

92. *Racial Isolation in the Public Schools* (Washington, DC: U.S. Commission on Civil Rights, 1967), pp. 86–87.

93. See, e.g., Loving v. Virginia, 388 U.S. 1 (1967).

94. Yick Wo v. Hopkins, 188 U.S. 356 (1886). Cases concerning jury discrimination, see, e.g., Turner v. Fouche, 396 U.S. 346 (1970), and municipal services discrimination, see, e.g., Hawkins v. Town of Shaw, 437 F.2d 1286 (5th Cir. 1971), *aff'd en banc* 461 F.2d 1171 (5th Cir. 1972), have focused on discriminatory application of ostensibly neutral policies.

95. Alexander v. Holmes County Board of Education, 396 U.S. 19, 20 (1969).

96. The possibility that tracking might produce such segregation apparently did not concern those who argued *Brown.* As Thurgood Marshall said: "I have no objection to academic segregation, only racial segregation. If they want to put all the dumb ones, White and Black, into the same school that is fine, provided they put all the smart ones, White and Black, into the same school." Jack Peltason, *Fifty-eight Lonely Men: Southern Federal Judges and School Desegregation* (New York: Harcourt, Brace Jovanovitch, 1961), p. 112.

97. Jefferson v. Hackney, 406 U.S. 535, 548 (1972).

98. The source of this argument remains United States v. Carolene Products Co., 304 U.S. 144, 152–153 n. 4 (1938): "[P]rejudice against discrete and singular minorities may be a special condition, which tends seriously to curtail the operation of those political processes ordinarily to be relied upon to protect minorities, and which may call for a correspondingly more searching judicial inquiry." That the claims of minorities do not always entitle them to such protection is made clear in Whitcomb v. Chavis, 403 U.S. 124, 153 (1971), where the Supreme Court characterized Black voters' claims of election district discrimination as embodying the disappointment of political losers, not warranting judicial intervention.

99. Hobson v. Hansen, 269 F. Supp. 401, 513 (D.D.C. 1967).

100. Hobson v. Hansen, at 497.
101. Hobson v. Hansen, at 513.
102. Hobson v. Hansen, 269 F. Supp. 401, 513 (D.D.C. 1967).
103. Hobson v. Hansen, at 514.
104. Larry P. v. Riles, 343 F. Supp. 1306 (N.D. Cal. 1972).
105. Larry P. v. Riles, at 1313.
106. Larry P. v. Riles.
107. Larry P. v. Riles, 343 F. Supp. 1306, 1314 (N.D. Cal. 1972).
108. Hannah v. Larche, 363 U.S. 442 (1969).
109. See, e.g., Warren Seavey, "Dismissal of Students: 'Due Process,'" *Harvard Law Review,* *70* (1957), 1406.
110. See Henry Foster, "Social Work, the Law and Social Action," *Social Casework, 45* (1964), 383–386. Robert O'Neill, "Justice Delayed and Justice Denied," *Supreme Court Review, 161* (1970), 184–195, identifies interests and values served by the due process hearing: a) accuracy and fairness, b) accountability, c) visibility and impartiality, d) consistency, and e) administrative integrity. O'Neill notes several governmental interests: a) collegiality and informality, b) flexibility in the dispensation of benefits, c) agency initiative, d) discretion and confidentiality, and e) minimization of expense — each of which is at least potentially impaired by the insistence on procedural formality.
111. Buss, "Procedural Due Process," p. 571.
112. Wisconsin v. Yoder, 406 U.S. 205 (1972).
113. Wisconsin v. Yoder, at 876; McMillan v. Board of Education, 430 F.2d 1145 (2d Cir. 1970), declares that: "If New York had determined to limit its financing of educational activities at the elementary level to maintaining public schools and to make no grants to further the education of children whose handicaps prevented them from participating in classes there, we would perceive no substantial basis for a claim of denial of equal protection." 430 F.2d at 1140.
114. Dixon v. Alabama State Board of Education, 294 F.2d 150 (5th Cir.), *cert, denied,* 368 U.S. 930 (1961); Wasson v. Trowbridge, 382 F.2d 807 (2d Cir. 1967): Goldwyn v. Allen, 54 Misc. 2d 94, 281 N.Y.S. 2d 899 (1967).
115. Mills v. Board of Education, 348 F. Supp. 866, 880 (D.D.C. 1972).
116. A comparison of the complexity and the importance of discipline and classification cases suggests the greater need of expert assistance — appointed, if necessary — in the latter cases. That retesting has revealed substantial school errors makes the need for such expert assistance all the stronger. See Smuck v. Hobson, 408 F.2d 175, 187 (D.C. Cir. 1969) (en banc): Stewart v. Phillips, Civ. No. 70–1199–F (E.D. Mass. 1971). See, e.g., Madera v. Board of Education, 386 F.2d 778 (2d Cir. 1967), *cert, denied,* 390 U.S. 1028 (1968).
117. Knight v. Board of Education, 48 F.R.D. 115 (E.D. N.Y. 1969).
118. Seymour Sarason, *The Culture of the School and the Problem of Change* (Boston: Allyn & Bacon, 1971).

Why Special Education Isn't Special

CARL MILOFSKY

As early as 1974, authors such as Carl Milofsky were critically examining the role of special education within the organizational structure of schools. Although special education was increasing in both size and sophistication, the results of research in this area disappointed Milofsky. In this article, Milofsky asserts that special education's failure to achieve optimal results for its students was due largely to the marginal status of special education professionals within schools and the district's administrative structures. He discovered that, far from reaching its goal of appropriately educating students with disabilities, special education was frequently used to alleviate problems such as discipline within schools. A major factor impeding program effectiveness was the failure of special educators to develop effective relationships with regular educators within their schools. Though dismayed by this finding, Milofsky documents successful school programs where regular and special educators worked closely together with the support of principals. These findings support a recurrent theme throughout this volume: the need to fundamentally restructure special education from its separate and marginal status — a theme that Thomas Skrtic deals with in depth in his 1991 article.

Many schoolchildren fail because they have one of a wide range of handicapping conditions. Kirk (1972) defines the "exceptional" child as one who deviates from the average or normal child: "1) in mental characteristics, 2) in sensory abilities, 3) in neuromuscular or physical characteristics, 4) in social or emotional behavior, 5) in communication abilities, or 6) in multiple handicaps to such an extent that he requires a modification of school practices, or special educational services, in order to develop to his maximum capacity" (p. 4). If this definition is broad, so are the special education programs that have been developed. The states of the arts of teaching, psychology, physiology, and medicine have not enabled special educators to diagnose with great specificity the causes of a child's learning problems or to design with much accuracy a program of instruction tailored to the child's needs. But several factors have encouraged people in these fields to acceler-ate their search.

First, the philosophy behind teaching special children has changed. Once thought ineducable, they are now viewed to benefit from instruction, al-though to varying degrees. The possibility of cognitive and emotional growth encourages professionals in the field to try to design better special education programs.

Second, many exceptional children used to go to private schools or special facilities offering different kinds of instruction for particular handicaps (Marver, 1974). They were not the public's responsibility. But increasingly there has been a movement to integrate special children into public schools. State and federal funds have been provided to public schools for the addi-tional services that special children require. Whether they are in self-con-tained classrooms within regular public schools or "mainstreamed" in regu-lar classrooms throughout the school, they need the attention and skills people trained to work with special children can provide. As a result, the demand for special education teachers, psychologists, and administrators in the public schools has increased markedly.

Finally, parents are becoming more informed about their handicapped child's right to a public education. Where parents are organized, they can provide pressure for better quality special education services within the public schools. For example, in Massachusetts the state legislature responded to organized parental pressure by passing Chapter 766 of the General Mas-sachusetts Laws, 1972, which provides for the most progressive public school special education program in the country (see also Kirp, Buss, & Kuriloff, 1974).

The results of this explosive growth in special education over the last quarter century (Keogh et al., 1972; Mackie, 1969), however, have been less than special. Evaluations of the effectiveness of such programs have shown few significant gains for children given special instruction or curricula. Ex-cept for severely mentally retarded children, who have responded to specific kinds of interventions,

> research concerning classes for children with more ambiguous handicaps —
> the educable mentally retarded, mildly emotionally disturbed and perceptually
> handicapped — reach quite different conclusions. Those programs do not
> tangibly benefit their students, whose equally handicapped counterparts
> placed in regular classes perform at least as well and without apparent detri-
> ment to their normal classmates. (Kirp, 1974, p. 19)

In part, special education's lack of success can be attributed to lack of knowledge about learning handicaps. It can also be explained by the severe shortage of trained special education teachers (Keogh et al., 1972; Rousseau & Schmidt, 1974). Many special education teachers have been pulled from the ranks of substitutes or have lacked the credentials to teach in regular classes. Degree programs in colleges of education have not produced sufficient numbers of special education teachers, or provided adequate in-service courses for regular teachers in charge of a special education class, although this situation seems to be changing. Moreover, special education classes in some schools have become "dumping grounds" for all the behavior- or discipline-problem children regular teachers cannot handle. Where this occurs, special education is strained even further to fit many different kinds of children, and its capacity for specialness for each child necessarily diminishes.

There is also an organizational explanation for the failure of special education. On an organizational chart, a bureau of special education, complete with its own teachers, psychologists, and administrators, frequently occupies a status equivalent to a division of elementary and secondary instruction. But special educators face chronic problems of access to regular school personnel and priorities. Unavoidably, the first commitment of the public schools is to the vast majority of students attending regular classes. Special education is a marginal enterprise. As such, its personnel face the same political obstacles to their access, power, autonomy, and program goals that many marginal enterprises in other organizations or systems confront. I contend that it is these obstacles, and the lack of recognition of and preparation for them, that undercut the effectiveness of special education programs in public schools today. This article attempts to document the extent to which regular teachers and administrators limit the ability of special educators to identify and screen children who will benefit from special education and to create and implement a range of appropriate special programs in schools. Evidence presented here comes from my observation of special education programs funded under the 1964 California Educationally Handicapped Minors Act (California Educational code, West's Annotated Codes, 1970), interviews with state and local program administrators, and observation of many meetings where students were evaluated and placed in special programs. These data are supplemented by the results of a survey of a large sample of special education teachers conducted in 1972 by Keogh et al.

Learning Disabilities and Administrative Dilemmas

At the core of problems public schools and special educators face is the difficulty of diagnosing educational handicaps (Grinspoon & Singer, 1972; Lambert & Grossman, 1964). In some cases, neurological defects can have striking effects:

> a) Sherwin is a slight, handsome, twelve-year-old boy. He is naturally quiet and introverted, so no one realized he was several years behind in reading skills

until an alert teacher of educationally handicapped (EH) children noticed him. Though Sherwin has been in a gifted class, attends summer institutes in entymology at a nearby college, can easily read words like "astronomy" and "exploration" and quickly tabbed me (correctly) as a sociologist, he cannot read words like "but," "and," or "in" because he has a perceptual handicap that causes him not to see letters. He can fill in the blanks when he reads "astronomy," but short words become alphabet soup, so he has never progressed beyond the second-grade level in reading achievement and has come to hate school.

b) Lars is a twelve-year-old boy who is extremely talkative and who looks precocious and intellectual with his floppy hair and dark-rimmed glasses. He gives anyone who will listen minute descriptions of how he will do each activity, what problems he foresees, and how he will overcome them. He is obviously bright but is terribly overactive. While he has some perceptual problems, his main learning difficulty is that he cannot sit in one spot long enough to do school work and is so hyperactive that he cannot be easily maintained in a regular class.

c) Erik, a ten-year-old boy, is Lars' opposite. He has been extremely quiet since he came to school, completely immersed in himself. It is hard to tell what his capabilities are or what the source of his behavior is. Teachers speculated that he was autistic during a school year in which he did not say a word. Much of his difficulty seems to stem from a chaotic and traumatic home life. Before his mute year in school he came home one day to find his mother's boyfriend dead in bed of an overdose of drugs. It took that year for him to begin to get over the shock. But he still often cannot remember his teacher's name and withdraws into a fantasy world as a teacher sits to read with him, only guessing at words and rarely reading.

The list could be extended considerably. In each case, children with apparently normal or superior capabilities are blocked by fairly specific incapacities.

Neurological problems are not always as clear as these I have mentioned. In many children, such handicaps are buried in school careers of disruptive failure or in quiet, often successful, coping with the problem. School officials guess that 20 percent to 30 percent of all children have such disabilities to some degree. But since teachers and parents rarely see reversal of numbers in writing or confusion of letters like *b, d, h, p,* and *q* as unusual, much less a sign of a neurological defect, children who have problems with reversals and closure often just struggle along. Teachers often insist that the problem should be corrected, but fail to offer advice on the cognitive devices a child could use to remember that his perception may be wrong and that he may have to make an adjustment before he writes. Highly motivated or intelligent children often work their way around such problems. Discussing neurological handicaps, one is surprised at the number of educated adults who say, "Oh yes, I used to do that." Children who are not greatly interested in school, however, or those who find it unpleasant and threatening, often do not work around their problems successfully. Minor neurological defects increase the risk that a child will become disruptive and will fail to learn.

Because neurological handicaps are worked into a child's way of adjusting to the demands of schooling, they are usually devilishly hard to find. A rebellious child, handicapped or not, generally does not perform well in school. It is hard to work with all the disruptive children in a school long enough and with enough rapport to decide whether their problems are caused by a neural lesion, slow cognitive maturation in some area, or other emotional or environmental variables. If a child's work seems to be average or better, school people may fail to screen her or him for some handicap that may be holding back even greater achievement.

The ambiguity of symptoms makes it difficult for school systems to select children for EH programs. The California program is limited to 2 percent of all children. But when a district has an average daily attendance of 40,000 students and just twenty psychologists who can spend only one or two days a week at each school, adequate screening is not possible. In the four districts I observed, only one of the state-mandated admissions and discharge committees spent more than an average of five minutes considering each child's problem and planning programs to address it before routinely passing them to an EH class. If there was space in a special education class, and if there was a 20-point discrepancy between a child's academic achievement and individually administered intelligence test scores, the psychologist's recommendation for placement was rarely questioned.

Not surprisingly, the children selected for special classes are predominantly the biggest troublemakers in each school. Children are selected because their teachers can no longer tolerate them in class and the principal has to find some solutions to the problems they have created. Removing a child from an escalating conflict situation can be important in limiting the educational and emotional damage it does to her or him. But deciding to remove children to EH classes depends mostly on administrative maintenance rather than concern for the child's development. The regular teacher and principal usually will not change their minds about placement, even if children are not benefiting from special education or if putting a particularly disruptive child in a special class will destroy the progress the other children in that class are making.

The effectiveness of EH classes varies, depending on the central administration of the district, the particular teacher conducting the class, the organizational stability of the school, and other factors. Some classes are models of successful intervention in the learning disabilities of children. These classes do not solely include behavior problems but, because of a successful screening program, include children whose classroom behavior suggests they could achieve at normal levels but are struggling with their schoolwork.

Other classes successfully resolve much of the frustration students feel and help them return to normal levels of school achievement, though it is not clear that this rehabilitation has anything to do with the identification and treatment of some learning disability they possess. Some classes do little for the academic achievement of children, but do manage to protect them from the frustration and anger of regular teachers. Here the classes function as crisis centers for their schools and include little successful teaching. In the least successful classes, the special program is in turmoil and was the victim of general hostility from the rest of the school.

This range of variation in special-class performance can be characterized by the difference in the way the special education teachers, their students, and the school psychologist relate to regular school personnel. In schools where principals understand something of the theory of teaching learning-disabled children, classes tend to be successful. In schools where regular teachers recognize the distinctive problems children with learning disorders have, where they do not see special classes solely as resources to lighten their teaching load or to remove difficult students from class, and where they are willing to accept additional responsibility to work with the special teacher and EH children, classes are likely to be more successful. In general, where regular school personnel do not strive to see the special class as a way of alleviating the organizational problems of the regular school administration, the special class is likely to be more successful. If the regular administration accepts that classes for the educationally handicapped are justified in their own terms, that is, that they will help students, and if it allows special classes to chart their own courses, they appear to be more successful.

Unfortunately, special education programs seem to exist to be subverted in some school districts. In many schools, regular teachers do not understand or support special education in general; therefore they cannot help by carefully screening trouble-making children from those who really need EH classes, by working closely with special teachers, or by welcoming EH children back into regular classrooms. In a survey of special educators, EH teachers found regular teachers unsympathetic to the needs of the special education class and unaccepting of EH students: only 22.2 percent of all EH teachers, and only 7.7 percent of those in predominantly Black districts, reported that regular teachers "understand" EH students; 48 percent of all regular teachers and 42.1 percent of those in predominantly Black districts are seen as accepting of EH students; other teachers were seen as supportive of special education by 47.5 percent of EH teachers; in Black districts, only 33.2 percent of the EH teachers saw other teachers as supportive. While EH teachers generally felt their students had definite defects of some sort, 32.7 percent saw prime benefits of EH classes to be improved social behavior, and 38.4 percent saw classes helping children to become "no problem [in a] regular class." In predominantly Black districts, the proportions were 46.2 percent and 53.8 percent (Keogh et al., pp. 66–88).

Special education programs can also be undercut by school administrators. Often supported with outside funds, these programs line the pockets of the general fund and in so doing justify their place in the school system. But when the goals of a program are displaced by the exploitation that goes on, one wonders why the programs are not simply terminated and the money distributed directly to the schools for operation of regular programs. One answer gained from the experience of the California Program for Educationally Handicapped Minors is that the administrative domination observed in these new programs, while unfortunate, occurs frequently in the early stages of the growth of new organizational bureaus. Although it may represent the beginnings of a *marginal* administration (Clark, 1956), it can also be a stage in the emergence of a distinctive organizational function and purpose.

In the years since EH programs were established, their personnel have faced two problems: developing the technical expertise necessary to help children and figuring a way of adjusting to the variety of political demands made by public school organizations. Their tasks have been difficult. Special educators have found that children with learning disabilities often have complicated problems dealing with school that have little to do with neurological handicaps: family problems, personality conflicts with school personnel, and careers of school disruption based on their early experiences of failure, to name a few. Special educators also have had to combat hostility from regular personnel who find the investment of money and personnel in a few children incongruous with the tradition of stretching educational dollars to cover the many other children in a school.

If they hold to their technical notion of what education for EH children ought to entail, special educators find themselves ignored and isolated by regular teachers and graced with few referrals. Special educators historically have had no place in the schools and usually they are treated distinctly as outsiders and intruders on the schooling process. To be effective, special educators have had to buy into the system, to give in to the exploitative efforts of regular school personnel because they have not known how to present their program so it would make sense in the context of the schools. While this can ease their isolation and gain them students, it can also undercut their autonomy and effectiveness. Both situations — isolation or exploitation — lead to few cases of special education classes successfully treating children and returning them to their regular classes. Understanding the current failure of programs for the educationally handicapped, however, demands understanding the causes and the extent of marginality for special education personnel.

An Outline of Special Educators' Roles

The School Psychologist

School psychologists serve counseling and assessment functions in schools. Most of them think the former is more important because they can help alter the disruptive careers of children before they develop a self-perpetuating cycle of conflict with school officials. Unfortunately, regular school personnel expect psychologists to spend most of their time on assessment. This is partly because the difficult counseling task is rarely done well in schools, and principals and teachers have little evidence of what it can accomplish (McIntyre, 1969). But it is largely because psychologists are seen as the experts who can test students and assess their abilities. As such, they are a major factor in the process of assigning children to special classes.

This process usually begins when a teacher tells the principal that a child is a behavior problem or is exhibiting some kind of learning difficulty that the regular teacher cannot overcome. The principal may first try to work the problem through with the teacher, but usually activates the next step of the process by filling out a form requesting that a psychologist examine the child.

In most California districts, psychologists are assigned to serve four or five schools. They spend one or two days a week at each school processing requests, observing classes, meeting with teachers and principals, and administering psychological tests to children. They also often spend their day looking for and visiting with parents. When the psychologist receives a request for services, he or she tries to meet with the teacher and principal as soon as possible. Some principals are what psychologists consider passive; that is, they refer many children to psychologists rather than supporting teachers to maintain difficult children in their classes or moving children to other classes when they cause problems. Other principals are considered independent; that is, they decide to place children in special classes and may use the psychologist only to validate that decision. The psychologist must try to get a sense of how the principal views special education placement and how urgent it is for a particular child.

If a child is a high-priority referral for the principal, the psychologist observes him or her in class, discusses the child's problems with the teacher and parents, and then gives the child intelligence and aptitude tests. The child is also seen by a speech therapist. At the same time, parents provide medical reports to the school nurse, who may contact the child's doctor and the hospital where he or she was born in search of medical problems that might affect learning. After these diagnostic steps are taken, the psychologist compiles a report on the child's problems. As the evaluation progresses, the psychologist, the principal, and relevant special education staff people informally decide where the child ought to be placed. When this decision is made, the psychologist makes a presentation to a district-wide screening committee that reviews all recommended special-class placements.

The permanent screening committee is composed of a special education administrator, a doctor or nurse, a psychologist, and perhaps one or two teachers. In addition, the psychologist, the school nurse, the school speech therapist, and occasionally other school officials attend the presentation. In most districts, the committee meeting makes few real decisions. The important ones have been made prior to the meeting. The committee serves primarily an organizational auditing function by ensuring that all necessary forms have been completed, that all steps have been taken, and that there is space for the child in a class. The committee also translates the psychologist's long report into language that fits the requirements of state laws about diagnosis and planning for treatment. As mentioned earlier, in the four districts I observed, only one committee spent more than an average of five minutes screening each child before assigning him or her to an EH program.

The organizational labeling process varies between districts and with the people involved. But in most schools, the psychologist has responsibility for deciding which children will be placed in special classes. Given this power, the psychologist could refuse to place children who would not clearly benefit from special programs. But decisions seldom are this clear cut. If a psychologist does not think a particular special education teacher is effective, he or she may be reluctant to refer children who have real learning problems to the class. On the other hand, a special class can be a useful resource for the school despite an ineffective teacher. Regular teachers get into battles of wills or have other emotional crises with some children, and all would benefit from separation. Since children often learn better (or at least are more comfortable) in the more intimate setting a special education class provides, regardless of whether they have learning deficiencies, a psychologist may use the special education class to resolve the problems he or she sees in regular classrooms.

If the psychologist is interested in helping children, he or she must have an ongoing, constructive relationship with regular teachers. If teachers have confidence in the sympathy, interest, and intelligence of the psychologist, many problems can be resolved before children develop serious secondary disturbances. For example, a psychologist reported one case where a child continually did inappropriate things like standing and talking in the middle of story time, giggling at the wrong time, and in many other ways disrupting the class. The teacher was irritated by the constant interruptions and saw this behavior as evidence that the child was slow. When the psychologist came to observe, it was clear to him that the child had normal intelligence but that he had trouble recognizing the intrinsic rules of the classroom situation. He also noted that the other children were usually as angry as the teacher at the disruptions and often told the boy to sit down and be quiet. The psychologist suggested to the teacher that if she were tolerant of the situation, the social pressure from other children might well solve the problem. He warned the teacher about the danger of provoking a confrontation and asked her to wait several months to see if things would clear up. The teacher was relieved, agreed to wait, and the problem did clear up. Without the confidence of the teacher, the psychologist could not have intervened as frankly as he did. The problem could have escalated, seriously damaging the boy's attitude toward school and making teaching more difficult for his teacher.

Psychologists do not easily establish rapport with regular personnel. Teachers resent the increasing proportion of the school budget spent on Ph.D.s who sit in offices with cushy jobs, never facing the firing line. School psychologists fit into this category of high-priced professionals whose value in cost-benefit terms can be questioned. Teachers argue that the money poured into specialists' salaries could be used to reduce class size, hire teacher aides, improve the playgrounds, or simply reduce taxes. Teachers and their unions are suspicious of special programs unless they see specialists in their school working and helping to solve real problems in a constructive way. Psychologists often feel vaguely uncomfortable, fearing they will suffer if funds for their programs stand between teachers and their raises. In one school, there were sixty-five members of the school staff, and only twenty-four were teachers. Teachers frequently complained about not knowing all these extra staff people, much less what they did. Not infrequently, an angry teacher would corner a visiting administrator of a special program, pressing him or her to detail where the $76.00 per gifted child in her class went and asking how to obtain some of the money for needed classroom resources.

Another important block to effective rapport between teachers and psychologists is the instability of psychologists' assignments in most districts. Special programs are always understaffed and psychologists overworked. District administrators often fill vacancies by shifting staff from one school to another. Distressingly often, even experienced staff have worked in their present school for only a short time. As a result, psychologists are unfamiliar with case histories, with the children already in special education classes in their jurisdiction, with the politics of the school, or with the strengths and weaknesses of regular and special education teachers. Thus, psychologists may find it difficult to weigh claims that particular children have problems or that particular teachers cannot tolerate too much conflict in their classes. But psychologists cannot seek needed information too aggressively; if they appear too suspicious, teachers will see them as patronizing and nosy featherbedders.

Psychologists, therefore, are outsiders, marginal to the local school. Lack of sure-footedness in school politics borne of frequent reassignments often forces psychologists to act with the interests of regular school administrative demands in mind rather than follow the postulates of clinical psychology. To some extent, such compromise is necessary in all school work. Successful student counseling hinges on managing attitudes, self-images, and practices of teachers and principals, as well as those of students. But the optimal mix between politics and psychology can only be achieved when regular school personnel think psychologists are effective. Since psychologists encounter frequent disruptions of their professional relationships, this confidence is hard to achieve. Frustrated in their strivings to build effective organizational roles, psychologists must buy into the organizational system by proving their interest or usefulness. This prevents them from being too critical or stingy with favors and can lead them to support the administrative order more than the needs of children. Their counseling role continually is subverted "for the time being."

Special Education Teachers

Special education teachers are isolated from each other because special education classes are dispersed throughout the school system. All teachers share many of the same strains, but teachers of the educationally handicapped are subject to unusual pressures. Children in special education classes often present serious discipline problems and, despite the teacher's best efforts, may not learn. Since the special education teacher's small amount of free time in school is spent with regular personnel who may not be aware of the unique problems of supervising a special class, the emotional support and task-related guidance necessary for gaining confidence on the job are often lacking.

Special education teachers are alienated from regular personnel. This is partly due to differences in the objectives and methods of their programs, but more important are differences in the status of the two groups in the organizational framework of the public school. Instructors in educationally handicapped programs are expected to be specialists, trained to handle unusually difficult teaching problems and to consult with regular teachers. But over the past quarter century, special education teachers have been largely untrained and ill-equipped to handle the educational problems set them. Among Keogh et al.'s (1972, pp. 22, 44) sample of teachers, only 18.9 percent of teachers for the educationally handicapped held special education credentials. Of the administrators sampled, 75 percent reported that they do not require regular teaching experience when they hire teachers for the educationally handicapped. Because of a nationwide shortage of trained special teachers (Rousseau & Schmidt, 1974), school districts have hired regular teachers for their educationally handicapped programs. Given the difficulties associated with teaching educationally handicapped children, experienced teachers rarely accept these posts. Teachers unable to find other jobs or substitutes seeking permanent positions are hired instead.

Often young and inexperienced, special education teachers are rarely accepted as specialists from whom regular teachers can seek advice or to whom they could entrust their most challenging teaching problems. One regular teacher with twenty years of experience felt that students with discipline and learning problems would have a better chance of resolving them in her class than if assigned to an incompetent special education teacher. Because of such attitudes, all special teachers have difficulty gaining legitimacy for their official role. But even when they are well-trained master teachers, special education teachers find it hard to gain acceptance from the regular school community. In a school I observed with such a master teacher, the students referred to the EH class were all behavior problems, not all of whom were diagnosed to have educational handicaps. I occasionally heard regular teachers sneer about those awful "little LDs" (learning deficiency students) or "MRs" (incorrectly labeling them mentally retarded). This prejudice against children in EH classes is extended to the special education teachers.

Perhaps the most isolating factor is that the school schedule does not often allow a special teacher to participate to any great degree in the interaction in the teachers' room. One can only appreciate the importance of this interaction as a device for mutual support after having worked in a classroom and taken part in lunchtime banter for several months (see McIntyre, 1969, pp. 48–55). It is extremely therapeutic for teachers to complain to each other about how difficult it is to teach Johnny or Sharon or to trade relevant anecdotes. Since most teachers in a primary school will have many of the same children through the years or will get to know all the brothers and sisters in a family, teachers can sympathize by relating tales about the same students or their siblings. While this can have the negative effect of setting up erroneous expectations based on the first teacher's or sibling's experience in school, it can be useful when done sensitively. Teachers can give each other helpful suggestions about handling specific students' problems or explain family difficulties that may influence how teachers interpret children's behavior in school.

The special education teacher who is cut off from such interaction loses many of the organizational benefits of the school but still must heed its constraints. If the special education teacher must hurry to another school during the regular lunch hour, he or she misses the incremental comparing of notes that spells out what teachers expect of each other. Both the special education and regular teachers miss the realization that their problems are similar. The special education teacher cannot participate fully when conflicts among teachers or between teachers and the principal develop. Alliances during such disagreements are important in cementing confidence among teachers (see Coser, 1956) and can pay important dividends later if a teacher needs to ask others for help in some difficult situation.

Exclusion from the coffee-room clique seems a trivial denial on the surface. But teaching is a naturally isolating and frustrating job under any circumstances. The special teacher receives little support from administrators or attention from the already harried psychologist. Unless a comforting audience of local teachers is available, the special teacher increasingly feels that he or she is failing the students, cannot handle their problems, must force them to work against their will, and is not contributing to the welfare of the school. He or she may lose a sense of reasonable goals and may have difficulty deciding what kinds of outcomes can be expected after a year of teaching.

As the special education teacher loses this sense of direction and confidence, he or she tends to be exploited by other people at the school. Where a special education teacher has not worked out a role through frequent informal interaction with other school personnel, he or she tends to take on more than an equal share. The special teacher is not protected by group norms that define how much is expected of a teacher. If a special education class has extra resources or fewer students than regular classrooms, then despite the special education teacher's conviction that he or she is working very hard at teaching, the principal and other teachers may disagree. To compensate for perceived advantages, they may ask special education teachers to do more around the school. Unless other teachers know from day-to-day exposure that the special teacher is working hard, he or she is likely to be assigned extra jobs. Ultimately, this sort of diversion can leave the special teacher with little time for his or her own teaching.

The following account a teacher gives of her struggle for independence illustrates how special education teachers can be exploited and suggests a solution to this problem. Miss Kerner had had no special education training but was hired in mid-year to teach EH children after having served as a substitute in the district. Her first teaching assignment was a typical discipline class, composed mostly of fifth- and sixth-grade boys who were considered troublemakers. She struggled with them during the spring while trying to learn the theories for training children with learning deficiencies. She soon began trying to educate regular teachers about the typical symptoms of mild neurological problems and instituted an after-school class for children who tended to reverse letters. Other teachers cooperated by sending students to her, and soon she had a class of thirty "normal" students from the one school. Teachers soon learned to identify children with the kinds of problems she could help resolve and found her an effective resource. They also became familiar with concrete strategies they could use in routine teaching to help children with less severe problems.

Despite this auspicious start, the principal assigned Miss Kerner to work as a curriculum consultant in an experimental program the school was undertaking. The assignment apparently stemmed from his observation that she liked working with regular teachers and wanted to keep children with learning problems in the regular classroom where possible. The assignment completely disrupted her teaching program, however, and represented a straightforward diversion of resources intended for special education. Although she was assigned to help a class that contained one EH student, she claimed that *that* student was the one least likely of all the EH students to benefit from individual help in the regular class. Instead, she felt that he would benefit most from the small-group work the learning-disabilities class allowed. The principal arranged her schedule so that she never had more than twenty minutes free at a time to work with her other learning-disabled students. The special class was destroyed by her assignment, though that class was her primary responsibility.

Furious at this exploitation, Miss Kerner began using every method she could think of to force the school to change her assignment. This was particularly difficult because the head of special education for the school district had agreed to the new arrangement. As she worked to fulfill her assigned responsibilities to her regular teaching team — she wanted to be sure that her regular teacher friends were not swamped with work because of her rebellion — Miss Kerner began organizing the parents of her students for an assault on the school board. Threatening lawsuits and ultimately forcing a state audit of the district's special education program, Miss Kerner finally forced her supervisors to allow her to arrange the schedule that best supported her special teaching responsibilities. The extra responsibilities were withdrawn the next fall. To her surprise, neither the other teachers nor the principal resented her action in the end and instead fully supported her role. Apparently, the episode served an educational function for other school personnel who now knew more clearly what Miss Kerner was supposed to be doing and what responsibilities fit with her job.

Miss Kerner's case is unusual because special education teachers are not usually taken advantage of so openly, nor are they often willing to fight for their professional rights. Perhaps, too, in a less flexible school district she would have been fired. It illustrates, however, that efforts to project new responsibilities on others is a fairly routine practice in public schools, and that assertiveness is a prerequisite for establishing the importance of one's professional activities. Special education teachers tend to be marginal in schools, and they are pushed to take on extra responsibilities. Since there is a high level of inexperience among special education teachers, and because they usually receive little professional support from other special education personnel or regular teachers, special education teachers have trouble defining the limits of their roles. Consequently, they find themselves overworked and feel they are not achieving what they are expected to do. Many leave special education positions as soon as the opportunity arises. This sense of failure supports a cycle of constant turnover, high levels of inexperience, lack of professional cohesion among special education teachers, and continued ineffectiveness of many classes.

Special Education Administrators

Special education administrations are typically overworked and understaffed. Their largest responsibility is to psychologists and special education teachers in the field. But the amount of routine administrative work that must be done often occupies most of their time. They must contact special education teachers at least every two or three weeks so attendance records can be kept up-to-date for the state's auditors and so materials can be ordered and special projects arranged. The central administration must keep abreast of the students whom psychologists are processing for the screening committee. Preparing for these meetings requires a prodigious amount of paperwork, most of which is required by state law. This must be coordinated with the fieldwork done by psychologists. These mundane tasks absorb virtually all of the time of the higher level administrators in special education departments.

While paperwork consumes much time, many administrative tasks are not performed successfully. While administrative organization and procedures are clear and orderly, conforming to state guidelines, 34 percent of all teachers and 46 percent of those in Black districts reported not receiving the program prescriptions for their students required by state law. Only 55 percent of students in educable mentally retarded classes (EMR, another special education program) in districts with mostly Black pupils had the required parental permission forms on file. While 80 percent of EH students received yearly reevaluations in accordance with state law, the percentage drops to 73 percent in Black districts; 47.8 percent of EMR students received reevaluations at least yearly (Keogh et al., 1972, pp. 55, 57, 72, 78, 84).

Bureaucratic details keep supervisors from actively helping teachers and psychologists work out substantive or political difficulties in the school. When supervisors visit, there is just enough time for the local personnel to share their troubles and for the central office representative to assure them that they are doing a good job. But since the special education division does not have a strong presence in the hierarchy of most school districts, these assurances are not helpful. A special education teacher is evaluated primarily by the regular school principal, who may have her or him removed from the school by writing a negative evaluation. Special education administrators cannot easily override a principal's rejection of a teacher. As a result, they have neither the inclination nor the expertise to advise local special education personnel about how they might define and protect their positions from the expansionist tendencies of the regular administration.

Indeed, the special education administration has its own difficulties maintaining its independence from the regular administration. The head of the division must wear two hats: one as the chief professional planner for special teaching and a second as the agent of the superintendent. These two roles often are in conflict. The assistant superintendent of special services must oversee the coordination of special and regular programs. While he or she must ensure that special programs are run with sufficient funds from outside sources, he or she may not be able to resist the demands of the superintendent or school board to use those funds for regular school needs.

This weakness in the top administration of special education is perhaps the key to the overall marginality of special education in public schools. The state audit of special education that Miss Kerner's action precipitated showed that in her district, 30 percent of special education money was used to pay for overhead, twice the amount acceptable under state guidelines. In addition, a building constructed from EH money was being used for regular classes. Following the audit, Miss Kerner's budget for teaching materials increased more than fivefold. Such excessive diversion of resources may be the exception, but observation of special education classes suggests they do not receive the yearly state expenditure of $1,880 per child.

Marginality and the Life Cycle of Bureaus

As these special education roles have emerged, their shape has, in many instances, been more strongly influenced by the demands of regular school administrations than by the goals of EH programs. While special education programs and personnel are intended to address the problems of children with psycho-linguistic learning disorders, those goals are clearly secondary in the operation of many programs. Student assignments, scheduling, curriculum structure, and psychologists' activities are not always planned best to meet the specific learning needs of EH children. Rather, they are oriented to help principals make teachers' lives easier and to keep regular schools running smoothly. The goals of the special education program are displaced and its activities become satellite programs, marginal to the regular program with little real content of their own.

In examining special educators' roles, however, such pessimism does not do justice to the achievements of some special educators. One psychologist I observed finds time to consult with teachers in their classrooms and makes constructive suggestions about how crises can be averted without removing a student from the classroom. Another assertive special education teacher was able to resist the exploitative tendencies of the regular structure and form constructive relationships with regular personnel. And in some districts, at least, the special education administration has retained enough fiscal integrity to offer substantial support to teachers of learning-disabled children. In these situations, special education programs were effective. They allowed intervention in careers of educational failure due primarily to perceptual or psychological problems.

It is my contention that special education programs are likely to succeed in situations where certain conditions are favorable. Those conditions are primarily related to what might be called *organizational maturity*. The apparent failure of many EH programs is due primarily to their inability to establish certain institutional qualities that allow a part of an organization (in this case, a bureau of special education) to pursue a distinctive purpose while maintaining mutually advantageous relationships with the larger organization (the regular school).

Throughout the earlier descriptions of special educators' roles, the most persistent inadequacy of personnel was that they did not know how to assert the need for their particular skill in the political context of the local school organization. Special educators do not have a strong sense of organizational *mission* (Selznick, 1957). Nor is their *technical rationality* sufficiently developed (Thompson, 1967). They do not know how to apply special education program guidelines to specific problems and relationships with other subdivisions of the school system. Special education functions are put aside in many cases because special educators allow themselves to be either dominated or *co-opted* (Selznick, 1966, pp. 217–226, 259–261).

These may add up to the same thing. If special educators show any hesitation or weakness, the regular administration defines a purpose for them. Special educators cannot defend themselves against this appropriation. With co-optation, special educators purposely set aside their personal goals to seek roles that regular educators will find important. Here, special educators strive to ingratiate themselves with the regular education structure, hoping that later they will be able to find ways of using their training and skills in an organizationally viable fashion. In both these situations, special educators abandon their programs because they do not know how to respond to the constraints and interferences of unfamiliar organizational situations. With experience, special educators could learn to combat interference from others in the public school organization and would increasingly manage to run their special education classes as they saw fit.

The literature of organizational theory documents that such a positive outcome is far from certain, however. The sort of organizational marginality special education is experiencing can be a first step in the emergence of an independent bureau. But it can also be a period of organizational uncertainty during which the program can either disintegrate or retain its marginality to the stronger organization (Clark, 1956). EMR programs suffered the latter type of status quo for many years, and this certainly could be the dominant pattern for EH programs (Goldstein, Moss, & Jordan, 1965, pp. 1–15).

There are a number of indications that EH programs will become relatively stronger in the coming years:

1. Since programs for EH students are based on an academic speciality in which disability is defined in terms of specific therapeutic techniques, improvement of these techniques will make identification and treatment of EH children more accurate and successful. As new knowledge about disabilities is communicated to special educators, it will become easier for them to distinguish children who are or are not appropriately placed in their classes.

2. More special education classes, especially in middle-class neighborhoods, have led to the emergence of active parents' groups, such as the California Association for Neurologically Handicapped Children, which monitor the special education programs of their school districts. As these groups gain experience in dealing with school districts, they sharpen their knowledge of how their children need to be taught. They can support the integrity of special programs and discourage schools from appropriating special educational resources.

3. Over time, more and more teachers will become experienced special education teachers. Gaining specific training will enable teachers to survive in their particular schools and also will broaden their sense of professionalism (Clark, 1956, pp. 148–150). New teachers will have a source of support to help them define their goals, improve their teaching techniques, and navigate the often troubled political waters of local schools.

Despite these strengthening factors, special education will have difficulty gaining full parity with regular education since the mission of public education as a whole is based on normal children and regular classrooms.

Supplemental Programs and the
Problems of Managing School Politics

I have argued that public school special education often fails to be special because it is marginal to the larger regular school organization and because special educators tend not to be sufficiently professional. From this perspective, the breakdown in programs may be seen as a predictable outcome of conflicts between professions and of growing organizational subdivisions.

In fact, the problem is deeper than this. Public schools are intensely political and, unless these politics are understood and accounted for in program planning, new programs that are organizationally subordinate will be exploited. Special educators have a highly developed professional structure and an elaborate technology. The problem is that their expertise can be used by school administrators to garner additional resources or take independence away from regular teachers. Unless they can prevent such subversion from occurring, they run the risk of alienating their regular colleagues and making them doubt the value of special education techniques.

To the extent that special education programs serve children with chronic and rather severe deficiencies, like those of Sherwin and Lars described at the beginning of this article, or that they handle primarily discipline problems, the observable effects of a special class may be minimal, despite psychological benefits to students (see Koppitz, 1971). Under these conditions, unless a special education teacher can gain the respect and confidence of regular educators, the special program is in danger of political domination.

One possible solution to reduce special education's alienation from regular programs is to integrate them. This approach, called mainstreaming, is at the core of the proposed California Master Plan for Special Education (California Assembly Bill 4640, 1973–1974 Regular Session). In it, special education teachers assist regular teachers by suggesting ways of working with handicapped children in regular classes. More cooperation and contact is established, and special instruction is provided. In one school observed for this study, a program was successfully mainstreaming blind children. However, unless special education teachers are carefully trained and are able to work with teachers as equals rather than as experts telling teachers how to do their jobs, it is doubtful that they would have fewer political problems with mainstreaming than they do now.

Two other solutions suggest themselves. First, professional training programs for all kinds of teachers, but particularly those preparing instructors and psychologists for special education programs, should recognize the centrality of organizational politics in schools. This concern has been largely lacking in research, as well as in teacher-training programs. Improving special educators' abilities to handle their relations with regular personnel is an important but long-term solution.

Second, perhaps special education as it is traditionally conceived is impossible and should be abandoned in favor of a system of organizational troubleshooters. They might be counselors trained in psychology and master teachers much like special educators, but their prime focus would be to help regular teachers identify and plan alternative courses of action when traditional school programs fail. By recognizing the importance of this role and providing sufficient flexibility to allow short-term changes in programs and class assignments, schools could ensure that difficult students receive appropriate instruction.

Solutions such as these are a long way from the student-centered, isolated rehabilitation programs that have dominated recent work on remediation of neurological handicaps. Education in this country generally means public education, however. If new teaching methods are to be introduced on a broad scale, the organizational problems likely to arise with their implementation must be thoroughly considered. Unless special education teachers and psychologists have access to children who are amenable to treatment, elaborate training techniques will do little good. And unless they are able to respond to complex community and administrative problems that produce classroom failure, oftentimes more severe than those emerging from neurological handicaps, special education personnel will never be sufficiently respected or allowed to do their work. In the past, failure to recognize these issues has prevented special education from being special in many schools. Unless they are incorporated into programs soon, we may expect a long wait for truly effective programs for neurologically handicapped children.

References

California Assembly Bill 4040, 1973–1974 Regular Session.

California Educational Code. (1970). West's Annotated Codes, Ch. 7.1, Sec. 6750.

Clark, B. R. (1956). *Adult education in transition: A study of institutional security.* Berkeley: University of California Press.

Coser, L. A. (1956). *The functions of social conflict.* New York: Free Press.

Goldstein, H., Moss, J. W., & Jordan, L. J. (1965). *The efficacy of special class training on the development of mentally retarded children* (U.S.O.E. Cooperative Research Project No. 619). Urbana: University of Illinois.

Grinspoon, L., & Singer, A. (1973). Amphetamines in the treatment of hyperkinetic children. *Harvard Educational Review, 43,* 515–555.

Keogh, B. K., et al. (1972). *Programs for educationally handicapped and educable mentally retarded pupils: Review and recommendations* (Technical Report SERP 1972-A11; Contract No. 4730 between the California State Department of Education and the University of California, Los Angeles). Los Angeles: University of California.

Kirk, S. A. (1972). *Educating exceptional children.* Boston: Houghton Mifflin.

Kirp, D. L. (1973). Schools as sorters: The constitutional and policy implications of student classification. *University of Pennsylvania Law Review, 121,* 705–797.

Kirp, D. L. (1974). Student classification, public policy, and the courts. *Harvard Educational Review, 44,* 7–52.

Kirp, D. L., Buss, W., & Kuriloff, P. (1974). Legal reform in special education: Empirical studies and procedural proposals. *California Law Review, 62,* 40–155.

Koppitz, E. M. (1971). *Children with learning disabilities: A five-year follow-up study.* New York: Grune & Stratton.

Lambert, N., & Grossman, H. (1964). *Problems determining the etiology of learning and behavior handicaps.* Sacramento: California Department of Education. (ERIC Document Reproduction Service No. ED 22269)

Marver, J. (1974). *An analysis of the allocation of state resources for exceptional children between public and private school programs.* Unpublished master's thesis, Graduate School of Public Policy, University of California, Berkeley.

McIntyre, D. (1969). Two schools, one psychologist. In F. Kaplan & S. B. Sarason (Eds.), *The psycho-educational clinic: Vol. 4.* Boston: Massachusetts Department of Mental Health.

Mackie, R. (1969). *Special education in the United States: Statistics, 1948–1966.* New York: Teachers College Press.

Rousseau, J., & Schmidt, K. (1974). 28,000 special ed jobs created. *Learning, 2*(8), 58–59.

Selznick, P. (1957). *Leadership in administration.* New York: Harper & Row.

Selznick, P. (1966). *TVA and the grassroots: A study in the sociology of formal organizations.* New York: Harper & Row.

Thompson, J. D. (1967). *Organizations in action.* New York: McGraw-Hill.

Data for this paper were gathered during two years of research on slow learning and school classification procedures. This work was partially funded by the Ford Foundation Funded Childhood and Government Project, Boalt Law School, University of California, Berkeley, and through the Project on Classification of Exceptional Children. The field work for this paper was done in San Francisco Bay Area schools as part of my work as a graduate student in the Sociology Department of the University of California, Berkeley.

This work would never have reached its current state without the accurate criticisms and patient interest of Professor David L. Kirp, Graduate School of Public Policy, University of California, Berkeley. Many thanks are also due my teachers, Barbara Heyns, Gloria Bradley, Hazel Gardiner, and the Hamilton Eleven, "those little LDs." Gail Saliterman has been very helpful in final preparation of the manuscript.

Engendering Change in Special Education Practices

MILTON BUDOFF

The genesis and initial implementation phases of Massachusetts' pioneering compre-
hensive special education law, Chapter 766, which was enacted in 1972, are detailed
by Milton Budoff in this 1975 article. The author, a participant in the advocacy
coalition that passed the law, traces the origins of the political foundation of the
special education reform movement back to concern over the inappropriate placement
of minority students and the failure to provide additional services to students appro-
priately placed. Much of the initial impetus for the law's passage resulted from
concerns about practices within the Boston Public Schools, which evolved into a
statewide coalition powerful enough to pass a sweeping special education law. The
new law incorporated the principles of individualization, mainstreaming, multidis-
ciplinary staffing, and due process review; these principles were later incorporated
into PL 94-142. Budoff continues to detail the extensive implementation problems
experienced in the first years of the law's enactment, including the continuation of
separate placements, the failure of the State Department of Education to provide
appropriate guidelines and training, and the imposition of cumbersome and coun-
terproductive regulations. However, he acknowledges that, overall, significant prog-
ress resulted from the new law. Budoff's piece is valuable, not only in its early
examination of persistent problems in the implementation of special education reform,
but also in its description of the role of advocacy in forcing change in special
education — a role that has grown and continues to have a major influence in
special education.

On July 18, 1972, the Massachusetts legislature passed Chapter 766, an educational bill of rights for the special needs child. As stated in the Preamble:

> This act is designed to remedy past inadequacies and inequities by defining
> the needs of children requiring special education in a broad and flexible
> manner . . . by providing the opportunity for a full range of special education
> programs for children requiring special education; by requiring that a program
> which holds out the promise of being special actually benefits children as-
> signed thereto.[1]

Harvard Educational Review Vol. 45 No. 4 November 1975

Chapter 766 prescribes an omnibus reform of the philosophy, structure, and practice of special education services. The law calls for comprehensive evaluation of the child, individualized and educationally effective programming, frequent reevaluations, strong parental involvement, an explicit due process system by which parents can appeal decisions, and advisory commissions of parents and professionals. All children between the ages of three and twenty-one, regardless of their degree of handicap, are entitled to an educational program in a setting that maximizes contact with their nonhandicapped peers.

The law is a truly radical piece of legislation that mandates many practices advocated by critics of public schools. While the law is aimed at the child with special educational needs, its philosophy is appropriate to the needs of all children who are, in fact, "special" in their idiosyncratic requirements. In a variety of ways, the law broadens the goals and responsibilities of education beyond a narrow focus on academic attainment. More critically, the regulations developed for the law attempt to specify how the principle of individualization is to operate in order to meet the needs of particular children and how schools are to be held accountable for educational outcomes.

The principles behind Chapter 766 should be applicable to educating all children. What is curious — and symptomatic of attitudes toward the handicapped held by educators, human service professionals, and the public — is that the law has come to be viewed in a dissociated manner as applicable only to the handicapped.

Few people would disagree with the goal of meeting handicapped children's needs. Yet Chapter 766 resulted predominantly from the sustained efforts of an informed, vociferous coalition of concerned citizens, child advocates, parents, and professionals against a largely unresponsive bureaucracy. This coalition had its roots in the grievances expressed by a group of low-income parents against the way schools were treating their special needs children. Together, the parents and their allies challenged educators with searching questions about how schools classify children, how parents are treated in this process, and what schools can do to select and deliver appropriate services without stigmatizing children. In what seemed like a rush of events, legislators responded to these concerns and acknowledged the need for radical reform of special education by passing Chapter 766.

This article first describes the series of events that made the public aware of the plight of children with special educational needs. It then discusses the provisions of the law and the transition process from signing the legislation to implementing it.

Chapter 766 is now in effect. Still, many of the vexing questions that sparked the drive for reform of special education remain unresolved. The final section of this article addresses the implications of the law and the problems that persist.

Consciousness Raising

The struggle for equal rights for handicapped children in Massachusetts was initiated as part of the more general struggle for equality by low-income and minority-group persons during the 1960s. Low-income children were sometimes called handicapped because diagnostic tests misclassified them. In other instances, low-income children were labeled mentally retarded as the only or most convenient way to shunt children with management and/or learning problems out of regular classrooms and into segregated special classes. What became evident, especially to the parents and neighbors of these children, was that the expectation that special classes would be "special-good" was not borne out: schools had little concern for the particular needs of children who required services beyond those available for regular students. Moreover, once assigned to the "dummy" class, children became the captives of prejudices that were expressed openly and often by their peers and the school staff. The children's under-education, social stigma, and considerable unhappiness became abundantly clear to the concerned parents. Feeling deceived and angry, the parents began to organize.

The anger over special education was expressed initially in the South End of Boston in 1968, when local residents issued a report entitled "End Educational Entombment." Suspecting that the schools were misdiagnosing minority-group children, they announced their intention to have local child guidance clinics reexamine twenty-two children to determine if they were indeed, as the schools claimed, mentally retarded. "End Educational Entombment II," issued one year later, indicated that sixteen of the twenty-two students were incorrectly placed and needed other kinds of treatment such as learning-disability classes, remedial reading, or speech help, which were denied them because their IQs were measured under 90. The report also identified some children who had substantial emotional problems that were contributing to their learning and behavior difficulties, and who thus required placement in classes for emotionally disturbed children.

During the next two years, the parents, aided by a lawyer, demanded that the Boston School Department and the Massachusetts Department of Education provide appropriate services for the sixteen misclassified children and reexamine all children in the city's special classes for the mentally retarded. At the time, these classes were the only alternatives to regular classrooms available throughout the system.

On September 30, 1969, the Boston School Committee responded to the report. It passed a series of resolutions that called for better testing practices; intensive in-service training programs for special class teachers and principals; and a Special Class Assistance Council to be composed equally of parents, mental health professionals, and community agency representatives. The council was to meet monthly to consult with the director of special classes and his subordinates and to assist in and insure implementation of this resolution. Concurrently, a state task force was appointed to review the records of children placed into special classes in Boston.

The School Committee resolutions had mixed results. Many of the sixteen children were either reintegrated into regular classes, although usually without benefit of a transitional program, or placed in one of the newly established classes for the emotionally disturbed. No training or testing programs were initiated. The Special Class Assistance Council was appointed, only to find itself with little power and less effectiveness.

The state review panel generated two dramatically different sets of findings. First, two members of the Massachusetts Bureau of Special Education conducted a perfunctory review and reported no problems in the placement of the twenty-two children. Then the two psychologists on the panel gained access to Boston's records. In contrast to the bureaucrats, they found gross violations of the state's minimal requirements for placing and monitoring children in special classes. They reported that the records of the twenty-two children showed no evidence of physical examinations, that some contained only IQ test scores, and that most did not contain required state forms. Yet the state director of special education concluded his investigation by saying that in each case, the placement of the child into a class for the mentally retarded was done properly. The review was never extended to other Boston children.

While the South End parents were seeking administrative redress, a task force of health and social service professionals, Boston school staff, and citizens were studying why large numbers of children in Boston were not attending school. It issued a report in October 1970, *The Way We Go to School: The Exclusion of Children in Boston,* which identified several excluded groups: truants, illegally suspended students, and students who lacked appropriate services.[2] It argued that the failure to provide services to many groups — Spanish-speaking children in particular — constituted a de facto exclusion and was, therefore, in violation of the state's requirement that the city provide an education to every child between six and sixteen years of age. In addition, the report described both the poor quality of services for the mentally retarded in special classes and the misclassification of minority-group children.

The task force report gained considerable publicity. Initially, the Boston School Committee responded by vigorously contesting the findings and defending the School Department's practices. Later, Boston schools offered some remedies, such as the expansion of bilingual classes for Spanish-speaking students. This expansion was hastened, though, by the requirements of a new state law largely inspired by the task force report.[3]

While the task force was looking into children's exclusion from schools, a group of psychologists was looking for an issue that would broaden the concerns of its professional association beyond guild matters. Wanting to stress psychologists' social contributions, the Board of Professional Affairs (BPA) of the Massachusetts Psychological Association (MPA) decided to focus on the misuse of IQ tests to evaluate Black children. In the fall of 1969, the BPA met with members of the Association of Black Psychologists (ABPsi). As in other cities, Boston's Black students were disproportionately represented in special classes for the educable mentally retarded. Approximately 60 percent of all special education students were Black, while only 25 percent of school enrollment was Black. A group of these psychologists, who had been actively involved with special education problems, began seriously to investigate what could be done about misclassification in schools — especially schools that traditionally had been unresponsive to criticisms of their treatment of Black and low-income children.

After months of discussing the problems involved in misclassification, the psychologists decided to explore the option of legal action. Although queasy about instituting a suit, the group conferred with a staff member of the Harvard Center for Law and Education, an agency involved in litigation on similar problems. A period of discussion and consultation ensued as the BPA and ABPsi sought to assess alternatives to legal action, as well as possible outcomes of a suit. At this time, an anti-poverty lawyer requested the psychologists' help in framing a court action on behalf of seven parents whose children needed special services. With this impetus, although with no little anxiety, the psychologists decided court action was necessary. They obtained approval from the BPA and helped the lawyers formulate a complaint, which they filed in Federal District Court on September 14, 1970. Because the South End parents still had received no relief from state authorities, they subsequently joined in the suit.

Pearl Stewart, mother of one of the twenty-two South End children, represented the class of parents against the Department of Educational Investigation and Measurement of the Boston School Department, represented by Acting Director Agnes Phillips. The formal complaint, *Stewart v. Phillips*, described two classes of plaintiffs: children who were misclassified in special classes for the mentally retarded, and those who were correctly placed in these classes but also required other services.[4] The defendants were the state Departments of Education and Mental Health and bureaus of the Boston School Department. The major argument in the suit was that the plaintiffs were denied due process because of inadequate evaluation, inappropriate placement, and ill-trained staff. Also included in the complaint was the issue of misuse of IQ tests with low-income and minority children. The plaintiffs requested that the court appoint a commission to suggest new evaluation and placement practices, and that it initiate a comprehensive program of supervision and retraining for the appropriate staff.

Interestingly enough, the need for staff retraining became all the more apparent after the complaint was formalized. Filing the suit made previously inaccessible information available to the plaintiffs' representatives, who discovered that the school psychometrists had little formal clinical training in dealing with special needs children and as a result commonly administered only routine achievement and intelligence tests.

The suit provoked a variety of responses from the professional societies, the school system, and the state commissioners. The professional societies were displeased that their members had gone to court. Although the legal action had been approved without dissent at the MPA's spring meeting, the leadership and even the BPA now hedged on the idea of taking such an active role as to sue on behalf of children's rights.

The Boston school system first reacted by abruptly ceasing to place students in classes for the mentally retarded, primarily because school principals were unwilling to assume responsibility for misplacement. Indeed, no one wanted this responsibility. The Special Class Department claimed that it was not responsible for the decision to place a child because it acted on the recommendations of the Department of Educational Investigation and Measurement (DEIM). Yet the DEIM claimed that it could not be held responsible since it merely evaluated test results and made recommendations. The DEIM's response to the suit was largely cosmetic: the testers, formerly known as research assistants, were renamed "psychologists."

Later the Boston School Department carried out a project funded by the state Bureau of Special Education to reevaluate all students in special classes for the mentally retarded. Conceding the possibility of misclassification was a new and positive step for both bureaucracies. However, the process was initiated less out of concern with children's needs than because the department had heard that special education regulations would change at the state level. For example, children with IQs above 79 were summarily reassigned from special classes to regular classes, with no provision for the process of transition.

At the state level, the commissioners of education and mental health were also feeling pressure from the suit. They offered to change the accreditation procedures for school psychologists and to revise the regulations for placement of and programs for the retarded. These regulations had remained unchanged since 1955, despite repeated complaints from psychologists and consumer groups. The groups that drafted new regulations included psychologists and lawyers who had worked on the original suit as well as staff from the two departments.

The resulting regulations represented a significant departure from past practices, one of which was a crucial element in the state's rapidly unfolding reform of special education. With their provisions for comprehensive assessment, mainstreaming, parent involvement, and equality of resources, the regulations set forth a radically new format for delivering special education services. Indeed, this format would later serve as the blueprint for Chapter 766.

One tenet of the new regulations was that the IQ score would no longer be the sole criterion for identifying the retarded child. For each child, a comprehensive assessment would include a recent physical examination; a psychological assessment of emotional status, general ability to learn (as measured by instruments other than IQ tests), and learning style; and an assessment of how the child functioned at home and in the community. After reviewing the data and performing any additional examinations deemed necessary, staff members would develop a comprehensive educational plan for the child. Basic to the planning would be the principle that students should participate as much as possible within the mainstream of the school.

The regulations accorded considerable emphasis to parental involvement. Under the old regulations, June promotion slips often only indicated to parents their children's new classroom assignments; the fact that these were special-class placements was not mentioned. Under the revised system, parents had to consent in writing before their child's examination process began, and they were to join in the assessment by telling school staff about the child's functioning outside school. Parents could also request a reevaluation for their child and could challenge his or her educational plan by appealing to regional and state boards. Of tremendous importance was the requirement that schools issue quarterly reports to parents and conduct annual reevaluations to ascertain a child's progress and to make changes in the educational plan.

Last, the regulations addressed the question of resources, requiring that facilities and materials for special classes be equal to those for regular classes. They also mandated a lower teacher/student ratio (1 to 8, or 1 to 12 with a teacher's aide) than the 1 to 18 ratio that was then common for educable mentally retarded classes.

Concurrent with the negotiation of the new regulations, another episode critical to the reform was unfolding. The legislature had upgraded the Bureau of Special Education to division level, creating the position of associate commissioner for special education. In the ensuing months, a broad range of consumer, professional, and child advocate groups was enlisted to influence the appointment made by the state Board of Education, an independent appointive body. Despite the fact that representatives from these groups were barred from the search committee, they initiated a national recruitment campaign for well-qualified candidates. Spurring their efforts was the perception — and later evidence — that the bureau director, a strong candidate for the post, had performed less than competently.

The efforts of these groups paid off. First, the appointment of the new administrator, a clinical psychologist and state special education consultant from California, represented a clear victory. An outsider to the Massachusetts system had simply never been considered before. Beyond the immediate outcome, the informal coalition responsible for the recruitment campaign, including such groups as the Massachusetts Association for Retarded Children, the Advisory Council for the Deaf, and the Association for Children with Learning Disabilities, had managed to organize itself into a formal, working coalition. The Coalition for Special Education was pleased that it had demonstrated the possibility of change in an unresponsive system.

Thus, by the end of 1971, the forces for change in special education had grounds for some optimism. A structure for reform appeared to be in place even though no arguments had been made in court. First, the innovative regulations for the mentally retarded would become the model for delivery of services to the emotionally disturbed and learning disabled. Second, the coalition expected that the new associate commissioner would be sympathetic to future reforms, since he owed his appointment largely to the activist groups' efforts. Finally, a citizens' committee, formed to advise the state Board of Education on special education, would also serve to support the associate commissioner. The committee's active involvement in the division's work would help introduce some openness and accountability into this bureaucracy.

Chapter 766

Although only a few individuals had initiated the efforts described in the previous section, within a few years they had built a force that was powerful enough to be one of the major factors in the passage of Chapter 766. Their efforts focused the public's attention on the need for special education reform and gave political stature to the issue. Another influence on the legislature was the "right to education" decision in *PARC v. Pennsylvania*.[5] Closer to home, the 1971 Massachusetts bilingual bill provided extra classes for the bilingual student, and its passage, due largely to citizen pressure, served as one impetus for the special education reforms.[6] The legislature took note of these new developments and their implications, but of particular interest to them was the convergence of political, consumer, and professional groups concerned with the needs of handicapped children. As a result, the legislature's education committee wrote an omnibus reform of the existing mélange of special education laws. Cosponsored by Michael Daly, chairman of the House Education Committee, and David Bartley, Speaker of the House of Representatives, the bill proposed a radical restructuring of the premises, philosophy, and practice of special education services. The bill entered the Massachusetts Code of Laws as Chapter 766.

At the core of Chapter 766 are the philosophy and model first enunciated in the revised regulations for the mentally retarded. Included in its scope are both philosophical and practical concerns: mainstreaming, delabeling, broadened eligibility, parental involvement, and assignment of legal responsibility for children with special educational needs to the local school districts. Equally important was the principle that the state would assume all extra costs of special education services.

The main philosophical underpinning of the law is mainstreaming, that is, placing the handicapped child in the least restrictive setting. This is translated to mean that the handicapped child is assigned into regular classrooms whenever possible. Any segregated classrooms within schools must have space and instructional materials equivalent to those of the regular classrooms; educational facilities and opportunities in institutions for special needs children must be as similar as possible to those offered in regular schools.

The law specifically abjures the use of categorical labels that stigmatize children. In the past, such labels were all the diagnostic process yielded. In contrast, Chapter 766 requires that a multidiscipline Core Evaluation Team (CET) assess each child's special needs and then prepare an appropriate individual educational plan. Along with instructional services, like tutoring in reading, a plan may include counseling, physical therapy, or psychotherapy for the child and/or the parents. Children are classified only in the sense that the CET selects from a range of program options (for example, periods away from the regular class or placement outside the public school).

With the emphasis on labeling removed, Chapter 766 opens the way for a dramatic expansion of eligibility for special services. The law takes the radical step of dealing with all children in actual or potential educational risk. Thus if a child is in danger at midyear of not being promoted, or indeed fails, he or she can be referred for services. Similarly, four other groups might be referred: 1) students suspended for more than five days in a quarter; 2) those absent more than fifteen days in a quarter without a medical excuse; 3) those who demonstrate distinct learning or behavior changes after an illness; 4) those considered delinquent.

Along with advances in meeting children's needs, Chapter 766 follows the model of the revised regulations for the mentally retarded described in the preceding section by prescribing an active role for parents. Parents must consent to the initial decision to evaluate their child; they contribute data for the evaluation; and they may participate in the conference to draw up the individual educational plan. If they do not agree with the plan, the examiner must give them a prompt hearing, followed, if necessary, by an appeal at the state level or in court. Once agreed upon, the plan must be monitored. If the evaluation team decides a child cannot be mainstreamed, it must specify to the parents what attainments the child must make before he or she can enter a regular classroom. The school must give parents quarterly reports on the child and annual reviews of the plan. Finally, parents also advise on policy formulation, since they hold half the seats on the regional and state advisory councils.

As significant as these new procedures are, the single most important principle established by the law is that the school district is responsible for all handicapped children of community residents, regardless of the degree of handicap. Districts are required to seek out all children aged three to twenty-one, evaluate their special needs, and provide suitable and educationally effective programs for them. The same legal responsibility covers the education, care, and treatment of all institutionalized children from a community. Prior to Chapter 766, the more severe the child's handicap, the more likely it was that parents would be shunted from agency to agency while their child would receive no service. Parents now have the legal right to demand that schools arrange suitable services for their children.

Transition Period

Chapter 766 was signed by Governor Francis Sargent on July 18, 1972, and became effective on September 1, 1974. The two-year transition period was to be devoted to redesigning the delivery system for special education services.

A number of tasks had to be completed. The Division of Special Education had to formulate regulations that would define acceptable practice at the school district level. Once developed, these regulations had to be reviewed and formally accepted by five other state agencies concerned with providing services to children: the Departments of Mental Health (DMH), Public Health, Welfare, Youth Services (for delinquent youth), and the Office for Children. These agencies would have to work cooperatively with the school districts to mobilize available resources on behalf of educationally needy children. A third task was the coordination of activities within the state Department of Education so that the resources and practices of each division within the department could be directed toward facilitating the special education reform. Finally, the Division of Special Education had to clarify the requirements set forth in the regulations and help the school districts prepare district and school staffs for implementation.

Two other issues required considerable energies from the understaffed division during the transition period. Legal responsibility for *all* children meant that school districts now had to create programs for children with moderate, severe, and multiple impairments. There are proportionately few such children in the population, and programs for them are costly. In many states, intermediate school districts or interdistrict collaboratives maintain the necessary facilities, serving the few children from each district who need them. In Massachusetts, before Chapter 766, these children were either excluded from school or served by state-aided private schools. The tradition of private school arrangements meant that there was no precedent for the interdistrict cooperation necessary to facilitate compliance with the law's commitment to public, mainstreamed education for these children.

A further problem was that responsibility for the state's school-aged institutional residents was to be transferred from the DMH to the division. The DMH had been severely criticized and successfully sued because of its inadequate care and training of mentally retarded residents. In addition to bruised egos and bitterness, the transfer threatened to create an administrative nightmare: a state department other than the administering agency would now assume prime responsibility for the education of institutionalized children. Some DMH staff had to be transferred to the Department of Education, and the DMH had to resolve difficult issues about the relationship between the education and training staffs and the direct-care personnel still on its rolls.

At the local level, the law required schools to design and deliver special education services for which there was no precedent and little existing knowledge in the field. Extending the schools' programming responsibility to children under five years and above sixteen years of age, the law significantly expanded services. High schools were disaster areas for children in special educational need — they provided few organizational formats beyond the segregated special class, even for mildly handicapped students. In short, to meet the challenge of serving all children, the schools needed at the very least a real sense of shared responsibility between the state and the districts. But this assurance was not forthcoming.

The time allotted for the transition period was clearly too short to achieve its complex goals. More important, the leadership of the Division of Special Education was indecisive, prone to generating confusion, and unable to draw up guidelines that would allow school districts to plan and budget for the impending, dramatic increases in staff. The overburdened state special education staff lacked an overall sense of the law's ramifications and was overwhelmed at the prospect of translating the law into practice. Consequently, it failed to develop a comprehensive, long-range plan that could serve as a guide for local implementation.

79

The several hundred school districts in the state varied considerably in the degree to which they already provided special education services. Some communities had excellent programs and required little more than new programs for the younger and older students now covered by the law. Other communities had been offering virtually no services to children with special educational needs. A plan would have enabled the districts to gauge their state of readiness and to figure out, in collaboration with state staff, how to phase in the programs mandated by the law. Since the advocacy coalition acknowledged the need for some type of phased implementation, such plans could have been debated publicly, with the effect that parents would have realized that not all systems would be prepared to offer an immediate, full range of services to their children.

Instead, the Division of Special Education offered many meetings but no written guidelines. The many mixed messages conveyed the division's confusion and its inability to address conceptually and plan for the complex law. For example, no definition of the child with special educational needs was ever established. Consequently, the districts had difficulty estimating the number of children potentially eligible for services, and they could not project staff needs for the first implementation year. The final regulations were so late in coming and rumors so rife as successive drafts were produced, that budgets for staff and other contracted costs — which had to be drawn up by district staff and approved by school committees during the year before the implementation date — could not be realistically formulated.

In fairness to the division, it should be noted that the legislature did not fund additional positions to help plan the transition; moreover, the woefully understaffed division was getting little cooperation in its planning efforts from the other state agencies, which jealously guarded their prerogatives, or within the state Department of Education. Concerned citizens and professionals, now joined by school personnel, were the ones who pressed for a constructive transition.

The process of developing regulations was paradigmatic of the failure of leadership that exacerbated the tensions and strains of the transition period. In keeping with the division's new stance of openness and responsiveness, task forces of professionals and concerned lay people were to be organized to develop prototype regulations for particular aspects of the law, such as typologies of educational need, program models, institutional programs, noninstructional intervention, staff requirements, and financing. Administrative procrastination, however, delayed the initial meetings for seven months. The task forces began meeting in January of 1973, and met without payment during the following four months. By June, each task force produced draft regulations for its particular area, and by September these were compiled into a complete set.

The associate commissioner, however, chose to largely ignore these draft regulations. Believing that providing guidelines was the responsibility of the division, he initiated a new, in-house effort at writing the regulations, using the work of the task forces merely as a resource. By now the constraints of time precluded additional substantive input from concerned professionals and citizens, even those who had voluntarily participated in the original formulations. The result was an increased sense of alienation, confusion, anger, and cynicism about the bureaucracy's efforts.

To counter the confusion and to gain additional planning time for the new service delivery system, the associate commissioner distributed a letter on October 10, 1973, indicating that the major activity for the first implementation year (1974–1975) would be comprehensive evaluation of referred and already-served children. The letter, suggesting a delay in implementation, aroused the ire of the consumer and advocate groups pressing for first-year programs that would serve the needs of children, not simply diagnose them.

Following this letter, and in the wake of the previous year's confusion, the Coalition for Special Education reasserted its pressure and began a process intended to force a more substantive and thoughtful response by the bureaucracy. During November, an implementation unit was formed within the division. It was specifically charged with developing final regulations quickly during the remaining year and establishing closer relationships with the school districts, the public, and the other state agencies involved in the reform. This group ultimately was to report directly to the commissioner of education. The advocacy coalition acted to press issues that had become blocked within the bureaucracy or had not been satisfactorily addressed there. For example, direct pressure from the coalition forced the Division of Occupational Education to develop guidelines for making vocationally relevant training opportunities available to the handicapped, whom this division had previously ignored. The implementation unit urged negotiations with DMH to insure constructive transitions in the institutions. The difficulties in such negotiations are illustrated by the fact that, one year after the implementation date for the law, the state agencies responsible for mental health and rehabilitation activities have still failed to mobilize their resources in support of the reform. Turf problems and the fantasy that state education appropriations could pay for services already legislatively funded through other state agencies have actually resulted in some reduction of services to handicapped children.

Concern about costs, anger about the lack of direction and guidance from the state department, and fear of legal actions resulted, in the spring of 1974, in an attempt to amend Chapter 766 to include a phase-in period. State education officials promoted this strategy to gain more time and to relieve themselves of immediate responsibility for district-level implementation. The movement to amend the law also gained the support of the legislative leaders, who were responsive to the confusion and uncertainty among mayors, city councilors, and school committee members in cities and towns around the state. The ostensible issue was the lack of initial funding for the new services: state reimbursement ordinarily becomes available in the November following the end of the school year in which expenses are incurred. City and town officials were genuinely concerned about costs for special education. This was a real concern, supported by a considerable past record of the legislature's failure to fund programs it had mandated. The unspoken issues, however, were the bureaucratic confusion, the unrealistic expectations of parents, and the districts' fears of legal actions.

The advocate groups were no happier than anyone else with the progress in preparing for implementation of the law. What is more, aware of the considerable anger of local school officials over the confusion that the law created, the advocate groups feared that the law might be amended to death. Thus, these groups renewed their efforts and persuaded the legislative leaders to withdraw their support from this process. Instead, David Bartley, Speaker of the House and cosponsor of the law, proposed a bill offering $26 million as an advance payment to the cities and towns against future reimbursement by the state.[7] The legislature quickly passed this bill. At the time, there was an expectation that subsequent legislation would award advance payments in the form of grants to local communities. However, the state's substantial fiscal problems precluded such action.

Despite the problems reflected in the move for an amendment, assignment to the implementation unit of the responsibility for transition activities had resulted in a more rapid, if erratic, pace in preparing for the date of the law's implementation. The regulations were finally approved by the Board of Education in June of 1974 after a herculean effort by a few dedicated persons. The other agencies whose written approval was required ratified these regulations during the early summer. The school districts received the 108 single-spaced pages of regulations just as students and faculty were dismissed for the summer. By the time schools would reconvene in September, the effective date of implementing Chapter 766 would be upon them.

Implications of Chapter 766

The main reason for the initial political success of Chapter 766 was that groups and individuals with a relatively diverse set of interests backed a law mandating services to meet the special needs of all children. Compared to this formidable coalition, initial opposition to the bill was feeble and half-hearted. Indeed, a considerable commitment to special education reform has developed. More than thirty state legislatures have passed comprehensive bills revising the delivery of special education services; of these bills, Chapter 766 is probably the most radical.

While the idea of changing the principles and practices of special education appears to be gathering nationwide momentum, the applicability of this reform to the education of *all* children has not been widely acknowledged. It is interesting to note that education critics outside special education have spoken of the need for many of the principles that Chapter 766 mandates: individualized and appropriate education for the child, effective treatment (accountability), parent involvement in determining their child's educational program, and parent participation in policy formulation. The promise of Chapter 766 is that by learning to define, understand, and address effectively the needs of children with serious educational and training problems, we can develop procedures for applying these principles to the education of all children.

Unfortunately, educators continue to treat handicapped children as separate from other children and therefore fail to perceive the wider implications of Chapter 766. Their attitudes are perpetuated by a poor understanding of what it generally means to call a child handicapped. For example, the large category of so-called learning-disabilities children includes few children who have bona fide, neurologically based learning problems; many children so designated have simply fared poorly in schools and thus read, write, or spell badly. These children are typically not separated from their peers for major segments of the school day, unlike the mildly retarded or emotionally disturbed child.

Most educators also fail to realize that over 85 percent of children diagnosed as mentally retarded are only mildly handicapped, with few discernible physical differences.[8] If one could develop a reasonable definition of mild emotional disturbance, a similar phenomenon would be evident. Indeed, many have argued that mild conditions of handicap are often school-generated, products of academic and behavioral demands of traditional schools and poor or inappropriate teaching. As has been discussed, many poor and minority-group children are misdiagnosed and labeled retarded when, in fact, they have learning and/or behavior problems. Special education reform, then, is a logical extension of the broader concern with the educational needs of all children who are ill-served by schools. Again, if educators recognized the relevance of Chapter 766's principles for school practice in general, perhaps the majority of such children would never have to drop into the special needs category at all.

This is not to say that the practices mandated by Chapter 766 are sufficiently refined to serve as a model for all education. Many problems remain: enormous knowledge gaps prevent an easy translation into practice of the principles that the law enunciates. Not only does the knowledge base in special education fail to provide clear guidance but, in addition, the regulations for Chapter 766 fail to address fundamental educational questions.

A glaring example of the way the regulations avoid knotty questions is the fact that they contain no definition of a child with special educational needs. Because the law proscribes labeling, children are categorized only to the degree by which they are mainstreamed; that is, by the program prototype to which they are assigned. There has been no uniform attempt to describe, however, the attributes or needs of a child that should dictate the choice of program prototype.

The weakness in the way regulations deal with the diagnostic process has its parallel in the process of developing an educational plan for the child. The myth developed and persists that a carefully defined plan, stated in explicit behavioral objectives, will somehow define meaningful immediate and longer term goals for the child and ipso facto, dictate the child's educational program. The process of describing behavioral objectives is a useful analytic exercise, for it forces the assessment staff to specify the critical attainments that would represent progress for the child. The theory underlying the use of behavioral objectives is that attainment or nonattainment of the goals will allow one to gauge the effectiveness of the educational treatment prescribed. Specification, however, does not necessarily lead to identification of the most appropriate goals. Until the general conceptual gaps are closed, the goals selected for the child may simply not be the most appropriate ones. Moreover, excessive pressure for specification may result in trivial, pseudo-mathematical statements that give the appearance of progress when, in fact, the changes demonstrated by the child may not relate to the longer term goals for that child.

Because of the difficulties in translating principle into practice (encountered especially during the transition period), the regulations for Chapter 766 elaborated cumbersome and complex procedures for school staffs to follow. School systems facing the threat of legal actions can become obsessed with meeting the letter of the regulations rather than pioneering practices to meet the spirit of the reform. The pressure for compliance, along with the state's listing of complex procedures, can throttle what little innovative energy school bureaucracies possess. One administrator has already complained that the "cumbersome paperwork of the evaluation process" required by Chapter 766 regulations puts local towns and school systems "into a strait jacket" and keeps them from helping special needs children.[9] The plaint deserves attention, for the effective provision of help to special needs children cannot be legislated by state assemblies nor adjudicated by courts.

Despite their conceptual confusion and their stultifying level of detail, the regulations do prescribe procedural mechanisms for deciding how to help children. Implicit in this procedural focus is the belief that, when there are no clear-cut or objective criteria for deciding an issue, a decision should be reached by consensus. Thus, the core evaluation team, like a trial jury or a legislative committee, is directed to operate by consensus. In effect, the regulations acknowledge that, since there are no clear-cut rules for deciding what is best for different kinds of children, there will inevitably be disagreements and mistakes. Thus the law mandates a review mechanism and an appeal procedure for parents who believe that their children have been placed inappropriately.

In the context of this approach to decisionmaking, there is an opportunity for child advocates to work constructively with school authorities. If they view the advocates as helpers, school personnel may learn to use them in the outreach effort for finding and helping children with special educational needs. However, advocates must preserve enough independence to take other actions if their informal attempts to work within the system fail. They must achieve a subtle balance, using their position outside the bureaucracy to help press for resources and programs that have been arbitrarily denied to particular children, while being mindful of the bureaucratic paralysis that may ensue if the pressure makes educators overly defensive.

At the state level, though, it seems advisable for child advocates to maintain an aggressive posture in the political arena. The radical reforms were achieved largely because of the concerted efforts of the active, informed, and vociferous Coalition for Special Education. Since there are considerable forces working to compromise significant features of Chapter 766, the continuing, active pressure of this coalition is still required to assure that each educationally needy child receives the benefits of the law.

One threat to Chapter 766 arises from political wrangling over finances. In Massachusetts, state reimbursement for special education programs is paid from a local aid fund before the cost of regular education services has been deducted. At a time when the state budget is under considerable pressure, a major target for reductions in expenditures may be the local aid to educational funds. A reduction in state support for regular education budgets may create a political backlash against special education by parents of nonhandicapped children, who fear cutbacks in services to their children.

Thus, the coalition still has political work to do. But holding the coalition together may prove as difficult as it is important. The coalition is still young, and groups that have only recently learned to cooperate with each other may revert to their old habit of competing for funds and services. Rather, they must continue to see the wisdom of cooperating to meet the needs of all children.

Within the coalition, the professional organizations were least able to mobilize themselves and were most timid about active involvement. In some instances, the professionals became hostile to the reform movement when activities reached the political level. The largely passive role of the professional organization — presumably those most concerned with meeting the needs of handicapped children — bears closer examination. It is important to understand whether the timidity of these organizations is endemic to middle-class organizations, whether it reflected narrow guild concerns, or whether it derived from professionals' discomfort at taking advocate positions that might be viewed as controversial or compromising to their sense of dignity.

Thus, the most difficult problem for advocates remains that of helping to translate the intent of the reform into results. They cannot do it alone; human-service professionals, particularly, must help to produce service-delivery systems relevant to the needs of their clients. The array of actors who must implement the Massachusetts law includes state and local administrators from a broad range of human-service, rehabilitation, and education agencies; child-assessment and instructional staffs in the local school districts; teacher unions;[10] university communities; parent-consumer and advocacy groups; and state and local governments. In considering how to orchestrate the efforts and participation of all these elements so that imaginative and useful outcomes emerge, one can begin to grasp the dimensions of the problem of implementation. If one also considers the idiosyncratic ego, power, and recognition needs of the individuals involved, it becomes clear that the process is an awesome one.

Thus, there are problems that remain to be solved and difficult tasks ahead for child advocates.[11] The process of change leading to Chapter 766 was not always pleasant for the people involved. But, by comparing special educational practices at the state and local levels seven years ago when the process began to those that will follow full implementation of the reform, one can see that the rewards have been immense. The legally mandated structure has been changed. It now remains to continue the work and to guarantee that the full benefits of the law reach the children.

Notes

1. Commonwealth of Massachusetts, Massachusetts General Laws, ch. 766, 1972.
2. Task Force on Children Out of School, *The Way We Go to School: The Exclusion of Children in Boston* (Boston: Beacon Press, 1971).
3. Commonwealth of Massachusetts, Bilingual Education Act, ch. 1005, 1971.
4. Stewart v. Phillips, Civ. Act. No. 70-1199-F (D. Mass., 1970).
5. Pennsylvania Association for Retarded Children (PARC) v. Commonwealth of Pennsylvania, 334 F. Supp. 1257 (E. D. Pa., 1971).
6. Commonwealth of Massachusetts, Bilingual Education Act, ch. 1005, 1971.
7. Commonwealth of Massachusetts, Massachusetts General Appropriations Act, ch. 431, 1974.

8. President's Panel on Mental Retardation, *A Proposed Program for National Action to Combat Mental Retardation* (Washington, DC: U.S. Government Printing Office, 1962), p. 5.

9. John Cullinane, "An Educator Looks at Chapter 766," *Boston Globe*, September 7, 1975.

10. The only extensive teacher-orientation effort was developed and implemented by the Massachusetts Teachers Association, the NEA affiliate that is the bargaining agent in many communities. In collaboration with a local college, they organized credit courses for teachers and helped them to understand the implications of the new law. Under a small grant from the state, working groups of teachers developed two series of booklets that were widely distributed throughout the state and provided the most useful materials produced during the transition period for regular and special education teachers.

11. Of particular concern to child advocates is the too-comfortable assumption that every parent will work in the child's best interest. Criteria must be developed that can guide the advocate as to when he or she should intervene on behalf of the child whose needs are being neglected by the parents. While one can resort to court action under various statutes relating to neglect, the processes are very cumbersome and demand extreme evidence of damage.

Preparation of this article was supported, in part, by grants OEG-0-8-080506-4597 and NE-G-00-3-0016 from the National Institute of Education. This article is a revised version of a paper entitled "Psycho-Educational Classification and Public Policy: Children's Rights," presented at a meeting of the American Psychological Association, New Orleans, August 1974.

Street-Level Bureaucrats and Institutional Innovation: Implementing Special Education Reform

RICHARD A. WEATHERLEY

MICHAEL LIPSKY

In this article, Richard Weatherley and Michael Lipsky report on a study they conducted on the initial implementation of the Massachusetts comprehensive special education statute, Chapter 766. The law, enacted in 1972, subsequently became a model for other state and federal special education legislation, including PL 94-142. Through their study, Weatherley and Lipsky discovered that, although the law was far-reaching and prescriptive, implementation patterns varied from community to community. In addition, the authors documented how the impact of coping mechanisms employed by school staff in handling the enormous demands of their jobs distorted implementation of the law. Though the patterns of response to these demands varied, the authors report how professionals charged with implementing the law constantly needed to rationalize, ration resources, and control uncertainties. Weatherley and Lipsky assert that policymakers must recognize the coping behaviors of what they refer to as "street-level bureaucrats" in order to discover which coping mechanisms coincide with preferred educational outcomes. This study is important not only in its early documentation of what have become consistent implementation problems in special education, but also in its development of the thesis that the cause of these problems does not reside solely in the policies themselves, but in the methods by which on-line implementers deal with the policies' demands, given limited resources and historical modes of response. This concept is developed further by the authors in their book Street Level Bureaucrats *(1977), which has been widely read and positively received by scholars and practitioners involved in social policy implementation.*

In 1972, the Comprehensive Special Education Law of Massachusetts, Chapter 766, was passed by the state legislature.[1] The law was to take effect in

September 1974. This measure, hailed as landmark legislation, mandates a significant departure from past practices in the education of children with any kind of physical, emotional, and/or mental handicap. Ours is a study of the first year of implementation of Chapter 766. It is an exercise in analyzing the introduction of innovative policy into public-service bureaucracies that process people on a mass basis.

This article focuses on one neglected but highly significant class of implementation contexts — the introduction of innovation into continuing practice. Rather than initiating new programs, providing new subsidies, or calling for new construction, Chapter 766 required adjustments in the behavior of public employees and in the working conditions established for them in their agencies. While we focus in this article on implementation of a statute affecting educational personnel, the class of implementation contexts into which our case study falls includes governmental efforts to change the work requirements not only of teachers, but also of police officers, welfare workers, legal-assistance lawyers, lower court judges, and health workers. These and other public employees interact with the public and make decisions calling for both individual initiative and considerable routinization. Such public employees share similar work situations.

These "street-level bureaucrats," as we have called them, interact directly with citizens in the course of their jobs and have substantial discretion in the execution of their work.[2] For such public workers, personal and organizational resources are chronically and severely limited in relation to the tasks that they are asked to perform. The demand for their services will always be as great as their ability to supply these services. To accomplish their required tasks, street-level bureaucrats must find ways to accommodate the demands placed upon them and confront the reality of resource limitations. They typically do this by routinizing procedures, modifying goals, rationing services, asserting priorities, and limiting or controlling clientele. In other words, they develop practices that permit them in some way to process the work they are required to do. The work of street-level bureaucrats is inherently discretionary. Some influences that might be thought to provide behavioral guidance for them do not actually do much to dictate their behavior. For example, the work objectives for public-service employees are usually vague and contradictory. Moreover, it is difficult to establish or impose valid work-performance measures, and the consumers of services are relatively insignificant as a reference group. Thus street-level bureaucrats are constrained but not directed in their work.

These accommodations and coping mechanisms that they are free to develop form patterns of behavior that become the government program that is "delivered" to the public. In a significant sense, then, street-level bureaucrats *are the policymakers* in their respective work arenas. From this perspective, it follows that the study of implementation of policy formulated at the federal or state level requires a twin focus. One must trace the fate of the policy in traditional fashion, from its authoritative articulation through various administrative modifications, to discover the ways this policy affects the context of street-level decisionmaking. At the same time, one must study street-level bureaucrats within their specific work context to discover how their decisionmaking about clients is modified, if at all, by the newly articulated policy. This turns the usual study of implementation on its head. Now the lowest levels of the policy chain are regarded as the makers of policy, and the higher level of decisionmaking is seen as circumscribing, albeit in important ways, the lower level policymaking context. The relationship between the development and implementation of policy is of necessity problematic since, in a sense, the meaning of policy cannot be known until it is worked out in practice at the street level.[3] Taking these considerations into account, we examine the school response to Chapter 766 in the context of the state-level development and articulation of policy.

The Massachusetts Comprehensive Special Education Law

The impetus for special education reform in Massachusetts and in other states derives from several related developments. First, university-based special educators have increasingly questioned the efficacy of special classes for many categories of children and have advocated a more generic and less segregated approach. While the issue is still being debated, available evidence suggests that special needs children do not necessarily learn better in special classes than in regular classes.[4] As one early critic of overreliance on special classes stated:

> It is indeed paradoxical that mentally handicapped children having teachers especially trained, having more money (per capita) spent on their education, and being enrolled in classes with fewer children and a program designed to provide for their unique needs, should be accomplishing the objectives of their education at the same or lower level than similar mentally handicapped children who have not had these advantages and have been forced to remain in the regular grades.[5]

Second, the process whereby children are evaluated, classified, and assigned to special classes has come under attack as being unduly arbitrary, culturally biased, and often motivated more by the desire to get rid of troublesome youngsters than to educate them. For example, a 1970 survey of special education programs in the Boston schools revealed a number of problems: an absence of uniform policy; failure to provide assessments and services required by state law; widespread misclassification of children of normal intelligence as retarded; use of special classes as dumping grounds, sometimes by rigging results of Stanford-Binet tests to justify exclusion of trouble-some children from regular classes; and denial of special services to those in need of them.[6]

A third concern has been the categorical approach to children requiring special education and the attendant use of labels as an aid to classification.[7] Categorical labels such as "emotionally disturbed," "retarded," "learning disabled," or "brain damaged," it is argued, call attention to a single pre-sumed deficit rather than to the child's developmental potential. Labels stigmatize the child as deviant or deficient without carrying any prescription for remedying the condition. Programs designed in response to such uni-dimensional labels are frequently themselves unidimensional (also reflecting in part the categorical approach to the training of special educators).[8] More-over, the categorical approach has led to the accretion of unrelated and frequently conflicting laws, programs, and school-reimbursement formulas for various categories of children. A history of legislative response to the lobbying efforts of parents organized in categorical interest groups has re-sulted in the favoring of certain groups over others and the neglect of those who may not fit into a recognized category.

The Massachusetts Comprehensive Special Education Law seeks to pro-vide a "flexible and uniform system of special education opportunities for all children requiring special education."[9] Such children are to be described generically as "children with special needs."[10] The law makes local school districts responsible for the education of all handicapped persons aged three to twenty-one, regardless of the nature or severity of the handicap, and requires the greatest possible integration of handicapped children into reg-ular class settings. This is to be accomplished through thorough assessment and planning for each handicapped child by an interdisciplinary team, with-out undue reliance on standardized tests. There are strong requirements for parent involvement and provisions for due process and appeal should a parent be dissatisfied with the outcome. Special education services are de-fined broadly to include social and medical services for the child, as well as family guidance and counseling for the parents or guardians.

Under prior funding arrangements, the state had paid 100 percent of the costs of institutional and special-school placements, but only 50 percent of most in-school services for the various categories of handicapped children. School committees (as local school boards are called in Massachusetts) therefore had faced strong disincentives to the development of local alter-natives to institutionalization. Chapter 766 proposed to alter this by requir-ing school systems to pay a share of the cost of institutionalization equal to the average per-pupil cost for children of comparable age within the local jurisdiction. Finally, the law provided for strengthening and decentralizing the state division of special education and defined its responsibilities vis-à-vis local jurisdictions in implementing the law.

The law was intended to produce significant change at all levels of the educational establishment — state, district, individual school, and classroom. Furthermore, it was expected both to alter and add to the workloads of all those responsible for special education. Our intent in studying the implementation of Chapter 766 was to examine the interaction between state-level policy and local implementation, and to observe the development of mechanisms to absorb the added workload and accommodate the resulting stresses, in order to assess these mechanisms' effects on implementation.

Methodology

The provisions of Chapter 766 took effect in September 1974. During the first year of implementation of the new law, we conducted interviews with school personnel at state and local levels and with a variety of others who played key roles in the passage of the legislation, the development of the regulations, or their implementation.

The major focus of our report is how the law affects the work situations of those at the local level ultimately responsible for its implementation — teachers, counselors, and specialists — and how the adjustments of these personnel to new work requirements affect implementation of the new law. Our concern is the processing of children rather than the content or quality of services and instruction. We studied the process of identification, referral, assessment, and educational plan development for children with special needs in three school systems. In these three systems, one of the investigators interviewed key officials responsible for special education, attended staff meetings, and reviewed pertinent documents during the 1974–1975 school year. A central component of the law is the assessment, by an interdisciplinary team, of children suspected to have special needs. One of the authors observed forty of these assessment meetings, called "core evaluations." All completed records of the 1,097 children evaluated in the three systems were reviewed, under procedures to safeguard confidentiality, for analysis of the salient referral, assessment, and outcome variables. These included the source of, reason for, and date of referral, as well as the ultimate disposition of the case.

Seven elementary schools, three in each of two school systems and one in the third, were selected for more intensive consideration. In these seven schools, personnel playing a role in implementing the law were interviewed, and follow-up interviews were held with teachers of all those children evaluated earlier in the school year. The major purpose of these teacher interviews

TABLE 1
Community and School Characteristics

	System A	*System B*	*System C*
Approximate enrollment	6,000	10,000	11,000
Per-pupil cost	$1,500	$1,400	$1,100
Pupil-teacher ratio (elementary)	16	15	20
Community median family income	$14,000	$10,000	$11,000
Percent workers professional, technical, managerial in community	45%	39%	22%

Source: Massachusetts Department of Commerce and Development, "City and Town Monograph" series, July 1973. This series is based on 1970 census data and 1971 and 1972 school reports. The statistics have been stated as approximations to discourage identification of the school systems.

was to determine what had transpired following the evaluations and development of educational plans for those children.

A comparison of community and school system characteristics is provided in Table 1.

The three systems, all in relatively large suburbs of Boston chosen to facilitate comparisons among cases, cannot be considered representative of the more than three hundred local school systems in Massachusetts. However, attendance at numerous meetings with school administrators from throughout the state confirmed to our satisfaction that the experience of these three systems with Chapter 766 has by no means been atypical.

The Implementation Context

The response of local systems was conditioned in large measure by what happened at the state level following passage of the law. While many conditions favored successful implementation, some that contributed to local implementation difficulties were the following: poor planning and management by the state division of special education; continued local uncertainty throughout the two-year planning period concerning program requirements and implementation deadlines; the failure to train regular classroom teachers to handle children with special needs; and, perhaps most serious, the failure of the legislature to guarantee adequate funding. These conditions exacerbated workload pressures within the schools, amplified discretion at the local level, and thereby contributed to assertions of unintended priorities in carrying out the law.

The Massachusetts Department of Education, like most other state departments of education, had long maintained a more or less passive stance toward local systems.[11] This had changed but slightly with the increase of federal funds for education in the 1960s. The state department had a reputation among local administrators as being inefficient, dominated by Boston interests, and, until the advent of Chapter 766, acquiescent to local determination. The state commissioner of education and legislative leaders recognized the need for change in the department's stance. The legislature more than doubled the budget of the Division of Special Education and provided for its decentralization into regional offices.[12] Yet, even the energetic new associate commissioner, Robert Audette, was limited by his own and the division's lack of managerial expertise, his firm commitment to a passive, regulatory role for the division, and the necessity to rely on incumbent staff accustomed to the old laissez-faire style. He was further hampered by a cumbersome process for bringing in new staff and an unrealistically low salary scale. These factors contributed to the recruitment of an enthusiastic but inexperienced staff, seen by local school officials as "anti-school," and the reliance on outside consultant firms.

Considerable time, effort, and money ($146,000) went into the development by an outside consultant of an operations manual for the child-evaluation procedure.[13] The manual, unveiled some ten weeks *after* the beginning of the 1974–1975 school year, proved so complex and unwieldy that, in response to vociferous protest, its use was soon made optional. Angry special educators actually considered a mass burning of the manual — nicknamed the "Red Devil" for its bright red cover and onerous contents — on the State House steps. Another manual specifically for administrators was not delivered until three and one-half months after the opening of school.

The two-year delay in implementation — the bill, it will be recalled, was signed into law in July 1972, to take effect as of September 1974 — while intended by the legislature for planning and preparation, was not utilized to full advantage. This failure was due in part to uncertainty as to whether full implementation would actually be required in September 1974. Postponement until September 1974 and phased implementation were advocated at various times during the planning period by the governor, the commissioner of education, the Association of School Superintendents, and even House Speaker David Bartley and Representative Michael Daly, the prime sponsors of the bill. Parent and advocacy groups strongly opposed phasing or postponement and threatened to file suit in the event that anything less than full implementation was approved. This debate over phased implementation continued until May 1974, undoubtedly causing many school officials to postpone gearing up until this crucial issue was resolved.

School officials also faced uncertainty about the funding of Chapter 766. While the law provides state support for local special education costs that exceed a school system's average per-pupil costs, state reimbursement is normally distributed in the November following the school year in which the funds have been expended. Thus, the school system must first raise and expend the funds and then wait for state reimbursement. In the case of Chapter 766, which was likely to increase costs considerably, this procedure would mean a substantial increase in local property taxes to pay for the new and expanded services. Under Massachusetts law, a school committee is autonomous; once it sets the school budget, the town is obliged to raise the necessary revenues. To complicate matters further, estimates of the first-year costs varied from the state Department of Education's $40 million to local town and school officials' $100 million.[14] In fact, no one knew what the costs would be. Schools could not predict how many children would be referred and evaluated or what specific services these children would require.

While the legislature finally allocated $26 million in advance funding to help the systems finance the initial year of Chapter 766, this only postponed the funding problem. Even prior to enactment of Chapter 766, the legislature had never fully funded the regular state program of aid to education. In the previous year, for example, localities received only 81.2 percent of what they were entitled to under the law.[15] Under Chapter 766, schools could expect to receive full state special education reimbursements, but, in the absence of greatly increased allocations by the legislature, these funds would be deducted from or "taken off the top" of the regular education reimbursements. As such, an increase in allocations was unlikely, and local school officials feared that the total state reimbursements would remain at about the same level but would simply be divided differently, with more going to special education and less to regular education programs. Since regular costs would certainly increase, towns would still have to raise property taxes to cover such increases — an unhappy prospect in a state already financing 75 percent of education costs through property taxes, a proportion exceeded by only two states.[16]

If state planning for implementation had been totally misguided or ineffective, there would be little point in discussing local-level implementation. Thus, it is particularly important to note that, in many ways, the circumstances for the implementation of Chapter 766 could be regarded as relatively auspicious, avoiding many of the problems often encountered in policy implementation.[17] First, the law was carefully researched, is clear and concise, and contains detailed, unambiguous regulations.

Second, Chapter 766 had strong constituent support and became in large measure a consumers' bill. Staff of the state legislature's Joint Committee on Education carefully orchestrated a broad-based lobbying effort that evolved into the Coalition for Special Education, an organization of thirty-three consumer and professional groups dedicated to the passage and implementation of this legislation.[18] Initial development of the regulations proceeded with considerable involvement of citizens. The division of special education organized ten task forces composed of parent and professional groups and others interested in the law. Each task force was charged with drafting a section of the regulations. After three full drafts and public hearings held throughout the state, the result was a 107-page document that set forth in clear language the law's requirements. The only opposition to Chapter 766 came from private school operators who feared a loss of students and revenue if the law were implemented. Public school administrators supported its intent, although they sometimes argued that Chapter 766 was unnecessary, since they were already doing what it would require. For example, one special education administrator stated in a memorandum to his superintendent, "Indeed, much of what is good in Chapter 766 has long been standard practice in [our town] and elsewhere — not infrequently in the teeth of opposition from the State, which today mandates what yesterday it forbade."

Third, the law provided sufficient resources to increase the bureaucracy's capacity to plan, coordinate, mobilize support for, direct, monitor, and assess implementation. The budget of the division of special education was more than doubled, from $350,000 for 1973 to $800,000 for 1974, thereby making available twenty-nine new staff positions.[19] Furthermore, the use of federal funds for contract services provided a means, amply used by the division, to recruit assistance for short-term tasks on short notice.

Finally, several oversight and monitoring mechanisms were established prior to the scheduled implementation of Chapter 766. A new state agency, the Office for Children, was established to coordinate, monitor, and assess services for children and generally serve as an advocate for their interests. It was assigned oversight responsibility for Chapter 766. Within the Division of Special Education, a Bureau of Child Advocacy was established to process appeals brought by parents under the law. And two private groups, the Massachusetts Advocacy Center and the Coalition for Special Education, jointly announced plans for monitoring compliance in each town. The threat of this monitoring effort helped ensure the compliance of local special education administrators, who often reacted with almost paranoid horror at the thought that an outside group of noneducators would seek to examine their performance.

Local-Level Responses

The major thrust of the Massachusetts Comprehensive Special Education Law, and what makes it truly innovative, is the requirement that children with special needs receive individualized assessment and treatment. This thrust is reflected in a number of provisions: the required assessment of children by interdisciplinary teams with parental involvement; the requirement that a specific educational plan be tailored to the needs of each child;

the replacement of generic descriptive labels by behaviorally specific inventories; and the accommodation, insofar as possible, of children with special needs in regular educational settings rather than in segregated classrooms. At the same time, certain provisions of the law are directed toward achieving uniform and nondiscriminatory treatment and comprehensive coverage of all children with special needs. As we will discuss later, these two aims of individualization and comprehensiveness are not entirely compatible in practice.

The requirements of the law created severe problems for local school districts. Extending school responsibility to persons aged three to twenty-one and requiring identification, assessment, and service provision to be accomplished in the first year posed challenges well beyond the capacity of any school system at the time. Special education administrators began the 1974–1975 school year without specific guidelines for constituting assessment teams, evaluating children, or writing educational plans. The regulations stipulated what needed to be done, but provided no blueprint for administering the process. Both the division and organized parent groups had taken an adversarial stance toward local schools, and, as a result, administrators feared numerous court suits and appeals, which they believed they would lose. Parents, for the first time, were to be involved in educational planning for their own children, thereby challenging the autonomy of educators. Schools were to provide social, psychological, and medical services that many educators believed to be well beyond the legitimate purview of educational institutions. There was considerable doubt that full state reimbursement would in fact be available to pay for such services, and the likely competition for resources within school systems threatened to exacerbate underlying tensions between regular and special education. Furthermore, each step in implementing the law called for numerous forms to be completed, creating an enormous paperwork burden.

Under Chapter 766, what had formerly been a simple procedure informally worked out by the teacher, the specialist, and perhaps the parents, now became a major team undertaking with elaborate requirements governing each step. The process officially begins with a referral for assessment that may be initiated by a parent, teacher or other school official, court, or social agency. Before that, however, "all efforts shall be made to meet such children's needs within the context of the services which are part of the regular education program."[20] The referral must document these efforts. Within five days of the referral, a written notice is to be sent to the parents informing them of the types of assessments to be conducted, when the evaluation will begin, and their right to participate in all meetings at which the educational plan is developed. Parents have the right to meet with the evaluation-team chairperson to receive an explanation of the reason and the procedure for the evaluation. The parent must give written consent for the evaluation and its individual components before the assessments may be initiated.

In the case of a full core evaluation, required when it is expected that a child will be placed outside of the regular class for more than 25 percent of the time, at least five assessments must be completed. An administrative representative of the school department must assess the child's educational status. A recent or current teacher must measure "the child's specific behavioral abilities along a developmental continuum, . . . school readiness, functioning or achievement, . . . behavioral adjustment, attentional capacity, motor coordination, activity level and patterns, communication skills, memory and social relations with groups, peers and adults." A physician must conduct a comprehensive health examination. A psychologist must provide an assessment, "including an individually appropriate psychological examination, . . . a developmental and social history, observation of the child in familiar surroundings (such as a classroom), sensory, motor, language, perceptual, attentional, cognitive, affective, attitudinal, self-image, interpersonal, behavioral, interest and vocational factors." A nurse, social worker, guidance counselor, or adjustment counselor must make a home visit and evaluate "pertinent family history and home situation factors." Additional assessments by psychiatric, neurological, learning-disability, speech, hearing, vision, motor, or any other specialists will be carried out if needed.[21]

For each assessment, a detailed written report of the findings must be forwarded to the chairperson of the evaluation team and frequently to the evaluating specialist's supervisor. After the individual assessments are completed, team members may, if they choose, come together in a pre-core meeting to discuss their findings. Finally, there is another team meeting with parents in attendance, in which the educational plan is developed. The educational plan must include a specific statement of what the child can and cannot do, his or her learning style, educational goals, and plans for meeting them during the following three, six, and nine months. This entire process, starting from the day the notification letter is mailed to the parents and ending with the completion of the educational plan, is to take no more than thirty days.

These requirements presented school personnel with an enormous increase in their workload in several ways. There were suddenly many more children to be evaluated. Many more individuals had to take part in each evaluation. Educational plans had to be written in much greater detail, completed faster, and circulated to a wider audience. Because team members had different schedules and other responsibilities, getting everyone together for a meeting became a difficult task. An evaluation of a child that might previously have taken two or three people a few hours to complete now took as many as ten to twenty hours for the chairperson and two to six hours for each of the other team members.

From the standpoint of implementation, the chief difficulty presented by Chapter 766 revolved around the tension between the requirements for an individualized approach to educating children and the strong pressures for mass processing created by requirements for comprehensiveness. This tension between individualization and mass processing is not unique; it is characteristic of many street-level bureaucracies that attempt to reconcile individualized service with high demand relative to resources. Since street-level bureaucracies, particularly schools, may not officially restrict intake, other means must be found to accommodate the workload. Workload pressures in the past were at least partially responsible for many of the abuses that Chapter 766 was intended to correct: special needs children were subjected to arbitrary assessment, being labeled and dumped into segregated special classes, exclusion, denial of appropriate services, and unnecessary institutionalization. The workload pressures did not disappear with passage of the law. If anything, they increased under the substantial burden of added demands.

School personnel put forth extraordinary efforts to comply with the new demands. However, under the current system of public education there was simply no way that everything required could be done with the available resources. In the following sections we examine the objectives of the law against the reality of its implementation. The behavior described below indicates the limits of school organization. It does not so much reflect negatively on school personnel as it demonstrates how new demands are accommodated into the work structure of people who consistently must find ways to conserve resources and assert priorities to meet, in some way, the demands of their jobs.

Mainstreaming

Martin J. Kaufman and associates summarize the case for mainstreaming as based on the belief that it will remove stigmas; enhance the social status of special needs children; facilitate modeling of appropriate behavior by handicapped youngsters; provide a more stimulating and competitive environment; offer a more flexible, cost-effective service in the child's own neighborhood; and be more acceptable to the public, particularly to minority groups.[22]

Chapter 766 requires that, to the maximum extent feasible, children with special needs be placed in regular education programs, even if for just a small fraction of the school day. If possible, special classes are to be located within regular school facilities.[23] This provision, designed to end the practice of segregating handicapped children, originally evoked fears that special

TABLE 2
Special Needs Children by Program Prototype

	October 1974	October 1975
Percent of special needs children in regular class with support (i.e., no time out)	35.9	19.8
Percent of special needs children in regular class with up to 25 percent time out	43.9	56.2
Percent of special needs children in regular class less than 75 percent of the time	20.2	24.0

Source: Data supplied to the author by an official of the Massachusetts State Department of Education.

classes would be closed and large numbers of difficult-to-manage children would be returned to regular classrooms.

The specter of hordes of handicapped children being loosed upon regular class teachers never materialized. To begin with, there were probably not that many children in full-time, self-contained, separate programs. Furthermore, the regulations contained a "grandfather clause," whereby all children in special programs as of September 1974 were presumed to be correctly placed unless evidence was presented to the contrary. Data obtained from an official of the state department of education indicate that children were actually shifted from less to more restrictive programs during the first year of implementation. In part, this shift probably reflects increased use of resource rooms. Ironically, by providing separate rooms staffed by specialists to provide special education services, school systems *decreased* the proportion of fully integrated children by sending them out of the regular classrooms for special help. Table 2 shows the percentage of special needs children in various programs as of October 1974, as implementation was getting under way, and as of October 1975, after implementation.

With regard to mainstreaming, the law's major impact follows from its procedural barriers proscribing the inappropriate assignment of children to self-contained classes. While several instances of active recruitment of children by special-class teachers were noted during the study, such instances were rare. This was true not only because of a lack of space in existing special classes, but also because of a genuine commitment to mainstreaming on the part of special education administrators and most special-class teachers. Chapter 766 provided special educators the necessary leverage with principals and other administrators to expand and revamp services. There was, however, evidence that a subtle kind of dumping was taking place: there appeared to be a wholesale shifting of responsibility for troublesome children from the regular class teacher to a specialist or resource-room teacher.

We observed many close working relationships between regular class teachers and specialists. Specialists would sometimes consult teachers on how to handle particular classroom problems and how best to work with individual children. Some efforts were made to coordinate learning in the regular class with the specialist's intervention program. However, the maintenance of such relationships requires time, which was in short supply. Far more frequently, the teacher had little contact with specialists, had no knowledge of the content of the educational plan, and demonstrated an attitude that the child's learning or behavior problem was the responsibility of someone else, namely, the specialist. Even when specialists sought to work closely with teachers, the pressures of increased caseloads and the vastly increased time spent in the assessment process prevented them from doing so. Thus the law, while limiting the segregation of handicapped children, resulted in a further compartmentalization of students needing special services and increased the danger that they might be stigmatized on the basis of their need for help from specialists outside the regular classroom.

More Efficient Identification and Processing

According to estimates from the state department of education, only 50 percent to 60 percent of children with special needs had been identified and provided services by Massachusetts schools prior to the passage of Chapter 766.[24] The present regulations require local education authorities to undertake a range of activities to identify children in need of special services, although there was no shortage of referrals from teachers and parents. The systems studied varied in the way they translated this requirement into action. System B derived more than half of its referrals from pre- and in-school screening, while screening accounted for but a small fraction of the other two systems' referrals. Furthermore, in all three systems, the kinds of disorders identified through screening were directly related to the specialty of the person doing the screening. For example, System B, which relied much more heavily on speech specialists to conduct screening than the other two systems, referred more than twice as many children for evaluation because of speech problems. In many instances, those doing the screening were actually referring children to themselves. That is, the speech specialist conducting screening would more than likely participate in the core evaluation and eventually treat the child. This overlap of functions suggests that the local systems need to guard not only against failing to identify children in need of special services, but also against unnecessarily recruiting children not in need of special services.

One measure of the relative efficiency of the assessment process is the time required to complete an assessment. The regulations require that the evaluation take place within thirty working days after the parents are informed, or in no more than thirty-five days after the child is referred. Despite substantial differences among the three systems with regard to procedures and staffing, there was surprising uniformity in the time taken to complete assessments. The mean number of months taken to complete the assessments was 6.9 in System A, 7.8 in System B, and 7.9 in System C — all considerably longer than the time permitted under the law and longer than the three months permitted until the plan must be signed by the parent. In Systems B and C, where data were available, only 11.9 percent and 21.2 percent of referrals, respectively, were completed within three months. This is an index of the overwhelming scope of the task confronting the schools.

Equity, Uniformity, and Comprehensive Coverage

Chapter 766 seeks to end arbitrary and discriminatory practices through an individualized approach to the classification and assignment of children with special needs. This is to be accomplished in a way that assures a measure of equity — equal treatment for children with the same needs — as well as responsiveness to parents and teachers. Fiscal constraints and the governance procedures of local school systems impose the additional requirements of accountability, efficiency, and fiscal integrity. These aims constitute conflicting bureaucratic requirements.[25] In the absence of specific guidance from the state department, the three school systems we analyzed pursued different strategies, each of which maximized one or more of these requirements at some sacrifice of the others. The differing approaches to the core evaluation process taken by the three systems warrant brief description.

System A, with the smallest enrollment, designated a psychologist, a social worker, and a learning-disabilities specialist already on staff as the primary core evaluation team. Several additional part-time specialists were hired to supplement this team, and existing school-based specialists and teachers were brought in when appropriate. This system has a strong tradition of principal and school autonomy and professionalism. Thus, while the primary team did conduct most of the evaluation in the central district offices, many evaluations were done in the schools, sometimes without the participation of any of the primary-team members. This two-tiered arrangement produced wide disparities among schools in the identification and assessment of children. The team and administrators adopted a largely reactive stance toward evaluation and, for the most part, simply processed referrals coming to them. Personnel at all levels rationalized this reactive posture with the belief that most children with special needs were already being served, and that the services provided by the system were superior to those found in most other systems.

System B hired an outside business consultant to design a procedure for central oversight of the work flow. New forms and other required documents were developed for personnel involved at each step of the referral and evaluation process. Central files made it possible to determine which forms were outstanding for any particular child. On the whole, the record-keeping system was excellent. Assessments and educational plans were forwarded to administrative supervisors to ensure central quality control. An aggressive case-finding effort was enhanced by the thorough orientation of teachers and principals. School psychologists were designated as chairpersons of the core evaluation teams, and, to accommodate this added responsibility, the number of psychologists was doubled. The procedures adopted by System B tended to be dominated by a concern for completing forms properly and speedily. As a result, assessment meetings were conducted hastily and with a minimum of genuine deliberation.

In System C, the largest of the three but with the smallest per-pupil expenditure, most evaluations were attended by the special education administrator or one of the program directors. Their presence assured a high degree of quality control. These administrators viewed their participation as a means of training school-based staff through their example and interactions in the meetings. The evaluations were regarded as belonging to the schools, and the chairpersons of the core evaluation teams had a much more varied array of backgrounds than chairpersons in the other systems. Whereas in Systems A and B the outcome of an evaluation was usually predetermined, System C held relatively few of the "pre-core" meetings in which team members would meet, usually without the parents, to discuss the assessments and educational plan. As a result, the core meetings in System C tended to be characterized by a great deal of give-and-take, a high level of parent involvement, and genuine group problem-solving. The deliberations were longer, with more people involved, and this system conducted a much higher percentage of full core rather than pre-core evaluations.

One indication of the differences in style among the three systems is shown in a comparison of numbers of persons involved and time spent in the core-evaluation meetings. Of meetings observed, the mean duration was forty-two minutes in System A, fifty in System B, and seventy-four in System C. The mean number of participants was 6 in System A, 5.7 in B, and 9.5 in C. While the three systems developed idiosyncratic procedures for identifying and processing special needs children, all confronted the same serious problem: no explicitly mandated system of priority in referral, assessment, or provision of services accompanied the requirement for uniform treatment of children with special needs. It seemed as if all children were to be processed at once without official regard to the seriousness of the individual situation; a child with multiple physical and emotional problems was to be processed no sooner than a child with a slight hearing impairment.

In practice, all three school systems made unofficial distinctions between routine and complex cases. Routine cases were viewed by school personnel as those in which the completion of the educational plan form was necessary in order to provide the services of a specialist. In these cases, an implicit decision would be made prior to referral that a service was needed. The evaluation was then viewed as a bureaucratic hurdle to be gotten over as quickly as possible, in some cases even without the supposedly mandatory participation of parents. Many of these meetings took on a contrived, routine character. The more complex cases were those in which the assessment of the child was in fact problematic — there was some disagreement among school personnel regarding the assessment or educational plan, considerable expense to the school system might be involved, or the parents were viewed as potential "troublemakers." Troublesome parents were those thought likely to disrupt the process by complaining, questioning, or rejecting recommendations of professionals, or those whose higher socioeconomic status suggested to school personnel that a threat might be forthcoming. The percentage of complex cases varied considerably among the three school systems. In System C, the majority of cases fell into this category, while in systems A and B complex cases constituted perhaps no more than 15 percent to 25 percent of the referrals.

In addition to making distinctions among kinds of referrals, the three systems employed a variety of unofficial rationing techniques to hold down the number of referrals. First, teachers sometimes failed to refer children despite evidence of problems that should have indicated the need for evaluation. Classroom teachers were deterred by the necessity of completing the forms and justifying their assessment of the problem to the principal and specialists. For some teachers, acknowledgment of a problem they could not handle themselves represented failure. They could look forward to the end of the school year when they would pass the children on to the next teacher in line; consequently, many tended to refer only those who were most troublesome. Second, a principal would occasionally dissuade parents from requesting a core evaluation with assurances that the child was doing fine or that services were already being provided. Third, referrals from teachers were submitted through the principal and/or specialist, and in a number of instances, the principal or specialist would simply fail to follow through. Finally, administrators sometimes gave instructions to cut back on referrals. In one of the systems, principals having the largest number of referrals were told by the central administration to curtail evaluations because of the costs of services being recommended.

In general, these rationing practices resulted from unsanctioned, informal categorization of potential referrals. Such categorization reflected the personal priorities of the individuals making the referral decisions. In weighing the relative costs and benefits of referring a child for core evaluation, individuals implicitly appeared to act on several criteria. Concern for the well-being of their children was without question the foremost consideration for the greatest majority of school personnel. Without such concern, implementation of Chapter 766 would have broken down completely, for in all three school systems, administrators and specialists kept the process going by working extraordinarily long hours under constant stress with little hope of catching up, at least during the first year or two.

The institutional rewards system provided another criterion. Some principals believed that they themselves would be at least informally evaluated on the number and handling of referrals. In System B and System C, principals were encouraged to refer; in System A they were not.

The degree to which children were creating problems for teachers or other personnel because of their disruptive behavior also affected decisions. Teachers interviewed generally stated that they referred the "loudest" children first. This general criterion was supported by an examination of the dates of referral for learning and behavior problems: in Systems B and C, where sufficient data were available, behavior referrals occurred with greatest frequency in the first three months of the school year.

The speed of processing tended to be affected by the position of the person making the referral. In general, parent and principal referrals, while accounting for a relatively small percentage of total referrals, were processed more rapidly than those from teachers.

Finally, the availability of services within the system influenced decisions. In one system, school-based specialists decided informally whether or not a child should be referred on the basis of the presumed solution rather than the presented problem. If they foresaw a need to buy the services of additional specialists, a quick evaluation would be held.

Both systems and individual schools varied in their rate of referral and processing. By the end of June 1975, System A had completed evaluations on approximately 3.8 percent of its students; System B, on 5.5 percent; and System C, on 2.8 percent.[26] Some individual schools in these systems did not refer and evaluate any children, while others processed many. Of the schools in Systems B and C that had evaluated at least five children, some completed nearly half of the evaluations within the required three-month period, while others completed none. There were also variations in the reasons for referral. Speech problems were the primary referral reason for about 20 percent of children evaluated in System B, only 5 percent in System A, and fewer than 2 percent in System C. While learning referrals were relatively constant across the three systems, ranging from 58.1 percent to 65.9 percent of referrals, behavior referrals constituted 22.2 percent in System A, 13.6 percent in System B, and 29.2 percent in System C.

Thus, a law and its administrative regulations, intended to produce uniform application of procedures, instead yielded wide variations in application. The chances of a child's being referred, evaluated, and provided with special education services were associated with presumably extraneous factors: the school system and school attended, the child's disruptiveness in class, his or her age and sex,[27] the aggressiveness and socioeconomic status of the parents, the current availability and cost of services needed, and the presence of particular categories of specialists in the school system.

Parent Involvement and Interdisciplinary Team Assessment

Chapter 766 seeks to regulate arbitrary and inappropriate classification and assignment of children by placing restrictions on the use of standardized tests and by requiring joint assessment and planning by an interdisciplinary team that includes parents. The net effect of these required procedures in the three systems has been greater involvement of parents, more careful assessment of children, and some genuine team decisionmaking. But, at the same time, both teachers and parents have played a secondary role to specialists in the evaluation process.

The impact of parent participation was as much a function of the team's anticipating pressures from parents as it was a response to their actual involvement. In numerous instances, parents made substantial contributions to the assessment or planning processes; however, school personnel frequently took actions aimed at placating or avoiding conflict with parents. For example, one of the authors observed administrators in a lengthy meeting developing a defensive strategy for handling an angry mother whose child's referral papers had been lost by school personnel. Their primary concern was not why the referral did not get processed, but rather how to absolve themselves of responsibility.

The parent was usually in the position of joining an ongoing group; generally, the core-evaluation team had met as a group during other assessments, and its members worked together on a continuing basis. The parent, in addition, might confront a sometimes unsubtle implication that the child and parent were somehow at fault for creating a problem. This was particularly true when the problem involved disruptive behavior or a learning difficulty of which the nature was not readily apparent. Perhaps defensive about their lack of time, training, and skills to work with special needs children, some teachers we observed assigned blame to parents and children, and they were frequently joined in this by other personnel. In fact, the deliberations in assessment meetings often revealed an underlying preoccupation with the assignment of blame. Here, for example, the teacher asked to describe a child's strengths and weaknesses responds with negatives:

> Academically, he is below grade; he has a short attention span and a severe learning disability, poor handwriting, poor work habits; his desk is disheveled, and he never puts anything away. His oral is better than his written work. He never gives others a chance. He is uncooperative, ignores school rules — due in part to his frustration with learning. He can't stay in his seat. He won't accept pressure. He is interested in smoking, drugs, and alcohol and has a security problem. He has difficulty with all the specialists. He fights. . . .

There were additional factors that put parents at a disadvantage. Often there were status differences between a poor or working-class parent and the middle-class professionals who might dress differently and speak a different language. The use of technical jargon lent an aura of science to the proceedings, making much of the discussion unintelligible to parents and, frequently, to teachers as well. One psychologist explained test results to a working-class parent in this way: "He is poor in visual-motor tasks. He has come up [improved] on sequencing-object assembly-completions, which may reflect maturation in addition to training — that is, his visual-motor improvement. . . ." In another meeting, a tutor began, reading from a report: "Reading, 2.1 level; comprehensive language skills, good; daily performance, erratic. He is the type of child with learning problems — he has difficulty processing short sounds, auditory sequencing, and so forth. The visual is slightly better than the auditory channel." In another meeting, a teacher and psychologist, trying to convince a reluctant parent that her child should be held back for a year, produced a computer printout showing the child's performance on test scores in comparison to other children the same age. The parent immediately capitulated.

The regulations governing the core-evaluation meeting call for assessments to deal equally with the child's capacities and strengths as well as with deficiencies. However, an assessment was principally the result of someone's concern about deficiencies. Furthermore, the assessment provided official certification that the child had "special needs" that required services over and above those provided for most other children. Most of the core evaluation was devoted to verifying the child's negative functioning through the recitation of test scores, anecdotal information, and observations. The presentation of negative data appeared to serve two functions. First, teachers frequently presented negative data about a child in an apparently defensive strategy aimed at absolving themselves of responsibility for the child's problem. Second, the negative assessment of a child might prepare the way to obtain parents' compliance with whatever plan school officials wished to impose.

Increased Services

While much of the controversy and effort in the first year's operation of Chapter 766 revolved around the assessment process, the ultimate goal of the law is the provision of services. School systems are required to provide whatever services are recommended by the core-evaluation team for an individual child, without being constrained by cost considerations. If appropriate services are unavailable, the school system must develop them or send a child at local expense outside the system where such services may be obtained. Because of its remarkable comprehensiveness, we might have expected this provision to break down in practice through informal imposition of cost or referral restrictions. Nonetheless, we may still legitimately inquire into the extent to which the spirit of the provision was honored.

The requirements immediately expanded the range of options for special education and did lead to some expansion and redesign of special education services. In some respects, however, the implementation of Chapter 766 actually resulted in a reduction of services, at least during the first year. One problem was the wholesale withdrawal of services to schoolchildren by the departments of welfare, public health, and mental health, the Massachusetts Rehabilitation Commission, and other state agencies. Special education administrators bitterly complained of instances in which services previously offered to children at little or no cost were now being withdrawn or offered on a fee basis.

Even more demoralizing for school personnel was the reduction of in-school specialist services, which resulted from the assignment of these specialists to complete core evaluations. In general, the specialists who were involved in assessment and educational plan meetings were the same persons who would be called upon to provide the recommended services. These specialists, along with other team members, faced two problems: the sheer volume of new assessments; and the vastly increased time required to test or otherwise evaluate a child, write up the assessment report, attend the team meetings, and write the educational plan. Specialists were caught in a particularly difficult bind. Their contribution was essential to the assessment process. At the same time, a conscientious discharge of these responsibilities meant less time available to work with children and more time spent completing forms. One specialist said, "It just kills me to walk by those kids with them saying, 'Aren't you coming to see us today?'"

The most frequent response to this overwhelming workload burden was to work harder and longer hours completing paperwork at home. The considerable personal strain on those engaged in implementation at the local level was apparent. While additional staff members were hired in all three systems, this increase in numbers was rarely sufficient to meet the increased demand. That the law was carried out as well as it was is due to the dedication of those at the local level whose extra efforts constituted a sizable hidden subsidy to the school system.

However, the magnitude of the workload often forced specialists to short-change the assessment process. When assessments could not be bypassed, they were routinized. Meetings became cursory. Parent signatures were obtained on blank forms to cut down the time required to get the signed educational plans returned. Educational plans, instead of providing individually tailored programs, were most often little more than road maps routing children to one or more specialists during the school day.

Earlier we discussed the rationing of attention to assessments in response to the overwhelming demand. For the same reason, special educators rationed the services they provided to children. One form of such rationing was that services that in previous years had been offered on an individual, one-to-one basis were now delivered to groups. This practice was rationalized on the grounds that group treatment is more beneficial, which of course it may be. However, it is hardly accidental that this theoretical breakthrough was coincident with the additional burdens placed on special education personnel by Chapter 766. Also, the number of hours a specialist would see a child per week was reduced. There was increased reliance on student trainees to fill service gaps. And, finally, initiation of services might simply be postponed until later in the school year.

Team members often failed to respond to very obvious service needs voiced by parents, particularly those involving counseling for emotional problems. For example, upon hearing the results of the testing of her child, a mother looked up and said: "You know I have another boy, William. He probably has that same problem, but they didn't give him those tests. I thought he was lazy and thoughtless, but he was afraid to go into third grade. He wanted to go back to second." The teacher responded, "There is nothing wrong with going back to second." This was the end of that discussion.

The relationship between classroom teachers and specialists is also a source of tension. The specialist can provide some relief for the teacher in handling a classroom problem; however, there are costs to the teacher in seeking such help. Classroom teachers resent the added paperwork burden involved in initiating referrals and the amount of time it takes to get specialists' services through the core evaluation process. They too may be intimidated by the specialists' technical jargon. Like parents, they may be unfamiliar with the assessment process and outnumbered in evaluation meetings.

There are several additional factors inherent in the respective situations of specialists and teachers that contribute to this tension. Classroom teachers and specialists have differing perspectives. Teachers often regard special needs children as contributing to their difficulties at work, whereas specialists regard these children as clients they were specifically trained to assist. Teachers have only one school year during which to accomplish their objectives for individual children or the class as a whole, but specialists can take a longer view. They may work with children over a period of years spanning the children's entire school careers. Thus a problem of some urgency to the teacher may be seen by the specialist as one that may be put off until some time in the future.

Status differences add to the tension. Specialists typically have qualifications as classroom teachers but also have additional education and certification and, in some cases, higher pay. Furthermore, specialists and teachers are responsible to different lines of authority. The classroom teacher is responsible to the principal, while the specialist reports to a program director or division head who is generally located both physically and administratively close to the top of the system's hierarchy.

An additional source of tension is the discrepancy between teachers' expectations and results. Teachers look to the assessment process to provide some relief from disruptive children, but this expectation frequently remains unsatisfied. Teachers reported that 58 percent of the children they referred for evaluation exhibited behavior problems. However, only 21 percent of these children were reported by the teachers to be getting any help either outside the school system or from the specialist within the system whose job it was to deal with behavior problems. Responsibility for children is also a source of conflict between classroom teachers and specialists. Teachers are subject to conflicting pressures. On the one hand, they may wish to relinquish responsibility for an individual child whom they view as disruptive. On the other hand, they may view themselves as having primary responsibility for the child and may resent intrusion from outsiders. One teacher put it this way:

> The first- and second-grade teachers here had a list of five or six kids who ought to be retained. However, the psychologist recommended promotion on the basis of IQ tests. Teachers are losing their identity. We used to have teacher aides here who were paid $100 a week and that worked fine. Now they hire tutors at $6.75 an hour.

Elimination of Labeling

The Chapter 766 requirement to discontinue the use of descriptive labels conflicts with the limited capacity of street-level bureaucracies to classify and differentially treat clients. Labels function as client-management aids and also help define worker-client relationships. Many classroom teachers and specialists were educated in an era when diagnosis ended with the assignment of a label, which in turn provided the sole basis for placement and treatment. Such terminology is not easily unlearned. Under the new regulations, there was some reduction in the use of labels and a very definite shift to individual behavioral descriptions. However, the use of labels persisted, as is indicated by the following statements made at assessment meetings:

> The Bender showed her to have an equivalent score of a five-year-old. However, I don't think she is a trainable.

> John was getting an awful lot of special help. He used to be, with an IQ under 50, according to state law, in a trainable class, but he has been in an educable class and has been progressing beyond what one would expect based on test scores alone.

Chapter 766's aim to eliminate labels was also foiled by federal requirements demanding continued use of the traditional designations. Thus, the State Division of Special Education compelled local school systems to report, as they had in the past, the numbers of and expenditures for children specifically classified as mentally retarded, physically handicapped, partially seeing, speech-hearing handicapped, emotionally disturbed, and learning disabled.

Even as old labels persisted, new ones were invented. When a psychologist and counselor were contrasting programs for "LD [learning-disabled] kids" and "our kids," the observer asked who "our kids" were. The psychologist replied, "Oh, they used to be called retarded." In another instance, one teacher said that she ran a program for "substantially independent" girls. When asked what that meant, she replied, "Well, we used to call it the EMH [educable mentally handicapped] class."

Conclusion

In September 1974, Massachusetts school systems confronted challenges to their management capabilities and to their deployment of personnel. They were obliged by the commonwealth to identify all pupils with special education requirements, including those not previously so classified. Moreover, this responsibility extended to a population both younger and older than the population the schools had previously had to serve. The systems were charged with assessing the special needs of children through consultation with a variety of specialists and with the complete involvement of parents. And they were responsible for designing individualized programs appropriate to those needs, regardless of cost. They were expected to do this with virtually no authoritative assertion of priorities and without firm assurance that they would be entirely reimbursed by the state for increased expenditures. Administrators were caught between the requirements to comply with the law, which they took quite seriously although the state's initial monitoring effort was much weaker than had originally been indicated, and the certainty that their school committees would rebel against expenditures that led to increased taxes. While they had the upport of parent groups and others actively concerned with special education, school administrators were dubious about this support because these groups tended to be unsympathetic to any approach that implied that a school system would do less than the law required.

Special education personnel thus experienced pressures to accomplish enormous tasks in a short period of time with no certainty of substantially greater resources. Many school systems had already been moving in the direction indicated by Chapter 766, but now they *had* to accomplish what had previously been a matter of voluntary educational policy. Under the circumstances, special education personnel had to cope with their new job requirements in ways that would permit an acceptable solution to what theoretically appeared to be impossible demands.

That the systems we studied processed hundreds of children while maintaining the levels of services they did provide is a tribute to the dedication of school personnel and to the coercive, if diffuse, effects of the law. However, in certain respects the new law, by dictating so much, actually dictated very little. Like police officers who are required to enforce so many regulations that they are effectively free to enforce the law selectively, or public welfare workers who cannot master encyclopedic and constantly changing eligibility requirements and so operate with a much smaller set of regulations, special education personnel had to contrive their own adjustments to the multiple demands they encountered.

While not, for the most part, motivated by a desire to compromise compliance, school personnel had to formulate policies that would balance the new demands against available resources. To this end, school systems, schools, and individuals devised the following variety of coping patterns.

They rationed the number of assessments performed. They neglected to conduct assessments; placed limits on the numbers that were held; and biased the scheduling of assessments in favor of children who were behavior problems, who were not likely to cost the systems money, or who met the needs of school personnel seeking to practice their individual specialties.

They rationed services by reducing the hours of assignment to specialists, by favoring group over individual treatment, and by using specialists-in-training rather than experienced personnel as instructors. They short-circuited bureaucratic requirements for completing forms and for following the procedures mandated and designed to protect the interests of parents. They minimized the potentially time-consuming problem of getting parents to go along with plans by securing prior agreements on recommendations and by fostering deference to professional authority.

In short, they sought to secure their work environment. As individuals, teachers referred (dumped) students who posed the greatest threat to classroom control or recruited those with whom they were trained to work. Collectively, they sought contractual agreements that the new law would not increase their overall responsibilities.

These responses are not unique to special education personnel, but are typical of the coping behaviors of street-level bureaucrats. Chapter 766 placed additional burdens of judgment on roles already highly discretionary.

The patterns of responses developed by educators to the multiple demands placed upon them effectively constituted the policy delivered to the public under the new law. Given the range of possible "solutions" to the demand-resource dilemma faced by Massachusetts educators, the solution derived by any single school system was not predictable. One system made qualitatively superior efforts to comply with the law, but ranked lowest among the systems studied in the number of assessments completed. The system that screened and assessed the most students was also the most inclined to routinize the assessment procedures and dilute the quality of service provisions. But, although the pattern of responses varied to some extent, there was a constant need to routinize, ration resources, control uncertainties, and define the task to derive satisfactory solutions to the new demands.

Despite shortcomings in implementation, the new law has contributed to making special education a general concern. It opens the process of categorizing special needs children to parents and to the scrutiny of special education interest groups. It articulates far-reaching objectives for school systems, retains local initiative, and forces a confrontation between school systems' responsibilities for general *and* special education. Chapter 766 heralds the day when all students, the quiet as well as the disruptive, the average as well as the exceptional, those who make good use of their potential and those who do not, will be responded to by the schools as individuals. In this respect, the first year of Chapter 766 should be analyzed not only for the ways in which the coping behaviors of school personnel perpetuate routinization of tasks and segmentation of the population. It should also be analyzed to discover which solutions to coping problems are most consistent with preferred educational objectives.

As the Massachusetts schools complete their third year of operation under Chapter 766, the situation has no doubt changed from the time of our field study. We cannot, however, predict that it has improved. The regulations have been somewhat revised to reflect the operating experience of the schools, and the Department of Education is attempting to audit local school systems' performance. The early crush of assessments we observed during the first year has no doubt subsided. However, we suspect that the pressure on school personnel to complete assessments has simply given way to pressure to implement, monitor, and revise the educational plans written earlier. If so, our analysis would suggest that these same personnel will now be forced to adopt coping mechanisms similar to those we have described as they attempt to deliver the educational services they prescribed earlier. Furthermore, in all likelihood the assessment and treatment routines and practices established under the press of that first hectic year are now firmly entrenched. As for cost considerations, school systems continue to be concerned about expenditures, but now try to assign many regular education items to the special education budget, since Chapter 766 expenditures have first claim in the state's educational-reimbursement program.

The recent enactment of federal special education reform and the likelihood that public pressure on the courts will eventually force nonparticipating states to adopt such reform suggests that close attention be paid to the Massachusetts experience. The Education for All Handicapped Children Act of 1975 (PL 94-142) raises the prospect that the kinds of implementation problems that plagued Massachusetts will be repeated across the country. For example, by requiring participating states to undertake more activities than Congress is likely to subsidize, the federal law appears to set the stage for the same kind of autonomous priority setting by individual communities that characterized the Massachusetts experience. This is perhaps the first lesson of the Massachusetts case. States attempting special education reform should expect to encounter problems similar to the ones discussed here if funding is uncertain and local communities must bear the brunt of costs.

There are other lessons for the implementation of laws that seek to change practice at the street level. An essential beginning in special education reform is the careful preparation of local personnel. Training classroom teachers to be better prepared and more confident in handling children with special needs is particularly important. Specialists need training in consultative skills so that they may better support classroom teachers. Unless roles are redefined and personnel prepared to meet new requirements, children will continue to be shunted from one specialist to the next with no one having responsibility for the whole child.

Second, rather than simply monitoring compliance with case-finding and assessment requirements, state departments of education should emphasize service provision and should exercise leadership in helping local systems establish, expand, and improve services. In Massachusetts, some local school systems were loath to share service innovations with other systems with which they competed for federal grant funds. The spirit of local independence and autonomy, perhaps at its strongest in New England towns, also impeded the kind of sharing and exchange that could have fostered joint solutions to implementation problems. Instead, each system invented its own evaluation-team model and way of controlling the paper flow and improvised numerous other responses to state requirements. At the federal level, the Bureau of Education for the Handicapped is giving priority to the development and dissemination of practical tools — a model evaluation manual and service prototypes, for example — that will help states get their programs under way. These may prove to be useful guides if they are not overtaken by events.

Third, it is often assumed that parents' interests are secured by parent participation. But our observations indicate that parents may be subjected to strong pressures from school personnel and may acquiesce in decisions not in the best interests of their children, despite the protection of the law. To properly safeguard the rights of children, each assessment team might include a volunteer or a staff member of another agency who would fill the role of child advocate.

Fourth, as implementation is substantially determined by the coping behaviors of those who have to carry out the new law, it would be useful to analyze these behaviors and reward those that most closely conform to preferred public objectives, while discouraging objectionable practices. Bureaucratic coping behaviors cannot be eliminated, but they can be monitored and directed.

Practical men and women charged with carrying out new legislation understandably and correctly seek appropriate responses, clarity in objectives and priorities, and certainty of support. Our analysis has focused on how school personnel respond when these matters are in doubt. But our findings do not mean that social reform legislation should be limited to mandating only that which street-level personnel can easily accomplish. On the contrary, much would be lost by reducing the scope of legislation to only that which can be readily accommodated. Rather than encouraging concentration of resources on a limited number of children, Chapter 766 cries out for increasing the scope of coverage. Preschoolers and post-high school minors have now become, by law, the responsibility of school systems. Parents may petition for special services and challenge schools' decisions about children's care. Indeed, the vision of many educators with whom we spoke was that the law would open the way to treating *every* child as deserving individual assessment and an individualized learning plan. This would be particularly true for the brightest students, generally thought to be a neglected group whose ordinary treatment in school provides suboptimal education and nurtures emotional problems. In short, the thrust of Chapter 766 is, if anything, to increase and expand services. But, as usually happens in most street-level bureaucracies, service providers are left to ration what legislatures and policymaking executives will not.

Concentrating too much on issues of coordination and phasing at the state level also misses the mark to some degree. This focus overlooks the role of law in giving legitimacy to conceptions of the social order and in directing people's energies toward objectives even if these objectives cannot be achieved completely in the short run. Thus, one can argue that the Massachusetts legislature was correct in advancing a law with a scope as broad as the needs of the children and young adults who were to be served. It is not at all obvious that the provision of special education services would have been more extensive or of better quality had the scope of the law been restricted. And one can argue that the parent and advocacy groups were correct in preventing the division of special education from asserting priorities: this kind of limitation not only would have contradicted the law, but also would have substituted state planning for local responsibility.

The case of special education in Massachusetts provides a sober lesson in how difficult it is to integrate special services for a stigmatized population, particularly when that population is attended by professional specialists, funded through separate channels, championed by people fearful that they will lose hard-won access to decisionmaking, and perceived to cause work-related problems for those responsible for managing the integration. In such a situation, the role of law in legitimizing new conceptions of the public order and in mobilizing resources should not be overlooked.

Notes

1. Chapter 766 of the Acts of 1972, The Commonwealth of Massachusetts.
2. This formulation is elaborated in Michael Lipsky, "Toward a Theory of Street-Level Bureaucracy," in *Theoretical Perspectives on Urban Politics*, ed. Willis D. Hawley and Michael Lipsky (Englewood Cliffs, NJ: Prentice-Hall, 1976), pp. 186–212.
3. The literature on policy implementation is considerable and growing rapidly. For two relatively recent reviews, see Erwin C. Hargrove, *The Missing Link: The Study of the Implementation of Social Policy* (Washington, DC: Urban Institute, 1975); and Donald Van Meter and Carl Van Horn, "The Policy Implementation Process: A Conceptual Framework," *Administration and Society, 6* (1974), 445–488.
4. See, for example, Orville G. Johnson, "Special Education for the Mentally Handicapped — A Paradox," *Exceptional Children, 29* (1962), 62–69; Howard L. Sparks and Leonard S. Blackman, "What Is Special About Special Education Revisited: The Mentally Retarded," *Exceptional Children, 32* (1965), 242–247; Lloyd M. Dunn, "Special Education for the Mildly Retarded — Is Much of It Justifiable?" *Exceptional Children, 35* (1968), 5–22; and Stephen M. Lilly, "Special Education: A Teapot in a Tempest," *Exceptional Children, 37* (1970), 43–49.

   For a summary of parent-instigated court challenges to testing, placement procedures, and special-class programming, see Sterling L. Ross, Jr., Henry G. DeYoung, and Julius S. Cohen, "Confrontation: Special Education Placement and the Law," *Exceptional Children, 38* (1971), 5–12.

   A more recent article provides an excellent exposition of mainstreaming, its antecedents, and the difficulties in implementing it: Martin J. Kaufman, Jay Gottlieb, Judith A. Agard, and Maurine B. Kukic, "Mainstreaming: Toward an Explication of the Construct," *Focus on Exceptional Children, 7* (1975), 1–12.
5. Johnson, "Special Education for the Mentally Handicapped," p. 66.

6. Task Force on Children Out of School, *The Way We Go to School: The Exclusion of Children in Boston* (Boston: Beacon Press, 1971).

7. For a detailed treatment of school classification, see David L. Kirp, "Schools as Sorters: The Constitutional and Policy Implications of Student Classification," *University of Pennsylvania Law Review, 121* (1973), 705–797.

8. See Burton Blatt and Frank Garfunkel, *Massachusetts Study of Educational Opportunities for Handicapped and Disadvantaged Children* (Boston: Massachusetts Advisory Council on Education, 1971), esp. pp. 273–284.

9. C. 766 §1.

10. C. 766 §9 (1).

11. K. Fred Daniel and Joseph W. Crenshaw, "What Has Been and Should Be the Role of State Education Agencies in the Development and Implementation of Teacher Education Programs (Both Pre- and In-Service)? A Review and Analysis of Literature," Washington, DC: U.S. Office of Education, Order No. OEC–0–71–3315, September 3, 1971.

12. Muriel L. Cohen, "Massachusetts to Fill 29 Special Education Jobs," *Boston Globe,* August 2, 1973. See also C. 766, §2, for a description of the powers and duties of the Division of Special Education.

13. An internal document of the Massachusetts Division of Special Education, "766 Update," May 1974, lists $146,000 of federal Title V funds as allocated to the child-assessment, or "core evaluation," process.

14. Mary Thornton, "Unfunded Chapter 766: Who Finally Will Foot the Bill?" *Boston Globe,* February 24, 1974; and James Worsham, "State Says Extra Ch. 766 Cost is $40 M, Not $100 M," *Boston Globe,* February 27, 1974.

15. Editorial, "Paying School Costs," *Boston Globe,* March 5, 1974.

16. Editorial, "Paying School Costs."

17. On some of the problems of translating legislation into practice mentioned here, see, for example, Edward C. Banfield, "Making a New Federal Program: Model Cities, 1964–1978," in *Policy and Politics in America,* ed. Allan P. Sindler (Boston: Little, Brown, 1973), pp. 124–158; Theodore Lowi, *The End of Liberalism* (New York: Norton, 1969); Martha Derthick, *New Towns In-Town* (Washington, DC: Urban Institute, 1972); and Jeffrey L. Pressman and Aaron B. Willdavsky, *Implementation* (Berkeley: University of California Press, 1973).

18. Milton Budoff traces the early development of support for special education in "Engendering Change in Special Education Practices," *Harvard Educational Review, 45* (1975), 507–526.

19. Cohen, "Massachusetts to Fill 29 Special Education Jobs."

20. Commonwealth of Massachusetts, Department of Education, "Regulations for the Implementation of Chapter 766 of the Acts of 1972: The Comprehensive Special Education Law," May 28, 1974 (henceforth referred to as "Regulations"), para. 314.0, p. 17.

21. The procedures for a full core evaluation are set forth in the "Regulations," para. 320.0, pp. 21–22. An intermediate core evaluation may be given, with the parent's approval, in those cases in which it is expected that the child will *not* be placed outside a regular class more than 25 percent of the time. It differs from the full core evaluation only in that fewer assessments are required. ("Regulations," para. 331.0, p. 34.)

22. Kaufman et al., "Mainstreaming," p. 2.

23. "Regulations," para. 502.10 (a), p. 58.

24. Mary Thornton, "Regulations on Special Education to Hike Taxes," *Boston Globe,* February 22, 1974. These estimates, it should be noted, were derived by applying the widely accepted national incidence figures of about 12 percent to the state's school population.

25. See James Q. Wilson, "The Bureaucracy Problem," *Public Interest, 6* (1967), 3–9.
26. Statewide, systems completed evaluations in a range from 2 percent to 20 percent.
27. The mean age of children evaluated varied from 12.6 years in System A to 7.5 in System B and 10.3 in System C. In all three school systems, males evaluated outnumbered females by between two and three to one.

The research on which this article is based was conducted under grants from the Russell Sage Foundation and the Bureau of Education for the Handicapped, Grant No. G00-75-0053. We are greatly indebted to the many people involved in special education affairs in Massachusetts who, despite severe time pressures, assisted with the study. We especially wish to thank Milton Budoff, Cynthia Gilles, and Frank Garfunkel for their support and encouragement in our undertaking this project, and Loren Dessonville and Lee Miringoff for their able assistance in the field research. This article is a revised and condensed version of a paper originally presented at the Annual Meeting of the American Political Science Association, Chicago, September 1976, and later issued as a working paper by the MIT-Harvard Joint Center for Urban Studies.

Part 2:
The Reassessment of Special Education

Beyond Special Education: Toward a Quality System for All Students

ALAN GARTNER

DOROTHY KERZNER LIPSKY

In one of the most widely disseminated articles in the history of special education, Alan Gartner and Dorothy Lipsky review the first decade of experience with the implementation of PL 94-142 and demonstrate that, contrary to legislative intent, the implementation of the act has resulted in increased segregation for students designated disabled. Although they acknowledge considerable progress in some areas, such as the provision of education to previously unserved populations, Gartner and Lipsky question the current referral, assessment, and placement processes, particularly as they apply to the so-called mildly disabled. Although procedural due process protection was incorporated into the law, the belief that such protection would lessen misdiagnosis and separation (see Kirp, ch. 1) is not supported by the authors' analysis. In addition to reporting an increased tendency toward segregation, Gartner and Lipsky document a variety of differing identification and placement processes, thus questioning the legitimacy of current practices. Along with reporting the failure of segregated practices in special education, they call for a revised educational system based on the values of inclusion and grounded in effective pedagogical practices. These authors have since articulated a new vision for special education in their book Beyond Separate Education *(1989), which continues to generate critical reflection in this area.*

> Thank you for your letter in which you ask about data concerning children who had been certified as handicapped and have returned to regular education.
>   While these are certainly very interesting data you request, these data are not required in State Plans nor has the Office of Special Education Programs collected them in any other survey.
> — *Letter to Alan Gartner from Patricia J. Guard, Deputy Director, Office of Special Education Programs, U.S. Department of Education, November 7, 1986*

The decision not to collect "interesting data" can conceivably be made for various reasons. For instance, policymakers may believe that the data are not important, or they may fear the results, or believe that the collection process is not worth the potential benefit. No doubt collecting decertification data might be difficult, and most likely would show an embarrassingly low level of return to general education. We believe, however, that the major reason such data are not collected has to do with beliefs and attitudes — some implicit, some explicit — generally held about the purposes of special education and about special education students.

The faults of current special education practice, as we will detail in the following pages, are myriad. It incorporates a medical view of disability that characterizes the disability as inherent in the individual and thus formulates two separate categories of people, handicapped and nonhandicapped, as useful and rational distinctions. This arbitrary division of students provides the rationale for educating students with handicapping conditions in separate programs, and even in completely separate systems.[1] The assumptions underlying separate programs have produced a system that is both segregated and second class.

The needs of students with handicapping conditions have led some parents and professionals to accept the notion of separate, if quality, education. We will argue that the current system has proven to be inadequate because it is a system that is not integrated, and that we must learn from our mistakes and attempt to create a new type of unitary system, one that incorporates quality education for all students.

It is our belief that the attitudes and assumptions about the disabled and disability require change, as do the inadequacies in general and special education practice. The need for such changes is both consequence and cause of a unitary system, thereby encouraging the production of an education model for all students — supple, variegated, and individualized — in an integrated setting.

While special education programs of the past decade have been successful in bringing unserved students into public education and have established these students' right to education, these programs have failed both to overcome the separation between general and special education and to make the separate system significant in terms of student benefits. This article first examines developments of the past decade, then analyzes the current failures, and, finally, formulates recommendations that will improve these programs in the future.

Background to the Law

There are many possible beginnings for a discussion of the current status of education of students with handicapping conditions. We start with *Brown v. Board of Education* (347 U.S. 483). In doing so, we wish to make three points:

1) to note the importance of education to the "life and minds" of children; 2) to set the framework concerning the inherent inequality of separate education; and 3) to recognize that advocacy efforts in the 1960s and 1970s on behalf of persons with disabilities were drawn from the context of the civil rights movement. One of the tactics that the disability rights movement learned from the Black civil rights movement was how to produce change in policies and practices through use of both the legal system and the legislature. Indeed, many see developments in special education as the logical outgrowth of civil rights efforts of an earlier period.

Between 1966 and 1974, a series of federal laws focusing on children with disabilities and the services they needed were enacted. Together, these laws can be seen as capacity building: preparing personnel, launching a set of discretionary grant programs, establishing the Bureau of Education for the Handicapped in what was then the U.S. Office of Education, providing capital funds, developing regional centers for deaf-blind children, and establishing authority for research and demonstration projects.

The concerns of adults with disabilities were addressed in the Rehabilitation Act of 1973. The Act provided a comprehensive program of vocational rehabilitation and independent living, established a federal board to coordinate and monitor access to public buildings and transportation, prohibited discrimination in employment, required affirmative action by federal agencies and federal contractors, and, almost as an afterthought, proclaimed a national mandate prohibiting discrimination against the handicapped by recipients of federal assistance (Section 504).[2]

Parents of children with disabilities were essential contributors in the legislative strategy and took the lead in litigation. Here the parent groups followed the precedent of *Brown* in its assertion of the essential importance of education. Two key decisions, *Pennsylvania Association of Retarded Citizens (PARC) v. Commonwealth* (334 F. Supp. 1257) and *Mills v. Board of Education* (348 F. Supp. 866), in 1971 and 1972, respectively, rejected reasons school districts had given for excluding students with handicapping conditions. In *PARC,* the federal district court overturned a Pennsylvania law that had relieved schools of the responsibility of enrolling "uneducable" or "untrainable" children. Basing its opinion on extensive expert testimony, the court ruled that mentally retarded children could benefit from education. In *Mills,* the federal district court ruled that a district's financial exigencies could not be the basis for excluding students with handicaps; they could not be made to take last place in the queue for funds.

The process of enacting PL 94-142, the Education for All Handicapped Children Act, began in the spring of 1974. Building both on the earlier legislative efforts and court cases, as well as a growing number of state laws extending the right to attend school to students with disabilities, Representative John Brademas (D-IN) introduced H.R. 7217; six months later Senator Jennings Randolph (D-WV) introduced S. 6. The Senate bill was passed by a vote of 83 to 10 on June 18, 1975, and the House bill by a vote of 375 to 44 on July 29. The key issues in the conference committee were: 1) funding levels, involving a cap on the number of students who could be counted as handicapped for funding purposes (as well as an internal cap on the number of learning-disabled students); 2) the respective roles of state education departments and local school districts; 3) services for children aged three to five; 4) the requirement of an individualized education plan (IEP) for each student; and 5) the date for full implementation of the law. The conference report was passed in the House on November 18 and in the Senate the next day with overwhelming majorities (only seven votes against in each chamber). After some suspense about whether President Gerald Ford would veto the bill because of its cost, he signed it into law ten days later.[3]

Public Law 94-142

As it presently exists, there is a duality inherent in PL 94-142. It contains a mixture both of attention to the needs of individual students and of provisions designed to solve problems that children with handicapping conditions experienced because the public school system, and other public agencies, failed to address the issue properly. One of its authors suggests that six basic principles are incorporated in the law: 1) the right of access to public education programs; 2) the individualization of services; 3) the principle of "least restrictive environment; 4) the scope of broadened services to be provided by the schools and a set of procedures for determining them; 5) the general guidelines for identification of disability; and 6) the principles of primary state and local responsibilities.[4]

In the previous decade, federal law, state statutes, and court decisions had begun to reduce the exclusion of children with disabilities from public education programs or the charging of their parents for services otherwise provided at no cost to nondisabled children. Often, exclusions were based on categorical statements about classes of "uneducable" children or in deference to professional judgments on a child's educability. The law eliminated this exclusion of children with disabilities: it stated in the unambiguous language of its title that "all handicapped children" were to be provided with a free public education. Henceforth, no child was to be rejected as uneducable.

Once students with handicaps were included in public education, Congress wanted to assure that each student, particularly one with severe handicaps, would receive services based upon individual need, not upon categories of handicap or pre-existing service offerings. The law explicitly required a multidisciplinary individual evaluation that was nondiscriminatory, and the development of an individualized education plan (IEP).

While each student's placement was to be individually determined, the law, in keeping with its philosophic acceptance of the concepts of "normalization," expressed a strong presumption that students with disabilities be placed in regular classes whenever possible, where they could receive specialized services as necessary.[5] Only when regular classroom placements did not meet individual students' needs would they be placed in separate classes or settings. This was expressed in the law's requirement that students be educated in the "least restrictive environment" (LRE).

The law, while rejecting the traditional medical model of disability, recognized that some of these students needed more than educational services alone to be successful in school.[6] Hence the concept of "related services" was developed, incorporating those services — including counseling, physical and occupational therapy, and some medical services — necessary to enable students to take advantage of and benefit from the educational program. In addition to describing the scope of services to be provided, the law established a process for determining students' handicapping condition, educational placement, and related services, which incorporated parental involvement and required substantial due process procedures and appeal rights.

During the course of the congressional debate, there was considerable dispute about the total number of students who would be eligible for services, and, foreshadowing a continuing issue, the number of those defined as having specific learning disabilities within that overall figure. For funding purposes, caps of 12 percent and 2 percent of the total school population, respectively, were set. Procedural guidelines were set for identification, assessment, and placement of students, with particular emphasis on nondiscrimination and procedural due process.

As was to be expected, the respective roles of the state and local educational agencies and the flow of money were key issues in the congressional consideration. While the House bill required that funds go directly to local educational agencies (LEAs), the Council of Chief State School Officers argued in favor of state responsibility for monitoring local school districts and gained a victory for the state educational agencies (SEAs). Funds were to flow through SEAs, with requirements that annual increasing percentages be passed on to the local level. Also, while recognizing that other state agencies might provide services to the students, particularly the severely impaired, the SEA had responsibility for assuring that the educational services were provided, regardless of who provided or paid for them or where the student received them.

The Current Situation

While there was considerable concern about the feasibility of implementing PL 94-142, and some difficulty in doing so at the compliance level, by and large it has been accomplished:

– Over six hundred and fifty thousand more students are being served now than when the law was enacted. During the 1985–1986 school year, somewhat over 4.37 million students received services under the provisions of PL 94-142.[7] This comprised approximately 11 percent of the total public school enrollment (a slight drop from the previous year), with percentages in some states pushing against the 12 percent cap. Generally, educators believe that few, if any, students needing services have not been identified.

– There has been a substantial increase in the funds devoted to special education, from $100 million in FY 1976 to $1.64 billion in FY 1985, for PL 94-142. However, the promised federal contribution (40 percent of the average per pupil cost by 1982) has never been met. Current figures are around 8.5 percent,[8] with states (54 percent) and local governments (37 percent) providing the difference.

– While there are some exceptions, such as students in prisons, from migrant families, and in some institutional settings, for the most part location of the student does not seem to be a factor in the availability of services. The overall responsibility of SEAs has been achieved, perhaps more so in special education than in other areas of SEA-LEA joint responsibility. With New Mexico's submission of a state plan in August 1984, all fifty states are presently participating under PL 94-142.

In these areas, the implementation of the law has been successful. And to turn now, more extensively, to areas of lesser achievement is neither to gainsay that achievement nor deny its rightness.

While considerations of each of the issues in the conduct of special education is required, we will focus here on only those areas in special education that have emerged as the most troubling. These include referral and assessment procedures, placement options, educational programs, Least Restrictive Environment (LRE), and parental participation.

Referral and Assessment Procedures

Perhaps no area in special education has received as much concern as have procedures used for the referral, assessment, and eventual placement of students. Together, these activities raise substantive issues: 1) cost, a key factor in the congressional capping of the number of students (at 12 percent) who could be counted for funding purposes; 2) professional judgment, particularly with regard to identification of students with learning disabilities; and 3) discrimination, as seen in the disproportionate number of minority and limited-English-proficient students referred for evaluation and placed in certain categories. These issues can be framed as a sequence of questions:

1. Who is being referred and on what basis?
2. What is the nature of the assessment?
3. What are the bases of the placement?
4. What is the likelihood, once a student is placed in a special education setting, that appropriate programs and services will be provided?
5. What is the likelihood, once these programs are provided, that the student will return to general education?

Aside from those students with obvious physical handicaps who are identified before entering a classroom, referral occurs, for the most part, "when student behavior and academic progress varies from the school norm. . . ."[9] The assumption in such cases is that there is something wrong with the student. In particular, referral is more likely to occur in cases where the student is a member of a minority group or from a family whose socioeconomic status varies from the district's norm.[10] Further,

> decisions about special education classification are not only functions of child characteristics but rather involve powerful organizational influences. The number of programs, availability of space, incentives for identification, range and kind of competing programs and services, number of professionals, and federal, state, and community pressures all affect classification decisions.[11]

Referral rates vary widely. This is apparent from examining two different sets of data from twenty-eight large cities. As a percentage of total student enrollment, referral rates range from 6 percent to 11 percent. The figures for assessment vary even more widely. For the same twenty-eight cities, the percentage of students who are referred and then placed in special education ranges from 7.8 percent to 91.8 percent.[12]

The most extensive study of the evaluation process reports that results are barely more accurate than a flip of the coin, with the evaluation process often providing a psychological justification for the referral.[13] The leading researchers conclude that current classification procedures are plagued with major conceptual and practical problems.[14]

While PL 94-142 includes eleven different classifications of handicapping conditions,[15] "most diagnoses of students placed in special education programs are based on social and psychological criteria. These include measured intelligence, achievement, social behavior and adjustment, and communication and language problems. Furthermore, many of the measuring criteria used in classification lack reliability or validity. . . ."[16] According to one observer, when test results do not produce the desired outcome, evaluators often change the yardstick: "If the test scores indicate the child is ineligible, but the teacher really feels the child needs help, we try to select other tests that might make the child eligible. . . ." The tests then become "a means of corroborating referral decisions. Testing, therefore, does not drive decisions but is driven by decisions."[17]

The major classification problems concern those students labeled as learning disabled. The number of students classified as learning disabled rose 119 percent between 1976–1977 and 1984–1985, at a time when the overall special education population rose 16 percent. The growth has been slowed in the past two school years. In 1985–1986, students labeled as learning disabled accounted for 42.8 percent of the students — aged three through twenty-one — receiving special education services.[18] The percentage of special education students labeled as learning disabled varied from 30 percent to 67 percent among the fifty states, and from zero percent to 73 percent among thirty large cities.[19]

In what can be fairly called a form of classification plea bargaining, this growth in those labeled as learning disabled has been accompanied by a decline (by some 300,000 between 1976–1977 and 1983–1984) in those labeled as mentally retarded. The Department of Education gently explains, "These decreases in the number of children classified as mentally retarded are the result of an increasing sensitivity to the negative features of the label itself and to the reaction on the part of local school systems to allegations of racial and ethnic bias as a result of the use of discriminatory or culturally biased testing procedures."[20]

The problem is not only the excessive numbers of students classified as learning disabled; there are even more troubling issues as to the accuracy of the label:

– More than 80 percent of the student population could be classified as learning disabled by one or more definitions presently in use.[21]

– Based upon the records of those already certified as learning disabled and those not, experienced evaluators could not tell the difference.[22]

– Students identified as learning disabled cannot be shown to differ from other low achievers with regard to a wide variety of school-related characteristics.[23]

– A study of special education in Colorado concluded: "The single most important finding is that more than half the children do not meet statistical or valid clinical criteria for the identification of perceptual or communicative disorders."[24]

Summarizing national data on the subject, the authors of one study remarked, "At least half of the learning disabled population could be more accurately described as slow learners, as children with second-language backgrounds, as children who are naughty in class, as those who are absent more often or move from school to school, or as average learners in above-average school systems."[25]

Such results are not surprising, given reports concerning the inadequacy and inappropriateness of the measuring instruments, the disregard of results in decisionmaking, and, often, the evaluators' incompetence and biases.[26] A decade later, there is nothing to warrant changing Nicholas Hobbs's assessment that the classification system of students with disabilities is "a major barrier to the efficient and effective delivery of services to them and their families and thereby impedes efforts to help them."[27] The standard for assessment, in special education as elsewhere, should be validity and reliability on a series of axes.

Placement Options

While referral and assessment procedures vary widely, and students are "placed" in special education programs based upon such discrepant outcomes, PL 94-142 is clear concerning least restrictive environment (LRE) criteria, namely, that "removal from the regular education environment" is to occur "only when the nature and severity of the handicap is such that education in regular classes with the use of supplementary aids cannot be achieved satisfactorily" [Sec. 612 (5) (B)]. There is, however, wide variability in the implementation of the federal law at the local level. This is shown in Table 1, which presents data showing the percentage of students with the four most frequent handicapping conditions who are placed in regular classes, the placement favored by the law. These four categories together account for 95 percent of all students classified as "handicapped."

Overall, 74 percent of special education students are in pull-out or separate programs. For each handicapping condition, the variation among states

TABLE 1

Percent of Students with Handicapping Conditions in Regular Classes

	All Conditions	Learning Disabled	Speech Impaired	Mentally Retarded	Emotionally Disturbed
U.S. average	69	78	96	31	44
State with highest percent in regular classes	90	99	100	84	88
State with lowest percent in regular classes	36	35	75	3	8

Source: Seventh Annual Report to the Congress on the Implementation of the Education of the Handicapped Act, Table 6C3.

is substantial. For the students labeled as learning disabled (LD), 16 percent are in regular classes, with a range from 0.06 percent to 98 percent — in effect, from a bare handful in Arizona to nearly all students in Alabama. For those students labeled as speech-impaired, the national average is 64 percent of the students in regular classes, ranging from zero percent in Mississippi to nearly all in Alabama. For those students labeled as mentally retarded (MR), the national average is 5 percent in regular classes, and ranges from zero percent in five states to 50 percent in New Hampshire. Finally, for those students labeled emotionally disturbed (ED), the national average is 12 percent in regular classes, and ranges from zero percent in four states to 74 percent in Alabama.

Such results indicate that students with seemingly identical characteristics qualify for different programs, depending on where they reside and how individuals on school staffs evaluate them. Most often, these are pull-out programs, despite evidence about their lack of efficacy.[28]

Patterns of service often appear to relate more to the systems of funding than to indices of pupil benefit. For example, each of the states with the highest percentage of the students in these four categories placed in regular classes used the same type of funding formula ("cost" basis), while in all but one case the states with the lowest percentage of students in the four categories in regular classes used another type of formula ("unit" basis).[29]

The consequence in New York, for example, was to reward LEAs for assigning students to more restrictive rather than less restrictive placements, and for assigning them outside of the public school system to private schools.[30] In other words, rather than encouraging and supporting the mandate of the law to place students in the least restrictive environment, current New York State Education Department practice rewards the opposite.

Some have argued that such funding practices explain both the growth of special education and the absence of decertification or the return of students to general education once they have met their IEP objectives in special education. While funding patterns no doubt have their consequences, we will argue that a set of attitudes is more important in producing the current pattern. Here it is sufficient to note that among twenty-six large cities, fewer than 5 percent of students in special education return to general education, with a range of zero percent to 13.4 percent.[31] No national figures, however, have been collected on the number of students who were certified as handicapped and who have returned to general education.

Educational Programs

The basic premise of special education is that students with deficits will benefit from a unique body of knowledge and from smaller classes staffed by specially trained teachers using special materials. We will address these assumptions of a segregated special education system in the concluding section of this article; here we cite recent research findings that support an integrated setting.

There is no compelling body of evidence that segregated special education programs have significant benefits for students. On the contrary, there is substantial and growing evidence that goes in the opposite direction.[32] In fifty recent studies comparing the academic performance of mainstreamed and segregated students with handicapping conditions, the mean academic performance of the integrated group was in the eightieth percentile, while the segregated students scored in the fiftieth percentile.[33]

A review of programs for academically handicapped students found no consistent benefits of full-time special education programs. Rather, it found full- or part-time regular class placements more beneficial for students' achievements, self-esteem, behavior, and emotional adjustment.[34] A study in one state found that 40 percent to 50 percent of students labeled as learning disabled did not realize the expected benefits from special education.[35]

In summarizing impediments to achieving national policy in the education of students with mild handicaps, a recent study rejects the prevalent "pull-out" strategy as ineffective, and concludes, "This split-scheduling approach . . . is neither administratively nor instructionally supportable when measured against legal requirements, effective schools research or fiscal consideration."[36]

A careful review of the literature on effective instruction strongly indicates that the general practice of special education runs counter to the basic effectiveness tenets in teaching behaviors, organization of instruction, and instructional support.[37] Furthermore,

> there appear to be at least three discrepancies between the suggestions for best practice and the observation of actual teaching practice for mildly handicapped students: (a) there is almost no instruction presented to these students that might be classified as involving high level cognitive skills, (b) there is a small amount of time spent in activities that could be considered direct instruction with active learner response and teacher feedback, and (c) students receive a low frequency of contingent teacher attention.[38]

While these shortcomings are true as well in general education classes, the needs of students appropriately classified as handicapped make the absence of the desired practices even more consequential.

At the classroom level, the time special education students spend on academic tasks is not greater than that for general education students: about forty-five minutes of engaged time per day.[39] And, most often, there is little qualitatively different in special education instruction in the areas of additional time on task, curriculum adaptation, diverse teaching strategies, adaptive equipment, or advanced technology. Classrooms, despite their small size, remain "teacher-centric."

The limited expectation for student learning in special education programs is reflected in the following results of a study of special education in large cities: 1) only seven of thirty-one cities evaluate "student achievement/ outcomes"; 2) only three of thirty-one cities conduct "longitudinal student outcome studies"; and 3) only nine of the twenty-four special education directors whose districts do not conduct such evaluations believe "student achievement/outcome studies" are needed.[40] Thus, combining the numbers of special education directors whose districts conduct such evaluations and those who do not, but say they are needed, fifteen of the thirty-one directors of large-city special education programs neither collect student outcome data nor believe that such evaluations are needed. While the failure to evaluate outcomes does not in and of itself indicate limited expectations, at the least it does indicate a lack of concern with outcomes, which we believe comes from limited expectations of student capacity.

Least Restrictive Environment

We have previously addressed the topic of separation in the context of instructional placement; in this section, we will focus on separation as one aspect of the overall least restrictive environment (LRE) mandate. The two are inextricably entwined: LRE placement is not a mandate in itself; rather, students are to receive services in an appropriate placement in the least restrictive environment.

This formulation is based on the premise that while many types of placement might be appropriate for a student, the one to be chosen should be the least restrictive, that is, the one that allows maximum integration of students with their peers. Putting it the opposite way, the Sixth Circuit Court of Appeals directed: in situations "where a segregated facility is considered superior, the court should determine whether the services which make that placement superior could feasibly be provided in a non-segregated setting. If they can, the placement in the segregated school would be inappropriate under the Act."[41] Further, the Department of Education has stated that the type of placement must not be based on any of the following factors, either alone or in combination: category of handicapping condition, configuration of the service delivery system, availability of educational or related services, availability of space, or curriculum content or methods of curriculum delivery.[42]

Despite such statements from the Office of Special Education and Rehabilitation Services, the reality in schools turns out to be far different. When the first figures were collected in 1976–1977, 67 percent of the students who were served under PL 94-142 were served in general classes, 25 percent in special classes. A decade later, the figures were essentially the same.[43] While overall there have been no changes in the direction of increasing the proportion of students receiving services in general education, the change has been in the opposite direction for the mentally retarded.[44]

The New York State Association for Retarded Children (NYSARC) has charged the State Education Department (SED) with failure to enforce the law, noting, among other charges, that in Nassau County on Long Island, "out of 320 special education classes, 308 are in segregated facilities." The response of the official charged with enforcing the law gives a somewhat peculiar reading to the SED's sense of its obligations here. "It's a question of where do you draw the line. . . . [While NYSARC is strongly in favor of placing students in integrated settings], many other people in New York State feel differently."[45] The continuing support in New York of its Board of Cooperative Education Services (BOCES), and similar intermediate units in other states, which cluster special education students in separate settings, no doubt will be an arena of future contention about the least restrictive environment.

An extensive study in Massachusetts not only mirrors the national data on the absence of integrated placements, but also reveals a significant trend toward more restrictive placements, especially in the past five years.[46] In its most recent report to Congress on the implementation of PL 94-142, the Department of Education, reporting on the eighteen states reviewed in the past year, indicated that "virtually every state had significant problems in meeting its LRE requirements. . . ."[47] Indeed, all eighteen states were out of compliance with the law in this area. Despite such findings, only seven states reported a need to improve their LRE performances.[48]

As we have learned in the area of race relations, integration is a more complex matter than achieving mere physical proximity. Not only are there administrative barriers when one organization operates its programs in the buildings of another, but there is also the day-to-day, period-to-period reality of the students' education. A unique analysis of "mainstreaming" in the Pittsburgh schools gives dramatic evidence of its actual limitations.[49] The district classifies approximately 6 percent of its students as mildly to moderately disabled, serving them in thirty-eight of the district's fifty-six elementary schools. Based on an examination of their academic schedules, "the percent of [special] students assigned to regular classes ranged from 3 to 7 percent. This means that over 90 percent of the mildly handicapped elementary students . . . were *never* assigned to regular education academic classes" (emphasis in the original).[50] Participation is limited in three ways: 1) scheduling students for fewer than the full number of periods in the week, 2) having students attend several different general education classes for the same subject, and 3) assigning students to inappropriate (by age or level) general education classes.[51] Thus, fewer than one-tenth of mildly handi-capped students participated in the mainstream, and of this small number, less than half participated in the mainstream class on a full basis. Given such program limitations, it is no surprise that only 1.4 percent of the students return to general education.[52]

In a review of mainstreaming in high schools, there was a large discrepancy between reported availability and actual utilization of general classroom education. Although special education teachers indicated that general classroom opportunities were available for their students with disabilities, according to the students' parents only one-third of the students were actually benefiting from this opportunity. Teachers cited the following impediments to mainstreaming special education students: 1) students lack entry-level skills required in general education classrooms; 2) general education classroom teachers resist mainstreaming efforts; and 3) supportive resources, such as modified curricula, are not available.[53]

Parental Involvement

Parents were central to the passage of PL 94-142 — to the enactment of prior and subsequent state laws as well as to the maintenance of strong regulations to implement them. While their rights are specifically cited in federal and state laws, parental involvement in student assessment, program development, and the evaluation of students' progress is limited.[54]

Research studies report that most parents are far from fulfilling their roles of providing information, participating in decisions, or serving as advocates.[55] One study reported that in 70 percent of the cases, parents provided no input to IEP development.[56] A more recent study reports that only half of the parents attended IEP meetings,[57] and that when they did, professionals believed they contributed little.[58] Other professionals suggest that perhaps parents "feel intimidated or are provided only limited opportunity" to become involved.[59] This point is emphasized in the most recent Department of Education report to Congress, which notes, "several studies have reported that in the majority of IEP conferences, the IEP was completely prepared prior to the meeting. . . ." The report concludes, "Presenting parents with what may appear to be decisions the school has already reached rather than recommendations, and the failure to directly communicate and provide appropriate opportunities for involvement, can obviously limit parent participation in the IEP decision making process."[60]

Parents of children with disabilities often feel as if they share their children's labels and are thereby perceived by others as part of the overall problem and in need of professional services for themselves.[61] Thus, should parents at an IEP conference express frustration or anger at the lack of educational or related services being provided to their children, professionals, rather than addressing the specific problem areas or providing the required services, are often quick to "diagnose" the parent as overwhelmed and over-protective and in need of psychological services to combat "their problems." If, on the other hand, parents lead an active life and have less time to devote to their children's education or therapeutic program than the professionals deem appropriate, this behavior is often diagnosed as a form of parental denial that requires psychological treatment for the family members. In addition:

> The belief that parents displace their anger onto the professional is a kind of "Catch-22." That is, whenever the parent disagrees with or confronts the professional, that behavior can be dismissed as an expression of inadequate adjustment, frustration, displaced anger, or a host of psychological problems. Any interpretation is possible other than that the parent may be correct![62]

The narratives of parents of children with disabilities repeatedly describe the power struggles surrounding their involvement in the students' education and the devaluing or denigration of their knowledge about their children.[63] Their concerns are often dismissed, their requests are often patronized, and their reports of the child's home behavior are often distrusted.[64] While not all parent-professional relationships are characterized by these factors, the pattern does appear to be endemic, in keeping with the historic role of the clinical or medical model in special education. Further, this attitude often leads to an over-valuing of the knowledge of so-called experts. Thus, professionals invariably refer children with problems and their parents to specialist rather than generalist service providers or mutual support groups. Summarizing the growing parent literature: "The narratives repeatedly express anger, frustration, and resentment . . . at the unnecessary burdens they and their children face because of social attitudes and behavior toward disabilities.[65]

A World of Disabling Attitudes

The National Council on the Handicapped, appointed by President Reagan, has reiterated what people with disabilities have been saying for years: their major obstacles arise from external rather than internal barriers. The Council cites with approval the statement of an expert United Nations panel:

> Despite everything we can do, or hope to do, to assist each physically or mentally disabled person achieve his or her maximum potential in life, our efforts will not succeed until we have found the way to remove the obstacles to this goal directed by human society — the physical barriers we have created in public buildings, housing, transportation, houses of worship, centers of social life and other community facilities — the social barriers we have evolved and accepted against those who vary more than a certain degree from what we have

been conditioned to regard as normal. More people are forced into limited lives and made to suffer by these man-made [*sic*] obstacles than by any specific physical or mental disability.[66]

Individuals with disabilities make the point even more directly:

In his classic article entitled "What does it mean when a retarded person says, 'I'm not retarded'?" Bogdan tells of people labelled retarded who say, "I have never really thought of myself as retarded. I never really had that ugly feeling deep down," and another who says, "The worst word I have been called is retarded." The single largest self advocacy organization of people labelled retarded calls itself "People First." Marsha Saxton, a person with Spina Bifida, reports, "As I see it, I'm not lucky or unlucky. I'm just the way I am. But I'm not disabled, I always thought. Or handicapped." Denise Karuth, who also has a physical disability, . . . writes, "Put your handkerchiefs away. I'm a lot more like you than you probably imagine." The message in each of these instances . . . is that a disability is only one dimension of a person, not all-defining and not inherently a barrier to being recognized as fully human.[67]

A quarter of a century ago, Erving Goffman addressed this issue. He wrote, "By definition, of course, we believe the person with a stigma is not quite human."[68] The point has been made more recently by Ved Mehta. "You see, we are confronted with a vast ignorance in the world about the handicapped [so that] they would not understand if we acted like normal people."[69]

In a variety of ways, persons with disabilities are neither treated like nor viewed as "normal people." More often, they are treated "specially" either for their own good or for someone else's, but always according to an externally imposed standard. From the many examples of this, two are noted here.

Airlines have asserted that for the safety of passengers who are blind (and sometimes, they argue, for the safety of nondisabled passengers), persons with disabilities *must* preboard, wait to deplane, sit in special seats and not in others, and receive special briefings. To the extent that any database is used to justify these requirements, it was created using blindfolded sighted persons in trial evacuations of planes. One need not suggest the likelihood that persons who are blind would be more rather than less able to maneuver in a smoky airplane than sighted persons (blindfolded or not!) to see that the requirements as to special treatment are both unnecessary and demeaning.[70]

The cases of "Baby Doe" in Indiana and "Baby Jane Doe" in New York have drawn considerable attention to professional attitudes toward disability and how they affect the treatment of newborns. Among the major issues raised is "quality of life." For example, in order to determine which babies with spina bifida should be provided "active vigorous treatment" as opposed to "supportive care only," doctors at the University of Oklahoma Health Sciences Center reported in 1983 on a formula they used to determine quality of life: QL = NE × (H + S). "QL" stands for quality of life; "NE" for natural endowment; "H" for contribution from home and family; and "S" for contribution from society.[71] Those infants for whom the equation predicted a high quality of life were given "active" medically indicated treatment; those for whom it predicted a low score received "no active" medical treatment: no surgery to close the spinal lesion or to drain fluid from the brain, no antibiotics to treat infection. "Of the 24 infants who did not get active, vigorous treatment, none survived. . . . All but one of the infants who received active, vigorous treatment survived. The exception was killed in an automobile accident."[72] What we have here, masquerading as an objective medical judgment, is a means test for care and a determination about one person's quality of life based on an outside person's assessment of a family's and society's "contribution."

Given public attitudes and policies such as these, persons with disabilities have increasingly developed a new perspective. This has been reflected recently in writings by disability-rights activists[73] and others in the independent-living movement. For them, "the problem of disability is not only of physical impairment but also of unnecessary dependence on relatives and professionals, of architectural barriers and of unprotected rights."[74] This formulation is echoed in the report of the first national survey of self-perceptions of Americans with disabilities:[75]

– An overwhelming majority, 74 percent, say they feel at least some sense of common identity with other people with disabilities. (Table 56)
– Nearly half, 45 percent, feel that disabled persons are a minority group in the same sense as Blacks and Hispanics. This figure rises to 56 percent of those disabled between birth and adolescence and 53 percent of those 44 years of age and younger. (Table 57)

This emerging and growing involvement of adults with disabilities can have a major impact in the field of special education. These individuals will be less likely to tolerate an educational system that fails to recognize the capabilities of handicapped students and to prepare them to deal with the realities of the outside world.

Special Education: Disabling Attitudes in Practice

It is the attitudinal milieu more than the individual's physical condition that influences society's response to persons with disabilities. An all-or-nothing concept of disability requires proof of total incapacity in order to gain entitlement to various benefit programs.[76] Further, the media portrays disabled persons as either the heroic individual or the pathetic cripple, rather than as a human being with a multiplicity of qualities. Together these images of disability burden policy, including the education of students with disabilities.[77]

This point was recognized by Justice William Brennan, writing for the Supreme Court in *School Board of Nassau County v. Arline,* who said, "Congress acknowledged that society's accumulated myths and fears about disability and disease are as handicapping as are the physical limitations that flow from actual impairment."[78]

Society's attitudes toward disability are deeply ingrained in professional practice. This is particularly evident in the social-psychological literature, where disability is based on the following assumptions: 1) disability is biologically based; 2) disabled persons face endless problems, which are caused by the impairment; 3) disabled persons are "victims"; 4) disability is central to the disabled person's self-concept and self-definition; and 5) disability is synonymous with a need for help and social support.[79]

Similar assumptions hold true in special education. Here the child and family are considered impaired, instruction is disability focused, professional personnel are often trained and certified to work with specific disabilities, and attention to societal issues is often considered too political and not the business of educational institutions. The assumptions underlying such beliefs can be tersely summarized: "1) Disability is a condition that individuals have; 2) disabled/typical is a useful and objective distinction; and 3) special education is a rationally conceived and coordinated system of services that help children labeled disabled. . . ."[80] This view of students labeled as handicapped, however, adversely affects expectations regarding their academic achievement. It causes them to be separated from standards and tests routinely applied to other students; to be allowed grades that they have not earned; and, in some states, to be permitted special diplomas.[81]

The rationale given for such watered-down expectations is that they are in the best interest of the child. Professionals often suggest that a child be placed in an environment where he or she will be "safe . . . because he would never be asked to do things there 'we know he cannot do.'" Many parents recognize, however, that a "safe" place may not be the best learning environment. Writing about their experience with Chicago-area schools, which identified their young son as being in need of special education, Lori and Bill Granger conclude:

> The trap of Special Education was now open and waiting for the little boy. It is a beguiling trap. Children of Special Education are children of Small Expectations, not great ones. Little is expected and little is demanded. Gradually, these children — no matter their IQ level — learn to be cozy in the category of being "special." They learn to be less than they are.[82]

Not only do "small expectations" excuse students from academic performance; they have also led state education departments, school systems, and the courts to excuse them from the social and behavioral expectations and standards set for other students. The medical or clinical model that under-girds special education inextricably leads to the belief that persons with a handicap, especially the severely disabled, are not capable of making choices or decisions. This conceptualization diminishes "our ability to see them as individuals capable of ever making a choice, let alone the right choice. Seldom, if ever, is the person with the handicapping condition involved in the process of determining how their behavior, or the behavior of those around them, will be modified. The end result is more control for the caregivers and less control for the person being cared for."[83] Having denied individuals with disabilities autonomy and decisionmaking authority — in effect denying them the respect given to people whom society respects — we then excuse their behavior, ascribing it to the disability.[84]

General Education

It is not special education but the total educational system that must change. The origin, growth, and shape of special education have in many ways been defined by general education and the attitudes and behaviors of mainstream educators toward students with handicapping conditions. Whatever the rationale or the benign purpose claimed, children with disabilities have been denied access to public education, or, when given access, have received an education that is not equal to that given other children.

The growth of special education in the past decade has occurred not only in response to the exclusion of students with handicapping conditions. Additional factors have fueled this growth, including: 1) cutbacks in Chapter I (formerly Title I) programs and other school remedial efforts that strained local school system resources (in the same period as and coincidental with the implementation of PL 94-142); 2) the development of remedial and pull-out programs for students with "problems" — slow learners, "disadvantaged," limited-English proficient (miscalled bilingual), new immigrants, and gay and lesbian students;[85] and 3) given the increased emphasis on accountability, the referral of "low achievers" to special education programs, thus excluding them from test-score analyses in school districts.

Another factor promoting exclusion has been a narrowing of the definition of what is considered "normal." In special education, "this often means referral based on race, sex, physical appearance, and socioeconomic status. . . ."[86] A recent study in ten states noted that referral occurs when student behavior and academic achievement vary negatively from the school norm, and for minority students, when their socioeconomic status is lower than the norm of the community.[87] Additionally, the role of school psychologists, given their training and the present educational philosophy, gives professional rationale for special education placements and for the ever-growing identification of deviant, or to use the more recent term, "at-risk" students.[88] The obverse of this has consequences for those students who remain in regular classroom programs. "Every time a child is called mentally defective and sent off to the special education class for some trivial defect, the children who are left in the regular classroom receive a message: no one is above suspicion; everyone is being watched by the authorities; nonconformity is dangerous."[89]

The problem is not special education or general education alone. "In a sense, regular and special education teachers have colluded to relieve regular teachers of responsibilities for teaching children functioning at the bottom of their class."[90] The pressure to "succeed" with high test scores, and with the very large class sizes that make individual attention extremely difficult, makes it more likely that teachers will seek uniformity of students rather than diversity. To put it more sharply, there is, in effect, a "deal" between special and general education. The former asserts a particular body of expertise and a unique understanding of "special" students, thus laying claim both to professional obligation and student benefit. The latter, because of the lack of skills and resources or prejudice, is often happy to hand over "these" students to a welcoming special education system. This includes not only those with the traditional handicapping conditions, but increasing numbers of students labeled "learning disabled," a category that, at present, incorporates such a multitude of students that, under one or another definition, it may incorporate as many as 80 percent of the general education student body. The "deal is sanctioned, on one hand, by the clinicians who provide an intrapsychic justification for the referral, and, on the other hand, by those in the role of advocacy who see increasing numbers of students in special education as providing evidence of their effectiveness."[91]

Next Steps

No discussion of a future education system for students with handicapping conditions can begin without acknowledgment of what has been achieved. As one of the PL 94-142 drafters writes, however:

> If the law has been massively successful in assigning responsibility for students and setting up mechanisms to assure that schools carry out these responsibilities, it has been less successful in removing the barriers between general and special education. It did not anticipate that the artifice of delivery systems in schools might drive the maintenance of separate services and keep students from the mainstream.[92]

A part of this separation is revealed in special educators' decrying the absence of attention to special education in the raft of national reports about education. Indeed, nearly an entire issue of *Exceptional Children* addressed this topic. The inattention to special education is described and the alleged trade-off between excellence and equity deplored.[93] Stephen Lilly suggests, however, that the reason special education is ignored is that "current special education policies and practices for students labelled mildly handicapped are neither conceptually sound nor of sufficient quality to be included in the 'ideal' educational system described by these authors." Thus, rather than deploring the inattention, he applauds it, saying that "until we are willing to examine our flawed assumptions about children and teachers and become integral members of the general education community, we cannot expect either to be featured in reform reports or to be involved in construction of the next era of public education in the United States."[94]

We have, in the preceding pages, examined some of the flawed assumptions about disability. Before turning to ideas for reform, this section will highlight some critiques of special education that are pertinent to the development of new designs. On the one hand, the Heritage Foundation has criticized the very premises of PL 94-142 by saying that it "rests on the questionable assumption that the responsibility for disabled individuals is primarily society's as a civil right," and has questioned its major program direction, saying that "public schools should not be required to educate those children who cannot, without damaging the main purposes of public education, function in a normal classroom setting."[95] At the opposite extreme, the National Coalition of Advocates for Students criticized the lack of access to education for various groups, including students with handicaps. They did so, however, without questioning "the underlying separateness of regular education and special education systems."[96]

A different level of critique is represented by those who argue that the current pattern of special education, by serving some inappropriately, "robs the genuinely handicapped of funds and services they need to deal with their very real problems."[97] In particular, for those labeled learning disabled, inappropriate expenditures are claimed, both in the cost of assessments and in the expense of providing low student-teacher ratios and individualized programs.[98]

In a seeming backlash against the poor quality of services for those with low-incidence handicaps, there is a call from some for a return to separate services. These include: a proposed resolution at the annual convention of the National Federation of the Blind to (re)establish specialized schools for the blind; a proposal from a group of superintendents of residential schools and state directors of special education to (re)establish residential schools for deaf and blind students;[99] the accreditation for the first time of a special education school by a regional accrediting association;[100] and the approval by the New York State Education Department for the construction of a segregated high school for students with physical disabilities.

While the return to more restrictive settings may be understood in light of current special education services, the more predominant reaction of professionals and parents is to propose reforms designed to preclude or limit services to inappropriately labeled students and/or to lower the "barriers" between general and special education.

While no one can argue for the inappropriate labeling of students, one can also empathize with the directors of special education programs who see such students "dumped" into their programs. More disturbing, however, are efforts to impose an arbitrary "cap" on the number of students referred, to cut a "bargain" with general education, or to tighten criteria. While "tightening eligibility criteria may seem to make the problem go away . . . the main effect might be either to a) redirect referred students into other categorical services or programs; or b) disguise as nonhandicapped the portion of students for whom technical eligibility cannot be demonstrated."[101]

Alternative Delivery System

An alternative way to serve students with mild and moderate handicaps is to integrate them into general education programs at the building level. Indeed, a number of states and districts are implementing experimental programs using such an approach, especially for students categorized as having "learning problems."[102] A report to the secretary of the U.S. Department of Education noted that present practices suffer from 1) fragmented approaches ("Many students who require help and are not learning effectively fall 'through the cracks' of a program structure based on preconceived definitions of eligibility. . . ."); 2) a dual system ("The separate administrative arrangements for special programs contribute to a lack of coordination, raise questions about leadership, cloud areas of responsibility, and obscure lines of accountability within schools."); 3) stigmatization of students (producing in students "low expectations of success, failure to persist on tasks, the belief that failures are caused by personal inadequacies, and a continued failure to learn effectively"); and 4) placement decisions becoming a battleground between parents and schools. In light of such practices, the panel called for experimental programs for students with learning problems, which incorporate increased instructional time, support systems for teachers, empowerment of principals to control all programs and resources at the building level, and new instructional approaches that involve "shared responsibility" between general and special education.[103]

While clearly an improvement over the present special education practice, this broad proposal nonetheless continues a dual-system approach for a smaller (more severely impaired) population.[104] As described a decade ago, such students will continue to be faced with consequences of negative attitudes and lowered expectations, with teachers making comparisons between them "in relation to degrees of handicap rather than comparing [their] skill levels to the criteria of nonhandicapped skill performance."[105]

The data in the earlier sections of this article concerning least restrictive environment and mainstreaming focused on students with mild and moderate handicapping conditions. This reflects both the preponderance of students in special education and the major emphasis in the research literature. There is, however, an increasing body of work concerning the integration of students with severe handicaps into regular schools.[106] The Association for Persons with Severe Handicaps (TASH) has been in the forefront of these efforts,[107] and a recent book gives guidance on the conduct of programs to integrate severely impaired students into regular programs,[108] as does a recent Council for Exceptional Children report.[109]

According to this research, the education of students with severe disabilities in an integrated setting requires first and foremost an attitude change from seeing the education of students with disabilities as different or "special" and the education of "nondisabled" students as normal and expected.

Major work in the integration of students with severe multiple disabilities in classes at age-appropriate schools has been carried out by the California Research Institute on the Integration of Students with Severe Disabilities (CRI). In the past five years, they have worked with over two hundred classes serving more than two thousand students with severe handicaps in twenty San Francisco Bay Area school districts. By integration, CRI means: 1) placement of classes in general school buildings that are the chronologically age-appropriate sites for the students; 2) a balanced ratio (from 5 percent to 20 percent) of such classes in a school; 3) structured opportunities for regular and sustained interactions between severely disabled and nondisabled students; 4) participation of the severely disabled students in all nonacademic activities of the school; and 5) implementation of a functional life-skills curriculum for severely disabled students. The rationale for educating students with severe disabilities in integrated settings is to ensure their normalized community participation by providing them with systematic instruction in the skills that are essential to their success in the social and environmental contexts in which they will ultimately use these skills. Thus, a key feature of the CRI model is the mixing of classroom, school, and community-based learning situations.[110]

This type of integration is a far cry from the "dumping" of students back into general education settings, rightly decried by parents and advocates after their long-fought battles. It is also vastly different from the segregated programs that have proven ineffective for many students.

A new framework for education is needed; its entire organization must be reconceptualized. Within this new framework, it would be appropriate to question programs of special education as a separate means of educating students who are deemed unable to profit from school simply because of their handicapping conditions. The growth in the numbers of those categorized as having handicapping conditions was coincidental with the post-Sputnik concern for American competitiveness in the Cold War; young people who failed to keep up with rising standards were categorized as "slow learners," "mentally regarded," "emotionally disturbed," "culturally deprived," and "learning disabled." There was a disproportionate percentage of students from minority and low-income families in the first four categories, while White and middle-class students constituted the bulk of students in the last category.

This discriminatory way of categorizing served the function of preserving class and skin-color privileges as the schools performed their assigned sorting function. And, in the current wave of school reform, "members of advantaged social groups will still advocate treating their failing children in ways that maintain their advantaged status as much as possible."[111] In essence,

> we are talking about the distribution of advantage and disadvantage in society through the differential provision of opportunities to acquire knowledge or to acquire the status that goes with having been exposed to a certain kind of knowledge. There is no question of simply doing it more or less effectively. Effectiveness in such situations only has a meaning when it relates to some set of recognized values or ideals.[112]

It is not simply a matter of using the present measurement instruments more sensitively or more discretely. Nearly three-quarters of a century ago, in a series of essays concerning the use of new IQ tests to measure officer candidates for World War I, Walter Lippmann wrote of his fear that these tests would be used to label children as inferior, and consign them to a second-class life. "It is not possible, I think, to imagine a more contemptible proceeding than to confront a child with a set of puzzles, and after an hour's monkeying with them, proclaim to the child, or to his parents, that here is a C-minus individual. It would not only be a contemptible thing to do. It would be a crazy thing to do. . . ."[113]

Drawing from an older history, one can learn from the experience on Martha's Vineyard in the eighteenth and nineteenth centuries, when it was the home of the highest concentration in the United States of people who were deaf. They were full participants in community life as workers, friends, neighbors, and family members:

> The fact that a society could adjust to disabled individuals, rather than requiring them to do all the adjusting, as is the case in American society as a whole, raises important questions about the rights of the disabled and the responsi-

bilities of those who are not. The Martha's Vineyard experience suggests strongly that the concept of a handicap is an arbitrary social category. And if it is a question of definition, rather than a universal given, perhaps it can be redefined, and many of the cultural preconceptions summarized in the term "handicapped," as it is now used, eliminated.

The most important lesson to be learned from Martha's Vineyard is that disabled people can be full and useful members of a community if the community makes an effort to include them.[114]

How then does one shape an educational system to include students with disabilities, one that is both consonant with and builds toward an inclusive society? Clearly, it is not done by taking students from the general education setting and labeling them as "deficient," nor is it done, as in special education, by focusing on the setting in which instruction takes place. Rather, research indicates that we must focus on the features of instruction that can produce improved learning for students.[115] Current practices, however, mean the "dumbing down" of the curriculum: "Instead of adapting instruction to individual differences to maximize common goal attainment . . . special education programs . . . in the extreme, become merely dead ends where common goals have been dropped altogether."[116]

An important step toward a restructured unitary system is expressed in a concept called "Rights without Labels": namely, the provision of needed services for students without the deleterious consequences of classification and labeling. A joint statement issued by the National Association of School Psychologists, the National Association of Social Workers, and the National Coalition of Advocates for Students suggests guidelines to encourage the education of (at least mild to moderately handicapped) students in general education settings.[117]

Regardless of the conceptual undergirding or the organizational arrangements of education for students with handicapping conditions, special education practice needs substantial improvement. In maintaining a separate special education system, however, no matter how refined or improved, education will continue to operate based on a set of organizational and individual assumptions that disabled and nondisabled youngsters require two distinct sets of services, which in turn require distinct funding, service delivery, and organization. While PL 94-142 requires educational services for students with handicapping conditions, it does not require a special education system.

There is an alternative to separate systems: a merged or unitary system. The conception of a unitary system requires a "paradigm shift," a fundamental change in the way we think about differences among people, in the ways we choose to organize schools for their education, and in how we view the purpose of that education.[118] It rejects the bimodal division of handicapped and nonhandicapped students, and recognizes that individuals vary — that single-characteristic definitions fail to capture the complexity of people. Moreover, it rejects the belief, common to all human services work that incorporates a medical or deviancy model, that the problem lies in the individual and the resolution lies in one or another treatment modality. The unitary system, in contrast, requires adaptations in society and in education, not solely in the individual:

> No longer would there be a need to approach differences in human capabilities or characteristics as disabilities on which to base categorical groupings. In a merged system, an individual difference in visual ability, for example, could be viewed as only one of numerous characteristics of a student, rather than the overriding educational focus of a student's life. . . . It would not dictate differential placement and treatment according to a categorical affiliation which is often inherent in the disabilities approach to education.[119]

In a merged or unitary system, effective practices in classrooms and schools would characterize education for all students. No longer would there be an education system that focuses on the limitations of "handicapped" students, a teacher's incapacity to teach students because of a lack of special credentials, or instruction that is determined by the label attached to students. Nor would blame be placed on students or on family characteristics. Rather, the focus would be on effective instruction for all students based on the belief that "substantial student improvements occur when teachers accept the responsibility for the performance of all their students and when they structure their classrooms so that student success is a primary product of the interaction that takes place there."[120]

At present, students are hampered in their intellectual growth by the lack of appropriate supports available to them and their families. Appropriate supports could include: assessment based on multidimensional axes; psychosocial evaluations directed toward instruction; instructional practices that utilize current research; classrooms and schools designed to incorporate effective schools research; enhanced staff and curriculum development; early intervention and transition programs; and postsecondary education, training, work, and community living options.[121] A new system means curriculum adaptations and individualized educational strategies that would allow both general and special education students to take more difficult courses. Another phenomenon that now distinguishes general from special education is that in general education, "in order to help young people make wise course choices, schools are increasingly requiring students to take courses that match their grade level and abilities. Schools are also seeing to it that the materials used in those courses are intellectually challenging." Moreover: "the more rigorous the course of study, the more a student achieves, within the limits of his capacity. Student achievement also depends on how much the school emphasizes a subject and the amount of time spent on it: the more time expended, the higher the achievement. Successful teachers encourage their students' best efforts."[122]

Fundamental to the work in school effectiveness (exemplified best by the late Ron Edmonds's efforts in New York City's public schools) is the principle that school improvement must involve both quality and equity. In other words, the results of school reform must benefit *all* students. The effective schools research identified five factors that characterize schools that achieve quality and equity: 1) high expectations for all students, and staff acceptance of responsibility for students' learning; 2) instructional leadership on the part of the principal; 3) a safe and orderly environment conducive to learning; 4) a clear and focused mission concerning instructional goals shared by the staff; and 5) frequent monitoring of student progress.[123] Work on effective instructional techniques, including teacher-directed instruction, increased academic engaged time, use of reinforcement, and individual instruction has paralleled much of the effective schools research.

While tutoring programs have involved students with handicaps for some time,[124] more recently, programs have been developed in which students with handicaps serve as tutors for other students with handicaps and for those without.[125] This serves to integrate students with handicaps, to promote respect for their capacity, and to enable them to learn by teaching.[126]

Recent reports on cross-cultural education can provide additional features worth emulating in a new unitary system. In Japan, for example, reports note the importance of clear purpose, strong motivation, and high standards; the importance of parental involvement and reinforcement between home and school; and the importance of maximum time devoted to learning and its effective use. Perhaps most central is the belief that differences in student achievement come not from innate differences in ability but from level of effort, perseverance, and self-discipline, each of which the school can encourage and teach.[127] While innate differences are limiting for some students appropriately labeled as handicapped, they are not limiting for most students in special education today.

In the United States, there is a body of "adaptive education" approaches and specific educational practice attuned to individual differences that have been shown to be effective for students with handicapping conditions.[128] Asserting the legal duty to provide effective schooling, lawyers at the Public Interest Law Center of Philadelphia put it succinctly: "Play school is out. Schooling is a profession. The law requires that practice in the schools measure up to the art of what has been demonstrated by the professional to be possible. What is done must be calculated to be effective."[129] In the Adaptive Learning Environments Model (ALEM) and similar programs, there is a design that integrates both those who are labeled as handicapped and those who are not and that benefits both.[130]

The ultimate rationale for quality education of students in an integrated setting is based not only on law or pedagogy, but also on values. What kinds of people are we? What kind of society do we wish to develop? What values do we honor? The current failure to provide a quality education to all students and the perpetuation of segregated settings expresses one set of answers to these questions. To change the outcome, we need to develop another set of values. As Walter Lippmann said in 1922, "If a child fails in school and then fails in life, the schools cannot sit back and say: 'You see how accurately I predicted this.' Unless we are to admit that education is essentially impotent, we have to throw back the child's failure at the school, and describe it as a failure not by the child but by the school."[131]

While there is neither agreement among educators nor commitment by policy-makers to a unitary system of quality education for all students, especially commitment in terms of money, we believe "we can, whenever and wherever we choose, successfully teach all children whose schooling is of interest to us. We already know more than we need in order to do this. Whether we do it must finally depend on how we feel about the fact that we haven't done it so far."[132]

Notes

1. Nomenclature in the field of disability is often confusing and changing. Generally, disability refers to the individual's condition, while handicap refers to the consequence in society. Thus, for example, the individual with quadriplegia is disabled by the paralysis of his or her legs, but handicapped by the absence of a ramp to the local library. In special education, however, given the title of the major federal law PL 94-142, "The Education for All Handicapped Children Act," the term "handicapped" is used synonymously with disabled. We will, therefore, use the terms "students with handicapping conditions" and "persons with a disability" interchangeably. We do not use the words handicapped or disabled, nor refer to a particular condition, such as deaf or blind, as an adjective. Rather than saying, "The deaf boy," we say, "The boy who is deaf." This makes the point that deafness is but one of the boy's characteristics, and not the most important.

2. For a study of the passage of Section 504, and the tortuous process of the issuance of regulations implementing it, see Richard K. Scotch, *From Good Will to Civil Rights: Transforming Federal Disability Policy* (Philadelphia: Temple University Press, 1984).

3. There is not one in-depth study of the law's development and passage. For a brief survey, see Roberta Weiner, *PL 94-142: Impact on the Schools* (Washington, DC: Capitol Publications, 1985).

4. Lisa J. Walker, "Procedural Rights in the Wrong System: Special Education Is Not Enough," in *Images of the Disabled/Disabling Images,* ed. Alan Gartner and Tom Joe (New York: Praeger, 1987), pp. 98–102.

5. Coined in 1959, normalization as a concept was introduced in the United States a decade later. Generally, it means giving people with disabilities opportunities to live in as normal a fashion as possible. See, in particular, R. B. Kugel and W. Wolfensber-

ger, *Changing Patterns in Residential Services for the Mentally Retarded* (Washington, DC: President's Committee on Mental Retardation, 1969), and W. Wolfensberger, *The Principle of Normalization in Human Services* (Toronto: National Institute on Mental Retardation, 1971).

6. The medical model views disability as located within the individual, and, thus, primary emphasis is devoted to the etiology or causes of conditions and the placement of persons in separate diagnostic categories. From this perspective, efforts to improve the functional capabilities of individuals are regarded as the exclusive solution to disability.

7. *Ninth Annual Report to the Congress on the Implementation of the Education of the Handicapped Act* (Washington, DC: U.S. Department of Education, 1987), Table EA1.

8. *Ninth Annual Report,* Table EJ1.

9. Walker, "Procedural Rights in the Wrong System," p. 105.

10. Among myriad studies, see especially Patricia Craig, *Status of Handicapped Students* (Menlo Park, CA: SRI, 1978), and *Barriers to Excellence: Our Children at Risk,* report of the National Coalition of Advocates for Students (New York, 1985).

11. B. K. Keogh, "Learning Disabilities: Diversity in Search of Order," in *The Handbook of Special Education: Research and Practice,* vol. 2, *Mildly Handicapped Conditions,* ed. Margaret C. Wang, Maynard C. Reynolds, and Herbert J. Walberg (Oxford: Pergamon, 1990).

12. *Special Education: Views from America's Cities* (Washington, DC: The Council of Great City Schools, 1986), Tables 8 and 9.

13. James E. Ysseldyke et al., "Generalizations from Five Years of Research on Assessment and Decision-Making," *Exceptional Education Quarterly, 4* (1983), 75–93.

14. James E. Ysseldyke et al., "A Logical and Empirical Analysis of Current Practice in Classifying Students as Handicapped," *Exceptional Children, 50* (1983), 160–166.

15. Deaf, deaf-blind, hard of hearing, mentally retarded, multihandicapped, orthopedically impaired, other health impaired, seriously emotionally disturbed, specific learning disabled, speech impaired, and visually handicapped.

16. Margaret C. Wang, Maynard C. Reynolds, and Herbert J. Walberg, "Rethinking Special Education," *Educational Leadership, 44* (1986), 27.

17. Richard White and Mary Lynne Calhoun, "From Referral to Placement: Teachers' Perceptions of Their Responsibilities," *Exceptional Children, 53* (1987), 467.

18. Keogh, "Learning Disabilities."

19. Betty Binkard, "State Classifications of Handicapped Students: A National Comparative Data Report," *Counter-Point 12* (1986), and *A Study of Special Education,* Table 2. Both the state and city data are for the 1984–1985 school year but are not strictly comparable.

20. *Seventh Annual Report to Congress on the Implementation of the Education of the Handicapped Act* (Washington, DC: U.S. Department of Education, 1985), p. 4.

21. James E. Ysseldyke, "Classification of Handicapped Students," in *Handbook of Special Education: Research and Practice,* vol. 1, *Learner Characteristics and Adaptive Education,* ed. Margaret C. Wang, Maynard C. Reynolds, and Herbert J. Walberg (Oxford: Pergamon, 1987).

22. W. A. Davis and L. A. Shepard, "Specialists' Use of Test and Clinical Judgment in the Diagnosis of Learning Disabilities," *Learning Disabilities Quarterly, 19* (1983), 128–138.

23. James E. Ysseldyke et al., *Similarities and Differences between Underachievers and Students Labelled Learning Disabled: Identical Twins with Different Mothers* (Minneapolis: University of Minnesota, Institute for Research and Learning Disabilities, 1979), and James E. Ysseldyke et al., "Similarities and Differences between Low Achievers and Students Classified as Learning Disabled," *Journal of Special Education, 16* (1982), 73–85.

24. Lorrie A. Shepard and L. A. Smith, *Evaluation of the Identification of Perceptual Communicative Disorders in Colorado* (Boulder: University of Colorado, 1981), p. 28.

25. Lorrie A. Shepard, L. A. Smith, and C. P. Vojir, "Characteristics of Pupils Identified as Learning Disabled," *Journal of Special Education, 16* (1983), 73–85.

26. Davis and Shepard, "Specialists' Use of Tests and Clinical Judgment in the Diagnosis of Learning Disabilities"; James E. Ysseldyke et al., "Technical Adequacy of Tests Used by Professionals in Simulated Decision-Making," *Psychology in the Schools, 17* (1980), 202–209; James E. Ysseldyke et al., "Declaring Students Eligible for Learning Disability Services: Why Bother with the Data?," *Learning Disability Quarterly, 5* (1982), 37–44; James E. Ysseldyke and B. Algozzine, "LD or Not LD: That's Not the Question!" *Journal of Learning Disabilities, 16* (1983), 29–31; James E. Ysseldyke and B. Algozzine, *Introduction to Special Education* (Boston: Houghton Mifflin, 1984).

27. Nicholas Hobbs, "An Ecologically Oriented Service-Based System for Classification of Handicapped Children," in *The Ecosystem of the "Risk" Child*, ed. E. Salzmeyer, J. Antrobus, and J. Gliak (New York: Academic Press, 1980), p. 274.

28. C. Carlberg and Kenneth Kavale, "The Efficacy of Special versus Regular Class Placement for Exceptional Children: A Meta Analysis," *Journal of Special Education, 14* (1980), 295–309. See also P. Johnston, R. L. Allington, and P. Afflerbach, "The Congruence of Classroom and Remedial Reading Evaluation," *Elementary School Journal, 85* (1985), 465–478.

29. "Funding formulas that create incentives for more restrictive and separate class placement or that support particular configurations of services based on special education teacher allocations maintain an inflexible program structure and fail to allow models that encourage students to remain in general classrooms with resource room or individualized help. . . . States that provide financial incentives for separate placements, or which traditionally have had dual systems of services, place students disproportionately in more restrictive placements." Walker, "Procedural Rights in the Wrong System," p. 110.

30. Based upon a study of the effects of the state's funding formulae on the New York City public schools conducted by Lynn Weikart, Chief Administrator, Office of Finance and Management, Division of Special Education, 1981–1983. The study found that the net cost to the school system — that is, program cost less state reimbursement — was greater when the student was placed in a more rather than less restrictive environment. In other words, while (generally) more restrictive placements cost more, the reimbursement was sufficiently greater so that the net cost to the school system favored more restrictive placements.

31. *Special Education*, Table 13. Again, these numbers must be viewed with some skepticism. Internal evidence suggests that the figures on students exiting from special education may, at least in some instances, be too high by at least half.

32. Dorothy Kerzner Lipsky and Alan Gartner, "Capable of Achievement and Worthy of Respect: Education for the Handicapped as if They Were Full-Fledged Human Beings," *Exceptional Children, 54* (1987), 61.

33. Weiner, *PL 94-142*, p. 42.

34. Nancy A. Madden and Robert L. Slavin, *Count Me In: Academic Achievement and Social Outcomes of Mainstreaming Students with Mild Academic Handicaps* (Baltimore: The Johns Hopkins University Press, 1982), p. 1.

35. R. Bloomer et al., *Mainstreaming in Vermont: A Study of the Identification Process* (Livonia, NY: Brador Publications, 1982).

36. George J. Hagerty and Marty Abramson, "Impediments to Implementing National Policy Change for Mildly Handicapped Students," *Exceptional Children, 53* (1987), 316.

37. William E. Bickel and Donna Diprima Bickel, "Effective Schools, Classrooms, and Instruction: Implications for Special Education," *Exceptional Children, 52* (1986), 489–500.
38. Catherine V. Morsink et al., "Research on Teaching: Opening the Door to Special Education Classrooms," *Exceptional Children, 53* (1986), 38.
39. James E. Ysseldyke, "Current Practices in Making Psychoeducational Decisions about Learning Disabled Students," *Journal of Learning Disabilities, 16* (1983), 226–233.
40. *Special Education,* Table 21.
41. *Roncker v. Walter,* 700 F. 2d 1058 (1983), *cert. denied,* 104 S. Ct. 196 (1983).
42. *Standards and Guidelines for Compliance with Federal Requirements for the Education of the Handicapped* (Washington, DC: Office of Special Education Programs, U.S. Department of Education, 1986), p. 24.
43. Walker, "Procedural Rights in the Wrong System," p. 104.
44. National Center for Education Statistics, *The School-Age Handicapped* (Washington, DC: Government Printing Office, 1985), p. 20.
45. "Special Ed Students Kept in Restrictive Environments, Disability Groups Say," *Education of the Handicapped* (29 October 1986), pp. 5–6.
46. *Out of the Mainstream: Education of Disabled Youth in Massachusetts* (Boston: Massachusetts Advocacy Center, 1987).
47. "Improved Special Education Monitoring Unearthing More Flaws, ED Says," *Education Daily* (21 April 1987), p. 3.
48. *Ninth Annual Report,* p. 166.
49. Janet Sansone and Naomi Zigmond, "Evaluating Mainstreaming through an Analysis of Students' Schedules," *Exceptional Children, 52* (1986), 452–458.
50. Sansone and Zigmond, "Evaluating Mainstreaming," p. 455.
51. The opportunity "to provide preparation periods for special education teachers . . . seems to be the decisive factors in these assignments." Sansone and Zigmond, "Evaluating Mainstreaming," p. 455.
52. *Special Education,* Table 13.
53. Andrew S. Halpern, "Transition: A Look at the Foundations," *Exceptional Children, 51* (1985), 483.
54. Despite myriad studies concerning PL 94-142, there has not been a systematic study nor an in-depth evaluation of parental involvement in the education of their children. Rick Rodgers, *Caught in the Act: What LEA's Tell Parents under the 1981 Education Act* (London: Centre for Studies on Integration in Education, 1986), is a model for this.
55. B. L. Baker and R. P. Brightman, "Access of Handicapped Children to Educational Services," in *Children, Mental Health, and the Law,* ed. N. D. Repucci, L. A. Withorn, E. P. Mulvey, and J. Monahan (Beverly Hills, CA: Sage, 1984), p. 297.
56. *A National Survey of Individualized Education Programs (IEPs) for Handicapped Children* (Triangle Park, NC: Research Triangle Institute, 1980).
57. C. A. Scanlon, J. Arick, and N. Phelps, "Participation in the Development of the IEP: Parents' Perspective," *Exceptional Children, 47* (1981), 373.
58. S. Goldstein, B. Strickland, A. P. Turnbull, and L. Curry, "An Observational Analysis of the IEP Conference," *Exceptional Children, 46* (1980), 278–286.
59. C. E. Meyers and Jan Blacher, "Parents' Perception of Schooling for Severely Handicapped Children: Home and Family Variables," *Exceptional Children, 53* (1987), 441.
60. *Ninth Annual Report,* p. 71.
61. See, for example, Philip M. Ferguson and Dianne L. Ferguson, "Parents and Professionals," in *Introduction to Special Education,* ed. Peter Knoblock (Boston: Little, Brown, 1987); Seymour B. Sarason and John Doris, *Educational Handicap, Public Policy, and Social History* (New York: Free Press, 1979); H. Rutherford Turnbull III and Alan P.

Turnbull, eds., *Parents Speak Out: Then and Now,* 2d ed. (Columbus, OH: Charles C. Merrill, 1985); Philip M. Ferguson and Adrienne Asch, "What We Want for Our Children: Perspectives of Parents and Adults with Disabilities," in *Schooling and Disability,* ed. Douglas Biklen, Philip M. Ferguson, and Allison Ford (Chicago: National Society for the Study of Education, 1989).

62. Dorothy Kerzner Lipsky, "A Parental Perspective on Stress and Coping," *American Journal of Orthopsychiatry, 55* (1985), 616.

63. Ferguson and Asch, "What We Want for Our Children."

64. A recent version of this is reported in Lori Granger and Bill Granger, *The Magic Feather* (New York: E. P. Dutton, 1986). Diagnosticians, having decided that the Grangers' child could not read, refused to heed the parents' report that he read at home; therefore, they failed to ask him to read, but rather only subjected him to batteries of tests to explain why he could not read.

65. Ferguson and Asch, "What We Want for Our Children."

66. "Report of the United Nations Expert Group Meeting on Barrier-Free Design," *International Rehabilitation Review 26* (1975), 3.

67. Douglas Biklen, "The Culture of Policy: Disability Images and Their Analogues in Public Policy," *Policy Studies Journal* (1987).

68. Erving Goffman, *Stigma: Notes on the Management of Spoiled Identities* (Englewood Cliffs, NJ: Prentice-Hall, 1963).

69. Ved Mehta, "Personal History," *The New Yorker, 60,* 53 (1985), 61.

70. A more recent law, PL 99-435, states: "No air carrier may discriminate against any otherwise qualified handicapped individual, by reason of such handicap, in the provision of air travel." Of course, the question here is the interpretation, should differential service be provided, as to whether it is "by reason of such handicap." *The Braille Monitor,* the National Foundation of the Blind's publication, provides extensive treatment of this topic from the perspective of an organization of the blind.

71. Richard Gross, Alan Cox, and Michael Pollay, "Early Management and Decision Making for the Treatment of Myelomeningocele," *Pediatrics* (1983).

72. Nat Hentoff, "The Awful Privacy of Baby Doe," *Atlantic Monthly* (1985), 59.

73. See particularly, Michelle Fine and Adrienne Asch, "Disability beyond Stigma: Social Interaction, Discrimination, and Activism," *Journal of Social Issues, 44* (1988), 3–22; William Gliedeman and William Roth, *The Unexpected Minority: Handicapped Children in America* (New York: Harcourt Brace Jovanovich, 1980); Harlan Hahn, "Paternalism and Public Policy," *Society* (1983), 36–42; Robert Funk, "Disability Rights: From Caste to Class in the Context of Civil Rights"; and Harlan Hahn, "Civil Rights for Disabled Americans: The Formulation of a Political Agenda," in *Images of the Disabled/Disabling Images,* ed. Alan Gartner and Tom Joe (New York: Praeger, 1987).

74. Gerben DeJong and Raymond Lifchez, "Physical Disability and Public Policy," *Scientific American, 248* (1983), 40–49.

75. Louis Harris and Associates, *Disabled Americans' Self-Perceptions: Bringing Disabled Americans into the Mainstream* (New York: Author, 1986).

76. National Council on the Handicapped, *Toward Independence: A Report to the President and to the Congress of the United States* (Washington, DC: Author, 1986), pp. 22–29.

77. For a description of these images as expressed in literature, the press, television, and the movies and a discussion of the ways in which the images play themselves out in policies in employment, education, health care, everyday living, and the treatment of newborns, see *Images of the Disabled/Disabling Images,* ed. Alan Gartner and Tom Joe (New York: Praeger, 1987).

78. "On Cases of Contagion," *New York Times,* 4 March 1987, p. A21.

79. Fine and Asch, "Disability beyond Stigma."

80. Robert Bogdan and J. Kugelmass, "Case Studies of Mainstreaming: A Symbolic Inter-actionist Approach to Special Schooling," in *Special Education and Societal Interests*, ed. L. Barton and S. Tomlinson (London: Croom-Helm, 1984), p. 173.

81. These are annotated "regular" diplomas which denote that the student has achieved the goals and objectives of her/his IEP. Such diplomas may reduce the pressure upon school districts to provide educational services that enable all students, including those labeled as handicapped, to earn a diploma.

    And where so-called minimum competency tests are used as diploma requirements, there are questions as to adequate notice, common courses of study, and the appropriateness of the competencies used, as well as test validity. Martha M. McCarthy, "The Application of Competency Testing Mandates to Handicapped Students," *Harvard Educational Review, 53* (1983), 146–164.

82. Granger and Granger, *The Magic Feather,* pp. 26, 27.

83. Doug Guess, Holly Anne Benson, and Ellin Siegel-Causey, "Concepts and Issues Related to Choice-Making and Autonomy among Persons with Severe Disabilities," *Journal of the Association for Persons with Severe Handicaps, 10* (1985), 83. The authors' suggestion that the opportunity for choice-making may have a positive effect upon an individual's learning appears to be correct. Analysis of programs involving persons with severe handicaps indicates that those which involve opportunities for choice are more effective; that is, increase the subject's learning. Alan Gartner, "TASH Reflects Changes," *TASH Newsletter* (October 1986), p. 12.

84. The approved process in carrying out disciplinary action for students with handicapping procedures involves the same clinical procedure which labeled the child; it must be used to determine whether the misconduct in question was a manifestation of the handicapping condition.

85. We favor the inclusion of all children in the public schools and believe that all can and should be educated in integrated settings. We oppose segregated schemes, such as that developed recently by the New York City Board of Education, which responded to the abuse of gay and lesbian students by setting up a separate and segregated school for them, rather than by meeting its obligation to provide safe settings for all students.

86. Walker, "Procedural Rights in the Wrong System," p. 105.

87. *A Policy-Oriented Study of Special Education's Service Delivery Systems Research* (Triangle Park, NC: Research Triangle Institute, 1984).

88. *School Psychology: A Blueprint for Training and Practice* (Minneapolis: National School Psychology Inservice Training Network, 1984), pp. 7–9.

89. Granger and Granger, *The Magic Feather,* p. xii.

90. Shepard, "The New Push for Excellence," p. 328.

91. Lipsky and Gartner, "Capable of Achievement," p. 59.

92. Walker, "Procedural Rights in the Wrong System," p. 109.

93. Marleen Pugach and Mara Sapon-Shevin, "New Agendas for Special Education Policy: What the National Reports Haven't Said," *Exceptional Children, 53* (1987), 295–299, and Mara Sapon-Shevin, "The National Education Reports and Special Education: Implications for Students," *Exceptional Children, 53* (1987), 300–307.

94. M. Stephen Lilly, "Lack of Focus on Special Education in Literature on Educational Reform," *Exceptional Children, 53* (1987), 326–327.

95. Heritage Foundation, "The Crisis: Washington Shares the Blame," *The Heritage Foundation Backgrounder* (Washington, DC: The Heritage Foundation, 1984), pp. 1, 12.

96. Sapon-Shevin, "The National Education Reports," p. 304.

97. Granger and Granger, *The Magic Feather,* p. xi.

98. *Special Education,* p. 52.

99. "Deaf, Blind Need Both Segregated and Mainstreamed Services, Experts Say," *Education Daily,* 9 December 1986, p. 4.

100. "Kennedy Institute First Special Ed School to Receive Accreditation," *Education Daily,* 26 November 1986, p. 2.

101. Michael M. Gerber, "The Department of Education's Sixth Annual Report to Congress on PL 94-142: Is Congress Getting the Full Story?" *Exceptional Children, 51* (1984), 213.

102. Margaret C. Wang, Maynard C. Reynolds, and Herbert J. Walberg, "Rethinking Special Education," *Educational Leadership* (1986), 26–31.

103. *Educating Students with Learning Problems — A Shared Responsibility,* A Report to the Secretary (Washington, DC: Office of Special Education and Rehabilitative Services, 1986), pp. 7–9.

104. See Susan Stainback and William Stainback, "Integration versus Cooperation: A Commentary on 'Educating Children with Learning Problems: A Shared Responsibility,'" *Exceptional Children, 54* (1987), 66–68.

105. L. Brown et al., "Toward the Realization of the Least Restrictive Educational Environments for Severely Handicapped Students," *AAESPH Review, 2* (1977), 198.

106. "Integration is *not* mainstreaming. . . . Children [with severe handicaps] who are integrated spend the majority of each school day in a special education classroom, although they join nonhandicapped peers for certain nonacademic activities. The education needs of the two groups are too disparate to warrant putting them together for academic activities. But integration provides a supportive environment in which nonhandicapped children and severely handicapped youngsters can play and grow as well as learn from one another." Mary Frances Hanline and Carola Murray, "Integrating Severely Handicapped Children into Regular Public Schools," *Phi Delta Kappan* (December 1984), 274.

107. Bud Fredericks, "Back to the Future: Integration Revisited," *TASH Newsletter, 13,* No. 6 (1987), 1.

108. Douglas Biklen, *Achieving the Complete School: Strategies for Effective Mainstreaming* (New York: Teachers College Press, 1985).

109. Susan Stainback and William Stainback, *Educating Students with Severe Handicaps in Regular Schools* (Reston, VA: The Council for Exceptional Children, 1985).

110. Wayne Sailor, Lori Goetz, Jacki Anderson, Pam Hunt, and Kathy Gee, "Integrated Community Intensive Instruction," in *Generalization and Maintenance in Applied Settings,* ed. R. Horner, G. Dunlap, and R. Koegel (Baltimore: Paul H. Brookes, 1988); Wayne Sailor, Ann Halvorsen, Jacki Anderson, Lori Goetz, Kathy Gee, Kathy Doering, and Pam Hunt, "Community Intensive Instruction," in *Education of Learners with Severe Handicaps,* ed. R. Horner, L. Meyer, and H. Fredericks (Baltimore: Paul H. Brookes, 1986).

111. Christine E. Sleeter, "Learning Disabilities: The Social Construction of a Special Education Category," *Exceptional Children, 53* (1986), 52.

112. F. Inglis, "Ideology and the Curriculum: The Value Assumptions of Systems Builders," *Policy Sciences, 18* (1985), 5.

113. Cited in Granger and Granger, *The Magic Feather,* p. v.

114. Nora Ellen Groce, *Everyone Here Spoke Sign Language: Hereditary Deafness on Martha's Vineyard* (Cambridge, MA: Harvard University Press, 1985), p. 108.

115. Sapon-Shevin, "The National Education Reports," p. 303.

116. R. E. Snow, "Placing Children in Special Education: Some Comments," *Educational Researcher, 13* (1984), 13.

117. The statement is available from the Advocacy Center for the Elderly and Disabled, 1001 Howard Avenue, New Orleans, LA 70113.

118. Thomas S. Kuhn, *The Structure of Scientific Revolutions* (Chicago: University of Chicago Press, 1962).

119. William Stainback and Nancy Stainback, "A Rationale for the Merger of Special and Regular Education," *Exceptional Children, 51* (1984), 109.

120. B. Algozzine and L. Maheady, "When All Else Fails, Teach!" *Exceptional Children, 52* (1985), 498.

121. Our focus in this article has been on school services. However, we cannot fail to note that whatever the many inadequacies of the education for students with handicapping conditions, services for those who have "aged out" of the PL 94-142 entitlement are far fewer. For example, a recent article notes that while approximately 50,000 mentally impaired students, those with IQs of 70 and below, leave schools each year, there are only "roughly 5,000 places in training and support programs nationwide. . . ." William Celis III, "Generation of Retarded Youth Emerges from Public Schools — But Little Awaits," *Wall Street Journal,* 16 January 1987, p. 25.

122. *What Works: Research about Teaching and Learning* (Washington, DC: U.S. Department of Education, 1986), p. 59.

123. Ronald Edmonds, "Effective Schools for the Urban Poor," *Educational Leadership, 37* (1979), 15–27, and "Some Schools Work and More Can," *Social Policy, 9,* No. 5 (1979), 26–31.

124. Joseph R. Jenkins and Linda M. Jenkins, *Cross Age and Peer Tutoring: Help for Children with Learning Problems* (Reston, VA: The Council for Exceptional Children, 1981).

125. R. T. Osguthorpe and T. E. Scruggs, "Special Education Students as Tutors: A Review and Analysis," *Remedial and Special Education, 7,* No. 4 (1986), 15–26.

126. Alan Gartner, Mary Conway Kohler, and Frank Riessman, *Children Teach Children: Learning by Teaching* (New York: Harper & Row, 1971).

127. *Japanese Education Today* (Washington, DC: U.S. Department of Education, 1987).

128. Margaret C. Wang and Herbert J. Walberg, eds., *Adapting Instruction to Individual Differences* (Berkeley, CA: McCutchan, 1985).

129. Frank J. Laski, Thomas K. Gilhool, and Stephen F. Gold, "A Legal Duty to Provide Effective Schooling," Adaptive Instruction Conference, 3 June 1983, p. 8.

130. Margaret C. Wang, Stephen Peverly, and Robert Randolph, "An Investigation of the Implementation and Effects of a Full-Time Mainstreaming Program," *Remedial and Special Education, 5* (1984), 21–32. The authors of this article were responsible for the introduction of the Adaptive Learning Environments Model (ALEM) program into the New York City public schools when, respectively, they were Executive Director and Chief Administrator for Program Development, Division of Special Education. We did this at the behest of the Chancellor, Frank J. Macchiarola, whose support of the program expressed his belief that all students can learn and that it was the obligation of the school system to enable that to happen. Basically, the ALEM program involved the full-time mainstreaming of students certified as handicapped in a program that adapted curricula to each student's needs, paced learning at an individual rate, and taught students to take responsibility for their own learning.

131. Walter Lippmann, "The Reliability of Intelligence Tests," *The New Republic* (1922), reprinted in *The I. Q. Controversy,* ed. N. J. Block and Gerald Dworkin (New York: Random House, 1976), p. 17.

132. Edmonds, "Some Schools Work and More Can," p. 29.

The Education for
All Handicapped Children Act:
Schools as Agents of Social Reform

JUDITH D. SINGER

JOHN A. BUTLER

In their article, Judith Singer and John Butler provide a very different analysis of the implementation of PL 94-142 than that provided by Gartner and Lipsky. Relying on their own extensive research of the EHA's implementation in five diverse school districts, the authors pose the question, "Has the EHA worked?" They avoid a simplistic answer by acknowledging that the inquirer's political orientation influences the response and discuss from various political perspectives the diverse views that can be developed about EHA's results. Singer and Butler go beyond a relativistic analysis, however, and draw conclusions that cut across political orientations. They contend that, despite EHA's shortcomings, the act has fostered: 1) a high level of procedural compliance, 2) dedication by school employees to the act's goals, and 3) an improvment in the quality of service from that which existed prior to the act. They conclude that EHA implementation demonstrates that a federal initiative can result in significant social reform at the local level.

The correspondence that follows this article — a letter to the editors of the Harvard Educational Review *written by James Lytle, a researcher for the Philadelphia Public Schools — takes strong exception to Singer and Butler's positive conclusions on PL 94-142 implementation. Lytle states that special education placement continues to negatively impact many students, particularly minorities. A response by Singer and Butler follows Lytle's letter.*

In 1977, the United States began implementation of PL 94-142, the Education for All Handicapped Children Act (EHA), requiring public schools to identify and then to provide special education services to all youngsters with educational, developmental, emotional, or physical disabilities.[1] Hailed as a "Bill of Rights" for children with handicaps, the law outlined a process whereby all children, regardless of the severity of their handicap, were assured the same educational rights and privileges accorded their nonhandicapped peers: "a free appropriate public education." EHA was to transform special education practice across the nation by bringing all states up to the standard that some states, prompted by court action and advocacy by handicapped rights groups, already had adopted.

After a decade of implementation, has EHA produced a real change in educational programming for handicapped children, or has it simply perpetuated a myth of social reform? Data collected in five major metropolitan school districts demonstrate that EHA has been an effective instrument of social reform through its direct influence on local special education programs. Despite severe budgetary and logistical constraints, school systems have managed to comply with EHA's regulations, and local special education directors have managed to negotiate with a wide range of competing interest groups to ensure implementation of the law's guarantees. This article also argues, however, that the effect of EHA on children has been less clear. Not only has it proven intrinsically difficult to evaluate the program's impact on children because of its individualized learning goals, but also, outcomes that have been measurable suggest that some children have been winners and others losers in the actual degree of entitlement the law confers.

How was EHA supposed to produce a change in educational practice? When first passed, the law included a panoply of requirements deemed necessary to make the entitlement a reality. In order to qualify for federal financial support under the new law, states and local school districts were required to: 1) identify all handicapped children of school age (5–18) and offer them educational services; 2) assess each handicapped child individually and formulate a written "individualized education program" (IEP); 3) ensure that handicapped students were placed in the "least restrictive environment" commensurate with their needs; 4) notify parents in writing about identification, evaluation, or school placement of their child and establish grievance procedures for parents wishing to contest a district decision; and 5) provide those "related services" required for children to benefit from special education.

Even though EHA was passed by sizable majorities in both House and Senate, it had detractors well before it became law. Prominent among them was President Gerald Ford, who signed the legislation only reluctantly, believing that it "promised more than the federal government can deliver." He spoke for many when he wrote that EHA contained "a vast array of detailed, complex and costly administrative paperwork and not educational programs." He signed the legislation only on the understanding that the law would not be fully implemented until 1978, by which time he hoped to see it revised to become an "effectual and realistic" program.[2]

Once launched, however, EHA took on a life of its own. Detailed regulations were written to reinforce EHA's specific requirements. Totaling 149 pages, these probably represented a high-water mark in federal attempts to standardize compliance with educational legislation.[3] And when, in 1982, the Reagan administration proposed revisions that would weaken the guarantees of EHA, the public response was so overwhelmingly negative that the proposals were quickly dropped.[4]

Even before it was implemented, EHA promised to be a fascinating case study of federal effort to influence state and local educational practice. First, federal requirements were extensive, yet new federal dollars were limited; this almost assured that there would be fireworks when the law was put into effect. How would local education agencies (LEAs) meet the new mandate without a substantial reallocation of existing dollars? Second, implementation of EHA required the active participation of a diverse range of interest groups stretching far beyond special education — regular education teachers, principals, administrators, parents, advocacy groups, and noneducational public agencies, including public and private health providers. How would the desires of these groups be balanced, and which groups would maintain the most control over children's educational programs? Third, because the law was based primarily on the precedents of civil rights legislation, little attention was given to the substance of special education curricula or the evaluation of outcomes for handicapped students. When all was said and done, what would happen to the children?

Finally, and more broadly, EHA embodied a classic paradox, pointed out by David Cohen, that has characterized all educational reform movements in the United States: "The scope of public responsibility, and thus the scope of government power, [has been expanded] in a political system designed to minimize the scope of public responsibility and restrain the exercise of public power."[5] How well, then, have the rights of the handicapped, so difficult to secure in the larger community and economic order, been secured in the schools?

All of these questions could have been anticipated in 1977, and all deserve to be asked again today with the benefit of ten years of evidence. In this article, we combine findings from our own study with the research literature on EHA, venture conclusions where warranted, and frame major issues that still seem to beg for resolution. We undertake this task with some humility, aware that our own values inevitably affect our choice of subtopics, and, at least to some degree, influence the interpretation of the findings.

Methodology

Our research project, the Collaborative Study of Children with Special Needs, was conducted from 1982 through 1985 in five major metropolitan

TABLE 1
Sociodemographic Characteristics of the Collaborative Study Sites

	Charlotte-Mecklenburg	Houston	Milwaukee	Rochester	Santa Clara County
Elementary school enrollment	38,003	116,070	38,407	18,846	65,552
Percent elementary school students receiving special education	7.6	7.9	10.6	13.4	9.4
Race/ethnicity of students					
Percent White	56.9	18.9	38.1	36.9	58.1
Percent Black	40.6	42.9	50.5	49.0	4.3
Percent Hispanic	0.0	35.0	7.5	11.3	26.6
1982 per pupil expenditure in dollars	2,570	2,696	4,242	4,228	3,080
1979 per capita income in dollars	7,814	8,857	7,104	6,492	9,545

Note: Data are for the 1983–1984 school year, except where noted.

school systems: Charlotte-Mecklenburg Schools, North Carolina; Houston Independent School District, Texas; Milwaukee Public Schools, Wisconsin; Rochester City School District, New York; and Santa Clara County Office of Education, California. Sites were selected so as to obtain geographic, socio-economic, and ethnic diversity both between and within districts, with the further constraint that they be situated in states with sizable special education populations (Table 1).

The initial data collection involved selecting stratified random samples of elementary school students receiving special education in each school system, interviewing their parents and teachers, and reviewing each child's school record. All special education students enrolled in grades K–6 in the fall of 1982 were eligible for inclusion, but we deliberately oversampled children with more serious and less prevalent mental or physical problems to obtain stable estimates for these groups.[6] Consent rates were very favorable (72 percent), and a total of 1,726 parents and 958 teachers were interviewed in the spring of 1983. Both sets of respondents were asked a wide range of questions focused on the student's functional status, school placement, and use of health and related services, as well as their own attitudes regarding the student's experience in school.

During the 1983–1984 school year, we conducted systematic key-informant interviews in each school system to create a qualitative information base on implementation. Key informants included the superintendent of schools, the special education director, the LEA budget director, school principals, special and regular education teachers, teachers' union representatives, parents, leaders of local advocacy groups, relevant health-care and social-service

TABLE 2

Who Is Served under EHA: National Trends from 1976–1977 through 1985–1986

	1976–77	1977–78	1978–79	1979–80	1980–81	1981–82	1982–83	1983–84	1984–85	1985–86
Number in Eligible										
Population (in 1000s)	44,322	43,566	42,549	41,632	40,969	40,096	39,655	39,144	38,561	39,353
Number Served (in 1000s)										
Total special education	3,692	3,751	3,889	4,005	4,142	4,198	4,255	4,298	4,315	4,317
Learning disabled	796	964	1,130	1,276	1,462	1,622	1,741	1,806	1,823	1,862
Speech impaired	1,302	1,223	1,214	1,186	1,168	1,135	1,131	1,128	1,129	1,128
Mentally retarded	959	933	901	869	829	786	757	727	708	661
Emotionally disturbed	283	288	300	329	346	339	352	361	372	376
Other severely impaired[a]	353	342	344	345	337	314	273	277	302	294
Percent of Total Population Classified as:										
Total special education	8.33	8.61	9.14	9.62	10.11	10.47	10.73	10.98	11.19	10.97
Learning disabled	1.80	2.21	2.66	3.06	3.57	4.05	4.39	4.62	4.72	4.73
Speech impaired	2.94	2.81	2.85	2.85	2.85	2.83	2.85	2.88	2.90	2.86
Mentally retarded	2.16	2.14	2.12	2.09	2.02	1.96	1.91	1.86	1.84	1.68
Emotionally disturbed	0.64	0.66	0.71	0.79	0.85	0.85	0.89	0.92	0.96	0.95
Other severely impaired[a]	0.81	0.79	0.82	0.83	0.83	0.79	0.69	0.70	0.78	0.75
Percent of Special Education Population Classifed as:										
Learning disabled	21.5	25.7	29.1	31.9	35.3	38.6	40.9	42.0	42.2	43.1
Speech impaired	35.3	32.6	31.2	29.6	28.2	27.0	26.6	26.2	25.9	26.1
Mentally retarded	26.0	24.9	23.2	21.7	20.0	18.7	17.8	16.9	16.4	15.3
Emotionally disturbed	7.6	7.7	7.7	8.2	8.4	8.1	8.3	8.4	8.6	8.7
Other severely impaired[a]	9.5	9.1	8.9	8.6	8.2	7.6	6.5	6.5	7.0	6.8

Source: Data are for children ages 3–21 in the 50 states and District of Columbia; for 1976–1977 through 1983–1984, National Center for Education Statistics, *The Condition of Education* (Washington, DC: U.S. Department of Education, 1985), Table 4.1, p. 182; and for 1984–1986, Office of Special Education and Rehabilitative Services, *Ninth Annual Report to Congress on the Implementation of the Education of the Handicapped Act* (Washington, DC: U.S. Department of Education, 1987), Table 2, p. 5.

[a]Other severely impaired includes children classified as hard of hearing, deaf, multihandicapped, orthopedically impaired, other health impaired, visually impaired, and deaf-blind.

personnel within the LEA and in other public agencies, and members of the school board. Information from these interviews shed light on school system dynamics and controversies, and helped narrow the range of speculation concerning determinants of some of the patterns we found in our quantitative analyses.

Because the systems in the Collaborative Study were not selected to be a national probability sample, inferences must be limited to the five systems themselves. However, the use of identical research methods in all five systems allows for the comparison of findings across districts and for the pooling of data when district differences do not dominate effects.[7] We believe that our findings reflect state and regional realities in many respects and thus would generalize to other large municipal school districts throughout the nation. To ensure an accurate national picture, though, we also report data provided by the U.S. Office of Special Education and Rehabilitative Services as part of its annual compliance reports to Congress.[8]

Patterns of LEA Compliance

When EHA went into effect in 1977, special education was already a major component of the U.S. public education system.[9] A total of 3.7 million elementary and secondary school students were receiving special education services, the special education teaching force numbered 179,000, and the federal government contributed $252 million to support program operations. As a result of EHA, special education has grown substantially. By 1986, as Table 2 shows, the number of children served had increased by 17 percent to 4.3 million, the number of teachers had increased by 54 percent to 275,000, and federal assistance had increased by 155 percent (in constant dollars) to $1.16 billion. However, as many local and state administrators would be quick to point out, the increase in federal contribution has lagged far behind program growth, so that it still represents less than 12 percent of excess expenditure on special education.[10]

How did all this change come about? From the outset, it was reasonable to assume that school districts would choose to be in minimal compliance with the new law while still maintaining preferred practice patterns and budget allocations. On the other hand, it was also reasonable to assume that a law this sweeping would indeed effect real change, at least some of it for the betterment of programs. In the following paragraph, we discuss how these two countervailing forces interacted to affect: 1) school districts' compliance with the procedural guarantees of the law, 2) the composition of the special education population, and 3) the form and substance of the special education program.

Procedural Compliance

By 1977, most states had begun to reform their special education laws; in some states, such as Massachusetts and Wisconsin, these laws were actually more stringent than the new federal law. Thus, in many states, the LEAs' task of bringing their rules and practices into conformance with federal regulations did not involve a radical departure from current law. Nevertheless, most districts found that EHA added visibility, impetus, and "teeth" to special education reforms, whether or not the basic provisions of the law were already embodied in state legislation.

Immediately after EHA was implemented, districts scrambled to comply with its procedural guarantees so as to obtain federal and state funds and avoid court action. Emphasis was placed on the identification and screening of eligible students, reduction of waiting times for placement, parent notification and involvement in the initial IEP conference, formulation of the IEP itself, and establishment of appeals procedures. To ensure full implementation of the law, state education agencies (SEAs) added evaluation personnel or reassigned existing personnel to evaluation functions.

Soon after procedures were established, they were refined and routinized by district staff and administrators. IEP forms were shortened and IEP conferences were redesigned so as to tie up less professional time. Centralized management information systems were created to keep track of children awaiting screening, evaluation, and placement. Guidelines for evaluating and placing children were issued from district offices to ensure homogeneity of implementation. By the early 1980s, provisions for ensuring EHA's procedural guarantees were well integrated into the education programs of all the districts studied. Moreover, no political force since that time, whether internal or external to the school bureaucracy, has undercut the fundamental rights provided by EHA. Visits to all five Collaborative Study sites in 1985–1986 indicated that a major shift had occurred in baseline assumptions and attitudes about the rights of handicapped students and that, despite severe fiscal constraints, the new set of procedures was likely to endure for the foreseeable future, supported by a well-established cadre of professionals and parents who had a strong interest in maintaining the new order.[11]

Implementation of EHA's procedural guarantees is therefore a success story of sorts. In the new law's first few years, a complex set of federally mandated procedures was carried out in recognizable form in many LEAs across the nation. Remaining, however, are nagging questions about whether excessive routinization and the pressure of budget cuts have diminished the potential benefits of the procedures. The scope of the IEP, at the center of the educational reform, is illustrative in this regard.

The IEP received the greatest initial attention from LEAs both because it was a readily measurable element of compliance and because it involved an appreciable departure from previous LEA practice. Although most special educators acknowledged the need for standardized procedures, many felt that the IEP's detailed objectives were too limiting and did not allow for midcourse correction. The specificity of the IEP also received close scrutiny from special education directors, who perceived it as a major point of vulnerability in compliance audits. Thus, many directors seized the opportunity to decrease the specificity of the IEP when, in 1981, Secretary of Education Terrel Bell said that IEPs were intended to be only "general benchmarks" and not specific instructional plans.[12]

Has the decreased specificity of the IEP diminished its utility? No, in the opinion of many teachers, who reported that the new IEPs gave them the latitude for professional judgment that was lacking before. This sentiment was echoed by psychologists and other diagnosticians who were now able to spend less time filling out forms and more time evaluating children and conducting therapy. However, some teachers complained that the new streamlined IEPs were so general that they were no longer helpful for planning instruction or measuring progress. There remains much difference of opinion on this issue, but it is clear that ten years into the law's implementation, school districts have begun to win the battle with EHA paperwork.

Who Receives Special Education?

As a percentage of total public school enrollment, the proportion of students receiving special education grew rapidly after implementation of EHA, from approximately 8 percent to approximately 11 percent nationally. By the early 1980s, however, the rate of growth slowed so that the 11 percent figure has been reasonably stable for several years, albeit with appreciable variations from state to state and LEA to LEA (Figure 1).[13] Almost all the growth in special education has been among two groups of children — those with the most and the least severe disabilities. For the former group, programs were added for small numbers of children with severe cognitive, emotional, or physical disabilities who had previously been institutionalized or in home care without any educational opportunities. Because these children were expensive to accommodate, they received considerable attention from educators and the press during EHA's early years. In fact, however, despite initial claims that there were hundreds of thousands of unserved children,[14] the number of children classified as seriously emotionally disturbed has increased by only 93,000 since 1976–1977, the number classified as mentally retarded (MR) has *decreased* by 298,000, and the number classified as physically handicapped, other health impaired, visually impaired, hearing impaired, or multihandicapped has *decreased* by 59,000 (Table 2).

Of far greater consequence has been the dramatic growth in the number of students classified as specific learning disabled (LD). In 1976–1977, LD students numbered approximately 800,000, representing 22 percent of the special education population nationally. In 1985–1986, they numbered 1.9 million, or 43 percent of the special needs students. As a proportion of total enrollment, the LD population grew from 1.8 percent in 1976–1977 to 4.7 percent in 1985–1986 (Table 2). Anticipating that LD would be a "soft" category, subject to variable interpretation, the original regulations proposed a 2 percent cap on the proportion of children so designated by any state. When this limit was judged too arbitrary, a flexible cap was established by which federal sources would recognize no more than 12 percent of total school enrollment as eligible for special education.

FIGURE 1

The Growth of Special Education during Ten Years of EHA (National Data)

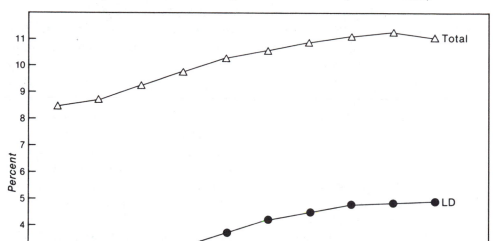

Legend:
Total = Total special education
LD = Learning disabled
SI = Speech impaired
MR = Mentally retarded
ED = Seriously emotionally disturbed
Other = Physical, sensory, health, and other impairments

In fact, the 12 percent cap has done little to restrict the growth of the LD category, for four reasons. First, few states serve as many as 12 percent overall. Second, districts with sufficient numbers of children in need have not been averse to exceeding the federal reimbursement limit, because reimbursement amounts are so low anyway. Third, the uniform reimbursement formulas used by some states have created an unintentional incentive to find LD children, because the generally lower cost of providing services for them permits part of their allocation to be used as a cross-subsidy. Finally, and perhaps most important, there have been strong ideological and practical reasons for designating children LD. These reasons include the desire not to stigmatize children with more traditional labels, the need for a convenient category for those reclassified from the MR category in the wake of court action and state legislation discouraging this designation, and the desire to obtain supplemental services for children at a time when other sources of support, such as Title I and funding for bilingual education, have been drying up.[15]

Aware of the LD problem, many LEAs and SEAs had begun by the early 1980s to question whether there should be a further increase in the number of children served, or even whether present levels of effort could be maintained. By 1983, at state and local initiative, several districts had moved to define eligibility more stringently: in order to qualify as LD, a student had to be seriously behind in grade level and had to have a severe discrepancy between academic performance and cognitive ability in at least one domain of school functioning.[16] This established a surrogate cap on the category in several districts, such as Houston, where the number of students designated as LD fell by 23 percent between 1984–1985 and 1985–1986. But because changes in selected districts have not been sufficient to control the size of the LD group nationally, this category is likely to receive increasing amounts of policy attention in the future.

Also likely to affect the size of the special education population is the imminent increase in public school enrollment. EHA was implemented when public school enrollments were declining for the first time in decades. Superintendents found themselves with fewer students to teach, but with more teachers than ever. Layoffs were one solution; another was the redeployment of existing personnel to other functions. It was easier to accommodate the needs of special students when other demands on the system were decreasing. The entry of the baby "boomlet" into the public schools, combined with projected teacher shortages, suggests that there will soon be additional pressures to control the size of the special education population.

Even without these pressures, however, the increases in the numbers of 5- to 18-year-olds served has not yet been mirrored in the numbers of 3- to 5-year-olds and 18- to 21-year-olds served. Most special educators would agree that these groups of children have as strong a claim on resources as those in elementary and secondary school — indeed, some would argue that early intervention services are essential from birth, as are aggressive follow-up services after high school vocational educational programs. EHA did not mandate services for these groups, but left them to be served at state option. The numbers of these children may soon increase, however, as a result of provisions included in the recently passed reauthorization of EHA.[17] The new law has created powerful financial incentives for states to offer special education services to preschoolers and has established a program to assist states in the provision of comprehensive and coordinated early intervention services for infants and toddlers. Federal monies may be the only way to ensure the provision of such services, for it was made clear during our key informant interviews that under budgetary constraints, it was these discretionary services that would be cut.

Program Structure and Content

Changes in the scope and comprehensiveness of services were initiated somewhat later than procedural reforms because they were generally more expensive, more difficult to monitor, and involved a larger element of LEA discretion. Changes were made in such matters as continuum of placement options, appropriate size of classes, training and personnel mix in special education, and provision of related services. These characteristics seem to have been at least as relevant to program quality as mandated procedural reforms, but they have remained highly dependent on the availability of resources. Hence staff training and program expansion have suffered more than procedural reforms from recent cutbacks.

Contrary to what might have been supposed, EHA did not radically change placement practices. Mainstreaming was not a new concept in most large LEAs by 1977, and many had already established philosophical preferences or doctrines on these matters. By 1977, over 90 percent of all special education students attended regular schools, and two-thirds received most of their instruction in regular classes (Table 3). This pattern reflected the preponderance of LD and speech-impaired children in the program, who, combined, often represented two-thirds to three-quarters of the local special education population. In fact, for MR students there has been a modest trend toward less integration, although this no doubt reflects more stringent thresholds for MR classification, which have been established during the same period.

Placement has often been constrained by available options. To the extent that changes in placement patterns have occurred, they have taken one of two general forms. For the severely handicapped, there has been movement from state facilities to public school facilities, from separate schools of all kinds into regular schools, and from private contract arrangements to publicly organized programs. Among the less severely handicapped, there has been movement toward more resource rooms, more noncategorical placements, and fewer self-contained classrooms.

Some districts have found that the mainstreaming ideology conforms with their desire for least-cost solutions. As one special education director remarked, "Mainstreaming is not always in the best interest of the child; sometimes, it is an economic decision." It is generally cheaper to place less severely handicapped students in regular classrooms as long as their teachers do not object too strenuously.[18] However, conscientious administrators have been aware that good mainstreaming almost always requires a more favorable teacher-student ratio, additional support staff, and pull-out arrangements for part of the day or week.[19] These often prove to be more expensive than self-contained classes.

TABLE 3

Where Are Special Education Students Placed under EHA:
Comparison of National Data for 1976–1977 and 1985–1986

Primary Handicap and School Year	Regular School		Special School	Other Environment[a]
	Regular Class	Special Class		
	Percent of Children in Placement[b]			
All special education students				
1976–77	68	25	5	2
1985–86	68	24	6	2
Speech impaired				
1976–77	91	8	1	0
1985–86	91	5	3	0
Learning disabled				
1976–77	81	17	2	0
1985–86	77	21	2	0
Emotionally disturbed				
1976–77	43	38	14	4
1985–86	46	33	13	7
Other severely impaired[c]				
1976–77	44	27	13	17
1985–86	44	37	6	13
Mentally retarded				
1976–77	39	51	9	1
1985–86	33	53	11	4

Source: Data are for children ages 3–21 in the 50 states and District of Columbia; for 1975–1976, the Bureau of Education for the Handicapped, First Annual Report to Congress on the Implementation of PL 94-142 (Washington, DC: U.S. Deprtment of Health, Education and Welfare, 1979), Table D–2.2; and for 1985–1986, the Office of Special Education and Rehabilitative Services, *Ninth Annual Report to Congress on the Implementation of the Education of the Handicapped Act* (Washington, DC: U.S. Department of Education, 1987), Table EC1, pp. E-45–46.

[a]Other environment includes public and private residential facilities, correctional facilities, hospital facilities,and homebound arrangements.

[b]Percentages may not add up to 100 percent because of rounding.

[c]Other severely impaired includes children classified as hard of hearing, deaf, multihandicapped, orthopedically impaired, other health impaired, visually impaired, and deaf-blind.

In the search for cost savings, LEA administrators have turned to cutting the major cost item within their control — personnel. Those first to go, especially in districts with strong union contracts, have been the younger but more appropriately trained special education teachers. Also vulnerable have been personnel whose services were not mandated by law. When layoffs have not been possible, personnel have been redeployed from less to more essential functions, with "essential" being defined from the school system's standpoint rather than from the child's or family's. One unfortunate result has been the loss of a wide range of support personnel and other noninstructional employees — precisely those who made entry into regular schools a successful experience for so many children early in EHA's implementation. This trend has been reinforced by the decision in numerous school districts to handle increased procedural demands by borrowing professional time from teachers and counselors to use for case management and administration. Social workers in several of the Collaborative Study sites, for example, were redeployed as IEP conference managers and no longer performed home visits.

One cost-cutting alternative generally not open to local administrators has been to cross-subsidize special education activities with funds from other federal accounts. For example, in her 1979 case study of the overlap between ESEA Title I and EHA, Beatrice Birman noted that most LEAs took such pains to differentiate EHA services from compensatory education services that artificial discontinuities were created, so that "students with slight speech or vision impairments could not participate in Title I academic programs."[20] Fear of federal audits thus stifled local creativity in combining funding sources.

Cross-subsidies have been an issue, however, in the provision of related services. Although EHA defines related services as those "services required to assist [children] . . . to benefit from special education," the law is somewhat ambiguous about their scope. Concerning payment for those services deemed necessary, LEAs have understood that as a practical matter the schools must pay. As a result, some public health, mental health, and health insurance organizations have withdrawn their financial support, allowing school resources to supplant their own.

For the most part, LEA dollars for related services have been spent, in descending order of total expenditure, on transportation, speech therapy, occupational and physical therapy (OT/PT), child counseling, medical diagnosis of various kinds, and school nursing services. Cost containment issues have been somewhat different in each domain. Transportation has been a particularly salient cost issue in large, geographically dispersed districts and small rural districts, although the impact of costs at the LEA level usually has been buffered by state or county contributions. The national trend among many LEAs since the early 1980s to return to a "local school" concept has been motivated in part by the desire to cap transportation costs.

Speech therapy and OT/PT have been provided largely at local option and represent an interesting case example of natural variation in LEA response. Because EHA is not explicit about who should receive such services, local decisions have tended to reflect not only objective indicators of need but also district wealth, the composition of IEP committees, and the political strength within the LEA of the professional groups delivering services. Two of the Collaborative Study sites, for example, have very extensive speech and language departments that existed well before EHA's implementation and have grown considerably since that time under the leadership of dedicated career bureaucrats with strong missionary zeal and good territorial instincts. When we remarked on the disproportionate number of students receiving speech therapy in one of those sites, the local special education director simply smiled and said, "That's not a battle I want to fight."

In the case of OT/PT, "the battle" has been somewhat more complicated because those prescribing the services have not always worked for the schools. Where cost has been an issue, LEA response has been first to narrow the eligible population and then to reduce the extent of service and the professional qualifications necessary for providing it. The provision of OT/PT has proved especially difficult in districts in which the local medical society perceives a threat to its authority when schools begin to determine who should receive therapy and how much therapy is appropriate. Physicians also have had an incentive opposite from that of the schools; that is, to enlarge the scope and duration of service. At least one Collaborative Study site encountered such a problem and had to institute its own "Medical Advisory Committee" so as to internalize and quell dissent among physicians.

Other related services are not major cost factors. In the five Collaborative Study sites, counseling was provided to 20 percent to 40 percent of all special needs children, but the majority of these had only one or two sessions with a therapist. Patterns of physician involvement and school nursing have not been altered much by EHA, except that many school systems have felt the need to hire a limited number of nurse practitioners or other mid-level health personnel to meet the needs of orthopedically and neurologically handicapped children, usually concentrated in self-contained or substantially separate and centralized locations.

In general, LEAs have been quite successful in containing special education costs. However, it remains easy to find critics who believe that, in a zero-sum competition for scarce educational resources, special education has assumed unwarranted priority over regular education.[21] In general, this argument has not galvanized widespread local dissent, even among the parents and teachers of regular students, because most individuals continue to believe in the importance of the new entitlement and perceive that special education has experienced cutbacks commensurate with cuts in other parts of the school budget. In fact, average per-child expenditure for special students in relation to average per-child expenditure for regular students is about where it was in 1977. The main difference today is that many more children with mild problems are at least nominally served, along with a few who have much more severe physical or mental problems. The main point of contention, therefore, is breadth of eligibility and not per-child cost. We will return to this topic below.

Maintaining Control over Special Interest Groups

Local interest group politics affect every major policy reform, and EHA has been no exception. Within LEAs, regular and special educators have differed in their goals and in their willingness to comply with specific provisions of the law. In the broader view, the negotiations between these two groups have been constrained by the interests of a diverse set of actors, including parents, teachers' unions, mental and public health agencies, and children's advocacy groups.

Control within the LEA

In each of the five school systems studied, the superintendent and the school board responded to EHA by restructuring, elevating, and expanding the powers of the special education unit within the LEA. The special education director of each district was a member of the superintendent's cabinet, and in two of the systems he or she was given control over the previously separate domain of pupil personnel services. Between 1976 and 1978, most special education departments also experienced sizable staff increases, creating a large group of professionals with a vested interest in the development and continuation of the program.

As special education directors gained more authority and responsibility, two predictable problems arose. One concerned how much discretionary authority they would be granted to develop school system policy in a largely uncharted domain. Superintendents and school boards generally prefer to respond to the complexities of new federal mandates by delegating them entirely to subunits directed by an expert. But because EHA was a high-visibility program with major budgetary implications and the potential for costly and continuing legal problems, it was difficult to delegate responsibility entirely. Instead, the most common pattern of bureaucratic conduct, at least during the first two years of the program, was one of constant interaction between the special education director, the superintendent, and other members of the superintendent's staff, with intermittent progress reports to the school board. Thereafter delegation increased somewhat and thus reduced the overtly political aspect of the special education director's role.

A more difficult problem facing special education directors was the need to control, at least to some degree, the actions of regular education administrators and teachers. For example, an IEP's recommendation of placing a handicapped child in a regular classroom could be carried out only with the approval of regular education personnel. Federal and state laws helped special education units to establish some measure of control, but counter-vailing priorities in regular education were predictable from the outset. Resolution often came through informal negotiations at the subdistrict level or at the individual school. For example, the role of an IEP team manager in several of the Collaborative Study sites involved meeting with principals before the IEP was formulated to see if a slot was available for a child whom special educators wished to mainstream for all or part of the week.

This mode of exerting control over regular education has given a great deal of discretionary power to those whom Richard Weatherley and Michael Lipsky have called "street-level bureaucrats" — teachers, principals, and specialists who interact on a daily basis with children and parents.[22] However, EHA's emphasis on procedural guarantees and federal monitoring has also given increased power to the LEA special education director, whose job it has been to focus on compliance-oriented activities. In essence, EHA has created a *dual* locus of organizational control, the LEA special education director's office and the "street level" of subjurisdictions and schools. It is the tension and interaction between these levels of authority, in the context of expanded legal obligations and discretionary power, that has determined the evolution of local special education policy. The polarity parallels the main contradiction inherent in EHA: its requirement, first, for uniform LEA procedures in observing the law, and second, for an individualized approach to the education of handicapped students.

The dual locus of control has been an effective management approach for special education directors. Centralized management information systems keep track of IEPs, children awaiting placement, services being received, and other data that might be needed for legal or monitoring purposes, quick-turnaround defense of special education priorities within the LEA, or public relations in the wider community. By contrast, decisions surrounding specific instructional activities have become or remained more decentralized. Special education directors have continued to decide the range of placement and service options for *categories* of handicapped children, but have willingly delegated decisions about appropriate mixes of instruction and related services for *individual* students. Special education directors in several districts admitted that delegation of discretionary decisionmaking to building-level personnel, who were at too low a level and too decentralized to draw fire, helped protect the overall special education unit from adverse political repercussions.

Control over Other Service Sectors

Another major issue facing special education directors has been the need to control, to the extent feasible, the contributions of other public service agencies, especially concerning the provision of related services such as

OT/PT and school nursing services sponsored by health departments, counseling services sponsored by mental health agencies, and hospital-based care for chronically ill children. Sharing of responsibility and cost, as mandated by EHA, has proved difficult because of the competing priorities, agendas, and accountability criteria of service providers outside public education. Formal arrangements for case coordination, pooling of information, and cost-sharing in the provision of related services remain the exception rather than the rule.

To fill the need for services, special education directors have fostered informal arrangements among private and public agencies, organizations, and individuals that have finessed questions concerning payment and control of case management. These informal agreements have created the forms of collaboration required to provide adequate services, especially for students with multiple handicaps or disabilities requiring routine interaction among educators and health or mental health professionals. However, because these informal arrangements are not open to public scrutiny in the same way as formal ones are, and because they require the dedication and entrepreneurial skills of one or more local actors, they tend to be idiosyncratic and difficult to replicate.

When agencies would not make informal arrangements, special education directors have resorted to other strategies to secure services for their students. In Santa Clara County, for example, the Crippled Children's Services Program of the California Department of Public Health had traditionally located its OT/PT facilities in county schools for physically handicapped children. When EHA was implemented, the schools increased the number of children recognized as eligible for OT/PT services. But health department authorities were reluctant to depart from their own eligibility criteria and professional judgment regarding the extent of therapy needed. State and federal intervention was required to adjudicate this bureaucratic boundary issue, and the health department now meets the school's needs.

Teachers' Unions

Teachers' unions had an obvious stake in the implementation of EHA because of the explicit provisions mandating IEP formulation, mainstreaming, and other time- or labor-intensive activities. Three of the school systems in the Collaborative Study had active teachers' unions. The two without unions have been freer to experiment with generic personnel, to adopt aggressive mainstreaming policies, and to use less expensive personnel for providing related services. For example, instead of involving a multidisciplinary team of social workers, guidance counselors, and psychologists in all placement decisions, the nonunionized Charlotte-Mecklenburg school district has used a "Student Support Specialist," a professional with a background in one of the three fields who has received in-service training in the remaining two.

Unionized districts, in contrast, have had to operate within much tighter constraints. Where unions have set out to be obstructionist or have denied that special education reform deserves priority, they have been quite successful in limiting innovative practice. For example, the union contract in one district specified that a teacher would spend a maximum of 15 minutes discussing a student referral, 15 minutes talking with a parent about the referral, and 30 minutes at an IEP meeting. Willingness to accept mainstreaming policies also has been used as a chip in wider contract negotiations. Union militancy is understandable, however, given the impact on regular classes that recent austerity measures instituted in many LEAs have had on class size, availability of ancillary personnel, and other factors that make it possible for teachers to teach.

Parents

The due process provisions of EHA, based in civil rights law, actually form an entitlement more for parents than for children. No previous education law has gone so far to mandate parent participation in school decisionmaking or to provide grievance procedures via both administrative hearings and the civil courts. The national special education law is a superb illustration of the theory, embodied in numerous federal educational reforms of the past twenty years, that parent participation is a necessary corrective for potential abuses of power by school authorities.

Not surprisingly, hopes for high levels of parent participation have proved no more realistic under EHA than under a range of other federal school reforms. Parents of handicapped children have been a diffuse interest group,

TABLE 4
Parent Participation in and Satisfaction with Special Education
in the Collaborative Study Sites

	Charlotte-Mecklenburg	Houston	Milwaukee	Rochester	Santa Clara County
Percent of parents attending the most recent IEP	42	40	45	32	95
Percent of parents satisfied with the overall education program	86	86	90	86	80
Percent of parents belonging to a parent group	4	3	3	6	6

and in four of the five Collaborative Study sites, fewer than 50 percent of the parents had attended their child's most recent IEP conference (Table 4). All five districts did have a limited number of vocal parent groups and a handful of (usually middle-class) parents who protested a placement decision or otherwise involved the district in grievance procedures. But the vast majority, especially low-income parents, have been generally passive in reference to the special education of their youngsters and uninvolved with other parents of handicapped children.

Some districts, however, have been effective in attaining parent participation. Almost 95 percent of the parents of special education students in Santa Clara County participated in their child's most recent IEP conference. Part of this high participation rate can be attributed to the relative affluence and higher parent education levels in the district: parents were able to make the time, were highly motivated to attend, and were not intimidated by the schools. But another factor was the willingness of many schools in the system to schedule IEP meetings at times convenient to parents, often outside regular school hours. Increased parent participation did come at a higher cost — more parents showed up at IEP meetings with a lawyer and a tape recorder — but their numbers were relatively small to begin with, and have diminished as precedents and procedures have become routinized.

Is it a failure in EHA's implementation that parent participation has not been greater? Surely socioeconomic differentials merit concern. But it remains a matter of dispute how central to the success of EHA parent participation really is. It is one matter to enfranchise parents and another to expect that they will wish to participate actively in their child's program. Our own parent interview data show a uniformly high level of parent satisfaction with their child's school program — more than 80 percent across all five districts reported satisfaction — exceeding the very positive ratings given by parents of children in the public schools as reported by the Gallup Poll.[23] The lesson seems to be that parents of public school students like what they are getting, and parents of special education students like it even more because of the individual attention their child receives. In this kind of political environment, it is difficult to argue that parents should be urged to become more militant in anticipating potential abuses, especially given the limited time that school teachers and administrators have to engage parents in depth.

Advocacy Groups

Parent organizations, disease-specific philanthropies, children's rights groups, legal aid organizations, and physicians' groups have all initiated activities to ensure full implementation of EHA. These efforts have played a major role in shaping the policy choices of special education directors in most districts; however, their impact has usually been idiosyncratic to local circumstances, influenced by a few key actors and organizations, a distinctive history of interaction between advocates and the LEA, and one or more influential court actions.

When considering the impact of these groups, a distinction must be drawn between parents as an interest group and advocates who have established themselves to represent parents. Although every district studied had several advocacy groups purporting to represent the parents of handicapped children, 6 percent or less of the parents interviewed in each school system reported being members of such groups (Table 4). There is no reason to assume that the issues raised by these groups did not reflect genuine parent concerns, but it is clear that parents of special needs children have not organized themselves as a cohesive political force. Lack of political organization may reflect low parental self-esteem and family isolation, but it also reflects the inherent fragmentation of the population of children we call handicapped. Although all have the same procedural rights, the educational needs of a learning-disabled child and those of a paraplegic child have little in common. This fact, combined with the strategic consideration that it is easier to organize around specific unmet needs than around a more abstract set of unmet procedural guarantees, almost assures that parents will be diverse and divided in their political expressions.

When parent groups have managed to organize, local special education directors have often controlled the groups' dissent by incorporating them, at least nominally, into the decisionmaking structure of the LEA. For example, in 1971, the external pressure of one key advocate led the Milwaukee School Board to establish the Exceptional Education Task Force, an independent advisory board. The task force successfully lobbied for statewide special education legislation, which passed in 1973, and from then until 1978 it continued to maneuver very effectively to negotiate the terms of program implementation under the new state law. As part of a reorganization of the special education unit in 1978, the special education director persuaded the school board and superintendent to make the task force an adjunct of his own department. This move to internalize dissent, combined with a decline in the energy of the task force itself, has considerably reduced the organization's effectiveness as a watchdog and its ability to marshal external pressure for change. In response to the specific requirement under EHA that every LEA establish a parent council, similar actions internalizing advocacy groups have occurred in three of the other Collaborative Study sites. Thus, the real effect of the parent councils has been to give greater power to special education directors.

On the other hand, some legal aid and legal rights organizations representing individual parents in grievance procedures or seeking test cases to establish policy in the higher courts have remained resolutely adversarial. These groups have been very influential in every LEA — each of the Collaborative Study sites had experienced at least one major court battle over EHA — and their costs have been considerable. According to the school district lawyers we interviewed, grievances raised by individual parents usually have concerned LEA unwillingness to place a child in a private school or provide supplemental services deemed essential by the parent. Class actions against school systems have tended to focus on waiting times for evaluation and placement, the inadequacy of placement options or services, and other instances of alleged skimping by LEAs in interpreting the procedural guarantees of the law.

In general, LEA practice has been influenced more by local and state court actions than by federal court actions. However, both state and federal decisions have only partially delineated what constitutes an "appropriate" education under the law. State-level opinions have sometimes been in conflict on this point. The few relevant Supreme Court cases since 1977 have established a climate of belief concerning what is likely to be acceptable local practice, but these decisions provide few specifics. For example, the 1982 *Rowley* decision,[24] which ruled that schools are not required to maximize every handicapped child's learning potential but only to provide opportunities commensurate with the opportunities provided for other children, was taken by most school districts as a signal that lower-cost placements and services would be permissible in many cases. However, the 1984 *Tatro* decision,[25] which ruled that schools were obligated to provide catheterization for a child with spina bifida, and the 1985 *Burlington* decision,[26] which ruled that the public schools must pay for private school tuitions if a private school is the appropriate placement, seemed to interpret more broadly the scope of services for which LEAs must pay.

Although major uncertainties continue to surround many aspects of legal compliance, test cases are fewer now than when EHA was first implemented. Not many organizations can sustain the expense of protracted court proceedings, and legal advocates are reluctant to initiate major class action suits in a political climate they perceive as increasingly hostile to broad interpretations of the law. Similarly, the grievances of individual parents tend to be fewer and to be tracked more readily into administrative hearings with well-established precedents to guide them. In the five communities we studied, legal and administrative actions to enforce compliance have waned dramatically. A predictable advocacy cycle therefore has been enacted: an initial flurry of activity, followed by institutionalization of the law, and, after ten years, the tendency among many groups to turn to other issues and priorities.

Winners and Losers

It is natural to suppose that EHA has benefited some children more than others. But do we know which ones they are, and do they tend to cluster in particular disability categories or socioeconomic groups? This question is more salient now than it was ten years ago when EHA first went into effect, because it is no longer sufficient to demonstrate compliance without also demonstrating program impact. For whom has EHA made a difference?

The first and most obvious response is that it has benefited those who would not previously have been eligible for free public special education and related services. In general, these are the most and the least handicapped, whose numbers have increased since the law went into effect. New eligibility for services establishes a strong *prima facie* case that these two groups have been among the winners, perhaps benefiting more than the traditional special education constituency, for whom schooling may have changed only marginally.

Predictably, children at the two extremes of the disability continuum also have proven the most controversial recipients of special education. Some doubt that "education" can be equated with the developmental needs of the severely impaired. As one teacher put it, commenting on the care of a seriously mentally retarded student with cerebral palsy, "I don't think it should be the role of public schools as a goal of learning to teach children to eat." This sentiment is echoed by some budget cutters who wish to restore essentially custodial arrangements for such youngsters, with minimal health supervision and little curriculum in learning. At the other end of the spectrum, some doubt the wisdom of defining children as learning disabled unless their condition has a specific organic etiology. The argument is that, because there is no adequate technology to differentiate the LD child from the child with more diffuse psychosocial or learning problems, we should not be enriching teaching arbitrarily for some and not for others. In general, however, both of these are minority views, not sufficient to dissuade the vast majority of school personnel and parents, inside and outside special education, that good things are happening for those children who never before were eligible for specialized instruction and services.

If previously ineligible students are one group of "winners" under EHA, are there others within the special education population? We would propose several different frames of reference within which to address this matter, each yielding somewhat different insights.

Who Is Most at Risk?

It makes little sense to consider who benefits most from an educational intervention without correcting for level of need or risk. This is the denominator in any social policy context. Some special education students have more severe handicaps than others, and expectations concerning the impact of school on these children must be adjusted accordingly. This recognition is at the base of EHA's rationale for individual assessment and programming. Similarly, however, even when children have disabilities that are of comparable severity or that result in similar degrees of functional limitation, they may still be more at risk of failure than other students because of family background or other factors associated with, but not resulting from, their handicap.

To determine the level of risk within the special needs population resulting from factors beyond the students' or schools' control, we examined the family background of the students participating in the Collaborative Study (Table 5). Many children receiving special education are clearly at a level of socioeconomic risk and family stress far beyond what the schools alone can reasonably be expected to address. For example, in four of the five systems studied, the mothers of one-third to over one-half of the special education students never graduated from high school; in the same four systems, almost half of the special education students lived with families whose total annual income was below 150 percent of the federal poverty line. In Rochester and Milwaukee, special education students were more likely to be living with a single mother or their grandparents than in a two-parent household and were more likely to have an unemployed or out-of-work parent heading that household than one who was working. It is clear that for many special needs children, having a handicap is only one, and not necessarily the most significant, factor shaping their life chances.

TABLE 5

Socioeconomic Risk Profiles of Special Education Students in the Collaborative Study Sites

Socioeconomic Risk Group	Charlotte-Mecklenburg	Houston	Milwaukee	Rochester	Santa Clara County
	Percent of Students in Socioeconomic Group				
Family income below 150 percent of poverty line	46	46	54	65	26
Not a two-parent household	43	36	54	57	24
Family income below $15,000 a year	41	33	48	58	22
Mother did not graduate from high school	35	53	42	54	24
Head of household does not have a full-time job	30	29	57	53	18

TABLE 6
Allocation of Special Education Expenditures in the Collaborative Study Sites

Primary Handicap	Mean Expenditure in Dollars	Percent of Special Education Population	Percent of Special Education Expenditures
Learning disabled	7,172	43	44
Speech impaired	5,414	27	21
Mentally retarded	7,853	15	16
Emotionally disturbed	8,204	11	13
Physically, hearing, visually or health impaired	10,791	4	7

Not all special education students within a given school district were at equal socioeconomic risk. Children with physical, sensory, or health impairments tended to come from more affluent, intact families than children with all other types of disabilities. This differential is probably due to the fact that these disabilities are not as likely to be environmentally linked, and that affluent parents will often send these children to public schools because of the special services provided under EHA. We conclude that, if one wishes to compare "winners" and "losers" among disability groups, it is essential to begin by acknowledging the very different levels of family need, disorganization, and stress that form the backdrop against which children's school experiences are enacted.

Many researchers have found that family background is associated with academic achievement, self-esteem, career aspirations, and psychosocial development — in short, all aspects of short-term and long-term development.[27] In the context of EHA, however, family background is also associated with access to the procedural guarantee of parent participation in the IEP process. Even after controlling for site differences in parent participation (as shown in Table 4), a White, married mother who had graduated from high school was 5.4 times more likely than a non-White, single mother who had not graduated from high school to have attended the most recent IEP conference held for her child. Hence, a program that gained enormous political support on the grounds that it was an entitlement for all, rather than a means-tested program for the neediest few, has conferred predictably different entitlements on middle-class and low-income children.

Per-Child Resource Allocation

Another way to think about winners and losers is in terms of resource expenditure. Which groups are receiving the lion's share of special education dollars? Let us consider this question first in its simplest form, then raise the issue of whether any meaningful judgment can be made about fairness, without adjusting for degree of functional impairment, priority in targeting, and effectiveness of marginal expenditure.

Our own per-child expenditure estimates suggest that, contrary to conventional wisdom, distribution of resources is more nearly equal across disability groups than might be imagined (Table 6). The stereotypical view is that the education of a handful of severely impaired children costs huge amounts of money, draining resources away from the many children in regular education and in the other categories of special education. In fact, because the most expensive students tend to be in the low prevalence groups, expenditures for these children do not dominate special education budgets. In the Collaborative Study sites, students with physical, hearing, visual, or other health impairments comprised 4 percent of the special education population and were allocated 7 percent of all special education dollars. For emotionally disturbed and mentally retarded children, the ratio of these two percentages was closer to one. This was true even though we estimated that services for some children cost in excess of $18,000 per year. Our evidence suggests that in large school districts such as the ones we studied, the rare case of the very expensive child tends to be canceled out by many less expensive cases. In fairness, however, it must be said that this analysis does not reflect the disparity that may arise when a very small district has responsibility for a very expensive child.

A final concern is to weight current patterns of per-child resource allocation in relation to consideration of fundamental values. Explicit in EHA and its regulations is the notion that priority should be given to children whose needs are greatest. From this, it is clear that the architects of the law believed that the more severe the child's disability, the more deserving he or she was of scarce public dollars. However, school personnel, physicians, and others have sometimes argued instead that the first dollar should go to the child most likely to benefit from it in terms of new learning, improved functional status, independence, or other outcome criteria. Imagine a four-cell table with high and low severity on one side, and high and low likely improvement or demonstrated effectiveness of educational services on the other; the issue is how to order the cells according to their claim on public resources. Clearly, the high-high cell comes first, and the low-low cell last, but in reality, most special education students fall into one of the other two cells in the table, making resource allocation choices a tradeoff between needs and education gains. The issue is especially complex because, although it is relatively easy to array children according to the severity of their disabilities, it is much harder to determine which children are likely to benefit the most from instruction and related services. This judgment involves prior consideration of the nature of benefits, which are themselves multidimensional.

Rich and Poor Districts

Because affluent districts can offer more services than poor ones, special education students who live in rich districts must be counted among the EHA winners. Although we performed cost analyses for only three districts, none of them among the most affluent in the country, differences in average per-pupil expenditures for special education were substantial: the expenditure for the average special needs student in Charlotte-Mecklenburg was $5,864, as compared with $7,482 in Milwaukee and $7,733 in Rochester.

What does a higher per-pupil expenditure buy? In some cases, it buys better-trained staff: 72 percent of the teachers interviewed in Rochester had master's degrees, compared with 38 percent of those in Charlotte-Mecklenburg and 32 percent of those in Milwaukee. In other cases, higher expenditure buys additional related services: almost 60 percent of the special needs students in Milwaukee and Rochester received speech therapy, compared with 45 percent in Charlotte-Mecklenburg. Variations are also a function of differences in the cost of living in different areas of the country. But regardless of the reasons for these variations, it remains clear that the particular school district in which a special needs child lives determines in large part the kind of education he or she will receive.

One very important set of additional benefits for handicapped children, which can be attained only outside the education sector, is access to health care. Sites with lower special education expenditures per pupil also tended to have lower rates of health insurance coverage and use of physicians. In Charlotte, for example, because of a very limited state Medicaid program, 31 percent of special education students whose families lived below the federal poverty standard were ineligible for public health insurance, and 34 percent had not seen a physician in the past year, as compared to 7 percent and 13 percent in Rochester. It is therefore important to assess not only the impact of EHA, but also that of a range of programs in the same state or LEA that may be related in generosity to programs offered in school.

Performance Gains

In a program with individualized learning goals, impact evaluation based on child assessments is intrinsically difficult. In order to evaluate a child's progress toward individual learning objectives, the researcher must first establish the child's measured baseline of performance in relevant domains, then identify indicators of progress and a schedule for assessing them, then devise a way to separate effects due to intervention from effects due to maturation and exogenous influences, and, finally, determine how to combine the resulting information on gains to produce a composite measure of success. This last step requires a framework for deciding what constitutes comparable dimensions of gain for children with disparate problems, as well as whether a child's advance, say, from 0 to 2 on a scale of 5 is as important as an advance from 3 to 5. Little wonder that this evaluation enterprise has proven impossible so far, notwithstanding the very useful clinical insights and partial information on individual children that the development and application of IEPs has fostered.

So how, for policy purposes, does one evaluate child performance gains in a real world of limited measurement technology? One approach is to rely on criterion-referenced measures specifically tailored to areas of desired improvement for each disability group. It is relevant to document, for example, how many LD children moved from being two grade levels behind in reading in the fall to less than one grade level behind in the spring. Also of interest might be gains in the number of physically handicapped children able to perform basic writing exercises or other combinations of motor and cognitive skills. Measures such as these are useful when combined with face-valid information from parents, teachers, and other professionals on satisfaction with the special education program, perceptions of child progress, and follow-up information on whether children complete school, take a first job, and retain employment over time. These approaches to evaluation focus not only on short-term school experience but also on long-term adaptation and functioning.

Lamentably, not much information from criterion-referenced testing or face-valid indicators is available at present, largely because it is costly and time-consuming to collect. Our own research has partial information of the second type, based on a cross section of parent and teacher impressions about the adequacy of the child's school program and how well the child appeared to have progressed by spring in reference to baseline functional and academic skills the previous fall. By these criteria, special education programs under EHA in the five sites received very high ratings of satisfaction from parents and of perceived improvements from teachers. However, such data are not derived from independent observers and therefore remain "soft." It is both a cliché and a profound truth to say that more research is needed on program effectiveness. Of course, no one should forget that program evaluation in regular education suffers from most of the same deficiencies and does so without having to deal with a philosophy of individual educational objectives.

Has EHA Worked?

It is characteristic of major pieces of social legislation that they permit internally consistent critiques from the right, the left, and the center. Evidence is marshaled selectively, according to the dictates of personal and political values, and the resulting view of the policy reflects a set of assumptions about the appropriate balance in the political order — between libertarian freedoms and government intervention, efficiency and equality, social investment and humanitarian concern, and local, state, and federal roles. Diverse views can be developed about EHA, with predictably different conclusions about whether the policy has failed or succeeded.

For conservative Americans it is easy to find evidence to support the concerns first expressed by President Ford when he nearly vetoed EHA in 1975. The law did indeed generate new paperwork; its authorization levels established expectations of federal financial support that Congress has never been willing to meet, shifting the financial burden for compliance to states and LEAs; it resulted in a comprehensive set of federal regulations that have been resented by many state and local authorities; and its procedural guarantees have often been cumbersome to carry out. Moreover, as a social investment, one billion or more federal dollars per year is a great deal to pay for a program whose benefits have yet to be demonstrated conclusively in terms of a reduced demand for social welfare services or other indicators that there is benefit to the larger society. The primary effect has been to expand special education, mainly via the LD category, to include a large number of children for whom specialized services may not be justified. Special education budgets have grown at a time when tax revenues have declined and costs of general education have risen. This trend has further intensified the competition with regular education for scarce resources that are badly needed to produce a literate and competent general population.

Such a critique can be extended and embellished, but its essential contours are familiar to most of us. The problem with the conservative argument is not so much in its particulars (though some, such as the zero-sum trade with general education, are exaggerated), but rather in the fundamental aspirations it reflects. For conservatives, the goal of a program for the handicapped is to prevent dependency, not to enhance the quality of lives. When viewed in this light, programs under EHA have generated little evidence of success except insofar as they have reduced the number of children in institutions and created better preconditions for handicapped children to acquire skills leading to self-sufficiency.

Radicals, from another standpoint, can make an equally forceful case that EHA has failed to meet expectations. After all, there is no evidence that EHA has done anything to change fundamental relationships or opportunities for the handicapped in our larger capitalist economic and social order. Handicapped persons have seldom been as productive or inexpensive as other workers. Along with poorly educated or otherwise disadvantaged segments of the population, they are part of a large underclass that the service-oriented economy of the United States largely ignores or attempts to contain by means of minimal social welfare programs. The main effect of EHA has not been to render the handicapped more employable or more likely to be productive adults — this is a matter far more directly influenced by labor supply and demand, employment rates, industrial growth, and other economic considerations. Instead, its effect has been that of an ideological ploy by those who control the country's economic order, acting via Congress and institutions of public education under a cloak of liberal rhetoric to placate the handicapped and extend the myth of equal opportunity to include this group, thereby letting the rest of us sleep more easily each night without having to concern ourselves with enduring social inequalities.

The liberal critique obviously differs from the conservative in its assumptions about the proper role of federal policy in trying to effect social change, and from the radical in its faith that incremental reforms via the schools can make a difference. From a liberal standpoint, EHA has been a success on several counts. It is a uniform national legal entitlement for all handicapped children and their parents regardless of income, and it has resulted in an egalitarian set of procedural guarantees in every public school system in the country. It has broadened access to public school for numerous children previously excluded and has moved others closer to the mainstream, shifting the basic opportunity structure of public education to give disabled children a fairer chance. It has infused significant, though not excessive, new funds and personnel into special education, with presumed improvements in teaching practice for the handicapped. And all this has been accomplished without unduly limiting state and local discretion to implement the law according to preferred practice patterns. Few other pieces of social legislation affecting children have conferred so many benefits on a needy group and done so without unintended negative consequences. Many of the important effects of the law have been impossible to measure, but this does not mean they have been inconsequential. EHA has fostered and reinforced a positive climate of belief and set of attitudes concerning the handicapped and has created opportunities for social and economic success, even if their aggregate effects are not yet demonstrable. The payoff of EHA as a social investment is enormous, especially given the modest national investment relative to what is spent in many other realms of domestic and foreign policy.

Along with the conservative and radical arguments, the liberal argument can lay claim to a wide range of relevant facts. Who, then, is right? Is there a single judgment to be rendered?

Twenty years ago, many individuals, regardless of political persuasion, would have flatly denied the feasibility of instituting in every school system in this country a program of individualized education, however imperfect, for 11 percent of the nation's children. Yet this was done within a few years of EHA's implementation. Regular education teachers, special education teachers, school administrators, and others at the local level have demonstrated a remarkable degree of dedication to the law's goals and an equally remarkable willingness to subsidize the program with their own efforts. Although initial enthusiasm has tapered off somewhat, special education under EHA continues to enlist independent support and to be a source of pride in almost every community, even among those who would not have lifted a finger to help the handicapped a decade ago.

We therefore conclude that the successful implementation of EHA has at least demonstrated that, for one group of children, a federal initiative *can* result in significant social reform at the local level. Although this reform came with an unwieldy set of administrative accountability requirements, federal demands have equilibrated rapidly with local capacity to respond, resulting in a basically workable system. Moreover, while some may argue that the reduction of administrative procedures and paperwork has resulted in a reduction of program quality, we believe that quality in general has improved to become substantially better than what was found in most districts a decade ago.

EHA has not succeeded, however, in providing a uniform entitlement for all handicapped children. Instead, the law has had differential results depending upon the district where the child happens to live and his individual family circumstances. School districts have differed dramatically in program expenditures, services, and personnel. Parent participation has been weak among those of low income and little education. Likewise, poverty, family disorganization, and stress are such powerful influences when compared to whatever transpires at school that one wonders whether a social reform based solely in the schools can countervail against formidable societal forces. Full realization of EHA as an entitlement will take place only if the schools increase their public outreach and if low-income children with handicaps are made jointly eligible under related social policies such as Medicaid and mental health legislation.

Nevertheless, EHA remains one of the most far-reaching pieces of societal legislation ever to benefit children. Since its enactment, it has successfully weathered a decade characterized by declining tax revenues, increasing school costs, and escalating doubts about the value and quality of public education. Yet the program continues to thrive under a broad umbrella of bipartisan support in Washington and a remarkable degree of public acceptance in local school districts. Notwithstanding variations in programs across states, districts, and children, it is this overall transformation of attitudes and practices that best reflects EHA's enduring impact at the local level.

Notes

1. The Education for All Handicapped Children Act (PL 94-142), 20 U.S.C. Sec. 1401 *et seq.* (1975).

2. Gerald Ford, as quoted by Robert Weiner in *PL 94-142: Impact on the Schools* (Arlington, VA: Capitol Publications, 1985), p. 20.

3. A detailed analysis of the history of federal disability policy is given in Richard K. Scotch, *From Good Will to Civil Rights* (Philadelphia: Temple University Press, 1984).

4. Marjorie Hunter, "Bell Ends Plan to Ease Some Rules for Education of the Handicapped," *New York Times,* 30 September 1982, p. A26.

5. David Cohen, "Policy and Organization: The Impact of State and Federal Educational Policy on School Governance," *Harvard Educational Review, 52* (1982), 474–499.

6. A more detailed account of the sampling procedure is given in Judith D. Singer, John A. Butler, and Judith S. Palfrey, "Health Care Access and Use among Handicapped Students in Five Public School Systems," *Medical Care, 24* (1986), 1–13.

7. David Greene and Jane L. David present a framework for analyzing data from multiple-site designs such as ours in "A Research Design for Generalizing from Multiple Case Studies," *Evaluation and Program Planning, 7* (1984), 73–85.

8. EHA explicitly mandated in Sec. 618(f)(1) that the U.S. Office of Special Education submit detailed annual reports to Congress on the progress being made in implementing the law. These reports provide data on numbers of children served, percentages of students in various disability categories and placements, provision of selected related services, and numbers of special education personnel. See, for example, Office of Special Education and Rehabilitative Services, *Ninth Annual Report to Congress on the Implementation of Public Law 94-142: The Education for All Handicapped Children Act* (Washington, DC: U.S. Department of Education, 1987).

9. Several factors contributed to the size of special education programs in 1977: 1) prior state legislation guaranteeing an education for all handicapped children; 2) Title VI of the Elementary and Secondary Education Act of 1965, which created the Bureau of Education for the Handicapped (later to become OSE) and launched a grant program to help states provide educational services to handicapped children; and 3) Sec. 504 of the Rehabilitation Act of 1973, which prohibited recipients of federal funds from discriminating on the basis of handicap.

10. Estimates of federal contributions to excess cost vary, but are uniformly low; see, for example, James Kakalik, William Furry, M. A. Thomas, and M. F. Carney, *The Cost of Special Education* (Santa Monica, CA: Rand Corporation, 1981).

11. Similar patterns were reported by Anne R. Wright, Rhonda Cooperstein, Ellen Renneker, and Christine Padilla in their four-year study of the implementation of EHA in twenty-two school districts from across the country, *Local Implementation of PL 94-142: Final Report of a Longitudinal Study* (Menlo Park, CA: SRI International, 1982); and by Barry G. Rabe and Paul E. Peterson in their study of the implementation of Title I and EHA in fourteen school districts, "Educational Policy Implementation: Are Block Grant Proposals Based on Out of Date Research?" *Issues in Education: A Form of Research and Opinion, 1* (1983), 1–29.

12. U.S. Department of Education, "Assistance to States for Education of Handicapped Children: Interpretation of the Individualized Education Program (IEP)," *Federal Register, 19* (January 1981), 5,460–5,474.

13. For additional analyses of the trends in the composition of the special education population, see Nicholas Zill, *The School-Age Handicapped* (Washington, DC: National Center for Education Statistics, 1985); Michael M. Gerber, "The Department of Education's Sixth Annual Report to Congress on PL 94-142: Is Congress Getting the Full Story?" *Exceptional Children, 51* (1984), 209–224; and Bob Algozzine and Lori

Korinek, "Where Is Special Education for Students with High Prevalence Handicaps Going?" *Exceptional Children, 51* (1985), 388–394.

14. During the 1975 hearings before the U.S. Senate Subcommittee on the Handicapped and U.S. House Subcommittee on Select Education, participants agreed on an estimate of 1.75 million unserved children (94th Cong., 1st Sess., 2 June 1975, Rep. No. 94–168).

15. The growth in the size of the LD category received attention from the General Accounting Office in their 1981 report on EHA, *Disparities Still Exist in Who Gets Special Education* (IPE-81-1, 30 September 1981), and from the National Association of State Directors of Special Education (NASDSE), *State/Local Communications Forum for Exploring Issues Related to PL 94-142* (Washington, DC: NASDSE, 1983).

16. A survey of these criteria is given in Cecil D. Mercer, Charlie Hughes, and Ann R. Mercer, "Learning Disabilities Definitions Used by State Education Departments," *Learning Disability Quarterly, 8* (1985), 45–55.

17. Education for the Handicapped Act Amendments of 1986 (PL 99-457).

18. The lower costs of full-time regular class placements as compared to all other placement options are documented in Ellen S. Raphael, Judith D. Singer, and Deborah K. Walker, "Per Pupil Expenditures on Special Education in Three Metropolitan School Districts," *Journal of Education Finance, 11* (1985), 69–88; also see Kakalik et al., *Costs of Special Education.*

19. A detailed analysis of the characteristics of special education classrooms is given in Judith D. Singer, John A. Butler, Judith S. Palfrey, and Deborah K. Walker, "Characteristics of Special Education Placements: Findings from Probability Samples in Five Metropolitan School Districts," *Journal of Special Education, 20* (1986), 319–337.

20. Beatrice Birman, *Case Studies of Overlap Between Title I and PL 94-142 Services for Handicapped Students* (Menlo Park, CA: SRI International, 1979), p. vi.

21. See, for example, John C. Pittenger and Peter Kuriloff, "Educating the Handicapped: Reforming a Radical Law," *Public Interest, 66* (1982), 72–96; or McCay Vernon, "Education's 'Three Mile Island': PL 94-142," *Peabody Journal of Education, 59* (1981), 24–29.

22. Richard Weatherley and Michael Lipsky, "Street-Level Bureaucrats and Institutional Innovation: Implementing Special Education Reform," *Harvard Educational Review, 47* (1977), 171–197.

23. Gallup, "The 15th Annual Gallup Poll of the Public's Attitudes Towards the Public Schools," *Phi Delta Kappan, 64* (1983), 33–47.

24. Rowley v. Hendrick Hudson School District, 102 S. Ct. 3034 (1982).

25. Irving Independent School District v. Tatro, 104 S. Ct. 3371 (1984).

26. Burlington School Committee v. Department of Education, 105 S. Ct. 1996 (1985).

27. Karl R. White presents a meta-analysis of much of this literature in "The Relation between Socioeconomic Status and Academic Achievement," *Psychological Bulletin, 91* (1982), 461–481. Although he argues that many authors have overstated the magnitude of the relationship, he does conclude that the average correlation is about .22.

Support for the preparation of this article and for some of the research presented in it was provided by the Robert Wood Johnson Foundation and the Commonwealth Fund. We thank Harriet S. Davidson for assistance with the key informant interviews, and Judith S. Palfrey, Deborah Klein Walker, Richard Murnane, and Steven R. Gordon for their advice on previous drafts of this article.

CORRESPONDENCE

Is Special Education Serving Minority Students?
A Response to Singer and Butler

JAMES H. LYTLE

The May 1987 issue of the *Harvard Educational Review* begins with an editorial decrying "the absence of public discussion on racism" and "the structured injustices that racism perpetuates." This is followed by an article by Judith Singer and John Butler on the Education for All Handicapped Children Act (EHA), in which the authors take the position that "few other pieces of social legislation affecting children have conferred so many benefits on a needy group and done so without unintended negative consequences."

The juxtaposition of these two arguments strikes me as cruelly ironic because, in my view, no recent piece of social legislation affecting children has so insidiously reinstitutionalized racist practices as has the EHA. Not only are minority children disproportionately represented in special education programs for the mildly handicapped — for example, Learning Disabled (LD), Mentally Retarded (MR), and Socially/Emotionally Disturbed (ED) — but the benefit of participation in these programs has yet to be demonstrated. By Singer and Butler's own admission, "not much information from criterion-referenced testing or face-valid indicators is available at present." But the reason is not that the information "is costly and time-consuming to collect." Rather it is because educators are reluctant to admit that programs for the mildly handicapped, despite enormous growth, have yet to demonstrate anything other than *negative* "benefits." Despite Singer and Butler's assertion to the contrary, evidence to support *this* position *is* available.

This evidence comes from a series of studies with which I have been directly involved — two for the Council of Great Cities Schools, a consortium of the nation's largest urban school districts, and over a dozen evaluation and management studies for the Philadelphia School District — as well as from observation in over one hundred classrooms for mildly handicapped students in Philadelphia. From the perspective this evidence affords, I would

The views expressed in this letter are those of the author and do not necessarily reflect the positions of the School District of Philadelphia or the Council of Great City Schools. Copies of the studies referred to are available from the Council and from Philadelphia's Office of Research and Evaluation.

Harvard Educational Review Vol. 58 No. 1 February 1988

like to address several points in the Singer and Butler article to which I take strong exception.

By restricting the sample in their study to students in grades K–6, Singer and Butler immediately overlook the most problematic issues involved in programs for the mildly handicapped — namely those of attendance, drop-out rates, discipline, career preparation, long-term academic growth, and high school completion, all of which compare unfavorably with the performance of regular education programs.

Although the authors touch briefly on the issue of Individualized Education Programs (IEPs), they clearly have spent little time studying them; otherwise, they would acknowledge that IEPs *for mildly handicapped students* reduce curriculum to drivel. Our research indicates that a majority of special education teachers in Philadelphia find entering students' IEPs of little or no value in planning instruction.

In their discussion of the "dramatic growth" in the number of students classified as LD, Singer and Butler suggest that districts are trying to cap LD enrollment by defining eligibility "more stringently," but that these changes "have not been sufficient to control the size of the LD group nationally." Although I would agree with their point, I think the evidence indicates that definitions of LD have little to do with program enrollment. In a study of eighteen of the Great Cities, conducted in the fall of 1984, we found that three cities in California that used the same definition and shared similar demographic characteristics had LD populations ranging from 2.5 percent to 6.2 percent of total enrollment. A recent internal analysis of Philadelphia's sub-districts produced similar variation: two districts with similar demographics had 4.5 percent and 9.2 percent of the school population enrolled in LD programs, respectively. In both instances, differences are most likely attributable to the idiosyncratic selection practices of special education administrators and psychologists. The results of an intensive study of Philadelphia's LD program conducted in the spring of 1984 support this interpretation. Over one-half of the psychologists interviewed said they would place students in LD programs regardless of whether or not the students met the qualification criteria if this were, in their view, the only way to get them help.

Singer and Butler make an unsubstantiated claim that local education agency (LEA) administrators have tried to control special education costs by cutting teaching positions, and that the "first to go . . . have been younger but more appropriately trained special education teachers." Through my work with Great Cities I know of no district dropping special education teachers; on the contrary, the problem is one of finding certified candidates to fill vacancies. Moreover, the implication that younger teachers are better trained than more experienced ones shows a serious misunderstanding of the real problems of special education. Given that most instruction for mildly handicapped students is in the remediation of basic skills, recent special education teacher candidates are generally poorly prepared for the job. Because they take so few courses in reading/language arts and mathematics pedagogy, not to mention science and social studies, they are unequipped to teach content. The problem is exacerbated by the fact that federal and state funding mechanisms provide program reimbursement only when handicapped students are taught by certified special education teachers. This policy results in such ludicrous practices as having secondary special education teachers draw straws to determine who will teach the science courses. One central explanation for the failure of programs for the mildly handicapped to provide demonstrable learning benefits is that special education teachers have been so inappropriately trained for the work they actually do.

Also, by focusing on grades K–6, Singer and Butler do not examine one of the most serious shortcomings of LEAs regarding services for special education students — access to career and vocational education. One would assume that since special education students are less likely to go on to higher education, they should be enrolled in greater proportion than regular education students in career and vocational programs. Yet twenty-one of twenty-eight major cities in the United States have proportionately *fewer* handicapped students than regular education students enrolled in such programs; for the twenty-eight cities combined, 11.3 percent of the handicapped students are in career and vocational programs, contrasted to 17.9 percent of regular education students. When one adds the additional consideration of minority over-enrollment in special education, the failure to provide career training for these students means that they emerge from school seriously undertrained for gainful employment.

Singer and Butler also fail to address the issue of providing psychiatric and mental health services for socially/emotionally disturbed students. Ironically, students assigned to ED programs because of serious behavior problems are provided only instructional services; they receive no direct or related mental health services to help them overcome the problems leading to their classification. In Philadelphia, for example, ED students at the secondary level are assigned to mixed groups including LD and MR students and are not provided other services.

With respect to levels of parental participation in EHA programs, Singer and Butler acknowledge that fewer than 50 percent of the parents in their study had attended their children's most recent IEP conference, and that low-income parents have been "passive in reference to the special education of their youngsters." But because their parental interview data show a "high level of parent satisfaction" in the five districts studied, they conclude that parental participation may not be "central to the success of EHA" and, moreover, that parents do not attend conferences because they are satisfied. Again, I believe their results are severely distorted because they examine only grades K–6. In an intensive study of the LD program in Philadelphia, we found that parental satisfaction declined as the children's length of time in the program increased. (Parents were also concerned that their children were frequently excluded from extracurricular programs.)

A more probably explanation for the failure of parents, particularly those with low incomes, to attend IEP conferences has to do with the dynamics of these meetings. Even for sophisticated parents, an IEP or placement conference can be intimidating. On one side is a school team, which can include the principal, counselor, nurse, psychologist, classroom teacher, and other specialists who are gathered to define the problem of the child. On the other side are the parents, or parent, who know all too well that their child has not been succeeding in school. Promises of smaller classes and individualized attention in such settings are hard for parents to resist. But how often in these conferences are the parents told that the chances are *less than 2 percent* that their child will ever again be a regular education student, and that the prospects of successfully completing high school will actually be diminished by accepting special education placement (speech and hearing placements excepted)? How many parents are aware that in making a referral, a classroom teacher has over a 50 percent chance of removing a "problem" child from his/her class? Another troublesome dimension of EHA is that a teacher referral immediately becomes a legally binding procedure *requiring* disposition. Yet teachers who make referrals have only a minimal obligation to document their attempts to help a child. Furthermore, the "problems" in an IEP conference virtually always reside in the child, not with the school or organization. By implication, at least some of the fault is that of the parents, as caretakers of the child.

Singer and Butler discuss the relationship between family background (that is, socioeconomic status) and access to the procedural guarantees of EHA. Regrettably, they do not address the more salient issues of race/ethnicity as they relate to special education classification. In Pennsylvania, mentally gifted (MG) is a special education category. Philadelphia has a total enrollment that is 64 percent Black, but only 37 percent of MG students are Black; 9 percent of the total enrollment is Hispanic, but only 2 percent of MG students are Hispanic. In the study of Great Cities LD programs mentioned earlier, we found that ten of the fourteen cities reporting racial distribution of enrollment had disproportionately high percentages of minority students in their LD programs. In the expanded 1986 Great Cities study of all special education programs, the participating special education directors all acknowledged that MR is the program in which minorities are most grossly overrepresented, but the issue was considered so sensitive that the study team chose not to collect racial/ethnic data. Conversely, placements for physical and severe handicaps tend to be almost exactly proportional to each city's student demographics. It should also be noted that boys are heavily over-represented in the LD and ED categories (in Philadelphia by a 7:3 ratio). This suggests that many "handicapped" boys are simply victims of early grade programs that emphasize academic and social skills for which they are not developmentally prepared.

Returning to the issue of the direct benefit/outcome of participation in programs for the mildly handicapped, we have conducted a series of evaluation studies in Philadelphia over the past three years to address these questions. In a large-scale study of LD programs in the spring of 1984, a review of student records (N = 865) indicated that students' mean IQ scores had *declined* one point from earliest to most recent IQ test. LD students in the sample were absent 50 percent more often than their regular education counterparts.

A 1985–1986 study of MR students at all levels found that those in high school had mean reading levels one year higher than the mean for elementary MR students, and math levels one-tenth of a year higher. A related study conducted in 1986–1987 examined various performance indicators for MR, LD, and S/ED enrolled in the secondary mixed category program. Their absence rates were twice those of regular education students — thirty days' average absence versus fifteen for regular education students. By comparing their current reading and mathematics levels with those of handicapped students in early grades, it was estimated that nine years of instruction had produced two years' growth for MR students, five years' growth for LD students (who must be of average intelligence), and four years' growth for ED students (who must also be of average intelligence).

In Philadelphia, 5.8 percent of students in regular education programs received high school diplomas in 1987, but only 3.3 percent of special education students in mildly handicapped programs completed high school. In the Great Cities study, the mean graduation rate was 3.8 percent, with a range of 0.4 percent to 13.2 percent; eighteen of twenty-six cities responding were below the mean. Special education directors in several cities indicated that the high school completion rate was distorted by the inclusion of speech- and hearing-disabled students.

I share this information from Philadelphia and the Great Cities because I know that our special education divisions are wrestling with the same problems. Beyond that, we in Philadelphia are committed to advocacy for children and to reforming the educational regulatory climate at federal and state levels, so that all of our children can be better served — sentiments shared by the Great Cities Schools. I have been forthcoming because the issues are too serious to remain unchallenged.

In this response I have argued that:

– EHA has reinstitutionalized racism through a new tracking system with the force of federal law and the pretense of science (diagnose, classify, prescribe).

– Programs for many mildly handicapped students have no clear benefit.

– IEPs are reductionist and of minimal utility.

– LD definitions do not relate to placement.

– Teachers for the mildly handicapped are poorly trained for what they actually do.

– Special education students are regularly taught content by teachers with little or no training in the subject of instruction.

– Related services, particularly career and vocational education and psychiatric services, are not adequately provided.

– Parent satisfaction declines over time.

– Referral/assignment and IEP meetings are loaded against parents, for whom informed consent is almost impossible — because the long-term effects of program participation are not discussed.

– Over 50 percent of referrals to Special Education lead to placements, and Special Education is unique among remedial programs because it permits regular education teachers to get rid of problem students at very little personal cost.

– Fewer than 2 percent of students placed in Special Education ever return to regular education — despite least restrictive environment/mainstreaming requirements.

– At least in America's large cities, Special Education classes for mildly handicapped students are disproportionately filled by minority students.

– Prospects of high school completion are lower for the mildly handicapped than for regular education students.

Given these conditions, I cannot conclude, as Singer and Butler do, that "good things are happening for those children who never before were eligible for specialized instruction and services." Most mildly handicapped students would clearly be better off in regular classes, with the enormous resources of Special Education redirected to help them succeed and to provide early intervention — so that those who follow will not suffer their fate.

This argument does *not* apply to severely and physically handicapped students who *have* benefited since the adoption of EHA from mainstreaming requirements, remarkable technological advances, and dramatically improved instructional techniques. The Great Cities Special Education directors take great pride in these students' accomplishments, but are bitter about being asked to deal with other students whom the regular education program cannot help. They do not pretend to have answers or solutions for the majority of the "mildly handicapped."

A problem with all the studies referred to, both those in Philadelphia and in the Great Cities, is that control groups are not acceptable options for developing or evaluating special education programs. To conclude that mildly handicapped students would be better off in regular education is simplistic. There is evidence, however, that regular education placement with strong support services does improve the probability of their success.

Singer and Butler Reply to Lytle:

We are in definite agreement with several of the comments made by James Lytle, and in two ways we feel his remarks are an important corrective to the emphasis of our article. On several other issues, however, we believe he is incorrect or has not produced convincing evidence in support of his views.

Lytle is concerned primarily with services for mildly impaired students; for the most part with those designated learning disabled (LD) and, to some extent, those designated emotionally disturbed (ED) and mentally retarded (MR). In the interest of conciseness, we will focus our comments primarily on these three groups, although it is important to note that Lytle makes only passing reference to students with speech impairments, a mildly disabled group that constitutes one quarter of the special education population, and he joins us in praising what has happened for those with severe impairments, many of whom were not in public schools at all prior to the enactment of PL 94-142.[1]

As mentioned in our article, we agree that there are major variations in the size of the LD population across states and school districts, and that these variations seldom reflect a "true" prevalence of some underlying disorder. LD remains a diffuse and socially constructed category. Even though we know that some of these children are genuinely dyslexic, dysgraphic, or have mild neurological disorders with an organic base, many of them are traditional "slow learners" or have problems that are psychosocial and environmental in origin. It is also clear that some teachers recommend an LD classification for pragmatic reasons. This often reflects the recognition that designating a child LD is one way — sometimes the only way — to get supplemental services and resources for the student.

Another point of agreement with Lytle is that Individualized Education Programs (IEPs), especially for students with learning disabilities, often can be either too diffuse — hence meaningless — or too technically detailed in psychological diagnosis without any accompanying indications for pedagogy. These problems are real, and reflect the fact that the study of learning disabilities is still in its infancy. But we do know more than we did twenty years ago about how to teach children with various specific learning problems, and we believe these gains should not be ignored even if their comprehension and implementation remain imperfect.

Lytle also is correct in pointing out how intimidating IEP meetings can be for parents. This is a point we made in our article as one likely explanation for major differences according to socioeconomic status and race in parent attendance at their child's most recent IEP conference. However, at least one district we studied was able to attain a 95 percent rate of parent participation, even among poor and minority parents, suggesting that meeting formats *can* be devised to be less intimidating. We hope that Lytle and others concerned about meaningful parent participation will develop policies that benefit from the experience of those districts that have the most fully empowered parents and have helped them gain their full entitlement under PL 94-142.

Lytle's point about the general inadequacy of programs for students with emotional problems is well taken. Although in the interest of brevity we did not present extensive data about programs for students with particular disabilities, evidence from our research suggests that there are serious gaps in services for students classified as emotionally disturbed: 39 percent had not seen a therapist in the previous year, 22 percent had only one to four sessions with a therapist, and 78 percent had been in separate special classes for all or most of the school day. Fewer children are classified as emotionally disturbed than are classified as learning disabled or mentally retarded, and states and school districts vary widely in numbers assigned to this classification, in part because of variations in ability to provide relevant services but also because of differences in willingness to pay for them. North Carolina, through its *Willy M.* provisions, is one state that has improved its strategies for meeting the needs of seriously emotionally disturbed children.[2] Others should reassess programs and policies in the immediate future.

Lytle comments that, by focusing on the K–6 group, we have taken a "best case." Things are much worse for older handicapped children in the schools, and many drop out before graduating from high school. This is an important point, which we mention in our article but perhaps not with sufficient emphasis. In hindsight, the architects of PL 94-142 probably were right in the early years of the law's implementation to target resources largely to elementary school and preschool youngsters. But an unintended consequence has been to reduce the pressure on junior high and high schools for better programs and services. These remain inadequate, we believe, despite recent efforts by federal and state authorities to allocate additional resources to transitional, vocational, and independent-living programs. Continuity of support across the age span remains a major challenge, especially in low-income communities such as the one Lytle serves.

Now for some frank differences of opinion. First, we do not agree that all strategies used for teaching students with learning disabilities have been an unmitigated disaster. Lytle's evidence from observational studies in Philadelphia notwithstanding, numerous research efforts in school settings do suggest that positive outcomes can and have been achieved for these children.[3] There is a tendency to be too gloomy about what is going on. Counsels of perfection are not helpful in an area in which incremental improvement is a positive achievement.

Second, we feel that Lytle misunderstood our points about the effects of cutbacks in many school districts on special education staffing patterns. We noted that: 1) fiscal austerity measures were indeed a factor for special education in the districts we studied and in many others between 1981 and 1985; 2) staff members most likely to be cut back or redeployed were "boundary spanning" personnel such as aides, social workers, psychologists, and others who bridged the worlds of school and home for the child but were not explicitly mandated by federal or state law; and 3) when the teaching force was cut or redeployed, it often happened that younger teachers were the first to be released or reassigned. We certainly would not argue that younger teachers are always more effective than older teachers for students with learning disabilities, only that their training has given them the benefit of the newest learning in a specialized field. The real problem Lytle may be pointing out is the inappropriate match between particular teacher training or competence and particular student needs, as well as the sheer size and composition of many classes, which can preclude success for even the most talented teacher.

Third, we believe that Lytle is incorrect when he suggests that less than 2 percent of all special education students ever return to regular education. Data from his own Council of Great City Schools study show that even in a single school year, an average of 5 percent of special education students return to regular education. In a follow-up study of 1,184 students in three Collaborative Study sites conducted two years after our initial data collection, we found that 17 percent returned to regular education, including 33 percent of those initially classified as speech impaired, 15 percent of those initially classified as learning disabled, and 9 percent of those initially classified as emotionally disturbed.[4] If these rates of return still seem low, it is important to remember that they are only annual and biennial estimates: the probability that a special education student will *ever* return to regular education is actually much higher. We conclude that, for many children, special education is not a one-way street.

Fourth, our data lend little support to the argument that PL 94-142 has "reinstitutionalize[d] racist practices." In fact, we were pleasantly surprised to find that, in four of the five major school systems we studied, each of which had substantial minority populations, there was no evidence of over-representation of minorities in any category of special education.[5] In the one district where we did find such a disparity, the deep concern of school administrators led them to take immediate corrective action. Data from the 1985–1986 school year on the racial and ethnic composition of the special education population in that district show no evidence of overrepresentation of minorities.

We share with Lytle and the editors of *HER* the certainty that racial prejudice manifests itself, in both subtle and not so subtle ways, in many of the nation's school systems and may in some instances result in unfair labeling and placement of minority children. It would not be surprising to discover that in Philadelphia, and perhaps in several other systems in the Great Cities consortium with histories of separate placements for children with learning disabilities, disproportionate numbers of minority youngsters are found in separate settings. This situation calls for immediate redress and reminds us that even the best-intentioned policy can be undermined. We found no evidence of such placement practices in any of our study sites. Had we found it, we certainly would not have ignored it.

Finally, we disagree with Lytle's conclusion that "most mildly handicapped students would clearly be better off in regular classes with the enormous resources of Special Education redirected to help them succeed. . . ." Our first problem with this conclusion is that it assumes that most children with learning disabilities are educated in substantially separate settings. In fact, national data presented in our article and data from the Collaborative Study presented elsewhere show that approximately three-quarters of all students classified as learning disabled spend all or most of their school day in a regular classroom.[6] Although placement practices do differ across districts (indeed, two of our sites, both of which participated in the Council of Great Cities Schools study, favored separate class placements for LD students), most mildly handicapped students across the country actually *are* substantially mainstreamed.

Our larger problem with Lytle's conclusion is that we question whether placement per se is the most important issue for children with learning disabilities. If there is compelling evidence of inferior treatment in separate classes, as Lytle apparently has found in Philadelphia, then such placements should be abolished. But, in some districts practicing separate placements for children with learning disabilities, this is not such an easy judgment to render.

Ultimately, we believe it is more important to focus on what actually happens to the learning-disabled child in his or her classroom, be it regular or special. The questions that interest us are: 1) Which setting is most likely to benefit the child? 2) Which supplemental curricula are most effective? 3) What is the best match between specific teacher training and credentials, on the one hand, and the specific needs of the child on the other? 4) What are the costs and benefits associated with being pulled out of the usual classroom? (Do children who are pulled out suffer discontinuities of peer friendship and informal learning? Do they fall behind in some areas as they gain in those taught in the pullout setting for part of the day or week?) We wish our own study could bring more information to bear on these subjects, and we note that the national research literature on these topics remains far from complete.

We are also troubled by Lytle's apparent conclusion that children with learning disabilities ought simply to be returned to regular classrooms. On this matter, he surely would agree that additional resources are needed. But how can the added help be provided unless a target group is identified, the qualifications of those who will provide the service are defined, and the general type of service is specified? Hence the need for an LD category or some equivalent surrogate, as well as at least a somewhat specialized set of credentials for those who would teach these children and some doctrine concerning appropriate curriculum.

We would argue that, short of abolishing the LD category altogether and refusing to offer any supplemental services, the LD designation under PL 94–194 has been about as flexible and nonstigmatizing as any means yet devised for compensatory education targeted to individual children. We also believe the national evidence, albeit incomplete, suggests that the benefits of supplemental services have, in general, far outweighed the detriment of any potential stigma or second-class treatment associated with the LD designation. We therefore do not share Lytle's enthusiasm for simply eliminating this category of service.

Lots of youngsters are now identified as having mild learning problems. Children and their parents do not seem especially daunted by this label; many, in fact, are relieved to have specific redress for problems long unattended. After all, compare these children to their mildly impaired predecessors in years past, some of whom would have been incorrectly labeled mentally retarded and others of whom would have been allowed to fail repeatedly in school without any specialized help.

The biggest risk for one who takes Lytle's position of placing the educational burden back on regular education is that it gives ammunition to the naysayers who would do nothing at all for children with mild learning disorders. For many of these critics, the real intent is to eliminate or reallocate supplemental funds from children with mild and remediable learning problems and to return to a pre-PL 94-142 world. Some of these same individuals also would be in favor of returning the most severely impaired children to separate institutional settings, simply to get these students out of the way of what they regard as the main business of schooling. We wish to take strong exception to this view, both because we believe that individualized instruction for children with special needs deserves supplemental support, and because we believe that in many school districts the goal of improved service for such children is being attained.

Notes

1. See Table 2 in Judith D. Singer and John A. Butler, "The Education for All Handicapped Children Act: Schools as Agents of Social Reform," *Harvard Educational Review, 57* (1987), 130.
2. Willy M. v. Hunt, Civ. Action No. CC78–0294 (W.D.N.C.), September 3, 1980, Second Set of Stipulations; February 20, 1981, Third Set of Stipulations.
3. See, for example, Bob Algozzine and Larry Maheady, eds., "In Search of Excellence: Instruction That Works in Special Education Classrooms," Special Issue, *Exceptional Children, 52* (1986); Nancy A. Madden and Robert E. Slavin, "Mainstreaming Students with Mild Handicaps: Academic and Social Outcomes," *Review of Educational Research, 53* (1983), 519–569; and Margaret C. Wang, "Mainstreaming Exceptional Children: Some Instructional Design and Implementation Considerations," *Elementary School Journal, 81* (1981), 195–221.
4. Additional details on this substudy can be found in Deborah Klein Walker, Judith D. Singer, Judith S. Palfrey, and John A. Butler, "Who Leaves and Who Stays in Special Education?: Findings from a Two-Year Follow-Up Study," *Exceptional Children, 54* (1988).
5. See "Health and Special Education: A Study of New Developments for Handicapped Children in Five Metropolitan Communities," *Public Health Reports, 101* (1986), 379–388. Additional unpublished analyses have also been done that examine over-representation within primary handicap groups.
6. These results are presented in Judith D. Singer, John A. Butler, Judith S. Palfrey, and Deborah Klein Walker, "Characteristics of Special Education Placements: Findings from Probability Samples in Five Metropolitan School Districts," *Journal of Special Education, 20* (1986), 319–337.

The Special Education Paradox: Equity as the Way to Excellence

THOMAS M. SKRTIC

In one of the most comprehensive and provocative articles to appear on special education, Thomas Skrtic addresses the dominant controversies within special education and applies a compelling analysis of the current state of special education from an organizational theory perspective. He begins by deconstructing the various discourses concerning special education as both a professional and institutional practice, and the role of public schools as a social practice. He addresses various fundamental assumptions, on which the current system is based: "Are mild disabilities pathological?" "Is diagnosis objective and useful?" "Is special education a rational system?" Answering none of these questions in the affirmative, he applies organizational theory to the role of special education in the nation's schools. From Skrtic's perspective, special education has become dysfunctional in the manner in which it attempts to deal with diversity. He argues that this failure will continue because the current bureaucratic school organizational structure, coupled with its professional culture, are inadequate and fail to meet the demands for equity and excellence. According to Skrtic, the current debates in special education miss this essential point. He calls for a total restructuring of schools and advocates for the establishment of "adhocracies" that would stress collaboration and active problem-solving among teachers. He argues that this type of organization would better prepare all students for the demands of the post-industrial United States by promoting inclusion, excellence, and equity.

> The final result of political action often, no, even regularly, stands in completely inadequate and often even paradoxical relation to its original meaning.
> — Max Weber, *Politics as a Vocation*[1]

Although the Education for All Handicapped Children Act of 1975 (EHA) marked the end of a successful policy revolution in which the spirit of mainstreaming was formalized in law, the special education community knew that if the law was to amount to anything more than "a comprehensive set of empty promises" (Abeson & Zettel, 1977, p. 115), an implementation

Harvard Educational Review Vol. 61 No. 2 May 1991

revolution would also have to be mounted and won (Abeson & Zettel, 1977; National Advisory Committee on the Education of the Handicapped, 1976; Weintraub, 1977). The strategy for winning the implementation revolution was to follow the letter of the law because special education professionals and advocates were convinced that the EHA "would only work if [they] and others made it work by using the procedures set forth in the law" (Weintraub, 1977, p. 114). At the time, of course, this appeared to be a prudent course of action. But the tragic irony is that the letter of the law has become the principal barrier to achieving the spirit of the law (see, for example, Gartner & Lipsky, 1987; Reynolds, Wang, & Walberg, 1987; Skrtic, Guba, & Knowlton, 1985; Stainback & Stainback, 1984; Walker, 1987).

Although no one in the special education community is questioning the spirit of the EHA, or the fact that some important implementation battles have been won, there is widespread concern that the implementation revolution has been lost (see, for example, Gartner & Lipsky, 1987; Reynolds, Wang, & Walberg, 1987; Stainback & Stainback, 1984; Will, 1986a). In fact, the sense of defeat is so pervasive that many of those who had been staunch supporters of the EHA are calling for a new revolution. This new revolution, which has come to be known as the Regular Education Initiative (REI), represents a number of proposals for achieving the spirit of the EHA for students with disabilities by extending its rights and resources to all students. Although there is opposition to the REI within the special education community, even its detractors agree that there are serious problems with the EHA and that, in principle, the REI has some appealing features (for example, Kauffman, Gerber, & Semmel, 1988; Keogh, 1988). However, those who oppose the REI are rightfully concerned that a new revolution could mean a loss of hard-won rights and, in the worst case, a full-circle return to the unacceptable conditions that existed before the EHA (Kauffman, 1988, 1989b; Kauffman, Gerber, & Semmel, 1988).

The REI debate parallels the earlier mainstreaming debate in at least three ways. First, in both cases, the ethics and efficacy of special education practices are criticized and a new approach is proposed. In the 1960s, the practices associated with the segregated special classroom were criticized for being racially biased, instructionally ineffective, and socially and psychologically damaging, and mainstreaming (and eventually the EHA) emerged as the solution (Abeson & Zettel, 1977; Christophos & Renz, 1969; Deno, 1970; Dunn, 1968; Johnson, 1962). In the current debate, the practices associated with mainstreaming and the EHA are under attack for virtually the same reasons (Heller, Holtzman, & Messick, 1982; Hobbs, 1980; Wang, Reynolds, & Walberg, 1987a), and the REI is being advocated as the new solution.

The second parallel is that both debates take place during a period of apparent reform in public education, the character of which is seen as consistent with the proposed special education reform. In the 1960s, advocates of mainstreaming argued that nascent structural reforms and instructional innovations in public education (for example, team teaching, open classrooms, individualized instruction) were consistent with the mainstreaming concept (Dunn, 1968). Today, the REI proponents are arguing that calls for school restructuring and the availability of new instructional technologies (for example, cooperative learning, teacher collaboration) are consistent with their reform proposals (Lipsky & Gartner, 1989a; Pugach & Lilly, 1984; Stainback, Stainback, & Forest, 1989; Wang 1989a,b; Wang, Reynolds, & Walberg, 1985, 1986).[2]

The third parallel explains the first two: both debates are forms of *naive pragmatism,* a mode of analysis and problem resolution that is premised on an unreflective acceptance of the assumptions that lie behind social practices. As such, naive pragmatism is "socially reproductive, instrumentally and functionally reproducing accepted meanings and conventional organizations, institutions, and ways of doing things for good or ill" (Cherryholmes, 1988, p. 151). Thus, the problem with the mainstreaming and REI debates is that their criticism stops at the level of special education practices; neither one questions the assumptions in which these practices are grounded. In the case of the mainstreaming debate, the result was that the new practices associated with the EHA and mainstreaming simply reproduced the special education problems of the 1960s in the 1980s (Skrtic, 1987a, 1988b). Moreover, although the REI debate implicates these assumptions and thus is less naive than the mainstreaming debate, it does not explicitly recognize the connection between special education practices and assumptions, and thus promises to reproduce the problems of the 1980s in the 1990s and beyond (Skrtic, 1988b, 1991).

It is a given, of course, that resolving social problems always requires one to be pragmatic. But being pragmatic in a just and productive way, in a way that does not merely reproduce and extend the original problems, requires a critical form of pragmatism, a mode of inquiry that accepts the fact that our assumptions themselves require evaluation and reappraisal (Cherryholmes, 1988). The advantage today is that revolutionary developments in the social disciplines are providing the conceptual and methodological insights for analyzing social practices from the perspective of their grounding assumptions.[3] Although the REI and mainstreaming debates are forms of naive pragmatism, by appropriating these insights and applying them to special education practices, it is possible to address the field's past and present problems in terms of *critical pragmatism,* a mode of analysis in which the grounding assumptions of social practices are themselves treated as problematic (Cherryholmes, 1988; Skrtic, 1991). Moreover, by conducting such an analysis of special education, and by extending it and its implication to public education per se, it is possible to address the broader question of educational reform in a way that reconciles the historical contradiction between the social goals of educational excellence and educational equity.

In subsequent sections I apply a form of critical pragmatism to three interrelated practices and their grounding assumptions.[4] The practices are: a) special education as a professional practice, b) special education as an institutional practice of public education, and c) public education as a social practice of our society. Because ultimately I am concerned with the legitimacy of public education, my approach is to subject it to an immanent critique, a form of criticism that asks whether public education's institutional *practices* are consistent with its democratic *ideals*. As such, I am interested in restoring the legitimacy of public education — that is, in transforming the real (actual practices) into the ideal — by forcing the reader to consider whether it is living up to its own standards.[5]

To carry out the immanent critique of public education, I conduct critical readings of three discourses, each of which surrounds, shapes, and legitimizes one of the three practices noted above. The discourses are: a) the REI debate in the field of special education, b) the discourse on school organization and adaptability in the field of educational administration,[6] and c) the discourse on school failure in the institution of public education. The purpose of reading the discourses critically is to deconstruct them — and thus the practices they legitimize — by exposing their silences, inconsistencies, contradictions, and incompleteness relative to their grounding assumptions.[7] The purpose of deconstructing the discourses and practices is to show that their grounding assumptions are inadequate and in need of reappraisal, that alternative assumptions are possible and desirable, and, most important, that choosing grounding assumptions is a political and moral act with implications for ethical practice and a just society.

The significance of the REI debate is that, when read critically, it provides the grounds to deconstruct special education as a professional practice, which, in conjunction with a critical reading of the discourse on school organization and adaptability, provides the grounds to deconstruct special education as an institutional practice of public education. The broader significance of deconstructing the institutional practice of special education is that, together with a critical reading of the discourse on educational excellence in general education, it deconstructs the discourse on school failure in the institution of public education.[8] Ultimately, without the legitimizing effect of the discourse on school failure, the immanent contradiction between its institutional practices and democratic ideals deconstructs twentieth-century public education and prepares the way for reconstructing it according to its traditional democratic ideals and the changing historical conditions of the twenty-first century.

The remainder of this article is divided into seven major sections. The first section is a genealogy of the twentieth-century discourse on school failure, which provides an overview of my basic argument and identifies the assumptions that ground the professional and institutional practices and discourses of public education — the assumptions that I believe need to be reappraised.[9] In the second section I deconstruct special education as a professional practice by showing that a critical reading of the REI debate delegitimizes its grounding assumptions. The third section is a critical reading of the discourse on school organization and adaptability. On the basis of this reading, I introduce an alternative way to conceptualize school organization and the problem of change, which I use in the fourth section to deconstruct special education as an institutional practice of public education. In the fifth section I combine my analysis of special education with a critical reading of the discourse on educational excellence in general education. My aim in this section is to show how these critical readings converge to delegitimize the discourse on school failure and, ultimately, to deconstruct the institution of public education. After section five, my focus shifts to reconstructing public education. In the sixth section I propose an alternative organizational configuration for schooling that is both excellent and equitable, and in the final section I consider the implications of this particular configuration for the emerging political and economic relevancies of the twenty-first century.

FUNCTIONALISM AND THE PROBLEM OF SCHOOL FAILURE

Functionalism, the dominant mode of theorizing in the social disciplines (Bernstein, 1976; Rorty, 1979) and the professions (Glazer, 1974; Schön, 1983), including general education (Bowles & Gintis, 1976; Feinberg & Soltis, 1985; Giroux, 1981), educational administration (Griffiths, 1983, 1988), and special education (Heshusius, 1982; Iano, 1986; Skrtic, 1986), presupposes that social reality is objective, inherently orderly, and rational, and thus that social and human problems are pathological (Foucault, 1954/1976, 1961/1973; Ritzer, 1980). As such, the functionalist worldview institutionalized the mutually reinforcing theories of *organizational rationality* and *human pathology* in society and in public education. As a result, when industrialization and compulsory school attendance converged to produce large numbers of students who were difficult to teach in traditional classrooms, the problem of school failure was reframed as two interrelated problems — inefficient organizations and defective students. This distorted the problem by largely removing it from the general education discourse and compartmentalizing it into two separate but mutually reinforcing discourses. The first one was in the developing field of educational administration, which, in the interest of maximizing organizational efficiency, was compelled to rationalize its orientation according to the precepts of scientific management (Callahan, 1962). The second was in the new field of special education, which emerged as a means to remove and contain the most recalcitrant students in the interest of maintaining order in the rationalized school plant (Lazerson, 1983; Sarason & Doris, 1979).

The discourses of all three fields are shaped by explicit presuppositions grounded in their respective foundations of professional knowledge, as well as by implicit presuppositions grounded in the social norms of human pathology and organizational rationality. Because its professional knowledge is grounded in scientific management, educational administration presupposes explicitly that school organizations are rational (Clark, 1985; Griffiths, 1983) and implicitly that school failure is pathological (Skrtic, 1991).[10] Conversely, special education's professional grounding in psychology and biology (medicine) means that it presupposes explicitly that school failure is pathological (Mercer, 1973; Skrtic, 1986) and implicitly that school organizations are rational (Skrtic, 1987a, 1988b). Given that its professional grounding is in psychology *and* scientific management (Cherryholmes, 1988; Oakes, 1985, 1986a,b; Spring, 1980), the general education discourse is grounded explicitly and implicitly in both presuppositions.

Taken together, these presuppositions yield four mutually reinforcing assumptions that shape the discourses and practices of all three fields and thus of public education itself. In the language of the special education discourse, these assumptions are that: a) disabilities are pathological conditions that students have, b) differential diagnosis is objective and useful, c) special education is a rationally conceived and coordinated system of services that benefits diagnosed students, and d) progress results from rational technological improvements in diagnostic and instructional practices (Bogdan & Knoll, 1988; Bogdan & Kugelmass, 1984; Mercer, 1973; Skrtic, 1986).[11] Inquiry in all three fields is dominated by functionalist methodologies (Griffiths, 1983, 1988; Lincoln & Guba, 1985; Poplin, 1987; Skrtic, 1986), which favor data over theory and assume, more or less, that empirical data are objective and self-evident (Churchman, 1971; Mitroff & Pondy, 1974). Thus, each discourse is a form of naive pragmatism that produces and interprets empirical data on student outcomes and school effects intuitively, according to the four taken-for-granted assumptions about disability, diagnosis, special education, and progress. This reproduces the status quo in all three fields, which reaffirms the four assumptions and, ultimately, reinforces the functionalist presuppositions of organizational rationality and human pathology in public education and society.

Thus, the institutional practice of special education (and the very notion of student disability) is an artifact of the functionalist quest for rationality, order, and certainty in the field of education, a quest that is both intensified and legitimized by the institutional practice of educational administration.[12] As such, special education distorts the problem of school failure and, ultimately, prevents the field of education from entering into a productive confrontation with uncertainty. And because uncertainty is a necessary precondition for growth of knowledge and progress in communal activities such as the physical sciences (Kuhn, 1970), the social sciences (Barnes, 1982; Bernstein, 1983), and the professions (Schön, 1983; Skrtic, 1991), the objectification and legitimization of school failure as student disability prevents public education from moving beyond its functionalist practices. The problem in special education and educational administration has been that, although both fields have experienced enough uncertainty to call their traditional practices into question, they have lacked a critical discourse for addressing their problems in a reflective manner (Bates, 1980, 1987; Foster, 1986; Skrtic, 1986, 1991; Tomlinson, 1982).[13] The problem in general education, however, is more fundamental. Not only has it lacked a critical discourse (Cherryholmes, 1988; Giroux, 1981, 1983; Sirotnik & Oakes, 1986), it has been largely prevented from having to confront uncertainty altogether, precisely because of the objectification of school failure as student disability. Ultimately, the problem is that this distortion of school failure prevents public education from seeing that it is not living up to its democratic ideals.

Public education in a democracy must be both excellent and equitable. If America was to avoid tyranny and remain free, Jefferson argued, public education must produce excellent (intelligent, imaginative, reflective) citizens and assure that "[persons] of talent might rise whatever their social and economic origins" (Greer, 1972, p. 16). The problem with the Jeffersonian ideal, however, is that its democratic ends are contradicted by the bureaucratic means that were used to actualize universal public education in this century. As such, the failure of public education to be either excellent or equitable can be understood in terms of the inherent contradiction between democracy and bureaucracy in the modern state (Weber, 1922/1978). Special education, then, can be understood as the institutional practice that emerged to contain this contradiction in public education. And because social institutions are best understood from their dark side — from the perspective of the institutional practices that emerge to contain their failures (Foucault, 1983) — special education is a particularly insightful vantage point for deconstructing twentieth-century public education. The paradox in all of this is that, when read critically, special education provides the structural and cultural insights that are necessary to begin reconstructing public education for the historical conditions of the twenty-first century and, ultimately, for reconciling it with its democratic ideals.

SPECIAL EDUCATION AS A PROFESSIONAL PRACTICE

Although the REI is generally thought of as a 1980s phenomenon, the first criticism of the EHA and mainstreaming, in the language of what was to become the REI, appeared in 1976 (Reynolds, 1976; Reynolds & Birch, 1977), barely a year after the EHA had been signed into law and nearly two full years before it was to become fully effective.[14] The next papers promoting the REI appeared in the early 1980s, and since then a body of supporting literature has been produced by four teams of writers whose names have become synonymous with the pro-REI position.[15] This literature contains two lines of argument: one against the current special education system, and one for certain general and special education reforms intended to correct the situation.

The arguments against the current system address an array of technical and ethical problems associated with the elaborate classification system required by the EHA, as well as instructional problems associated with the pull-out approach implied by mainstreaming. Although the reforms for addressing these problems are unique to particular teams of REI proponents, all four teams agree that the EHA and mainstreaming are fundamentally flawed, particularly for students who are classified as mildly to moderately handicapped (hereafter, mildly handicapped); that is, students classified as learning disabled, emotionally disturbed, and mentally retarded, who make up over two-thirds of the 4.5 million students served under the law.[16] Although the field's initial reaction to the REI was mixed, a full-blown controversy developed in 1988 when several leading figures in the three mild disability subfields published a *tour de force* response criticizing the REI.[17] Since then, the controversy has become a heated debate over the ethics and efficacy of the current system of special education on the one hand, and the wisdom and feasibility of the REI reform proposals on the other.[18]

Criticism of the Current System

The debate over current practices is important because it is implicitly a debate over the adequacy of special education's grounding assumptions, which are recast below in the form of questions.

Are Mild Disabilities Pathological?

Although the debate has been quite heated, there is virtually no disagreement on this point.[19] Both the REI proponents (Gartner & Lipsky, 1987; Pugach & Lilly, 1984; Stainback & Stainback, 1984; Wang, Reynolds, & Walberg, 1986, 1987b) and opponents (for example, Braaten, Kauffman, Braaten, Polsgrove, & Nelson, 1988; Bryan, Bay, & Donahue, 1988; Council for Children with Behavioral Disorders, 1989; Kauffman, Gerber, & Semmel,

1988; Keogh, 1988) agree that there are students for whom the mildly handicapped designation is an objective distinction based on a pathology, but that because of a number of definitional and measurement problems, as well as problems related to the will or capacity of teachers and schools to accommodate student diversity, many students identified as mildly handicapped are not truly disabled in the pathological sense, a situation that is particularly true for students identified as learning disabled. Moreover, both sides in the debate agree that there are additional students in school who remain unidentified and thus unserved; while some of these students have mild pathological disabilities, there are others who do not but nonetheless require assistance. Although the REI proponents recognize that many of these students, including those who have or are thought to have mild disabilities, present difficult problems for classroom teachers, their point is simply that neither the general education system nor the special education system is sufficiently adaptable to accommodate their individual needs (for example, Gartner & Lipsky, 1987; Pugach & Lilly, 1984; Wang, Reynolds, & Walberg, 1986), a point with which most REI opponents agree (Bryan, Bay, & Donahue, 1988; Kauffman, 1988; Kauffman, Gerber, & Semmel, 1988; Keogh, 1988).[20]

Is Diagnosis Objective and Useful?

The REI proponents argue that differential diagnosis does not result in objective distinctions, either between the disabled and nondisabled designations or among the three mild disability classifications (Gartner & Lipsky, 1987; Stainback & Stainback, 1984; Wang, Reynolds, & Walberg, 1986, 1987a). As noted above, the REI opponents generally agree that the disabled-nondisabled distinction is not objective. Moreover, they also agree that distinctions among the three mild disability classifications are not objective because, in addition to measurement and definitional problems, the process for making these decisions in schools is "embedded in a powerful economic, political, and philosophical network" (Keogh, 1988, p. 20; see also Council for Children with Behavioral Disorders, 1989; Gerber & Semmel, 1984; Hallahan & Kauffman, 1977; Kauffman, 1988, 1989a,b).

On the matter of the utility of differential diagnosis, the REI proponents argue that there are no instructionally relevant reasons for making the disabled-nondisabled distinction, or for distinguishing among the three mild disability classifications. Their point is that all students have unique learning needs and, moreover, that students in the three mild disability classifications, as well as those in the other special needs classifications, can be taught using similar instructional methods (for example, Lipsky & Gartner, 1989a; Reynolds, Wang, & Walberg, 1987; Stainback & Stainback, 1984, 1989; Wang, 1989a,b; Wang, Reynolds, & Walberg, 1986, 1987a). Here, too, most of the

REI opponents agree, admitting that "effective instructional and management procedures will be substantially the same for nonhandicapped and most mildly handicapped students" (Kauffman, Gerber, & Semmel, 1988, p. 8; see also Gerber, 1987; Hallahan & Kauffman, 1977).[21]

Is Special Education a Rational System?

The REI proponents argue that the only rational justification for the existence of the special education system is that it confers instructional benefit on students who are designated as handicapped (Lilly, 1986; Lipsky & Gartner, 1987; Reynolds, 1988; Reynolds, Wang, & Walberg, 1987; Stainback & Stainback, 1984; Wang, Reynolds, & Walberg, 1987a), a position with which the REI opponents agree (Kauffman, Gerber, & Semmel, 1988; Keogh, 1988). On this basis, the REI proponents believe that, given the weak effects of special education instructional practices and the social and psychological costs of labeling, the current system of special education is, at best, no more justifiable than simply permitting most students to remain unidentified in regular classrooms and, at worst, far less justifiable than regular classroom placement in conjunction with appropriate in-class support services (Lipsky & Gartner, 1987, 1989a; Pugach & Lilly, 1984; Stainback & Stainback, 1984; Wang, Reynolds, & Walberg, 1987a). Thus, the REI proponents reject the idea that special education is a rational system.

Although none of the REI opponents argue that special education has been shown to lead to direct *instructional* benefit (see, for example, Keogh, 1988; Hallahan, Keller, McKinney, Lloyd, & Bryan, 1988), some of them argue that the handicapped designation is beneficial in a *political* sense.[22] That is, they justify the current system of special education on the political grounds that it targets otherwise unavailable resources and personnel to designated students. Such targeting, they argue, is essential if these students are to receive instructional assistance in the context of the resource allocation process in schools (Council for Children with Behavioral Disorders, 1989; Kauffman, 1988, 1989b; Kauffman, Gerber, & Semmel, 1988). As noted, the REI opponents recognize that to be justifiable, special education must confer instructional benefit on designated students, and that, at present, special education interventions do not confer such benefits. In effect, then, the REI opponents who justify special education on political grounds are saying that, although special education is not an instructionally rational system in its current form, it is a politically rational system. This is so, they maintain, because the nonadaptability and political inequality of the general education system makes the pull-out logic of mainstreaming and the targeting function of the EHA absolute necessities if designated students are to receive instructional assistance in school, even though the assistance they receive does not appear to be effective.

As we will see below, in response to the question of the nature of progress, the REI opponents (including those who justify special education on political grounds) argue that the special education system can be improved incrementally through additional research and development. Thus, their position on the nature of special education cannot be separated from their position on the nature of progress in the field. In effect, when their positions on the third and fourth assumptions are considered together, the REI opponents are saying that, although special education is not an instructionally rational system *at present,* it is a politically rational system that can be rendered instructionally rational *in the future,* given the assumption of the possibility of rational-technical progress. Thus, let us say for present purposes that the REI opponents are arguing that special education *is* an instructionally rational system, given the caveat that, to be rational in an instructional sense, rational-technical progress *must* be possible.[23]

Is Progress Rational and Technical?

This question asks whether progress can be made under the current system through incremental technological improvements in its associated diagnostic and instructional practices. The REI proponents argue that the diagnostic and instructional practices of the current system are fundamentally flawed and thus cannot and should not be salvaged. They believe that these practices and the entire system must be replaced through a fundamental restructuring of the special and general education systems (Lilly, 1986; Lipsky & Gartner, 1987, 1989a; Pugach & Lilly, 1984; Reynolds, Wang, & Walberg, 1987; Stainback & Stainback, 1984; Stainback, Stainback, & Forest, 1989), which is an argument against the possibility of rational-technical change. Although the REI opponents recognize that there are serious problems with the current special education system, they believe that incremental progress is possible through additional research and development aimed at improving special education diagnostic and instructional practices while maintaining the current system (Braaten, Kauffman, Braaten, Polsgrove, & Nelson, 1988; Bryan, Bay, & Donahue, 1988; Council for Children with Behavioral Disorders, 1989; Hallahan, Keller, McKinney, Lloyd, & Bryan, 1988; Kauffman, 1988, 1989b; Kauffman, Gerber, & Semmel, 1988; Keogh, 1988; Lloyd, Crowley, Kohler, & Strain, 1988). This, of course, is an argument for the possibility of rational-technical change.

At this point in the critical reading, the REI proponents and opponents reject the two grounding assumptions associated with the presupposition of human pathology, the explicit disciplinary grounding of special education's professional knowledge and practice since the field's inception. Moreover, the REI proponents also reject the two assumptions associated with the normative presupposition of organizational rationality. Thus, by rejecting the field's entire framework of grounding assumptions and presuppositions, the arguments of the REI proponents deconstruct special education as a professional practice. However, by arguing that special education is a politically (if not an instructionally) rational system that can be improved in a rational-technical manner, the REI opponents retain the third and fourth assumptions and thus hold out some hope for the legitimacy of the field.

Although the REI proponents and opponents agree that the field's grounding assumptions about the nature of disability and diagnosis are inadequate, their disagreement over the nature of special education and progress has resulted in total disagreement over an appropriate course of ameliorative action. On one hand, the REI proponents believe that, given the negative evidence on the ethics and efficacy of special education practices and the nonadaptability of the general education system, a completely new system should be formed by restructuring the two systems into a single adaptable one. On the other hand, the REI opponents believe that, negative evidence on the adequacy of special education notwithstanding, the current system and its associated practices should be retained for political purposes, given the nonadaptability of the general education system and the fact that special education practices can be improved. Thus, the REI debate turns on the question of whether school organizations can and will be restructured into the adaptable system envisioned by the REI advocates.

The REI Proposals

There are four REI proposals, each of which, to one degree or another, calls for eliminating the EHA classification system and the pull-out approach of mainstreaming. Each also proposes restructuring the separate general and special education systems into a new system in which, depending on the proposal, most or all students who need help in school are provided with in-class assistance.[24] Although the REI proponents generally agree that this restructured system should be "flexible, supple and responsive" (Lipsky & Gartner, 1987, p. 72), a "totally adaptive system" (Reynolds & Wang, 1983, p. 199) in which professionals personalize instruction through "group problem solving . . . shared responsibility, and . . . negotiation" (Pugach & Lilly, 1984, p. 52), they disagree on which students should be integrated into the new system on a full-time basis.[25]

Whom to Integrate?

Each of the four teams of REI proponents believe that all students currently served in compensatory and remedial education programs, as well as every other student who needs help in school but is not currently targeted for it, should remain in the regular classrooms of the restructured system on a full-time basis and receive whatever assistance they need in those classrooms. Where they differ, however, is with respect to which students currently classified as handicapped under the EHA should be served in this manner.

The Lilly and Pugach proposal is the least inclusive. In addition to those students noted above, it includes only "the vast majority of students served as 'mildly handicapped'" (Lilly, 1986, p. 10) under the EHA, whereas students with moderate, severe, and profound disabilities would be taught by special educators in separate settings within regular school buildings.[26] The Reynolds and Wang proposal is somewhat more inclusive in that it maintains that "most students with special learning needs" (Wang, Reynolds, & Walberg, 1985, p. 13; Reynolds & Wang, 1983) should be in these regular classrooms on a full-time basis, while reserving the option of separate settings for some students, presumably those with severe and profound disabilities.[27]

The Gartner and Lipsky proposal includes all students currently served under each EHA classification, except those with the most severely and profoundly handicapping conditions. These students would receive their primary instruction in separate classrooms located in regular, age-appropriate school buildings (Gartner & Lipsky, 1987). Finally, in what is the most inclusive proposal, Stainback and Stainback (1984) argue for the integration of all students, including those with the most severely and profoundly disabling conditions, while recognizing the need to group students, "in some instances, into specific courses and classes according to their instructional needs" (p. 108).

What to Merge?

Although the strategy for creating the adaptable system necessary to implement the REI proposals is most often characterized as a merger of the general and special education systems, only the Stainback and Stainback and Gartner and Lipsky proposals actually call for a merger of the two systems at the classroom level.[28] The other two teams propose a merger of instructional support personnel above the classroom level. Toward this end, Reynolds and Wang (1983) propose eliminating the categorical special needs pull-out programs through a two-step merger. The first merger is within special education, among the programs serving the three traditional mild disability classifications. The second is between this merged or noncategorical special education program and the other "compensatory services that are provided for disadvantaged, bilingual, migrant, low-English-proficiency, or other children with special needs" (1983, p. 206). Supported by paraprofessionals, these generic specialists form a school-based support team that works "mostly in the regular classrooms . . . to supply technical and administrative support to regular classroom teachers" (1983, p. 206).[29]

The Lilly and Pugach proposal merges the special education resource and support programs that currently provide services "for the mildly handicapped, and primarily for the learning disabled" (Pugach & Lilly, 1984, p. 54) with the traditional general education support service of remedial education.[30] They recognize the need for support services, but propose a single, coordinated system of services based in general education and provided largely in regular classrooms, rather than the current array of special pull-out programs (Lilly, 1986; Pugach & Lilly, 1984). Although the Reynolds and Wang and Lilly and Pugach proposals modify the current notion of instructional support services by replacing the categorical pull-out approach with a noncategorical or remedial model of in-class support services, both of them retain the traditional notion of a classroom, in the sense of one teacher with primary responsibility for a group of students.[31]

Although the Stainback and Stainback proposal calls for merger at the classroom level, it actually merges general and special education subject areas, not special education and general instructional programs or personnel. It calls for disbanding special education programs and integrating the residual personnel into the general education system according to an instructional specialization. Each teacher in this system would have "a strong base in the teaching/learning process" (Stainback & Stainback, 1984, p. 107) and a particular specialization in a traditional general education subject (for example, science or reading) or a special education subject (for example, supported employment), and each would work individually in a separate classroom (Stainback & Stainback, 1987a; Stainback, Stainback, & Forest, 1989). As with the first two proposals, this one provides support services above the classroom level. Here, however, the support personnel are organized as subject-area specialists rather than generic specialists, which modifies the current categorical pull-out approach by replacing it with in-class subject area support services. As in the case of the other two support services models, this one retains the traditional notion of a classroom in which one teacher has primary responsibility for a group of students (see Stainback & Stainback, 1984, 1987a).

The Gartner and Lipsky proposal calls for a merged or unitary system in which education is "both one and special for all students" (Lipsky & Gartner, 1987, p. 73). Such a system would mean the complete abandonment of a separate special education system for students with mild to moderate disabilities. Although in their original proposal Gartner and Lipsky also emphasized the support services level (Gartner & Lipsky, 1987), in a recent clarification and extension (Lipsky & Gartner, 1989a) they emphasize the classroom level by linking their proposal for a restructured system to the excellence movement in general education, which is, for them, the effective schools movement (Edmonds, 1979; Lezotte, 1989). As such, their basic assertion is that, through broad adoption of the principles and practices identified in the effective schools research, "the education of students labeled as handicapped can be made effective" (Lipsky & Gartner, 1989a, p. 281). They build their case for the effective schools approach by combining Edmonds's (1979) assertion that, if some schools are effective, all schools can be effective, with Gilhool's (1976) parallel assertion about effective integration of students with disabilities. They conclude that effective schools, and thus effective education for students labeled handicapped, is a matter of will and commitment on the part of teachers and schools to adopt the principles and practices contained in the effective schools literature.[32]

Reactions to the REI Proposals

The REI opponents argue against the possibility of an adaptable system on historical and political grounds and conclude that special needs have not, are not, and simply cannot be met in regular classrooms. Kauffman (1988) and others (Council for Children with Behavioral Disorders, 1989) argue that, historically, the separate special education system emerged precisely because of the nonadaptability of regular classrooms and that, since nothing has happened to make contemporary classrooms any more adaptable (see Keogh, 1988), the REI most likely will lead to rediscovering the need for a separate system in the future. In their political or microeconomic criticism of the REI reform proposals, Kauffman, Gerber, & Semmel (1988; see also Gerber, 1988b; Gerber & Semmel, 1985) argue that "teachers, whether in regular or special class environments, cannot escape the necessary choice between higher means [that is, maximizing mean performance by concentrating resources on the most able learners] and narrower variances [that is, minimizing group variance by concentrating resources on the least able learners] as long as resources are scarce and students differ" (Gerber & Semmel, 1985, p. 19, cited in Kauffman, Gerber, & Semmel, 1988, p. 10). This is true, they argue, "whenever a teacher instructs a group of students . . . [except] when new resources are made available or more powerful instructional technologies are employed" (Kauffman, Gerber, & Semmel, 1988, p. 10).

Although these are compelling arguments, they ignore the fact that the REI proposals call for creating a system of adaptable classrooms by making new resources available and introducing more powerful instructional technologies, the exact conditions that can narrow group variances without negatively affecting class means, according to the microeconomic argument itself. Thus, these are not arguments against the REI proposals; implicitly, they are compelling arguments against the traditional notion of a classroom. In fact, by arguing that both regular and special education classrooms are nonadaptable in a microeconomic sense, the REI opponents make a stronger case against the current system of special education than the REI proponents. Moreover, by arguing that the regular classroom has not changed and that neither it nor the special classroom can change, the REI opponents contradict their position on the possibility of rational-technical change, and thus their implicit support of the third and fourth assumptions.[33]

As we have seen, on the question of the adequacy of the current system of special education, the REI proponents reject all four of the field's grounding assumptions, while the opponents reject the two about disability and diagnosis but retain the two about special education and progress. In their criticism of the REI proposals, however, the REI opponents reverse their position on the two assumptions about special education and progress, and thus implicitly agree with the REI proponents that all four of the field's grounding assumptions are inadequate. At this point, then, the arguments for and against the field's current practices and those against the REI proposals reject all four grounding assumptions and thus deconstruct special education as a professional practice. Nevertheless, although the deconstruction of special education appears to be complete, we will see in a subsequent section that the REI proponents reverse their position on the third and fourth assumptions as well.

As we know, in their criticism of the current system the REI proponents argue against the rationality of special education (and thus of the traditional organization of schools). However, when their reform proposals are considered from an organizational perspective (see below), they actually reproduce and extend the traditional organization of schools and call for a rational-technical approach to change. Thus, both sides in the REI debate reject the first two assumptions and thus the presupposition of human pathology that serves as the field's explicit disciplinary grounding, but they are contradictory and inconsistent about the third and fourth assumptions and thus about the presupposition of organizational rationality that serves as the field's implicit normative grounding. Therefore, let us reserve judgment on whether the arguments in the REI debate deconstruct special education as a professional practice until we have considered the notion of organizational rationality in greater depth.

In the following section, I address the legitimacy of the presupposition of organizational rationality by way of a critical reading of the discourse on school organization and adaptability in the field of educational administration. On the basis of this reading, I introduce two alternative ways to conceptualize school organization and the problem of change, which I combine in subsequent sections to carry out my deconstructions of the institutional practice of special education and the discourse on school failure, as well as my deconstruction and reconstruction of the institution of public education.

THE DISCOURSE ON SCHOOL ORGANIZATION
AND ADAPTABILITY

Generally speaking, there are two sources of insight into school organization and adaptability: the prescriptive discourse of educational administration, and the theoretical discourse of the multidisciplinary field of organization analysis. The field of educational administration is grounded in the notion of scientific management, an extremely narrow view that presupposes that organizations are rational and that organizational change is a rational-technical process (Burrell & Morgan, 1979; Scott, 1981). Although scientific management is a purely functionalist approach for organizing and managing industrial firms, it was applied to schools and other social organizations during the social efficiency movement at the turn of the century (Callahan, 1962; Haber, 1964), and has remained the grounding formulation of educational administration ever since.[34]

The theoretical discourse of organization analysis is grounded in the social disciplines and thus, in principle, provides a much broader range of perspectives on organization and change. Ultimately, however, the theories produced in the field of organization analysis are shaped by the various modes of theorizing or paradigms that have been available to and, more important, historically favored by social scientists (Burrell & Morgan, 1979).[35] Because functionalism has been the favored mode of theorizing in the social sciences, the theoretical discourse on organization, like the prescriptive discourse of educational administration, has been dominated by the functionalist paradigm, and thus by the presupposition of organizational rationality (Burrell & Morgan, 1979). However, over the past thirty years, the same revolutionary developments in the social disciplines that were noted previously have produced a number of new theories of organization that are grounded in other modes of social theorizing that had been underutilized in organizational research.[36]

One important substantive outcome of these developments has been a shift in emphasis on the question of the nature of organization and change itself. Whereas the functionalist notion of rational organizations (that is, prospective and goal-directed) and rational-technical change had been the exclusive outlook in organization analysis, many of the newer theories are premised on the idea that organizations are nonrational entities (that is, quasi-random, emergent systems of meaning or cultures) in which change is a nonrational-cultural process (Pfeffer, 1982; Scott, 1981). Methodologically, the trend in organization analysis, as in the social sciences generally, has been away from the traditional foundational notion of one best theory or paradigm for understanding organization. Thus, the contemporary discourse in organization analysis is characterized by theoretical diversity

(Burrell & Morgan, 1979; Pfeffer, 1982; Scott, 1981) and, at the margins at least, by an antifoundational methodological orientation (Morgan, 1983).[37]

Drawing on these substantive and methodological developments, the following analysis considers school organization and adaptability from two general frames of reference that, together, include several theories of organization and change drawn from each of the modes of theorizing found in the social disciplines. The *structural* frame of reference includes configuration theory (Miller & Mintzberg, 1983; Mintzberg, 1979) and what will be referred to as "institutionalization theory" (Meyer & Rowan, 1977, 1978; Meyer & Scott, 1983). By combining these two theories, we can understand school organization as an inherently nonadaptable, two-structure arrangement. The *cultural* frame of reference includes what will be referred to as paradigmatic (Brown, 1978; Golding, 1980; Jonsson & Lundin, 1977; Rounds, 1979, 1981) and cognitive theories of organization (Weick, 1979, 1985), which, when combined, provide a way to understand school organizations as cultures or corrigible systems of meaning. The two frames of reference are presented separately below and then integrated in the next major section where the relationship between organization structure and culture is used to reconsider the four grounding assumptions of special education as an institutional practice of public education.[38] Although the reader no doubt will begin to see in the following analysis some of the organizational implications that I will emphasize in subsequent sections, at this point I will refrain from commenting on those implications. My aim here is merely to set the stage for the sections to follow.

The Structural Frame of Reference[39]

The central idea in configuration theory is that organizations structure themselves into somewhat naturally occurring configurations according to the type of work that they do, the means they have available to coordinate their work, and a variety of situational factors. Given these considerations, school organizations configure themselves as professional bureaucracies (Mintzberg, 1979), even though in this century they have been managed and governed as machine bureaucracies (Callahan, 1962; Meyer & Rowan, 1978; Weick, 1982). According to institutionalization theory, organizations like schools deal with this contradiction by maintaining two structures: a material structure that conforms to the technical demands of their work and a normative structure that conforms to the cultural demands of their institutionalized environments. By combining the insights of configuration theory and institutionalization theory, school organizations can be understood in terms of two organizations, one inside the other. On the outside, their normative structure conforms to the machine bureaucracy configuration, the structure that people expect because of the social norm of organizational rationality. On the inside, however, the material structure of schools conforms to the professional bureaucracy configuration, the structure that configures itself around the technical requirements of their work.

Differences between the Machine and Professional Bureaucracies

The differences between the two organizations stem from the type of work that they do and thus the way they can distribute it among workers (division of labor) and subsequently coordinate its completion. Organizations configure themselves as machine bureaucracies when their work is simple; that is, when it is certain enough to be *rationalized* (or task-analyzed) into a series of separate subtasks, each of which can be prespecified and done by a different worker. Because it can be completely prespecified, simple work can be coordinated by standardizing the work processes through *formalization,* or the specification of precise rules for doing each subtask. Organizations configure themselves as professional bureaucracies when their work is complex; that is, when it is ambiguous and thus too uncertain to be rationalized and formalized. Because their work is too uncertain to be broken apart and distributed among a number of workers, division of labor in the professional bureaucracies is achieved through *specialization.* That is, in the professional bureaucracy (which typically does client-centered work) clients are distributed among the workers, each of whom specializes in the skills that are needed to do the total job with his or her assigned client cohort. Given this form of division of labor, complex work is coordinated by standardizing the skills of the workers, which is accomplished through *professionalization,* or intensive education and socialization carried out in professional schools.

The logic behind rationalization and formalization in the machine bureaucracy is premised on minimizing discretion and separating theory from practice. The theory behind the work rests with the technocrats who rationalize and formalize it; they do the thinking and the workers simply follow the rules. Conversely, specialization and professionalization are meant to increase discretion and to unite theory and practice in the professional. This is necessary because containing the uncertainty of complex work within the role of a particular professional specialization requires the professional to adapt the theory behind the work to the particular needs of his or her clients (Schein, 1972). In principle, professionals know the theory behind their work and have the discretion to adapt it to the actual needs of their clients. In practice, however, the standardization of skills is circumscribed; it provides professionals with a finite repertoire of standard programs that are applicable to a finite number of contingencies or presumed client needs. Given adequate discretionary space (see below), there is room for some adjustment. However, when clients have needs that fall on the margins or outside of the professional's repertoire of standard programs, they either must be forced artificially into the available programs or sent to a different professional specialist, one who presumably has the right standard programs (Perrow, 1970; Weick, 1976). A fully open-ended process — one that seeks a truly creative solution to each unique need — requires a problem-solving orientation. But professionals are performers, not problem solvers. They perfect the programs they have; they do not invent new ones for unfamiliar contingencies. Instead of accommodating heterogeneity, professionals screen it out by squeezing their clients' needs into one of their standard programs or by squeezing them out of the professional-client relationship altogether (Segal, 1974; Simon, 1977).

An organization's division of labor and means of coordination shape the nature of interdependency or coupling among its workers (March & Olsen, 1976; Thompson, 1967; Weick, 1976). Because machine bureaucracies distribute and coordinate their work by rationalizing and formalizing it, their workers are highly dependent on one another and thus, like links in a chain, they are tightly coupled. However, specialization and professionalization create a loosely coupled form of interdependency in the professional bureaucracy, a situation in which workers are not highly dependent on one another. Because specialization requires close contact with the client and professionalization requires little overt coordination or communication among workers (everyone knows roughly what everyone else is doing by way of their common professionalization), each professional works closely with his or her clients and only loosely with other professionals (Weick, 1976, 1982).

Managing Professional Bureaucracies Like Machine Bureaucracies

Given the prescriptive discourse of educational administration and the social norm of organizational rationality, traditional school management (Weick, 1982) and governance (Meyer & Rowan, 1978; Mintzberg, 1979) practices force school organizations to adopt the rationalization and formalization principles of the machine bureaucracy, even though they are ill-suited to the technical demands of doing complex work. In principle, this drives the professional bureaucracy toward the machine bureaucracy configuration because, by misconceptualizing teaching as simple work that can be rationalized and formalized, it violates the theory/practice requirement and discretionary logic of professionalization. Thus, by separating theory and practice and reducing professional discretion, the degree to which teachers can personalize instruction is reduced. Complex work cannot be rationalized and formalized, except in misguided ways that force the professionals "to play the machine bureaucratic game — satisfying the standards instead of serving the clients" (Mintzberg, 1979, p. 377).

Fortunately, however, the imposition of rationalization and formalization does not work completely in school organizations because, from the institutionalization perspective, these structural contingencies are built into the outer machine bureaucracy structure of schools, which is decoupled from their inner professional bureaucracy structure where the work is done. That is, the outer machine bureaucracy structure of schools acts largely as a myth that, through an assortment of symbols and ceremonies, embodies the rationalization and formalization but has little to do with the way the work is actually done. This decoupled arrangement permits schools to do their work according to the localized judgments of professionals — the logic behind specialization and professionalization — while protecting their legitimacy by giving managers and the public the appearance of the rationalized and formalized machine bureaucracy that they expect.

But decoupling does not work completely either because, from the configuration perspective, no matter how contradictory they may be, misplaced rationalization and formalization require at least overt conformity to their precepts and thus circumscribe professional thought and action (Dalton, 1959; Mintzberg, 1979). Decoupling notwithstanding, managing and governing schools as if they were machine bureaucracies increases rationalization and formalization and thus decreases professional thought and discretion, which reduces even further the degree to which teachers can personalize instruction.

Similarities between the Machine and Professional Bureaucracies

Even though they are different in the respects noted above, the machine and professional bureaucracies are similar in one important way: both are inherently nonadaptable structures because they are premised on standardization. All bureaucracies are performance organizations; that is, structures that are configured to perfect the programs they have been standardized to perform. Of course, the standardization of skills is intended to allow for enough professional thought and discretion to accommodate client variability. However, even with adequate discretionary space, there is a limit on the degree to which professionals can adjust their standard programs and, moreover, they can only adjust the standard programs that are in their repertoires. In a professional bureaucracy, coordination through standardization of skills itself circumscribes the degree to which the organization can accommodate variability. A fully open-ended process of accommodation requires a problem-solving organization, a configuration premised on inventing new programs for unique client needs. But the professional bureaucracy is a performance organization; it screens out heterogeneity by forcing its clients' needs into one of its existing specializations, or by forcing them out of the system altogether (Segal, 1974).

Because bureaucracies are performance organizations, they require a stable environment. They are potentially devastated under dynamic conditions, when their environments force them to do something other than what they were standardized to do. Nevertheless, machine bureaucracies can change by restandardizing their work processes, a more or less rational-technical process of rerationalizing their work and reformalizing work behavior. However, when its environment becomes dynamic, the professional bureaucracy cannot respond by making rational-technical adjustments in its work because its coordination rests within each professional, not in its work processes. At a minimum, change in a professional bureaucracy requires a change in what each professional does, because each professional does all aspects of the work individually and personally with his or her clients. Nevertheless, because schools are managed and governed as if they were machine bureaucracies, attempts to change them typically follow the rational-technical approach (Elmore & McLaughlin, 1988; House, 1979), which assumes that changes in, or additions to, the existing rationalization and formalization will result in changes in the way the work gets done. Of course, this fails to bring about the desired changes because the existing rationalization and formalization are located in the decoupled machine bureaucracy structure. However, because such changes or additions require at least overt conformity, they act to extend the existing rationalization and formalization. This, of course, drives the organization further toward the machine bureaucracy configurations, which reduces teacher thought and discretion even further, leaving students with even less personalized and thus even less effective services.

Even though schools are nonadaptable structures, their status as public organizations means that they must respond to public demands for change. From the institutionalization perspective, schools deal with this problem by using their outer machine bureaucracy structure to deflect change demands. That is, they relieve pressure for change by signaling the environment that a change has occurred, thereby creating the illusion that they have changed when, in fact, they remain largely the same (Meyer, 1979; Rowan, 1980; Zucker, 1981). One way that school organizations signal change is by building symbols and ceremonies of change into their outer machine bureaucracy structure, which, of course, is decoupled from the actual work. Another important signal of change is the ritual or decoupled subunit. Not only are the two structures of schools decoupled, but the various units (classrooms and programs) are decoupled from one another as well. As we know from the configuration perspective, this is possible because specialization and professionalization create precisely this sort of loosely coupled interdependency within the organization. As such, schools can respond to pressure for change by simply adding on separate classrooms or programs — that is, by creating new specializations — to deal with the change demand. This response acts to buffer the organization from the change demand because these subunits are decoupled from the rest of the organization, thus making any substantive reorganization of activity unnecessary (Meyer & Rowan, 1977; Zucker, 1981).

The Cultural Frame of Reference

Organization theorists working from the cultural frame of reference think of organizations as bodies of thought, as schemas, cultures, or paradigms. Their theories are premised on the idea that humans construct their social realities through intersubjective communication (see Berger & Luckmann, 1967). As such, the cognitive and paradigmatic perspectives on organization and change are concerned with the way people construct, deconstruct, and reconstruct meaning and how this relates to the way action and interaction unfold over time in organizations. Cognitive theories emphasize the way people create and recreate their organizational realities; paradigmatic theories emphasize the way organizational realities create and recreate people. Together, these theories reflect the interactive duality of the cultural frame of reference — people creating culture and culture creating people (Pettigrew, 1979).

Organizations as Paradigms

Paradigmatic theorists conceptualize organizations as paradigms or shared systems of meaning. They are concerned with understanding the way existing socially constructed systems of meaning affect and constrain thought and action in organizations. From this perspective, an organizational paradigm is a system of beliefs about cause-effect relations and standards of practice and behavior. Regardless of whether these paradigms are true, they guide and justify action by consolidating disorder into an image of orderliness (Brown, 1978; Clark, 1972). From this perspective, organizational change requires a paradigm shift, which is difficult because the paradigm self-justifies itself by distorting new information so it is seen as consistent with the prevailing view. Nevertheless, when sufficient anomalies build up to undermine the prevailing paradigm, a new one emerges and action proceeds again under the guidance of the new organizing framework (Golding, 1980; Jonsson & Lundin, 1977).[40]

One way that anomalies are introduced into organizational paradigms is when values and preferences in society change. However, to the degree that the new social values are inconsistent with the prevailing paradigm, resistance emerges in the form of political clashes and an increase in ritualized activity, which act to reaffirm the paradigm that has been called into question (Rounds, 1979; see also Lipsky, 1975; Perrow, 1978; Zucker, 1977). Another way that anomalies are introduced is through the availability of technical information that indicates that the current paradigm is not working, which can bring about a paradigm shift in one of two ways (Rounds, 1981). The first way is through a confrontation between an individual (or a small constituency group), who rejects the most fundamental assumptions of the current paradigm on the basis of information that the system is not working, and the rest of the organization's members, who are acting in defiance of the negative information to preserve the prevailing paradigm. The second way is when an initially conservative action is taken to correct a generally recognized flaw in what is otherwise assumed to be a viable system. Here, the corrective measure exposes other flaws that, when addressed, expose more flaws, and so on, until enough of the system is called into question to prepare the way for a radical reconceptualization of the entire organization.

Organizations as Schemas

From the cognitive perspective, an organization is a cognitive entity, a paradigm or human schema, "an abridged, generalized, corrigible organization of experience that serves as an initial frame of reference for action and perception" (Weick, 1979, p. 50). That is, although an organizational paradigm orients the thought and action of its members, the members are active in creating and recreating the paradigm. Through activity, selective attention, consensual validation, and luck, people in organizations unrandomize streams of random experience enough to form a paradigm that — correct or not — structures the field of action sufficiently so that meaningful activity can proceed (Weick, 1979, 1985). Members' sampling of the environment, and thus the paradigms they construct, are shaped by prior beliefs and values, which act as filters through which they examine their experiences. Moreover, activity in organizations, which from the cognitive perspective is the pretext for sense-making, is shaped by material structures like formalization, professionalization, and bureaucracy itself. These structural contingencies shape members' organizational realities because they influence the contacts, communication, and commands that they experience and thus affect the streams of experience, beliefs, values, and actions that constitute their organizational paradigms. Furthermore, the paradigm and its values and beliefs also "constrain contacts, communication, and commands. These constraints constitute and shape organizational processes that result in structures" (Weick, 1979, p. 48). Thus, from this perspective, organization is a mutually shaping circularity of structure and culture. Depending on where one enters the circle, organization is a continuous process in which structural contingencies shape the work activities or organizational members, which in turn shapes the members' value orientation and thus the nature of the organizational paradigms they construct to interpret the organization's structural contingencies.

From this perspective, school organizations are "underorganized systems" (Weick, 1985, p. 106), ambiguous settings that are shaped and reshaped by values and beliefs (see also Cohen, March, & Olsen, 1972). Change occurs in such contexts when organizational members believe, correctly or not, that a change in the environment was caused by their own actions. Although this may be an error, when environments are sufficiently malleable, acting on a mistaken belief can set in motion a sequence of activities that allows people to construct the reality that the belief is true. From the cognitive perspective, confident action based on a presumption of efficacy reinforces beliefs about efficacy contained in the paradigm. For good or ill, things are done in certain ways in ambiguous, underorganized systems because people believe their assumptions and presuppositions. And, because believing is seeing in these settings, things change when these beliefs change (Weick, 1985).

Thus, the very underorganized nature of schools that prevents change from a structural perspective is the precise condition that makes change possible from a cultural perspective. Under conditions of increased ambiguity and uncertainty, the presuppositions that underwrite the prevailing paradigm are called into question. Change occurs when someone or something introduces new presuppositions that explain the ambiguity and thus reduce the uncertainty (Brown, 1978; Golding, 1980; Rounds, 1981; Weick, 1979). The recognition of an important, enduring ambiguity — an unresolvable anomaly in the prevailing paradigm — is an occasion when an organization may redefine itself. From the cultural perspective, organizations like schools are human constructions grounded in values. Schools change when apparently irresolvable ambiguities are resolved by confident, forceful, persistent people who manage to convince themselves and others to adopt a new set of presuppositions, which introduces innovation because the values embedded in these presuppositions create a new set of contingencies, expectations, and commitments (Weick, 1985).

SPECIAL EDUCATION AS AN INSTITUTIONAL PRACTICE

The structural and cultural frames of reference on school organization and adaptability are combined in this section and used to reconsider the four grounding assumptions relative to special education as an institutional practice of public education. The first three assumptions are addressed below. Following that, the fourth assumption is considered by way of an organizational analysis of the EHA and the REI proposals.

School Organization, Student Disability, and Special Education[41]

The participants in the REI debate reject the assumptions that mild disabilities are pathological and that diagnosis is objective and useful, recognizing instead that many students are identified as handicapped simply because they have needs that cannot be accommodated in the regular classrooms of the general education system. This contradiction can be understood from an organizational perspective by redescribing student disability as an organizational pathology resulting from the inherent structural and cultural characteristics of traditional school organizations.

Structurally, schools are nonadaptable at the classroom level because professionalization ultimately results in "convergent thinking, in the deductive reasoning of the professional who sees the specific situation in terms of the general concept" (Mintzberg, 1979, p. 375). Given a finite repertoire of standard programs, students whose needs fall outside the standard programs must be forced into them or out of the classroom, a situation that is compounded by the rational-technical approach to school management, which, by introducing unwarranted rationalization and formalization, reduces professional thought and discretion and, thus, the degree to which teachers can personalize their standard programs. The same phenomenon can be understood culturally by thinking of the standard programs as a paradigm of practice that persists because anomalies are distorted to preserve its validity. The principal distortion, of course, is the institutional practice of special education, which reaffirms the paradigm by removing students for whom it does not work. In effect, this prevents teachers from recognizing anomalies in their paradigms and thus, ultimately, removes a valuable source of innovation from the system.[42] Moreover, rationalization and formalization compound and further mystify the situation because they conflict with the values that ground the paradigm and thus increase ritualized activity, which further reduces thought and personalization.

Thus, whether we think of schools from the structural or the cultural frame of reference, the implication is that the first two grounding assumptions are inadequate and incomplete. In organizational terms, student disability is neither a human pathology nor an objective distinction; it is an organizational pathology, a matter of not fitting the standard programs of the prevailing paradigm of a professional culture, the legitimacy of which is artificially reaffirmed by the objectification of school failure as a human pathology through the institutional practice of special education.

The participants in the REI debate reject the assumption that special education is an instructionally rational system and recognize that, at best, it is a politically rational system for targeting otherwise unavailable educational services to designated students, even though the targeting process stigmatizes the students and the services do not necessarily benefit them instructionally. This contradiction can be understood from an organizational perspective by reconceptualizing the institutional practice of special education as an organizational artifact that emerged to protect the legitimacy of a nonadaptable bureaucratic structure faced with the changing value demands of a dynamic democratic environment.

Even though specialization, professionalization, rationalization, and formalization make schools nonadaptable structures, these organizations maintain their legitimacy under dynamic social conditions by signaling to the public that changes have occurred through symbols, ceremonies, and decoupled subunits. As such, the segregated special classroom emerged in conjunction with compulsory school attendance to preserve the legitimacy of the prevailing organizational paradigm by symbolizing compliance with the public demand for universal public education.[43] Structurally, special education is not a rational system; it is a nonrational system, an institutional practice that functions as a legitimizing device. Culturally, it distorts the anomaly of school failure and thus preserves the prevailing paradigm of school organization, which ultimately reaffirms the functionalist presuppositions of organizational rationality and human pathology in the profession of education and in society.[44]

School Organization and Progress

Both sides in the REI debate agree that most mild disabilities are not pathological and that diagnosis is neither objective nor useful. As such, the arguments put forth in the debate reject the presupposition of human pathology as a grounding for the institutional practice of special education. However, the two sides disagree over an appropriate course of action because of a conceptual confusion about the nature of special education and progress resulting from the presupposition of organizational rationality. As we have seen, this confusion among the REI opponents is evident in their defense of the current system of special education and their criticism of the REI proposals. The same sort of confusion among the REI proponents can be illustrated at this point by considering their reform proposals from an organizational perspective, which I will turn to after analyzing the EHA. Before considering either reform measure, however, it will be helpful to introduce a third organizational configuration.

The Adhocracy

As we know, the professional bureaucracy is nonadaptable because it is premised on the principle of standardization (of skills), which configures it as a performance organization for perfecting standard programs. Conversely, the adhocracy configuration is premised on the principle of innovation rather than standardization and, as such, configures itself as a problem-solving organization for inventing new programs. It is the organizational form that configures itself around work that is so ambiguous and uncertain that neither the standard programs nor the skills for doing it are known (Mintzberg, 1979).[45]

Perhaps the best example of this configuration is the National Aeronautics and Space Administration (NASA) during its Apollo phase in the 1960s. Given its mission to put an American on the moon, it configured itself as an adhocracy because at that time there were no standard programs for this sort of manned space flight. At that point in its history, NASA had to rely on its workers to invent and reinvent these programs on an ad hoc basis — on the way to the moon, as it were. Although NASA employed professional workers, it could not use specialization and professionalization to distribute and coordinate its work because there were no specialties that had perfected the standard programs for doing the type of work that was required, and thus no professional fields whose existing repertoires of standard programs could contain its uncertainty. As such, during its Apollo phase, NASA's division of labor and means of coordination were premised on *collaboration* and *mutual adjustment*, respectively.

Under such an arrangement, division of labor is achieved by deploying professionals from various specializations on multidisciplinary project teams, a situation in which team members work collaboratively on the team's project and assume joint responsibility for its completion. Under mutual adjustment, coordination is achieved through informal communication among team members as they invent and reinvent novel solutions to problems on an ad hoc basis, a process that requires them to adapt, adjust, and revise their conventional theories and practices relative to those of their colleagues and the teams' progress on the tasks at hand (Chandler & Sayles, 1971; Mintzberg, 1979). Together, the structural contingencies of collaboration and mutual adjustment give rise to a *discursive coupling* arrangement that is premised on reflective thought, and thus on the unification of theory and practice in the team of workers (Burns & Stalker, 1966). By contrast, during its current Space Shuttle phase, NASA configures itself as a professional bureaucracy (Romzek & Dubnick, 1987), a performance organization that perfects a repertoire of standard launch and recovery programs that were invented during its Apollo phase. This transfiguration from the adhocracy to the professional bureaucracy configuration begins when the organization assumes that it has solved all or most of its problems and thus that the programs it has invented can be standardized and used as solutions in the future. The difference between the two configurations is that, faced with a problem, the adhocracy "engages in creative effort to find a novel solution;

the professional bureaucracy pigeonholes it into a known contingency to which it can apply a standard program. One engages in divergent thinking aimed at innovation; the other in convergent thinking aimed at perfection" (Mintzberg, 1979, p. 436).

Finally, under the organizational contingencies of collaboration, mutual adjustment, and discursive coupling, accountability in the adhocracy is achieved through a presumed community of interests — a sense among the workers of a shared interest in a common goal, in the well-being of the organization with respect to progress toward its mission — rather than through an ideological identification with a professional culture (professional bureaucracy) or a formalized relationship with an organization (machine bureaucracy) (Burns & Stalker, 1966; Chandler & Sayles, 1971; Romzek & Dubnick, 1987). Thus, rather than the *professional-bureaucratic* model of accountability that emerges in two-structure configurations like schools, the organizational contingencies of the adhocracy give rise to a *professional-political* mode of accountability, a situation in which work is controlled by experts who, although they act with discretion, are subject to sanctions that emerge within a political discourse among professionals and client constituencies (Burns & Stalker, 1966; Chandler & Sayles, 1971).[46]

The Education for All Handicapped Children Act

From an organizational perspective, the basic problem with the EHA is that it attempts to force an adhocratic value orientation on a professional bureaucracy by treating it as if it were a machine bureaucracy.[47] The EHA's ends are adhocratic because it seeks a problem-solving organization in which interdisciplinary teams of professionals and parents collaborate to invent personalized programs, or, in the language of the EHA, individualized educational plans (IEPs). But this orientation contradicts the value orientation of the professional bureaucracy in every way, given that it is a performance organization in which individual professionals work alone to perfect standard programs. Culturally, this value conflict produces resistance in the form of political clashes, which undermine the ideal of collaboration, as well as an increase in ritualized activity, which, by further mystifying the prevailing paradigm of practice, intensifies the problem of professionalization and thus deflects the ideals of problem solving and personalization.[48] Moreover, because the EHA's means are completely consistent with the value orientation of the machine bureaucracy structure — rationalization of instruction programs (see below) and formalization of procedures — the EHA extends and elaborates the existing rationalization and formalization in schools. Structurally, this both decouples the adhocratic ends of the EHA from the actual work and further reduces professional thought and discretion, a process that intensifies professionalization and thus reduces personalization. This results in even more students who fall outside the standard programs, many of whom must be identified as handicapped to protect the legitimacy of the prevailing paradigm. Moreover, because there is a legal limit on the number of students who can be identified as handicapped under the EHA, as well as a political limit on the amount of school failure society will tolerate, the EHA, in conjunction with other rational-technical reforms associated with the excellence movement, helped to create the new "at-risk" category of student causalities, which, at this point, is decoupled from both general education and special education.[49]

Because the EHA requires at least overt conformity, a number of symbols of compliance have emerged, two of which are important for present purposes. The symbol of compliance for programs that serve students with severe and profound disabilities is the traditional decoupled subunit, the segregated special classroom. These programs are simply added to the existing school organization and, to one degree or another, decoupled from the basic operation. Because the nature of the needs of the students in these programs is beyond the standard programs of any single profession and thus requires an interdisciplinary approach, their efficacy depends on school organizations providing the team of professionals that is required. Beyond this, these programs have very little to do with the basic school operation.[50]

The symbol of compliance for most students identified as mildly handicapped is the resource room, a new type of decoupled subunit. From an organizational perspective, the resource room is even more problematic than the special classroom because it violates the logic of the professional bureaucracy's means of coordination and division of labor.[51] Under the mainstreaming model, the responsibility for the student's instructional program is divided among one or more regular classroom teachers and a special education resource teacher. This contradicts the division of labor because it requires that the student's instructional program be rationalized and assigned to more than one professional. Of course, this is justified implicitly on the assumption that the professionals will work collaboratively to integrate the program. But the collaboration required to integrate the student's instructional program contradicts the logic of professionalization and thus the loosely coupled form of interdependency among workers. Because professionalization locates virtually all of the necessary coordination within the teacher, there is no need for collaboration in schools, and thus it rarely occurs.[52]

Given the adhocratic spirit of the EHA, it was intended to decrease the effects of student disability by increasing personalized instruction and regular classroom integration. However, given the bureaucratic value orientation of schools and of the procedural requirements of the law itself, the result has been an increase in the number of students classified as disabled, a disintegration of instruction, and a decrease in personalization in regular and special classrooms.[53]

The Regular Education Initiative Proposals[54]

The problem with the REI proposals is that each of them reproduces and extends the value contradictions of the EHA. This is so because, even though they reject the two assumptions associated with the notion of human pathology, ultimately they retain the assumptions that school organizations are rational and that changing them is a rational-technical process. In organizational terms, the result is that, although the REI proposals call for an adhocratic value orientation, they retain the professional bureaucracy inner configuration of schools and extend their machine bureaucracy outer configuration. They retain the professional bureaucracy configuration because, by retaining the classroom teacher, each proposal retains a specialized division of labor and a professionalized means of coordination — a combination that yields loose coupling and thus deflects the ideal of collaboration.

In principle, as long as the work in schools is distributed through specialization and coordinated through professionalization, there is no need for teachers to collaborate. Collaboration emerges when work is distributed on the basis of a collaborative division of labor and coordinated through mutual adjustment, an arrangement that is premised on a team approach to problem solving and yields a form of interdependency premised on reflective discourse. Although the Reynolds and Wang, Lilly and Pugach, and Stainback and Stainback proposals call for collaborative problem solving between a classroom teacher and a support services staff, by retaining the notion of a classroom and placing the support services staff above it, they actually extend the rationalization and formalization of the machine bureaucracy configuration and thus undermine the ideals of problem solving and personalized instruction. That is, placing the support staff above the classroom teacher implies that the theory of teaching is at the support level while the mere practice of teaching takes place in the classroom, an administrative arrangement that maintains the misplaced convention of separating theory from practice. Moreover, this politicizes and thus undermines the ideal of collaboration, because placing support personnel above the practice context makes them technocrats rather than support staff (Mintzberg, 1979). In an actual machine bureaucracy, technocrats are the people with the theory; they control and define the activities of the other workers. This is not collaboration in an organizational sense; it is bureaucratic control and supervision. In professional bureaucracies, where the notion of a technocracy within the organization violates the logic of professionalization (Mintzberg, 1979), technocrats are resisted, particularly change agents and other school improvement personnel (Wolcott, 1977).

The same problems are inherent in the Gartner and Lipsky proposal, which retains the regular classroom and proposes to make it effective for all students by implementing the principles of effective schools research through school improvement projects. Here the assumption is that the theory of effective teaching, which is known by the school improvement and effective schools specialists apart from and prior to the classroom context, is contained in the principles identified in effective schools research and that implementing these principles in the practice context is simply a matter of the teacher making a commitment to follow them. In principle, imposing such standards from above, their apparent efficacy in some other context notwithstanding, can only lead to an extension of existing rationalization and formalization, and thus to an increase in ritualized activity. Ultimately, this leads to an increase in professionalization and a corresponding decrease in personalization.[55] Finally, the Stainback and Stainback proposal compounds both of these problems. Not only does it retain the notions of a classroom and the separation of theory and practice, thus politicizing and undermining the ideals of collaboration and problem solving, but by creating a system of individual subject area specializations, it disintegrates the student's instructional program across even more teachers than the mainstreaming approach. Ironically, the REI proposal that promotes total integration of students implies a virtually complete disintegration of instruction.

Although the arguments put forth in the REI debate reject the assumption of human pathology and thus represent progress relative to the mainstreaming debate, the outcome is the same. The adhocratic values of the REI proponents are distorted by the bureaucratic value orientation of school organization. Moreover, because they retain the presupposition of organizational rationality, their adhocratic ends are deflected by the bureaucratic value orientation of their own proposals.

Earlier in the analysis we saw that a critical reading of the REI debate rejected the presupposition of human pathology and thus left the legitimacy of special education as a professional practice hanging on the adequacy of the presupposition of organizational rationality. At this point, however, we have seen that a critical reading of the discourse on school organization and adaptability, in conjunction with an organizational analysis of the EHA and the REI proposals, rejects the presuppositions of human pathology and organizational rationality. Such a reading deconstructs special education, both as a professional practice and as an institutional practice of public education. In terms of the adequacy of its grounding assumptions, special education cannot be considered a rational and just response to the problem of school failure.

The Special Education Paradox

THOMAS M. SKRTIC

PUBLIC EDUCATION AND THE DISCOURSE
ON SCHOOL FAILURE

To this point in the analysis we have been concerned with special education, first as a professional practice from the vantage point of the REI debate, then as an institutional practice from the perspective of school organization and adaptability. The focus of this section is the implications of the deconstruction of special education for the discourse on school failure and, ultimately, for the legitimacy of the institutional practice of public education. Considering these implications, however, will require broadening the analysis to include the voice of the general education community and what it has to say about school failure from the perspective of educational excellence. If we think of the mainstreaming and REI debates in special education as two debates within a broader discourse on educational equity, and the effective schools and school restructuring debates in general education as two debates within a broader discourse on educational excellence, we can begin to see how the equity and excellence discourses parallel, mirror, and, ultimately, converge upon one another.[56]

The first parallel is that the initial debate within each discourse is an extreme form of naive pragmatism that merely reproduces the problems it sets out to solve. As in the case of mainstreaming and the EHA, the new practices that emerged out of the effective schools debate reproduced the original problems (Clark & Astuto, 1988; Cuban, 1983, 1989; Slavin, 1989; Stedman, 1987; Timar & Kirp, 1988; Wise, 1988). The second parallel is that the failure of the first debate within each discourse gives rise to the second debate, which, although it is less naive, is also a form of naive pragmatism that promises to reproduce current problems in the future. As we will see below, although the restructuring debate is less naive than the effective schools debate, it does not explicitly recognize the connection between general education practices and the four assumptions. As such, like the REI debate in special education, it promises to reproduce the general education problems of the 1980s in the 1990s and beyond (see Cuban, 1983, 1989; Skrtic, 1991; Wise, 1988). Although the restructuring debate parallels the REI debate in this second respect, the effects of this pattern in the two debates are mirror images of one another.

As we know, the REI debate implicates school organization in the problem of student disability. Thus, the first way that the two debates mirror each other is that, by pointing to the emergence and persistence of homogeneous grouping — curriculum tracking, in-class ability grouping, and compensatory pull-out programs — as an indication of deep structural flaws in traditional school organization (Cuban, 1989; Oakes, 1985, 1986a,b; Stedman, 1987; Wise, 1988), the restructuring debate implicates student disability in the problem of school organization. The second way that the REI and re-

235

structuring debates mirror each other is that, although both of them reject two of the four assumptions and question the other two, in the final analysis they retain the assumptions that they question. We saw this pattern for both the REI proponents and opponents relative to the assumptions about the rationality of school organization and change. The mirror image of this contradiction in the restructuring debate is that, although it rejects the two assumptions about the rationality of school organization and change, it questions but retains the two assumptions about the nature of school failure and diagnosis. That is, although it criticizes the institutional practice of tracking, and even the overrepresentation of minority students in certain special education programs, it does not criticize special education as an institutional practice (see Goodlad, 1984; Oakes, 1986a,b; Sizer, 1984), and thus retains the assumptions that school failure is pathological and that diagnosis is objective and useful.[57]

The restructuring debate does not recognize special education as a form of tracking because its criticism of homogeneous grouping stops at the point of presumed pathology, which is the third and, for present purposes, most important way that the two debates mirror one another. Whereas the REI debate rejects the presupposition of human pathology but retains that of organizational rationality, the restructuring debate rejects organizational rationality but retains human pathology. The significance here, of course, is that the two debates — and thus the discourses on excellence and equity in public education — converge to reject both of the functionalist presuppositions that ground the twentieth-century discourse on school failure, and thus they deconstruct it.

The broader significance of the deconstruction of the discourse on school failure is that it provides the grounds for an immanent critique of the institution of public education. That is, confronted with the fact that its practices are neither excellent nor equitable, public education must account for itself without recourse to the distorting and legitimizing effects of the functionalist discourse on school failure. Ultimately, to be able to continue making the claim that it embodies the Jeffersonian ideal of democratic education, public education must reconstruct itself to be both excellent and equitable.

EXCELLENCE, EQUITY, AND ADHOCRACY

We can turn from deconstruction to reconstruction by considering the moments of truth contained in the convergence between excellence and equity in the REI and restructuring debates. As we know, the REI proponents call for virtually eliminating the regulatory requirements of the EHA. The corresponding argument among the proponents of restructuring is for eliminating scientific management as the approach to administration and change (for example, Boyer, 1983; Cuban, 1983, 1989; Goodlad, 1984; Oakes, 1985, 1986a,b; Sirotnik & Oakes, 1986; Sizer, 1984; Wise, 1988). In organizational terms, the first convergence is that both sets of proponents are arguing for the elimination of rationalization, formalization, and tight coupling — the misplaced structural contingencies of the machine bureaucracy. The second convergence is between the REI proponents' arguments for merging the general and special education systems and the arguments of the restructuring proponents for merging the various general education tracks. Here, both sets of proposals are calling for the elimination of specialization, professionalization, and loose coupling — the structural contingencies of the professional bureaucracy configuration. In practical terms, both sets of proponents seek an adaptable system in which increased teacher discretion leads to more personalized instruction through collaborative problem solving among professionals and client constituencies (Boyer, 1983; Cuban, 1983, 1989; Goodlad, 1984; McNeil, 1986; Oakes, 1985; Sizer, 1984). Of course, because the restructuring proponents retain the assumption of pathology, there are differences between the two sets of proposals. But these are differences in degree, not in kind. In organizational terms, the participants in both debates are arguing for the introduction of collaboration, mutual adjustment, and discursive coupling — the structural contingencies of the adhocratic form. In principle, both sets of reform proposals require an adhocratic school organization and professional culture.

The REI opponents' position on equity is that, given the nonadaptability of regular classrooms and school organizations, the targeting function of the EHA and the pull-out logic of mainstreaming must be maintained for political purposes, diagnostic and instructional inadequacies notwithstanding. The moment of truth in this position is the argument that, as long as resources are constant and students differ, no teacher, whether in a general or special education classroom, can escape the necessary choice between excellence (higher class means) and equity (narrower class variances), unless more powerful instructional technologies are available. In organizational terms, this is true because the structural contingencies of rationalization and formalization circumscribe a finite set of resources relative to a prespecified set of activities and outcomes, while those of specialization and professionalization circumscribe a finite repertoire of standard programs relative to a finite set of presumed client needs. Thus, students whose needs fall on the margins or outside of these standard programs must be either squeezed into them or squeezed out of the classroom. Given the inevitability of human diversity, a professional bureaucracy can do nothing but create students who do not fit the system. In a professional bureaucracy, all forms of tracking — curriculum tracking and in-class ability grouping in general education, as well as self-contained and resource classrooms in special, compensatory, remedial, and gifted education — are organizational pathologies created by specialization and professionalization and compounded by rationalization and formalization. Students are subjected to — and subjugated by — these practices because, given their structural and cultural contingencies, traditional school organizations cannot accommodate diversity and so must screen it out.

The problem with the REI opponents' argument, however, is that it assumes that nonadaptability is inherent in schooling, rather than in its traditional bureaucratic organization. Student diversity is not an inherent problem for school organizations; it is only a problem when they are premised on standardization and thus configure themselves as performance organizations that perfect standard programs for known contingencies. As we have seen, the adhocratic form is premised on innovation. It configures itself as a problem-solving organization for inventing novel programs for unfamiliar contingencies. Regardless of its causes and its extent, student diversity is not a liability in a problem-solving organization; it is an asset, an enduring uncertainty, and thus the driving force behind innovation, growth of knowledge, and progress.

The problem with the REI and restructuring proposals in this regard is that, although their ends require the adhocratic configuration, their means reproduce the professional bureaucracy configuration. This is so because, by retaining the notion of a classroom, they retain a specialized division of labor, a professionalized means of coordination, and thus a loosely coupled form of interdependency. Both reform approaches eliminate rationalization and formalization — and thus the misplaced machine bureaucracy outer structure of schools — while retaining specialization and professionalization — and thus the professional bureaucracy inner structure.

From an organizational perspective, the argument for eliminating rationalization and formalization is an argument for uniting theory and practice in the professional. The problem with this move in the REI and restructuring proposals, however, is that by retaining the professional bureaucracy configuration, they unite theory and practice in the *individual professional* rather than in a *team of professionals*.[58] From a structural perspective, innovation is "the building of new knowledge and skills, [which] requires the combination of different bodies of existing ones" (Mintzberg, 1979, p. 434). This requires a division of labor and a means of coordination that "break through the boundaries of conventional specialization," creating a situation in which "professionals must amalgamate their efforts [by joining] forces in multidisciplinary teams, each formed around a specific project of innovation" (Mintzberg, 1979, pp. 434–435). From a cultural perspective, repertoires or paradigms of practice are social constructions; innovation occurs when new paradigms emerge through confrontations over uncertainty within social groups (Brown, 1978; Rounds, 1981; Weick, 1979). From an organizational perspective, professional innovation is not a solitary act; when it does occur, it is a social phenomenon that takes place within a reflective discourse.

The problem of uniting theory and practice in the individual professional can be illustrated by considering the genealogy of special education as a professional and institutional practice.[59] The first special classroom teachers were general education teachers who thus had to invent new programs for students who, by definition, had needs that fell outside their repertoires of standard programs. Moreover, because special classrooms were decoupled from the machine bureaucracy structure and thus were relatively free from its rationalization and formalization, theory and practice were united in the special classroom teacher. However, because these teachers were decoupled from other regular and special classroom teachers and thus lacked the structural contingencies of collaboration, mutual adjustment, and discursive coupling, they were denied the structural conditions necessary for the emergence of an adhocratic mode of professional practice. The inadequacy of special education practices throughout this century illustrates the problem with freeing teachers from the outer machine bureaucracy structure of school organizations while retaining the inner professional bureaucracy structure. Although such a move may permit teachers to invent new repertoires, it will not assure that the repertoires they invent will be any more effective, ethical, or, in the long run, much different from what they had been doing before being set free.[60]

From a structural perspective, the REI and restructuring proponents are right about eliminating the rationalization and formalization associated with scientific management and the EHA. At a minimum, achieving their adhocratic ends will require merging theory and practice. However, if merging theory and practice is to have the adhocratic effects they desire, they will have to do more than merge general education tracks and the general and special education systems in the ways that they have proposed. Achieving their adhocratic ends will require merging theory and practice *in conjunction with* eliminating specialization and professionalization. This will require eliminating the classroom, which, in structural terms, is an organizational artifact of the structural contingencies of the professional bureaucracy configuration and, in practical terms, the principal barrier to the introduction of collaboration, mutual adjustment, and discursive coupling, the structural contingencies of the adhocracy configuration. Furthermore, from a cultural perspective, achieving their adhocratic ends will require that an adhocratic professional culture emerge and be sustained within public education. To emerge, such a culture will require the structural contingencies of the adhocratic form. To be sustained, it will require an enduring source of uncertainty because, as we saw in the case of NASA, without problems to solve, adhocracies revert to bureaucracies.[61]

In political terms, the institution of public education cannot be democratic unless its practices are excellent and equitable. In organizational terms, its practices cannot be excellent and equitable unless school organizations are adhocratic. In structural and cultural terms, school organizations cannot be adhocratic — and thus cannot be excellent, equitable, *or* democratic — without the uncertainty of student diversity. In the adhocratic school organization, educational equity is the precondition for educational excellence.

HISTORY, EDUCATION, AND DEMOCRACY

Although the evidence on educational excellence, equity, and adaptability is overwhelmingly negative, there are schools that are relatively effective, equitable, and adaptable, including some that have met or surpassed the intent of the EHA and the spirit of mainstreaming.[62] One way to explain this contradictory evidence theoretically is to think of schools as ambiguous, underorganized systems that are shaped by values. Of course, given the organizational history of public education, the value orientation of school organizations and their members tends to be bureaucratic. On occasion, however, someone, some group, or some event increases ambiguity enough to cast doubt on the prevailing paradigm and, under conditions of increased ambiguity, someone or some group, acting on a different set of values, manages to decrease the ambiguity by redefining the organization for themselves and others. In fact, it is just this sort of organizational phenomenon that one finds in successful schools. Their success turns on human agency, on the values, expectations, and actions of the people who work in them.[63] Schools can be effective, equitable, and adaptable, but when they are, they are operating more like adhocracies than bureaucracies. And they are operating this way because the people in them are thinking and acting more like problem solvers than performers. They are acting and thinking this way because someone or some group reduced uncertainty by reframing an ambiguous situation in terms of adhocratic values, a subtle process of deconstruction and reconstruction in which organizational members construct a new set of structural and cultural contingencies for themselves and their clients.

Although such an interpretation of today's successful schools provides further support for the adhocratic form, it does not account for the fact that the traditional industrial-era definitions of excellence and equity that have shaped the research on successful schools are losing their relevance with the emergence of post-industrialism. To assess the implications of post-industrialism for public education and the adhocratic form, it will be helpful to consider the arguments put forth in the social reconstruction debate, one of several debates within the progressive education movement earlier in this century (see Kliebard, 1988; Kloppenberg, 1986).

The proponents of social reconstruction were concerned that bureaucracy was distorting democracy. As Weber (1922/1978) explained, democracy and bureaucracy grow coincidentally because actualizing democratic government requires the bureaucratic administrative form. The problem is that, although democracy is supposed to be dynamic, the bureaucracy on which it depends resists change, a problem that, for Weber, was the central and irresolvable fact of the modern state. In *The Public and Its Problems,* Dewey (1927/1988b) argued that, although industrialization had intensified the problem of bureaucracy, it also provided an opportunity to recover democracy. According to Dewey (1899, 1927/1988b), the problem of bureaucracy is intensified by industrialization because it places more of life — particularly work and education — under the bureaucratic form. This reduces the need for problem solving and discourse, which stunts the growth of reflective thought and, ultimately, undercuts the ability of the public to govern itself. The opportunity posed by industrialization was that it created an expanding network of social interdependencies that Dewey (1929–1930/1988a) believed made possible and begged for a way of developing a new sense of *social* individualism to replace the *possessive* form of individualism of the eighteenth and nineteenth centuries.

For Dewey (1897, 1916, 1927/1988b) and other progressive reformers (see Kloppenberg, 1986), the only meaningful response to the problem and opportunity of the industrial era was to restore the public for democracy through a cultural transformation, which was to be actualized by instituting progressive education in the public schools. Dewey's (1897, 1899, 1916) notion of progressive education was particularly well-suited to this end because, as a pedagogy grounded in the antifoundational epistemology of American pragmatism, it was premised on the belief that education in a democracy should both cultivate a sense of social responsibility by developing an awareness of interdependency, and engender a critical attitude toward received knowledge by promoting an appreciation of uncertainty. The problem, of course, was that the value orientation of progressive education is pluralistic and adhocratic, which contradicts the individualistic and bureaucratic value orientation of public education. Thus, the circularity in the progressive argument for transforming society through education was and still is that:

> If the problems facing society can be traced to its individualism . . . and reform must proceed by means of education, how can reformers get around the

awkward fact that the educational system is imbued with precisely the values that they have isolated as the source of the problem? (Kloppenberg, 1986, p. 377)

No one grasped the circularity problem better than Weber (1922/1978). Whereas the problem of an unreflective public lay in the contradiction between democracy and bureaucracy in the modern state, he argued that the circularity of trying to solve it through education meant confronting an even greater problem in the logic of modernity itself: the contradiction among democracy, bureaucracy, education, and professionalization. Weber explained that the ever-increasing push to further bureaucratize government and the economy creates the need for more and more experts and thus continually increases the importance of specialized knowledge. But the logic of expertise contradicts democracy because it creates "the struggle of the 'specialist' type of man against the older type of 'cultivated' man" (1922/1978, p. 1090). And since the progressive project is premised on restoring democracy by educating the cultivated citizen, it is stymied because public education itself becomes increasingly bureaucratized in the interest of training specialized experts. Thus, democracy continues to decline, not only because the bureaucratic form resists change, but because the cultivated citizen continues to disappear. As more of life comes under the control of the professional bureaucracy's standard problem solutions, the need to solve problems and to engage in discourse diminishes even further. This tendency stunts the growth of reflective thought in society and in the professions, which not only undercuts the ability of the public to govern itself democratically, but also the ability of the professions to see themselves critically.

The advantage today is that post-industrialism is premised on an even greater and more pervasive form of interdependency and social responsibility. Whereas the network of social interdependencies of industrialization stopped at the boundaries of industrial organizations themselves, post-industrialization extends the network into the very core of the post-industrial organization form (Drucker, 1989; Naisbitt & Aburdene, 1985; Reich, 1983). The key difference is that industrial organization depended on the machine bureaucracy configuration and thus on the separation of theory and practice and an unreflective, mechanical form of interdependency among workers. However, post-industrial organization depends on the adhocratic form; on collaboration, mutual adjustment, and discursive coupling, and on a political form of accountability premised on a community of interests among workers, managers, and, ultimately, among the organization's members, consumers, and host community (Drucker, 1989; Mintzberg, 1979; Reich, 1983, 1990).

Reich (1990, p. 201) characterized the adhocracies of the post-industrial economy as "environments in which people can identify and solve problems for themselves," as contexts in which individual skills are integrated into a group. . . . Over time, as group members work through various problems . . . they learn about each others' abilities. They learn how they can help one another perform better, what each can contribute to a particular project, and how they can best take advantage of one another's experience. (Reich, 1990, p. 201)

The system of education needed for the post-industrial economy is one that prepares young people "to take responsibility for their continuing education, and to collaborate with one another so that their combined skills and insights add up to something more than the sum of their individual contributions" (Reich, 1990, p. 202). As such, educational excellence in the post-industrial era is more than basic numeracy and literacy; it is a capacity for working collaboratively with others and for taking responsibility for learning (Drucker, 1989; Naisbitt & Aburdene, 1985; Reich, 1983). Moreover, educational equity is a precondition for excellence in the post-industrial era, for collaboration means learning collaboratively with and from persons with varying interests, abilities, skills, and cultural perspectives, and taking responsibility for learning means taking responsibility for one's own learning and that of others. Ability grouping and tracking have no place in such a system because they "reduce young peoples' capacities to learn from and collaborate with one another" and work against developing a community of interests, a situation that is precluded unless "unity and cooperation are the norm" in schools (Reich, 1990, p. 208).

Given the relevancies of the post-industrial era, the successful school is one that prepares young people to work responsibly and interdependently under conditions of uncertainty. It does this by promoting in its students a sense of social responsibility, an awareness of interdependency, and an appreciation of uncertainty. It achieves these things by developing its students' capacity for experiential learning through collaborative problem solving and reflective discourse within a community of interests. The successful school in the post-industrial era is one that produces cultivated citizens by providing all of its students with the experience of a progressive education in an adhocratic setting. Given the emerging historical conditions of the twenty-first century, and the fact that democracy *is* collaborative problem solving through reflective discourse within a community of interests, the adhocratic school organization provides more than a way to reconcile the social goals of educational excellence and educational equity. It provides us with an opportunity to resume the critical project of American pragmatism in public education and, thus, with another chance to save democracy from bureaucracy.

Notes

1. Max Weber (1919/1946, p. 117).
2. Although the special education community has responded favorably to what is being referred to as the school restructuring phase (see Elmore, 1987; notes 8 and 56) of the excellence movement, the push for higher standardized test scores during the early phase of the excellence movement (see Wise, 1988) was viewed negatively (see Pugach & Sapon-Shevin, 1987; Shepard, 1987).
3. The developments in the social disciplines include the general trend away from objectivism and toward subjectivism (see, e.g., Bernstein, 1976; Schwartz & Ogilvy, 1979) and, more important, the reemergence of antifoundationalism (see, e.g., Bernstein, 1983; Lyotard, 1979/1984; Skinner, 1985). Whereas social inquiry historically has been dominated by the objectivist conceptualization of science and the foundational view of knowledge and thus by a monological quest for the truth about the social world, contemporary scholars are calling for dialogical social analysis — an antifoundational discourse open to multiple interpretations of social life (see, e.g., Bernstein, 1983; Rorty, 1979; Riceour, 1981). The reemergence of antifoundationalism has led to a revival of interest in philosophical pragmatism, particularly in the work of John Dewey (see Antonio, 1989; Kloppenberg, 1986) and his contemporary appropriators (e.g., Rorty, 1979, 1982), as well as increased attention to the work of contemporary Continental philosophers like Derrida (1972/1982a) and Foucault (1980). An important methodological outcome of these developments has been the emergence of new antifoundational methodologies and the reappropriation of older ones (see notes 4, 5, 7, and 9). A second important outcome has been the emergence of the text as a metaphor for social life (Geertz, 1983), which implies a mode of social analysis that views human and institutional practices as discursive formations that can be read or interpreted in many ways, none of which is correct in a foundational sense, but each of which carries with it a particular set of moral and political implications. Among other things, social analysis under the text metaphor studies that which conditions, limits, and institutionalizes discursive formations; it asks how power comes to be concentrated in the hands of those who have the right to interpret reality and define normality (Dreyfus & Rabinow, 1983; see notes 4, 5, 7, and 9).
4. My version of critical pragmatism uses four antifoundational methodologies (see note 3): two reappropriated ones, immanent critique and ideal type (note 5), and two newer ones, deconstruction (note 7) and genealogy (note 9). Given its grounding in philosophical pragmatism, critical pragmatism does not seek "truth" in the foundational sense; it is, rather, a form of edification (see Cherryholmes, 1988; Rorty, 1979). As used here, it is a mode of inquiry that, by forcing us to acknowledge that what we think, do, say, write, and read as professionals is shaped by convention, helps us avoid the delusion that we can know ourselves, our profession, our clients, "or anything else, except under optional descriptions" (Rorty, 1979, p. 379). Critical pragmatism is "the same as the 'method' of utopian politics or revolutionary science (as opposed to parliamentary politics or normal science). The method is to redescribe lots and lots of things in new ways, until you . . . tempt the rising generation to . . . look for . . . new scientific equipment or new social institutions" (Rorty, 1989, p. 9). For an extended discussion of my version of critical pragmatism, see Skrtic (1991). For a somewhat different version, see Cherryholmes (1988).
5. Immanent critique is more than a method of analysis. Historically, from Hegel and Marx to more contemporary emancipation theorists in the social disciplines (e.g., Horkheimer, 1974) and education (e.g., Giroux, 1981), it has been understood as the driving force behind social progress and change, a process driven by the affinity of humans for attempting to reconcile their claims about themselves (appearances) with

their actual social conditions (reality) (Hegel, 1807/1977; Kojeve, 1969). It is an emancipatory form of analysis in that it is intended to free us from our unquestioned assumptions about ourselves and our social practices, assumptions that prevent us from doing what we believe is right (Antonio, 1981; Schroyer, 1973). As a method, however, immanent critique does not on its own provide a way of identifying the ideals or actual conditions of social phenomena. For this I will use Max Weber's (1904/1949) method of ideal types.

The ideal-typical analytic is premised on the idea that the meaning of social phenomena derives from the cultural significance (value orientation) behind human and institutional action. As such, ideal types are exaggerated mental constructs (developed from empirical and theoretical knowledge) for analyzing social phenomena in terms of their value orientation. They are not "true" in a foundational sense; they are mental constructions used as expository devices (Dallmayr & McCarthy, 1977; Mommsen, 1974; Ritzer, 1983). I use ideal types extensively in the article to draw out and emphasize the explicit and implicit value orientations in the discourses and practices considered, particularly in the characterizations of school organization that are used in the second half of the paper (see notes 38 and 39).

6. I use the term educational administration in both a narrow sense (to refer to the field and practice of educational administration) and a broad sense (to refer to the fields and practices of educational policy and educational change, or school improvement or educational reform), inclusive of the role played by persons in the fields of educational administration (narrow sense), including special education administration. By the discourse on school organization and adaptability I mean the discourse on these topics in the field of educational administration (both senses), as well as in the broader discourse on organization and change in the multidisciplinary field of organization analysis (see Scott, 1981; notes 34 and 37). I use "school organization and adaptability" rather than "school organization and change" to refer to this discourse because I am interested in the capacity for change at both the microscopic level of the individual professional and the macroscopic level of the entire organization (see notes 35 and 36).

7. Deconstruction is Derrida's (1972/1982a,b) method of reading texts by focusing on their margins (silences, contradictions, inconsistencies, and incompleteness) rather than on their central ideas or arguments. Although Derrida deconstructs philosophical texts, the method of deconstruction has been applied broadly to the texts of the social sciences and professions, including professional, institutional, and social practices and discourses (see Cherryholmes, 1988; Hoy, 1985; Ryan, 1982; Rorty, 1989). Whereas traditional analyses purport to enable us to read or interpret a text, discourse, or practice (as an accurate or true representation of the world), deconstruction tries to show that interpretation is a distinctively human process in which no single interpretation ever has enough cognitive authority to privilege it over another (see Derrida, 1972/1982a).

8. I use terms like general education, regular education, and regular classroom in reference to the typical kindergarten through twelfth grade program within public education. Although I recognize that these terms often carry "decidedly neutral or even negative connotations" (Lilly, 1989, p. 143) for professional educators outside the field of special education, I use them for ease of presentation only, particularly where clarity demands that I distinguish between general education and special education professionals, practices, and discourses, as well as between education in a broad sense (the entire field or institution of education) and education in a narrow sense (the kindergarten through twelfth grade program).

Although I use the term special education in the narrow sense of the professional field (or institutional practice) of special education, the implications of much of what

I have to say in the first half of the paper apply equally well to students in the other special needs programs (e.g., compensatory, remedial, and migrant education), as well as students who are tracked in one way or another within the general education programs (see note 12). In the second half of the article references to the other special needs programs and tracking practices in general education are made explicit. By "the discourse on educational excellence" in the field of general education I mean what general educators think, do, say, read, and write about educational excellence, a discourse that (over the past decade) can be understood in terms of two related debates — what I will refer to as the "effective schools" and "school restructuring" debates (see note 56). Although it plays a key role in special education classification practices under the EHA, I have not included the field of school psychology in the present analysis. For a separate treatment, see Skrtic (1990a).

9. Genealogy is Foucault's (1980, 1983) approach for analyzing what conditions, limits, and institutionalizes social practices and discourses. He used genealogy to study "the way modern societies control and discipline their populations by sanctioning the knowledge claims and practices of the human sciences: medicine, psychiatry, psychology, criminology, sociology and so on" (Philip, 1985, p. 67; Foucault, 1961/1973, 1963/1975, 1975/1979). The key difference between genealogy and traditional historical analysis is that the genealogist is far less interested in the events of history than in the "norms, constraints, conditions, conventions, and so on" (Dreyfus & Rabinow, 1983, p. 108) that produced them.

10. My use of the qualifiers "explicit" and "implicit" here is a bit misleading. It is more accurate to think of all three discourses as being grounded in unquestioned presuppositions. Explicit here refers to the idea that certain presuppositions are an explicit part of the profession's knowledge tradition relative to other ones that are merely implicit norms in society. This problem will come up again (see note 19) because the degree of implicitness and explicitness of guiding assumptions is a key part of the subject matter of this type of inquiry (see notes 4, 5, 7, and 9).

   Although one could argue that the field of educational administration implicitly assumes that school failure is pathological on the grounds that historically it has avoided topics on school effects and student outcomes (Bridges, 1982; Erickson, 1979), human pathology is explicit in the conceptualization of administration that grounds the field. The Getzels-Guba model of administration (Getzels & Guba, 1957), "the most successful theory in educational administration" (Griffiths, 1979, p. 50), is, in part, an extension of Barnard's (1938) conceptualization of administration (Campbell, Fleming, Newell, & Bennion, 1987) that assumes a cooperative (rational) organization in which uncooperativeness is pathological (Burrell & Morgan, 1979).

11. The same assumptions in the language of the general education and educational administration discourses are that: a) school failure is a (psychologically or sociologically) pathological condition that students have, b) differential diagnosis (identification by ability, need, and/or interest) is objective and useful, c) special programming (homogeneous grouping in general education tracks and segregated and pull-out classrooms in special, compensatory, gifted, and remedial education) is a rationally conceived and coordinated system of practices and programs that benefits diagnosed students, and d) progress in education (increases in academic achievement and efficiency) results from incremental technological improvements in differential diagnosis and intervention practices and programs (see Bridges, 1982; Cherryholmes, 1988; Erickson, 1979; McNeil, 1986; Oakes, 1985, 1986a,b; Sirotnik & Oakes, 1986; Spring, 1980).

12. Although I am emphasizing the institutional practice of special education here, we will see in subsequent sections that, from an organizational perspective, all practices that group or track students in general education (e.g., in-class ability grouping,

curriculum tracking), as well as the other institutional practices that remove students from the general program (e.g., compensatory, gifted, remedial education), are artifacts of functionalist assumptions about organizational rationality and human and social pathology.

13. Although the introductory discussion dichotomized the mainstreaming debate and the REI debate as if there were a period between them when the field was completely certain about the adequacy of mainstreaming and the EHA, it is more accurate to think of the field of special education as being in a more or less constant state of self-criticism since the early 1960s. Criticism subsided somewhat during the period shortly before and after the enactment of the EHA, but it did not disappear (see, e.g., Keogh & Levitt, 1976; MacMillan & Semmel, 1977; Reynolds, 1976; Reynolds & Birch, 1977). The field of educational administration (narrow sense) has been in a constant state of self-criticism since at least the early 1950s (Clark, 1985; Cunningham, Hack, & Nystrand, 1977; Griffiths, 1959, 1983, 1988; Halpin, 1970; Halpin & Hayes, 1977; Hayes & Pharis, 1967; Spring, 1980). Driven by the persistent anomaly of little or no substantive change or improvement in public education, the field of educational change or school improvement has been characterized by the same sort of self-criticism since the early 1960s (Elmore & McLaughlin, 1988; House, 1979; Lehming & Kane, 1981; note 36).

14. Hallahan, Kauffman, Lloyd, and McKinney (1988), key opponents of the REI, argue that the concept first appeared in Reynolds and Wang (1981), which, in revised form (Wang, Reynolds, & Walberg, 1985, 1986), subsequently received formal recognition from Madeleine C. Will (1985, 1986a,b), the Assistant Secretary for the Office of Special Education and Rehabilitative Services in the Reagan administration. This is an important connection because, in subsequent criticism of the REI, a major argument has been that it is "entirely consistent with Reagan-Bush policies aimed at decreasing federal support for education, including the education of vulnerable children and youth" (Kauffman, 1989a, p. 7). Although Wang (Wang & Walberg, 1988), a key proponent of the REI, agrees that Will (1986a) provided the original policy statement for the REI, she contends that the REI itself is grounded in empirical evidence on the inadequacies of the current system contained in Heller, Holtzman, and Messick (1982); Hobbs (1975, 1980); and Wang, Reynolds, and Walberg (1987a). Thus, the REI opponents tend to characterize the REI as a political outcome of conservative ideology, while the proponents characterize it as a logical outcome of empirical research. Nevertheless, it is perhaps more accurate to think of it as a logical outcome of Maynard Reynolds's liberal strategy of "progressive inclusion" (Reynolds & Rosen, 1976), the idea that the entire history of special education is or should be one of incremental progress toward more normalized instructional placements. In 1976, Reynolds, one of the architects of the "continuum of placements" model that underwrites mainstreaming (Reynolds, 1962; see also Deno, 1970) and a key REI proponent, rejected the pull-out logic of mainstreaming in favor of making "regular classrooms . . . more diverse educational environments, [thus reducing] the need to . . . use separate . . . educational environments" (Reynolds, 1976, p. 8). He proposed to do this "through the redistribution of resources and energies, through training, and, finally, through the redistribution of students" (1976, p. 18). Thus, although there probably is a moment of truth in both the REI proponents' and opponents' characterizations of the motivation behind the REI, Reynolds formulated the concept and started the debate before either the empirical data were available or the conservative ideology held much sway in Washington.

15. Besides Will's (1984, 1985, 1986a,b) statements on or related to the REI, and several attempts to place the REI in perspective (e.g., Davis, 1989; Davis & McCaul, 1988; Lieberman, 1984, 1988; Sapon-Shevin, 1988; Skrtic, 1987a,b, 1988b), the vast majority

of the literature promoting the REI has been produced by eight individuals working either alone or in teams of two (or, at times, with other colleagues). I will refer to them as REI proponents according to the following two-person teams: a) Maynard Reynolds and Margaret Wang (Reynolds, 1988; Reynolds & Wang, 1981, 1983; Reynolds, Wang, & Walberg, 1987; Walberg & Wang, 1987; Wang, 1981, 1988, 1989a,b; Wang & Reynolds, 1985, 1986; Wang, Reynolds, & Walberg, 1985, 1986, 1987a,b, 1988, 1989; Wang & Walberg, 1988); b) M. Stephen Lilly and Marleen Pugach (Lilly, 1986, 1987, 1989; Pugach & Lilly, 1984); c) Susan Stainback and William Stainback (Stainback & Stainback, 1984, 1985a,b, 1987a,b, 1989; Stainback, Stainback, Courtnage, & Jaben, 1985; Stainback, Stainback, & Forest, 1989); and d) Alan Gartner and Dorothy Kerzner Lipsky (Gartner, 1986; Gartner & Lipsky, 1987, 1989; Lipsky & Gartner, 1987, 1989a,b). The analysis of the REI proponents' arguments against the EHA and for their REI proposals is based on virtually all of the literature cited in a) through d) above, as well as some additional related work done by these authors and others, as noted.

16. In their criticism of the current system of special education, all four teams of REI proponents refer, more or less, to a common body of EHA implementation research, virtually all of which is reviewed or cited in Wang, Reynolds, and Walberg (1987a) and Gartner and Lipsky (1987). The 4.5 million figure represents an increase of about 20 percent in the number of students identified as handicapped since 1976–1977, much of which has resulted from increases in the number of students identified as learning disabled, a classification that currently represents over 43 percent of all students identified as handicapped and that, despite attempts to tighten eligibility criteria, has increased over 140 percent since 1977 (U.S. Department of Education, 1988; Gerber & Levine-Donnerstein, 1989). In addition to these three classifications, the mildly handicapped designation includes students with mild forms of speech and language problems and students with physical and sensory impairments that are not accompanied by other severely disabling conditions, such as severe mental retardation (Reynolds & Lakin, 1987). When these additional students are included in the count, estimates of the proportion of students considered mildly handicapped range from 75 percent to 90 percent of those students classified as handicapped in school (Algozzine & Korinek, 1985; Shepard, 1987; Wang, Reynolds, & Walberg, 1989).

17. The first published reactions to the REI (Lieberman, 1985; Mesinger, 1985) were decidedly negative, but focused exclusively on Stainback and Stainback (1984). These were followed by reactions from three subgroups within the field that, although sensitive to current problems and generally supportive of reform, merely called for more information (Teacher Education Division of the Council for Exceptional Children, 1986, 1987), proposed a mechanism for interpreting information and building a consensus (Skrtic, 1987b), or specified several preconditions of reform (Heller & Schilit, 1987). Neither these reactions nor those of others who have criticized the REI in part (e.g., Davis, 1989; Davis & McCaul, 1988; Lieberman, 1984, 1988; Sapon-Shevin, 1988; Skrtic, 1987a, 1988b) or in whole (e.g., Vergason & Anderegg, 1989) have had much impact on the course of events. The controversy over the REI began with the publication of a special issue of the *Journal of Learning Disabilities* (*JLD*) in 1988 and has been sustained by several other articles since then that have been written by some of the same authors. Together, the *JLD* articles and these other pieces include: a) Braaten, Kauffman, Braaten, Polsgrove, & Nelson (1988); b) Bryan, Bay, & Donahue (1988); c) Council for Children with Behavioral Disorders (1989); d) Gerber (1988a, 1988b); e) Hallahan, Kauffman, Lloyd, and McKinney (1988); f) Hallahan, Keller, McKinney, Lloyd and Bryan (1988); g) Kauffman (1988, 1989a,b); h) Kauffman, Gerber, and Semmel (1988); i) Keogh (1988); j) Lloyd, Crowley, Kohler, and Strain (1988); k) McKinney and Hocutt (1988); and l) Schumaker and Deshler

(1988). My analysis of the REI opponents' assessment of the adequacy of the current system of special education and their criticism of the REI proponents' proposals for reform is drawn from the literature cited in a) through j) above, as well as from some additional work done by these authors and others, as noted.

18. The controversial nature of the current debate and the degree to which it has divided the field is clear in some of the more recent encounters in the literature. In these pieces the REI advocates characterize the opponents as segregationists (Wang & Walberg, 1988) and compare the current system of special education to slavery (Stainback & Stainback, 1987b) and apartheid (Lipsky & Gartner, 1987), whereas the REI opponents characterize the proponents as politically naive liberals and the REI as the Reagan-Bush "trickle-down theory of education of the hard-to-teach" (Kauffman, 1989b, p. 256).

19. There is no argument over the fact that most disabilities in the severe to profound range are associated with observable patterns of biological symptoms or syndromes, and are thus comprehensible under the pathological model (Mercer, 1973). In any event, the issue relative to these students, as in the case of the students identified as mildly handicapped, is whether they are being served adequately and ethically under the current system (see note 25). In most cases, students classified as mildly handicapped, and particularly those classified as learning disabled, emotionally disturbed, and mildly mentally retarded, do not show biological signs of pathology (Algozzine, 1976, 1977; Apter, 1982; Hobbs, 1975; Mercer, 1973; Rhodes, 1970; Rist & Harrell, 1982; Ross, 1980; Schrag & Divorky, 1975; Skrtic, 1988b; Swap, 1978).

It should be clear that the participants in the REI debate are not speaking explicitly to the four assumptions (see note 10). Indeed, that is the problem with the debate, as noted. Thus, from this point on in the article (including endnotes), I will at times omit the qualifiers "implicit" and "explicit" when discussing the implications of REI proponents' and opponents' arguments for the four grounding assumptions, particularly when including them is cumbersome, as it is in this section because the discussion includes two other levels of implicitness. First, there is the nature of agreement (implicit or explicit) between the REI proponents' and opponents' assessments of current practices, a level I will retain in text. Second, there is the nature of the unquestioned presuppositions that ground the field (explicit in the professional knowledge tradition or an implicit social norm) (see note 10), which I will not retain in text. So, when I say that the REI proponents or opponents "reject" or "retain" an assumption or presupposition, it should be understood that they do so implicitly. The same will hold true (relative to the four assumptions) for the arguments of the participants in the effective schools and school restructuring debates in general education, which will be addressed in subsequent sections (see notes 8 and 56). In all cases where it seems necessary for clarity, however, I will use the qualifiers in the text or in a note.

20. A further argument of the REI proponents relative to the nonadaptability of the general education system is that the existence of the special education system is a barrier to the development of a responsive capacity within general education, both in public schools and in teacher education (Lilly, 1986, 1989; Pugach, 1988; Pugach & Lilly, 1984; Reynolds, 1988). This assertion relative to public schools is addressed extensively in subsequent sections from an organizational perspective (see also Skrtic & Ware, in press). For my position on this assertion relative to teacher education, see Thousand (1990).

On the related matter of the attribution of student failure, both the REI opponents and proponents agree that an exclusively student-deficit orientation is inappropriate. Although some of the REI opponents argue that the proponents lean too far toward an exclusively teacher-deficit orientation (Kauffman, Gerber, & Semmel, 1988; Keogh,

1988), the REI proponents clearly recognize the responsibility of the student in the learning process (Gartner, 1986; Walberg & Wang, 1987; Wang, 1989b).

21. The only REI opponent who makes a case for the potential instructional relevance of differential diagnosis considers it to be an empirical question that, if answered in the negative, should signal the discontinuance of the practice of differential diagnosis and the categorical approach to special education (Keogh, 1988). Although Bryan, Bay, and Donahue (1988, p. 25) do not make an explicit argument for the instructional relevance of differential diagnosis, by arguing that "one cannot assume that any two learning disabled children would be any more similar than a learning disabled child and a normally achieving child, or a normally achieving child and an underachieving child" they actually make an implicit argument against the instructional utility of differential diagnosis and thus implicitly agree with the REI proponents' position that all students have unique learning needs and interests, even those within the traditional mild disability categories.

22. Although there is general agreement among the REI opponents that the instructional effectiveness of special education interventions has not been demonstrated, two arguments are put forth in favor of instruction delivered in special education settings. The first one is that teachers in general education are unable to meet the diverse needs of students with learning disabilities in their classrooms (Bryan, Bay, & Donahue, 1988). The second argument rests on the speculation that more powerful instructional techniques might be more easily implemented in special education settings than in regular classrooms (Hallahan, Keller, McKinney, Lloyd, & Bryan, 1988; see also Hallahan & Keller, 1986).

23. The argument that the current system is politically rational cannot be divorced from the argument that progress is rational-technical because, although targeting students for services that are instructionally ineffective at present but will be rendered effective in the future may be politically justifiable, targeting them for ineffective services that will not be rendered effective in the future is not justifiable, politically or ethically (see note 33).

    As for the question of whether special education is a rationally coordinated system of services, the REI proponents argue that it is coordinated with neither the general education system nor with the other special needs programs. They characterize the entire special needs enterprise, including the special education system, in terms of disjointed incrementalism — a collection of disjointed programs, each with its own clients, personnel, administrators, budget, and regulations, which have been added to schools incrementally over time (Reynolds & Birch, 1977; Reynolds & Wang, 1983; Reynolds, Wang, & Walberg, 1987; Wang, Reynolds, & Walberg, 1985, 1986). Although the REI opponents are generally silent on the issue of coordination, Kauffman, Gerber, and Semmel (1988) respond by linking it to their argument for the political rationality of the current system. Although they recognize the lack of coordination, they consider it to be an unavoidable consequence of the politically rational targeting function of the EHA, a function that is fundamental to the very notion of categorical programs.

24. Although she has been a major figure in the REI debate, Will (1985, 1986a, 1986b) has not offered a specific proposal as such (see notes 14, 15, 27, and 28).

25. This issue actually separates the four teams of REI advocates into two camps. The Gartner and Lipsky and Stainback and Stainback teams have distanced themselves from the other two teams and from the REI itself, noting that, while it has resulted in some positive momentum for reform, ultimately it is merely "blending at the margin" (Lipsky & Gartner, 1989a, p. 271) because it maintains two separate systems. For Stainback and Stainback (1989, p. 43), the REI concept is too restrictive because it "does not address the need to include in regular classrooms and regular education

those students labeled severely and profoundly handicapped" (see also notes 19 and 27).

26. The Lilly and Pugach proposal excludes students classified as mildly handicapped who have "developmental learning disabilities" (Pugach & Lilly, 1984, p. 53), that is, learning disabilities that are presumed to be pathological (Kirk & Chalfant, 1983).

27. Reynolds and Wang reserve the option of separate settings because they believe that "surely there will be occasions to remove some students for instruction in special settings" (Wang, Reynolds, & Walberg, 1985, p. 13). Will's (1986a) position in this regard is similar to those of Lilly and Pugach and Reynolds and Wang, in that her version of a restructured system continues to rely on separate instructional settings for some students, a position that has been criticized by Stainback and Stainback (1987b) and Gartner and Lipsky (1987, p. 385) as perpetuating "a dual system approach for a smaller (more severely impaired) population."

28. Each team of REI proponents, as well as Will (1986a,b), takes a unique stance on this point, both in terms of the degree to which general and special education should be merged and the level or levels of the institution of public education at which merger should take place. Although neither Will nor any of the four teams of proponents speaks to each of the following levels, taken together they address changes at or have implications for: a) the U.S. Department of Education, b) research and development centers, c) teacher education programs, d) local education agencies, e) school buildings, and f) classrooms. Although she is somewhat contradictory on the matter (see Gartner & Lipsky, 1987; Stainback & Stainback, 1987b; note 27), Will (1986a, p. 415) calls for "enhanced component parts," better cooperation, and shared responsibility between the two systems at all levels, particularly at levels a) and e); she does not, however, call for outright merger of the two systems at any level. In the analysis of these proposals in text, the notion of merger is addressed at the building and classroom levels only (see notes 29 and 30).

29. Above the regular classroom teachers and generic specialists, Reynolds and Wang (1983) propose a merger of district-level consultants who would provide the classroom teachers and generic specialists with consultation and training on generic topics (Wang, Reynolds, & Walberg, 1985).

30. In addition to merging special and remedial education at the building level, the Lilly and Pugach plan (Pugach & Lilly, 1984, p. 54) proposes a merger at the level of teacher education. Their plan would merge "what is now special education for the mildly handicapped [in departments of special education] with what are currently departments of elementary and secondary education or curriculum and instruction" (p. 53) for the purpose of "providing instruction of the highest quality . . . for advanced preparation of support services specialists at the graduate level" (p. 54), as well as undergraduate instruction for persons in preparation for the role of regular classroom teacher.

31. Other than the recommended use of more powerful instructional technologies — such as cooperative learning, curriculum-based assessment, and peer tutoring (Lloyd, Crowley, Kohler, & Strain, 1988; Thousand & Villa, 1988, 1989) — and professional problem-solving mechanisms — such as teacher assistance teams (Chalfant, Pysh, & Moultrie, 1979) and collaborative consultation (e.g., Pugach, 1988) — the primary difference at the classroom level is that students who would have been removed under the current system remain in the classroom on a full-time basis where they, their teachers, and any other students who need assistance are provided with in-class support services.

32. Drawing on the work of Edmonds (1979), Gilhool (1976, 1989), Allington and McGill-Franzen (1989), and Lezotte (1989), Gartner and Lipsky argue that a) all students, including those with special needs, can learn effectively from the same peda-

gogy; b) this generic pedagogy is known and available in the principles and practices contained in the effective schools research; and c) these principles and practices are replicable through school improvement programs. Ironically, although they argue that effective education for students labeled as handicapped is a matter of will and commitment on the part of teachers and schools, Gartner and Lipsky call for reformulating the EHA into a new mandate "that requires a unitary system [that] is 'special' for all students." That is, they call for transforming the EHA into "an effective schools act for all students" (1989a, p. 282).

33. The explicit historical and political arguments against the possibility of change presented in Council for Children with Behavioral Disorders (1989), Kauffman (1988), and Kauffman, Gerber, and Semmel (1988) contradict the implicit arguments for the possibility of incremental change through research and development presented in Braaten, Kauffman, Braaten, Polsgrove, and Nelson (1988); Bryan, Bay, and Donahue (1988); Council for Children with Behavioral Disorders (1989); Hallahan, Keller, McKinney, Lloyd, and Bryan (1988); Kauffman (1988); Kauffman, Gerber, and Semmel (1988); Keogh (1988); and Lloyd, Crowley, Kohler, and Strain (1988). It is obvious, of course, that by contradicting their position on the possibility of rational-technical change, the REI opponents reverse their position on the fourth assumption. However, this also reverses their position on the third assumption because, on political and ethical grounds, their position on the third and fourth assumptions cannot be separated (see note 23).

34. There was an attempt in the mid-1950s to ground educational administration (narrow sense) in the theoretical discourse of the social sciences (Griffiths, 1959; Hayes & Pharis, 1967), but it failed (Cunningham, Hack, & Nystrand, 1977; Halpin, 1970; Halpin & Hayes, 1977). As a result, the field continues to be grounded in the prescriptive discourse of scientific management (Clark, 1985; Griffiths, 1983; Spring, 1980). Although this orientation has been criticized by persons in the field (e.g., Clark, 1985) and others (e.g., Spring, 1980), and arguments from within the field for a critical orientation have emerged (e.g., Bates, 1980, 1987; Foster, 1986), the field continues to be dominated by the prescriptive discourse of scientific management and by functionalist conceptualizations of organization, administration, and inquiry (Clark, 1985; Griffiths, 1988; Lincoln, 1985).

35. These modes of theorizing can be understood in terms of two dimensions of metatheoretical assumptions: a) an objectivism-subjectivism dimension that corresponds to various presuppositions about the nature of science, and b) a microscopic-macroscopic dimension that reflects various presuppositions about the nature of society. Counterposing the two dimensions forms four modes of theorizing or paradigms of social scientific thought: a) functionalism (micro-objectivist), the dominant mode in the West; b) interpretivism (micro-subjectivist); c) structuralism (macro-objectivist); and d) humanism (macro-subjectivist) (Burrell & Morgan, 1979; Ritzer, 1980, 1983). Each paradigm represents a unique way to understand the social world, including organization and change (Burrell & Morgan, 1979; Morgan, 1983). In terms of the theoretical discourse in the field of organization analysis, the objectivism-subjectivism dimension corresponds to assumptions about the nature of action in organizations, ranging from the objectivist notion of rational action to the subjectivist notion of nonrational action. The microscopic-macroscopic dimension corresponds to assumptions about the level at which organizational activity is most appropriately analyzed, ranging from theories that emphasize organizing processes at the micro-level of individuals and small groups to those that emphasize organization structure at the macro-level of total organizations (Pfeffer, 1982; Scott, 1981).

36. One major development has been a series of paradigm shifts. Referring to the four paradigm matrix in note 35, the three shifts include: a) one in the 1960s from the

micro-objectivist to the macro-objectivist paradigm, b) one in the 1970s at the micro-scopic level of analysis from the micro-objectivist to the micro-subjectivist paradigm, and c) one in the 1980s at the macroscopic level of analysis from the macro-objectivist to the macro-subjectivist paradigm (Burrell & Morgan, 1979; Pfeffer, 1982; Scott, 1981). A related development has been the emergence of several theories that implic-itly or explicitly bridge paradigms (see Skrtic, 1988b, 1991), each of which facilitates the integration of theoretical insights from two or more paradigms (see note 38). Although educational administration (narrow sense) continues to be dominated by the rational-technical perspective on organization and change, there has been a shift in the field of educational change from the rational-technical to the nonrational-cul-tural perspective on change (House, 1979). This shift has been driven by three decades of uncertainty surrounding the apparent inability to actually bring about meaningful change in school organizations (Boyd & Crowson, 1981; Cuban, 1989; Elmore & McLaughlin, 1988; Lehming & Kane, 1981; Wise, 1988). As a result, the nonrational-cultural perspective increasingly has become the favored outlook on change (e.g., Goodlad, 1975; House, 1979; Sarason, 1971/1982; Sirotnik & Oakes, 1986; notes 37 and 38).

37. In the interest of space, I conduct my deconstruction of the discourse on school organization and adaptability in the field of educational administration indirectly. That is, I spend most of the available space in this section on the antifoundational interpretation of school organization and adaptability that I will use in subsequent sections to deconstruct the institutional practice of special education, the discourse on school failure, and the institution of public education. Nevertheless, virtually everything that is presented in this section and the ones to follow can be read as a deconstruction of the discourse on school organization and adaptability in the field of educational administration because it delegitimizes the presupposition of organi-zational rationality, the explicit grounding of the field of educational administration. For a more direct deconstruction of the discourse on school organization and adapt-ability in the field of educational administration, see Skrtic (1988b, 1991). For addi-tional critical analyses that can be read as deconstructions, see Bates (1980, 1987), Foster (1986), House (1979), and Sirotnik and Oakes (1986).

38. The structural and cultural frames of reference do not correspond to the rational-technical and nonrational-cultural perspectives (see notes 35 and 36). Indeed, the particular combination of theories in each frame of reference was selected to avoid this dichotomy, as well as those between objectivism-subjectivism and microscopic-macroscopic. This is the sense in which the present analysis is antifoundational and dialogical. Such an analysis gives a voice to a variety of perspectives, while recognizing that none of the perspectives, including its own, are "true" in a foundational sense (see Skrtic, 1988b, 1991, in press).

39. Throughout this section all of the material relative to configuration theory (e.g., nature of work, division of labor, coordination of work, interdependency or coupling among workers) is drawn from Mintzberg (1979) and Miller and Mintzberg (1983), except where noted otherwise. All of the material relative to institutionalization theory (e.g., material and normative structures, decoupled structures and subunits, and myth, symbol, and ceremony) is drawn from Meyer and Rowan (1977, 1978) and Meyer and Scott (1983), except where noted otherwise.

Within both the structural and the cultural frames of reference I treat each theory and the images of organization and change that emerge from them (and from combining them) as ideal types (see note 5), as exaggerated mental constructs for analyzing traditional school organization in terms of its value orientation. My aim in this section of the paper is to combine these ideal types to form two larger ideal types — one structural and one cultural. In subsequent sections I combine the structural and cultural ideal types into a larger ideal type and use it to carry out my deconstruction and reconstruction of public education.

40. The process of organizational change from this perspective is similar to a Kuhnian (1970) paradigm shift: long periods of stability that are maintained by the self-reinforcing nature of the organization's current paradigm (what Kuhn would call the long period of normal science) and occasional periods of change in which unreconcilable anomalies eventually destroy the prevailing paradigm (what Kuhn would call revolutionary science and the shift to a new paradigm).

41. Other than a few citations that clarify and extend my theoretical arguments on organization and change, virtually all of the citations in this section refer to empirical and interpretive evidence that supports the theoretical claims made in text.

42. For empirical evidence that teachers rarely view their instructional practices as a potential source of the problem in special education referrals, and that the special education referral and classification process is oriented to place the blame for failure on the student rather than on the standard programs in use, see Bennett and Rogosta (1984), Sarason and Doris (1979), White and Calhoun (1987), and Ysseldyke, Thurlow, Graden, Wesson, Algozzine, and Deno (1983).

43. For historical evidence on the conditions under which the special classroom emerged, see Lazerson (1983) and Sarason and Doris (1979). For empirical evidence on the disjunction between the special classroom and the rest of the school enterprise, see Deno (1970), Dunn (1968), Johnson (1962), and Reynolds (1962). See Chandler and Plakos (1969), MacMillan (1971), Wright (1967), and Mercer (1973) for empirical evidence on the overrepresentation of students from minority groups in segregated special classrooms after *Brown v. Board of Education* (1954), which, of course, is another example of the use of the special classroom to protect legitimacy. Indeed, the organizational isolation of the special classroom and the overrepresentation of students from minority groups in these classrooms were two of the major arguments for the EHA (Christophos & Renz, 1969; Deno, 1970; Dunn, 1968; Johnson, 1962). From an organizational perspective, the problem of over-representation of students from minority groups in special education classrooms and programs, both before (e.g., Christophos & Renz, 1969; Dunn, 1968) and after the EHA (e.g., Heller, Holtzman, & Messick, 1982), can be understood as school organizations using an existing decoupled subunit to maintain legitimacy in the face of failing to meet the needs of disproportionate numbers of these students in regular classrooms.

44. In organizational terms, although special education is a nonrational system, it is a politically rational system in two opposite senses: it protects students from the nonadaptability of school organizations, in the REI opponents' sense; and it protects school organizations from the uncertainty of student diversity, in the sense developed here. I will return to these ideas, and particularly to the moment of truth in the REI opponents' political justification for special education, in subsequent sections.

45. Recognition of the adhocratic configuration, or what were called "organic" organizations, occurred in the 1960s (Pugh, Hickson, Hinnings, MacDonald, Turner, & Lupton, 1963). Because these organizations operated in dynamic, uncertain environments, where innovation and adaptation were necessary for survival, they configured themselves as the inverse of the bureaucratic form (Burns & Stalker, 1966; Woodward, 1965). Mintzberg (1979) called them adhocracies following Toffler (1970), who popularized the term in *Future Shock*.

46. Although I will not pursue the issue of accountability in any great depth here, the mode of accountability that emerges in the adhocracy represents an alternative to the two extreme positions on accountability that have shaped the current debate on school restructuring, what Timar and Kirp (1988, p. 130) called the "romantic decentralist" (i.e., professional) and the "hyperrationalist" (i.e., bureaucratic) modes of

accountability (see also Murphy, 1989; Timar & Kirp, 1989), as well as Conley's (1990, p. 317) middle ground "constrained decisionmaker" position. Modes of accountability are shaped by the logic of the division of labor, means of coordination, and form of interdependency in organizations. There is no way out of the professional-bureaucratic dilemma as long as schools are configured as professional bureaucracies. The constrained decisionmaker position merely tries to strike a balance between the two extremes while leaving the current configuration of schools intact. The key to accountability in the adhocracy is that it avoids all three positions by assigning responsibility to groups of professionals, thus politicizing discretion within a discourse among professionals and client constituencies. For a somewhat more extended treatment of this topic, see Kiel and Skrtic (1988) and Skrtic (1991); see also note 58.

47. The EHA is completely consistent with the third and fourth assumptions; it is a rational-technical mechanism for change that assumes that schools are machine bureaucracies — that is, organizations in which worker behavior is controlled by procedural rules and thus subject to modification through revision and extension of formalization and supervision (see Elmore & McLaughlin, 1982). Its requirements for classification, parent participation, individualized educational plans, and least restrictive environment placements are perceived to be new technologies for diagnosis and intervention. Moreover, its requirement for a comprehensive system of personnel development, what Gilhool (1989, p. 247) called "probably the most important provision of the act," assumes that "there [are] known procedures for effectively educating disabled children," and that the problem is simply that "the knowledge of how to do so [is] not widely distributed." This, of course, assumes the possibility of rational-technical change through dissemination of practices and training (see notes 35 and 36).

48. For empirical and interpretive evidence on the degree to which the EHA has resulted in an increase in political clashes, a decrease in collaboration, and an increase in the number of students identified as handicapped, see note 15 and Bogdan (1983); Lortie (1978); Martin (1978); Patrick and Reschly (1982); Singer and Butler (1987); Skrtic, Guba, and Knowlton (1985); and Weatherley (1979). For empirical and interpretive evidence that the EHA's adhocratic goal of personalized instruction contradicts its bureaucratic means of uniform procedures, see Singer and Butler (1987); Skrtic, Guba, and Knowlton (1985); and Wright, Cooperstein, Renneker, and Padilla (1982). For empirical and interpretive evidence that special education has itself conformed to the two-structure, machine-professional bureaucracy configuration to deal with this contradiction, see Singer and Butler (1987); Skrtic, Guba, and Knowlton (1985); and Weatherley (1979). As Singer and Butler noted, the EHA "has created a *dual* locus of organizational control," an arrangement in which information necessary for "legal or monitoring purposes, quick-turnaround defense of special education priorities . . . or public relations in the wider community" are managed centrally in the office of the special education director; whereas instructional decisions "have become or have remained more decentralized" in the hands of professionals (p. 139).

49. On the rational-technical nature of the excellence movement (note 56), see Bacharach (1990), Cuban (1983), Meier (1984), Resnick and Resnick (1985), and Wise (1988). For example, Wise (1988, p. 329) characterized it generally as "state control, with its emphasis on producing standardized results through regulated teaching." See Cuban (1989) on the relationship among school reform, the at-risk category, and the graded school, "the core processes" of which are "labeling, segregating, and eliminating those who do not fit" (p. 784). The graded school, of course, is the traditional school organization, that is, the actual case of the idealized professional bureaucracy configuration presented here.

50. The degree of decoupling, as well as the availability of the requisite personnel, depends in large measure on the local history of special education services, which reflects the value orientation embedded in political cultures at the state, local, and school organization levels. For empirical and interpretive evidence on this point see McDonnell and McLaughlin (1982); Skrtic, Guba, and Knowlton (1985); Noel and Fuller (1985); and Biklen (1985). Although there are exceptions (Biklen, 1985; Thousand, Fox, Reid, Godek, & Williams, 1986), students classified as having severe and profound disabilities and the professionals who serve them continue to be located in segregated classrooms, a matter of great concern in the work of Stainback and Stainback (see note 15) and others (e.g., Biklen, 1985; Thousand, Fox, Reid, Godek, & Williams, 1986). When these classrooms are located in regular school buildings, they follow the organizational form of the traditional decoupled subunit, which historically has existed as an adhocratic space outside the bureaucratic configuration of general education. The needs of the students in these programs typically are so variable that the notion of a standard program is virtually precluded. Moreover, the complexity of the diagnostic and instructional problems is so great that interdisciplinary collaboration is essential. Given the extreme ambiguity and complexity of the work in these programs, the fact that they are decoupled from the machine bureaucracy structure, and the degree to which collaboration, mutual adjustment, and discursive coupling characterize the work (see Sailor & Guess, 1983), these programs are prototypical of the adhocratic form in public education. See Skrtic (1991) for an extended discussion of this point.

51. Although regular classroom placement to the maximum extent possible is required for these students under the EHA, they are identified as handicapped because they cannot be accommodated within existing standard programs in particular regular classrooms (Skrtic, Guba, & Knowlton, 1985; Walker, 1987). As such, depending on the degree to which the particular school is more adhocratically or bureaucratically oriented, mainstreaming for these students more or less represents symbolic integration, primarily in nonacademic classrooms and activities. For empirical and interpretive evidence on this point, see Biklen (1985); Carlberg and Kavale (1980); Skrtic, Guba, and Knowlton (1985); and Wright, Cooperstein, Renneker, and Padilla (1982).

52. In principle, teachers working collaboratively in the interest of a single student for whom they share responsibility violates the logic of loose coupling and the sensibility of the professional culture (Bidwell, 1965; Mintzberg, 1979; Weick, 1976) and thus, in principle, collaboration should not be expected to any meaningful degree in professional bureaucracies. At a minimum, mainstreaming and the resource room model require reciprocal coupling (Thompson, 1967), which is not the type of interdependency that specialization and professionalization yield. For empirical evidence that collaboration among regular teachers and between regular and special education teachers is rare, fleeting, and idiosyncratic in the professional bureaucracy, see Bishop (1977); Lortie (1975, 1978); Skrtic, Guba, and Knowlton (1985); Tye and Tye (1984); and notes 48 and 53.

53. Although the adhocratic ends of the EHA are distorted because of the bureaucratic nature of the law and its implementation context, schools appear to be complying with its procedural requirements because of the adoption of practices that, although they may be well-intended and in some respects may actually result in positive outcomes, serve largely to symbolize (e.g., IEPs and resource rooms) and ceremonialize (e.g., IEP staffings and mainstreaming) compliance with the letter of the law rather than conformance with its spirit. For empirical evidence on the symbolic and ceremonial nature of the IEP document and staffing process, resource room programs, and mainstreaming, see Carlberg and Kavale (1980); Gerardi, Grohe, Benedict, and Coolidge (1984); Schenck (1980); Schenk and Levy (1979); Ysseldyke, Thurlow,

Graden, Wesson, Algozzine, and Deno (1983); and notes 51 and 48. Moreover, from a policy perspective, symbolic compliance with procedural requirements can lead monitors and implementation researchers to faulty conclusions. For example, Singer and Butler (1987, p. 151) observed that "federal demands have equilibrated rapidly with local capacity to respond," and thus concluded that the EHA demonstrates that "a federal initiative *can* result in significant social reform at the local level." Although they are correct in asserting that such equilibration has resulted in "a basically workable system" (p. 151), they fail to recognize that equilibrium is largely a process of institutionalizing the necessary symbols and ceremonies of compliance (Rowan, 1980; Zucker, 1977, 1981), which, given the contradiction between their bureaucratic orientation and the EHA's adhocratic ends, renders the system workable for school organizations but not necessarily for the intended beneficiaries of the federal initiative.

54. Citations for the proposals of the four teams of REI proponents have been omitted in this section. The proposals analyzed here are those described in the section "Special Education as a Professional Practice" and its corresponding notes. The same format is followed in the remainder of the article for references to the REI proponents' and opponents' arguments for and against the REI and the current system of special education, as well as for the REI proponents' reform proposals.

55. For empirical evidence that the excellence movement has resulted largely in extensions of rationalization and formalization, see Clark and Astuto (1988), Timar and Kirp (1988), and note 49. For empirical evidence that the excellence movement, in general, and the effective schools movement (see note 56), in particular, have increased ritualization and professionalization and decreased personalization, see Cuban (1983, 1989), Slavin (1989), Stedman (1987), and Wise (1988). For example, Cuban noted that, under the effective schools formula, curriculum and instruction in many schools have become more standardized and thus less personalized. The problem is that advocates of effective schools, although well meaning, "seldom [question] the core structures of the graded schools within which they [work]. Their passion was (and is) for making those structures more efficient" (Cuban, 1989, p. 784).

56. By the "effective schools" debate I mean the earlier phase of the excellence movement, which was shaped by the thinking in *A Nation at Risk* (National Commission on Excellence in Education, 1983) and generally seeks excellence through means that are quantitative and top-down: quantitative in that they simply call for more of the existing school practices; top-down in that their bureaucratic value orientation turns the goal of higher standards into more standardization for producing standardized results (e.g., Wise, 1988; notes 49 and 55). The proponents of this approach do not question traditional school organization, they simply want to make it more efficient (e.g., Cuban, 1989; notes 49 and 55). By the "school restructuring" debate I mean the more recent phase of the excellence movement, which was shaped by the thinking in books like *High School* (Boyer, 1983), *A Place Called School* (Goodlad, 1984), and *Horace's Compromise* (Sizer, 1984). The participants in this debate (see, e.g., Bacharach, 1990; Clark, Lotto, & Astuto, 1984; Cuban, 1983, 1989; Elmore, 1987; Elmore & McLaughlin, 1988; Lieberman & Miller, 1984; McNeil, 1986; Oakes, 1985; Sergiovanni & Moore, 1989; Sirotnik & Oakes, 1986; Wise, 1988) generally seek excellence through means that are qualitative and bottom-up: qualitative in that they call for fundamental changes in the structure of school organizations; bottom-up in that they call for an increase in professional discretion, adult-adult collaboration, and personalization of instruction.

57. Although tracking as such is criticized, neither students labeled handicapped nor special education as an institutional practice receive much attention in the restruc-

turing debate or the effective schools debate (Lilly, 1987; Pugach & Sapon-Shevin, 1987; Shepard, 1987).

58. The best articulation of this position within the restructuring debate is Schön's (1983, 1987, 1988, 1989) argument for developing reflective practitioners by eliminating the "normal bureaucratic emphasis on technical rationality" (Schön, 1983, p. 338) in schools and thus permitting teachers to become "builders of repertoire rather than accumulators of procedures and methods" (1988, p. 26). Although Schön clearly recognized that the reflective practitioner requires a reflective organization (Schön, 1983, 1988), he conceptualized the reflective practitioner as an individual professional engaged in a monological discourse with a problem situation, rather than a team of professionals engaged reflectively in a dialogical discourse with one another. As such, Schön retains the structural contingencies of specialization and professionalization and thus the professional bureaucracy configuration. For a deconstruction of Schön's notion of the reflective practitioner, see Skrtic (1991).

Beyond the problem of innovation, eliminating rationalization and formalization while retaining specialization and professionalization creates a professional mode of accountability, which places virtually all decisions about the adequacy of practice in the hands of individual professionals. From an organizational perspective, this is a problem in a structural sense because the convergent thinking and deductive reasoning of professionals and professions means that they tend to see the needs of their clients in terms of the skills they have to offer them (Mintzberg, 1979; Perrow, 1970; Segal, 1974). In a cultural sense, professionals and professions tend to distort negative information about their paradigms to make it consistent with their prevailing paradigms of practice (see, e.g., Brown, 1978; Rounds, 1979, 1981; Weatherley & Lipsky, 1977; Weick, 1985; see also note 46).

59. For genealogies (note 9) of special education's professional knowledge, practice, and value orientation, see Skrtic (1986, 1988a, 1991). For histories of special education see, for example, Lazerson (1983), and Sarason and Doris (1979).

60. For evidence on the ethics and efficacy of special education practices before the EHA, see note 43. For evidence on these practices after the EHA, see notes 15, 17, 48, 51, and 53.

61. See Cherryholmes (1988) for a discussion of critical pragmatism (note 4) as a mode of professional practice and discourse in public education. See Skrtic (1991) for a discussion of it as a means of developing and sustaining an adhocratic professional culture. Critical practice is "continual movement between construction of a practice . . . and deconstruction of that practice, which shows its incompleteness and contradictions. . . . Critical discourse is continual movement between the constitution of a methodology designed to [construct, deconstruct, and reconstruct practices] and subsequent criticism of that approach" (Cherryholmes, 1988, pp. 96–97). The goal of critical pragmatism is education or self-formation (Gadamer, 1975), a pedagogical process of remaking ourselves as we think, write, read, and talk more about our practices and discourses.

62. For the negative evidence on educational excellence, equity, and adaptability see, for example, Cuban (1979), Edgar (1987), Elmore and McLaughlin (1988), Goodlad (1984), Lehming and Kane (1981), McNeil (1986), Oakes (1985), Sizer (1984), and note 15. For empirical and interpretive evidence that some schools are more effective, equitable, and adaptable than others, as well as discussions of contributing factors, see Berman and McLaughlin (1974–1978); Brophy (1983); Clark, Lotto, and Astuto (1984); Goodlad (1975); Lieberman and Miller (1984); McNeil (1986); and note 63. For the same type of evidence and discussions relative to the EHA and mainstreaming, see Biklen (1985); Skrtic, Guba, and Knowlton (1985); Thousand, Fox, Reid, Godek,

and Williams (1986); Wright, Cooperstein, Renneker, and Padilla (1982); and note 63.

63. For empirical and interpretive evidence on the place of human agency in successful schools, see Biklen (1985); Brophy (1983); Clark, Lotto, and Astuto (1984); Lieberman and Miller (1984); McNeil (1986); Singer and Butler (1987); Skrtic, Guba, and Knowlton (1985); and Thousand, Fox, Reid, Godek, and Williams (1986).

References

Abeson, A., & Zettel, J. (1977). The end of the quiet revolution: The Education for All Handicapped Children Act of 1975. *Exceptional Children, 44*(2), 115–128.

Algozzine, B. (1976). The disturbing child: What you see is what you get? *Alberta Journal of Education Research, 22,* 330–333.

Algozzine, B. (1977). The emotionally disturbed child: Disturbed or disturbing? *Journal of Abnormal Child Psychology, 5*(2), 205–211.

Algozzine B., & Korinek, L. (1985). Where is special education for students with high prevalence handicaps going? *Exceptional Children, 51*(5), 388–394.

Allington, R. L., & McGill-Franzen, A. (1989). Different programs: Indifferent instruction. In D. K. Lipsky & A. Gartner (Eds.), *Beyond separate education: Quality education for all* (pp. 75–97). Baltimore, MD: Paul H. Brookes.

Antonio, R. J. (1981). Immanent critique as the core of critical theory: Its origins and developments in Hegel, Marx, and contemporary thought. *British Journal of Sociology, 32*(3), 330–345.

Antonio, R. J. (1989). The normative foundations of emancipatory theory: Evolutionary versus pragmatic perspectives. *American Journal of Sociology, 94*(4), 721–748.

Apter, S. J. (1982). *Troubled children, troubled systems.* New York: Pergamon Press.

Bacharach, S. B. (Ed.). (1990). *Education reform: Making sense of it all.* Boston: Allyn & Bacon.

Barnard, C. I. (1938). *Functions of the executive.* Cambridge, MA: Harvard University Press.

Barnes, B. (1982). *T. S. Kuhn and social science.* New York: Columbia University Press.

Bates, R. J. (1980). Educational administration, the sociology of science, and the management of knowledge. *Educational Administration Quarterly, 16*(2), 1–20.

Bates, R. J. (1987). Corporate culture, schooling, and educational administration. *Educational Administration Quarterly, 23*(4), 79–115.

Bennett, R. E., & Ragosta, M. (1984). *A research context for studying admissions tests and handicapped populations.* Princeton, NJ: Educational Testing Service.

Berger, P. L., & Luckmann, T. (1967). *The social construction of reality.* New York: Doubleday.

Berman, P., & McLaughlin, M. W. (1974–1978). *Federal programs supporting educational change* (Vols. 1–8). Santa Monica, CA: Rand Corporation.

Bernstein, R. J. (1976). *The restructuring of social and political theory.* Philadelphia: University of Pennsylvania Press.

Bernstein, R. J. (1983). *Beyond objectivism and relativism: Science, hermeneutics, and praxis.* Philadelphia: University of Pennsylvania Press.

Bidwell, C. E. (1965). The school as formal organization. In J. G. March (Ed.), *Handbook of organizations* (pp. 972–1022). Chicago: Rand McNally College Publishing.

Biklen, D. (1985). *Achieving the complete school: Strategies for effective mainstreaming.* New York: Columbia University Press.

Bishop, J. M. (1977). Organizational influences on the work orientations of elementary teachers. *Sociology of Work and Occupation, 4,* 171–208.

Bogdan, R. (1983). Does mainstreaming work? is a silly question. *Phi Delta Kappan, 64,* 425–434.

Bogdan, R., & Knoll, J. (1988). The sociology of disability. In E. L. Meyen & T. M. Skrtic (Eds.), *Exceptional children and youth: An introduction* (pp. 449–477). Denver: Love Publishing.

Bogdan, R., & Kugelmass, J. (1984). Case studies of mainstreaming: A symbolic interactionist approach to special schooling. In L. Barton & S. Tomlinson (Eds.), *Special education and social interests* (pp. 173–191). New York: Nichols.

Bowles, S., & Gintis, H. (1976). *Schooling in capitalist America.* New York: Basic Books.

Boyd, W. L., & Crowson, R. L. (1981). The changing conception and practice of public school administration. In D. C. Berliner (Ed.), *Review of research in education* (pp. 311–373). Itasca, IL: F. E. Peacock.

Boyer, E. L. (1983). *High school.* New York: Harper & Row.

Braaten, S. R., Kauffman, J. M., Braaten, B., Polsgrove, L., & Nelson, C. M. (1988). The regular education initiative: Patent medicine for behavioral disorders. *Exceptional Children, 55*(1), 21–27.

Bridges, E. M. (1982). Research on the school administrator: The state of the art, 1967–1980. *Educational Administration Quarterly, 18*(3), 12–33.

Brophy, J. E. (1983). Research in the self-fulfilling prophesy and teacher expectations. *Journal of Educational Psychology, 75*(5), 631–661.

Brown v. Board of Education (1954). 347 U.S. 483, 74 S.Ct. 686, 98 L.Ed. 873.

Brown, R. H. (1978). Bureaucracy as praxis: Toward a political phenomenology of formal organizations. *Administrative Science Quarterly, 23*(2), 365–382.

Bryan, T., Bay, M., & Donahue, M. (1988). Implications of the learning disabilities definition for the regular education initiative. *Journal of Learning Disabilities, 21*(1), 23–28.

Burns, T., & Stalker, G. M. (1966). *The management of innovation* (2nd ed.). London: Tavistock.

Burrell, G., & Morgan, G. (1979). *Sociological paradigms and organizational analysis.* London: Heinemann.

Callahan, R. (1962). *Education and the cult of efficiency.* Chicago: University of Chicago Press.

Campbell, R. F., Fleming, T., Newell, L. J., & Bennion, J. W. (1987). *A history of thought and practice in educational administration.* New York: Teachers College Press.

Carlberg, C., & Kavale, K. (1980). The efficacy of special versus regular class placement for exceptional children: A meta-analysis. *Journal of Special Education, 14,* 295–309.

Chalfant, J., Pysh, M., & Moultrie, R. (1979). Teacher assistance teams: A model of within-building problem solving. *Learning Disabilities Quarterly, 2,* 85–86.

Chandler, J. T., & Plakos, J. (1969). *Spanish-speaking pupils classified as educable mentally retarded.* Sacramento: California State Department of Education.

Chandler, M. D., & Sayles, L. R. (1971). *Managing large systems.* New York: Harper & Row.

Cherryholmes, C. H. (1988). *Power and criticism: Poststructuralist investigations in education.* New York: Teachers College Press.

Christophos, F., & Renz, P. (1969). A critical examination of special education programs. *Journal of Special Education, 3*(4), 371–380.

Churchman, C. W. (1971). *The design of inquiry systems.* New York: Basic Books.

Clark, B. R. (1972). The organizational saga in higher education. *Administrative Science Quarterly, 17,* 178–184.

Clark, D. L. (1985). Emerging paradigms in organizational theory and research. In Y. S. Lincoln (Ed.), *Organizational theory and inquiry: The paradigm revolution* (pp. 43–78). Beverly Hills, CA: Sage.

Clark, D. L., & Astuto, T. A. (1988). *Education policy after Reagan — What next?* (Occasional Paper No. 6). Charlottesville: University of Virginia, Policy Studies Center of the University Council for Educational Administration.

Clark, D. L., Lotto, L. S., & Astuto, T. A. (1984). Effective schools and school improvement: A comparative analysis of two lines of inquiry. *Educational Administration Quarterly, 20*(3), 41–68.

Cohen, M. D., March, J. G., & Olsen, J. P. (1972). A garbage can model of organizational choice. *Administrative Science Quarterly, 17*(2), 1–25.

Conley, S. C. (1990). Reforming paper pushers and avoiding free agents: The teacher as a constrained decision maker. In S. B. Bacharach (Ed.), *Education reform: Making sense of it all.* Boston: Allyn & Bacon.

Council for Children with Behavioral Disorders. (1989). Position statement on the regular education initiative. *Behavioral Disorders, 14,* 201–208.

Cuban, L. (1979). Determinants of curriculum change and stability, 1870–1970. In J. Schaffarzick & G. Sykes (Eds.), *Value conflicts and curriculum issues.* Berkeley, CA: McCutchan.

Cuban, L. (1983). Effective schools: A friendly but cautionary note. *Phi Delta Kappan, 64*(10), 695–696.

Cuban, L. (1989). The "at-risk" label and the problem of urban school reform. *Phi Delta Kappan, 70*(10), 780–784 and 799–801.

Cunningham, L. L., Hack, W. G., & Nystrand, R. O. (Eds.). (1977). *Educational administration: The developing decades.* Berkeley, CA: McCutchan.

Dallmayr, F. R., & McCarthy, T. A. (1977). *Understanding and social inquiry.* Notre Dame, IN: University of Notre Dame Press.

Dalton, M. (1959). *Men who manage.* New York: Wiley.

Davis, W. E. (1989). The regular initiative debate: Its promises and problems. *Exceptional Children, 55*(5), 440–446.

Davis, W. E., & McCaul, E. J. (1988). *New perspectives on education: A review of the issues and implications of the regular education initiative.* Orono, ME: Institute for Research and Policy Analysis on the Education of Students with Learning and Adjustment Problems.

Deno, E. (1970). Special education as developmental capital. *Exceptional Children, 37*(3), 229–237.

Derrida, J. (1982a). *Dissemination* (B. Johnson, Trans.). London: Athlone Press. (Original work published 1972)

Derrida, J. (1982b). *Margins of philosophy* (A. Bass, Trans.). Chicago: University of Chicago Press. (Original work published 1972)

Dewey, J. (1897). My pedagogic creed. *School Journal, 54*(3), 77–80.

Dewey, J. (1899). *The school and society.* Chicago: University of Chicago Press.

Dewey, J. (1916). *Democracy and education.* New York: Macmillan.

Dewey, J. (1988a). Individualism, old and new. In J. A. Boydston (Ed.), *John Dewey: The later works, 1925–1953.* Vol. 5: 1929–1930 (pp. 41–123). Carbondale: Southern Illinois University Press. (Original work published 1929–1930)

Dewey, J. (1988b). The public and its problems. In J. A. Boydston (Ed.), *John Dewey: The later works, 1925–1953.* Vol. 2: 1925–1927 (pp. 235–372). Carbondale: Southern Illinois University Press. (Original work published 1927)

Dreyfus, H. L., & Rabinow, P. (Eds.). (1983). *Michel Foucault: Beyond structuralism and hermeneutics.* Chicago: University of Chicago Press.

Drucker, P. F. (1989). *The new realities.* New York: Harper & Row.

Dunn, L. M. (1968). Special education for the mildly retarded — Is much of it justifiable? *Exceptional Children, 35*(1), 5–22.

Edgar, E. (1987). Secondary programs in special education: Are many of them justified? *Exceptional Children, 53,* 555–561.

Edmonds, R. (1979). Some schools work and more can. *Social Policy, 9*(5), 26–31.

Elmore, R. F. (1987). *Early experiences in restructuring schools: Voices from the field.* Results in Education series. Washington, DC: National Governors Association.

Elmore, R. F., & McLaughlin, M. W. (1982). Strategic choice in federal education policy: The compliance-assistance trade-off. In A. Lieberman and M. W. McLaughlin (Eds.), *Policy making in education: Eighty-first yearbook of the National Society for the Study of Education* (pp. 159–194). Chicago: University of Chicago Press.

Elmore, R. F., & McLaughlin, M. W. (1988). *Steady work: Policy, practice, and the reform of American education.* Santa Monica, CA: Rand Corporation.

Erickson, D. A. (1979). Research on educational administration: The state-of-the-art. *Educational Researcher, 8*(3), 9–14.

Feinberg, W., & Soltis, J. F. (1985). *School and society.* New York: Teachers College Press.

Foster, W. (1986). *Paradigms and promises: New approaches to educational administration.* Buffalo, NY: Prometheus Books.

Foucault, M. (1973). *Madness and civilization: A history of insanity in the age of reason* (R. Howard, Trans.). New York: Vintage/Random House. (Original work published 1961)

Foucault, M. (1975). *The birth of the clinic: An archeology of medical perception* (A. M. Sheridan Smith, Trans.). New York: Vintage/Random House. (Original work published 1963)

Foucault, M. (1976). *Mental illness and psychology.* Berkeley: University of California Press. (Original work published 1954)

Foucault, M. (1979). *Discipline and punish: The birth of the prison* (A. M. Sheridan Smith, Trans.). New York: Vintage/Random House. (Original work published 1975)

Foucault, M. (1980). *Power/knowledge: Selected interviews and other writings, 1972–1977* (C. Gordon, Ed.; C. Gordon, L. Marshall, J. Mepham, & K. Soper, Trans.). New York: Pantheon Books.

Foucault, M. (1983). The subject and power. In H. L. Dreyfus & P. Rabinow (Eds.), *Michel Foucault: Beyond structuralism and hermeneutics* (pp. 208–226). Chicago: University of Chicago Press.

Gartner, A. (1986). Disabling help: Special education at the crossroads. *Exceptional Children, 53*(1), 72–79.

Gartner, A., & Lipsky, D. K. (1987). Beyond special education: Toward a quality system for all students. *Harvard Educational Review, 57*(4), 367–390.

Gartner, A., & Lipsky, D. K. (1989). *The yoke of special education: How to break it.* Rochester, NY: National Center on Education and the Economy.

Geertz, C. (1983). *Local knowledge: Further essays in interpretive anthropology.* New York: Basic Books.

Gerardi, R. J., Grohe, B., Benedict, G. C., & Coolidge, P. G. (1984). I.E.P. — More paperwork and wasted time. *Contemporary Education, 56*(1), 39–42.

Gerber, M. M. (1987). Application of cognitive-behavioral training methods to teach basic skills to mildly handicapped elementary school students. In M. C. Wang, M. C. Reynolds, & H. J. Walberg (Eds.), *Handbook of special education: Research and practice. Vol. 1: Learner characteristics and adaptive education* (pp. 167–186). Oxford, Eng.: Pergamon Press.

Gerber, M. M. (1988a). Tolerance and technology of instruction: Implications for special education reform. *Exceptional Children, 54*(4), 309–314.

Gerber, M. M. (1988b, May 4). Weighing the regular education initiative: Recent calls for change lead to slippery slope. *Education Week,* pp. 36, 28.

Gerber, M. M., & Levine-Donnerstein, D. (1989). Educating all children: Ten years later. *Exceptional Children, 56*(1), 17–27.

Gerber, M. M., & Semmel, M. I. (1984). Teacher as imperfect test: Reconceptualizing the referral process. *Educational Psychologist, 19,* 137–148.

Gerber, M. M., & Semmel, M. I. (1985). The microeconomics of referral and reintegration: A paradigm for evaluation of special education. *Studies in Educational Evaluation, 11,* 13–29.

Getzels, J. W., & Guba, E. G. (1957). Social behavior and the administrative process. *School Review, 65,* 423–441.

Gilhool, T. K. (1976). Changing public policies: Roots and forces. In M. C. Reynolds (Ed.), *Mainstreaming: Origins and implications* (pp. 8–13). Reston, VA: Council for Exceptional Children.

Gilhool, T. K. (1989). The right to an effective education: From *Brown* to P.L. 94–142 and beyond. In D. K. Lipsky & A. Gartner (Eds.), *Beyond separate education: Quality education for all* (pp. 243–253). Baltimore, MD: Paul H. Brookes.

Giroux, H. A. (1981). *Ideology, culture, and the process of schooling.* Philadelphia: Temple University Press.

Giroux, H. A. (1983). Theories of reproduction and resistance in the new sociology of education: A critical analysis. *Harvard Educational Review, 58*(3), 257–293.

Glazer, N. (1974). The schools of the minor professions. *Minerva, 12*(3), 346–364.

Golding, D. (1980). Establishing blissful clarity in organizational life: Managers. *Sociological Review, 28,* 763–782.

Goldman, J., & Gardner, H. (1989). Multiple paths to educational effectiveness. In D. K. Lipsky & A. Gartner (Eds.), *Beyond separate education: Quality education for all* (pp. 121–139). Baltimore, MD: Paul H. Brookes.

Goodlad, J. I. (1975). *The dynamics of educational change.* New York: McGraw-Hill.

Goodlad, J. I. (1984). *A place called school: Prospects for the future.* New York: McGraw-Hill.

Greer, C. (1972). *The great school legend: A revisionist interpretation of American public education.* New York: Basic Books.

Griffiths, D. E. (1959). *Administrative theory.* New York: Appleton-Century-Crofts.

Griffiths, D. E. (1979). Intellectual turmoil in educational administration. *Educational Administration Quarterly, 15*(3), 43–65.

Griffiths, D. E. (1983). Evolution in research and theory: A study of prominent researchers. *Educational Administration Quarterly, 19*(3), 201–221.

Griffiths, D. E. (1988). Administrative theory. In N. J. Boyan (Ed.), *Handbook of research on educational administration* (pp. 27–51). New York: Longman.

Haber, S. (1964). *Efficiency and uplight: Scientific management in the progressive era, 1890–1920.* Chicago: University of Chicago Press.

Hallahan, D. P., & Kauffman, J. M. (1977). Categories, labels, behavioral characteristics: ED, LD, and EMR reconsidered. *Journal of Special Education, 11,* 139–149.

Hallahan, D. P., Kauffman, J. M., Lloyd, J. W., & McKinney, J. D. (1988). Introduction to the series: Questions about the regular education initiative. *Journal of Learning Disabilities, 21*(1), 3–5.

Hallahan, D. P., & Keller, C. E. (1986). *Study of studies for learning disabilities: A research review and synthesis.* Charleston: West Virginia Department of Education.

Hallahan, D. P., Keller, C. E., McKinney, J. D., Lloyd, J. W., & Bryan, T. (1988). Examining the research base of the regular education initiative: Efficacy studies and the adaptive learning environments model. *Journal of Learning Disabilities, 21*(1), 29–35; 55.

Halpin, A. W. (1970). Administrative theory: The fumbled torch. In A. M. Kroll (Ed.), *Issues in American education.* New York: Oxford University Press.

Halpin, A. W., & Hayes, A. E. (1977). The broken ikon, or What ever happened to theory? In L. L. Cummingham, W. G. Hack, & R. O. Nystrand (Eds.), *Educational administration: The developing decades* (pp. 261–297). Berkeley, CA: McCutchan.

Hayes, D., & Pharis, W. (1967). *National conference of professors of educational administration.* Lincoln: University of Nebraska Press.

Hegel, G. W. F. (1977). *Phenomenology of spirit.* Oxford, Eng.: Clarendon Press. (Original work published 1807)

Heller, K., Holtzman, W., & Messick, S. (1982). *Placing children in special education: A strategy for equity.* Washington, DC: National Academy of Sciences Press.

Heller, W. H., & Schilit, J. (1987). The regular education initiative: A concerned response. *Focus on Exceptional Children, 20*(3), 1–6.

Heshusius, L. (1982). At the heart of the advocacy dilemma: A mechanistic world view. *Exceptional Children, 49*(1), 6–13.

Hobbs, N. (1975). *The futures of children: Categories, labels, and their consequences.* San Francisco: Jossey-Bass.

Hobbs, N. (1980). An ecologically oriented service-based system for the classification of handicapped children. In E. Salzinger, J. Antrobus, & J. Glick (Eds.), *The ecosystem of the "risk" child* (pp. 271–290). New York: Academic Press.

Horkheimer, M. (1974). *Eclipse of reason.* New York: Seabury. (Original work published 1947)

House, E. R. (1979). Technology versus craft: A ten-year perspective on innovation. *Journal of Curriculum Studies, 11*(1), 1–15.

Hoy, D. (1985). Jacques Derrida. In Q. Skinner (Ed.), *The return of grand theory in the human sciences* (pp. 83–100). Cambridge, Eng.: Cambridge University Press.

Iano, R. P. (1986). The study and development of teaching: With implications for the advancement of special education. *Remedial and Special Education, 7*(5), 50–61.

Johnson, G. O. (1962). Special education for the mentally handicapped — A paradox. *Exceptional Children, 29*(2), 62–69.

Jonsson, S. A., & Lundin, R. A. (1977). Myths and wishful thinking as management tools. In P. C. Nystrom & W. H. Starbuck (Eds.), *Prescriptive models of organizations* (pp. 157–170). New York: Elsevier North-Holland.

Kauffman, J. M. (1988). Revolution can also mean returning to the starting point: Will school psychology help special education complete the circuit? *School Psychology Review, 17,* 490–494.

Kauffman, J. M. (1989a). *The regular education initiative as Reagan-Bush education policy: A trickle-down theory of education of the hard-to-teach.* Austin, TX: Pro-Ed Publishers.

Kauffman, J. M. (1989b). The regular education initiative as Reagan-Bush education policy: A trickle-down theory of education of the hard-to-teach. *Journal of Special Education, 23*(3), 256–278.

Kauffman, J. M., Gerber, M. M., & Semmel, M. I. (1988). Arguable assumptions underlying the regular education initiative. *Journal of Learning Disabilities, 21*(1), 6–11.

Keogh, B. K. (1988). Improving services for problem learners: Rethinking and restructuring. *Journal of Learning Disabilities, 21*(1), 19–22.

Keogh, B. K., & Levitt, M. L. (1976). Special education in the mainstream: A confrontation of limits? *Focus on Exceptional Children, 8,* 1–11.

Kiel, D. C., & Skrtic, T. M. (1988). *Modes of organizational accountability: An ideal type analysis.* Unpublished manuscript, University of Kansas, Lawrence.

Kirk, S. A., & Chalfant, J. D. (1983). *Academic and developmental learning disabilities.* Denver: Love Publishing.

Kliebard, H. M. (1988). The effort to reconstruct the modern American curriculum. In L. E. Beyer & M. W. Apple (Eds.), *The curriculum: Problems, politics, and possibilities* (pp. 19–31). Albany: State University of New York Press.

Kloppenberg, J. T. (1986). *Uncertain victory: Social democracy and progressivism in European and American thought, 1870–1920.* New York: Oxford University Press.

Kojeve, A. (1969). *Introduction to the reading of Hegel.* New York: Basic Books.

Kuhn, T. (1970). *The structure of scientific revolutions* (2d ed.). Chicago: University of Chicago Press.

Lazerson, M. (1983). The origins of special education. In J. G. Chambers & W. T. Hartman (Eds.), *Special education policies: Their history, implementation, and finance.* Philadelphia: Temple University Press.

Lehming, R., & Kane, M. (1981). *Improving schools: Using what we know*. Beverly Hills, CA: Sage.

Lezotte, L. W. (1989). School improvement based on the effective schools research. In D. K. Lipsky & A. Gartner (Eds.), *Beyond separate education: Quality education for all* (pp. 25–37). Baltimore, MD: Paul H. Brookes.

Lieberman, A., & Miller, L. (1984). *Teachers, their world and their work: Implications for school improvement*. Alexandria, VA: Association for Supervision and Curriculum Development.

Lieberman, L. M. (1984). *Preventing special education . . . for those who don't need it*. Newton, MA: GloWorm Publications.

Lieberman, L. M. (1985). Special education and regular education: A merger made in heaven? *Exceptional Children, 51*(6), 513–516.

Lieberman, L. M. (1988). *Preserving special education . . . for those who need it*. Newton, MA: GloWorm Publications.

Lilly, M. S. (1986, March). The relationship between general and special education: A new face on an old issue. *Counterpoint, 6*(1), p. 10.

Lilly, M. S. (1987). Lack of focus on special education in literature on education reform. *Exceptional Children, 53*(4), 325–326.

Lilly, M. S. (1989). Teacher preparation. In D. K. Lipsky & A. Gartner (Eds.), *Beyond separate education: Quality education for all* (pp. 143–157). Baltimore, MD: Paul H. Brookes.

Lincoln, Y. S. (Ed.). (1985). *Organizational theory and inquiry: The paradigm revolution*. Beverly Hills, CA: Sage.

Lincoln, Y. S., & Guba, E. G. (1985). *Naturalistic inquiry*. Beverly Hills, CA: Sage.

Lipsky, D. K., & Gartner, A. (1987). Capable of achievement and worthy of respect: Education for handicapped students as if they were full-fledged human beings. *Exceptional Children, 54*(1), 69–74.

Lipsky, D. K., & Gartner, A. (Eds.). (1989a). *Beyond separate education: Quality education for all*. Baltimore, MD: Paul H. Brookes.

Lipsky, D. K., & Gartner, A. (1989b). School administration and financial arrangements. In S. Stainback, W. Stainback, & M. Forest (Eds.), *Educating all students in the mainstream of regular education* (pp. 105–120). Baltimore, MD: Paul H. Brookes.

Lipsky, M. (1975). Toward a theory of street-level bureaucracy. In W. D. Hawley, M. Lipsky, S. B. Greenberg, J. D. Greenstone, I. Katznelson, K. Orren, P. E. Peterson, M. Shefter, & D. Yates (Eds.), *Theoretical perspectives on urban politics* (pp. 196–213). Englewood Cliffs, NJ: Prentice-Hall.

Lloyd, J. W., Crowley, E. P., Kohler, F. W., & Strain, P. S. (1988). Redefining the applied research agenda: Cooperative learning, prereferral, teacher consultation, and peer-mediated interventions. *Journal of Learning Disabilities, 21*(1), 43–52.

Lortie, D. C. (1975). *Schoolteacher: A sociological study*. Chicago: University of Chicago Press.

Lortie, D. C. (1978). Some reflections on renegotiation. In M. C. Reynolds (Ed.), *Futures of education for exceptional students: Emerging structures* (pp. 235–243). Reston, VA: Council for Exceptional Children.

Lyotard, J. F. (1984). *The postmodern condition: A report on knowledge*. Minneapolis: University of Minnesota Press. (Original work published 1979)

MacMillan, D. L. (1971). Special education for the mildly retarded: Servant or savant? *Focus on Exceptional Children, 2*(9), 1–11.

MacMillan, D. L., & Semmel, M. I. (1977). Evaluation of mainstreaming programs. *Focus on Exceptional Children, 9*(4), 1–14.

March, J. G., & Olsen, J. P. (1976). *Ambiguity and choice in organizations*. Bergen, Norway: Universitetsforlaget.

Martin, E. (1978). Preface. In M. C. Reynolds (Ed.), *Futures of education for exceptional students* (pp. iii–vi). Reston, VA: Council for Exceptional Children.

McDonnell, L. M., & McLaughlin, M. W. (1982). *Education policy and the role of the states.* Santa Monica, CA: Rand.

McKinney, J. D., & Hocutt, A. M. (1988). The need for policy analysis in evaluating the regular education initiative. *Journal of Learning Disabilities, 21*(1), 12–18.

McNeil, L. M. (1986). *Contradictions of control: School structure and school knowledge.* New York: Methuen/Routledge & Kegan Paul.

Meier, D. (1984). "Getting tough" in the schools. *Dissent, 31,* 61–70.

Mercer, J. (1973). *Labeling the mentally retarded: Clinical and social system perspectives on mental retardation.* Berkeley: University of California Press.

Mesinger, J. F. (1985). Commentary on "A rationale for the merger of special and regular education." *Exceptional Children, 51*(6), 510–512.

Meyer, J. W., & Rowan, B. (1977). Institutionalized organizations: Formal structure as myth and ceremony. *American Journal of Sociology, 83,* 340–363.

Meyer, J. W., & Rowan, B. (1978). The structure of educational organizations. In M. W. Meyer (Ed.), *Environments and organizations* (pp. 78–109). San Francisco: Jossey-Bass.

Meyer, J. W., & Scott, W. R. (1983). *Organizational environments: Ritual and rationality.* Beverly Hills, CA: Sage.

Meyer, M. W. (1979). Organizational structure as signaling. *Pacific Sociological Review, 22*(4), 481–500.

Miller, D., & Mintzberg, H. (1983). The case for configuration. In G. Morgan (Ed.), *Beyond method: Strategies for social research* (pp. 57–73). Beverly Hills, CA: Sage.

Mintzberg, H. (1979). *The structuring of organizations.* Englewood Cliffs, NJ: Prentice-Hall.

Mitroff, I. I., & Pondy, L. R. (1974, September/October). On the organization of inquiry: A comparison of some radically different approaches to policy analysis. *Public Administration Review,* pp. 471–479.

Mommsen, W. J. (1974). *The age of bureaucracy: Perspectives on the political sociology of Max Weber.* New York: Harper & Row.

Morgan, G. (Ed.). (1983). *Beyond method: Strategies for social research.* Beverly Hills, CA: Sage.

Murphy, J. T. (1989). The paradox of decentralizing schools: Lessons from business, government, and the Catholic Church. *Phi Delta Kappan, 70*(10), 808–812.

Naisbitt, J., & Aburdene, P. (1985). *Re-inventing the corporation.* New York: Warner Books.

National Commission on Excellence in Education. (1983). *A nation at risk: The imperative for educational reform.* Washington, DC: U.S. Government Printing Office.

Noel, M. M., & Fuller, B. C. (1985). The social policy construction of special education: The impact of state characteristics on identification and integration of handicapped children. *Remedial and Special Education, 6*(3), 27–35.

Oakes, J. (1985). *Keeping track: How schools structure inequality.* New Haven: Yale University Press.

Oakes, J. (1986a). Keeping track, Part 1: The policy and practice of curriculum inequality. *Phi Delta Kappan, 68*(1), 12–17.

Oakes, J. (1986b). Keeping track, Part 2: Curriculum inequality and school reform. *Phi Delta Kappan, 68*(2), 148–154.

Patrick, J., & Reschly, D. (1982). Relationship of state educational criteria and demographic variables to school-system prevalence of mental retardation. *American Journal of Mental Retardation, 86,* 351–360.

Perrow, C. (1970). *Organizational analysis: A sociological review.* Belmont, CA: Wadsworth.

Perrow, C. (1978). Demystifying organizations. In R. C. Sarri & Y. Hasenfeld (Eds.), *The management of human services* (pp. 105–120). New York: Columbia University Press.

Pettigrew, A. (1979). On studying organizational cultures. *Administrative Science Quarterly, 24*(4), 570–581.

Pfeffer, J. (1982). *Organizations and organization theory.* Marshfield, MA: Pitman.

Philip, M. (1985). Michel Foucault. In Q. Skinner (Ed.), *The return of grand theory in the human sciences* (pp. 65–81). Cambridge, Eng.: Cambridge University Press.

Poplin, M. S. (1987). Self-imposed blindness: The scientific method in education. *Remedial and Special Education, 8*(6), 31–37.

Pugach, M. (1988). The consulting teacher in the context of educational reform. *Exceptional Children, 55*(3), 266–277.

Pugach, M., & Lilly, M. S. (1984). Reconceptualizing support services for classroom teachers: Implications for teacher education. *Journal of Teacher Education, 35* (5), 48–55.

Pugach, M., & Sapon-Shevin, M. (1987). New agendas for special education policy: What the regular education reports haven't said. *Exceptional Children, 53*(4), 295–299.

Pugh, D. S., Hickson, D. J., Hinnings, C. R., MacDonald, K. M., Turner, C., & Lupton, T. (1963). A conceptual scheme for organizational analysis. *Administrative Science Quarterly, 8*(4), 289–315.

Reich, R. B. (1983). *The next American frontier.* New York: Penguin.

Reich, R. B. (1990). Education and the next economy. In S. B. Bacharach (Ed.), *Education reform: Making sense of it all* (pp. 194–212). Boston: Allyn & Bacon.

Resnick, D., & Resnick, L. (1985). Standards, curriculum, and performance: Historical and comparative perspectives. *Educational Researcher, 14*(4), 5–20.

Reynolds, M. C. (1962). A framework for considering some issues in special education. *Exceptional Children, 28*(5), 367–370.

Reynolds, M. C. (1976, November 22–23). *New perspectives on the instructional cascade.* Paper presented at the conference "The Least Restrictive Alternatives: A Partnership of General and Special Education," sponsored by Minneapolis Public Schools, Special Education Division, Minneapolis, MN.

Reynolds, M. C. (1988). A reaction to the JLD special series on the regular education initiative. *Journal of Learning Disabilities, 21*(6), 352–356.

Reynolds, M. C., & Birch, J. W. (1977). *Teaching exceptional children in all America's schools.* Reston, VA: The Council for Exceptional Children.

Reynolds, M. C., & Lakin, K. C. (1987). Noncategorical special education: Models for research and practice. In M. C. Wang, M. C. Reynolds, & H. J. Walberg (Eds.), *Handbook of special education: Research and practice. Vol. 1: Learner characteristics and adaptive education* (pp. 331–356). Oxford, Eng.: Pergamon Press.

Reynolds, M. C., & Rosen, S. W. (1976, May). Special education: Past, present, and future. *Education Forum,* pp. 3–9.

Reynolds, M. C., & Wang, M. C. (1981, October). *Restructuring "special" school programs: A position paper.* Paper presented at the National Invitational Conference on Public Policy and the Special Education Task of the 1980s, Racine, WI.

Reynolds, M. C., & Wang, M. C. (1983). Restructuring "special" school programs: A position paper. *Policy Studies Review, 2*(1), 189–212.

Reynolds, M. C., Wang, M. C., & Walberg, H. J. (1987). The necessary restructuring of special and general education. *Exceptional Children, 53*(5), 391–398.

Rhodes, W. C. (1970). A community participation analysis of emotional disturbance. *Exceptional Children, 36,* 306–314.

Ricoeur, P. (1981). *Paul Ricoeur: Hermeneutics and the human sciences* (J. B. Thompson, Ed. & Trans.). Cambridge, Eng.: Cambridge University Press.

Rist, R., & Harrell, J. (1982). Labeling and the learning disabled child: The social ecology of educational practice. *The American Journal of Orthopsychiatry, 52*(1), 146–160.

Ritzer, G. (1980). *Sociology; A multiple paradigm science.* Boston: Allyn & Bacon.

Ritzer, G. (1983). *Sociological theory.* New York: Alfred A. Knopf.

Romzek, B. S., & Dubnick, M. J. (1987). Accountability in the public sector: Lessons from the Challenger tragedy. *Public Administration Review, 47*(3), 227–238.

Rorty, R. (1979). *Philosophy and the mirror of nature.* Princeton, NJ: Princeton University Press.

Rorty, R. (1982). *Consequences of pragmatism.* Minneapolis: University of Minnesota Press.

Rorty, R. (1989). *Contingency, irony, and solidarity.* Cambridge, Eng.: Cambridge University Press.

Ross, A. O. (1980). *Psychological disorders of children.* New York: McGraw-Hill.

Rounds, J. (1979). *Social theory, public policy and social order.* Unpublished doctoral dissertation, University of California, Los Angeles.

Rounds, J. (1981). *Information and ambiguity in organizational change.* Paper presented at the Carnegie-Mellon Symposium on Information Processing in Organizations, Carnegie-Mellon University, Pittsburgh, PA.

Rowan, B. (1980). *Organizational structure and the institutional environment: The case of public schools.* Unpublished manuscript, Texas Christian University, Fort Worth.

Ryan, M. (1982). *Marxism and deconstruction.* Baltimore, MD: The Johns Hopkins University Press.

Sailor, W., & Guess, D. (1983). *Severely handicapped students: An instructional design.* Boston: Houghton Mifflin.

Sailor, W., Halvorsen, A., Anderson, J., Goetz, L., Gee, K., Doering, K., & Hunt, P. (1986). Community intensive instruction. In R. Horner, L. Meyer, & H. Fredericks (Eds.), *Education of learners with severe handicaps* (pp. 251–288). Baltimore, MD: Paul H. Brookes.

Sapon-Shevin, M. (1987). The national education reports and special education: Implications for students. *Exceptional Children, 53*(4), 300–307.

Sapon-Shevin, M. (1988). Working towards merger together: Seeing beyond distrust and fear. *Teacher Education and Special Education, 11*(3), 103–110.

Sarason, S. B. (1971/1982). *The culture of the school and the problem of change* (orig. ed. 1971; rev. ed. 1982). Boston: Allyn & Bacon.

Sarason, S. B., & Doris, J. (1979). *Educational handicap, public policy, and social history.* New York: The Free Press.

Schein, E. H. (1972). *Professional education.* New York: McGraw-Hill.

Schenck, S. J. (1980). The diagnostic/instructional link in individualized education programs. *Journal of Special Education, 14*(3), 337–345.

Schenck, S. J., & Levy, W. K. (1979, April). *IEP's: The state of the art — 1978.* Paper presented at the annual meeting of the American Educational Research Association, San Francisco, CA.

Schön, D. A. (1983). *The reflective practitioner: How professionals think in action.* New York: Basic Books.

Schön, D. A. (1987). *Educating the reflective practitioner: Toward a design for teaching and learning in the professions.* San Francisco: Jossey-Bass.

Schön, D. A. (1988). Coaching reflective practice. In P. Grimmett & G. Erickson (Eds.), *Reflection in teacher education.* New York: Teachers College Press.

Schön, D. A. (1989). Professional knowledge and reflective practice. In T. Sergiovanni & J. Moore (Eds.), *Schooling for tomorrow: Directing reforms to issues that count.* Boston: Allyn & Bacon.

Schrag, P., & Divorky, D. (1975). *The myth of the hyperactive child.* New York: Pantheon.

Schroyer, T. (1973). *The critique of domination.* Boston: Beacon Press.

Schumaker, J. B., & Deshler, D. D. (1988). Implementing the regular education initiative in secondary schools: A different ball game. *Journal of Learning Disabilities, 21*(1), 36–42.

Schwartz, P., & Ogilvy, J. (1979). *The emergent paradigm: Changing patterns of thought and belief.* Menlo Park, CA: SRI International.

Scott, R. W. (1981). *Organizations: Rational, natural, and open systems.* Englewood Cliffs, NJ: Prentice-Hall.

Segal, M. (1974). Organization and environment: A typology of adaptability and structure. *Public Administration Review, 34*(3), 212–220.

Sergiovanni, T. J., & Moore, J. H. (Eds.). (1989). *Schooling for tomorrow*. Boston: Allyn & Bacon.

Shepard, L. A. (1987). The new push for excellence: Widening the schism between regular and special education. *Exceptional Children, 53*(4), 327–329.

Simon, H. A. (1977). *The new science of management decision*. Englewood Cliffs, NJ: Prentice-Hall.

Singer, J. D., & Butler, J. A. (1987). The Education for All Handicapped Children Act: Schools as agents of social reform. *Harvard Educational Review, 57*(2), 125–152.

Sirotnik, K. A., & Oakes, J. (1986). *Critical perspectives on the organization and improvement of schooling*. Boston: Kluwer-Nijhoff Publishing.

Sizer, T. R. (1984). *Horace's compromise: The dilemma of the American high school*. Boston: Houghton Mifflin.

Skinner, Q. (Ed.). (1985). *The return of grand theory in the human sciences*. Cambridge, Eng.: Cambridge University Press.

Skrtic, T. M. (1986). The crisis in special education knowledge: A perspective on perspective. *Focus on Exceptional Children, 18*(7), 1–16.

Skrtic, T. M. (1987a). An organizational analysis of special education reform. *Counterpoint, 8*(2), 15–19.

Skrtic, T. M. (1987b). The national inquiry into the future of education for students with special needs. *Counterpoint, 7*(4), 6.

Skrtic, T. M. (1988a). The crisis in special education knowledge. In E. L. Meyen & T. M. Skrtic (Eds.), *Exceptional children and youth: An introduction* (pp. 415–447). Denver: Love Publishing.

Skrtic, T. M. (1988b). The organizational context of special education. In E. L. Meyen & T. M. Skrtic (Eds.), *Exceptional children and youth: An introduction* (pp. 479–517). Denver: Love Publishing.

Skrtic, T. M. (1990a, August 10–14). *School psychology and the revolution in modern knowledge*. Paper presented at the American Psychology Association Convention, Boston, MA.

Skrtic, T. M. (1990b). Social accommodation: Toward a dialogical discourse in educational inquiry. In E. G. Guba (Ed.), *The paradigm dialog: Options for inquiry in the social sciences* (pp. 125–135). Beverly Hills, CA: Sage.

Skrtic, T. M. (1991). *Behind special education: A critical analysis of professional knowledge and school organization*. Denver: Love Publishing.

Skrtic, T. M. (in press). Toward a dialogical theory of school organization and adaptability: Special education and disability as organizational pathologies. In T. M. Skrtic (Ed.), *Exploring the theory/practice link in special education: A critical perspective*. Reston, VA: Council for Exceptional Children.

Skrtic, T. M., Guba, E. G., & Knowlton, H. E. (1985). *Interorganizational special education programming in rural areas: Technical report on the multisite naturalistic field study*. Washington, DC: National Institute of Education.

Skrtic, T. M., & Ware, L. P. (in press). Reflective teaching and the problem of school organization. In E. W. Ross, G. McCutcheon, & J. Cornett (Eds.), *Teacher personal theorizing: Issues, problems, and implications*. New York: Teachers College Press.

Slavin, R. E. (1989). PET and the pendulum: Faddism in education and how to stop it. *Phi Delta Kappan, 70*(10), 752–758.

Spring, J. (1980). *Educating the worker-citizen: The social, economic, and political foundations of education*. New York: Longman.

Stainback, S., & Stainback, W. (1984). A rationale for the merger of special and regular education. *Exceptional Children, 51*(2), 102–111.

Stainback, S., & Stainback, W. (1985a). *Integration of students with severe handicaps into regular schools*. Reston, VA: Council for Exceptional Children.

Stainback, S., & Stainback, W. (1985b). The merger of special and regular education: Can it be done? A response to Lieberman and Mesinger. *Exceptional Children, 51*(6), 517–521.

Stainback, S., & Stainback, W. (1987a). Facilitating merger through personnel preparation. *Teacher Education and Special Education, 10*(4), 185–190.

Stainback, S., & Stainback, W. (1987b). Integration versus cooperation: A commentary on educating children with learning problems: A shared responsibility. *Exceptional Children, 54*(1), 66–68.

Stainback, S., & Stainback, W. (1989). Integration of students with mild and moderate handicaps. In D. K. Lipsky & A. Gartner (Eds.), *Beyond separate education: Quality education for all* (pp. 41–52). Baltimore, MD: Paul H. Brookes.

Stainback, S., Stainback, W., & Forest, M. (Eds.). (1989). *Educating all students in the mainstreaming of regular education.* Baltimore, MD: Paul H. Brookes.

Stainback, W., Stainback, S., Courtnage, L., & Jaben, T. (1985). Facilitating mainstreaming by modifying the mainstream. *Exceptional Children, 52*(2), 144–152.

Stedman, L. C. (1987). It's time we changed the effective schools formula. *Phi Delta Kappan, 69*(3), 215–224.

Swap, S. (1978). The ecological model of emotional disturbance in children: A status report and proposed synthesis. *Behavioral Disorders, 3*(3), 156–186.

Teacher Education Division of the Council for Exceptional Children. (1986, October). *Message to all TED members concerning The National Inquiry into the Future of Education for Students with Special Needs.* Reston, VA: Author.

Teacher Education Division of the Council for Exceptional Children. (1987). The regular education initiative: A statement by the Teacher Education Division, Council for Exceptional Children. *Journal of Learning Disabilities, 20*(5), 289–293.

Thompson, J. D. (1967). *Organizations in action.* New York: McGraw-Hill.

Thousand, J. S. (1990). Organizational perspectives on teacher education and school renewal: A conversation with Tom Skrtic. *Teacher Education and Special Education, 13*(1), 30–35.

Thousand, J. S., Fox, T., Reid, R., Godek, J., & Williams, W. (1986). *The homecoming model: Educating students who present intensive educational challenges within regular education environments* (Monograph No. 7–1). Burlington: University of Vermont, Center for Developmental Disabilities.

Thousand, J. S., & Villa, R. A. (1988). *Enhancing success in heterogeneous classrooms and schools* (Monograph 8–1). Burlington: University of Vermont, Center for Developmental Disabilities.

Thousand, J. S., & Villa, R. A. (1989). Enhancing success in heterogeneous schools. In S. Stainback, W. Stainback, & M. Forest (Eds.), *Educating all students in the mainstream of regular education.* Baltimore, MD: Paul H. Brookes.

Timar, T. B., & Kirp, D. L. (1988). *Managing educational excellence.* New York: Falmer Press.

Timar, T. B., & Kirp, D. L. (1989). Education reforms in the 1980's: Lessons from the states. *Phi Delta Kappan, 70*(7), 504–511.

Toffler, A. (1970). *Future shock.* New York: Bantam Books.

Tomlinson, S. (1982). *A sociology of special education.* Boston: Routledge & Kegan Paul.

Tye, K. A., & Tye, B. B. (1984). Teacher isolation and school reform. *Phi Delta Kappan, 65*(5), 319–322.

U.S. Department of Education (USDE), Office of Special Education and Rehabilitative Services. (1988). *Annual report to Congress on the implementation of the Education for all Handicapped Children Act.* Washington, DC: Author.

Vergason, G. A., & Anderegg, M. L. (1989). Save the baby! A response to Integrating the Children of the Second System. *Phi Delta Kappan, 71*(1), 61–63.

Walberg, H. J., & Wang, M. C. (1987). Effective educational practices and provisions for individual differences. In M. C. Wang, M. C. Reynolds, & H. J. Walberg (Eds.), *Handbook of special education: Research and practice. Vol. 1: Learner characteristics and adaptive education* (pp. 113–128). Oxford, Eng.: Pergamon Press.

Walker, L. J. (1987). Procedural rights in the wrong system: Special education is not enough. In A. Gartner & T. Joe (Eds.), *Images of the disabled/disabling images*. New York: Praeger.

Wang, M. C. (1981). Mainstreaming exceptional children: Some instructional design and implementation considerations. *Elementary School Journal, 81,* 195–221.

Wang, M. C. (1988, May 4). A promising approach for reforming special education. *Education Week,* pp. 36, 28.

Wang, M. C. (1989a). Accommodating student diversity through adaptive instruction. In S. Stainback, W. Stainback, & M. Forest (Eds.), *Educating all students in the mainstream of regular education* (pp. 183–197). Baltimore, MD: Paul H. Brookes.

Wang, M. C. (1989b). Adaptive instruction: An alternative for accommodating student diversity through the curriculum. In D. K. Lipsky & A. Gartner (Eds.), *Beyond separate education: Quality education for all* (pp. 99–119). Baltimore, MD: Paul H. Brookes.

Wang, M. C., & Reynolds, M. C. (1985). Avoiding the "catch-22" in special education reform. *Exceptional Children, 51*(6), 497–502.

Wang, M. C., & Reynolds, M. C. (1986). "Catch 22 and disabling help": A reply to Alan Gartner. *Exceptional Children, 53*(1), 77–79.

Wang, M. C., Reynolds, M. C., & Walberg, H. J. (1985, December 5–7). *Rethinking special education.* Paper presented at the Wingspread Conference on the Education of Students with Special Needs: Research Findings and Implications for Policy and Practice, Racine, WI.

Wang, M. C., Reynolds, M. C., & Walberg, H. J. (1986). Rethinking special education. *Educational Leadership, 44*(1), 26–31.

Wang, M. C., Reynolds, M. C., & Walberg, H. J. (Eds.). (1987a). *Handbook of special education: Research and practice. Vol. 1: Learner characteristics and adaptive education.* Oxford, Eng.: Pergamon Press.

Wang, M. C., Reynolds, M. C., & Walberg, H. J. (1987b, October 1–3). *Repairing the second system for students with special needs.* Paper presented at the Wingspread Conference on the Education of Children with Special Needs: Gearing Up to Meet the Challenges of the 1990s, Racine, WI.

Wang, M. C., Reynolds, M. C., & Walberg, H. J. (1988). Integrating the children of the second system. *Phi Delta Kappan, 70*(3), 248–251.

Wang, M. C., Reynolds, M. C., & Walberg, H. J. (1989). Who benefits from segregation and murky water? *Phi Delta Kappan, 71*(1), 64–67.

Wang, M. C., & Walberg, H. J. (1988). Four fallacies of segregationism. *Exceptional Children, 55*(2), 128–137.

Weatherley, R. (1979). *Reforming special education: Policy implementation from state level to street level.* Cambridge, MA: MIT Press.

Weatherley, R., & Lipsky, M. (1977). Street-level bureaucrats and institutional innovation: Implementing special education reform. *Harvard Educational Review, 47*(2), 171–203.

Weber, M. (1946). Politics as a vocation. In H. H. Gerth & C. W. Mills (Eds. & Trans.), *From Max Weber: Essays in sociology* (pp. 77–128). Oxford, Eng.: Oxford University Press. (Original work published 1919)

Weber, M. (1949). "Objectivity" in social science and social policy. In E. A. Shils & H. A. Finch (Eds. & Trans.), *The methodology of the social sciences.* New York: Free Press. (Original work published 1904)

Weber, M. (1978). *Economy and society* (G. Roth & C. Wittich, Eds.; E. Fischoll et al., Trans.) (2 Vols.). Berkeley: University of California Press. (Original work published 1922)

Weick, K. E. (1976). Educational organizations as loosely coupled systems. *Administrative Science Quarterly, 21*(1), 1–19.

Weick, K. E. (1979). Cognitive processes in organization. In B. M. Staw (Ed.), *Research in organizational behavior* (Vol. 1, pp. 41–74). Greenwich, CT: JAI Press.

Weick, K. E. (1982). Administering education in loosely coupled schools. *Phi Delta Kappan, 63*(10), 673–676.

Weick, K. E. (1985). Sources of order in underorganized systems. In Y. S. Lincoln (Ed.), *Organizational theory and inquiry: The paradigm revolution* (pp. 106–136). Beverly Hills, CA: Sage.

Weintraub, F. J. (1977). Editorial comment. *Exceptional Children, 44*(2), 114.

White, R., & Calhoun, M. L. (1987). From referral to placement: Teachers' perceptions of their responsibilities. *Exceptional Children, 53*(5), 460–468.

Will, M. C. (1984). Let us pause and reflect — But not too long. *Exceptional Children, 51*(1), 11–16.

Will, M. C. (1985, December). *Educating children with learning problems: A shared responsibility.* Paper presented at the Wingspread Conference on the Education of Special Needs Students: Research Findings and Implications for Policy and Practice, Racine, WI.

Will, M. C. (1986a). Educating children with learning problems: A shared responsibility. *Exceptional Children, 52*(5), 411–416.

Will, M. C. (1986b). *Educating children with learning problems: A shared responsibility. A report to the secretary.* Washington, DC: U.S. Department of Education.

Wise, A. E. (1988). The two conflicting trends in school reform: Legislated learning revisited. *Phi Delta Kappan, 69*(5), 328–333.

Wolcott, H. F. (1977). *Teachers versus technocrats: An educational innovation in anthropological perspective.* Eugene, OR: Center for Educational Policy and Management.

Woodward, J. (1965). *Industrial organizations: Theory and practice.* Oxford, Eng.: Oxford University Press.

Wright, A. R., Cooperstein, R. A., Renneker, E. G., & Padilla, C. (1982). *Local implementation of P.L. 94–142: Final report of a longitudinal study.* Menlo Park, CA: SRI International.

Wright, J. S. (1967). *Hobson vs. Hansen: Opinion by Honorable J. Skelly Wright, Judge, United States Court of Appeals for the District of Columbia.* Washington, DC: West Publishing.

Ysseldyke, J., Thurlow, M., Graden, S., Wesson, C., Algozzine, B., & Deno, S. (1983). Generalization from five years of research on assessment and decision-making: The University of Minnesota Institute. *Exceptional Education Quarterly, 4,* 75–93.

Zucker, L. G. (1977). The role of institutionalization in cultural persistence. *American Sociological Review, 42,* 726–743.

Zucker, L. G. (1981). Institutional structure and organizational processes: The role of evaluation units in schools. In A. Bank & R. C. Williams (Eds.), *Evaluation and decision making* (CSE Monograph Series No. 10). Los Angeles: UCLA Center for the Study of Evaluation.

I would like to thank Dwight Kiel and Linda Ware for their helpful comments on an earlier draft of this article.

Part 3:

*From Theory
into Practice*

Understanding Reading Disability: A Case Study Approach

PETER H. JOHNSTON

Concurrent with the growth of special education during the past two decades has been increased concern for the phenomenon of dyslexia. As Peter Johnston points out, there are major differences in educational opinion concerning etiology and praxis in regard to reading failure. Some reading experts assume that reading problems arise from some individuals' slowness in processing verbal information. This assumption leads them to prescribe remedial strategies that stress development of compensatory strategies to circumvent the unremediable slowness. Other experts, however, argue that reading failure stems from underdeveloped higher level mental processes; this view holds that the cause of reading problems can be attacked directly through teaching of strategic and metacognitive thinking skills. According to Johnston, however, missing from this debate over theory and practice is a careful examination of reading problems as they truly exist; he argues that the reading disability literature is lacking in studies of dyslexic individuals' actual, real-world reading processes. In this article, Johnston uses three case studies of adult men to examine the psychological and social determinants of their failure to read. Using these men's self-reports of their reading histories and current reading processes, Johnston describes how certain factors — anxiety, maladaptive thinking strategies, conflicting motives, and causal attributions — both give rise to and reinforce their difficulties in deciphering the written word. This research report contributes to our understanding of dyslexia by offering a richer, more complex perspective on this disability; it also demonstrates the power of qualitative methodology in special education research.

These are the words of an adult disabled reader and his wife:

> *Mrs. Wilson:* I can remember one night our then little girl, who's now a teenager — we were taking her to the emergency room . . . OK . . . on the way to the emergency room, though — as sick as she was — she was reading the billboards to him, saying different things, "Oh Daddy, look at," and so on and so forth. And when we got her situated that night and came home, he said, "You know I cannot believe that this little first grader can read words off those

Harvard Educational Review Vol. 55 No. 2 May 1985

billboards and I can't." And he said to me, "How am I going to explain this to her when she comes home and says, 'Daddy, what's this?'"

Mr. Wilson: And I was totally . . . I never . . . and it's only happened to me once. I was jealous of my own child . . . jealous so bad that I was . . . really felt it . . . . in my whole life. The jealousy that I felt for her . . . and of course it was over within a second, but . . .

Jack Wilson went to school through the eighth grade, has normal intelligence, and as a mere infant mastered the extraordinarily complex task of learning the English language. Why is it that he, along with roughly 14 million other Americans like him, cannot read (Weber, 1975)? Does he, as most current theories argue, have a fundamental processing deficit that stands between him and literacy but did not prevent him from learning spoken language? In this article, I will use three case studies to argue that there are more likely interpretations that have been systematically ignored because of an essentially reductionist approach to the investigation of reading failure. I will argue that case studies involving examination of the individual's goals, motives, and situations should play a much larger role in research into reading failure.

Theories of reading failure currently center on two major differences between good and poor readers. The first is that people with reading problems process verbal information more slowly than others. Models based on this difference are represented, for example, by the work of Sternberg and Wagner (1982), Vellutino (1983), and Wolford (1981). The second difference is in the area of higher mental processes such as strategic and metacognitive (conscious and planful) behavior. Models that fall into this category are in a substantial minority (Crowder, 1983) and have been described by Ceci (1982), Clay (1979b), and Johnston and Winograd (1983).

Major differences exist between the underlying assumptions and the nature of the research from these two schools of thought and in their educational implications. The theories based on differences in processing speed involve characteristics that are resistant to alteration through education, whereas the models based on differences in higher mental processes describe characteristics that potentially can be changed with education.

These differences are similar to the state/trait tension in personality psychology. The trait notion places a stable and internal characteristic at the root of the problem; the goal of researchers, therefore, is to explain between-subject variability and differences in average performances between groups. The alternative to this, represented by the "state" notion, seeks to explain the variability of individual performance across situations. In this case, the expected cause is less long term and more amenable to instruction than when the trait notion is the guiding one.

Processing limitations and neurological factors as explanations of reading failure are based on a trait orientation that accepts inappropriate strategies as unchangeable and tries to work around them. Alternative explanations stress learning strategies, which are thought of as hypotheses and methods used by learners in different learning situations. These models suggest that the source of reading problems is a lack of strategies, inadequate strategies, and inappropriately generalized strategies. Other problems relate to a deficient or discrepant knowledge base on which the strategies operate. The educational solution, then, is to modify or teach learning strategies and discourage the use of ineffective approaches. By contrast, trait-oriented analysis accepts inappropriate strategies as unchangeable and tries to work around them.

The learning-strategies approach, because it allows for individual diversity, is best studied at the individual level. This argument in favor of case studies over group studies has arisen in several different areas of psychology and education. In clinical psychology, for example, the argument has focused on the problem of the individuality of the client versus the generality of the syndrome (see, for example, Allport, 1962, 1966; Bem & Allen, 1974; Browning & Stover, 1971; Mischel, 1984). Behavioral psychology has made extensive use of single-subject research procedures, but until recently, cognitive psychologists have generally avoided the use of case studies.

There has always been some support for the case studies in reading. The first one reported was by Morgan (1896), which described "a case of congenital word-blindness." In 1938, Olson made the following two statements about case studies in the *National Society for Studies in Education Yearbook*: "From the point of view of prediction and control of the growth and the behavior of an individual, the case study is the most scientific method now known. . . . The case study in relation to education is a method with a respectable past and a promising future" (Olson, pp. 329–332). However, forty-seven years later, this "future" has not been realized. Clinical reading programs still have a slender research base (Arter & Jenkins, 1978). With few exceptions (see, for example, Coles, 1984), cognitive scientists in the field of reading have not accepted case studies as sources of data for expanding theory and practice. *Reading Research Quarterly*, the major research journal in the field, has not published a single case study in its entire history. This amounts to a gross imbalance in methodology.

This article explores the nature of reading disability through the use of case studies of adult disabled readers. Case studies were used on the assumption that there can be substantial individual differences in experience and in important dimensions of behavior (both overt and covert) that are as critical as the commonalities between individuals. Adult disabled readers were selected, rather than younger disabled readers, because they have an important advantage: adult disabled readers have conscious access to many more mental processes than do younger reading-disabled children (Brown & Day, 1983). Thus they can partially overcome the problem frequently noted in the literature, that less mature readers are less aware of and less able to report on their own mental activity (see, for example, Gambrell & Heathington, 1981; Hare & Pulliam, 1980; Winograd & Johnston, 1982). Reading-process data and the subjects' reports about their present and past experiences learning to read are presented as data sources to suggest non-neurological explanations for reading failure and the difficulties encountered by adults learning to read.

I suggest that some proportion of adult reading disability results from a combination of conceptual difficulties, rational and irrational use of self-defeating strategies, and negative affective responses. Further, since adult disabled readers represent the maturity of reading failure, we might use these behaviors as indicators of the final form of younger disabled readers' behavior. Employing Vygotsky's (1978) perspective on psychological research, I will argue that an understanding of reading failure cannot be gained through fragmented analyses of the speed of performance of various isolated mental acts out of the context of their social and motivational environment and antecedents.[1] Rather, a useful understanding will only emerge from an integrated examination of the cognitive, affective, social, and personal history of the learner.

Method

Subjects

The subjects in this study were adult males, here called Jack, Bill, and Charlie, ages forty-five, twenty-six, and forty-three, respectively. According to the Analytical Reading Inventory (Woods & Moe, 1981), their approximate reading levels at referral were second grade (Jack), third grade (Bill), and early kindergarten (Charlie). Jack and Charlie remained in school until eighth grade, while Bill continued until eleventh grade. Although no formal intelligence tests were administered, the occupational levels to which these men had risen, in spite of their reading failure, were evidence of their functioning within the normal range of intelligence.[2]

Procedures

Individual instruction sessions with each of these people were tape-recorded with his permission. Sessions ranged from forty-five minutes to two hours, and the data presented in this article are largely drawn from eight sessions with each person. Sessions involved interactive assessment, spontaneous and elicited introspection and retrospection, and elicited think-aloud reports and oral reading performance. The conclusions made in this article are drawn from a combination of all these sources from comparable information produced by more than one person.

Verbal reports remain a controversial data source. Recent work, however, suggests that under certain conditions such reports can yield important, valid information (for example, Afflerbach & Johnston, 1985; Ericsson & Simon, 1980, 1984). It is particularly important to note that the retrospective accounts reported here describe traumatic experiences, like the one described at the beginning of this article. For such recollections, it is likely that the recollection of the basic event is valid, while the details of the event may or may not be. In any case, these subjects' retrospective reports are unlikely to have been distorted in line with specific theoretical orientations, such as might be the case with some previous work (for example, Simpson, 1979).[3]

Results and Discussion

The data relate to a variety of different theoretical frameworks, each of which can be used to help explain why intelligent and otherwise socially adept adults have failed to learn to read. Implicit are some suggestions for prevention and remediation of reading failure. The data have been organized within the general categories of 1) conceptual problems, 2) strategies, 3) anxiety, 4) attributions, and 5) goals and motivation. Each section contains data along with a discussion of their relevance to theories of and remedies for reading failure.

Conceptual Problems

Several types of data suggest that some of these readers' difficulties arise from or are compounded by misconceptions or missing conceptions about various aspects of reading. A minor but interesting example is Bill's pronunciation of "dwindle" as "windle." Did he simply not see the first letter? When asked to repeat it and explain, he noted that the *d* looked as though it ought to be silent. Another example is that Charlie was unable to perform phonemic segmentation of words, a difficulty that must have caused severe conceptual problems as he worked his way through the phonic worksheets with which he was supplied in an earlier adult education remedial program, since knowledge of phonemic segmentation is a prerequisite for analyzing letter/sound relationships.

Other examples are found in retrospective accounts of early reading experiences:

> *Bill:* Through first and second grade I can remember memorizing the books. I didn't read the stories, I would memorize them.

P.J. (Peter Johnston): Did you know that wasn't really reading?

Bill: No.

P.J.: Or did you think that was what it was all about?

Bill: At the time, yes.

Similarly, Jack comments:

> I can remember first grade . . . I couldn't figure out what they were doing and
> it never really caught up with me . . . I never really could understand . . . how
> do these kids know these letters? I know those letters made words, but how do
> they know them?

And again later:

> I had learned symbols . . . and 1 and 2 and 3, which were symbols . . . and 1
> is one, 2 is — even two numbers together will make a number. . . . But that
> just . . . you know . . . so I wanted that for five-letter words. . . . yet . . . like I
> had this idea that . . . I was going to know just by looking at it, you know. . . .
> But there's no way you could possibly take all the words in the dictionary and
> just learn them by sight. Of course the teacher would hold these flash cards
> out and everybody would be hollering the words, and I don't know what the
> heck is going on, you know, what's she doing, you know . . . how do they know
> the word?

Suppose that intelligent individuals such as Bill, Jack, and Charlie developed the notion that reading is largely remembering. They may continue to be at least moderately successful until the second or third grade, by which time the materials would be too difficult for them. To reveal their ignorance at that point would be socially stressful. Additionally, because the erroneous beliefs sometimes seem related to success, they are difficult to give up, much the same way that gambling beliefs and behaviors are difficult to erase. Merritt (1972) has noted this potential for partial reinforcement to make erroneous reading behaviors and concepts about print difficult to eliminate.

That reading difficulty can arise from, and be maintained by, conceptual errors is suggested by Downing's (1972) work on cognitive clarity and is very much in line with the work of Canney and Winograd (1979), Horn, Powers, and Mahabub (1983), and Massaro and Hestand (1983), which show substantial conceptual differences between more and less able readers. An important example of such difficulty is provided by Charlie. In our initial session, Charlie consistently recognized all but four letters of the alphabet and about twenty words. Quite quickly he eliminated the remaining letter confusions *b-d, q-b, d-b,* and *h-r,* and learned another fifteen self-selected words. He could not, however, distinguish two of these words from each other — *street* and *sewer.* Since these were the only words beginning with *s,* his identification of them seemed heavily reliant on the first letter. In one session, these two words were placed one above the other, and Charlie was asked, "In what ways are these two words different? How do they look different from one another?" He stared at the two words for fourteen seconds before responding, "This one's got five and this one's got six." His response suggests at least two particular *conceptual* difficulties: inattention to spatial orientation and to letter sequence. This conceptual interpretation differs from the more frequent perceptual interpretations. Although both explain the failure to detect stimulus differences, the perceptual explanation blames physical or physiological differences while the conceptual explanation attributes the problem to differences in knowledge of what is important and, hence, the allocation of attention. Several writers have noted the fact that both of these conceptual difficulties represent developmental discontinuities (Clay, 1979a; Merritt, 1972). Neither concept is salient for most of children's learning prior to their encountering print.

Clay's (1979b) work on the prevention and remediation of reading failure fits well with a conceptual interpretation. Clay strongly suggests the importance of early detection of erroneous or restricted development of concepts about print and print processing. Once an inappropriate concept is learned or an appropriate one not learned, further instruction that presupposes an understanding of that concept may be not only wasteful but also destructive because of the resultant experience of failure and its emotional consequences (Abramson, Garber, & Seligman, 1980; Dweck, 1975; Johnston & Winograd, 1983; Merritt, 1972).

Retrospective accounts of schooling practices, as in Bill's "flash card" story, suggest that such conceptual difficulties may have been at the root of the problem for these readers. Consider also Bill's response to the question, "How did they teach you to read in the beginning?":

> That was Mrs. X. Stories were repetitious. It was easy. We just memorized them. Any time I used to have to stand up in class, I read great. Y'know . . . I got great marks and stuff. I remember that.

Thus, in this instance, the reading failure was possibly linked to early instructional practices and to the failure to detect a defective concept about reading.

Strategy

Another source of reading difficulty may be the strategies used by these individuals. These can be divided into two categories: general coping strategies used to "get through the day," and strategies used exclusively when reading is required.

General coping strategies Society places a strong emphasis on literacy. This emphasis is not so much a high, positive value as an expectation that people will be literate. Adults who are not literate are painfully aware that they are considered inadequate. Bill, Jack, and Charlie each said that if people learned about his reading problems they would think of him as stupid. This social stigma has several ramifications, some of which are affective and will be discussed later. One ramification that is relevant here, however, is that these adults' behaviors are strongly motivated by the immediate problem of avoiding exposure as "stupid." This behavior reinforces the unsuccessful and unrewarding behaviors noted previously and ensures that any reading skills they do have receive little, if any, practice. As a result, skills do not become automatic, and there is little experimentation with strategies that create flexibility in reading.

Unlike some cognitive difficulties, reading failure cannot be ignored because the demands for literacy are too pervasive. Disabled readers have two choices for dealing with their problem. They can try to fix it, or they can accept it and try to cope with it. Even in their early school years, Bill, Jack, and Charlie were all very good at devising coping strategies that used their strengths to compensate for their weaknesses. This approach began, at least for two of them, quite early. These are some of the coping strategies that they remember using:

> *Bill:* Oh you . . . sit there scared that the teacher's going to call on you. You become a class clown . . . you can . . . either that or I could . . . I remember a lot of things I used to do, especially in eleventh grade. I had one teacher. . . . I used to walk her out to the car and everything. I'd proposition her all the time. She loved it. I got a . . . I walked out of it with a B average and I didn't do any homework and I didn't do anything in class. . . . But also you sit right up the front of the class too; you don't sit in the back . . . back is. . . . They pick on the kids in the back. Since about third or fourth grade I haven't even done anything.

> *P.J.:* But you've read some stuff.

> *Bill:* Any teacher who teaches her class says verbally what has to be learned. All you have to do is pay attention.

> *P.J.:* Can you remember a point where you realized that memorizing wouldn't work anymore?

> *Bill:* Yes, quite a few of them . . . I was afraid to say anything. It was easier to bluff.

Listening for oral instructions and bluffing are effective only for attaining short-term survival goals but are self-defeating in terms of the long-term goal of learning to read.

As these individuals became adults, they adopted several other coping strategies. One such strategy was to find alternative, nonprint information sources. For example, Bill participates in business meetings for which and at which he must read material. His strategy is to be sure to spend some time "shooting the breeze" with other participants before the meeting to pick up the gist of things. At the meeting he says nothing until asked for his opinion, by which time he has been able to gain enough information to respond. He reported that this also makes him appear conservative and thoughtful. Charlie reads the prices on gas pumps to get the right gas in his car and truck. He cannot read the words but uses the price hierarchy as his information source. Unlike many readers for whom the price is not so relevant, he always remembers the current prices. This method is not without risk, since diesel fuel has thrown him off a couple of times and he has put some diesel in his truck.

This avoidance of print is frequently supported by family and friends. Each of the people referred to in this article had such support. For example, Jack's wife typed reports and read occasional reports to him. Bill noted that in school "I had a lot of girls who helped me . . . even in class . . . if I didn't know what was going on and all of a sudden I'd be called on, the answer would be there. Someone would be there to help me."

In general, Jack, Bill, and Charlie took a preventive approach to the problem, which involved systematically excluding print from their lives. The goal of their behavior was never to be caught in a situation in which they might be expected to read. This meant avoiding print at all costs in any potentially social situation. Thus, even though they may have wanted to learn to read, they systematically missed opportunities to practice decoding. This avoidance of print must be taken into account in explanations of reading failure that place causal emphasis on speed of processing and on automaticity differences between more and less able readers (see, for example, Sternberg & Wagner, 1982).

Reading strategies For some, there are practical constraints on print avoidance. For example, two of these people had reached career positions — one in management — that required them to read. Invariably, the material that they were required to read was extremely difficult for them — far beyond their available reading skill. In order to handle such material, they were forced to invoke a different pattern of reading strategies from those used by normally developing readers.

The two men who could read to some degree dealt with the problem of having to read in similar ways. The next section will document their dominant strategies in this situation and contrast them with strategies used by younger, competent readers.

Both Jack and Bill make extensive use of their general knowledge and the context of a given word or phrase in order to figure it out. These context-driven strategies are characteristic of high-progress readers. Most importantly, they predict and they self-correct; however, the big difference between these adults and younger, high-progress readers is that more able readers use a balance of context and text when they arrive at a word they do not understand. Jack and Bill, on the other hand, rely excessively on context-utilization strategies that they have overdeveloped to the point that their strengths have become their weaknesses. That is, often these strategies are relied upon even when the context and their general knowledge are totally inadequate, and when they actually are capable of using a more efficient print-driven strategy, such as making use of the letter-sound relationship.

There are numerous ways to combine strategies to figure out words not instantly recognized. Forms of phonic analysis can be combined with forms of context strategy, such as rereading the previous context or reading ahead to the end of the sentence. When mature efficient readers reach an unfamiliar word, they tend to use some form of phonic analysis, usually in conjunction with prediction (Holdaway, 1979). Rereading or reading ahead are usually tried only upon the failure of the other more efficient methods. Rereading is a particularly expensive strategy because it disrupts the flow of thought (Collins & Smith, 1982).

Bill's response, when confronted with an unknown word, is to use approximately the following sequence:

– read (or skim) to the end of the sentence (or several sentences);
– reread the sentence (or smaller or larger segment);
– consult memory for association (sometimes the first strategy used);
– and use letter/sound relationships (last resort).

This sequence of strategies is likely to be the reverse of that used by efficient readers; the least efficient strategies are used first. But although inefficient, they frequently give the reader enough to continue. For example, when Bill encountered the word *Charlene,* his thinking went as follows:

Bill: Charlotte — Charlene [long pause].

P.J.: Is it Charlotte or Charlene? How would you know? How would you figure it out?

Bill: It's Charlene.

P.J.: How did you know?

Bill: Because I have a Charlene . . . ah . . . working for me at work.

P.J.: OK. But how would you be able to figure it out from the letters?

Bill: *l-e-n-e* /ēn/ it looks to me.

P.J.: What would Charlotte end with?

Bill: e-t.

The text-driven strategies — his weakness — are avoided, even when they are available. The strategy he used here was to fall back on memory.[4]

Sometimes strategy implementation is less systematic. For example, Jack might simply look at different words for a clue:

> *Jack:* Yeah . . . because know what? I wanted to bounce off those other words, to get that word without trying to sound the word right, without even realizing it. Why do I do that to myself? I do, though. You know, I do it self-consciously. But that's just what I was doing . . . trying to make these words tell me what this word is.

Again, this avoidance of text-driven strategies ensures that they will not be developed and certainly will not become automatic.

The extent to which this use of strengths to compensate for weaknesses dominates and distorts the reading process can be demonstrated by examining running records of Bill's reading. His reading bore many of the characteristics of what Coltheart, Patterson, and Marshall (1980) have called "deep dyslexia," in which readers frequently substitute synonyms while reading, allegedly because of neurological factors. For example, in one instance he substituted *cab* for *taxi* in the first sentence of a story. Other substitutions in that story were *tires/wheels, motor/engine,* and *walked/stepped.* The explanation for this behavior turned out to be more straightforward than "deep dyslexia." While Bill's *taxi/cab* substitution appears to have been done with insufficient context, the context was in fact more than sufficient. When he "read" the word taxi, his eyes were halfway down the page. There are two forms of evidence for this. The first is from his own reports that suggest that Bill's problem is strategic rather than neurological.

> I scan ahead to where I'm going to have trouble with . . . I often . . . I'm reading the sentence, but my mind is deciphering that word before I get to it. Or trying to figure out what that word is.
>
> I've got to slow down when I read because my eyes will go faster than my mind. That's another thing I've had to learn to do. When I first started trying to get myself to read, I'd read over something; then, when I'd stop and read over it slow, it would be totally different.

The second form of evidence comes from analysis of oral reading with and without an intervention to prevent the use of this read-ahead strategy. An index card was prepared with a one-quarter- by three-quarter-inch piece cut from the top left corner. Bill was asked to read using this card to mask all but the word being read. This intervention was alternated for brief periods of time with normal reading without the card: a few minutes without the card, a few minutes with the card, then a few minutes without the card again, and so on. This type of design produced the pattern shown in Figure 1.

Forcing Bill to focus his attention on the print detail of the word being read increased his accuracy, decreased both the number and extent of his

FIGURE 1
The Effects of a Self-Controlled Masking Card on Oral Reading Behaviors

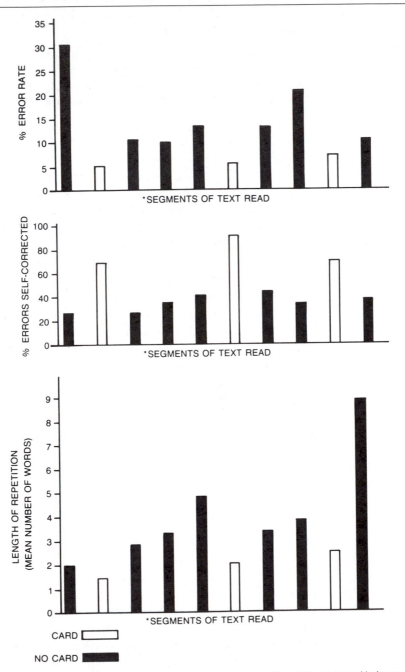

Segments of text were read with and without the use of a card masking all but the word being read. These text segments were not identical in length. Longer segments were broken into smaller units of similar length. The average number of words per segment was 134.

repetitions, and increased his self-correction rate. Bill normally did not decode even those words that he could readily figure out, a behavior that hampered the development of automatic decoding. Thus, his distorted reading strategies were self-perpetuating. Indeed, the order in which he used strategies seemed to be automatic. It was only with great determination and considerable frustration that Bill was able to resist rushing the masking card along to the end of the line. Often he was not able to resist. As he noted when asked how far ahead of his voice his eyes had traveled:

> *Bill:* I used to be way ahead. I'm making myself slow down. Wherever my eyes are looking I try and read the words. That was a . . . that's very hard for me to do.

> *P.J.:* OK. So you knew that before you were actually reading about . . . saying . . . this, you were looking here.

> *Bill:* My eyes were about at least four words ahead all the time.

One consequence of Bill's approach to reading was that his attention was divided. He allocated some of his attention to the difficult word well before his voice arrived at the problem. This is very similar to efficient readers' eye-voice span, except that Bill seemed to allocate a far greater proportion of attention to the impending problem than would a normal reader who uses the eye-voice span largely to plan articulation of already-read text. Apparently, the competing demands on Bill's cognitive resources caused increasing interference with oral reading, evidenced by increasing pauses between words as the difficult word was approached (see Figure 2). He also noted this verbally:

> *Bill:* I was concentrating on that word [*mantel*] before I got to it. I was reading, but that's the word I was going to stumble on.

> *P.J.:* Do you know where you started worrying about it?

> *Bill:* I think when I hit *scientists* I already glanced back down to *mantel*. . . . I know I hit it back up in here someplace, too, when I was worried about it. There was *mantel* someplace else in here.

This voice print supports the verbal report. When Bill's voice was at point A, his eyes had already reached point B (the problematic word *mantel*). As his voice approached the word that he was still working out, the processing conflict between oral production of the words already read and the difficult word to be decoded produced increasing hesitations between words. As noted in the verbal report, a similar pattern of hesitations preceded the first use of the term *mantel* (Point C), including a false start at the word. Also worth noting is Bill's substitution of *heavy* for *deep* in a segment produced orally while presumably attending to the upcoming problem word.

FIGURE 2
Voice Print Showing the Location and Extent of Pauses
between Words as Read by Bill

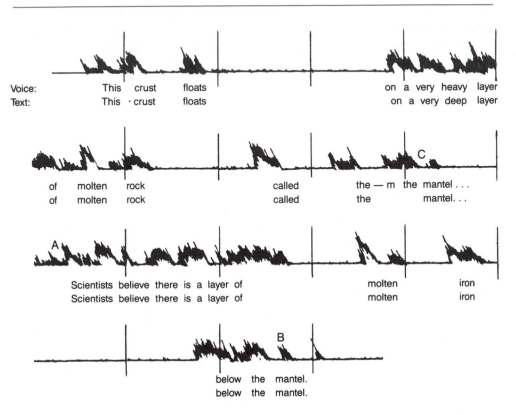

Note: When Bill's voice is at point A, his attention is already focused on point B. Similarly, his attention is focused on point C some time before his voice arrives at that point. The substantial hesitations preceding points B and C (the problematic word "mantel") are apparently caused by interference between the demands of voice production and decoding.

Upon further inquiry it became apparent that Bill was very strong in what Sternberg (1984) would call "global planning." Upon turning a page, his first step was to scan the page for difficult words so that he knew where they were located and could allocate attention appropriately ahead of time. Next, he began reading the page to himself before uttering the first word. Thus, there was a marked pause after each page was turned. I checked this on several occasions by turning the page and covering it within seconds, asking how many problem words were on the page and where they were. Bill was able to respond quite accurately. He also described this behavior:

> I initially started . . . I would take something and look at it . . . I've got to read this. I'd look down the whole thing and say, "Holy shit! I've got about six of them I'm going to run into" . . . and . . . in my mind I'd be worrying about those six as I started to read down.

Jack, too, had extremely well-developed predictive skill through the use of context. This sometimes led him into trouble because he maintained his view over that of the author. Consider his comments on his (mostly silent) reading of a book:

> *Stone Fox* . . . did not like the illustrations in that book at all. It didn't do me . . . these illustrations . . . I ignored them totally because I wanted my own visual idea of who the characters were and I don't know if that's wrong . . . but, see, that sometimes gets me messed up, though, with reading. Well, I get so involved with my visual . . . in my thoughts of what's going on . . . and then projecting ahead that I get overwhelmed and I shut down on reading . . . because everything's forced at once and I can't concentrate on decoding, see? So what happens to me . . . I've got to calm myself down and say, "Forget now what's going to happen two pages from now."

Jack's comments are very similar to Bill's, and the pattern of reading performance obtained with and without the masking card (shown in Figure 1) was also very similar to Bill's. From observation and self-report, it seems that silent reading differed from oral reading largely because neither Jack nor Bill read line by line down the page. Their eyes skipped back and forth, and more sections of the text were missed.

This overuse of meaning-driven strategies is interesting in the light of findings on the differences between more and less able readers, and more and less intelligent students. That the individuals described here are intelligent is attested to by their considerable ability to use partial information (see, for example, Resnick & Glaser, 1976; Sternberg & Wagner, 1982) and their extensive global planning (Sternberg, 1984). Indeed, it is their intelligent response to a perceived problem that appears to prevent them from developing normal reading behaviors. These data, at least for these particular readers, speak against the explanation of reading failure posed by Wolford (1981), which lays the blame on failure to use partial information. On the other hand, these data lend support to a model of reading failure such as that presented by Ceci (1982), which emphasizes problems with higher level processing and differences in purposeful, rather than automatic, processing. Although Crowder (1983) notes that such a model is at variance with most other models of disability, it may deserve greater consideration.

A further problem with Bill, Jack, and Charlie's reported or observed reading strategies is in their specificity. Some of their strategies were devised for certain tasks and are of no use beyond those tasks. For example, Bill had trouble with the word *were,* often confusing it with *when.* He expressed his solution strategy: "Is, was, when, were — I just say that and I get it." He used this same strategy on three different occasions during the sessions. Its success, however, is restricted to the one task and cannot be generalized to other problems. It is not clear how it works, but its continued operation prevents the development of more functional, more widely applicable strategies.

Consider also the case described earlier of Charlie attempting to describe the differences between the two words *street* and *sewer*. His response was, "This one's got five and this one's got six." Charlie was then shown that street had two *e*'s next to each other — which he indicated he had not detected — as well as some other characteristics. Subsequently he reliably distinguished between the two words and consistently reported that the *ee* was the basis of his discrimination (after *s* for the initial distinction). The task confronting this intelligent and otherwise successful man required that he combine knowledge that he already had — distinguishing letters and patterns — with comparative skill that he already had in an essentially nonverbal task, the diagnosis and repair of pumps and related mechanical and electrical equipment. He was simply not seeing the words. While motivated to learn to read, he typically did not apply his available knowledge and skill to the task, and even when he did he used inflexible and restrictive problem-solving strategies, strategies that are uncharacteristic of this generally resourceful person.

Thus, Charlie has developed isolated knowledge about a number of things. For example, he knew that adding an *s* to his christian name resulted in a friend's surname, and he could write this. However, he could not apply the principle of adding an *s* to other words to produce new or altered words. Generalizing such a simple example requires practicing independently, taking the risk of applying it in a new context, and having rich sources of feedback to define the limits of generalizability.

Anxiety

As discussed earlier, the risk of being seen as stupid caused Charlie, as it probably causes other adults like him, to systematically avoid practice and feedback. There may be other explanations of this behavior, too, such as anxiety.[5]

Charlie: j-a . . . uh . . . j's . . . ah . . . getting nervous now.

P.J.: Can you write it?

Charlie: Oh boy . . . had it down last night. Ain't that something. I just had it in my head; that's why I brought it up. Boy, I can't believe this . . .

Bill: I started sounding it out and stuff, but I started saying, "Hell, I know what this goddamn word is, how come I can't say it?"

In my view, the effect of anxiety in reading difficulty cannot be overestimated, although its circular causal properties are difficult to demonstrate. Charlie, the most severely reading disabled of the three discussed here, is a very fit and healthy forty-three-year-old who had been taking medication for high blood pressure since he was thirty-two. My first session with him is illustrative. His wife had made the initial contact for him to see me. I was to meet him at an appointed place. He arrived ten minutes early, left, and called his wife to tell her I had not shown up. When we later met, his anxiety was apparent in several ways. When I gave him the preprimer word list from the Analytical Reading Inventory (Woods & Moe, 1981), he could read only two words. He was flushed and wringing his hands under the table. Later in the session, after some success with words like *stop,* he was able to recognize, one at a time, more of these words. However, additional specific occurrences provided further evidence that anxiety caused problems. When asked to write *men's* he wrote *mem,* immediately scribbled it out, then wrote *me,* scribbled that out even more quickly, and then wrote *m,* and with trembling hand, admitting to nervousness, he was unable to write any more. Later, after experiencing some success, he was able to write this word unprompted. The next time his performance deteriorated in this manner, he noted his nervousness and indulged in extensive self-recrimination. His wife told me the next day that he had gone to a bar on his way home and "got smashed — he's never had to expose himself like that before."

The debilitating nature of such anxiety can also be seen in the self-reports, where Jack finally works out a word.

P.J.: That was fairly hard work.

Jack: Yes, it was.

P.J.: Because it's not that long, really. You've got much harder words up there.

Jack: I know it.

P.J.: Why do you think you had trouble like that?

Jack: I know one thing. I was getting . . . for some reason something triggered me off before this that I was starting to get tense . . . and I could see, I could feel myself shutting down. Like when I get this way I can feel my whole self tense . . . and I'm not absolutely, not even been . . . I'm not even . . . at one point there I wasn't even being able to . . . I had to force myself to concentrate because everything was going.

This stress may be greater for adult poor readers than for younger poor readers or for other adults facing difficult tasks because they have a longer history of stressful associations. For example:

Jack: What it is, it's the old feelings. It's like, y'know, well . . . something will trigger it. Like when I was a kid in school and they would ask me the first day,

I would be in a first . . . say, a new class, and they would ask me to read, and the teacher didn't know that I couldn't read. Well, those feelings still can come back to me, and it's like a feeling . . . never . . . I can't even begin to explain. It's like you completely feel isolated, totally alone, and when that sets in . . . course, I don't get it now like I did then . . . but it's still that quaint feeling will come over me, and if I . . . if it overwhelms me . . . it . . . it . . . it takes you right up . . . you know, and you do, you shut right down.

I think it's more my emotions and my feelings, and, of course, it's a catching-up part. You know, it's like everything that has happened to me through the years all of a sudden comes all floating back, and it's like a crash. You know, your mind can go back and reach out and grab all those terrible, terrible . . .

If I took . . . if . . . you know . . . like, I would have to take my time. It wouldn't come automatically, but if I was . . . kept myself calm . . . I could read it. Get myself . . . the least bit nervous . . . could not read it. If you wrote it in script, forget it [although he can write script letters).

Everything would go blank. I could not pull . . . I could not get anything out of it. It would just completely . . . could not function . . . could not function . . . could not organize my mind to make it, to read it.

These comments reflect a very severe form of anxiety, severe enough to be called a neurosis. Indeed, Merritt (1972) has described reading failure in just these terms. He notes the similarity between the characteristics of reading-disabled children and the behavior of animals who have suffered experimentally induced neurosis (although such research would no longer be acceptable). These include resistance to entering a learning situation, fear responses (trembling, hiding, attempting to escape from the learning situation), inability to resist making incorrect responses, compulsive responding, regressive behavior, loss of the ability to delay a response, and changes in social behavior, such as symptoms of suspicion, aggressiveness, and refusal to join the flock (Hilgard & Marquis, 1964; Masserman, 1950).

The general level of anxiety with which these adults must live is evident from comments throughout this article, but for some it is exacerbated by having to deal with individuals who take pleasure in tormenting them.

Bill: He [previous immediate supervisor] used to like to go through the dictionary to find words to drive me nuts. It drove me nuts because I couldn't even pronounce half of them and that was his specialty . . . so he'd write up the log at night. . . . There'd be important things I had to know, and he'd sit there for half an hour going through the dictionary, so that means I had to sit there for an hour and a half. [Bill talks about the "Webster."] It's fantastic, the words and stuff that are in there . . . it's not that . . . but you can go through it and find words that will drive you nuts, you know. Well, he used to sit there and do it. . . . Well, he's a coordinator now. [Laughs.] He used to always tell me, "You just remember you're number two," and I just used to laugh.

That such stress was also present in their school experiences is evidenced in these retrospective descriptions:

Charlie: You'd have to stand up and read your book or something, and if I couldn't read or something I'd just pass it on to the next kid.

* * *

Bill: I never learned anything through the whole class because two kids used to sit in back of me and beat on me all the time. Whenever I told the teacher she would . . . this is what sticks in my mind . . . when I would go up to the teacher crying she told me I was a crybaby and go sit down or go in the corner. So I got punished, which I never understood, for being hurt.

* * *

Jack: Last week of school vacation was my traumatic week, thinking about how I had to go back into the new grade with my old classmates but with a new teacher, and have to tell her that I don't know how to read. Oh . . . it was terrible . . . so . . . I was cubbied in that little spot in my desk and there I can remember it; and it was like the third day and it was my turn to read and everybody said, "He doesn't know how to read." And she just says "next" and all . . .

If they didn't say "test" I could do it. I know it. If, you know . . . because that was another thing. Tests . . . tests to me . . . tell me that it was a test . . . you know . . . that would devastate me. . . . You'd have to tell me that . . . the word "test" . . . and my heart beats in my throat. . . . Now th . . . uh . . . this [present tutor] that I have now, I think she was aware of that and never would say "test." "We'll do this today," and I think my little trigger in my mind . . . course, I'm always thinking beyond, you know. I would say, this is a test, I know it is . . . to myself.

As noted above, these anxiety reactions seem almost literally to shut down the reader's mind. Interestingly, this same kind of reaction can be brought on by success.

Jack: I would start reading, and I would have to be very careful that all of a sudden I would get this flash on my mind: "My God, you're reading." The minute that happened — shut down.

It also seems that this effect can be quite general:

Jack: I was getting physically tired from reading. . . . Like, I'll start reading and this tiredness comes right over my mind. I almost feel that if I read another word it's going to break. You know . . . the eyes get heavy and I start shutting down, and if I just take a break when that happens — put the book down for awhile, maybe get a glass of water, just do something — then go back to it, it'll come back.

However, there appears to be an additional effect, which is

. . . and I hate even telling you this, but I need to learn the sounds of syllables and to be able to construct. . . . and I was avoiding it so much because I'm afraid of it . . . you know . . . you get these little . . . I don't understand why I'm afraid of it.

Further evidence of this avoidance of print detail is provided by this comment from Jack about television credits:

> I have actually witnessed myself . . . though . . . in the last few weeks . . . I can turn that right off . . . I have the . . . I don't know it's control or what, but I can actually . . . I can either make myself read it or look at it just like it is.

Together, these reactions — a general avoidance of print detail and a shutting down of processing under stress — could produce a condition of almost literal "word blindness" when reading is required. This would make learning to read a very difficult feat indeed.

Attributions

While anxiety seems very important, at least as important are the causes to which these individuals attribute their failure. Their attributions represent helpless (Dweck, 1975) or passive (Johnston & Winograd, 1983) responses to learning failure. These examples are illustrative:

> *Charlie:* And I went to some program, too. I was in the special class up there for reading and writing, and it seemed the same way there. I was . . . just couldn't pick it up in my head or learn or anything. So I don't know what . . . ah . . . myself . . . I said to myself, I know I'm not going to . . . ah . . . I'm not going to know anything on that sheet because I'm full blank.
>
> *P.J.:* Mmmmm.
>
> *Charlie:* Just like an idiot.
>
> * * *
>
> *Bill:* Because you feel stupid . . . because they're smarter than you, and if you say anything then you're lower than them . . . idiot can't read, y'know.
>
> * * *
>
> *Jack:* I worry that people will think I'm stupid.
>
> *P.J.:* Do you think to yourself, maybe I am?
>
> *Jack:* Yes.

Consider the consequences of these attributions. They imply a stable, internal, global factor beyond the learner's control: low intelligence. This attribution is highly unmotivating and is probably the most detrimental to learning (Dweck, 1975).

Where do these attributions come from? These comments suggest some possible sources:

> *Jack:* Everyone . . . you know . . . [who] didn't bring in their homework would be punished. "Jack, it's all right." They didn't do nothing if I didn't have my homework, there'd be nothing said to me. So then finally it was like a knife — it was almost like a piercing pain in my head when she said it to me, "Jack, you don't have to worry about doing your homework anymore."

The boys [Jack's sons] started to have the trouble, I blamed myself for their problem . . . which . . . figuring that it was hereditary . . . you know . . . dunce-o-me.[6]

An interesting change occurred in Jack's attribution as his reading improved. The following two statements represent a shift from helpless, unmotivating attributions to more active, motivating ones with some consequent side effects.

Jack: [initial interview] What's wrong with me that I have this problem?

Jack: [after considerable improvement] I don't know if I should say this or not, but the last few months I felt a little resentment towards my mother because of the instruction, and that bothers me. I sort of at some point say, "Well, why didn't she intervene or why didn't she do whatever she could have done to make this not happen to me?" Because . . . see . . . prior to now I have always felt that there is a possibility that something was wrong. You know, maybe I was retarded. I think that was always in the back of my mind and that's a hard thing to live with.

According to the extensive literature on teacher-student interaction reviewed recently by Allington (1983), Brophy (1983), Hiebert (1983), and Johnston and Winograd (1983), teachers treat less able students quite differently from more able students and, in doing so, implicitly tell the less able students that they are *constitutionally* less able. This attribution of failure to a cause for which there is little hope of a cure is profoundly unmotivating.

These attributions also follow from society's equating literacy with intelligence. Bill's awareness of this is evident when he finally admits his problem to some co-workers. The evidence lies in his attempts to legitimate his problem as a real entity separate from intelligence. Note in the following quotation his use of the term "dyslexia," which has now had considerable public exposure, and his reference to the university and the term "doctor."

Bill: It's funny . . . you start to . . . a lot of people . . . I says, "I'm going to [university name] . . . for . . . I've had some problems reading." I say "dyslexia" . . . just . . . y'know. They say, "Well, what's the problem?" and I say, "Well, I skip lines and sentences and, y'know, I get lost after about a page or so." There's a lot of people . . . it's . . . I always thought that . . .

P.J.: Oh, you thought you were alone?

Bill: Yeah! It . . . ah . . . *Doctor* — I get the title in there — "I go up and see Doctor Johnston," y'know. "Well, what's it cost anyway?" And I says, "Well, he's doing it for free." Y'know . . . and . . . ah . . . you hear the same problem I had. "How can I get help?" and "Jeez . . . you think he'd take me in?" I didn't realize it was that . . . ah . . . y'know . . . these guys are . . . well, I'm in supervision and that's probably crazy, them looking up at me and having problems, but these are maintenance men who have to read the manuals to fix the equipment, and they're stumbling through the manuals.

Bill: Like this weekend — the weekend before — is when I started talking to people. Well, once I talked to about three of them and got the same answer. We're all standing in a group. I was . . . y'know . . . when you throw out "dyslexia," well, that opens it up, y'know . . . and I don't feel bad talking about it.

These comments highlight the extreme loneliness felt by these individuals. Each thinks that he is virtually the only person with the problem. The comments also reveal a legitimate function for the term "dyslexia." While of little functional use in the scientific description of reading failure, it has a liberating social value in separating the concepts of literacy and intelligence.

Goals and Motivation

Charlie had considerable motivation for learning to read. He was being pushed at his primary job to accept a promotion that would pay more but add paperwork, and at his part-time job his excuses for not reading — "forgot my glasses," and so on — were wearing thin. His army reserve friends had given him a very difficult time for missing all the promotion tests and hence never being promoted. Why, then, did he not seek assistance in solving his problem? There are several overlapping reasons for this. First, he noted the importance of secrecy. If people were to know that he could not read, they would think him stupid and not value his opinion. His desire to avoid being considered "marginal" to society, and his conflict between concealing his reading problem versus accepting and revealing it have been likened to the dilemma of the homosexual "coming out" (Charnley & Jones, 1979). (The psychology of such decisions has been described by Musgrove, 1977.) A second reason behind Charlie's failure to seek assistance was his view of learning to read as a long-term goal, and, given his attributions, potentially an unattainable one. In the meantime, he had more immediate pressures from his two jobs and his social commitments.

Goal conflicts such as these cause these adults to feel constantly ambivalent about striving to learn to read. At different times, depending on the context, different goals assume different priorities, but usually the shorter term goals take precedence. The aggregate effect on learning to read is generally negative. For example, Bill commented:

I tried going to [a reading clinic]. Before I even went down and talked to them and . . . ah . . . I just . . . I don't know why . . . I just . . . I was on my way to it . . . do the rest of the stuff . . . just . . . ah . . . never went back.

Bill is not alone in this. The dropout rate from adult basic education courses in the United States is about one-third (Hunter & Harmon, 1979). Cook (1977) also notes that even the threat of loss of welfare payments for failure to attend such courses produced a turnout of only 2.6 percent of those affected.

Nicholls (1983) describes a distinction between motivation in ego-involving and task-involving situations. The distinction hinges on whether the central goal is to protect or enhance one's ego, or to complete a task, or solve a problem. Since the consequence of demonstrating an inability to read is highly ego-involving, the response is often self-defeating. For example, the shift from task-involvement to ego-involvement can be seen in this example from Bill:

> Your eyes have to move in a certain way on the paper so that when I started . . . you'd actually try to read it and you'd stumble through the paper and you notice they're staring at you. So then all of a sudden you're not reading . . . your eyes are just moving through the lines down the paper.

Nevertheless, Bill wanted so much to read that he tried several strategies on his own:

Bill: At work I had to learn to read.

P.J.: How did you do it?

Bill: Wasn't easy. I had to use the dictionary. I had to look up words.

P.J.: In order to look up in the dictionary you had to know how to read some.

Bill: That's where my biggest problem was . . . finding out where the words were in the dictionary. I had to look up . . . well, that isn't right . . . but it sounds like this . . . so if that sounds like this, then it should be over on this page in the dictionary. You know, it sort of breaks up the words for you.

In the dictionary a lot of definitions are hard because I couldn't read what the definition of the word was. But in the Webster, the one I have . . . it's what . . . the college dictionary . . . it usually has four or five meanings. If somewhere during the paragraph I can find one of the meanings to figure out what the word is, or pretty much. So, if I couldn't sound it out I could get a rough meaning of what the word was. Another thing I did in the last two years . . . *Sesame Street* . . . watch that with my kids. You see that? Mr. /ch/ or whatever.

On the satellite I'd find a lot of French movies, or whatever, that I could really not give a shit about, that had American on the bottom, and I'd go through them until I'd get real lost in the movie.

These efforts are all self-imposed, task-involving situations. This same intelligent and persistent person, in an ego-involving situation, reacts differently, as can be discerned from Bill's reaction to the suggestion that he read to his own children, ages five and eight:

> I actually tried that but my eight-year-old started pointing out my mistakes, so that was that — never did that again.

Others' reactions to one's success can also affect motivation.

Bill: That one [book] I struggled through. I haven't read in a long time. Reading . . . the first time . . . my wife was in . . . I says, "Well, I've finished the book." She says "Well, OK." I says, "You don't understand. That's the first time I've read through a whole book." [Laughs.] She goes . . . she . . . she didn't think it was any big deal, she didn't. Well, that bothered me a little bit. But then after that I picked up this one. I read that in one night because . . .

P.J.: Was it easier going, or motivation was high, or . . .

Bill: Motivation was high.

Success in this case had a greater effect on motivation than the external feedback. The extreme emotional impact of realized success was expressed by Jack after he had been in the program for a considerable time and was reading at a seventh-grade instruction level:

P.J.: I thought of you when watching *Return of the Jedi*. It has subtitles.

Jack: [excited] You know . . . you know, I saw that and you know what? I realized after a while that I was reading them. I wasn't always finishing before they took it off the screen, but I was reading them. I used to avoid looking at the words, and I couldn't watch foreign movies. But I got such an incredible feeling . . . it was like . . . it's hard to explain. I get the same feeling when they play the Star Spangled Banner — sort of choked up.

Jack's motivation to learn was heightened by his perspective on the free tuition he was receiving in the university reading clinic.

Jack: I think it's a fantastic thing for the simple fact you got two people that are meeting for the same purpose. We're both there to learn . . . um . . . there's no pay involved. The teacher wants to get something out of this as well as the student.

P.J.: But is that what you think helped you best?

Jack: Yes . . . because . . . we're on the same level and I have to achieve for her as well as myself because if I don't achieve I'm gonna make her look like she's failing. . . . Like, see, I have went through the game at work of your paying somebody and I don't want to sound like . . . but it's monetary, when you're paying them, so, you know, do you really have to do it? I don't have to do it then . . . because you're paying them to do it for you. I think it's a fantastic thing.

On the other hand, there were frequent motivational conflicts. For example, these men occasionally expressed concern over the increased responsibility that improved reading skill might engender. If they were to improve they might be *expected* to read, even by those who are close to them and know that they have difficulty. Some of these motives may be quite subtle and difficult to gather evidence for. For example, after making good progress in the clinic, Jack reached a plateau at a sixth- to seventh-grade level where he has remained for nearly two semesters. The reasons for this have not been caught on tape and cannot be presented verbatim. However, conversations suggest that they include the fact that to an unemployed male, regular contact with a concerned female tutor is not something to be given up easily. Additionally, Jack seems to have deduced that if, after forty-five years, he finally does become literate, then he always could have become literate. To admit this would force him to contemplate what might have been, and his struggle with this is not an easy one.

Conclusion

In this article I have tried to present a multifaceted yet integrated picture of adult reading failure. The complex set of conditions within which these individuals operate is inextricably interwoven with their cognitive activity. As noted earlier in Footnote 1, this perspective is more in line with the work of Vygotsky and of Activity Theory than with the bulk of current research on reading failure. For example, with rare exceptions, the affective and motivational dimensions of reading failure are conspicuous mainly for their absence from current research and causal explanations.

Past attempts at explanations of the differences between good and poor readers have tended to dwell on the minutiae of mental operations without considering either the psychological or social contexts within which they occur. Diverse reader goals have also been given short shrift. Consistent with Activity Theory, in this article I have argued that such impoverished models are dangerous in that diagnoses that follow from them will favor factors less modifiable through education than those described here. Rather than the neurological and processing deficit explanations currently in vogue, we need to consider more seriously explanations that stress combinations of anxiety, attributions, maladaptive strategies, inaccurate or nonexisting concepts about aspects of reading, and a huge variety of motivational factors. Although these aspects are most likely to exist in combination, I suspect that each alone is powerful enough to engender some degree of reading failure. Given the structure of teacher-student interactions (Allington, 1983; Brophy, 1983; Hiebert, 1983) and the present competitive social context equating literacy with intellect, it is perfectly reasonable to suppose that these factors are likely to cause or catalyze problems for many children.

The consequences of such an emphasis on educationally modifiable components strongly suggest, in contrast to most current models of reading disability, that reading failure can be prevented. Indeed, we have evidence that this is the case. Clay (1979b) has shown that children whose reading development is not proceeding normally can be identified after they have been in school for six months to a year. Intensive one-to-one instruction to clarify their misconceptions and accelerate the development of independent reading processes allows them to return to the regular instructional program in thirteen to fourteen weeks on the average. These students need no further assistance (Clay, 1979b, 1982). The interpretation also suggests that the longer a reading problem goes undetected, the more difficult it will be to remedy. Thus, the emphasis is on early detection of reading difficulty, a suggestion that runs counter to some current practices that focus assessment at the end of schooling in an accountability model.

Most current explanations of reading difficulties focus on the level of operations, devoid of context, goals, motives, or history. While some work has focused on the context of reading failure rather than mental operations (McDermott, 1977; Mehan, 1979), there has been little effort to integrate these two dimensions. The consequent explanations of reading failure are sterile and have resulted in more or less terminal diagnoses of reading failure. Until we can integrate the depth of human feeling and thinking into our understanding of reading difficulties, we will have only a shadow of an explanation of the problem and ill-directed attempts at solutions.

Notes

1. This approach to the study of cognitive processes has previously been suggested by the Activity Theory model of cognitive research (Leontiev, 1979; Vygotsky, 1978; Wertsch, 1979; Zinchenko & Gordon, 1979). Activity Theory allows for three levels of activity — activities, actions, and operations — each of which is distinctive yet inseparable from the other two. In this model of human behavior, complex patterns of activities are considered to be the highest level of analysis. Motives and emotions are the major concern at this level of investigation because they drive the activity. At the second level of analysis (action), behavior is seen as organized around goals which are devised to be compatible with the motives. Operations are the third and lowest level of analysis. These more isolated component behaviors are selected to attain goals under particular conditions. Thus, operations are defined with respect to the context in which a goal is given.
2. I based this assumption on Sternberg's model (1984) of intelligence and on the American Association of Mental Deficiency adaptive behavior criteria.
3. Compare these individuals' naiveté with the personal recollections of Simpson (1979). Prior to writing her book, Simpson studied psychology at both undergraduate and graduate levels and had read a substantial amount of literature on the topic from a particular theoretical orientation. It would be hard to avoid distortions in these recollections to fit the subsequent understanding of the problem. Nonetheless, Simpson's work is excellent in its use of cases to build an understanding of the difficulties faced by individuals with literacy problems.
4. These observations should not, indeed cannot, be interpreted as suggesting a need for intensive phonics instruction as the remedial technique. For a relevant discussion the interested reader should refer to Holdaway (1979).
5. See references to attribution theory literature (for example, Butkowsky & Willows, 1980; Dweck, 1975; Johnston & Winograd, 1983; Weiner, 1972) discussed later in this article.
6. Jack's blaming himself could increase anxiety over the children's reading, which might then be translated into stress on them.

References

Abramson, L. Y., Garber, J., & Seligman, M. E. P. (1980). Learned helplessness in humans: An attributional analysis. In J. Garber & M. E. P. Seligman, *Human helplessness: Theory and applications* (pp. 3–34). New York: Academic Press.

Afflerbach, P., & Johnston, P. (1985). On the use of verbal reports in reading research. *Journal of Reading Behavior, 16,* 307–322.

Allington, R. L. (1983). The reading instruction provided readers of differing reading abilities. *Elementary School Journal, 83,* 559–568.

Allport, G. W. (1962). The general and unique in psychological science. *Journal of Personality, 30,* 405–422.

Allport, G. W. (1966). Traits revisited. *American Psychologist, 21,* 1–10.

Arter, J. A., & Jenkins, J. R. (1978, January). *Differential diagnosis — prescriptive teaching: A critical appraisal.* (ERIC Document Reproduction Service No. ED 150 578)

Bem, D. J., & Allen, G. (1974). On predicting some of the people some of the time: The search for cross-situational consistencies in behavior. *Psychological Review, 81,* 506–520.

Brophy, J. E. (1983). Research on the self-fulfilling prophecy and teacher expectations. *Journal of Educational Psychology, 75,* 631–661.

Brown, A. L., & Day, J. (1983). Macrorules for summarizing strategies: The development of expertise: *Journal of Verbal Learning and Verbal Behavior, 22,* 1–44.

Browning, R. M., & Stover, D. O. (1971). *Behavior modification in child treatment: An experimental and clinical approach.* Chicago: Aldine-Atherton.

Butkowsky, I. S., & Willows, D. M. (1980). Cognitive-motivational characteristics of children varying in reading ability: Evidence for learned helplessness in poor readers. *Journal of Educational Psychology, 72,* 408–422.

Canney, G., & Winograd, P. (1979). *Schemata for reading and reading comprehension performance.* (Tech. Rep. No. 120.) Urbana, IL: Center for the Study of Reading. (ERIC Document Reproduction Service No. ED 169 520)

Ceci, S. J. (1982). Extracting meaning from stimuli: Automatic and purposive processing of the language-based learning disabled. *Topics in Learning and Learning Disabilities, 2,* 46–53.

Charnley, A. H., & Jones, H. A. (1979). *The concept of success in adult literacy.* Cambridge, Eng.: Huntington.

Chi, M., & Koeske, R. (1983). Network representation of a child's dinosaur knowledge. *Developmental Psychology, 19,* 29–39.

Clay, M. M. (1979a). *Reading: The patterning of complex behaviour* (2d ed.). Auckland, New Zealand: Heinemann.

Clay, M. M. (1979b). *The early detection of reading difficulties: A diagnostic survey with recovery procedures* (2d ed.). Exeter, NH: Heinemann.

Clay, M. M. (1982). *Observing young readers: Selected papers.* Exeter, NH: Heinemann.

Coles, G. S. (1984). Adult illiteracy and learning theory: A study of cognition and activity. *Science and Society, 47,* 451–482.

Coltheart, M., Patterson, K., & Marshall, J. (1980). *Deep dyslexia.* London: Routledge & Kegan Paul.

Collins, A., & Smith, E. (1982). Teaching the process of reading comprehension. In D. K. Detterman & R. J. Sternberg (Eds.), *How and how much can intelligence be increased* (pp. 173–185). Norwood, NJ: Ablex.

Cook, W. D. (1977). *Adult literacy education in the United States.* Newark, DE: International Reading Association.

Crowder, R. G. (1983). *Psychology of reading: A short survey.* New York: Oxford University Press.

Diener, C., & Dweck, C. (1978). An analysis of learned helplessness: Continuous changes in performance, strategy and achievement cognitions following failure. *Journal of Personality and Social Psychology, 36,* 451–462.

Downing, J. (1972). The cognitive clarity theory of learning to read. In V. Southgate (Ed.), *Literacy at all levels* (pp. 63–70). London: Ward Lock Educational.

Dweck, C. S. (1975). The role of expectancies and attributions in the alleviation of learned helplessness. *Journal of Personality and Social Psychology, 31,* 674–685.

Ericsson, K. A., & Simon, H. (1980). Verbal reports as data. *Psychological Review, 87,* 215.

Ericsson, K. A., & Simon, H. (1984). *Protocol analysis: Verbal reports as data.* Cambridge, MA: MIT Press.

Flower, L., & Hayes, J. (1978). The dynamics of composing: Making plans and juggling constraints. In L. Gregg & I. Steinberg (Eds.), *Cognitive processes in writing* (pp. 31–50). Hillsdale, NJ: Erlbaum.

Gambrell, L. B., & Heathington, B. S. (1981). Adult disabled readers' metacognitive awareness about reading tasks and strategies. *Journal of Reading Behavior, 8,* 215–222.

Hare, V., & Pulliam, C. (1980). College students' metacognitive awareness of reading behaviors. *Yearbook of the National Reading Conference* (pp. 226–231). Washington, DC: National Reading Conference.

Harris, K. R. (1982, March). *The effects of cognitive training on private speech and task performance during problem solving among learning disabled and normally achieving children.* Paper presented at the annual meeting of the American Educational Research Association, New York.

Hiebert, E. (1983). An examination of ability grouping for reading instruction. *Reading Research Quarterly, 13,* 231–255.

Hilgard, E. R., & Marquis, D. G. (1961). *Conditioning and learning.* London: Methuen.

Holdaway, D. (1979). *The foundations of literacy.* New York: Ashton Scholastic.

Horn, M. D., Powers, J. E., & Mahabub, P. (1983). Reader and nonreader conceptions of the spoken word. *Contemporary Educational Psychology, 8,* 403–418.

Hunter, C., & Harman, D. (1979). *Adult illiteracy in the United States.* New York: McGraw-Hill.

Johnston, P., & Winograd, P. (1983, December). *Passive failure in reading.* Paper presented at the annual meeting of the National Reading Conference, Austin, TX.

Leont'ev, A. (1979). The problem of activity in Soviet psychology. In J. V. Wertsch (Ed.), *The concept of activity in Soviet psychology* (pp. 37–71). Armonk, NY: Sharpe.

Massaro, D. W., & Hestand, J. (1983). Developmental relations between reading ability and knowledge of orthographic structure. *Contemporary Educational Psychology, 8,* 174–180.

Masserman, J. H. (1950). Experimental neuroses. *Scientific American, 182,* 38–43.

McDermott, R. P. (1977). Social relations as contexts for learning. *Harvard Educational Review, 47,* 198–213.

Mehan, H. (1979). *Learning lessons.* Cambridge, MA: Harvard University Press.

Meichenbaum, D. (1977). *Cognitive behavior modification.* New York: Plenum Press.

Merritt, J. E. (1972). Reading failure: A re-examination. In V. Southgate (Ed.), *Literacy at all levels* (pp. 175–184). London: Ward Lock Educational.

Mischel, W. (1984). Convergences and challenges in the search for consistency. *American Psychologist, 39,* 351–364.

Morgan, W. P. (1896). A case of congenital word-blindness. *British Medical Journal, 2,* 1378.

Musgrove, F. (1977). *Margins of the mind.* London: Methuen.

Nicholls, J. (1983). Conceptions of ability and achievement motivation: A theory and its implications for education. In S. Paris, G. Olson, & H. Stevenson (Eds.), *Learning and motivation in the classroom* (pp. 211–237). Hillsdale, NJ: Erlbaum.

Olson, W. C. (1938). General methods case study. In G. M. Whipple (Ed.), *The scientific movement in education* (The 37th Yearbook of the National Society for the Study of Education, Part II, pp. 329–332). Bloomington, IL: Public School Publishing.

Resnick, L. B., & Glaser, R. (1976). Problem solving and intelligence. In L. B. Resnick (Ed.), *The nature of intelligence* (pp. 205–230). Hillsdale, NJ: Erlbaum.

Sidman, M. (1960). *Tactics of scientific research.* New York: Basic Books.

Simon, H. (1980). Problem solving and education. In D. Tuma & F. Reif (Eds.), *Problem solving and education* (pp. 81–96). Hillsdale, NJ: Erlbaum.

Simpson, E. (1979). *Reversals: A personal account of victory over dyslexia.* Boston: Houghton Mifflin.

Sternberg, R. J. (1984). What should intelligence tests test? Implications of a triarchic theory of intelligence for intelligence testing. *Educational Researcher, 13,* 5–15.

Sternberg, R. J., & Wagner, R. K. (1982). Automatization failure in learning disabilities. *Topics in Learning and Learning Disabilities, 2,* 2–11.

Torgeson, J. K. (1977). The role of nonspecific factors in the task performance of learning-disabled children: A theoretical assessment. *Journal of Learning Disabilities, 10,* 27–34.

Vellutino, F. (1983). Childhood dyslexia: A language disorder. In H. R. Myklebust (Ed.), *Progress in learning disabilities* (Vol. 5, pp. 135–173). New York: Grune & Stratton.

Vygotsky, L. S. (1962). *Thought and language.* Cambridge, MA: MIT Press.

Vygotsky, L. (1978). *Mind in society.* (M. Cole, V. John-Steiner, S. Scribner, & E. Souberman, Trans.). Cambridge, MA: Harvard University Press.

Weber, R. M. (1975). Adult illiteracy in the United States. In J. Carroll & J. Chall (Eds.), *Toward a literate society* (pp. 147–164).

Wertsch, J. (1979). The concept of activity in Soviet psychology: An introduction. In J. Wertsch (Ed.), *The concept of activity in Soviet psychology* (pp. 3–36). Armonk, NY: Sharpe.

Weiner, B. (1972). *Theories of motivation.* Chicago: Rand-McNally.

Winograd, P., & Johnston, P. (1982). Comprehension and the error detection paradigm. *Journal of Reading, 14,* 61–76.

Wolford, G. (1981, April). *Reading deficits: Are they specific to reading?* Paper presented at the meeting of the Society of Research in Child Development, Boston.

Woods, M. L., & Moe, A. J. (1981). *Analytical reading inventory* (2d ed.). Columbus, OH: Merrill.

Zinchenko, V. P., & Gordon, V. M. (1979). Methodological problems in the psychological analysis of activity. In J. V. Wertsch (Ed.), *The concept of activity in Soviet psychology* (pp. 72–133). Armonk, NY: Sharpe.

I am indebted to "Bill," "Charlie," and "Jack" for their extensive contributions to my understanding of reading failure. This article has also benefited from comments by Richard Allington, James Fleming, Rose-Marie Weber, and Peter Winograd.

The Deaf as a Linguistic Minority: Educational Considerations

TIMOTHY REAGAN

"Hearing impaired/deaf" is one of the "handicapping conditions" listed in EHA. As such, all deaf students are entitled to special educational services as needed. In this article, Timothy Reagan argues that, although EHA has ensured comprehensive educational services for the deaf, the disability-focused perspective of EHA also endorses a very limiting view of deafness. He describes the deaf community in the United States as a distinct group with its own languages and cultural norms, as well as networks for self-help and political and social action. Moreover, the deaf community is alive with debate over issues of language, education, and relationships with the mainstream culture. In the context of this book on special education in the United States, Reagan's article demonstrates vividly how viewing individuals and groups as "handicapped" not only restricts our expectations of them, but also often belies the realities of their lives.

> What is it like to "hear" a hand?
> You have to be deaf to understand.
> . . . .
> What is it like to comprehend
> Some nimble fingers that paint the scene,
> And make you smile and feel serene
> With the "spoken word" of the moving hand
> That makes you part of the world at large?
> You have to be deaf to understand.
>
> — Willard J. Madsen, "You Have to Be Deaf to Understand"[1]

The last thirty years have seen remarkable changes in the educational system of the United States, not the least of which have been those affecting social and linguistic minorities. The 1954 *Brown v. Board of Education*[2] Supreme Court decision provided the legal basis for widespread desegregation in the schools and an end to the long tradition of separate and unequal education for Blacks and Whites in U.S. society.[3] Nevertheless, some twenty years later, meaningful racial integration is still an unrealized ideal in many parts of the nation.

In 1974, the *Lau v. Nichols*[4] decision expanded the coverage of the doctrine of "equal educational opportunity" to include the provision of "affirmative steps" for minority-language children unable to function in school in English.[5] While the Court did not specify that bilingual programs were the only acceptable way school districts might meet the educational needs of non-English-speaking students, the "*Lau* remedies," initially issued by the Department of Health, Education and Welfare (HEW) in the summer of 1975, clearly favored the implementation of bilingual education programs.[6]

In a 1979 decision in Ann Arbor, Michigan, the educational problems faced by speakers of Black English were addressed for the first time by a court of law.[7] The *King* decision recognized Black English as a viable and legitimate variety of English and acknowledged that the learning problems of many poor Blacks may be partly linguistic in nature.[8] The decision, however, was far from radical.[9] Indeed, it recommended such approaches as in-service sociolinguistic training for teachers, rather than the development of bilingual or bidialectical programs for speakers of Black English.[10] Still, the rights of those whose native language is a specific nonstandard variety of English were recognized in *King,* and future judicial challenges may conceivably apply similar criteria to other nonstandard varieties of English.[11] We see, then, an expansion of concern with and sensitivity to the special educational needs and problems of minority students, especially linguistic minorities. The rights of one sizable linguistic minority group, however, have been overlooked throughout this period, probably through a combination of ignorance, bias, and a generally unrecognized history of oppression. I am referring to the deaf.[12]

Commonly identified as simply "handicapped," little attention has been given to the deaf as a cultural and linguistic minority group with distinctive educational needs. The federal law that defined special education in the United States, PL 94-142, has been used, rather than *Lau,* to provide the legal basis for contemporary developments in the education of the deaf. This has resulted in widespread misunderstanding of the deaf in educational circles, as well as of pedagogical approaches in deaf education that, were they to be directed toward any other minority-language population in the United States, would be condemned by educators and policymakers alike. This article provides an analysis of the cultural and linguistic aspects of the deaf community, of the education of the deaf as a cultural and linguistic minority, and of alternative approaches in the education of the deaf. It also offers arguments for the provision of bilingual education programs for the deaf.

Linguistic Situation

Although small numbers of the deaf use speech and lipreading as their primary means of communication, the vast majority rely on a variety or combination of varieties of sign language and manual "codes."[13] In general, three major types of signing are used by the deaf in the United States: American Sign Language (ASL), Pidgin Sign English (PSE), and different kinds of Manually Coded English (MCE). The distinctions among them have important educational consequences.

ASL is the language used by the deaf and is, in fact, the single "most effective signal of membership in the deaf community."[14] It has been the focus of a great deal of linguistic study since the 1960 publication of William Stokoe's landmark work, "Sign Language Structure."[15] ASL's linguistic features are now understood, at least in fairly broad outline. It is a language in every sense of the word, relying on visual, rather than auditory, encoding and decoding. ASL has a complex, rule-governed phonology, syntax, and morphology.[16] For example, each sign contains at least five distinct parameters that delimit its meaning. These parameters are handshape(s), movement of hand, position/location of hand, palm orientation, and facial expression and other body movement(s).[17] These parameters, which also affect meaning in most other sign languages, function in ASL roughly as phonological distinctions do in oral languages.[18] Figure 1 shows how a change in one or more of the parameters can result in the formation of a different sign.[19]

Although ASL has traditionally been considered the low-status variety of signing (as contrasted with those varieties that more closely approximate English) by both the deaf and hearing worlds,[20] this negative attitude appears to be changing.[21] Undoubtedly, "deaf pride" has played a role in this change, which has been further encouraged by the preparation of new instructional materials for the teaching of ASL to hearing individuals.[22] As ASL becomes increasingly accepted as a "legitimate" foreign language in colleges and universities, and continues to gain recognition by hearing individuals, this change is likely to become even more profound.

An interesting sociological feature of ASL is that, unlike other languages, it is passed on more commonly from child to child — usually in residential schools for the deaf — rather than from parent to child. Indeed, since only an estimated 12 percent of deaf children have deaf parents, it can be argued that "for close to 90 percent of the deaf population, the group language [ASL] and sociocultural patterns are not transmitted from parent to child."[23] Further, ASL provides a language of "group solidarity" not generally shared with hearing individuals.[24] Its use is almost never allowed in formal or educational settings, a fact that has important social and pedagogical implications and to which we will return.[25]

FIGURE 1
Changes in the Parameters That Result in a Different Sign

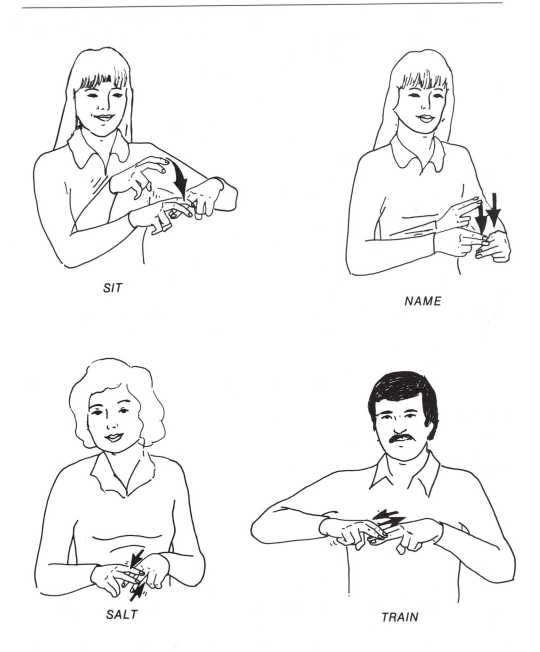

SIT

NAME

SALT

TRAIN

These illustrations are from *A Basic Vocabulary: American Sign Language for Parents and Children,* by Terrence J. O'Rourke. Copyright © 1978 by T. J. Publishers, Inc., Silver Spring, MD.

FIGURE 2
Overlapping Continua of the Three Major Types of Signing

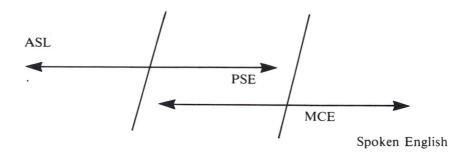

Pidgin Sign English refers to a range of different types of signing that incorporate varying amounts of ASL and English in a pidgin system. In general, PSE can be defined as the use of ASL signs in English word order.[26] Words that have no ASL equivalents (such as *the, a,* and so on) may be fingerspelled in PSE, but this is not required. PSE serves as a bridge between the deaf and hearing individuals who know some sign language but who may or may not know ASL.[27] It is commonly used in the education of the deaf at the intermediate, secondary, and postsecondary levels[28] — for example, at Gallaudet College.[29]

Manually Coded English (MCE) encompasses a number of very different systems designed to represent visually the English language. The systems of MCE include Seeing Essential English (SEE I), Signing Exact English (SEE II), Linguistics of Visual English (LOVE), Cued Speech, and Fingerspelling (including the Rochester Method).[30] The key is that MCE is a manual *code* used to transmit English, rather than a language in and of itself.[31] This is no doubt one of the principal arguments in favor of its use, as Gerilee Gustason notes: "The most important principle of Manual English systems is that English should be signed as it is spoken for the deaf child to have linguistic input that would result in his mastery of English."[32] This aspect of MCE, together with its ease of acquisition for hearing individuals, helps to explain its popularity in both preschool and primary education.[33] Nevertheless, the use of MCE in early childhood education, while pedagogically superior to an oral (that is, nonmanual) approach, has not been particularly effective in providing an adequate education for the deaf.

These three major types of signing can be conceptualized as falling along two overlapping continua.[34] If viewed as a continuum ranging from the most

FIGURE 3
Lexical and Syntactic Variations in Sign Varieties of the English Sentence

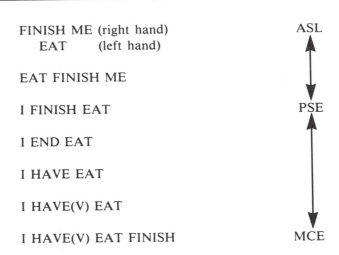

FINISH ME (right hand)
EAT   (left hand)   ASL

EAT FINISH ME

I FINISH EAT   PSE

I END EAT

I HAVE EAT

I HAVE(V) EAT

I HAVE(V) EAT FINISH   MCE

From James Woodward, "Sociolinguistic Research on American Sign Language: A Historical Perspective," in *Sign Language and the Deaf Community: Essays in Honor of William C. Stokoe,* ed. Charlotte Baker and Robbin Battison (Silver Spring, MD: National Association of the Deaf, 1980), p. 123. Printed by permission of the publisher.

private, exclusive to the deaf, to the most public, common to most of U.S. society, the types of signing can be envisioned as shown in Figure 2.

Since ASL and English are not historically related languages — in the way that English and German are, for example — we must use two overlapping lines, rather than a single line, to represent the range of sign systems. As a pidgin, PSE incorporates enough syntactic, semantic, and morphological variation to fall along both continua, and hence can be seen as mediating between the two distinct linguistic communities. Figure 3 provides an illustration of how the continua between ASL and MCE function for the English sentence "I have eaten."

The result of this range of signing systems has been what Stokoe has called "sign language diglossia."[35] The term *diglossia,* coined by Charles Ferguson in the late 1950s,[36] is normally used to describe a situation in which "two varieties of a single language exist side by side throughout the community, with each having a definite role to play."[37] Commonly, the two varieties of the language are the literary and colloquial, as in the differential usage in Greece of *katharevusa* (the *H,* or high-status, variety) and *dhimotiki* (the *L,* or low-status, variety).[38] Joshua Fishman has expanded this definition of diglossia, suggesting that diglossia may also refer to a situation in which two different languages are used for different functions in a community.[39]

Within Fishman's broader definition, the situation for the deaf community in the United States is diglossic.[40] Sign varieties approximating English are the *H* varieties, while ASL serves as the *L* variety.[41] James Woodward clearly explicates the situation: "As in other diglossic situations, the literary variety (English) is used in formal conversations in church, in classrooms, for lectures, and so on. The colloquial variety (ASL) is used in smaller, less formal, more intimate conversations. English is considered superior to ASL, and ASL is regarded as ungrammatical or nonexistent."[42] The diglossic situation of the deaf community is likely to remain, but the relative status of English to ASL, as noted earlier, appears to be changing. Few today would consider English innately superior to ASL, and no one could now justifiably maintain a belief in the supposed "ungrammaticality" of ASL.

Cultural Situation

The deaf constitute a unique subculture in U.S. society. Although many of the characteristic features of the deaf subculture are linguistic, or at least partially linguistic, in nature, other important cultural values, attitudes, and traditions are present as well. One of the more significant features of deaf life has been the role played by residential schools for the deaf in the maintenance and transmission of deaf culture.[43] As we noted earlier, this is one of the principal ways in which the deaf differ from other minority groups, because it means that the culture is, in most instances, passed on from child to child. Four general features demarcate the deaf subculture.

Language

Language generally plays a key role in cultural and ethnic identification, and this is especially true for the deaf. Membership in the deaf community is contingent upon communication competence in ASL, which thus serves a dual function as both the community's vernacular language and its principal identifying characteristic.[44] Given the diglossic nature of language use in the deaf community, ASL serves in many instances as an effective barrier to hearing people's access to the deaf subculture.[45] As Kathryn Meadow has noted about language in general, "It can serve as a cohesive, defining source of pride and positive identification and simultaneously as a focus for stigma and ridicule from members of the majority culture."[46] This is clearly the case with respect to ASL, though, again, the hearing world's resistance to ASL appears to be changing.

Group Identification

The deaf community in the United States perceives itself as a distinctive group in both social and linguistic terms, and is generally recognized as a distinctive population by the dominant society, though perhaps not a culturally distinct one. Interestingly, there are significant differences in how the parameters of the group are established and how that grouphood is evaluated.

In the hearing world, distinctions based on the extent to which an individual can hear (for example, hearing vs. hard-of-hearing vs. deaf) are seen as reasonably significant. Further, hearing-impaired individuals are commonly "valued" based on the extent to which they can hear. In the deaf community this is not the case. Rather, the degree or extent of hearing loss is simply not regarded as a criterion for membership in the deaf community so long as there is some degree of hearing loss.[47] Indeed, Carol Padden notes that "there is one name for all members of the cultural group, regardless of the degree of hearing loss: Deaf. In fact, the sign DEAF can be used in an ASL sentence to mean 'my friends,' which conveys the cultural meaning of 'Deaf.' "[48]

Endogamy

The maintenance of endogamous marriages is often seen by cultural and ethnic groups as a key to their survival. Among the deaf, intermarriage appears to be the most typical pattern. Estimates for the rate of endogamous marriage in the deaf community range from 86 percent to well over 90 percent.[49] By these estimates, the deaf are significantly more endogamous than most other contemporary U.S. cultural and ethnic groups.

Organizational Network

Lastly, the network of voluntary organizations that serves the deaf community is comparable to that serving any other cultural or ethnic group in U.S. society.[50] In addition to the National Association of the Deaf (NAD) and the various state associations of the deaf, there are social clubs, sports teams, the "Deaf Olympics," the National Theatre of the Deaf, and a host of others. This is especially significant given Padden's observation that "deaf people consider social activities an important way of maintaining contact with other deaf people."[51] In short, such organizational networks help both to maintain the cohesiveness of the group and to serve the companionship needs of group members.

The deaf, then, do indeed appear to constitute a subcultural community in contemporary U.S. society. Figure 4 shows the classification and significant features of the deaf community. This same diagram, with only minor

FIGURE 4
Classifications and Significant Features of the Deaf

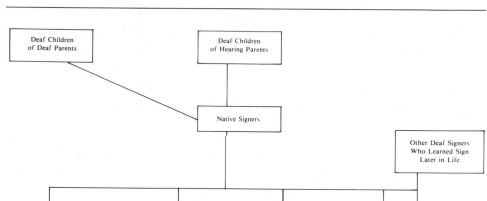

This figure is adapted from Lilian Lawson, "The Role of Sign in the Structure of the Deaf Community," in *Perspectives on British Sign Language and Deafness,* ed. Bernice Woll, James Kyle, and Margaret Deuchar (London: Croom Helm, 1981), p. 168. Printed by permission of the publisher.

modifications, has been used to describe the deaf community in Great Britain and could presumably be applied to a number of other nations as well.[52]

Competing Approaches in the Education of the Deaf

Historically, the major controversy in the education of the deaf in the United States has been the debate between the oralists and the manualists.[53] The oralists, working in the tradition of Alexander Graham Bell,[54] have emphasized the need for deaf children to acquire competence in English, as manifested in lipreading and the ability to produce speech. Signing is discouraged and generally not allowed in schools.[55] At the present time, approximately one-third of the educational programs for the deaf in the United States use the oral approach.[56] Such programs are ideologically similar to traditional, pre-*Lau* approaches to non-English-speaking minority groups whereby children were commonly punished for using their native language.

Manualists, on the other hand, have advocated a combination of speech and signing (in English word order) in the classroom. The role and extent of signing, however, even in the manual approach, has tended to be limited. Rather than using ASL, the manualists favor sign systems that approach English syntactically, so that speech and signs can be used together.[57] As Woodward has noted, "Until recently, there has never been any question that the language code in the classrooms should approach English; the question has been through what channel could English be best represented and understood."[58]

A new wrinkle appeared in the oral-manual controversy in the late 1960s, however, as total communication gained popularity in deaf education.[59] Like so many other educational slogans, "total communication" gained widespread support because it could mean so many different things to so many different people.[60] Commonly, total communication meant that "no change in philosophy took place; to all other methods, techniques, training, and curricula, signs were merely added."[61] This is especially interesting in view of the fact that NAD has specifically defined the term as "a philosophy of communication which implies acceptance, understanding, and use of all methods of communication to assist the deaf child in acquiring language and the deaf adult in understanding."[62] In short, while there may have been greater acceptance of sign language in the education of the deaf, there was hardly a revolution in deaf education. Total communication has been used to mean nothing more than the "simultaneous method" in many programs.[63] In schools it has not engendered the acceptance, understanding, or use of sign languages in general, or of ASL in particular.

Bilingual Education and the Deaf

Despite widespread international support for initial mother-tongue approaches in education, bilingual education programs in the United States have been far from popular.[64] Empirical evidence for the effectiveness of such programs is often ambiguous.[65] The successes of early immersion programs for Anglophone students in Canada are commonly used to support calls for similar English as a Second Language programs for minority-language students in this country.[66] There is some agreement that initial mother-tongue programs are most likely to be effective where children come from lower socioeconomic status (SES) backgrounds, where they may not be proficient in their native language, where their native language has low social status, and where teachers in regular classrooms are of a different ethnicity or language background.[67]

These criteria suggest that the deaf might be an ideal population for bilingual education programs. While the social-class background of the deaf population is quite varied, an increasing percentage of the school-age deaf population is coming from minority and lower SES backgrounds.[68] More significant, though, is the generally low SES that the deaf as a community continue to face in U.S. society as a result of social and economic discrimination. The question of the deaf child's native language is difficult because, for the deaf child, "home language" and "native language" are not necessarily synonymous, except in the rare cases where a deaf child is born to deaf, ASL-using parents. In any event, visual rather than auditory languages are the natural communicative approach for the deaf child. Taking this into account, and recognizing both the role of ASL in the deaf community and the artificial nature of MCEs, it is reasonable to treat the deaf child *as if* his/her native language were ASL. This means, of course, that in the vast majority of cases the child will not be proficient in the native language. We have already discussed the traditionally low social status accorded ASL in both the deaf and hearing worlds. With respect to the ethnicity and language backgrounds of the teachers, there is a classic colonial model in the education of the deaf in which great resistance to the hiring of deaf professionals persists. Further, the control of deaf education, at all levels, is firmly in the hands of hearing individuals.

The need for the deaf child to learn to cope with and function in both the hearing and deaf cultures would make a bicultural — as well as a bilingual — approach especially desirable. Indeed, the deaf have a uniquely powerful argument for such programs. Nevertheless, despite the strong arguments in favor of a bilingual-bicultural approach in the education of the deaf, only a few individuals have proposed such programs, and their audience has been limited for the most part to those already immersed in and sympathetic to studies of deaf culture and the linguistics of ASL.[69] Furthermore, few of their proposals have been published, and even these have reached a narrow audience.[70] Educators involved with bilingual education, minority studies, and multicultural education, on the other hand, have generally tended to ignore the deaf, save in discussion about Blacks, Latinos, and so forth, who happen also to be deaf. The notion that being deaf in and of itself might have important cultural and linguistic implications appears to have been overlooked. Woodward correctly claims that "the Deaf community has had a more difficult time overcoming inferiority stereotyping by the majority culture than other minority groups, since deaf people are viewed as a *medical* pathology."[71]

In the development and implementation of a bilingual-bicultural program for the deaf, two conditions would have to be met.[72] First, ASL — *not* PSE or some form of MCE — would have to be not only allowed but encouraged in the classroom. This would require reeducating teachers of the deaf as well as others, but the rewards would almost certainly be worth the effort. Second,

315

members of the deaf community would need to be active and, ideally, co-equal partners in the control, administration, and teaching of the pro-grams.[73] Given the resistance even to the hiring of deaf teachers in many schools, this would require significant amounts of time, effort, and pressure.[74] To do otherwise, however, would be to allow an essentially imperialistic approach to the education of a sizable minority group in the United States to continue unabated. Such a path cannot, I believe, be condoned.

This approach does not mean that the acquisition of English skills should be eliminated or minimized in the education of the deaf. English remains the written language of the deaf community and is an indispensable key to the hearing world. The question, instead, has to do with the best way for the deaf student to acquire English and, with the educational role of ASL, the language of the deaf community. It is time to recognize the deaf as a cultural and linguistic community and to reject the view of deafness as an exclusively physiological condition. Perhaps, in time, hearing people may even come to realize how much they have to learn from the deaf. Perhaps, someday, we will understand what it means to " 'hear' a hand."

Notes

1. Original poem printed by permission of the author.
2. Brown v. Board of Education, 347 U.S. 483 (1954).
3. See Richard Kluger, *Simple Justice: The History of Brown v. Board of Education and Black America's Struggle for Equality* (New York: Vintage Books, 1975). Also of interest is Meyer Weinberg, *A Chance to Learn: A History of Race and Education in the United States* (Cambridge, Eng.: Cambridge University Press, 1977).
4. Lau v. Nichols, 414 U.S. 563 (1973).
5. See Herbert Teitelbaum and Richard J. Hiller, "Bilingual Education: The Legal Mandate," *Harvard Educational Review, 47* (1977), 138–170.
6. The "*Lau* Remedies" originally appeared as "H.E.W. Memorandum on 'Task Force' Findings Specifying Remedies Available for Eliminating Past Educational Practices Ruled Unlawful Under Lau v. Nichols, Summer, 1975."
7. See Center for Applied Linguistics, *The Ann Arbor Decision: Memorandum Opinion and Order & The Educational Plan* (Arlington, VA: Author, 1979); and *The Ann Arbor Black English Case,* ed. Arthur Brown (Gainesville, FL: John Dewey Society, 1980).
8. Martin Luther King Junior Elementary School Children v. Ann Arbor School District Board, Civil Action No. 7–71861 (E.D. Mich. 12 July 1979).
9. See Geneva Smitherman, " 'What Go Round Come Round': *King* in Perspective," *Harvard Educational Review, 51* (1981), 40–56.
10. Smitherman, " 'What Go Round Come Round' "; Walt Wolfram, "Landmark Decision Affects Black English Speakers," *The Linguistic Reporter, 22* (1979), 1, 6–7.
11. See Walt Wolfram, "Beyond Black English: Implications of the Ann Arbor Decision for Other Non-Mainstream Varieties," in *Reactions to Ann Arbor: Vernacular Black English and Education,* ed. Marcia Farr Whiteman (Arlington, VA: Center for Applied Linguistics, 1980), pp. 10–23.
12. See Harlan Lane, "A Chronology of the Oppression of Sign Language in France and the United States," in *Recent Perspectives on American Sign Language,* ed. Harlan Lane

and Francois Grosjean (Hillsdale, NJ: Erlbaum, 1980), pp. 119–161; Edward L. Scouten, *Turning Points in the Education of Deaf People* (Danville, IL: Interstate, 1984); and Donald F. Moores, *Educating the Deaf: Psychology, Principles, and Practices* (Boston: Houghton Mifflin, 1978), pp. 27–64.

13. Barbara M. Kannapell and Paul E. Adams, *Orientation to Deafness: A Handbook and Resource Guide* (Washington, DC: Gallaudet College Press, 1984), ch. 4, pp. 9–10.

14. Carol Erting, "Language Policy and Deaf Ethnicity in the United States," *Sign Language Studies, 19* (1978), 139.

15. William Stokoe, "Sign Language Structure: An Outline of the Visual Communication Systems of the American Deaf," *Studies in Linguistics: Occasional Papers, 8* (1960); also of interest is William Stokoe, Dorothy Casterline, and Carl G. Croneberg, *A Dictionary of American Sign Language* (Washington, DC: Gallaudet College Press, 1965).

16. Stokoe, "Sign Language Structure"; Charlotte Baker and Carol Padden, *American Sign Language: A Look at Its History, Structure, and Community* (Silver Spring, MD: T. J. Publishers, 1978); and Ronnie Wilbur, "The Linguistic Description of American Sign Language," in *Recent Perspectives on American Sign Language,* pp. 7–31.

17. Based on Kannapell and Adams, *Orientation to Deafness,* ch. 4, p. 3. See also Robbin Battison, "Signs Have Parts: A Simple Idea," in *Sign Language and the Deaf Community: Essays in Honor of William C. Stokoe,* ed. Charlotte Baker and Robbin Battison (Silver Spring, MD: National Association of the Deaf, 1980), pp. 35–51.

18. See, for example, Margaret Deuchar, *British Sign Language* (London: Routledge & Kegan Paul, 1984), ch. 3.

19. See also Martin L. A. Sternberg, *American Sign Language: A Comprehensive Dictionary* (New York: Harper & Row, 1981).

20. See Kathryn P. Meadow, "Sociolinguistics, Sign Language, and the Deaf Sub-Culture," in *Psycholinguistics and Total Communication: The State of the Art,* ed. T. J. O'Rourke (Washington, DC: American Annals of the Deaf, 1972), pp. 19–33; William Stokoe, "Sign Language Diglossia," *Studies in Linguistics, 21* (1970), 27–41; and James Woodward, "Some Sociolinguistic Aspects of French and American Sign Languages," in *Recent Perspectives in American Sign Language,* pp. 103–118.

21. See Kannapell and Adams, *Orientation to Deafness,* ch. 4, p. 3.

22. Kannapell and Adams, *Orientation to Deafness.* Good examples of such materials are Charlotte Baker and Dennis Cokely, *American Sign Language: A Teacher's Resource Text on Grammar and Culture* (Silver Spring, MD: T. J. Publishers, 1980); Elaine Costello, *Signing* (Toronto: Bantam, 1983); Louie J. Fant, Jr., *Ameslan: An Introduction to American Sign Language* (Northridge, CA: Joyce Media, 1972); and Tom Humphries, Carol Padden, and T. J. O'Rourke, *A Basic Course in American Sign Language* (Silver Spring, MD: T. J. Publishers, 1980).

23. Erting, "Language Policy and Deaf Ethnicity," p. 140.

24. James Woodward, *How You Gonna Get to Heaven If You Can't Talk With Jesus: On Depathologizing Deafness* (Silver Spring, MD: T. J. Publishers, 1982), p. 33.

25. See Kannapell and Adams, *Orientation to Deafness,* ch. 4, p. 3.

26. See Judy Reilly and Marina L. McIntire, "American Sign Language and Pidgin Sign English: What's the Difference?" *Sign Language Studies, 27* (1980), 151–192; and James C. Woodward, Jr., "Some Characteristics of Pidgin Sign English," *Sign Language Studies, 3* (1973), 39–60.

27. Woodward, "Some Characteristics of Pidgin Sign English."

28. Kannapell and Adams, *Orientation to Deafness,* ch. 4, p. 4.

29. Gallaudet College is significant here because it is the only liberal arts college for the deaf in the world.

30. For SEE I, see David Anthony, ed., *Seeing Essential English* (Greeley: University of Northern Colorado, 1971); see also Paul W. Ogden and Suzanne Lipsett, *The Silent*

Garden: Understanding the Hearing Impaired Child (New York: St. Martin's Press, 1982), pp. 109–118; and Jerome D. Schein, *Speaking the Language of Sign: The Art and Science of Signing* (Garden City, NY: Doubleday, 1984), pp. 64–77. For SEE II, see Gerilee Gustason, D. Pfetzing, and E. Zawalkow, *Signing Exact English: Seeing Instead of Hearing* (Rossmoor, CA: Modern Sign Press, 1972); see also Anthony, *Seeing Essential English.* For LOVE, see Dennis Wampler, *Linguistics of Visual English* (Santa Rosa, CA: Santa Rosa City Schools, 1971); see also Gustason, Pfetzing, and Zawalkow, *Signing Exact English.* For Cued Speech, see R. O. Cornett, *Cued Speech: A New Aid in the Education of Hearing Impaired Children* (Washington, DC: Gallaudet College, 1966); see also Wampler, *Linguistics of Visual English.*

31. See Baker and Cokely, *American Sign Language,* pp. 65–71; Ogden and Lipsett, *The Silent Garden,* pp. 110–111; and Schein, *Speaking the Language of Sign,* pp. 64–66.

32. Gustason as quoted in Kannapell and Adams, *Orientation to Deafness,*, ch. 4, p. 5.

33. Kannapell and Adams, *Orientation to Deafness,* ch. 4, p. 5.

34. This is not the way the ASL–English continuum is commonly presented. Normally, the two languages are shown as two extremes of a single continuum. This is problematic, as explained in the text. For examples of the more general usage, see Baker and Cokely, *American Sign Language,* p. 77; Ogden and Lipsett, *The Silent Garden,* pp. 110–111; Carol Padden and Harry Markowicz, "Cultural Conflicts Between Hearing and Deaf Communities," in *Proceedings of the Seventh World Congress of the World Federation of the Deaf* (Silver Spring, MD: National Association of the Deaf, 1976), pp. 407–411; and Woodward, "Some Sociolinguistic Aspects of French and American Sign Languages."

35. See Stokoe, "Sign Language Diglossia," p. 1.

36. See Charles A. Ferguson, "Diglossia," *Word, 15* (1959), 325–340; see also James Woodward, "Sociolinguistic Research on American Sign Language: A Historical Perspective," in *Sign Language and the Deaf Community,* pp. 119–122.

37. Ferguson, "Diglossia," p. 1.

38. Ferguson, "Diglossia," pp. 2–5.

39. See Joshua Fishman, "Bilingualism With and Without Diglossia: Diglossia With and Without Bilingualism," *Journal of Social Issues, 23* (1967), 29–38.

40. See Woodward, "Sociolinguistic Research," p. 120.

41. Woodward, "Sociolinguistic Research," p. 120.

42. Woodward, "Sociolinguistic Research," p. 120.

43. See Kathryn P. Meadow, "The Deaf Subculture," *Hearing and Speech Action, 43* (1975), 16–18; and Arden Neisser, *The Other Side of Silence: Sign Language and the Deaf Community in America* (New York: Knopf, 1983), pp. 281–282.

44. See Erting, "Language Policy and Deaf Ethnicity," pp. 139–140; Harry Markowicz and James Woodward, "Language and the Maintenance of Ethnic Boundaries in the Deaf Community," *Communication and Cognition, 11* (1978), 29–37; Meadow, "The Deaf Subculture"; Meadow, "Sociolinguistics, Sign Language, and the Deaf Sub-Culture"; and Padden, "The Deaf Community and the Culture of Deaf People," in *Sign Language and the Deaf Community,* pp. 89–103; and Padden and Markowicz, "Cultural Conflicts Between Hearing and Deaf Communities."

45. See Meadow, "The Deaf Subculture," p. 17; Woodward, *How You Gonna Get to Heaven,* pp. 32–33.

46. Meadow, "The Deaf Subculture," p. 17.

47. See Erting, "Language Policy and Deaf Ethnicity," p. 140; and Padden, "The Deaf Community and the Culture of Deaf People," pp. 95, 99–100.

48. Padden, "The Deaf Community and the Culture of Deaf People," p. 100.

49. See, for example, *Family and Mental Health Problems in a Deaf Population,* ed. John D. Rainer, Kenneth Z. Altshuler, and Franz J. Kallmann (New York: New York State

Psychiatric Institute, Columbia, 1963); and Jerome D. Schein and Marcus Delk, *The Deaf Population of the U.S.* (Washington, DC: Gallaudet College Press, 1974).

50. Erting, "Language Policy and Deaf Ethnicity," p. 140; Kannapell and Adams, *Orientation to Deafness,* ch. 2, pp. 48–49; and Meadow, "The Deaf Subculture," p. 16.

51. Padden, "The Deaf Community and the Culture of Deaf People," p. 97.

52. See Lilian Lawson, "The Role of Sign in the Structure of the Deaf Community," in *Perspectives on British Sign Language and Deafness,* ed. Bencie Woll, James Kyle, and Margaret Deuchar (London: Croom Helm, 1981), pp. 166–177.

53. Woodward, *How You Gonna Get to Heaven,* p. 15.

54. See Scouten, *Turning Points in the Education of Deaf People,* pp. 152–166, 383–384.

55. Kannapell and Adams, *Orientation to Deafness,* ch. 4, p. 7.

56. Kannapell and Adams, *Orientation to Deafness,* ch. 4, p. 7.

57. Woodward, *How You Gonna Get to Heaven,* p. 15.

58. Woodward, *How You Gonna Get to Heaven,* p. 15.

59. See Scouten, *Turning Points in the Education of Deaf People,* pp. 326–330.

60. For an excellent discussion of educational "slogans," see B. Paul Komisar and James E. McClellan, "The Logic of Slogans," in *Language and Concepts in Education,* ed. B. Othanel Smith and Robert H. Ennis (Chicago: Rand McNally, 1961), pp. 195–214.

61. Neisser, *The Other Side of Silence,* p. 4.

62. Quoted in Kannapell and Adams, *Orientation to Deafness,* ch. 4, p. 8.

63. See Kannapell and Adams, *Orientation to Deafness,* ch. 4, p. 6; Moores, *Educating the Deaf,* p. 16.

64. See, for example, *Mother Tongue Education: The West African Experience,* ed. Ayo Bamgbose (Paris: UNESCO, 1976); *Issues in International Bilingual Education: The Role of the Vernacular,* ed. Beverly Hartford, Albert Valdman, and Charles R. Foster (New York: Plenum, 1982); and UNESCO, *The Use of Vernacular Languages in Education* (Paris: UNESCO, 1953).

65. See, however, Timothy Reagan, "Bilingual Education in the United States: Arguments and Evidence," *Education and Society, 2* (1984), 131–135; and Rudolph C. Troike, *Research Evidence for the Effectiveness of Bilingual Education* (Rosslyn, VA: National Clearinghouse for Bilingual Education, 1978).

66. Of interest here is Merrill Swain and Sharon Lapkin, *Evaluating Bilingual Education: A Canadian Case Study* (Clevedon, Avon: Multilingual Matters, 1982).

67. See Christina Bratt Paulston, "Ethnic Relations and Bilingual Education," *Working Papers in Bilingualism,* No. 6 (Toronto: Ontario Institute for Studies in Education, 1975); G. Richard Tucker, "The Linguistic Perspective," in *Bilingual Education: Current Perspectives,* Vol. II (Arlington, VA: Center for Applied Linguistics, 1977), pp. 1–40. Also of interest is Iris C. Rotberg's "Some Legal and Research Considerations in Establishing Federal Policy in Bilingual Education," *Harvard Educational Review, 52* (1982), 149–168.

68. See *The Hispanic Deaf: Issues and Challenges in Bilingual Special Education,* ed. Gilbert L. Delgado (Washington, DC: Gallaudet College Press, 1984), p. 28.

69. See Barbara M. Kannapell, "Bilingualism: A New Direction in the Education of the Deaf," *The Deaf American, 26* (1974), 9–15, and "Personal Awareness and Advocacy in the Deaf Community," in *Sign Language and the Deaf Community,* pp. 105–116; Barbara Luetke-Stahlman, "Using Bilingual Instructional Models in Teaching Hearing-Impaired Students," *American Annals of the Deaf, 128* (1983), 873–877; Raymond Stevens, "Education in Schools for Deaf Children," in *Sign Language and the Deaf Community,* pp. 177–191; William C. Stokoe, Gallaudet College, "An Untried Experiment: Bicultural Education of Deaf Children," Unpublished manuscript, 1975; and James Woodward, "Some Sociolinguistic Problems in the Implementation of Bilingual Education for Deaf Students," in *Second National Symposium on Sign Language Research and Teach-*

ing, ed. Frank Caccamise and Doin Hicks (Silver Spring, MD: National Association of the Deaf, 1980).

70. Woodward, "Some Sociolinguistic Problems."
71. Woodward, *How You Gonna Get to Heaven,* p. 11.
72. Woodward, *How You Gonna Get to Heaven,* p. 22.
73. Woodward, *How You Gonna Get to Heaven,* p. 33.
74. See also Hugh T. Prickett and J. T. Hunt, "Education of the Deaf — The Next Ten Years," *American Annals of the Deaf, 122* (1977), 365–381.

HER has used the lowercase "d" for the word deaf in this article. However, it is the common practice in the deaf community to distinguish between the *d*eaf (in an audiological sense) and the *D*eaf (in a sociocultural sense). We wish to note that the author made this distinction in his original manuscript.　　— Ed.

Communication Unbound:
Autism and Praxis

DOUGLAS BIKLEN

During the past twenty years, Douglas Biklen has combined expertise in special educational praxis and qualitative research to critique our understanding of "best practice" in teaching students with disabilities. In 1988 and 1989, Biklen traveled to Melbourne, Australia, to study the work of Rosemary Crossley and her colleagues at the Dignity through Education and Language Communication Centre, who had developed a new method of communicating with students labeled autistic. Biklen discovered that through the center's "facilitated communication" procedure — a method that uses an electronic keyboard and the supportive touch of a teacher to encourage student expression — autistic students demonstrated that they had rich, complex inner lives that they could share articulately. Biklen, greatly impressed by his interactions with these students, wrote this report, which details Crossley's methods, the startling insights he gained into the lives of persons with autism through her methods, and the challenges his insights offer to commonly held understandings of autism. Knowing full well the controversy generated by Crossley's work — contradicting, as it does, current theories regarding autism — Biklen offers this rich ethnographic description as a goad to educators to reevaluate their work with autistic individuals.

Jonothan Solaris cannot speak. David Armbruster can say a few words, usually unintelligible.[1] Both are young adolescents classified as autistic. I first met them in Melbourne, Australia, at the Dignity through Education and Language (DEAL) Communication Centre, an independent, government-funded organization established by educator Rosemary Crossley and her colleagues to assist people who are unable either to talk or to do so clearly. Jonothan seemed full of nervous energy and he got up from his seat frequently. His way of walking on the balls of his feet was akin to prancing. David gazed at the ceiling light, reaching toward it with his hands. Both boys relied heavily on peripheral vision. Even when spoken to, I felt like they listened to me "sideways." Also, their facial expressions didn't correspond with the conversation, although David smiled a lot.

I was not surprised by how either of them appeared. Theirs were the behaviors of autism. But what I did not anticipate was that their communication with me would assault my assumptions about autism and ultimately yield important lessons for education.

On the day of my visit, Jonothan and David were present to demonstrate a method that Crossley had developed called "facilitated communication." I spent fifteen or twenty minutes speaking with David's mother and several DEAL staff members, occasionally directing my statements to Jonothan and David. Then, when Crossley asked if they had anything to tell me, Jonothan began to type on a Canon Communicator (a small electronic typing device with a dot matrix tape output). With a staff member's hand on his shoulder, Jonothan typed, "ILIKEDOUGGBUTTHHEISMAAD."[2] Seeing what Jonothan had written, Crossley asked why he thought I was "maad," whereupon he typed, "HETALKSTOMELIKEIMHUMAN." By "MAAD" he had meant "crazy."

Jonothan and David produced only a few sentences in the several hours that we were together. But when they typed, they did so fairly quickly, without hesitation, and independently (with just the hand on the shoulder). I asked David and Jonothan if I could take some pictures of them communicating. I explained that people in the United States would be interested in seeing what they were doing. They both agreed, typing "y" for "yes" on their Canons. David added, "NOSEY PEOPLE TO EVEN WANT TO SEE ME." Unlike Jonothan, he had put in spaces between the words. During this session, Crossley described the method of facilitated communication that had allowed David and Jonothan to communicate. In the midst of her enthusiastic and lengthy discourse, David revealed his sense of humor, typing, "TURN HER OFF."

Crossley's first attempt at facilitation with a person with autism had been Jonothan, not an "easy" student. For over a month he had resisted typing. When I asked him what had finally caused him to communicate on a regular basis, he did not answer. Then, several minutes later, he typed, "IMNOTVERYQUITRHIGHTNOWBECIGOTSATONBYROSIE." Translated, he said, "I'm not very quiet right now because I got sat on by Rosie." Hearing this, Crossley asked, "Do you mean that literally or metaphorically?" Jonothan responded by typing "MET."

Jonothan's easy grasp of this abstract concept, "metaphorical," and David's facile sarcasm struck me as extraordinary. The content of their communication was "normal," not what one expects from children with autism. A year and a half earlier I had been similarly, if not so vividly, shocked by a letter from Australia that described Crossley's success in using a new technique to allow people with autism to communicate. The letter claimed that Crossley was eliciting "high-level" communication from her students. "Sophisticated written (typed) communication at sentence level," I was told. I didn't know what to think about this claim. It seemed conceivable to me that Crossley and her colleagues had happened on a *few* people with autism for whom such communication was possible. But it made no sense that people with autism who had been classified as severely intellectually disabled would have normal or even near-normal literacy skills. By definition, people with autism who do not speak or who speak only a small range of phrases are referred to as "low functioning" and are thought to have a severe intellectual disability as well (Rutter, 1978). Of course, one possible explanation was that Crossley's students were actually mildly disabled; in other words, perhaps they had autism but were among the group commonly called "high functioning." This term is often applied to those people with autism who have usable, easily understood speech. Yet the letter described the method as working with students who typically might be called "low functioning," and included some who were previously thought to be severely intellectually disabled. The letter about Crossley was baffling, so much so that, whether consciously or not, I put it out of my mind for a year and a half. But when I knew I would be in Melbourne I arranged to visit DEAL. Then, seeing David and Jonothan type sophisticated thoughts, I could not ignore the many questions their communication posed.

How, why, and with whom does facilitated communication work? Does facilitated communication work anywhere or is it more effective in certain settings, under specific educational or social conditions, and with certain people more than with others? If there were preferred conditions, how would these compare to prevailing notions about "good" schooling? Presumably, the DEAL students themselves would be able to comment on many issues, such as how society treats them and how they want to be treated. Would the DEAL students change as a result of their newfound communication and, if so, how? Equally important, would the ability to communicate lead to changes in their families, schools, and other environments? Did the success of students like David and Jonothan portend a dramatic transformation in how we think about and define autism?

In July of 1989, seven months after the session with Jonothan and David, I returned to Melbourne to study Crossley's work more systematically. I observed nearly all the students Crossley worked with both at DEAL and in the community over a four-week period. I also observed the two part-time speech therapists working with other children at DEAL, interviewed parents, and visited schools. My discussion in this article is based upon communication efforts by twenty-one individuals served by the Dignity through Education and Language Centre.[3] All twenty-one are nonspeaking or speak only with echolalic expressions (echoes of phrases they have previously heard); all have been labeled autistic or display autistic behaviors. Observations and interviews were audio-recorded; thus students' typed words were recorded as facilitators read them aloud.

Origins of Crossley's Discovery

Crossley's discovery of literacy skills among nonspeaking people or people who have disordered speech because of autism and other developmental disabilities occurred by accident. During the 1970s, when she worked at the St. Nicholas Institution, she had used hand support or arm support to help people with cerebral palsy achieve greater control over their movements, to slow them down, *and* to give them more likelihood of hitting an intended target (for example, a switch, key, button, letter, or picture on a board). The method was controversial (Crossley & McDonald, 1980) because it raised the possibility that the people's choice of letters from a language board, for example, might reflect the facilitator's rather than the learner's choice. The controversy ultimately subsided somewhat when, through message-passing tests (for instance, Crossley left the room and returned to facilitate communication about something that had transpired in her absence), the Supreme Court of Victoria sided with Crossley, recognizing the students as authors of such communication (Crossley & McDonald, 1980). Application of this method to people with autism and similar conditions was unplanned although, Crossley now believes, logical. She began with Jonothan.

By every account, Jonothan was a handsome but challenging child. He was not toilet trained. He fidgeted. To get things, he simply grabbed them. He did not look people in the eye. He nearly skipped when walking, on the balls of his feet. He had a history of fits of screaming, regurgitating food, scratching, and running away from people. In March of 1985, when Jonothan was seven, Rosemary Crossley invited his mother to leave him with her for an afternoon. That afternoon, after watching Jonothan's stereotyped repetitive play with a squeeze mop, Crossley managed to settle Jonothan on her sofa, first interesting him in a speech synthesizer and then in a Canon Communicator. With wrist support, he pressed buttons that she touched. Occasionally he pressed buttons without any assistance. She typed "JONOTHAN," followed by "MUM," and then asked him for "Dad." He went straight to the D, without wrist support and then to A, where he hesitated.

"I think he completed 'DAD' with no prompting but with wrist support," she wrote later in her notes that day. If she had "prompted" him, she would have actually moved his wrist toward the letter or letters; instead, she merely supported his wrist as he moved his hand toward the letters. She typed "JONATHAN," whereupon he typed "JON*O*THAN." Crossley later checked the spelling with his mother. Jonothan had been correct. Crossley asked him if the mop was a plane when he was playing with it. He typed "MOP." She guided him through the entire alphabet on the keyboard, then asked him what letter the word good starts with. He pressed G. She asked how many fingers she had on one hand. He pressed 5. She asked how many on two hands; he pressed 10. "If you took 5 from 10, how many would you have left?" she then asked. He typed 5. She continued, 5 plus 3? He gave 8. For 3 plus 4, he pressed 6. She said try again. He got 7. She observed, over time, that Jonothan often veered to the side of a character at the last moment, resulting in a typographical rather than a cognitive error, presumably the result of cerebellar damage to judgment of distance. Crossley asked if Jonothan had anything he would like to say. He spelled "STOP." He was reluctant to finish the word; he made several tries and erasures before completing it.

Coincidentally, on the afternoon I interviewed Crossley about how she had discovered that this method worked with Jonothan, he came to visit DEAL. Crossley told him that we had just been talking about the first time he had typed on the Canon. She asked him if he remembered what his first word had been. As she asked the question, she held out a Canon Communicator. Independently, he typed "DAD." Then he typed, "JONOTHAN NOT JONA-THAN." This is one child who remembers his first words.

When Jonothan's mother returned to Crossley's home that afternoon in 1986, Crossley presumed that Jonothan wanted to show her what he had been doing. But, in Crossley's words, "he completely gummed up . . . [He] was quite unable or unwilling to give so much as a 'yes' or 'no' with her there." Jonothan's inability to communication with his mother continued until she died in 1989. While Jonothan communicates with several other people now, much of it independently or with only a hand on the shoulder, his communication with his mother was basically unsuccessful, a fact she found "discouraging."

Why people who regularly communicate independently with a few people but not at all or only with support to the wrist and forearm with others is mysterious. Is it difficult for some students to communicate with people with whom they feel a close personal bond? In other words, is it harder to reveal yourself and your skills to those whose judgment you especially value? Are some people better at facilitation than others? Must the student believe that the person is an effective facilitator? Is the willingness or ability to communicate with particular people reflective of the "autistic" quality of wanting order and sameness?

Observations of First Assessments

Among the DEAL students I observed were people whom Crossley was seeing for the first time. They included school-age children and young adults, and ranged in age from five to twenty-three. Like my first meeting with Jonothan and David, these first sessions startled me. Crossley's assessment of Louis is a case in point.

Louis is twenty-four years old, with reddish-brown hair and gold metal-rimmed, rectangular-shaped glasses with thick lenses. He was wearing a black-and-white sweater, black jeans, and white tennis shoes when we met him at an adult training center (ATC) — ATCs are considered one step less demanding than sheltered workshops, which are designed specifically for people with disabilities who are presumed unable to work in competitive employment but capable of working under supervision, albeit often at less than average productivity rates and for less than the minimum wage. People who attend ATCs are generally considered too disabled to qualify for admittance to a sheltered workshop. Louis had very little facial expression. He does not speak, except for a few phrases that seem involuntarily uttered and are out of context. As he entered the room where Crossley was to conduct the assessment, he said: "Excuse me. Get mommy on the bus. Excuse me," which didn't make sense to me. Attempts at answering his statements by saying, for example, "There is no need to be excused, you are fine," did not quiet him. He repeated the phrase.

Crossley introduced herself and me to Louis, who sat between us. She described her work to him as helping people who don't speak find other ways to communicate. She apologized in advance for her assessment approach: "Louis, I ask people a lot of really silly questions." She commenced the session by asking him to press down on various pictures on a talking computer, a children's toy with a voice output that requests the person using it to press various pictures or letters and which announces the user's choice, for example, "Right, that's the apple."

As Crossley asked questions, tears began to roll down Louis's face. He was crying silently. She reassured him, telling him that she would do it with him. She held her hand on top of Louis's right arm. In response to the command, "Press the red car," Louis put his index finger on it and Crossley helped him push it down. Louis was moving slowly. He seemed tentative. The machine instructed him to find the circle, which he did. He followed with correct answers to square, triangle, circle, and triangle. He hit them all, five of five.

Crossley changed the display page on the talking computer. This time he was asked for the small rectangle. Louis started to go for the big one. She held him back and said, with emphasis, "*Small* rectangle." He then went for it correctly. She reassured him, "Yes." Louis had struggled with the demands of the machine; with Crossley's help he had gotten the right answers. When asked for the "big square," Louis hesitated. As he hovered over it, Crossley encouraged him, "Go on, you've got it." He did. Next he was asked, "Find the small yellow rectangle." His hand wobbled between the brown triangle and blue circle. Crossley pulled him back and Louis uttered the words, "That one," and hit the small yellow rectangle.

The next screen displayed a picture of grass, a tree, a car, a house, and a cat. He pressed the car on demand. He got the tree. The he was asked to locate the word "tree" as distinct from the picture. He did. Again he got five out of five. On another screen he had to choose pictures to go with the words "yacht," "fish," "dog," "girl," "bird," and "boy." For "girl" he started to move away from the picture of a girl. Crossley pulled his hand back and asked, "Where are you going?" With the exception of this help, he pressed the words independently.

The next sheet included only words. When Crossley asked Louis to identify the clock, his finger seemed to drop to flower. She said, "Hold on," and asked, "Can you point to clock?" He did. She followed by asking him to point to the words "hand," "eye," and "fish." He identified each. For these, she was holding the top of his sleeve above his wrist. Louis was seemingly expressionless throughout. Next, Crossley read five sentences aloud to Louis and asked him to find words in the sentences, including, for example, "our," "on," "and," "is," and "the." He got them all. She was pleased. "Terrific. That's great, mate," she declared.

Finally, she switched to a page displaying the alphabet and asked Louis to point to specific letters, including, for example, "v," "g," "a," and "z." He got them all. Less than half an hour had elapsed and Crossley was ready to introduce Louis to the Canon Communicator. At this point, I wrote in my notebook, "He's sailing." Except for minor stumbling with the geometric figures, Louis had cruised through the questions. Also, he now had a slight smile at the corner of his mouth. He had relaxed.

Crossley showed Louis the Canon and went through the alphabet and numbers with him. "For starters," she asked, "can you type your name?" At this point, her hand was stretched out flat, on top of, but not actually touching, his. He typed "LOUIS." As he finished, she asked if there was anything else he wanted to say. Louis started typing again. First he typed an "O," then "PC." Crossley pulled his hand back from the keys, saying, "I'm not sure I follow. Let's start over." This time he typed "POCCO." She was confused. Then we realized what he was typing. *Pocco* is his last name. He was still responding to Crossley's first request, to type his name.

Crossley asked again if there was anything else Louis wanted to say. He typed, "IM NOT RETARDED," to which she remarked, "No, I don't think you are. Keep going." Louis continued, "MY MOTHER FEELS IM STUPID BECAUSE IH [he back-spaced this and crossed out the *h*] CANT USE MY

VOICE PROPERLY." A tear rolled down his left cheek as he typed. And Crossley said to me and to Louis, "A lot of people believe that what people say is what they're capable of."

Louis was not done. He typed, "HOW MUCH IS A CANON?"

"They're dear," Crossley answered.

"I SAVE A BIT BUT NOT ENOUGH," Louis typed.

Crossley explained that she would continue to work with Louis in conjunction with the Adult Training Center and that she would try to get him a Canon. Then she congratulated him on his work in the session and said to me, for Louis to hear, "Anybody who starts off typing 'I'm not retarded' isn't retarded. First rule!"

The words of other first-time communicators, meaning those who communicated neither with echolalia or by physical manipulation of objects, were no less astonishing. One young man typed "I CAN READ" for his first sentence. He had learned to read by being around words and by watching television. Crossley's students and their parents typically report that the students had had incidental exposure to language through television, magazines, and books, or with labels on foods and other items. Some were reported to have been in formal reading programs as part of early intervention and developmental training efforts. Yet until Crossley elicited typing from them, the assumption for all of them was that they had *not* learned to read.

Margaret, a seventeen-year-old young woman referred to DEAL by an autism center, also surprised me with her performance in her first session at DEAL. Except for the word "no" and an approximation of "hello," she is mute. During a two-hour assessment session, though I addressed her several times, she never once looked at me. Her first sentence, typed independently, save Crossley's hand on her shoulder, was a question: "CAN I COME AGAIN?" Sessions with younger children were often much shorter, with the students unable or unwilling to cooperate for such long stretches.

Doubts: Facilitation or Manipulation?

Despite the seeming ease with which Crossley assesses some new students, she and her colleagues admit that communication is not always so easily facilitated. Initially, it has often proved difficult for students to communicate with more than one or two facilitators, especially when they are new to DEAL. They may refuse to communicate at particular moments, in particular situations, with certain people, or for specific time periods as, for example Jonothan did. Some are independent in some situations, but dependent or noncommunicative in others, whether with the same or other people. Some then will produce obviously incorrect information. Related to this, facilitators often find themselves inadvertently cueing their nonspeaking partners to letters and therefore to words or statements. This is particularly true with people who are just learning to communicate by typing with facilitation. Occasionally, people who have previously demonstrated excellent facility will type only repetitions of specific letters and phrases or will produce unintelligible sequences of letters or words. All of the people I observed typing "independently," with just a hand on the shoulder, did not type as well or sometimes at all for me alone or for other new facilitators. Jane Remington Gurney, a speech therapist at DEAL, recounted that she worked with several students for "months," unsure whether the students' output was anything more than a reflection of her own manipulation of their arms. She recalled that ". . . gradually I began to receive words from clients that were not in my vocabulary, were phonetically spelled or were . . . spelled better than I could spell." She also found that when she tried "too hard" she was even less successful.

Several facilitators, including speech therapists, teachers, and parents, encountered difficulty in identifying the source of certain communication: either it had been generated by the person being supported or by their own unconscious selection or cueing. They reported instances where they had believed the communication to be genuine, only to discover that it reflected their own subtle cues. I asked a teenager, Bette, for example, "What is your full name? Is it Beth, Elizabeth, or Bette?", to which she answered "Elizabeth." She also declared that she prefers the name Bette. Later I learned that her full name is Beth and that her family and friends call her Bette. Another student, Geraldine, gave a staff member her family's address incorrectly. Such miscues have caused facilitators to wonder about the validity of other communication. Were the words the students' own? Or were they the facilitators'? Or were there perfectly reasonable explanations for the "incorrect" communication? Did Bette think "Elizabeth" sounded better and therefore claim it as her name? Did Geraldine not know her address and decide simply to provide any address in order to at least answer the question asked? Or had she heard the address previously — was this a typed version of echolalia, like the advertising jingles that people with autism have been known to type? Both girls who provided "incorrect" information in these instances communicated independently in other conversations, with only the support of a hand on the shoulder or a finger touching the thread of a sweater.[4]

Within the professional community there has also been a mixed reception to Crossley's work. In 1988, an ad hoc group of psychologists, speech specialists, educators, and administrators calling themselves the "Interdisciplinary Working Party" issued a critique of "assisted communication" (Interdisciplinary, 1988). The Working Party report cited major contradictions between the nature of communication content being claimed for people with autism and prevailing theories of autism. A letter and assessment statement on DEAL prepared by staff of the Victorian Autistic Children's Association, Eastern Centre, stated, for example, "Well recognized characteristics of autism bring into question much of the assisted communication of autistic children" (p. 91). The assessment, dated September 1, 1987, argues that children with autism would need "far more time to learn the task procedure" than just the brief moments given by Crossley, that the children would have a hard time remembering the sequence of letters they had typed into the Canon Communicator ("short-term sequential memory tasks are particularly difficult for autistic children"), and that Crossley's prompts of counting to ten or saying "Get on your bike" would cause students with autism to forget the task and instructions. This evaluation of Crossley's work also stated that "the sentence structure used by all the children via assisted communication was not characteristic of the 'different' language used by autistic children." Only the most advanced would be capable of using "I"; they would not typically be able to use the word "by" correctly; and "why" questions would "involve cognitive processes well beyond the ability of all but a few autistic children" (p. 93). The Working Party report led to a state government inquiry entitled *Investigation into the Reliability and Validity of the Assisted Communication Technique* (Intellectual Disability Review Panel, 1989).

The Review Panel report noted that people with intellectual disabilities are "extremely susceptible to influence by people who may be unaware of the extent to which they may be influencing decisions." The panel's charge was to ensure clients' "maximum control" of decisions — in other words, communication and the decisions made on the basis of communication. The panel argued, "Given the conflict that the 'assisted communication technique' has engendered and the consequences for the client if doubt exists about his/her communication," it was essential for any disputes over communication to be resolved (p. 18).

In the Review Panel's studies of facilitated communication, the findings were equivocal. The study involved two different procedures, one in which people were given questions that were the same as those given to the facilitator and different from those given the facilitator (the facilitator wore earphones that transmitted the same or different information). The second procedure involved message passing. In this latter approach, people were given gifts. The facilitator did not know about the gifts. The people were then asked to tell the facilitators what they had been given. Since the Review Panel chose not to describe its subjects in any detail, the conclusions others are able to draw from the study are limited. The results of both parts of the study were summarized by the Review Panel in the following manner:

The validity of the communication while using the "assisted communication technique" was demonstrated in four of the six clients who participated in the two studies. Under controlled conditions the data clearly indicated that the communication of one of the three clients was validated using the "assisted communication technique." The communication of the three clients who participated in the message passing exercise was also validated. The validity of the remaining two clients' communication when using the "assisted communication technique" was not established. However, the absence of data on these occasions does not automatically imply that the clients are not capable of communication. In all three cases of the controlled study, client responses were influenced by the assistant. Influence occurred with a client who demonstrated valid, uninfluenced responses to other items. It appeared that a given assistant could influence some client responses and leave others uninfluenced. (p. 40)

The Panel also noted that assistants appeared unaware of when they might be influencing communication. Also, some of the uninfluenced correct responses were correct in general information (category) but were not as specific as anticipated. The Panel concluded that the two parts of the study had produced support from those who claimed facilitated communication had validity *and* for those who doubted it.

Behavior and the Person

The behaviors of people labeled autistic are often unusual and appear to reflect lack of attention and/or awareness of social and communication cues and/or severe intellectual disabilities. Perhaps it is such behaviors, including the on-again, off-again ability or willingness of students to communicate, that cause some people to worry that facilitated communication is no more real than a Ouija board.

Polly is a fifteen-year-old high school student who attends regular tenth-grade classes. Before being mainstreamed for the first time in ninth grade, Polly had attended a special school for students with severe disabilities. As her mother rushed to catch her up on math and other school content areas, Polly grasped concepts quickly. Given a subtraction problem that would yield only a negative answer, Polly hesitated momentarily and then typed, "BUT IT IS LESS THAN NAUGHT." I asked one of the teachers to describe Polly's best and worst days at the high school. The teacher explained that Polly had attended the school for three months before being willing or able to communicate with her, and that her "best day" was "when she typed for me!" The "worst" day was when Polly climbed a tree and pulled her skirt up over her head. Another bad day was when Polly urinated in the playground. Her mother believes Polly was testing whether the school would accept her *and* that she was saying, "Look, I'm retarded — do you still want me?"

Polly has several behaviors that are not uncommon for a person labeled autistic, including a tendency to walk on the balls of her feet and sometimes clap her hands together. At school, she will occasionally pace from her locker about fifteen feet to the top of the steps and back. She has had a habit of picking up items such as a wad of dried gum off the ground and putting it in her mouth; if asked, however, she'll stop this particular behavior. When she's seated, she sometimes places her hands between her legs and rocks forward. When she types on the Canon or on an electric typewriter she frequently appears to be looking off into space, horizontally rather than forward. When I would meet her at school or at DEAL I would extend my hand to shake hers. As I grasped her hand, she would pull back, smiling.

Another DEAL student, Bette, could be observed typing independently while simultaneously grimacing and nervously flicking her fingers between words. On one occasion she wanted to stop doing fill-in-the-blanks type "set work" and demonstrate to her parents that she could say what she wanted. She typed the words, "LET ME SHOW THEM WHAT I CAN REALLY DO." As she finished typing, she slapped the table hard. It was startling and incongruous. At home, her mother explains, even since Bette has begun to type with her mother's facilitation, "it's a little bit puzzling that . . . she can . . . have these intelligent thoughts, and yet she will . . . wet . . . the bed or [do] something like that. It's puzzling for us." Bette often needs to be prompted to keep eating or to use a bathroom; otherwise she will sometimes not eat and has toileting accidents. The same seems true of her communication. She will not initiate it. But when her mother, her teacher, or a DEAL staff person begins a conversation with her and provides some support, such as a hand on her sleeve, she will usually communicate.

Such unusual behavior was typical of the people I observed. When I reached out to shake Amanda's hand as I was saying goodbye for the day, she reeled back on the sofa, made a high-pitched scream and put one leg up in the air as her arms reached backward. Another student, Robert, smacked himself on the head with his open hand in the middle of a communication exercise. Then he typed to Crossley, "IM NERVOUS." When she asked him, "Are you prepared to fight your nerves?", he responded, "IM FINE." Tommy, age twelve, screamed intermittently while typing. His typed communication was quite normal. Joshua, age six, cried sharp, high-pitched cries off and on during the session. When he typed, he did so quickly. He would type the letter "z" repetitively unless stopped. At the same time, he could answer questions that Crossley posed. She asked him what a cowboy does and he answered, "RIDES." He typed the letters very quickly. Eric had a habit of clipping the output tape off the Canon Communicator. As he typed, he occasionally stopped to slap the table and kick at it. He also kept repeating over and over "McDogs," which his mother said meant McDonalds. It appeared to be echolalic speech.

A young man, Paul, had sores and scratches on his face one day when he came to DEAL. When Crossley asked him what had happened, he responded enigmatically, typing, "I hurt my face. I bashed myself. I do things I don't want to." Throughout the session he held a handful of cloth strips. He brushed the ends of these against his nose and face. He moaned while writing captions for a cartoon and also scrunched his face into a severe grimace. In the middle of the writing, Paul got up from his chair, reached under his black sweater and ripped his undershirt off. When Crossley asked, "Now Paul, what brought that on?", he responded, "I felt hot." Later his mother told me that when she has asked him why he grabs pieces of cloth, he has responded, "Because I can't help myself."

Edward, a high school student who is mute, implied that he could use his behavior calculatingly, refusing to type for his teachers and teaching assistants, holding out for his mother to be his facilitator. When Crossley asked him what he thought his teachers should do about him, he responded with humor: "SHOOT ME."

Autism as We Have Understood It

My initial difficulty in understanding and *accepting* the claim that children with autism who were mute or highly echolalic could be literate was undoubtedly influenced by what I knew about autism. Results from Crossley's work challenged current theories; she was getting results that no one else had.

The literature on autism is complex and sometimes contentious. (For discussions of the controversies, see, for example, Donnellan, 1985; Rimland, 1964; and Rutter, 1968.) Hypotheses about its cause have ranged from the psychogenic (Bettelheim, 1967), in which mothers are blamed for treating their children so coldly as to cause them to turn inward, to the physiological (Ornitz & Ritvo, 1968; Wetherby, 1984). Yet for all the struggles waged about the "true" nature of this baffling condition or set of behaviors, there is a great deal of agreement about the behavior of people labeled autistic. Autism is characterized by problems of speech, language, and communication, including mutism, echolalia, and perseverative speech, difficulties with social interaction, stereotyped activity, a seeming concern for sameness or constancy of order, and lack of response or unusual response to external events or actions (see, for example, Rutter, 1978; Wetherby, 1984). There is less unanimity, however, about the implications of the behavior.

Language behaviors associated with autism include delay in the development of language and atypical expressions of language. Capturing the range of communication (or absence of it) that characterizes people labeled autistic, over a decade ago Wing summarized the work of Kanner (1943, 1971), Rutter (1968, 1978), and Eisenberg (1956), concluding that "simple stereotypes of the less able child have their counterparts in the elaborate repetitive routines and the stereotyped speech of the more able children" (Wing, 1978, p. 40). When some children labeled autistic develop more elaborate speech, she notes, "it is characterized by very special abnormalities, suggesting that it is learned by rote without understanding of the rich and subtle associations of words" (p. 40) — in other words, what we might call delayed, transplanted, or recurrent echolalia. Children with autism are assumed to have difficulty understanding abstract concepts "such as time, color, size, and feelings. . . . Questions such as who, what, where, when, and why are confusing" (Schopler, Reichler, & Lansing, 1980, p. 29).[5]

To use an analogy from electronics, the brain of a person with autism has been characterized more like a tape recorder and playback device than a computer. Those who display echolalia typically produce words that are phonologically correct, but which appear to be repetitions of other people's phrases or chunks of phrases rather than the person's own creation (Baltaxe & Simmons, 1977; Tager-Flusberg, 1981a,b). A number of such children echo television advertisements, seemingly without linking the words to content. Often, they repeat phrases heard much earlier, producing a delayed echo. Prizant (1983) calls such learning and expression a "gestalt style of language acquisition," a "gestalt mode of cognitive processing," and "gestalt forms" of expression.

Until fairly recently, the assumption has been that though the range of children labeled autistic includes some who perform in the normal range, those who do not communicate or who communicate only very limited numbers of echolalic phrases, often seemingly out of context, and who have a variety of other unusual and seemingly asocial behaviors in the main are not smart (see, for example, Bartak, Rutter, & Cox, 1977; James & Barry, 1983; and Ricks & Wing, 1975). Language in the form of stereotyped phrases, incorrect semantics, and the ability of some children to "parrot back long phrases" (Schopler, Reichler, & Lansing, 1980, p. 29) were presumed to be the trademarks of incompetence. If they used words appropriately, this was thought to result from "accidental operant conditioning because these words are closely connected with rewards, especially food" (Ricks & Wing, 1975, p. 209).

More recently, Prizant and Rydell have suggested that the language of people with autism occurs along a continuum from little or no symbolic or abstract activity to higher-order thinking and therefore more normal language, though they caution that even in its most flexible form, echolalic language "rarely approaches the flexibility of 'normal' language forms and use" (1984, p. 191). It is presumed that "highly echolalic autistic people use echoes as a means of engaging in ongoing discourse" (Paul, 1987, p. 77), the facility of which is tempered by their less-than-normal comprehension/communicative knowledge (Mirenda & Schuler, 1988, p. 25). In a discussion of echolalic expression, Wetherby (1984) hypothesizes that the person with autism relies on the limbic system for language, accounting for the person's "proficient use of communication to achieve environmental needs, and deficient use of communication for social purposes" (p. 29); more complex, intentional communication would require cortical control.

Other important developments in recent years concern eye use and communication methods. Assumptions about poor eye contact, for example, are being challenged by the growing realization that people with autism may not lack eye-to-face contact, but may use it differently than "normal" people (Mirenda, Donnellan, & Yoder, 1983; see also Rutter, 1978). Additionally, a wide array of communication literature supports teaching alternative modes of communication to people whose speech is limited. Wetherby (1984), for example, advocates gestural rather than vocal communication training for people with severe autism. She believes that instruction in manual language builds on existing strengths; "the autistic child's use of communicative gestures (for example, giving, pointing, pushing away, head shaking, and nodding) should be the primary consideration in language intervention and should form the foundation for teaching words, whether through speech or signs" (p. 31). Similarly, Schuler and Baldwin (1981) also note that nonspeech methods allow easier, quicker access to communication where there has been a breakdown in speech: "Techniques that can be used effectively to teach nonspeech responses, such as prompting or 'molding,' by guiding the student's hands through the required responses can't be used to teach speech" (p. 250).

Despite these changing perspectives on autism, scholars continue to ask several questions similar to the ones Kanner (1943, 1971) raised thirty years after his original elaboration of the condition or set of behaviors. Is autism attended by a global intellectual deficit? Is autism a combination of specific acquisition/detection or receptive deficits? Is it reflective of processing deficits? Does autism reflect some other problems?

An Alternative Interpretation of Unusual Communication

In light of the natural language produced by Crossley's students through typing, we are compelled to search for an alternative explanation for their mutism and unusual speech. The obvious interpretation is that they have a neurologically based problem of expression. In other words, their difficulty with communication appears to be one of praxis rather than cognition.

Here, I use the term *praxis* not as a technical term, but merely to refer to the problem of people with autism speaking or enacting their words or ideas. In contrast with the recording and playback metaphor used earlier, that person's speech ability is more like a "dedicated" computer or language device, capable of expressing phrases that have already been introduced aurally; the more advanced version of this speech-output device can select segments of phrases and join them with others, though it generally lacks the program to "output" verb tense and pronouns correctly. With facilitation, the person can bypass his or her problem of verbal expression and type natural language.

By saying that the person with autism has a problem with praxis, we do *not* presume a deficit in understanding, but rather in expression. This interpretation also presumes that while there may be peculiarities in vision and learning, such as involuntary attention to light or acute sensitivity to certain sounds, these do not necessarily reflect or create cognitive problems.

There is a small body of generally ignored literature on educational methods that, at minimum, does not contradict and may well support this praxis theory. In the late 1960s, two pediatricians in upstate New York employed the Edison Response Environment (ERE), "a cubicle enclosing a multiphase electric typewriter, projector, and programming device that could respond to or direct the user in a variety of ways," also called the "talking typewriter" (Goodwin & Goodwin, 1969), to teach children with disabilities, including learning disabilities and physical disabilities. Sixty-five of their students had been diagnosed as autistic. Some students who were generally nonspeaking, except for some nonfunctional or echolalic speech, produced individual words and echolalic-like phrases. In some instances, the typing was followed by speech development. One child, for instance, is described as using the ERE

> in a sporadic and explosive fashion, often dashing up the stairs and into the booth in which it was installed, sometimes falling down en route, jumping up on the chair, lifting up the plastic lid and typing a few keys, then tearing off the paper and rushing downstairs. This continued over a period of several months. Efforts to slow him down were only partially successful. (p. 558)

One day, this student, Malcolm, seemed to change. He typed his name and then the word "cow" and left the room. On subsequent visits he seemed to recognize letters and words, "but still did not talk." He was four at the time. With his acquisition of words, he also began to talk. "At eight, he has a large vocabulary, speaks intelligently with slight articulation defect, and is doing well in the second grade of a home instruction program" (p. 558). Another student, John, also with obvious autism, first produced only stereotyped typing. His teacher had described him as "hyperactive, jams food in his mouth, laughs in a peculiar cackle, won't mind, pushes other children, mimics, screams, never says I" (p. 560). At the Goodwins's clinic he typed labels or sign names, for example "UTICA CLUB" (a regional beer) and "WORK ZONE AHEAD." Later, John successfully completed the fifth grade.

It is difficult to discern from the Goodwins's notes and article how unusual or typical of their total subject group these students may have been. Many of the children with whom they worked remained institutionalized, were placed in special schools, or stayed at home with no education. In their concluding remarks on the ERE treatment and studies, the Goodwins argued that the ERE did not cause the students' intelligence, but rather provided the means of expressing their intelligence: "The E.R.E. was the instrument that showed us abilities not measured by conventional psychological tests" (1969, p. 562).

Another approach to teaching academic and communication skills seems to have coincidentally built upon and confirmed the Goodwins's experiences. In her book *Effective Teaching Methods for Autistic Children,* Oppenheim (1974) describes "hand-over-hand" work with autistic children as a crucial aspect of first efforts at manual communication with students at the Rimland School for Autistic Children. Oppenheim's approach apparently used hand writing rather than typing, but the support she provided closely resembles Crossley's facilitated communication. She concluded that "the autistic child's difficulties with writing stem from a definite apraxia just as the non-verbal child's troubles with articulation do when speech finally develops" (p. 54). This communicative apraxia to which she referred has been described in a rare autobiographical account by Temple Grandin, a person with autism: "Up to this time, communication had been a one-way street for me. I could understand what was being said, but I was unable to respond. Screaming and flapping my hands was my only way to communicate" (Grandin & Scariano, 1986, p. 21). To overcome the student's apparent problem with "motor expressive behavior," Oppenheim found that it was "usually necessary to continue to guide the child's hand for a considerable period of time" (p. 54). She reported:

> Gradually, however, we are able to fade this to the mere touch of a finger on the child's writing hand. "I can't remember how to write the letters without your finger touching my skin," one nonverbal child responded when he was asked why he would not write unless he was touched. (p. 55)

Oppenheim concluded that students' problem with communication was "not recognition, but rather execution, in retaining the mental image of required motor patterns. Ultimately . . . finger-touching can be eliminated, and the child does write without it, *although some children want the touch of a finger on some other bodily surface such as the head, in order to write*" (Oppenheim, 1974, p. 55, emphasis mine).

Typing overcomes many of the difficulties of hand writing by simplifying the communication motion to pointing at or pressing letters or numerals. Oppenheim used some pointing at pictures and multiple-choice captions and some typing, although it appears that she used typing mainly with the students whose "eye-hand coordination is sufficiently developed" (p. 58). Some educators have encouraged the use of language boards or symbol systems as other accessible means of communicating, but typing has the advantage of giving people access to nonprogrammed, non-preselected communication symbols (for instance, the alphabet and numbers) — and, the communication becomes their own.

Like the Goodwins, Oppenheim presumes a potential competence in her students, no matter how stereotyped or unusual their behavior. She suggests that teachers ignore the behaviors and focus on teaching academics:

> The immaturities and/or deficiencies in the child's general functioning — including the fact that the child may be nonverbal or noncommunicative — should never be used as an index of the likelihood of his being able to absorb and benefit from teaching at higher cognitive levels — specifically, his ability to learn reading, writing, and mathematics. (1974, p. 90)

Principles of Facilitated Communication

Crossley's interactions with nonspeaking and aphasic people reflect a certain attitude.[6] Like Oppenheim and the Goodwins, she expects her students to communicate. She seems to admire them. She anticipates their producing interesting or even unique statements. Table 1 shows the attitudinal dimensions of facilitated communication.

Facilitated communication practices vary considerably with the student's disability, behavior, style of interaction, personality, and other factors. Consequently, the method is not a uniform approach to teaching or supporting communication that can be used with each person, but rather a range of skills as described in Table 2.

Conversational Communication: A Maintenance Session

One Saturday morning, four students who communicate with facilitation (a facilitator gives wrist, arm, or hand-on-shoulder support) gathered at DEAL for a "maintenance" session.[7] Jane Remington Gurney, a speech therapist, had arranged an activity to focus the group. "It's your task to find out as much as you can about Doug," she explained. She wanted them to practice interviewing, to "try to get . . . [their] questions out as quickly as" they could "in the most direct way." This skill, she believed, would help them engage in school classroom discussions more effectively, allowing them to ask questions before "the teacher's passed on to the next thing." She asked the students to figure out signaling devices to indicate when they wanted their printouts from the Canon Communicators read aloud by their facilitators. Polly was to put up her hand. Amanda would speak the word "ready." Peter would make a sound that approximates "ya." And Bette would tap the table where she was typing. Peter has a severe tremor and required arm support as he typed.

Amanda, Beth, and Polly did most of their typing independently, with support by a hand on a shoulder, or hand on a sleeve, leg, or elsewhere. Jane began the interview by telling the group that my full name is "Professor Doug Biklen."

Amanda spoke first: "Professor of what?" she asked.

"Of special education," I explained, "at Syracuse University, in Syracuse, New York."

Peter asked me what I thought about "each area of Australia." I said that I had not actually seen each area, but that Queensland had beautiful fish, warm weather, and overly conservative politics. I was admittedly clichéd about Sydney, calling it gorgeous but "too fast moving," and a little more detailed on Melbourne, singling out its array of ethnic restaurants, beautiful flowers, Victorian architecture, and a quaint but efficient tram system.

Amanda then asked, "Why are you here?"

I explained my interest in facilitated communication.

Next, Polly, who had heard me lecture several days earlier on the topic of integrating students with disabilities in typical schools, challenged me. "You put emphasis on integration," she noted. "What really does integration have to offer to some terribly retarded people?" Her question was a variation on the theme "I'm not retarded," and at the same time a question about what I believe.

"It offers the chance to be seen as an ordinary person. Of course that depends on other people being able to see them in this way," I responded.

"You must be so idealistic," she accused me.

"I think I'm optimistic," I countered. "I think if I were to call my attitudes 'idealistic' I would be . . . saying that I don't quite believe them."

Amanda entered the conversation, seeming to argue at once with Polly and with society. "Too mean to judge people by ability," she typed.

I returned to Polly's original question: "I don't know if it's fair to call someone 'so terribly disabled.'"

Peter returned us to personal details. "Are you married?" he had typed.

"I am," I answered.

"What's your wife's name?" he asked.

"Sari," I told him.

"Funny name," Peter commented, with a loud, nearly laughing sound.

TABLE 1
Attitudinal Dimensions of Facilitated Communications

Presentation/Intention

1. Don't patronize people with nervous jokes, excessive familiarity, or babying. Be candid.
2. Be reasonably vulnerable and self-effacing (e.g., make note of your own errors, personal limitations, etc.).
3. Be apologetic about the assessment process. Invariably it involves asking questions that are too simple for the person being queried; apologize for speaking about the person in front of him or her (e.g., when asking a speaking person something about the person who is nonspeaking).
4. Being a dynamic support means being able to suborn your own ego or, at the very least, being able to carry on a two-sided conversation rather than imposing a one-sided, dominant relationship. You have to be comfortable touching, being close to people, and supporting without taking over.
5. Don't use labels; e.g., talk about "students like so-and-so," rather than referring to people as having a particular disability.

Assumptions/Beliefs

6. Assume the person's competence. "It's far better to overestimate than underestimate a person's ability."
7. Believe communication is important; conveying this belief will help convey to the person that you see him or her as important, as your peer, as someone worthy of being "heard." Respond to what is typed as if it were spoken.

"I prefer to call it unusual," I joked.

Amanda returned the conversation to ideas. "Tell me how really retarded people get people to see them as ordinary human beings," she typed.

"We might ask the question differently," I countered. "Why is it that so-called ordinary people do not see people who are so-called 'really retarded' as ordinary?"

Amanda found my question a non-answer: "That gives me the question back, not answer it," she complained.

"What I meant by posing another question was to say that maybe the problem of gaining acceptance is not . . . owned by people labeled different but is a problem for those who do the labeling."

"Most people need proof," Polly declared. "How can the disabled meet such a gauntlet?"

Polly seemed to be challenging my ideas about the social construction of reality specifically concerning disabilities, but also agreeing with me — the gauntlet is not the disability as much as it is society's demand for proof that people meet a standard of normality.

Amanda accused me of being glib: "If you had that problem you would believe that the problem was yours."

I didn't give up the argument, though in retrospect I could have been more sympathetic and less chidingly argumentative. "I guess I'm saying that all of us need to force society to abandon the gauntlet. And I do consider it a problem of mine," I added.

"Not realistic," Polly insisted.

TABLE 2
Facilitated Communication Practices

Physical Support

1. Attend to the person's physical location: feet on ground, typing device slanted (e.g., at 30-degree angle), stabilized table, non-slip pad under device and person, relaxed atmosphere, etc.
2. Initially, and only where necessary, provide physical supports under the forearm, under or above the wrist, or by helping a person to isolate the index finger to facilitate use of communication aid.
3. Pull back the hand or arm after each choice so that the person takes enough time to make a next selection and also to avoid repeating selections.

Being Positive

4. Progress through *successful* choices of pictures, words, sentences, letters, name spelling, first sentence, pulling back, and reminding the person of the question or request whenever an incorrect or nonsensical choice is about to be made. Use semantic common sense (e.g., *n* does not come after *w*). In other words, help the person avoid errors.
5. Provide encouragement verbally and avoid telling the person that he or she has made an error or mistake during assessment (i.e., Don't say "No," "That was wrong," or "Incorrect"). Relate to the person naturally, conversationally.
6. Be direct and firm about the tasks: the need for practice, staying on task, focusing eyes, etc. Redirect the person to the tasks (e.g., "I'm going to count to 10—1, 2, 3,...10" or "You know the house rules, work before play").

Other Support

7. Keep your eyes on both the person's eyes and on the target (e.g., letter keys). This helps you identify and prevent errors caused by hand/eye coordination problems. It also helps you monitor whether the person is attending to the task.
8. Facilitated communication often requires the facilitator to do several tasks at once, for example, carrying on a verbal conversation with the person being assisted or with others in the room, watching the person's eyes, looking at the printed output, thinking of the next question or activity and at the same time keeping your mind on the present activity, and so forth, in addition to providing physical support and encouragement.

Achieving Communication/Overcoming Problems

9. Communication is a process, including support, fading, training receivers, etc. It is important to see it as a process and to recognize that people generally get better (i.e., faster and more independent) at it over time. Ongoing support increases a person's speed; thus, independence is balanced by need for speed. Encourage lots of practice; practice builds accuracy and speed!
10. If a person is not communicating, is producing nonsensical communication, or is producing questionable or wrong communication (e.g., when you doubt the communication and believe that it might be you, the facilitator, who is initiating the choices of letters and words), revert to set, structured curricula (e.g., fill in blanks, math drills).
11. Look for small differences in communication style or behavior, such as 1) radial ulnar instability— when a person's index finger swings to one side when approaching a letter, thus consistently getting a typographical error; 2) habitual, meaningless repetitions of certain letters; or, 3) the tendency to revert to familiar, echolalic words or phrases.
12. Stop stereotyped utterances by ignoring them and focusing on the task of manual communication.
13. Ignore "behavior" such as screeches, hand slapping on desk, pushing desk away, and getting up by asking, for example, "What's the next letter you want?"

Curriculum

14. Don't use teaching or communication situations to "test" the person (e.g., "Is this a cup or a dollar bill?").
15. Give the student choices of work to do.
16. Use interesting materials: cartoons to be filled in, caption-less magazine pictures, crossword puzzles, and other activities that would not offend adults, teenagers, or other age groups with whom you are working.
17. Don't start communication work by focusing on the expression of feelings; wait for feelings to come. Allow the person with whom you are working to initiate feelings at his or her own choosing.
18. Get nonspeaking people working together; group sessions can be encouraging and motivating as well as interesting to people who are developing familiarity with facilitated communication. It is often helpful for facilitators (also called receivers) to work with other than their usual partners in group sessions.

At this point, Peter reentered the conversation, relating our discussion of acceptance to his own situation. Peter lives in an institution for people presumed intellectually disabled. "Do you really feel there's a future for us out of institutions?" he asked.

"Yes, absolutely," I responded, "for everyone."

"You'll still have to make concessions," Polly typed.

"What do you mean by concessions?" I asked.

Jane tried to turn us away from the conversation to something more concrete. "Let me just remind you people to stick to the task which is to find out something about Doug."

Of course they were finding out a lot about me, albeit what I believe rather than the usual details.

Responding to my question about concessions, Polly explained, "Unless people suborn their own wishes, it will fail." In other words, people with disabilities can only be accepted if society makes accommodations.

I agreed. The state builds roads for car drivers and airports for people who want to fly. These seemed analogous; "society can take communication seriously; it can encourage facilitated communication by training communicators and by making communication devices available." Similarly, I offered, "Society can organize schools to serve *all* students."

Polly was unconvinced. She brought in economics: "You are illogical because there is no profit in disability."

At this point, Bette asked a seemingly unrelated question. She wanted to know if she would ever be able to communicate. Peter told her she did "not have to worry."

Amanda, still focused on the airports analogy, accused me of naiveté: "That falls down," she reasoned, "because people can worry about us but still not have enough money to build airports." Society might insist on funding airports before human services.

Amanda then returned the conversation to Bette's question about talking. Speaking to Peter, she declared, "To you it may not be, but to me it is and I think it is to Bette, to [a] person who wants to be like others."

Next, Amanda questioned my thoughts on deinstitutionalization. "Have you thought about people wanting to be in institutions?" she challenged.

"I believe in self-determination," I told her. "People should have choices. My experience has been that when people have the option to live outside the institution, they choose it. But society often doesn't create those options."

As I spoke, Polly was writing about Bette's desire to speak. I was now getting used to this on-again-off-again style of conversation, delayed by the timing of speaking through typing devices. Polly had typed, "Not important [to speak] if you have typing. Just tell yourself that daring to reach out is more important."

Jane interjected a bit of humor: "Now who is idealistic?"

Now it was Bette's turn. "I want to ask Doug if people like me will ever be normal . . . able to do more things that other people do?" I told her that I considered her normal in the sense that she has good ideas, lots of interests, especially an interest in other people, and that other people could come to see what I saw.

I am not sure if this comment triggered Peter's next remark or whether his statement was just a general sally. He asked, "Why do you make people believe they can do the impossible?"

"There is a consistency about this conversation," I joked. "I'm constantly being told by school people that I'm 'unrealistic' [in reference to school integration], by which they mean 'We don't want to hear what you say' or 'It's not going to work.' And then I come here and you say the same thing, except you are saying, 'They are not going to let it work.'"

Jane came to my defense. "Is this the way the group really feels or the way you've been conditioned to feel by the response you've had?"

Peter answered, "I've tried for thirteen years to be normal and I'm still where I started."

Polly typed that she did not object to the principle of integration, "but the distaste that has to be broken down in each case."

"Why am I arguing with all of you?" I asked.

Bette returned the conversation to the question about being normal. "I do not think that. I am not able to do many things." Then she asked, "Can Doug be out of America for very long?" — that is, would I be around to facilitate her communication, and to be a friend?

Polly typed about her own struggle for integration and acceptance. "Some really terrible kids have no responsibility." Her mother explained that Polly was referring to the fact that the other students in her school don't have to forge their way in school or society; they can fool around, make nuisances of themselves, and act immature. Polly added that she and other students with autism have a responsibility "thrust on us. Just want to be like those terrible kids."

I told her I understood.

Ever the detail person, Peter asked me if I make a lot of money. Bette asked if my job makes me happy. I answered "yes" to both.

Finally, Amanda gave in and joined my side of the integration argument. "Help get the skeptics to think like you. We are so cheesed [fed up]. At least I am."

The Question of Proof

Inevitably, an element of my examination of facilitated communication involved looking for proof that the words were the students' own. Proof took two forms: 1) some students were able to type independently, either without physical contact or with a hand on the shoulder, leg, thread of the sleeve, or other location; and 2) for those who lacked independent communication, the nature of communication varied across individuals, despite the fact that a single facilitator might be facilitating; there were facial expressions, verbal noises, including laughter, or other signs of a person's understanding of communication; and/or in some instances, the content of the communication suggested that it *really* came from the person communicating, not from the facilitator.

Instances of independent communication were numerous. A dozen students were observed typing phrases independently. Six of them communicated independently (without hand support on the arm or hand) much of the time, with at least two different facilitators. Of those who typed independently less often or not at all, nearly all had only recently been introduced to facilitated communication. Yet, one of the people who was independent had only recently been introduced to facilitated communication. While it is possible in any instance of facilitation involving the forearm, wrist, or hand for the person's communication to be influenced by a facilitator, presumably such instances could be double-checked at another time without support if they were particularly important. Independent communication of a similar level of literacy and content to that which was observed being physically facilitated was taken as validating a person's communication.

Petrov is an adolescent who attends a school for deaf and hearing-impaired students. He wears hearing aids, but he is not deaf. For years, people assumed he was deaf. As I observed him in a class at the deaf school in which other students were all either profoundly deaf or hearing impaired, Crossley held just the cloth of his sweatshirt, not even resting her hand on his shoulder. He typed answers to math problems. I asked why he had hearing aids. He typed, "I excuse myself, helping myself by pretending to be deaf." In sociological terms, he was "managing stigma"; his reasoning seems to be that his hearing aids imply a hearing loss that explains his not speaking and also suggests that his absence of speech is not due to an intellectual disability. He had typed this independently, but the originality and unexpected character of his answer also seemed a kind of "proof" that the words were his.

In instances where the person did not type independently, without support under the forearm or on the hand, there was often evidence that the person worked independently. Brian, for example, has little affect in his expression. Yet he has a slight smile at appropriate moments. In my conversations with him, his mood and comfort changed as we communicated.

Initially, his responses to me were quite formal. He said, for example, "I AM ACHIEVING A GREAT DEAL ALREADY AND I AM HOPING TO ACHIEVE MUCH MORE." His teacher told me it took her six months of trying before she became able to facilitate for Brian. She held her hand on his. When I asked what it was like before he learned to type, he abandoned his formalism: "IT WAS HELL AND I COULD NOT EVEN BEGIN TO MAKE MY NEEDS KNOWN." At one point, his teacher and Crossley left the room. I asked Brian if his mother and father would be coming to the center to talk to us or if just one of his parents was coming. I asked him to type "B" for both or "O" for one. He typed "B." Both arrived a little while later. Toward the end of our conversation, with his father facilitating him in his conversation, Crossley asked Brian if he had anything he wanted to say to her. He responded, "I'VE TALKED A LOT ABOUT YOU [he had been speaking with me]. I DON'T NEED TO TALK *TO* YOU." Characteristically, Brian's face displayed its usual nearly expressionless facade, with just a slight smile at the corner of his mouth. Independently, Brian turned off the Canon.

Clearly, the level of proof for those people who were not communicating independently was less "ironclad." Yet, the indicators that communication was the person's own were strong enough, in my view, to justify the continuing assumption of its validity.

Conclusion

The implications of the DEAL students' communication are enormous. Among other things, it forced me to redefine autism. While the students in this study included some who previously had been thought of as severely intellectually disabled and autistic, they demonstrated unexpected literacy skills. The Saturday morning group, for example, instead of querying me about the concrete facts of my life, were far more focused on my beliefs. They chose to converse about concepts. Each of them obviously engages in internal conversations; each had thought about the issues we discussed. Also, they had chosen to speak about their feelings. Obviously their problem was neither in cognition nor affect. Rather, their difficulty has been in sharing what they know and feel.

Readers of this article will naturally ask, "Will facilitated communication allow all people labeled autistic to communicate at high levels of literacy?" This question is not easily answered. First, the category of autism, like many disability categories, is not as precise or as uniformly applied as we might imagine or desire. A broad range of behaviors are defined as autistic, with the result that people who seem quite different from one another share the label of autism. Second, it is of course not possible to prove that *all* people so labeled will achieve a particular level of communication. We can learn about their potential only through practice. Third, it is quite possible, even expected, that within the group of those categorized as autistic there will be a very wide range of intellectual ability, as there is in the general population. Nevertheless, it is especially noteworthy and encouraging that among those for whom facilitated communication has allowed high levels of literacy and numeracy are people who were previously presumed to be among the "lowest" intellectually functioning persons labeled autistic.

Before they could communicate, these students were evaluated primarily by their repertoires of unusual behaviors. Now that they *do* communicate, schools, families, and society ask: Will the stereotyped and other behaviors associated with autism diminish or even disappear as students become more fluent communicators? This is not known. While there is observational evidence that some bizarre behaviors decline — Polly does not make a habit of climbing trees at her high school and pulling her skirt up — others persist. Paul did rip his teeshirt off during a communication session, and he still clutches strips of cloth, occasionally brushing them against his face; Polly still puts objects in her mouth, but less often than in previous years; and Bette still slaps her work table periodically. It is noteworthy that at the time of these observations, Bette had begun communicating fluently only a few months earlier and Paul was living in a locked ward of an institution where he had no opportunities to communicate. Crossley believes that students who have been able to use facilitated communication at home and in school over a period of months and even years demonstrate fewer unusual behaviors than when they first came to DEAL. "We never could have mainstreamed [in school] so many of the students if they hadn't changed," she argues.

The question of how much acceptance Crossley's students will find in their families and schools cannot be separated from their behavior or from the perceptions and attitudes of people around them. Students in Polly's high school English class regularly volunteer to be in discussion groups with her; the teacher says they recognize that Polly has creative ideas about the readings they discuss. But she still does not have classmates whom she considers her friends. Polly told me that she worries about the idea of possibly having friends. She has not yet had one, other than her mother, her siblings, Rosemary Crossley, and people like herself who use facilitated communication. She is afraid. "I don't know what to feel," she told me. David Armbruster said he wanted girls at his school to stop "mothering" him. "I want a girlfriend," he declared. Not surprisingly, the degree to which DEAL students can or will reach out and communicate to others seems to depend on how others receive them.

Awareness of that fact pervades Crossley's work. She embraces the age-old, but not always honored, belief in students' capacity to learn and express themselves. From her first interaction with students, where she uses no-fail and always open-ended assessments, to her unstructured dialogues with students about their lives, she engages them, speaking personally and directly to them, never patronizing. Her purpose, after all, is not to test their competence but to find ways for them to reveal their competence. She warns us against the persistent tendency to impose low expectations on students. Their poetry, their letters, and their statements are the text of her work and comprise both the product and the material of her teaching.

Perhaps more than most students, the students described in this article *demand* an education-through-dialogue approach, where teachers and students learn from each other and where schooling validates personal expression. It is as if this group of people, labeled autistic, by *not* communicating except with certain facilitators and in certain, supportive circumstances, is saying what all students at one time or another have said, if less obviously: We will reveal ourselves, we will show our creativity, when we feel appreciated, when we are supported.

Notes

1. In the tradition of ethnographic research, all students have been given pseudonyms to protect their privacy.
2. Jonothan left out spaces between words and repeated several letters without correcting the errors, although he later demonstrated the ability to put in spaces and to make his own corrections; the Canon Communicator is like any electric typewriter such that if the person typing lingers on a key, it will produce the same letter more than once.
3. In all I observed twenty-seven people, nine of whom were being seen by DEAL staff for the first time and who had not previously communicated more than single words or signs or echolalic phrases. The six people observed at DEAL that are not included in this account had a variety of other disabling conditions, including Down Syndrome, cerebral palsy, and other physical and intellectual disabilities.
4. Crossley's recommendation in instances of doubt over the communication is for facilitators to return to "set work" in which the correct answers are known, at least until the person's facility with communication increases and becomes more independent.
5. The assumption has been that children with autism are unable "to analyze and categorize both linguistic and nonlinguistic data" (Menyuk, 1978, p. 115). This inability has been thought to limit the person's "performance in certain intellectual tasks and social adaptation" (pp. 114–115). Consistent with this interpretation, Wing explains the apparent "social avoidance and poor eye contact . . . as arising from the absence of any mechanism for understanding the environment" (Wing, 1978, p. 41).
6. The principal differences between Crossley's approach and that of most other educators of children with autism is her addition of hand-over-hand, wrist, or arm facilitation in the initial stages of typed communication *and* the expectation that students are capable of sophisticated communication.
7. As with all observations and interviews, this session was audio-recorded. Since facilitators spoke the students' words aloud, it was possible to develop a verbatim transcript of the entire conversation.

References

Baltaxe, C. A. M., & Simmons, J. Q. (1977). Bedtime soliloquies and linguistic competence in autism. *Journal of Speech and Hearing Disorders, 42,* 376–393.

Bartak, L., Rutter, M., & Cox, A. (1977). A comparative study of infantile autism and specific developmental receptive language disorders. III. Discriminant function analysis. *Journal of Autism and Childhood Schizophrenia, 7,* 383–396.

Bettleheim, B. (1967). *The empty fortress: Infantile autism and the birth of the self.* New York: Free Press.

Crossley, R., & McDonald, A. (1980). *Annie's coming out.* New York: Penguin.

Donnellan, A. M. (Ed.). (1985). *Classic readings in autism.* New York: Teachers College Press.

Eisenberg, L. (1956). The autistic child in adolescence. *American Journal of Psychiatry, 112,* 607–612.

Goodwin, M. S., & Goodwin, T. C. (1969). In a dark mirror. *Mental Hygiene, 53,* 550–563.

Grandin, T., & Scariano, M. M. (1986). *Emergence labeled autistic.* Novato, CA: Arena Press.

Intellectual Disability Review Panel. (1989). *Investigation into the reliability and validity of the assisted communication technique.* Melbourne: Department of Community Services, Victoria.

Interdisciplinary Working Party on Issues in Severe Communication Impairment. (1988). *DEAL Communication Centre Operation. A Statement of Concern.* Melbourne: Author.

James, A. L., & Barry, R. J. (1983). Developmental effects in the cerebral lateralization of autistic, retarded, and normal children. *Journal of Autism and Developmental Disorders, 13,* 43–55.

Kanner, L. (1943). Autistic disturbances of affective contact. *Nervous Child, 2,* 217–250.

Kanner, L. (1971). Follow-up study of eleven autistic children originally reported in 1943. *Journal of Autism and Childhood Schizophrenia, 1, 2,* 119–145.

Menyuk, P. (1978). Language: What's wrong and why. In M. Rutter & E. Schopler (Eds.), *Autism* (pp. 105–116). New York: Plenum Press.

Mirenda, P., & Schuler, A. L. (1988). Augmenting communication for persons with autism: Issues and strategies. *Topics in Language Disorders, 9,* 24–43.

Mirenda, P. L., Donnellan, A. M., & Yoder, D. E. (1983). Gaze behavior: A new look at an old problem. *Journal of Autism and Developmental Disorders, 13,* 397–409.

Oppenheim, R. (1974). *Effective teaching methods for autistic children.* Springfield, IL: Charles C. Thomas.

Ornitz, E. M., & Ritvo, E. R. (1968). Perceptual inconsistency in infantile autism. *Archives of General Psychiatry, 18,* 76–98.

Paul, R. (1987). Communication. In D. J. Cohen, A. M. Donnellan, & R. Paul (Eds.), *Handbook of autism and pervasive development disorders* (pp. 61–64). New York: John Wiley & Sons.

Prizant, B. M. (1983). Language acquisition and communication behavior in autism: Toward an understanding of the "whole" of it. *Journal of Speech and Hearing Disorders, 48,* 286–296.

Prizant, B. M., & Rydell, P. J. (1984). Analysis of functions of delayed echolalia in autistic children. *Journal of Speech and Hearing Research, 27,* 183–192.

Ricks, D. M., & Wing, L. (1975). Language, communication, and the use of symbols in normal and autistic children. *Journal of Autism and Childhood Schizophrenia, 5,* 191–221.

Rimland, B. (1964). *Infantile autism.* New York: Appleton-Century-Crofts.

Rutter, M. (1968). Concepts of autism: A review of research. *Journal of Child Psychology and Psychiatry, 9,* 1–25.

Rutter, M. (1978). Etiology and treatment: Cause and cure. In M. Rutter & E. Schopler (Eds.), *Autism* (pp. 327–335). New York: Plenum Press.

Schopler, E., Reichler, R. J., & Lansing, M. (1980). *Individualized assessment and treatment for autistic and developmentally disabled children.* Baltimore: University Park Press.

Schuler, A. L., & Baldwin, M. (1981). Nonspeech communication and childhood autism. *Language, Speech, and Hearing Services in Schools, 12,* 246–257.

Tager-Flusberg, H. (1981a). On the nature of linguistic functioning in early infantile autism. *Journal of Autism and Developmental Disorders, 11,* 45–56.

Tager-Flusberg, H. (1981b). Sentence comprehension in autistic children. *Applied Psycholinguistics, 2,* 5–24.

Wetherby, A. M. (1984). Possible neurolinguistic breakdown in autistic children. *Topics in Language Disorders, 4,* 19–33.

Wing, L. (1978). Social, behavioral, and cognitive characteristics: An epidemiological approach. In M. Rutter & E. Schopler (Eds.), *Autism.* New York: Plenum Press.

I wish to thank the following people for reading and commenting on drafts of this manuscript: Sari Knopp Biklen, Janet Bogdan, Robert Bogdan, Katharine Butler, Rosemary Crossley, Alison Ford, Peter Knoblock, Luanna Meyer, Patricia Mirenda, Linda Milosky, Missy Morton, Shridevi Rao, and Nina Saha. Thanks also to Lou Heifetz for his review of a prospectus for the article and to Dianne Woods of the World Rehabilitation Fund for her support throughout the project.

Research for this article was accomplished with support in part from the World Rehabilitation Fund's International Exchange of Experts (WRF/IEEIR), which in turn is funded by the National Institute on Disability and Rehabilitation Research (NIDRR). The article reflects the author's views and not necessarily those of WRF/IEEIR or NIDRR.

Tipping the Balance

JOSEPH CAMBONE

In this article, Joseph Cambone describes a small classroom of young children at a residential treatment center and their teacher, "Anne." Through a year-long series of conversations with Cambone, which focused on videotapes he had made of her class, Anne describes her ongoing search to understand and teach her five students. Because these children have severe emotional and behavioral problems that cause them to act out verbally and physically, teaching them is a constant challenge. Yet as Anne reveals through her dialogue with Cambone, the dramatic, stark issues of these students rivet her attention, thoughts, and caring. Step-by-step, Anne and her class are able to settle into an ever more cohesive group in which teaching and learning are possible. In describing this classroom situation in extremis, Cambone reveals some universals about the teaching process and child development. Although most teachers do not encounter the intense behavior problems Anne faces daily, they are likely to find her concerns and thought processes familiar. Similarly, while few children have experienced the traumas these students have, or share the intensity of their fears and angers, these five children's struggles to learn, grow, and develop a sense of competence should be well-known to any teacher of young children. This article is an example of what teachers of special students can accomplish when they go beyond labels and preconceived notions of human limitations.

> Especially in times of darkness,
> that is the time to love, that an act of love might
> tip the balance.
>
> — Aeschylus

Chaos

"I was some of the problem. My expectations were wrong." It is early October a week after the lesson took place, and we are getting ready to watch it together on the videotape I have made. Anne sits with her Diet Coke, I with my pad and video paraphernalia. It is our first meeting together, and I am struck (as I will be throughout our months of videotaping lessons and talking about them afterwards) by how honestly self-critical she is. "I remember thinking that I was glad we would see this on videotape," she says with a little laugh. She seems nervous, perhaps even embarrassed, about watching together what was clearly a difficult lesson. I had anticipated that. What I had not anticipated was her curiosity. More than anything, she is curious. She wants to see for herself where she made her errors, how she was part of the problem. For that opportunity, she is glad.

But I am puzzled: how could she have been the problem? I had obviously seen the lesson differently through the lens of the camera. These children are so difficult to manage, and the lesson seemed such a reasonable one to attempt! This group of five boys is the youngest in the long history of this residential treatment center. By all accounts, they are the most violent and disturbed for their age.*

Six-year-old Jeremy was born in a state institution and already has been in nearly ten foster homes. Small and thin, his dark hair is cut in a spiky brush-cut top that sets off his pale olive skin; he is cute, spunky, and talkative. Adults and children alike are drawn to him. But he is frequently confused and frustrated by almost all social situations and often becomes physically assaultive or sexually provocative.

Paul is seven. He and his family have been homeless until just recently, and there is evidence that he has been sexually abused in one of many shelters. This school is the first place that he has lived for any extended period of time. His round, deep-brown face is full of expression; his large almond-shaped eyes are always wide with what seems to be confusion and panic — and sometimes, thankfully, the glee of a little boy. He is known by almost all of the adults in the school by now, because his tantrums have been so exceedingly violent, frequent, and prolonged.

Six-year-old Steve had also been sexually abused before his adoption. Unlike the other boys, he is not a child who has tantrums often. Instead, he becomes oppositional, automatically shouting "NO!" at small requests or even when offered opportunities for fun. Often he sits, jaw set in his long, delicate face, brows furrowed, eyes squinting, whispering obscenities and taunts at the other boys. He is the only boy at grade level in his school work.

Samuel, eight years old, is a unique child, with average intelligence but pervasive neurological difficulties. In one-to-one situations he is sweet and affectionate, never hesitating to hug adults or tell them how much he loves them. But he has spent very little time in classrooms or with groups of any kind. He is given to screaming episodes at the slightest provocation, leaving adults and students alike wondering at the cause.

---

* I have changed the names of all adults and children to protect their confidentiality. However, to faithfully depict their experience, I have purposely retained their language.

Blond, blue-eyed, freckled Jamie is five years old, full of energy and continually on the move. He is unable to sit still for more than a few seconds at a time, always bumping into others, teasing and taunting them, poking his fingers at their sides. His activity level can escalate rapidly, easily disrupting the whole class; he is placed in "time-out" frequently. He is bright and verbal and quite engaging.

None of the boys has spent substantial time in school. Taken on their own, they are difficult to manage, demanding, and impulsive — put together, they interact explosively, provoking each other in a variety of ways, fighting, striking out at adults, throwing furniture and objects, and running away. Whenever I have seen the five together, chaos has not been far away. I thought the lesson went pretty well, considering the boys' behavior. . . .

"Was this a bad lesson?" I betray my incredulity through my tone of voice. She laughs her laugh, intelligent and perceptive, always with the slight touch of apology, and answers, "Well, this was not as good a lesson as it could have been!" She explains:

> In terms of the process of a teacher . . . this has been a really hard group for me 'cause I've needed to change a lot of the things I'm doing. I'm constantly critiquing what I'm doing. And the group has been so out of control most of the time! On one level I know that a lot of other people who have been here at the school even longer than I have said, "Oh my God! I can't believe that group!" And "I don't know how you deal with them every day." And "This is the most difficult group I've ever had in the art room!" And blah blah blah! So I know it's not me. But at the same time I'm constantly knowing that I *do* need to change what I'm doing and that there are things that I can change to make it better. So I'm sort of constantly replaying that in my head.

Her eagerness to be self-critical seems layered, like so much of what she does; perhaps being self-critical helps fend off the impulse to blame the boys for their difficulties, as others sometimes do. Given their extremely troublesome behavior, it is easy to blame them. Perhaps, too, she is self-critical because she knows that, in a way, she is in the spotlight; people are watching closely and with a certain amazement at how she'll handle the most difficult group they've seen in years.

Yet, the self-analysis goes much deeper, to what being a teacher means to her. Anne believes that being self-analytical is part of the "process of being a teacher." This process involves constantly reevaluating assumptions about what works and what does not work in the classroom, not settling on one method; rather, developing curriculum *in response to* the children. Anne believes that this year's plans cannot be based on last year's students.

So she is "glad" as we watch the tape of the lesson — glad for the opportunity to think over her assumptions, glad to think over her methods. And I am glad for the opportunity to watch her think as we begin to watch the videotape together:

Cathy's voice is getting tighter. It's the third week of school and already Anne has given this new teaching intern plenty of responsibility. The boys are getting restless, whispering, fidgeting on the L-shaped bench that wraps around the far left corner under the windows. There are usually five boys in the group, but Jeremy has already been removed from the room for trouble. Anne is setting up a new lesson and has not given them her full attention for just over a minute. The boys' energy is palpable, unfocused. She pulls the table out and puts the apples on it before them.

The PAUSE button gets pushed. "I wasn't well organized enough. I mean that is an immediate hindsight reaction. . . ." At first I think she is referring to having the apples ready and the table in place. But she is referring to her disorganized mind-set: she wasn't planning for the right children. "I've done this lesson at least twice before with other groups and the kids loved it. They were totally motivated to eat the apples . . . it was fun, a great lesson! . . . I sort of was stupid in saying '. . . I can just do it off the top of my head!'" She watches the frozen action on the screen. ". . . I didn't really think enough about how different this group is from last year's — just how because it was successful last year . . . !"

She has focused on her interior organization for the lesson, while I have focused on how not being ready with materials causes tension to mount in the room. Ordinarily, a teacher can take at least sixty seconds or so of class time to arrange supplies for an activity, but not in this class — trouble begins brewing in those sixty seconds. Any time spent talking instead of doing something tempts fate; transitions between activities can be tortuous. I begin to understand her comments about organization. If she can move the boys smoothly from activity to activity, keeping them focused on objects by using their hands and eyes, she can divert their attention away from their own thoughts or each other. Nevertheless, it has to be the right activity. I push PLAY.

Samuel, strange and distant, starts making gulping noises, moving his head forward and back like a chicken when it walks. "Samuel, I can't put in a good sticker for you until you're not making noises. Samuel, look at me." Cathy is trying to regain his attention. He doesn't hear, lost in his own rhythm. Anne is moving quicker now but says nothing. Paul and Jamie are laughing together on the bench, mostly ignoring Cathy. Jamie makes small kung-fu gestures. Paul laughs at the gestures Jamie uses and makes a few of his own. Jamie laughs and ups the ante; leaning back in his chair, he spreads his legs and pretends to play with his penis.

Over the voices on the tape, Anne comments on Samuel. "It's very frustrating to figure out what to do with him! His biggest problem is being over-stimulated, and he's in a group of extremely acting-out kids. The other kids are probably scary. . . ." She isn't sure he should remain in the class — maybe this school is the wrong place for him, maybe he needs something even more specialized. And Jamie is such a baby, not even six years old. He is so bright and eager, but over-run with impulses. She sees him play with his penis and wishes she could just let it pass by without comment. "It's something that [seems unimportant]. He plays with his penis on top of his pants . . . in some ways it is not atypical for a five-year-old. But with this group and knowing him. . . ." Cathy, who is less experienced, and less philosophical, seems frantic:

> *"Jamie, it looks to me that you need to go to time out." He leans toward her, purses his lips, sticks his tongue out a little, and makes a growling noise. Samuel mimics him, although he makes no sound. The defiance is contagious and Paul starts fidgeting wildly. Karen, the milieu therapist who is the third member of this team, takes Jamie by the hand and leads him out. Jamie hesitates and looks at Anne and says, "Ohhhh! What am I gonna do?" He seems befuddled. Was I doing something wrong, he seems to say; what did I do? "But when can I get my 'good' sticker?" he whines as he is withdrawn from the room. Anne turns to the remaining boys, face set in a serious look.*

When a child does something like Jamie did, something that she thinks in itself is minor or manageable but could upset the others, she is distressed. "How much do you send one kid away from the group for something you think might upset the others in the group?" She returns to this question again and again, unable to answer it. The tension of this uncertainty about what approach to take marks the first weeks of school.

> *By now, Paul is in motion again, kneeling on his bench on all fours, swaying his buttocks back and forth. He is a ball of energy, but when he sees the adults' attention shift from Jamie back to him he jumps into a perfect sitting position.*
>
> *"Today we're going to talk about apples," she begins. She stands behind the table and puts out four different types of apples. The three boys give her rapt attention, as if they'd never seen an apple before. "Who can tell me something about these apples?" Hands shoot up in a great start to the lesson. Samuel says, "There's a red one, a green one, and [pointing to a golden delicious apple] a white one." "So they have different what . . . ?" Samuel: "Colors." Anne: "Paul, what can you tell me about these apples?" He leaps off his bench and lurches toward the apples, leaning in as he goes. "No, stay in your seat, you'll get to touch them later." "But I have to show you!" He is pleading, he can't say it without touching. But she just continues speaking to the boys about the lesson. He inches backwards and sits down.*
>
> *Fully animated, he points at one, leaning forward, twisting in his seat, trying to find something important to say about the apple. His hand is outstretched, feeling the apple in the air as she calls on him again. "What can you tell me*

about these apples?" "They got skin on 'em? And stems?" Am I on the right track? he seems to ask as he works himself up to standing on one leg, knee still on the bench. His movement is getting larger; he can't sit still. "Good job, Paul." Now standing, he starts to sway, swinging his arms and hands up and down in the front of his body, then around to his back, then in front again. A little louder, "They have skin all around them." Anne acknowledges quickly, "Yes, they have skin all around them." Paul, voice filled with drama, "To make them warm!"

"What are you thinking?" I ask, hitting PAUSE. "Just how constantly in motion he is, that he has not been still once! . . . He's doing okay . . . although he is moving so fast . . . would it help him, would it be better or worse to make him stop and sit still?" She has him involved. His energy is ample but she is keeping it within boundaries. She makes a decision: "Right now, Paul moving his body around a lot is a minor problem compared to Paul being typically aggressive. It's sort of like saving my battles." She is constantly vigilant, watching them closely, collecting information, and sorting it on the fly.

She simply gestures to him to sit. Paul climbs back on the bench and kneels on it, facing away from the group, his head as a third point touching the bench. Samuel starts moving in his chicken motion, stops, starts again. Is he paying attention? "I like the red one and the dotted one," Steve says. Paul, up and moving again toward the apples asks, "You mean this one?" Anne loses none of her own momentum as she points and says, "Back on your seat, Paul." Once again he returns and lies across the bench.

The idea for the lesson is to use the senses to experience what is different and what is the same about apples. "We're going to see how they look, how the apples smell, how the apples feel, how the apples taste . . . ," she says. Paul is on the move again. "Sit down," she says calmly and firmly without missing a beat. "This is a McIntosh. We're going to pass the apple around, and we're going to look with our eyes and say some words that tell what a McIntosh apple looks like."

Steve holds the apple and smiles. "It's cold!" he says. "There's a word for what it feels like. Remember that. But right now let's look at how it looks." She has a chart ready to write down words that tell how it looks, then feels, smells, and tastes. But it is too late, she has given them the apple to hold and the wheel's in motion. Paul takes the apple, gazing dreamily out the window as he rubs it between his hands, then smooths it against his face. "Now you guys are looking and feeling," Anne says aloud to herself. It's a statement of fact — things are already happening differently from what she planned. In truth, they are not "looking" at all, they are feeling. She planned a structured, sequential lesson on the five senses; they're interested only in feeling.

She tries again to focus them, to redirect the lesson, to organize their learning. "I want boys to remember to look with their eyes. Now who can tell me a word about how this apple looks." Steve has caught on. He says, "It's red." Samuel says, "It's juicy." But Anne is concentrating on getting the squirming Paul back on track. "Paul, what's a word about how the apple looks?" "It looks funny!" He is on his knees in front of her in a flash. "This could be a mouth and this could be a head." This time she lets him stay. After all, he has told her what it looks like. "Yes, but what color is it?" she asks. "It's red." Steve complains that he had already said that. No one hears him over Paul so he says, barely audible, his eyes slitted and angry, "It looks like a bum!" Paul has moved back to the bench and is walking on it like a crab with excitement. The tone in the room has changed but she isn't yet sure why. "I need everybody sitting quietly on the bench and eyes on me." There is a brief moment of stillness.

When her simple request to sit quietly works, Anne decides not to make a big deal about everyone talking at once. She just stops and regroups. She wants to get on with the lesson and give each boy a chance to participate, but she needs a moment to get a handle on the tone of the room. She did not hear Steve's comment, and Samuel's was overshadowed by Paul's voice as well, but she picked up on the change in tone, a shift away from exuberance and toward agitation. "Tone" is important to many of her decisions. It is an indication of the group's mood and level of tolerance. When she is made confident by the group's tone that they are doing well, she knows she can give an individual boy a little more latitude in his behavior, as she has with Paul. She draws on "knowledge of the individual kids and knowledge of the group dynamics. . . . If I feel like [a boy is] doing something that is going to set off the rest of the group, it's gotta stop right away. And if it looks like it's something that nobody else is paying attention to and the kid is still with what is going on, then I might let it go." But in this case she misreads the tone, misunderstands why it has shifted, misses that the constant motion and commotion seem to be masking the boys' underlying confusion about what she wants. The tension is mounting among the children. They are offering ideas, talking about the apples. What does she want? They are mumbling what is important to them — "it's cold," "it's juicy" — but she is trying to focus them on seeing. Samuel is squirming and Steve has turned around in his seat, yawning, inattentive. She has lost them somehow.

After the lesson she realizes her error — the lesson was not suited for them. "We needed to cut out like twenty-five steps. . . . I've always taught the youngest kids who were emotionally disturbed and learning disabled and I felt like I had already pared everything down to the barest minimum. With this group, I need to go twenty steps below that." But in the moment, she wants to push them: "I'm used to pushing kids to that next level of thinking.

. . . But the task I was asking them to do didn't make sense. I mean forget the difference between the eyes and the hands! Save the five senses for another lesson! That's a prerequisite skill they don't have yet." In this case, she has misjudged, has pushed too hard too soon, and the delicate balance of control was quickly lost.

> *"Paul, can you say what the apple looks like?" He jumps up and comes to her. She lets it go. He kneels. "There are little green spots and flat on the bottom. Flat here, flat here, and here it's busted." "Good job Paul, now sit down." Paul, the showman, takes a bow before the group. Steve has been trying to speak again and gets pre-empted by Paul. Samuel giggles. Steve has been continually thwarted by Paul's misbehavior and when Paul, perpetual motion on the bench, bounces around the bench toward Steve, Steve punches him in the side. Not hard, just enough. Paul hits him back. Anne is firm, calm. "Now Steve and Paul, each of you have three minutes to sit quietly and we're not going to go on until you're finished." The room bursts into pandemonium.*
>
> *Anne's mind races to meet the crisis.*

"It's moving so quickly and I don't feel I have time to think about what I'm saying. . . ."

> *Paul leaps up to run from the room but Cathy grabs him. Samuel starts rocking back and forth, head like a rag doll. Paul is yelling, "Fuck you, leave me alone, fuck you." "Paul, you have to the count of three to be back on your bench or you will leave the classroom. One, two . . ." Paul stops screaming and cursing, smiles at his classmates, cocky. Samuel gets quiet but then laughs and seems like a willing participant in the misbehavior. "Now the whole group is going to sit." When they hear this, the room bursts into chaos again. Paul grabs his crotch wildly and starts shouting suggestive words. Samuel laughs hysterically. Paul lifts his shirt and displays his stomach provocatively to Samuel, sing-songing, "BELLYBUTTON!!" Anne takes his arm and begins to remove him.*

"He's going to do something either dangerous or so outrageous that it is going to cause more of a problem."

> *Samuel starts to make noises. As Paul moves past the table with the apples on it, he picks one up and, still shouting sexual epithets for the boys, throws it at the wall. Anne takes both arms and walks him to time-out. Steve jumps from his chair and runs for the apple.*

"This shouldn't be happening. I'm a bad teacher! If this is happening in my classroom I should be able to have better control than this!!"

> *Samuel starts shrieking "FUCKER" over and over while he starts rocking. Finally, he jumps up and tries to run away.*

"Can't we do anything to shut him up! He has good reason to be anxious . . . but we can't even be supportive!"

Cathy catches his arm, tries to hold Samuel and to get Steve back in his chair at the same time. Anne, at the other side of the room, has Paul pinned in a chair.

"An adult needs to put hands on him and physically stop him because otherwise he's going to run out of the classroom, knock something over, or do something potentially dangerous!"

He is kicking her and attempting to head-butt her, screaming.

"There's a part of me that is dealing with the physical reality — of not being able to physically put Paul down."

Karen returns Jamie to the room at just this moment.

". . . this is a stupid time to bring Jamie into the room!"

Apparently, he has calmed down. Karen leaves Jamie in a chair on the far side of the room, takes Samuel from Cathy, and leaves the room with the shrieking Samuel. At the same time, Anne sees that Paul cannot remain and removes him from the room to the Crisis Center. Steve remains, looking innocent, on the bench.

"I can't remember whether Steve had been part of the initial problem or not. It all happened so quickly."

The class is over in ten minutes. It takes another thirty minutes to calm the children down and get on with the day. As we finish the tape, Anne is visibly frustrated, struggling to find what is going wrong, why she can't teach in the way she knows best and interact therapeutically with the boys as she has done in the past. "So much is happening at once . . . I need to be juggling so many things at once!" In the end, she circles back to where she began: "I was some of the problem. My expectations were wrong."

Insight

The huge old oak stands majestic in the center of the sprawling lawn, its last leaves driven away by the first rainy day of November. The manicured lawn, stretching gradually up the hill from the tree to the large, beige Victorian mansion, is dying green and sepia, and the last struggling marigolds are beginning to fade in the big barrel planters along the walks. Even in the rain, the campus is pretty. Sitting on a bluff over the river, the property was once a wealthy dairy farm. Now it is a school for emotionally disturbed boys, and the barn, with a copper weather vane atop its cupola, has been tastefully refitted for offices. The old carriage house matches the main house in style and color and is used as a crisis center. The very modern school building sits farther back on the property, near the pasture that stretches up and out, rolling away toward the river; it is conservation land filled with birds. The mansion itself, called The House, is a residence for the boys, and although the inside is revamped for that purpose, the exterior retains its original grace. Canadian geese fly overhead, leaving the river behind for the winter, and I breathe it all in as I amble up the walk, past Anne's classroom window, to my appointment with the principal to speak about Anne's work.

"FUCK YOU!"

Paul's voice pushes through the wall and crashes into the landscape. Samuel's piercing wail follows. Furniture is pushed over, and Paul's obscenities fuse with Samuel's sustained cries. I think about the video session Anne and I have planned for that afternoon, the conversations we will have, and the struggle she is involved in. I look one more time at the lovely campus and take another, deeper breath.

In the staff room at lunchtime, Anne is propped on the end of her seat, leaning toward her colleagues, talking rapidly, loudly, her food half eaten. Her usually pale face is drained further of color, tears fill her eyes. She is furious. Whatever I overheard an hour before led to something even more serious. I've never seen her angry — even when the children are outrageously provocative, she remains calm, her voice measured. I hesitate to ask what has happened and instead watch her two teacher colleagues listen carefully, offer words of encouragement, and validate her feelings of frustration and anger. They are good listeners, long practiced at "giving space," letting anger wind down before trespassing with their own thoughts and opinions. Yet it is clear that they are not listening out of obligation. They are sincere, they share her worry about the children, and they share many of her beliefs about teaching practice.

Almost in unison, all three look up at the clock. It is 11:55. By 11:56 they are gone. As always, they must be ready when the boys return from lunch, ready to maneuver them smoothly into the afternoon activity. Predictability, consistency, and challenge are words they use to explain their work, conditions they believe are requirements for these children. But making those beliefs manifest puts tremendous pressure on them; it requires them to wolf down meals, communicate economically, and quickly move on — even though they are personally upset. The heart of this school beats fast, pushes hard; it is difficult not to get caught up in the rapid-fire thinking, talk, and movement. Invariably, within twenty minutes of arriving, my pulse is racing, too.

At 3:00 that afternoon, Anne is still upset as she tells me the story. It began at "wake-up." The boys were resistant to getting out of bed and doing their morning routines. Breakfast was disagreeable, and by the time they reached the classroom, Anne, Cathy, and Karen had a difficult time settling the boys in. They had a full day ahead: reading, math, and writing, as usual. But a special event was planned for the morning. The "Animals as Intermediaries" folks were coming. These people are a group of naturists who come to the school with live, usually wild, but injured animals as part of a schoolwide science program. Today they brought a field mouse and a dog. Anne had high hopes for this period. When they had come the week before, the activity was a great success. But today, Jeremy, in a rage because Steve got to hold the dog's leash and he did not, picked up a stapler and threw it at the dog, beginning a chain of problems that reverberated throughout the morning. Karen took Jeremy to the crisis center, where this behavior escalated, and before long, Jamie was removed by Cathy for misbehavior as well.

Left alone with the three remaining boys, Anne continued with the planned curriculum and moved on into Big Books period. Big Books are just that: three feet tall, colorful, with large type. They are the basis for multiple language and reading activities. This is usually a successful time for all, but today the negative momentum of the morning pushed hard against the fun of Big Books. Steve ended up in time-out, Paul began running around the room, climbing on the window sill, and Samuel began to shriek, "because that's what he does whenever someone else is having trouble." Refusing to sit down when he was told to, Paul became physically abusive toward Anne, requiring her to hold him in a chair. When his behavior became even more assaultive, kicking and head-butting her, she attempted to put him in a full restraint, in which the child is maneuvered into a position where he cannot move his body, thus preventing harm to himself and others. He proved too wild and strong for her, and she was unable to control him. In the back of her mind, she knew the other two boys were watching closely to see if she could safely restrain Paul, and she knew she could not. She pulled back and let him run out of the room. The situation had shaken her and the other boys badly. "That was an upsetting scene because the other kids were watching me not be in control, physically in control of this situation. And then he [Paul] was running around campus being out of control."

To make matters worse, about five minutes after Paul was finally calmed down, his therapist insisted on having her regularly scheduled meeting with him, even though he had just assaulted a teacher and run around campus. Against Anne's strong objection, the therapist relieved Paul from his consequences and took him to get his lunch — in front of the boys who have just seen him assault their teacher. Anne was outraged. She tells me:

> [He] sort of pranced into the lunchroom and got his lunch and all the other boys sort of looked at him and said "he just hit a teacher and ran around campus, what is he doing here?" And it was really very confusing. I was very angry because I didn't agree with that happening. So that was sort of the straw that broke the camel's back. Here was this child who had just done, in my mind, the two worst things he could have done! And there he was. And so I told his therapist to take him out of the lunchroom, that he couldn't be there,

that he couldn't be near other boys and that I didn't want boys in my class to see him at all right now. And it was a little bit tense.

She laughs a laugh that almost apologizes for her passion. But she is extremely serious: how can she be expected to make her classroom a safe place to learn if everyone doesn't give the children the same message about their behavior? These children can't differentiate the therapy session from the classroom; all adults are the same to them, and what the therapist sees as unconditional positive regard for Paul seems to seven-year-old Paul like getting off the hook. Anne's argument is quite persuasive, it has the force of belief, and her frustration is real.

Anne's frustrations are mounting. She is frustrated because it is already November and the chaos is continuing, frustrated that she can't deal with the children individually and therapeutically because so many things happen at once, frustrated that she cannot keep everyone safe, and particularly frustrated when she sees adults not working as a team. That, in fact, is the "straw that broke the camel's back."

Even though the feeling of chaos claims the balance of the day, there is a difference in the class. I had felt the difference earlier as I taped her lesson, felt that she might be making inroads into the chaos. Yet, it is evident as we begin to watch the tape together that she is not yet feeling any positive difference. The class still feels like bedlam to her. But it is clear to me that she is more confident about how to proceed. Closely watching her work with the children as she responds to whatever surprises they toss at her, I realize how intellectually agile she is. She enters a given period with a plan and a terminal goal, but her intellectual and emotional stance is open and ready: What will they do? What will they say? How will I respond so that I can keep them moving toward the goal and not lose them to anger or frustration? Each situation the boys present is a fresh problem to be solved in a series of steps toward a final goal. She draws on her earlier repertoire of activities, but she applies them in new ways, for different purposes.

Her work is not just responsive in the moment, though. Threaded through her talk about the class and evident in her actions with the boys are three principles that she has extracted from the chaos: these boys, individually, are clearly capable of higher intellectual and behavioral functioning; the problems they are presenting are group-management problems; the schedule of the day must be altered accordingly. By keeping these three ideas in mind, she limits the field of possible approaches: focus on their individual strengths, work to improve their interaction skills, and modify their environment to enhance their strengths and promote healthier interaction.

Three children and three adults sit huddled on the bench together, first an adult, then a child, then an adult, child, adult, child. Jeremy and Paul, she explains to Cathy and Karen, and for the ears of the three remaining boys, have been separated for the remainder of the day for their violent behavior.

I'm surprised. The remainder of the day? "[I am] trying to preserve the classroom space as a safe, calm space. Even if that means that four out of five need to leave it and then gradually come back one at a time. . . . But this . . . space needs to be preserved as a place where learning happens and where crazy behavior can't happen. . . ." I think back to her recurring dilemma: "How much do you send one kid away from the group for something you think might upset the others in the group?" She seems to have made a decision about how to proceed — make the classroom a place of learning and pull them back one at a time. This is a methodological decision that reflects Anne's adjustment to who these children are and the ways they think — they are young, inexperienced in school, and still unsure of what is required of them, and they are easily confused by what others say and do. She has decided to structure the environment in unambiguous, stark terms. The group-management problems can be resolved only if the children understand the environmental requirements: in this class, we learn; in this class, we do not act crazy. It is simply stated, over and over, in word and deed. It is for this reason that she is angry with Paul's therapist. By giving the message that consequences for violence could and will be suspended by one adult, but not another, the therapist undermines Anne's efforts.

Anne is finishing a read-aloud book. All five children seem mellow and affectionate. Jamie sees me and my video camera and comes up to look. Anne suggests that if the boys are interested and do a good job cleaning up and getting ready for the next period, I will demonstrate the camera. They hop to it, the transition goes smoothly, and one by one they sit on my lap and film their teachers and classmates. Then, just as easily, they hop back to their benches and begin writing class.

Anne shows them a large manila envelope, addressed and ready to go. It is a thank-you letter to a museum they had toured the week before. "Remember yesterday we wrote a thank-you letter to the Children's Discovery Museum. I got a big envelope. . . ." In it she put the oversized card that they had written as a group the day before. She tells them how she addressed the envelope and will send it. It is a brief lesson in letter writing. Quickly, she moves on and shows them the book they had made yesterday filled with the photos taken at the museum. On every page, a boy had pasted a photo of himself doing some fun thing at the museum. Under each photo he dictated a short sentence about what he did. "Here's Steve's picture. It says 'Steve liked the chain-reaction room!' And there's Samuel's picture, and it says, 'Samuel is jumping on the giant water bed!'" As she reads the caption under each picture, they give her all their attention, giggling with glee when their picture comes up.

"They said what to write and I *wrote* it, and they could *read* it," she says with excitement. "It was a record of their experiences: Jamie liked this, Paul liked this, Jeremy liked this. . . ." There is a remarkable difference in the presentation of this book from the presentation of lessons earlier in the year — the apples, for instance. Here, the short lesson is focused directly on the boys, what they thought, felt, saw, and did. The children laugh, ask questions, make comments. This way of doing things makes sense to them. They are in positive frames of mind. Characteristically, Anne decides to push them a little, to try something they don't like as much, and she pulls out the easel to begin a group lesson. She is always looking for an opportunity to push them harder, to acclimate them to school-like activities, to shift the balance in favor of academics.

> *"We'll keep this on the shelf in our room so that if you want to show anyone about our trip, you can." Anne sets up the easel as she speaks, "I thought that it is nice to have things to show about special things you've done. And this morning we did something special. Who can remember some of the things that we did this morning when the animals came to the class . . . ?" At the slightest hint of a structured lesson, where questions will be asked and answers required, the boys' anxiety level goes up. Samuel starts rocking and making low noises; Jamie whines and sprawls on the bench. Cathy goes to Jamie, Anne to Samuel. Each talks quietly to the boys and they sit up. But Jamie is still fidgety. "I don't want to do this," he complains. Anne pushes ahead and asks Samuel what he liked about this morning. "I liked patting the dog." Anne writes the sentence on the easel. Not to be outdone, Jamie's hand shoots up. "I'm glad you've thought of something you liked, Jamie. What did you like?" His words spill from his mouth, he has so much he liked. "Wait, wait," says Anne with a smile, "let me get all this down!"*
>
> *They finish recording all the fun things they did. The lesson lasts less than three minutes. Anne gives them paper and markers and they draw pictures of what they remember, dictate sentences about the pictures to Anne, then copy what she has written under the pictures themselves.*

I run down with Anne what I've learned in the first moments of taping: the boys were able to look through my camera without incident, they have gone to a museum in another town on a field trip, and have engaged in a short lesson that, a month ago, would have led to a disruption. "How is it you were able to accomplish these things two days in a row?" First she reminds me the period would never have been successful if all five children had been present. She would have had to do everything differently in that case. Then, as she speaks, she seems to be putting a name on what she has been doing, has been knowing, but did not yet put into words. "[I could do it] because there were these really salient things. We had gone on this trip and had this experience with the animals. They had been powerful or exciting or different experiences. It seemed like too good an opportunity to pass up! . . . I wanted to capitalize on these things and get them to do this . . . If they're gonna be able to do it [writing] at all, they'll be able to do it best when there's something they're really excited about." She has decided that, in part, managing the behavior of the group means getting them interested in what they are doing in class. The more they are interested, the more leverage she has to keep them out of trouble and in the group.

Using "salient" things makes the difference. She has searched for and located what excites the boys in school, and has put more of the same in their way. Yet "salience" does not translate to doing whatever they want — an activity may be fun, but not salient. For Anne, salient activities are interesting to the boys *and* fulfill her academic or social goals for them as well. Her goals are clear. In the case of language arts, the older three boys (whom she considers first graders) will be writing stories on their own by June. The younger, kindergarten-aged boys will be dictating stories. From the beginning of September "that's been the same goal. My feelings about how realistic it is go up and down a little bit." She laughs. Sometimes it seems she laughs because her words sound absurd to her own ears, her beliefs and hopes incongruous in the current situation. Perhaps she should be happy with the small accomplishments and forget the terminal goals. "I'm too product-oriented!" she says, and laughs again.

Finding the salient content for her classes is important, but the day's organization is equally important to managing the group's behavior. Keeping them interested alone will not solve her problem of group management; when and how they do activities is just as important. Very early in the year, she decided that the afternoon schedule was too intense for these young children. With the slightly older children she had taught in the past, a half-hour each of language arts, science, and social studies activities made sense. For this year's youngsters, these artificial differentiations by content area didn't make sense. She believed the more important skills were learning to use language, to listen, to function as a group, and do group lessons, at least for now. Science, social studies, and writing became the materials she used, but what really mattered to Anne was ". . . balancing out each individual kid's academic, cognitive potential versus their behavioral, social needs . . . figuring out how to get them to do what they are capable of doing, [and] at the same time keeping them in a group and having reasonable behavioral expectations for the group. . . ." She still had their academic goals in mind, but, "I needed to find a way to get all those experiences and all those goals done differently." And so she abandoned her formal writing period, as well as formal science and social studies, replacing them with a series of structured experiences in which the emphasis was less on content and more on group process. The activities she chose were still academic, but more spontaneous, more dependent on the prevailing moods of the class. The afternoon began to look more like preschool or kindergarten and less like first or second grade.

The five boys loved being read to and would remain calm and attentive all through a picture book. So she read books about Pilgrims and Fizzwiggle the Cat. They enjoyed filmstrips too, especially about insects or dinosaurs. They loved to draw. After each activity the boys drew pictures and made things with their hands. All around the room hung drawings of Pilgrims and dinosaurs, insects and cats. Yet underneath each drawing or on a label beneath a string of clay beads were always words — a sentence about the artwork. The early creations were labeled in an adult's neat hand; the later ones gradually gave way to the prehensile scrawl of kindergartners, silent testimony to the slow progression of the year, to "taking turns a little bit, not trying to accomplish all as quickly as I might have last year, by doing sometimes language art things, sometimes science things, sometimes social studies things. But the goals are still there. . . ."

Anne had set her goals for them long ago, it just has been unclear how to get to those goals. She is used to older children, and to setting goals for first and second graders. These children are kindergartners; the types of things she can teach, the ways she prefers to teach don't seem to work. Yet she is making slow progress. She can keep three in the room at one time, sometimes without fights. Slowly, one by one, she will bring them back into the classroom. She can regroup them after a terrible morning and lead a productive afternoon. But the activity must be salient. She can cover some content with them. She just has to be flexible about when and how. She has to have the freedom to maneuver the schedule to match the mood.

Regression

"Yak! Yak! He's a Lego maniac!!
Yak! Yak! He's a Lego maniac!!
Yak! Yak! He's a Lego maniac!!"

Over and over, for nearly ten minutes, Jamie chants the phrase. He is flung across Anne's lap and she holds him tightly, a rag doll, spent from anxiety, awaiting his state social worker's visit. The worker does not visit unless there is news, usually bad news: "We can't find your mommy." "We can't find your daddy." "We have a new foster home." "You'll be moving to a residential school." He doesn't know what Anne knows, that they have found his mommy and daddy and she has sent him some presents. She wants him back, is going to fight the state, which wants to put him up for adoption. This news will only overwhelm him more.

Anne is overwhelmed, too. As the weeks of struggle have turned into months, it is harder to hold on to the belief that she can make a difference, harder to resist being tipped into despair. And so she labors to balance herself between despair and belief. Now, she sits silently and Jamie chants his mantra in his futile battle to focus on one thing instead of the million thoughts and worries that are rushing at his mind. She is not unlike him. The desperate events of the past months rush at her and she does battle with them, she forces them into perspective by reminding herself why she does. She is thinking, she tells me later, about nothing in particular and everything that has happened, numb and anguished at the same time.

The past two weeks have been a complete regression back to less than zero. And until two days ago, pretty literally no teaching academics happened at all in the classroom. Two of the boys, Jeremy and Steve, we found out, have been involved in fairly extensive sexual activity on the weekends with one another. Both of them were pretty much basket cases for about two weeks and practically unable to be in class at all. [When they are in class] . . . the severity of [their] sexual and aggressive acting out [is so disruptive to others, that] Jamie has also, pretty much [been] unable to be in school. And with that much going on, Samuel, of course, spends a lot of time shrieking and has a lot of difficulty because things were pretty chaotic. So for almost two weeks I did little else than restrain kids all day. And it was really miserable, and really awful.

I finally felt that we were *getting* somewhere, like we are progressing toward some of the goals, that we were doing better as a group, and then everything fell apart, and it didn't make any sense, and I couldn't understand why. And then finding out why, having one of the boys disclose some of these things that were going on, on the one hand made it feel better because at least there was a reason for it! You know, it wasn't me, it wasn't the classroom, it wasn't just out of the blue!! But it also felt really bad. It was like we couldn't even keep these kids safe! That things were happening that are making their lives worse while they're in residential care! And that felt yukky — even though it wasn't my personal thing. It left me feeling very unhopeful about Jeremy's prognosis, very disheartened.

In choosing to work with these kinds of kids, clearly I'm not just interested in academic teaching. I'm interested in social/emotional growth of kids. So I expect that some proportion of my time is gonna be spent dealing with social/emotional behavioral issues with kids and not just with teaching. But there is that part of it that feels like, "Well for two weeks all I did was restrain kids, I didn't have a classroom, I wasn't a teacher!" You know, I planned all this great curriculum that I didn't get a chance to do. . . . The neat curriculum isn't as important to me as how the kids are doing altogether. It's frustrating to feel like you're working so hard to plan . . . here I am, I revamped all these things, I have all these new ideas and we're not even getting to try them because everyone is out of control all the time. And that feeling of like, I said in the beginning of the year, I said to my team who were new [this year], at Thanksgiving we're really going to see improvement. We didn't. That was wrong.

For pretty much two weeks I've thought about the kids twenty-four hours a day. I've gone home and had dreams about them and felt very hopeless. It was a little bit better at the end of this week, 'cause better things started happening the past couple of days. At the same time that this is happening, I found out about a kid who graduated from here last year whose parents are about to terminate his adoption. And there was like a kid who wow! Here was one of our success stories! I had just told one of the parents of one of the kids in my class about this wonderful [story]: This boy came when he was seven and a half, graduated when he was ten and went to public school and he was doing so much better. Look how there is hope and success! And here his life is falling apart! And Jeremy is back to sucking the dicks of his friends when he is out of eyesight for ten seconds! And he is being really violent and really aggressive. And on one level it made me feel really hopeless and it's really shitty to feel hopeless about six-year-olds! And it's really hard to maintain the kind of energy that it takes to do this work when you're not feeling hopeful about it.

I guess I remind myself of the times when I feel hopeful, of the good things that can happen, and of my real belief that things will get better. I don't think I can fix them. I think I can help be part of making them healthier people. And if I didn't think that, I don't think I would do this kind of work. I think it's one of the reasons I like working with younger kids. . . . I wonder sometimes, especially with some of the more damaged kids how much of that damage can be undone. The damage is there and it's always going to be there. But he's *six years old*! I'd like to think that all the time and effort and energy that's going into everything, that I'm doing and that others are doing with him is going to mean that ten years from now he can lead some sort of productive, more normal life where he is not completely overrun by sexual and aggressive impulses 80 percent of the time! So I think . . . that [the] definition of success is different. . . . I've felt differently about it at different points in my professional growth. I feel differently about it for different kids. And it's really hard with such young kids to project what the ultimate hope might be for what they might be like.

I think [I have] high standards and push the kids and maybe cause more behavioral problems 'cause I'm pushing them to do things. It wouldn't be worth doing that if they were always going to be at a place like this for their whole lives. Like *who cares,* you know, how much socially appropriate behavior they learn, and if they learn how to read and do math and those kind of things! I think that there is always in the back of my head the thought and the hope that at some point down the road they're gonna go to some more normal setting. Whether they're gonna be adopted and stop living here or they go back to a public school at some point. Or that they stay at a place like this and are more successful there. You know or whatever. That there is a goal, that each one of these kids is capable of more higher functioning.

"Yak! Yak! He's a Lego maniac!!
Yak! Yak! He's a Lego maniac . . ."

Progress

"Guess what? Our first book is about to be published!" She sits before the group, her voice full of excitement. Just one minute before, she had begun the transition from read-aloud time to writing. Everyone had enjoyed the book, had been huddled together on the bench, like puppies warming themselves against each other. Yet when Anne announced the transition, Paul threw himself back on the bench, spread his legs and started gesturing to his anus. Jeremy started yelling at him to stop. Jamie began yelling his request to get a book. Samuel started screaming. In a flash, without speaking, the three adults moved into action. Paul was removed to a chair on the other side of the room; Jeremy, refusing to move to time-out, needed to be quickly lifted off the bench and carried out. An adult sat next to Samuel and touched his arm and he quieted. As quickly as the disruption began, it was over. Paul was brought back to his seat — he had regained control quickly. Jeremy remained in the time-out chair but listened to what was going on. As if nothing has happened, Anne begins what will be a positive lesson.

> *"Guess what? Our first book is about to be published! Samuel decided that he was going to write about his dog and he wrote 'Samuel and His Dog.' Then he thought of a lot of different things all about his dog and he wrote them in his book. Samuel, can you come here and sit next to me while I show them your book? 'My dog lived in the forest. My dog likes bones. . . . My dog's name is Sunshine!' "*

By early January, Anne had reinstituted a formal writing time at the boys' request. The first time one of the boys asked to write a book was during a free choice period back in November (free choice comes at the end of every day; if they have done all their school work, they can choose an activity of their own to do). Given their great love for read-aloud, it did not come as too big a surprise. Anne did not leap on the opportunity then; instead she "let this excitement keep on building on its own. A couple of months from now I will introduce it as a formal activity because they will be excited." She also waited because they still could not sit at a table together in November. They could listen to books, loved listening, in fact, but if they moved to work at tables everything fell apart. She still needed to work on their ability to spend time together as a group.

> *The tone of the class seems very different. She finishes reading Samuel's book and begins to explain how boys can publish books they've written. She demonstrates how the books are constructed, with contact-paper-covered cardboard serving as a book jacket, shows how to glue the pages. She shows them the press-on letters they can use on the front for a title. Each page, she reminds them, must be illustrated as well. The explanation takes time and they sit*

paying attention. Occasionally, Paul bounces on his seat and Anne stops for a moment. "I'm going to wait until everyone pays attention." Paul immediately quiets down and gives his attention to the activity. "When each boy finishes his story, he can do this to his story to publish it." They like that idea a lot!!

Anne divides the group in two; Jamie and Jeremy go with Cathy, the others remain with her. This is a chronological division, the younger children will not be required to write. If they want to write, they can. What is important is for them to tell stories and have Cathy write them down. However, Anne believes that the other three boys need to begin to do their own writing and not just tell stories. She feels a pressure to get them to do first-grade work, but not at the expense of their learning to dislike writing. She worries about this being their first writing experience. She wants to guarantee that it is positive. Hence they can write about whatever they choose and illustrate with the pictures they love to draw. Anne will then type their stories and ready them for "publication." Each finished story means the class has an "Author of the Day" who sits with the teacher in front of the group and has his story read. Only positive comments are allowed from the audience. Within a few weeks, fifteen or so books have been "published" and sit on the class book-shelf, to be taken out and read aloud, over and over again.

Paul dances to his chair at the table, swaying his buttocks back and forth. "Paul, go back to your bench. And when I see you sitting the right way you can come up to the table." He sits for a brief moment while she settles Steve in. "OK, Paul, you can come over." He runs across the room and leaps on his chair. One leg goes up on the tabletop and he starts to climb. Anne calmly tells him to sit correctly and keeps reading from Steve's story of yesterday. "'Steve and Karen have a snow ball fight.' That's good. Think about what you want to write today." Steve is not in a very good mood, it seems. When Anne turns to help Paul, Steve mumbles an obscenity toward Paul under his breath. Anne tells him to go back to his bench and to sit for a minute for speaking that way. As he leaves the table, he pretends to spit on Paul's work. Paul retaliates and pretends to spit on Steve's work. "Now you have one minute on your bench as well." Paul erupts verbally, "He fuckin' spit on my fuckin' paper!" "Well," says Anne calmly, almost nonchalantly, "that doesn't mean you should do the same thing." "Loud-mouth," says Steve toward Paul. I tense up and focus the camera closely on what will be a violent episode . . . nothing. They both sit back and wait quietly while Anne turns her attention to Samuel, who has ignored this whole altercation, busily readying the pieces of his publishable book.

No screaming, no desks pushed over, no fists flying. Has she "fixed" them, I ask myself.

Steve moves his legs up underneath himself cross-legged. Paul does the same. Steve folds his hands, Paul does the same. One sticks out his tongue, the other sticks out his tongue. Anne and Samuel continue to talk about his story; they are laughing together and having fun, talking about the illustration that he needs to do. Miraculously, both Steve and Paul abandon their taunting and watch Anne. She finally brings Paul back to the table, opens his book with him and beings to read it. "What does this say?" she asks. He reads a page to her. "What will come next?" she asks. He falls to the work and starts writing his sentence. She has two of them working now. "Okay, Steve, now you can come to the table. What do you want to write about you and Karen today?"

Earlier in the year, she had to send them out of the room for difficult behavior, get fun things happening in the room, then bring them back one at a time. Now she can accomplish this same thing with them remaining in the room. ". . . It just took longer than I expected to get them acclimated into being in a classroom. I think in some ways, when I do look back on the year as a whole, I will say the first three months were spent getting the kids comfortable with the concept of being civilized in a classroom setting. It took that long to have them feel safe in a class and be able to contain themselves well enough to start doing anything else."

They do seem to feel safer, seem more confident in Anne, calmer in the environment. They seem to know what they are doing, the activities make sense. And it is clear that Anne feels good about them. Her frustration is not apparent, her body seems more relaxed, her voice almost gentle. Since safety and control no longer dominate the period, she can begin to push a little harder to get the boys to produce. For each boy, the issue to push on is different.

"Steve, what do you want to write?" "Me and Karen . . . uh . . ." He hands her a paper and demands she write down what he is saying. "You know what, Steve, I don't have to write the word 'Karen,' you can copy it from right here." He flares up, "NO, you write Karen!!!" She ignores him, he is being obstinate, and she refuses to help. He takes it out on Paul. "Pussy!" he says at Paul, who just keeps working. Anne points to Steve's bench, and he goes there quietly. Samuel, in the meantime, is calling for her attention. He wants to show his drawing of his dog. It is just a bunch of legs in space. "Where is his body?" she asks. "I don't want to draw a body," Samuel replies. "Well, it's gonna be awfully hard for people to understand your picture, then." He draws another picture, but now only a body and no legs! "Now where are the legs?"

When she brings Steve back to the table, she still quietly insists that he copy words that he already knows or are written for him somewhere else in his story. As soon as he has trouble with a word that he doesn't yet know or hasn't written before, she is there to write it down. With Samuel she continues to insist that he make a dog with legs, and the correct number of legs as well. The conversations overlap, the boys interrupt her, she deals with three questions at once. Instead of safety and control problems, these are new and welcome troubles, problems she is more accustomed to dealing with. Now that they are engaged in their work, they all want her attention simultaneously, they want their questions to be answered first, they cannot wait. This is, to her, "the classic writing time. Writing time in all of my classes felt that way, even with kids who can write and were further along. I know they are all working on their own thing and they all need my help all the time. They have no ability to understand you need to be helping other people as well. I pretend to be listening to all three of them constantly all of the time." She thinks about the problems that Steve is having today, his easy frustration and impatience with the task and with her. She wonders if it is because she is doing something wrong.

> *She lets Steve dictate a difficult sentence. "Anne . . . Anne . . . Anne," Samuel calls in his drooping whine. She responds, finally, when she has finished with Steve. But no sooner has she turned to Samuel than Steve is demanding from her that she spell the word "to." She moves back immediately and spells it. But he makes an error writing it, tries to erase, tears his page. "See! This fuckin' paper. . . ." She tries to help, suggests he tape the tear. "I hate you. . . . I'm going to stab you . . . no tape. . . . I want you to erase that damn letter!!!" Behind him Samuel is droning over and over, "I'm on my last page, Anne . . . I'm on my last page, Anne . . . I'm on my last page, Anne." Paul asks for help. She speaks with Samuel, she answers Paul's question, she tapes Steve's page . . .*

The PAUSE button gets pushed on the video machine. "At this point I was upset that Steve was getting as frustrated as he did, partly, I feel, with the way the writing program is set up, nobody should be getting frustrated. Partly, I was feeling that I was moving too fast with Steve in terms of what he was doing. But then I wasn't sure if his frustration was because I was moving too fast or if it was because he was having a cranky, needy day and even if it was not too hard for him, he would be feeling that way."

I smile to myself, and think back to September: "I was some of the problem. My expectations were wrong." I am amazed that she is being self-critical, now. Steve is being nasty even though she is being as helpful as seems possible. But it is a part of her personality, a drive within her, part of her "process of being a teacher." She believes these boys are capable, that learning for them should be fun, creative, exciting; it should focus on strength and health, not pathology. Teaching skills and competencies, she says, can be the most therapeutic thing of all. Yes, I think, for the teacher and the taught.

Belief

When I get out of my car on this April morning, about twenty boys are running up to class to begin their school day. Jostling, teasing, and generally doing what young boys do, they all race ahead of Samuel, who is struggling hard, and failing miserably, at doing what young boys generally do. His parents have tried to dress him "*a la mode.*" He has new sneakers, a good windbreaker; he is holding a backpack along with the books that didn't fit in it, and straining to get his Walkman over his ears. All the while, he is trying to run and keep up with the others. But the Walkman slips off his head and falls to the ground. When he bends to reach for it, his books fall from his hand and the backpack follows. He flops on the sidewalk, not yet warmed after winter, and tries to reassemble his "look." His lack of coordination would be farcical if it were not so real.

In the front office, I pass young Jamie. He is angry as he walks with his therapist. "Where can I buy a gun?" he asks her. "I really need a gun!" His words smash against my ears like cymbals. My eyes meet his therapist's and she smiles wanly, takes him by the hand, and walks on.

I look at the children and I think about Anne and the work she does. How sustaining the power of belief must be for her! Although her resolve wavers, she believes in the children, in their ability to heal. She is convinced, truly, that she *must* make a difference. "I wonder sometimes, especially with some of the more damaged kids, how much of that damage can be undone. The damage is there and it's always going to be there. But he's *six years old!*" She possesses a kind of love for the children, some might say a foolish love, that keeps her pushing against the weight of their troubles, always trying to tip the balance in their favor.

I would like to acknowledge Dr. Sara Lawrence Lightfoot, Donald Freeman, and Dr. Richard Small for their insightful critiques of earlier drafts of this portrait. Especially, I would like to thank "Anne" for generously fitting me into her already busy schedule, and for engaging in the reflective process with such vigor.

The Learning-Disabilities Test Battery: Empirical and Social Issues

GERALD S. COLES

Since the implementation of the Education for All Handicapped Children Act (EHA), the fastest growing and by far the largest category of special education students has been the group labeled "learning disabled." A relatively new concept in the 1970s when current special education legislation was promulgated, learning disabilities were widely seen by special educators as an explanation for school failure that was not attributable to social, emotional, or generalized cognitive deficits. The hope at the time was to look more carefully at the neurological makeup of learning-disabled individuals in order to determine more precisely the organic causes of school failure and, perhaps, better ways to overcome them. Gerald Coles, writing in 1978, critically examines the notion of learning disabilities. He analyzes the ten most widely used instruments for determining learning disabilities — perceptual, intelligence, and neurological tests — and finds them wanting in terms of validity and reliability. Given the slim empirical basis for identifying learning disabilities, Coles questions why educators so earnestly believe in the label, learning disabled. He argues that school personnel, buttressed by medical authority, have come to rely on biological explanations to explain the failures of schools to meet students' diverse learning needs. He contends that, in reinterpreting institutional deficits as inherent deficits of children, educators mistakenly dedicate their resources to remediating individuals' assumed learning disabilities instead of reforming inadequate school practices. Through the 1980s, Coles continued to develop this critique as the phenomenon of learning disabilities became even more established within public education. His The Learning Mystique *(1989) offers a comprehensive challenge to the label, learning disabled.*

Efforts to solve the problems of learning disabilities have experienced a period of growth unparalleled by almost any other specialized field. Although the subject of learning disabilities was virtually unheard of ten or fifteen years ago, today education, psychology, and medicine are all contributing to its growing body of literature, with which one can barely keep abreast. The press and television keep learning disabilities constantly before the public's attention, and it has become a fertile field of specialization for students seeking a marketable degree and for industries seeking new markets.

As the field has grown, however, so too has criticism of it. Learning-disabilities specialists have been the target of a widely sold demythologizing critique (Schrag & Divoky, 1975), and many of them, admitting that from its inception the field has been rife with ambiguities and contradictions, are demanding less confusion and greater clarity (Gomez, 1967; Orlando & Lynch, 1974; Silver, Note 1). Recent publications (Glenn, 1975; Hammill, 1976; Orlando & Lynch, 1974) have raised sobering questions about the prescribed diagnostic and therapeutic guidelines. Although the profession appears to be secure, there is little doubt that it is now feeling the strains of controversy and the need for reassessment.

One reassessment that must be made concerns the special knowledge the field claims to possess. The special knowledge of learning-disabilities specialists, and, indeed, the special knowledge on which the entire field rests, is the ability to diagnose the presence of learning disabilities in children and prescribe effective programs of treatment. Using a medical model and equipped with their own black bag of diagnostic instruments, the learning-disabilities specialists, sometimes together with other specialists, examine child patients. If they think there are learning disabilities, they write authoritative diagnoses stating that, based on the results of certain tests, it has been determined that the children have neurological problems that impede learning. Parents and teachers will be likely to accept these findings as true. Because the children have been given a set of seemingly scientific and valid tests, the conclusions must also be valid. The children, now proclaimed to be learning disabled, begin the remedial path toward cognitive competence.

Although many professionals in the field believe that they possess special knowledge, much of the current debate revolves around the basic question of whether or not the field can back up its claims to knowledge with valid empirical evidence. The answer rests in large part on the nature of the learning-disabilities test battery — the set of tests used to determine the quantity and quality of learning disabilities in children. Certainly subjective clinical experience and preclinical research on cognitive functioning are important diagnostic tools, but the test battery itself, with its objective, formally validated instruments, is the core of the learning-disabilities diagnosis. The battery provides credibility to the conclusions and recommendations of the learning-disabilities professional.

The central tests in a learning-disabilities battery evaluate perception, language, intelligence, and neurological function. Although the tests are often categorized as dealing with separate areas, they often overlap because they are all designed to fit a single model of neurological impairment based upon the accepted definition of learning disabilities first formulated by the National Advisory Committee on Handicapped Children in 1968:

> Children with special learning disabilities exhibit a disorder in one or more of the basic psychological processes involved in understanding or using spoken or written languages. These may be manifested in disorders of listening, thinking, talking, reading, writing, spelling, or arithmetic. They include conditions which have been referred to as perceptual handicaps, brain injury, minimal brain dysfunction, dyslexia, developmental aphasia, etc. They do not include learning problems which are due primarily to visual, or motor handicaps, to mental retardation, emotional disturbance, or to environmental disadvantage. (p. 4)

It is apparent that this definition has its limitations. What a learning disability is remains extraordinarily vague; it is primarily a definition by exclusion. The specific conditions mentioned, such as dyslexia, are no more precisely defined than the encompassing term "learning disabilities," and by excluding environmental disadvantage, it limits attention to middle- and upper-class children. Nonetheless, what remains essential to the definition, and to this discussion as well, is that a learning disability is defined in terms of an organic and neurological dysfunction of the cerebral processes. The purpose of a learning-disabilities test battery is to determine whether or not a minimal neurological dysfunction is impeding the child's ability to learn under otherwise normal conditions.

Although a standard learning-disabilities battery does not exist, the guidelines in handbooks and texts for setting up a battery are all similar, and the inclusion of certain tests is fairly standard. An individual learning-disabilities battery will, of course, vary according to the problems a child is suspected of having, an examiner's preference for particular tests, and the resources of an agency. Nonetheless, it is possible to describe a representative battery.

The Learning-Disabilities Battery

The ten most frequently recommended tests and evaluations suggested for a learning-disabilities battery in authoritative publications of the past ten years (Arena, 1967; Bannatyne, 1971; Meier, 1976; Millman, 1970; New Jersey Association for Children with Learning Disabilities, 1974; Phipps, 1976–1977) are the Illinois Test of Psycholinguistic Abilities, the Bender Visual-Motor Gestalt Test, the Frostig Developmental Test of Visual Perception, the Wepman Auditory Discrimination Test, the Lincoln-Oseretsky Motor Development Scale, the Graham-Kendall Memory for Designs Test, the Purdue Perceptual-Motor Survey, the Wechsler Intelligence Scale for Children, a neurological evaluation by a neurologist, and an electroencephalogram. On the assumption that their empirical support is as scientifically sound and at least as good as that for other tests with a similar purpose, these specific, frequently recommended tests will be discussed as examples of generic categories, such as tests of visual-auditory processing. In so doing, we can explore the quality of the information a learning-disabilities specialist obtains by using these instruments and procedures, knowing that authorities in the field regard them as the best that are available.

This review is based on a thorough examination of the literature (Buros, 1972, 1974). Particularly useful was a bibliographic search performed by the National Library of Medicine's retrieval service. Although the research actually cited is selective rather than exhaustive, it has been chosen as representative of conclusions reached within the body of validation research. Where validation studies for a test or procedure have been numerous, some have been omitted as redundant. Where a review of a particular test has been cited, the evidence reported is drawn from the total research on the test related to learning disabilities. Numerous papers are available on each of these tests and procedures, but studies dealing with the learning disabled represent only a small portion of the total number of validation studies because the majority deal with special groups — psychiatric patients, juvenile delinquents, the physically disabled, and the mentally retarded.

Validation studies testing the presence of learning disabilities frequently use retarded readers as a means of identifying children who are learning disabled. (In this article, "retarded readers" refers to normally intelligent children reading below grade level, not to mentally retarded readers.) Using this approach, investigators assume that, although retarded reading can have many causes, if environmental deprivation is excluded, a significantly large group have problems attributable to faulty neurological processing — they are learning disabled. Consequently, it is assumed that retarded readers, because they are certain to include some neurologically impaired children among them, will perform differently on learning-disabilities tests. Clearly, this assumption is not necessarily valid, but it was thought to be necessary to avoid a logical dilemma in trying to identify subjects as "learning disabled." The identification could be made either through an exclusionary process, that is, by excluding exogenous, sensory, and mental-retardation factors that are not regarded as causing learning disabilities, or through learning-disabilities tests. Both methods for identification are logically faulty: the exclusionary because it does not positively identify a child as learning disabled; the testing because positive classification is based on the learning-disabilities tests, which themselves are under investigation.

While most people understand that retarded readers are not necessarily learning disabled, they sometimes overlook the converse — that learning-disabled children are not necessarily retarded readers. An individual might be learning disabled and still have adequate reading skills; his problems can lie in other areas such as speaking or writing. Despite this, the overwhelming number of children identified as learning disabled in either schools or clinics are poor readers; they may or may not have other language difficulties. For this reason, most studies dealing with children who have been identified as learning disabled have used reading level as the criterion by which to distinguish the learning disabled from the non-learning-disabled.

Perceptual Tests

The Illinois Test of Psycholinguistic Abilities (ITPA) (Kirk, McCarthy, & Kirk, 1968) purports to measure those input, processing, and output abilities that underlie language development; it is perhaps the most frequently used learning-disabilities test. The research on the relationship between the ITPA and academic achievement has been reviewed by Newcomer and Hammill (1975). They included studies of children classified as learning disabled or as retarded readers, and they tabulated correlation coefficients for each of the twelve ITPA subtests, the composite score, and the indices of reading, spelling, and arithmetic. A .35 median coefficient was accepted as indicating significant correlation. The following results were the same whether the subjects had been categorized as retarded readers or learning disabled.

With regard to the question of which tests could predict reading success, only three subtests — Auditory Association, Grammatic Closure, and Sound Blending — and the composite score reached the minimal level of predictive significance; and of these, only Grammatic Closure retained a significant relationship with reading in studies that controlled for intelligence, a variable closely correlated with the ITPA. For spelling, only Grammatic Closure was significantly related under general conditions, but when intelligence was controlled for, even that coefficient did not reach a practical level of significance. Similar results were obtained for arithmetic, to which neither subtests nor composite score were related when mental ability was partialed out. In short, "nine of the twelve ITPA subtests lack predictive validity for any aspect of academic achievement studied" (p. 735), and two of the three remaining subtests, as well as the composite score, dropped below practical significance when intelligence was controlled.

The Grammatic Closure subtest remained significantly correlated with reading achievement when intelligence was controlled, but its psycholinguistic value was questioned by the reviewers. Although the test is a measure of standard English morphology, "linguistic measures of this type are highly influenced by sociological factors such as race and social class, variables which have extensive influence on school performance" (p. 736).

A second part of Newcomer and Hammill's review examined the diagnostic validity of the ITPA by determining how well the test distinguished between good and poor readers. Research results were tabulated to see which subtests distinguished between good and poor readers in at least 50 percent of the studies. When IQ was not controlled, only Grammatic Closure and Sound Blending met this criterion; when mental ability was controlled, neither the subtests nor the composite score reached the 50 percent level for successful discrimination of good from poor readers.

The Bender (Bender, 1938) is a visual-motor perception test which claims to measure neurological development and dysfunction. Although it has a forty-year history and has become a standard test in the learning-disabilities battery, the Bender presents a conflicting research picture of its usefulness in cognitive and educational assessment. A number of studies report that the test successfully distinguishes "learning disabled" and poor readers from normal controls (Henderson, Butler, & Gaffney, 1969; Keogh & Smith, 1967; Koppitz, 1970; Larsen, Rogers, & Sowell, 1976; Norfleet, 1973; Thweatt, 1963), but others adduce considerable evidence that proves the contrary (Ackerman, Peters, & Dykman, 1971; Hartlage & Lucas, 1976; Lachmann, 1960; Nielsen & Ringe, 1969; Obrzut, Taylor, & Thweatt, 1972; Robinson & Schwartz, 1973; Wikler, Dixon, & Parker, 1970).

An example of the former category is the longitudinal study in which Keogh and Smith (1967) found that the Bender was a good predictor of future academic success, particularly for success in the upper elementary grades when administered in kindergarten. When the kindergarten Bender scores were divided into high, average, and low groups, the investigators found that the better the score, the more likely the child would be reading at grade level in sixth grade. However, the investigators also found that when the Bender was administered later — in the middle or upper elementary grades — it did not correlate consistently with academic success.

Inconsistent results were reported by Chang and Chang (1967), when they established a correlation between academic achievement and the Bender for second-grade children but not for third graders. Furthermore, the authors noted that the magnitude of the correlation between the Bender and reading scores for the second-grade children "was relatively the same as those reported in the literature for pupils of this age with average ability" (p. 53).

An example of research concluding that the Bender is a poor diagnostic instrument is Robinson and Schwartz's study (1973). These authors administered the Bender to children entering first grade; they then retested them with the Bender and a reading-achievement test at the end of the first grade and again at the end of the third. The investigators found no correlation between initial Bender scores and reading-achievement scores at the end of the two grades, even though the relative success on the Bender was generally the same for the children at the beginning and end of the three-year test period. Further, when the ten worst readers were compared with the remaining fifty-four children on the Bender and other visual-perception tests, no significant differences between the two groups were found.

One question that often complicates the interpretation of learning-disability findings concerns the extent to which emotional rather than neurological problems influence test results. In an attempt to clarify this issue, Lachmann (1960) hypothesized: "If reading disability reflects a lag or retardation in perceptual-motor development, retarded readers should show significantly less mature performance on the Bender than either a comparable group of normal readers or a group of emotionally disturbed children who have normal reading ability" (p. 427). To test the hypothesis, three groups were selected: retarded readers, normal readers with a record of emotional problems, and normal readers with no record of emotional problems. Test results showed that the retarded readers scored significantly lower than the normal readers with emotional problems. Related findings come from a study by Ackerman, Peters, and Dykman (1971), which found no correlation between Bender scores and scores of neurological status based on a neurological examination. It seems clear from these studies that the Bender is tapping more than neurological development and dysfunction.

Another factor compounding the problem of assessing the Bender, as well as interpreting the ITPA, is that the studies usually do not partial out intelligence. In one that did (Henderson, Butler, & Gaffney, 1969), the authors found that the Wechsler Intelligence Scale for Children (WISC) was a better predictor of reading and arithmetic achievement than was the Bender, and they concluded "that if intelligence is partialed out the Bender adds very little or nothing to the prediction of reading and arithmetic achievement" (p. 270).

Questions of etiological interpretation have been raised by supporters of the test, including Koppitz (1970), who standardized Bender scoring. Koppitz acknowledged that the same test results can be obtained from children who are brain damaged, are slow maturers, or who have brain tumors, emotional problems, or problems of "unknown origin." Nonetheless, though a specific cause for test performance may be impossible to ascertain, Koppitz advises that, when children "reveal the same 'signs' of cortical malfunctioning as do brain damaged children," they "should be treated as if they were brain damaged" (p. 430). Obviously, this conclusion violates the canons of learning-disabilities diagnoses, for one might as easily advise that, whenever brain-damaged children perform the same as non-brain-damaged children, they should be treated as though they had normal brains.

The Frostig Developmental Test of Visual Perception (Frostig, Lefever, & Whittlesey, 1964) is said to provide a perceptual quotient that indicates each child's level of visual-perception development. Research on the Frostig has not, however, supported the use of the test as a predictor of reading success.

Only in studies of first-grade children can strong support for the test be found (Bryan, 1964; Frostig, Lefever, & Whittlesey, 1964; Gamsky & Lloyd, 1971). Although some studies give evidence of correlations between some of the subtests and academic achievement (Olson, 1966; Olson & Johnson, 1970), by and large, research has shown that beyond the first-grade level, the Frostig rapidly decreases in usefulness and is not an accurate predictor of reading achievement (Ashlock, 1963; Black, 1976; Colarusso, Martin, & Hartung, 1975; Frostig, Lefever, & Whittlesey, 1964; Liebert & Sherk, 1970; Nielsen & Ringe, 1969; Olson, 1966; Robinson & Schwartz, 1973; Rosen, 1966). The entire assumption of the test has been challenged by some researchers who now conclude that the Frostig measures intelligence and not different functions (Corah & Powell, 1963; Gamsky & Lloyd, 1971).

Another approach to assessing the Frostig test is through the Frostig Visual Perception Training Program used to remedy "perceptual" problems diagnosed with the test. Comparisons of children trained with this program and other children working solely with regular reading materials show that the Frostig-trained children usually score higher on the Frostig perceptual test, but their scores are not significantly different from those of other children on standardized reading tests (Buckland & Balow, 1973; Cohn, 1966; Jacobs, 1968).

The usefulness of the Wepman Auditory Discrimination Test (Wepman, 1958), an instrument designed to assess the ability of children to discriminate between sounds, has been reported both by the author of the test (Wepman, 1960) and by other researchers. Goetzinger, Dirks, and Baler (1960), for example, compared fifteen poor readers from a clinic with fifteen good readers from regular classes. Matched for chronological age and intelligence, the poor readers were found to have scores that were significantly inferior to those of the good readers on the Wepman. Support for the Wepman as a diagnostic instrument can also be found in a study by Lingren (1969). The study matched readers attending a remedial reading clinic with a group of normal readers on sex, IQ, and chronological age. The author reported that eight of the twenty disabled readers, but none of the twenty normal readers, were below the test norms on the Wepman.

Mixed test results were obtained in a study with fourth-grade pupils (Hafner, Weaver, & Powell, 1970). The Wepman correlated significantly with the reading-vocabulary portion but not the reading-comprehension portion of a reading-achievement test. It is difficult to interpret these results because the paper does not provide information on the relative achievement levels of students on the reading subtests. It does not, however, seem that auditory-discrimination ability is related to two major cognitive components of reading comprehension: reasoning and word knowledge in context.

Flynn and Byrne (1970) conducted one of the few studies on learning-disabilities tests that looked closely at the influence of socioeconomic levels. They used the Wepman and other auditory-perception tests with third-grade children, and their results showed that advanced readers, those who scored at a 4.2 or higher grade level in reading, scored significantly better on the Wepman than did poor readers, who scored at a 2.2 or lower grade level in reading. When the subjects were divided along socioeconomic lines, the results were mixed. The advanced readers in high and low economic levels were not significantly different, but the poor readers in the low economic group performed significantly worse on the Wepman than did those in the high economic group, suggesting some degree of environmental influence. Unfortunately, an adequate interpretation of the auditory abilities of good and poor readers in this study is not possible: when the investigators examined the youngsters for intelligence, they found significant differences for total and verbal IQ scores, with the advanced readers more than one standard deviation above the retarded readers, regardless of socioeconomic level. As a result, it is not clear how auditory-discrimination problems are related to overall cognitive development.

Findings that cast doubt on the value of the Wepman were reported by Larsen, Rogers, and Sowell (1976), who failed to find significant differences on the Wepman between learning-disabled and normal groups, ages eight and one-half to ten and one-half. When they divided the learning-disabled children into two subgroups — one a grade below their expected reading level and the other two grades below — the Wepman did not significantly distinguish between them. Goetz (1971) used the Wepman with first graders and found no correlation between test scores and reading achievement.

Research on the remaining perceptual tests is not as extensive as it has been for the ITPA or the Bender. Enough studies, however, have been made to appraise the validity of these tests, and their conclusions are in line with those already described.

Pyfer and Carlson (1972) used the Lincoln-Oseretsky Motor Development Scale (Sloan, 1955) to test children with learning problems because the test "is one of the few standardized instruments that includes both fine and gross motor tasks arranged in order of difficulty for school-aged groups" (p. 292) and, presumably, because they considered it a good measure of perceptual-motor dysfunction. The results failed to support the perceptual-motor explanation of learning disabilities, however, because the learning-disabled group did not significantly differ from the normative standards of the tests.

Another investigation (Hurwitz, Bibace, Wolff, & Rowbotham, 1972) compared the Lincoln-Oseretsky test performance for learning-disabled, delinquent, and normal children. In contrast to the results of Pyfer and Carlson, the learning-disabled group scored significantly lower than the normal children on this test, but so did the juvenile delinquents, making it difficult to know the extent to which the test reflects emotional or neurological problems.

Another study using the Lincoln-Oseretsky to examine the relationship of motor proficiency and reading retardation produced less ambiguous results. Lewis, Bell, and Anderson (1970) studied the motor and reading skills of a group of one hundred junior high school males and found that, on the basis of their overall test scores, 71 percent of the youngsters could be correctly categorized as retarded or adequate in reading.

The Graham-Kendall Memory for Designs Test (Graham & Kendall, 1960) is another measure of perceptual-motor development. Evidence that "reading retardation is related to visual-motor development as measured by the Graham-Kendall" was reported by Walters (1961). When thirty-five second-grade children were divided into high and low reading groups, the mean scores on the Graham-Kendall were positively correlated with reading success. Similarly, a study (Lyle, 1968) of fifty-four retarded readers and fifty-four normal readers found that the Graham-Kendall differentiated significantly between them. When IQ was partialed out, the Graham-Kendall scores for the two groups were still significantly different. Lyle concluded that because the Graham-Kendall system is based "upon empirically determined differences in the reproductions of designs of brain-injured and normals [and] also discriminates between retarded readers . . . and matched controls, reading retardation may be a symptom of minimal cerebral dysfunction" (p. 853).

Contrasting results were obtained by Wikler, Dixon, and Parker (1970), who used the Graham-Kendall and several other instruments with twenty-two children referred to an outpatient clinic for academic and behavior problems. The subjects were matched with a control group for school achievement. The results of the Graham-Kendall, as well as of the Bender and the Minnesota Percepto-Diagnostic Test, showed that the performance of these children was significantly below that of the controls. The test did distinguish them as learning disabled; the degree to which the test reflected neurological as opposed to emotional problems again remained moot.

The last of the recommended perceptual-motor tests, the Purdue Perceptual-Motor Survey (Roach & Kephart, 1966), has, like the Frostig, been used as an instrument to prescribe follow-up remediation plans developed by one of the authors of the test (Kephart, 1960). In a massive epidemiological study in eight Rocky Mountain states, undertaken to determine the nature and extent of learning disabilities among school children, Meier (1971) found "no data on . . . the Purdue tests which warrant mentioning, since the [learning-disabled] and control children performed about equally well on the test" (p. 11). The effect of the remedial program on reading achievement was equally unimpressive (Falik, 1969; Fisher, 1971; McBeath, 1966).

Intelligence Tests

The very question of the relationship between intelligence and learning disabilities involves a contradiction. On the one hand, a child classified as learning disabled is by definition of near-average, average, or above-average general intelligence and therefore does not have intelligence problems. A child with educational problems and lower-than-average intelligence is considered to be retarded rather than neurologically impaired. The IQ test is only included in a learning-disabilities battery to confirm that the child does not have general intelligence problems and therefore might be learning disabled.

On the other hand, there is evidence that while the IQ scores of children classified by schools as learning disabled are often not low enough to categorize them as retarded, the majority are below the mean of the general population (Hallahan & Kauffman, 1977). In a survey of over 3,000 learning-disabled children, Kirk and Elkins (1975) found that their median IQ was 93 and that 35 percent of them had IQs below 90. In practice, many children appear to be diagnosed as learning disabled for reasons other than those in accord with the strict learning-disabilities definition.

In addition, the argument has been advanced that an IQ test can help to diagnose learning disabilities through evaluation of subtest scores and disparities. For example, in research on the Wechsler Intelligence Scale for children (WISC) (Wechsler, 1949), a discrepancy of fifteen points between verbal and performance scales was said to be indicative of minimal brain dysfunction (Black, 1974; Holroyd & Wright, 1965). The relevance of this conclusion to learning disabilities is not apparent. In Black's study, for example, even though the children with a discrepancy of fifteen points or greater did show a greater incidence of neurological abnormalities, no significant differences in reading, spelling, or arithmetic achievement were discerned between these children and those without a discrepancy. In a later study, Black (1976) found that the percentage of children with minimal brain dysfunction having a fifteen-point verbal-performance discrepancy was consistent with normal probabilities for the chronological age of the subjects. Other studies have also found no significant differences in verbal-performance scales between learning-disabled and normal children (Black, 1973; Kallos, Grabow, & Guarino, 1961; Rudel & Denckla, 1976).

Whether or not an IQ test can help diagnose learning disabilities is a question that has previously been asked in studies of WISC subtests given to poor readers. They found low scores for information, coding, vocabulary, arithmetic, and digit-span subtests (Belmont & Birch, 1966; Farr, 1969) and some subtest patterns related to basic-skills retardation (Ackerman, Dykman, & Peters, 1976; Huelsman, 1970); but the findings were not consistent for groups or individuals, and attempts to interpret them have been minimal. Huelsman (1970), after reviewing investigations of WISC subscore patterns and then conducting his own investigation, concluded that future research "should be directed toward defining the possible significance of differences in WISC scores rather than toward pattern identification which seems relatively useless" (p. 549).

The significance of WISC scores remains obscure if for no other reason than that correlations between WISC subtests and reading disability have left questions of causation unanswered. It is not clear whether WISC results reflect language, perceptual-motor, or academic problems; whether reading achievement is a consequence of abilities comprising intelligence; or whether both reading achievement and WISC scores reflect a third factor (Farr, 1969). Finally, there is little evidence that analysis of IQ test performance contributes to practical remediation plans for academic problems (Farr, 1969; Pikulski, 1975).

Neurological Tests

When an evaluation of a child suspected of being learning disabled proceeds from the learning-disabilities specialist to the neurologist — the ultimate expert in assessing neurological dysfunction — two assessments are usually made: a neurological examination for "soft signs" (sometimes called equivocal or borderline signs) and an electroencephalogram (EEG).

In contrast to an EEG, which may record abnormal brain-wave patterns, soft signs are physical characteristics and responses that are not clear indications of brain damage but are developmentally abnormal and are thought to constitute minimal brain dysfunction (MBD). Among these soft signs are fine and gross motor-coordination deficiencies, mixed and confused laterality, strabismus, defective or slow speech development, short attention span, poor balance, gait disturbance, inadequate muscle tone, and general awkwardness.

Learning-disabilities studies investigating neurological dysfunction, as expressed in soft signs, have generally used two procedures: the first distinguishes between groups by the extent of their neurological dysfunction and then examines their respective differences on measures of academic achievement; the second classifies groups by academic achievement and then seeks evidence of differences in neurological impairment through a neurological assessment.

To date, research shows that neurologists are no closer than learning-disabilities specialists to establishing a relationship between minimal neurological dysfunction and learning problems. Claims of neurological deficiencies in academically retarded children have been reported, but the majority of this research has been marred by serious methodological shortcomings or by omission in the published studies. For example, Millman (1970) reported that in his clinic, where over 50 percent of the referrals are for academic failure, twenty-one of the fifty cases reviewed "were seen as having minimal brain dysfunction" (p. 92). Apart from these summary figures, however, and a few similar ones, Millman does not discuss the criteria used for his assessment. No analysis is made of the relationship between MBD and academic problems, nor is there a single word on the relationship between MBD and nonacademic problems.

A study by Eaves and Crichton (1974–1975), which first identified children according to signs of neurological impairment, reported a correlation between neurological dysfunction and learning problems, but unfortunately omitted important methodological information. The investigators followed up sixty-six children originally diagnosed as having MBD to determine the relationship between original diagnosis and subsequent grade attainment. Eaves and Crichton state, without describing their diagnostic criteria, that at the time of the original evaluation, 85 percent of the children showed unequivocal signs of brain dysfunction, according to neurological and psychological examinations. Their follow-up showed that the greater the extent of MBD diagnosed in the original evaluation, the greater the likelihood that the child would be below the expected grade level. Conclusions from the study are tenuous because the authors mention, but fail to examine, possible correlations between emotional problems, medication, or actual academic achievement and grade attainment.

A more substantial follow-up study (Dykman, Peters, & Ackerman, 1973) of children already diagnosed as learning disabled did describe both its original and follow-up evaluative criteria. The follow-up, done approximately five years after the original diagnosis, found that at age fourteen, these children continued to have significantly lower academic achievement levels and significantly greater neurological impairment than had normal children identified in the original evaluation. One serious methodological problem in the study was that the investigators who performed the neurological examination of the children had apparently been told beforehand which of the children had been categorized as learning disabled. Other researchers have recognized this potentially biasing factor, and they have performed "blind" examinations of subjects and controls.

Support for the relationship between neurological dysfunction and learning disabilities was also reported by Cohn (1961). Having first distinguished between groups of children according to their academic achievement, he reported significantly more abnormal neurological signs among a group with reading and writing difficulties than among the normally achieving children.

Unfortunately, the author did not indicate whether or not the neurological examinations were blindly administered.

Minimally positive results favoring the neurological hypothesis were reported by Adams, Kocsis, and Estes (1974) in a study of fourth graders categorized as either learning disabled, borderline disabled, or normal according to a formula of expected, as opposed to actual, academic achievement. Following this group division, seven soft signs were selected for the study, primarily because research reports had identified them as useful in diagnosing learning disabilities. Of these seven soft signs, only diadachokinesia, a hand-control motor function, and graphesthesia, the sensory ability to recognize figures "written" on the skin, produced reliable distinctions between learning classifications, but even these were not consistent when sex was considered: for example, significant differences in diadachokinesia in the dominant hand were found for males but not females, and the reverse was true for the nondominant hand. A significantly greater incidence of graphesthesia was found for learning-disabled girls than for learning-disabled boys. Although the two signs "were significantly different in the learning-disabled group as compared to the control group, the magnitude of the differences was not great enough to make it helpful in differentiating the two groups clinically" (p. 618).

A study of Boshes and Mykelbust (1964) divided eighty-five academic underachievers into three groups according to neurological status — negative, suspect, or positive. The neurologist who examined the children had no knowledge of the clinical history of the subjects. When the authors compared the results of the academic-achievement tests, they found no significant differences among the groups in silent or oral reading, syllabification, auditory blending, or spelling.

Another study, also dividing groups of children according to the results of an examination for suspected neurological signs, used nine separate neurological and visual-motor status comparisons. Edwards, Alley, and Snyder (1971) reported that they found no significant differences in academic achievement among the groups and concluded that the results provided "no evidence that a diagnosis of minimal brain dysfunction based on the pediatric neurological evaluation . . . is a useful predictor of academic achievement" (p. 20).

In a blind study by Mykelbust (1973), in which children were first grouped according to a learning-disability formula based on intellectual and academic criteria, no differences in neurological status were found between learning-disabled and academically successful children when they were classified as either neurologically normal or abnormal by pediatric neurologists. Nor did any one of the 137 neurological signs used in the examination significantly distinguish between the groups. Only when the total number of signs was compared were the groups significantly different, with the learning-disabled group having the greater number. It is important to note, however, that a large number of soft signs were found in the control group as well: the totals were 528 and 475, respectively.

Black (1973) investigated two samples of children with reading disorders, one with evidence of neurological dysfunction, and another group with no such evidence, but who were matched for age, grade placement, and IQ. When he compared the two groups for various measures of academic performance and intellectual skills he found no appreciable differences between the groups on various measures of academic performance and intellectual skills. The author concluded that "differentiating learning disabled children as demonstrating or not demonstrating neurological dysfunction is not especially useful when the primary concern is cognitive function . . . academic achievement . . . [or] remediation" (pp. 315–316).

The question of the influence of intelligence on neurological assessments has been examined by Routh and Roberts (1972). Eighty-nine children referred to a child-development specialist were examined by a multidisciplinary team using behavioral, academic, and neurological measures. Correlations were found for a number of variables, including significant relationships between academic achievement and neurological soft signs; however, none of these relationships held up when age and IQ were partialed out.

These studies are typical of investigations that have failed to find a significant relationship between neurological functioning and academic achievement. Similar results have been reported elsewhere by Ayers (1968); Black (1974); Henderson, Butler, and Gaffney (1969); Rie, Rie, and Stewart (1976); and Wikler, Dixon, and Parker (1970).

In a review of EEG studies, Freeman (1967) concluded that the EEG does not relate conclusively to academic achievement, psychiatric and emotional problems, hyperactivity, or other behavioral difficulties. Since that review, EEG studies have continued to show mixed results, producing more negative than positive evidence of their diagnostic usefulness.

When comparing EEG abnormalities in learning-disabled children to a control group with normal academic achievement selected from the same schools, Ayers and Torres (1967) found significantly more abnormalities in the learning-disabled children. The investigators also found a significant correlation between the EEG findings and reading achievement in a related analysis. Another study (Black, 1972), also favoring the use of the EEG, found a significantly greater incidence of EEG abnormalities among retarded readers than among normal readers.

Largely unfavorable results were reported by Meier (1971) in his extensive epidemiological study of learning disorders. He found "considerable numbers" (p. 10) of abnormalities for both learning-disabled and control groups, and only in convulsive-type tracing did the learning-disabled group have a significantly higher number.

Hartlage and Green (1971) examined the EEG records and academic-achievement scores for 114 children. EEG and achievement testing were done independently, and the administrators of one test had no knowledge of scores on the other test. The children were divided into several groups with different EEG records. When compared with achievement-test scores, no significant differences were found among the groups.

Mykelbust (1973) studied the EEG records of children categorized as learning disabled, borderline disabled, and normal. The EEG records were read without the investigator's knowing in which group the child had been placed. Mykelbust found no significant differences between the learning-disabled and control groups but, surprisingly, more significantly abnormal EEG records among the borderline group.

In the study by Wikler, Dixon, and Parker (1970), children referred for scholastic and behavior problems had significantly more EEG abnormalities than the matched control group. No differences between the two groups were found in reading, spelling, or arithmetic achievement tests.

EEG studies, such as that by Wikler, Dixon, and Parker, are complicated by their failure to select only children with learning problems. When other factors, such as emotional problems, are not accounted for, interpretation of EEG results is difficult because, to date, the EEG results among children grouped for various behavior and psychological problems have proved to be indistinguishable from each other (Dubey, 1976).

Evaluation of the Learning-Disabilities Thesis

Taken as a whole, the tests used in a representative learning-disabilities battery fail to demonstrate that children categorized as learning disabled are neurologically impaired. Some research validating the intent of each test is available, but the predominant finding in the literature suggests that each test fails to correlate with a diagnosis of learning disabilities. The evidence from studies using formal neurological examinations of learning-disabled children is especially damaging to the neurological impairment explanation. Surely, if the neurological thesis were to find support anywhere, it would find it in the techniques and science available to neurologists. Unfortunately for those who have held this thesis, studies of borderline symptoms, soft signs, have uniformly failed to contribute to the diagnosis of academic underachievement.

One factor preventing these studies from reaching definitive conclusions is that the research contains numerous methodological deficiencies, some of which have already been noted. Because elaboration of these deficiencies would require another paper, I can mention only briefly a few serious examples, the most salient, perhaps, being the failure to identify personal characteristics essential to the definition of learning disabilities. More often than not, children with emotional problems were either not distinguished from those without, or they were distinguished only on subjective criteria, such as a teacher's assessment. Frequently, children were classified as learning disabled solely because they were underachievers, or were referred to clinics for sundry other reasons. Similarly, many of the investigations failed to account for, and partial out, additional variables such as intelligence, age, social class, and race.

Related to these methodological shortcomings is the issue of construct validity — that is, the empirical assurance that a test measures the attribute it is said to measure. Test construct validity is assumed in most of the studies, and they do not incorporate the multi-method, multi-trait matrix recommended for establishing construct validity (Cronbach, 1970). However, a number of the above studies incorporate either more than one trait or more than one method, and consequently contain evidence that might affect conclusions about the construct validity of the learning-disabilities test. This evidence, as we have seen, frequently does not support construct validity. Some studies, for example, show inconsistencies among similar learning-disabilities tests in their effectiveness in distinguishing learning-disabled from non-learning-disabled students or good readers from poor ones. Other studies looking at more than one trait found that the predictability of a learning-disability test fell below statistical significance when intelligence was partialed out. In investigations in which a learning-disabilities test could divide students into high- and low-scoring groups, the students could not be separated by commensurate academic-achievement scores. Still other studies found learning-disabilities tests that failed to distinguish significantly between retarded readers presumed to have neurological problems and normal readers presumed to have emotional problems. All of these results raise questions about construct validity: whether the tests measure the neurological-learning constructs specialists claim they measure; whether a neurological process, modality, or other variables determine the test results; and whether the constructs in the learning-disabilities tests are sound, but the concept of the neurologically impaired academic underachiever is not.

Added to the difficulty of judging the construct validity of these tests is the discrepancy between what authors of tests claim these tests measure and what the learning-disabilities authorities say they measure. The majority of test developers do maintain that their instruments or procedures fit into a model of neurological and perceptual-motor dysfunctions, and this presumption prevails among learning-disabilities authorities for all the tests they recommend in the representative battery. A few test authors, however, do not purport to measure neurological dysfunction. Wepman (1958) states that his test is a diagnosis of auditory-discrimination ability only; he does not claim that the test specifically identifies the learning disabled or that auditory-discrimination problems are neurological in origin. Similarly, in the test-administration manual, Frostig, Lefever, and Whittlesey (1964) express the "hope" that "the test may eventually become a useful tool in the diagnosis of brain damage" (p. 12), but add this caveat: "Although experience has shown that brain damage often seriously affects perceptual ability, the test does not at present presume to measure organic dysfunctions" (p. 13).

Another methodological deficiency — and one that is extraordinary in view of the large number of studies that have been done — is that apparently no study examines the teaching and school environment of learning-disabled children to see how the quality of their education might have contributed to, if not actually created, the difficulties they encounter in acquiring basic skills. Despite the literature critical of teaching and its effect on children participating in learning-disabilities studies, the quality of the instruction these children receive is always assumed to be adequate — as well it must be if it is to accord with the definition of learning disabilities cited previously.

The evidence appears, therefore, to point to the conclusion that the tests do not measure neurological dysfunctions in learning-disabled children, but that methodological inadequacies prevent us from drawing this conclusion with certainty. These same methodological problems do, however, provide support for the position that we do not know what these tests measure. Even if all of the tests were significantly correlated with academic achievement, we would still not have much evidence to demonstrate that the etiology of the test performance was neurological, emotional, pedagogical, developmental, or attributable to any number of other factors. Controlling for and identifying these factors is clearly a difficult undertaking, but this undertaking should be within the scope of our present investigatory skill. Unfortunately few of the studies reported here have acknowledged the complexity of their task, and fewer still have used procedures that adequately take it into account.

This review has concentrated on individual tests and not on a composite profile analysis, in large part because the literature on these tests has assumed that each part of the battery has the strength to stand on its own, independent of the whole battery. The intent, and the claim, of most of the tests is that each one of them is able to discern a learning disability that the instrument or procedure has identified in validation studies. Furthermore, for most tests throughout the battery — in particular the ITPA, the Bender, the EEG, and the neurological workup — the objective is not to look for a specific aspect of neurological dysfunction, but to find a general expression of minimal neurological problems. Therefore, it is appropriate to evaluate the battery with respect to the diagnostic power of each test. However, another more practical reason for reviewing the tests individually is that the majority of studies on learning-disabilities diagnosis have investigated only one or a few tests, and seldom have composite profiles been empirically evaluated.

What does the battery reveal when cumulative deficits are evaluated? The answer to that question is that, as of now, we do not really know. The research available suggests that when the evidence is in, we will not be any closer to finding support for the neurological-deficit claim than we are presently. In two major analyses of the test profiles of MBD children (Crinella, 1973; Routh & Roberts, 1972), no single abnormal syndrome related to academic underachievement was found; subclusters of MBD characteristics were no more than tentative hypotheses based on a few subjects; the largest group of children had no subcluster patterns; and many of the subclusters had no characteristics that were necessarily indicative of neurological dysfunction.

Given the lack of empirical support for these tests, whether used individually or collectively, we may well ask why these tests have been used to draw conclusions about children and to classify them. Although we have not discussed the chronological development of the research for these tests, it should be apparent by now that their validity has always been questionable. Yet, in spite of the speculative nature of these tests, learning-disabilities professionals have acted, not as if they had tests that required abundant field assessments before their value could be judged, but rather as if they had in their hands diagnostic instruments that could lay bare the cognitive processes of a child's mind. In books, manuals, and courses, these and similar tests have been presented as mature tools for a mature profession. The lack of scientific foundation for the learning-disabilities battery, in contrast to ubiquitous recommendations for its use, forces the conclusion that, by replacing science with assertion, analysis with alchemy, and modesty with hyperbole, the learning-disabilities battery appears to have sprung fully formed out of the heads of learning-disabilities professionals like Athena out of Zeus.

It might be argued that, even if these tests do not possess the substantial validity claimed for them, they nevertheless can, in combination with clinical experience, be useful in helping a learning-disabilities specialist diagnose a child's problems with some degree of certainty. Learning-disabilities specialists can do this skillfully, it might be said, because they diagnose and try to find remedies for the educational problems of numerous children and, in the process, have acquired a body of skills and insights; the specialist, so it is argued, is not merely an automaton mindlessly recording test results and prescribing cures. The merit of this position can be assessed by looking both at the diagnosis and at the remedies the specialist prescribes.

With respect to diagnosis, the state of knowledge reviewed in this article suggests that the diagnostic judgments of a learning-disabilities specialist are caught up in evidential and logical weaknesses from which they cannot be extricated without considerable qualification. If, for example, a specialist suspects a child has a learning disability, the evidence or clinical impression upon which the judgment is based comes either from a test battery, from experience with related cases, or from both. The research on the battery suggests that at best a clinician will have only enough evidence to suspect that a child has a learning disability. Without question, a suspicion is of valuable clinical use, but it nonetheless remains a suspicion; it cannot be used as if it were firm knowledge. As for the knowledge a specialist might have acquired as a result of work with related cases, again the diagnosis of these previous related cases was based either on objective evidence or on clinical impressions and conclusions. But if little or no objective evidence is available in the current case, how could it have been available in earlier ones? And if the present diagnosis is based on clinical impressions and conclusions, on what were these based? If they were based on previous clinical experience, which was not based on objective research, the clinician becomes ensnared in an infinite regression of previous diagnostic experience that never once rested on a solid, empirical foundation.

If the claim is made that clinical knowledge is based on the remedial treatment and elimination of a suspected learning disability, the evidence for such a claim is also quite meager. We have seen that in experiments where the dysfunction itself was treated, there was little success. For example, when Frostig materials were used to remedy learning disabilities by treating the processing difficulties, no related improvement in learning resulted. It is possible that, even though the etiological diagnosis was correct, the program's attempt to treat the neurological dysfunction directly was incorrectly devised and therefore failed. The point of this present discussion, however, is that experiments that treat the disabilities have not decisively corroborated the explanation of learning disabilities as an organic disorder. A typical problem, for example, arises in the use of cerebral stimulants to correct a learning disability diagnosed as organic in origin. The theory has been that, if the medication improves learning performance, then ipso facto its success demonstrates the organic etiology (Satterfield, 1975). The drug most commonly used in this approach has been Ritalin (methylphenidate). To date, the evidence has not fully supported the contention that this medication does improve leaning; recent studies have, on the contrary, shown that children achieve less academically, as measured by objective achievement tests, when using Ritalin than when not (Rie, Rie, & Stewart, 1976; Rie, Rie, Stewart, & Ambuel, 1976). Thus we return to the question of how clinicians know that a child has a learning disability, and the answer is that, at present, they can at best suspect its existence. Neither logic nor empirical evidence allows us to go beyond that suspicion.

Without question, many youngsters have been diagnosed as learning disabled and have worked with clinicians and teachers who have demonstrably improved their academic abilities. But it is not evident that this improvement was the result of anything more than the proper application of the remedial techniques themselves and sympathetic treatment of the children and the specific symptoms they might have. These techniques have been and are now being used successfully with children in remedial clinics, regardless of the causes of their failure to learn. Within this process, it has yet to be demonstrated that certain remedial techniques work better for learning-disabled retarded readers than for non-learning-disabled retarded readers, or vice versa. The same may be said for published remedial materials. It might well be that the remedial techniques used for a specific academic problem actually treat a neurological dysfunction that is causing the problem and that the techniques are equally successful, whatever the cause, but this remains a hypothesis. What is more certain is that the success of learning-disabilities specialists in remedying the problem results from their ability to use general remedial techniques and not from their special knowledge of neurological dysfunction.

Do problems of minimal neurological dysfunction exist that impede academic learning? At present, the evidence in support of the thesis is far from compelling. While it cannot be said that no evidence exists, the entire field of learning disabilities has an empirical foundation too frail for the ponderous structure that has been erected upon it. I would suggest that, while there appears to be evidence that among some persons, a minimal neurological dysfunction does play a contributory role in impeding learning, that role is relatively minor and becomes influential only in combination with other factors. Before valid and useful diagnoses can be made, we must discover what exactly constitutes a minimal neurological dysfunction. Furthermore, we have no evidence to substantiate the claim that neurological dysfunctions are a major factor in inhibiting academic achievement.

If we continue to use the term "learning disability" at all, it should be restricted to its narrow neurological definition and not be made synonymous with educational deficiencies resulting from an entire spectrum of causes (Bannatyne, 1971).

Certainly the issue of etiology is important, for without an answer to the question of why some children fail to learn, remedial education will continue to be a bastion of liberal education ministering to generation after generation of poorly developed casualties. The evidence persists, however, that the predominant cause of educational underachievement, whether viewed historically (Cippolla, 1969), internationally (Carnoy, 1974; UNESCO, 1976), or nationally (Greer, 1973; Bowles & Gintis, 1976), is social-class injustice, with such corollaries as racial and ethnic discrimination contributing heavily. Educators concerned with etiology might better turn their attention to these primary social factors that find expression in educational practice, family relations, and the child's sense of self, and which, if eliminated, would produce the most noticeable degree of educational improvement.

Social Context of the Learning-Disabilities Test Battery

In the concluding portion of this article I would like to make a few remarks about the learning-disabilities test battery within a broader context than I have considered thus far. Up to this point, my analysis has been primarily empirical; some conceptual leaps will therefore be necessary. But this is done for a reason: to concentrate only on the empirical evidence itself runs the risk of operating only within the "givens," of reifying the "universe of discourse" of this field. In particular, we risk narrowly concentrating on specific instruments or on the specific tasks that learning-disabilities specialists perform. Neither the battery, the term "learning disability," nor the learning-disabilities specialist exists in a vacuum. We must go beyond the empirical "facts" to historical and social analysis to uncover the origins and meanings of the facts and to evaluate them properly. Marcuse (1964) has observed that

> thought — any mode of thinking which is not confined to pragmatic orientation within the status quo — can recognize the facts and respond to the facts only by "going behind" them. . . . [The] factors in the facts . . . become data only in an analysis which is capable of identifying the structure that holds together the parts and processes of society and that determines their interrelation. (pp. 185, 190)

The learning-disabilities battery has been developed partly in an attempt to provide a rational way of understanding children whose inability to learn appears otherwise inexplicable. These children do not remember words from one day to the next; they constantly reverse letters and words; after five minutes of work they are squirming and anxious to do something else. Nothing seems to help them, so they appear to many educators to have neurological problems of perception, memory, or motor control.

But these inexplicable problems and the genuinely useful remediation that learning-disabilities specialists perform still do not fully explain the emergence of the battery. Researchers as far back as Samuel Orton in the 1920s have been concerned with the issue of neurological impairment. We still have to explain why the learning-disabilities battery has been unleashed only in the past decade or so. Obviously, it was not because the field struck empirical gold.

The reason, I believe, lies to a great extent in our social system — a system now requiring vast structural changes to remedy its present state of instability. Unable to make these changes, and in an effort to make unassailable its deteriorating institutions, the system, in its own defense, has generated and nurtured the growth of such fields as learning disabilities — providing, in other words, biological explanations for problems that require social solutions.

As Allan Chase (1977) has documented, these biological explanations have been used to explain social maladies in times of social instability since the beginning of the nineteenth century. Beginning with Malthus and continuing with Galton, Spencer, Goddard, and others, biological analyses have been used to provide an ostensibly scientific explanation for social problems such as poverty and crime. But, in Chase's words, these have actually been pseudoscientific claims put forth with neither scientific knowledge to support them nor available research data to refute them. More than mere viewpoints in scientific debates, these explanations have served the ideological purpose of justifying social and economic inequities and of bolstering the malfunctioning social order. This "biologizing" of social problems has posited organic casualties for poverty, aggression, and violence, as well as for educational underachievement (Anderson, 1972; Delgado, 1971; Jensen, 1969; Mark & Ervin, 1970; Wilson, 1975).

The ideological functions of particular biological explanations have been noted in a number of recent analyses. For example, in addressing the definition of mental illness, Thomas Scheff (1975) remarked:

> The concepts of mental illness in general — and schizophrenia in particular — are not neutral, value-free, scientifically precise terms but are, for the most part, the leading edge of an ideology embedded in the historical and cultural present. . . . The concept of illness and its associated vocabulary — symptoms, therapies, patients, and physicians — reify and legitimate the prevailing public order. . . . The medical model of disease refers to culture-free processes that are independent of the public order. (pp. 6–7)

Similarly, in an examination of IQ testing, Kamin (1974) discussed the political uses of the IQ test and concluded:

> The IQ test in America, and the way in which we think about it, has been fostered by men committed to a particular social view. That view included the belief that those on the bottom are genetically inferior victims of their own immutable defects. The consequence has been that the IQ test has served as an instrument of oppression against the poor — dressed in the trappings of science, rather than politics. The message of science is heard respectfully, particularly when the tidings it carries are soothing to the public conscience.

> . . . The poor, the foreign-born, and racial minorities are shown to be stupid. They are shown to have been born that way. The underprivileged are today demonstrated to be ineducable, a message soothing to the public purse as to the public conscience. (p. 2)

Corresponding analyses reducing social problems to medical or biological problems have been made by other writers (Braginsky & Braginsky, 1971; Chorover, 1974; Foucault, 1965; Szasz, 1970; Tobach, 1974).

Within this framework, we can begin to understand both the emergence and the major function of the concept of learning disabilities. By positing biological bases for learning problems, the responsibility for failure is taken from the schools, communities, and other institutions, and is put squarely on the back, or rather within the head, of the child. Thus, the classification plays its political role, moving the focus away from the general educational process, away from the need to change institutions, away from the need to rectify social conditions affecting the child, and away from the need to appropriate more resources for social use toward the remedy of a purely medical problem. It is a classic instance of what Ryan (1972) has called "blaming the victim." That is, it is an explanation of a social problem that attributes its cause to the individual failings, shortcomings, or deficiencies of the victims of the problem. Balow (1971) referred to this shifting of responsibility when, in a paper critical of giving neurological explanations for reading problems, he asked rhetorically:

> If reading disability is at root a medical problem, why is it that the vast preponderance of serious cases come from those geographic areas where the home, community, and school environment are most hostile to academic learning? Why are up to 60 percent of slum area children and only two percent of suburban children severe reading disability cases? (p. 517)

Coupled with this biological emphasis, several additional influences have emerged that help to nurture the claims attributed to the learning-disabilities test battery. One influence is the pharmaceutical industry, which, through heavy promotional work aimed at professionals from education, psychology, and medicine, has fostered the use of cerebral stimulants as a means of treating learning-disabled children (Schrag & Divoky, 1975). Precise marketing information on these drugs is difficult to obtain, but the figures on Ritalin, the major stimulant prescribed, suggest that their distribution and sales have been, and remain, substantial. According to IMS America (Note 2), a pharmaceutical data-collection firm, approximately 396,000 prescriptions for Ritalin were written by private physicians for young patients examined in their offices in 1972. The number climbed to 480,760 by 1974, then jumped the following year to 608,660. In 1976, perhaps because of a good deal of widely publicized critical attention directed toward Ritalin, the number dropped to approximately 422,000. The decrease in prescriptions since the mid-seventies suggests that Ritalin is being prescribed more cautiously, but when these figures are compared with the total number of prescriptions filled by pharmacies, a different picture emerges. For example, in a one-year period during 1972–1973, 623,000 prescriptions for Ritalin were filled by pharmacists; for the first ten months of 1977, the figure was 1,463,000, with a projected annual total of approximately 1,800,000. The figures therefore indicate that, while the number of children for whom Ritalin was prescribed for the first time might be approximately the same in 1972 and 1977 and might have declined from 1975 to the present, the total number of youngsters taking Ritalin has increased during the five-year period.

These figures are insufficient for a thorough analysis because of the difficulty in obtaining data. They do not include, for example, prescriptions written in clinics, the size of prescriptions, how many were new and how many refills. Unquestionably, the past and current use of Ritalin is substantial. It is equally unquestionable that the learning-disabilities test battery supplies the "objective" documentation used to justify prescribing this medication. Without these and similar tests, the pharmaceutical companies would be hard pressed to demonstrate the existence of a neurologically impaired population in need of cerebral stimulants.

Another influence supporting the test-battery claims — more psychosocial than economic, although for many clinicians it has economic advantages as well — is the prestige of the biomedical professions. As Friedson (1970) has observed, the characteristics that mark a "profession" are its claims of "knowledge of an especially esoteric, scientific, or abstract character" and of work that is "extraordinarily complex and nonroutine, requiring for its adequate performance extensive training, great intelligence and skill, and highly complex judgment" (pp. 106, 153–154). Of all professional groups, it is the medical profession that has the clearest claim to this kind of prestige and authority, particularly in its prerogative to diagnose, treat, and direct treatment. Thus, in a professional relationship where there is the opportunity to share assumptions about the biological nature of a "disorder," the closer a profession comes to acquiring the terminology and characteristics of the medical profession, the more that profession can increase its prestige and "its position in the class structure and in the market place" (p. 153).

It is my firm impression that educators, consciously or not, have attempted to enhance their profession, which otherwise has only moderate social status. They have sought affiliation with the medical world not only because multidisciplinary work is valued, but also because it provides them with an aura of greater knowledge, authority, and importance. And who can blame them? How mundane to tell someone you teach remedial reading. How awesome to announce that you do clinical work with minimally brain-dysfunctional children, more dyslexic than dyscalculic, who are benefiting from methylphenidate.

Admittedly, my impression is unprovable and is derived only from work in clinics and association with special education, but similar observations have been made by researchers studying the effects of medical hierarchical relationships in other fields. In psychiatric hospitals, for example, it has been noted that psychiatrists, who have the most power and prestige in the hierarchy, are the ones whose relationships with, attitudes toward, and diagnoses of patients serve as models for the nonmedical professionals and staff below them (Rosenhan, 1973). An illustration of this, where psychiatric language is employed by low-level staff to explain the actions of inmates, is furnished by Belknap (1956): "In the usual case of this kind [a mental patient breaks a rule], such things as impudence, insubordination, and excessive familiarity are translated into more or less professional terms, such as 'disturbed' or 'excited,' and presented by the attendant to the physician as a medical status report" (p. 170).

There is, of course, a dialectic in these relationships that produces resistance and opposition. In the previous illustration, sharing the language of the physician signifies both affiliation with those in power and acknowledgment of the disparity in power — a disparity that always contains potential antagonism. In the case of learning-disabilities specialists, tensions appear to be commensurate with the controversy that exists within the specialty as a whole. I have known a number of learning-disabilities specialists and clinical staff who give little credence to neurological interpretations of academic underachievement, but who continue to diagnose children in those terms because they believe that their superiors expect this kind of diagnosis. To do otherwise would place the diagnostician's professional competence and standing in jeopardy. Others have reluctantly diagnosed children as neurologically impaired primarily because only with this diagnosis could children be placed in a Neurologically Impaired (NI) class that had a better curriculum than they could obtain in a regular classroom. Their view of the NI classroom was not that it was particularly good at remedying problems of neurological impairment, but that it used a method of instruction beneficial to all kinds of underachievers.

There is little question that eventually the tests reviewed here will be discarded; the evidence against them is mounting. The central question is really whether recognition of the invalidity of these tests will result in abandonment of an untenable professional dogma, or whether it will merely result in the test battery being replaced by other equally questionable instruments. I have sketched the context of the test battery because I believe the answer lies in the political and social realm and not in the worth of other less well-known instruments that are standing in the wings; these tests, in any case, do not yet exist. The future of the learning-disabilities test battery will depend upon how we answer the following questions: How catastrophic then will it be for dependent industries, institutions, and professionals to acknowledge that, so far as we can tell, Johnny's neural connections are intact? If we do not "blame the victim," where then does the blame lie?

Notes

1. Silver, L. B. (1977). *Minimal brain dysfunction or whatever: A plea for clarity.* Unpublished manuscript.
2. IMS America Limited. (1977). Copyright market statistics used with permission of publisher. Ambler, PA.

References

Ackerman, P. T., Dykman, R. A., & Peters, J. E. (1976). Hierarchical factor patterns on the WISC as related to areas of learning deficit. *Perceptual and Motor Skills, 42,* 583–615.

Ackerman, P. T., Peters, J. E., & Dykman, R. A. (1971). Children with specific learning disabilities: Bender test findings and other signs. *Journal of Learning Disabilities, 4,* 437–446.

Adams, R. M., Kocsis, J. J., & Estes, R. E. (1974). Soft neurological signs in learning disabled children and controls. *American Journal of Disabled Children, 128,* 614–618.

Anderson, C. (1972). *Society pays: The high costs of minimal brain damage in America.* New York: Walker.

Arena, J. I. (Ed.). (1967). *Management of the child with learning disabilities: An interdisciplinary challenge.* San Rafael, CA: Academic Therapy.

Ashlock, P. A. (1963). *Visual perception of children in the primary grades and its relation to reading performance.* Unpublished doctoral dissertation, University of Texas.

Ayers, F. W. (1968). *Central nervous system function in children with reading problems.* Unpublished doctoral dissertation. University of Minnesota.

Ayers, R., & Torres, F. (1967). The incidence of EEG abnormalities in a dyslexic and a control group. *Journal of Clinical Psychology, 23,* 334–336.

Balow, B. (1971). Perceptual-motor activities in the treatment of severe reading disability. *Reading Teacher, 24,* 513–525.

Bannatyne, A. (1971). *Language, reading and learning disabilities: Psychology, neuropsychology, diagnosis and remediation.* Springfield, IL: Charles C. Thomas.

Belknap, I. (1956). *Human problems of a state mental hospital.* New York: McGraw-Hill.

Belmont, L., & Birch, H. G. (1966). The intellectual profile of retarded readers. *Perceptual and Motor Skills, 22,* 787–816.

Bender, L. (1938). A visual-motor gestalt test and its clinical use. *American Orthopsychiatric Association Research Monograph, 3.*

Black, F. W. (1976). Cognitive, academic, and behavioral findings in children with suspected and documented neurological dysfunction. *Journal of Learning Disabilities, 9,* 182–187.

Black, F. W. (1972). EEG and birth abnormalities in high and low perceiving reading-retarded children. *Journal of Genetic Psychology, 121,* 327–328.

Black, F. W. (1973). Neurological dysfunction and reading disorders. *Journal of Learning Disabilities, 6,* 313–316.

Black, F. W. (1974). WISC verbal-performance discrepancies as indicators of neurological dysfunction in pediatric patients. *Journal of Clinical Psychology, 30,* 165–167.

Boshes, B., & Mykelbust, H. R. (1964). A neurological and behavioral study of children with learning disorders. *Neurology, 14,* 7–12.

Bowles, S., & Gintis, H. (1976). *Schooling in capitalist America.* New York: Basic Books.

Braginsky, D. D., & Braginsky, G. M. (1971). *Hansels and Gretels: Studies of children in institutions for the mentally retarded.* New York: Holt, Rinehart & Winston.

Bryan, Q. R. (1964). Relative importance of intelligence and visual perception in predicting reading achievement. *California Journal of Educational Research, 15,* 44–48.

Buckland, P., & Balow, B. (1973). Effect of visual perceptual training on reading achievement. *Exceptional Children, 39,* 299–304.

Buros, O. K. (1972). *The seventh mental measurements yearbook.* Highland Park, NJ: Gryphon Press.

Buros, O. K. (1974). *Tests in print.* Highland Park, NJ: Gryphon Press.

Carnoy, M. (1974). *Education as cultural imperialism.* New York: McKay.

Chang, T., & Chang, V. (1967). Relation of visual-motor skills and reading achievement in primary-grade pupils of superior ability. *Perceptual and Motor Skills, 24,* 51–53.

Chase, A. (1977). *The legacy of Malthus: The social costs of the new scientific racism.* New York: Knopf.

Chorover, S. L. (1974). The pacification of the brain. *Psychology Today, 7,* 59–69.

Cippolla, C. M. (1969). *Literacy and development in the West.* Baltimore: Penguin Books.

Cohn, R. (1961). Delayed acquisition of reading and writing abilities in children. *Archives of Neurology, 4,* 153–164.

Cohn, R. I. (1966). Remedial training of first grade children with visual perceptual retardation. *Educational Horizons, 45,* 60–63.

Colarusso, R., Martin, H., & Hartung, J. (1975). Specific visual-perceptual skills as long-term predictors of academic success. *Journal of Learning Disabilities, 8,* 651–655.

Corah, N. L., & Powell, R. J. (1963). A factor analytic study of the Frostig developmental test of visual perception. *Perceptual and Motor Skills, 16,* 59–63.

Crinella, F. M. (1973). Identification of brain dysfunction syndromes in children through profile analysis: Patterns associated with so-called minimal brain dysfunction. *Journal of Abnormal Psychology, 82,* 33–45.

Cronbach, L. J. (1970). *Essentials of psychological testing.* New York: Harper & Row.

Delgado, J. M. W. (1971). *Physical control of the mind: Toward a psychocivilized society.* New York: Harper & Row.

Dubey, D. R. (1976). Organic factors in hyperkinesis: A critical evaluation. *American Journal of Orthopsychiatry, 46,* 353–366.

Dykman, R. A., Peters, J. E., & Ackerman, P. T. (1973). Experimental approaches to the study of minimal brain dysfunction: A follow-up study. *Annals of the New York Academy of Science, 203,* 93–108.

Eaves, L. D., & Crichton, J. U. (1974–1975). A five-year follow-up of children with minimal brain dysfunction. *Academic Therapy, 10,* 173–180.

Edwards, R. P., Alley, G. R., & Snyder, W. (1971). Academic achievement and minimal brain dysfunction. *Journal of Learning Disabilities, 4,* 134–138.

Falik, L. H. (1969). The effects of special perceptual-motor training in kindergarten on reading readiness, and on second-grade performance. *Journal of Learning Disabilities, 2,* 385–402.

Farr, R. (1969). *What can be measured?* Newark, DE: International Reading Association.

Fisher, K. L. (1971). Effects of perceptual-motor training on the educable mentally retarded. *Exceptional Children, 38,* 264–266.

Flynn, P. T., & Byrne, M. C. (1970). Relationship between reading and selected auditory abilities of third-grade children. *Journal of Speech and Hearing Research, 13,* 725–730.

Foucault, M. (1965). *Madness and civilization.* New York: Random House.

Friedson, E. (1970). *Professional dominance: The social structure of medical care.* New York: Atherton.

Freeman, R. D. (1967). Special education and the electroencephalogram: Marriage of convenience. *Journal of Special Education, 2,* 61–73.

Frostig, M., Lefever, W., & Whittlesey, J. (1964). *Development test of visual perception.* Palo Alto, CA: Consulting Psychologist Press.

Gamsky, N. R., & Lloyd, F. W. (1971). A longitudinal study of visual perceptual training and reading achievement. *Journal of Educational Research, 64,* 451–454.

Glenn, H. (1975). The myth of the label: Learning disabled child. *Elementary School Journal, 75,* 357–361.

Goetz, E. (1971). Hearing growth and reading. *Claremont Reading Conference, 35,* 120–126.

Goetzinger, C. P., Dirks, D. D., & Baer, C. J. (1960). Auditory discrimination and visual perception in good and poor readers. *Annals of Otology, Rhinology, and Laryngology, 69,* 121–136.

Gomez, E. H. (1967). Minimal cerebral dysfunction (maximum neurological confusion). *Clinical Pediatrics, 6,* 589–591.

Graham, F. K., & Kendall, B. S. (1960). *Memory for designs test.* Missoula, MT: Psychological Test Specialist.

Greer, C. (1973). *The great school legend.* New York: Viking Press.

Hafner, L. E., Weaver, W. W., & Powell, K. (1970). Psychological and perceptual correlates of reading achievement among fourth graders. *Journal of Reading Behavior, 2,* 281–290.

Hallahan, D. P., & Kauffman, J. M. (1977). Labels, categories, behaviors: ED, LD, EMR reconsidered. *Journal of Special Education, 11,* 133–134.

Hammill, D. D. (1976). Defining learning disabilities for programmatic purposes. *Academic Therapy, 12,* 29–37.

Hartlage, L. C., & Green, J. B. (1971). EEG differences in children's reading, spelling and arithmetic abilities, *Perceptual and Motor Skills, 32,* 133–134.

Hartlage, L. C., & Lucas, T. L. (1976). Differential correlation of Bender-Gestalt and Beery visual motor integration test for black and for white children. *Perceptual and Motor Skills, 43,* 1039–1043.

Henderson, N. B., Butler, B., & Gaffney, B. (1969). Effectiveness of the WISC and Bender-Gestalt test in predicting arithmetic and reading achievement for white and non-white children. *Journal of Clinical Psychology, 29,* 206–212.

Holroyd, J., & Wright, F. (1965). Neurological implications of WISC and Bender-Gestalt test in predicting arithmetic and reading achievement for white and non-white children. *Journal of Consulting Psychology, 29,* 206–212.

Huelsman, C. B., Jr. (1970). The WISC subtest syndrome for disabled readers. *Perceptual and Motor Skills, 30,* 535–550.

Hurwitz, I., Bibace, R. M., Wolff, P., & Rowbotham, B. (1972). Neuropsychological function of normal boys, delinquent boys, and boys with learning problems. *Perceptual and Motor Skills, 35,* 387–394.

Jacobs, J. N. (1968). An evaluation of the Frostig visual perception training programme. *Educational Leadership, 25,* 332–340.

Jensen, A. R. (1969). How much can we boost IQ and scholastic achievement? *Harvard Educational Review, 39,* 1–123.

Kallos, G. L., Grabow, J. M., & Guarino, E. A. (1961). The WISC profile of disabled readers. *Personnel and Guidance Journal, 39,* 476–478.

Kamin, L. J. (1974). *The science and politics of IQ.* New York: Wiley.

Keogh, B., & Smith, C. (1967). Visuo-motor ability for school prediction: A seven year study. *Perceptual and Motor Skills, 25,* 101–111.

Kephart, N. C. (1960). *The slow learner in the classroom.* Columbus, OH: Merrill.

Kirk, S. A., & Elkins, J. (1975). Characteristics of children enrolled in the child service demonstrations centers. *Journal of Learning Disabilities, 8,* 630–637.

Kirk, S. A., McCarthy, J. J., & Kirk, W. D. (1968). *Illinois test of psycholinguistic abilities.* Urbana: University of Illinois Press.

Koppitz, E. M. (1970). Brain damage, reading disability and the Bender-Gestalt test. *Journal of Learning Disabilities, 3,* 429–433.

Lachmann, F. M. (1960). Perceptual-motor development in children retarded in reading ability. *Journal of Consulting Psychology, 24,* 427–431.

Larsen, S. C., Rogers, D., & Sowell, V. (1976). The use of selected perceptual tests in differentiating between normal and learning disabled children. *Journal of Learning Disabilities, 9,* 32–37.

Lewis, F. D., Bell, D. B., & Anderson, R. P. (1970). Relationship of motor proficiency and reading retardation. *Perceptual and Motor Skills, 31,* 395–401.

Liebert, R., & Sherk, J. (1970). Three Frostig visual perception subtests and specific reading tasks for kindergarten, first and second grade children. *Reading Teacher, 24,* 130–137.

Lingren, R. H. (1969). Performance of disabled and normal readers on the Bender-Gestalt, Auditory Discrimination Test, and visual-motor matching. *Perceptual and Motor Skills, 29,* 152–154.

Lyle, J. G. (1968). Performance of retarded readers on the Memory-for-Designs Test. *Perceptual and Motor Skills, 26,* 851–854.

Marcuse, H. (1964). *One-dimensional man.* Boston: Beacon Press.

Mark, V. H., & Ervin, R. F. (1970). *Violence and the brain.* New York: Harper & Row.

McBeath, P. M. (1966). *The effectiveness of three reading preparedness programs for perceptually handicapped kindergartners.* Unpublished doctoral dissertation, Stanford University.

Meier, J. H. (1971). Prevalence and characteristics of learning disabilities found in second grade children. *Journal of Learning Disabilities, 4,* 1–16.

Meier, J. H. (1976). *Developmental and learning disabilities: Evaluation, management, and prevention in children.* Baltimore: University Park Press.

Millman, H. L. (1970). Minimal brain dysfunction in children: Evaluation and treatment. *Journal of Learning Disabilities, 3,* 89–99.

Mykelbust, H. F. (1973). Identification and diagnosis of children with learning disabilities: An interdisciplinary study of criteria. *Seminars in Psychiatry, 5,* 55–77.

National Advisory Committee on Handicapped Children. (1968). *Special education for handicapped children* (First Annual Report). Washington, DC: U.S. Department of Health, Education, and Welfare.

New Jersey Association for Children with Learning Disabilities. (1974). *Handbook on learning disabilities.* Englewood Cliffs, NJ: Prentice-Hall.

Newcomer, P. L., & Hammill, D. D. (1975). ITPA and academic achievement: A survey. *Reading Teacher, 28,* 731–741.

Nielsen, H. J., & Ringe, K. (1969). Visuo-perceptive and visuo-motor performance of children with reading disabilities. *Scandinavian Journal of Psychology, 10,* 225–231.

Norfleet, M. A. (1973). The Bender-Gestalt as a group screening instrument for first grade reading potential. *Journal of Learning Disabilities, 6,* 383–388.

Obrzut, J. E., Taylor, H. D., & Thweatt, R. C. (1972). Reexamination of Koppitz developmental Bender scoring system. *Perceptual and Motor Skills, 34,* 279–282.

Olson, A. V. (1966). School achievement, reading ability and specific perception skills in the third grade. *Reading Teacher, 19,* 490–492.

Olson, A. V., & Johnson, C. I. (1970). Structure and predictive validity of the Frostig developmental test of visual perception in grades one and three. *Journal of Special Education, 4,* 49–52.

Orlando, C., & Lynch, J. (1974). Learning disabilities or educational casualties? Where do we go from here? *Elementary School Journal, 74,* 461–467.

Phipps, P. M. (1976–1977). Learning disabilities and teacher competencies. *Academic Therapy, 12,* 225–230.

Pikulski, J. J. (1975). Assessing information about intelligence and reading. *Reading Teacher, 29,* 157–163.

Pyfer, J. L., & Carlson, B. R. (1972). Characteristic motor development of children with learning disabilities. *Perceptual and Motor Skills, 35,* 291–296.

Rie, H. E., Rie, E. D., & Stewart, S. (1976). Effects of methylphenidate on underachieving children. *Journal of Consulting and Clinical Psychology, 44,* 250–260.

Rie, H. E., Rie, E. D., Stewart, S., & Ambuel, J. P. (1976). Effects of Ritalin on underachieving children: A replication. *American Journal of Orthopsychiatry, 46,* 313–322.

Roach, E. G., & Kephart, N. C. (1966). *The Purdue perceptual-motor survey.* Columbus, OH: Merrill.

Robinson, M. E., & Schwartz, L. B. (1973). Visuo-motor skills and reading ability: A longitudinal study. *Developmental Medicine and Child Neurology, 15,* 281–286.

Rosen, C. L. (1966). An experimental study of visual perceptual training and reading achievement in first grade. *Perceptual and Motor Skills, 20,* 979–986.

Rosenhan, D. L. (1973). On being sane in insane places. *Science, 179,* 250–258.

Routh, D. K., & Roberts, R. D. (1972). Minimal brain dysfunction in children: Failure to find evidence for a behavioral syndrome. *Psychological Reports, 31,* 307–314.

Rudel, R. G., & Denckla, M. B. (1976). Relationship of IQ and reading score to visual, spatial, and temporal matching tasks. *Journal of Learning Disabilities, 9,* 169–178.

Ryan, W. (1972). *Blaming the victim.* New York: Vintage.

Satterfield, J. H. (1975). Neurophysiologic studies with hyperactive children. In D. P. Cantwell (Ed.), *The hyperactive child.* New York: Spectrum.

Scheff, P., & Divoky, D. (1975). *The myth of the hyperactive child.* New York: Pantheon Books.

Sloan, W. (1955). *Lincoln-Oseretsky test of motor development.* Chicago: Stoelting.

Szasz, T. A. (1970). *The manufacture of madness.* New York: Dell.

Thweatt, R. C. (1963). Prediction of school learning disability through the use of the Bender-Gestalt test: A validation study of Koppitz's scoring technique. *Journal of Clinical Psychology, 19,* 216–217.

Tobach, E. (Ed.). (1974). *The four horsemen: Racism, sexism, militarism and social darwinism.* New York: Behavioral Publications.

UNESCO. (1976). *The experimental world literacy programme: A critical assessment.* Paris: UNESCO Press.

Walters, C. E. (1961). Reading ability and visual-motor function in second grade children. *Perceptual and Motor Skills, 13,* 370.

Wechsler, D. I. (1949). *Wechsler intelligence scale for children.* New York: Psychological Corporation.

Wepman, J. (1958). *Wepman auditory discrimination test.* Chicago: Chicago Language Research Associates.

Wepman, J. (1960). Auditory discrimination, speech and reading. *Elementary School Journal, 3,* 325–333.

Wikler, A., Dixon, J. F., & Parker, J. B. (1970). Brain function in problem children and controls: Psychometric, neurological, and electroencephalographic comparisons. *American Journal of Psychiatry, 125,* 94–105.

Wilson, E. O. (1975). *Sociobiology: The new synthesis.* Cambridge, MA: Harvard University Press.

Screening, Early Intervention, and Remediation: Obscuring Children's Potential

ANNE MARTIN

After several years as a teacher of older children, Anne Martin returned to teaching kindergarten and found that in the intervening years, an increased emphasis on early diagnosis and intervention had transformed the life of the kindergarten classroom. Special education pull-out programs caused fragmentation of individual students' school lives and made it more difficult to develop a cohesive classroom community. Moreover, special educators' concern for discovering and treating children's learning deficits — which were often given intimidating, coldly medical labels — placed undue emphasis on weaknesses rather than on appreciation and acknowledgment of strengths. In this article, Martin uses many concrete examples from her classroom to illustrate problems brought on by early diagnosis and intervention; she also offers an alternative approach. Based on the "Staff Review" procedure developed at the Prospect School in North Bennington, Vermont, Martin describes a process in which teachers collaborate to produce a rich understanding of individual children within the context of their whole lives in schools. In an example of this method, Martin describes how one teacher, feeling defeated by a student's extreme behaviors and her special education team's inability to offer useful support, found renewed hope, energy, and concrete strategies through focused sharing with a group of colleagues. It is Martin's belief that many of the solutions to students' problems lie within the caring community of the classroom headed by a teacher who is part of a caring community of other teachers and professionals.

The correspondence that follows this article — a letter written by Karyn Gitlis on behalf of the Tempe (Arizona) Elementary School Speech-Language Pathologists and a response from Martin — indicates the strong reaction many special educators may have to Martin's argument.

As a teacher of primary-grade children in a suburban public school system, I have become increasingly concerned with both the theory and the delivery of special needs services to children at school. The current national trend is to give "screening tests" to entering children, to depend heavily on test results in creating Individualized Education Plans (IEPs) for children iden-tified as having problems, and to give special services according to a rigid body of rules and regulations. State laws based on PL 94-142, the Education for All Handicapped Children Act, were presumably set up to permit "early intervention" and to make sure all children in need would have equal op-portunity for special services. Unfortunately, although these laws are well intentioned, they have had consequences far from their originally stated aims, and I have been repeatedly dismayed and angered by their effects on the lives of children. While mandated screening procedures and education plans may work well in some cases of physical or other extreme disabilities, I think they have had a demonstrably negative influence on our views of children's potential and our views of children and teaching altogether. In my discussion of these issues, I am drawing mainly on what I know best: my own classroom experience. While I am aware that my experience is limited, it is probably not so different from the experiences of countless other teach-ers in other places.

When I returned to teaching kindergarten several years ago, having worked with older children in the meantime, I was amazed at how expecta-tions for entering children had changed in that fifteen-year span. I found that beginning students were supposed to be "ready" for school, whereas my whole training in early childhood education and my prior experience as a kindergarten teacher had led me to assume that it was precisely in kinder-garten that children *became* ready for school. But now, in class, children were supposed to learn "skills" through formal lessons, which might include work-sheets and workbooks. They were being screened either before entering school or during the first weeks of kindergarten, and any child who did not do well on the screening test was the subject of a concern that was commu-nicated to parents. These young children, often not five years old, were being sorted out and categorized with little allowance for the infinite variety of their learning styles and developmental patterns. This is not how I saw kindergarten at all.

Entering kindergarten is a big step for five-year-old children, whether they have previously attended nursery school or whether this is their first school experience. They are now in "real" school where they are part of a large student body, perhaps joining older siblings in the same building. Within a large group under the care of one teacher, they are expected to become self-controlled in behavior and gain some independence in their learning. In a thoughtful kindergarten program, children are challenged and stretched intellectually through carefully chosen materials and activities, encouraged to express their own ideas and thoughts through many media, and helped to deal with social issues like friendship, conflict, and cooperation.

A flexible kindergarten program can accommodate wide diversity in children's backgrounds, maturity, temperaments, interests, talents, abilities, and skills. In this important introduction to school, every child should have the chance to grow, to be appreciated, and to learn to be a contributing member of a group. It seems, however, that schools are increasingly unwilling to accept all children and to adjust to their particular needs. I remember one meeting of kindergarten teachers in which the suggestion was made that we should visit all the preschools in our district to identify and head off problem children before they registered for kindergarten. But even without such extreme measures, our entering children tend to be labeled and pigeonholed through screening and testing procedures.

Early in the school year, I was asked to meet with school personnel who had administered a screening test to my new kindergarten children during the first weeks of school. To my surprise, test results indicated that fully half of my young students were considered to be "at risk" in one or more crucial developmental areas. One of my brightest students was said to be possibly learning disabled, and my most skilled artist deficient in fine motor ability. My most cooperative learner was "oppositional" and displayed "negative attitudes." There were lists of names under the headings of "gross motor concerns," "LD [Learning Disabled] risks" and "needing fine motor practice." The more I remonstrated and gave counterevidence (I was already starting to *know* these children, after all), the more I was met by grave, implacable insistence on the validity of the judgments, although we all agreed that a one-time test at the beginning of a new school experience was likely to yield inaccurate information. I became increasingly frustrated and strident in the face of the accusations, both explicit and implied, that I was closed-minded and not sufficiently attuned to children's needs. Even though I knew that getting angry and alienating colleagues was not a productive strategy, I felt I had to assert my values against what seemed to me a constricting view of children's potential.

This confrontation was not a new situation. I had repeatedly rejected not only the particular instrument of our screening tests (which happens to be one that I find especially objectionable), but the whole idea of sorting our children into categories and giving them numerical scores for isolated skills. I have maintained that there is no way that a twenty-minute contact and a set of test scores can adequately describe a child's potential to learn. All children come to school as complex persons with their own unique backgrounds and sets of experiences. For me the fascination of each new school year is the gradual revelation of this complexity as I observe the children and develop a relationship with each child and the whole group. It is only through living in the classroom together that we start to understand one another and begin to get a sense of each other's strengths and vulnerabilities. Yet when it comes down to meetings about students, especially those including parents, it is the test scores and the recommendations of "support service" personnel that are generally given far greater weight than teacher observations. My main quarrel with special services is that the whole thrust is to identify weaknesses and concentrate on problems, instead of focusing on strengths and consciously supporting those strengths in order to encourage growth in all areas.

The language used to describe children in professional reports, whether written by school personnel or by outside clinicians, may seem to be just current professional jargon, but its implicit meanings are actually highly significant.[1] For instance, the phrase "children at risk" has become a familiar one, picked up frequently by the media in reference to a variety of problems like poverty, hunger, lead poisoning, AIDS, or teenage pregnancy. The words have a dramatic ring that catches people's attention. The expression "children at risk" is explicitly a prediction of danger and implicitly a call for immediate strong action to avert disaster. Obviously, some of the issues where children are seen to be at risk are actually life-and-death matters. In schools, however, the phrase can be casually applied to almost any concern, from trivial matters such as a handwriting deficiency to the possibility of total school failure.

In an article entitled "A Generation at Risk,"[2] a prediction of failure is made for a large part of America's entering class of students:

> Not only is the class of 2000 smaller than many of its predecessors, reflecting the low birthrates of recent years, but it could easily turn out to be less prepared for college or the workplace. That is because the generation now in kindergarten, more than any before it, is dominated by children whose circumstances — poverty, an unstable home, a non-English-speaking background or membership in a minority group that historically has performed below average academically — make them statistically more likely to fail in school.

Not only does this article hold the extraordinary assumption that belonging to a minority group or having a non-English-speaking background almost guarantees failure, but it conveys a sense of hopelessness about our society's ability to adjust to differences in the school population. As the report comments, a teacher can look at the admittedly "bright young faces" of new kindergartners, and "within a few months, she can predict pretty well who among these children is going to succeed and who will fail." If children are identified as "at risk," it is easy to give up on them early on.

Often children are now labeled "at risk," where formerly they might have been described as children who are not performing well in school. To say that a child is having some problems with certain aspects of school invites an examination of how the classroom could adapt to the child's difficulties. To say that a child is "at risk" invites predictions of dire consequences that easily become self-fulfilling prophecies. The label "at risk" tends to eclipse attempts to learn, patiently, to know the child better before suggesting solutions, in favor of prescribing immediate and often inappropriate measures. If and when "interventions" are not successful, it is easy to place blame on the extent of the damaging conditions rather than an ineffective response by the school.

Where remedial services are available, schools tend to be in such a rush to jump in with "early intervention" that young children hardly get a chance to set in motion their own ways of learning before teachers are warned of their learning problems. For example, before Laurie even entered my kindergarten, I was told to look for serious difficulties.[3] It seemed that she had been tested during the summer and that a meeting was scheduled for the second week of school to discuss her learning deficiencies. I managed to hold off the meeting for several weeks, since I wanted to get to know Laurie before we held the discussion. What I saw was a little girl who loved books and language, who played with other children, who separated from her mother easily and followed routines well, who was clearly interested in discussions, in topics of study, in written symbols, and the world around her. In short, I saw no problems. It seemed that Laurie had had some emotional difficulties at nursery school in late spring, after a traumatic family experience. In the aftermath, Laurie was given several cognitive tests, whereupon it was suddenly discovered that she had trouble in sequencing and ordering information that was "not meaningful." The report read in part:

> Laurie's best performance, which was advanced for her age, was her recall of story details which required memory for extensive, meaningful verbal information. Notably, when recall required verbal information that did not have a context — verbal and number series — she was less skilled. . . . It appears at this time that Laurie's memory is enhanced when the information is verbal and meaningful. This has implications for Laurie's "listening" skills.

I would have thought that the implication would be to develop her strong talent and interest in literature, listening to stories and storytelling so that she could learn in a meaningful context. But the recommendation was that she should receive help in the learning center three times a week, in light of the fact that, besides the trouble in processing information, she also lacked "automaticity" in naming numbers and letters and in printing them. This child was not yet five when she was tested and expected to know numbers and letters, which the tester termed "school readiness information." Since when do we expect kindergarten children to enter school with the school skills they are coming in to learn? The upshot of our meeting with a roomful of professionals was that if Laurie didn't have special services now, she might suffer "in the third grade," and then it would have been our neglect in kindergarten that caused the problem. I felt that we had plenty of time to let Laurie find herself, and that instead of making possibly self-fulfilling predictions of failure in the third grade, we should respond to problems if and when they arose. It was left up to an understandably perplexed parent to decide which course would be best for the child.

Another child, who had been speaking English for only a year and a half, entered kindergarten with a thick sheaf of test results and clinical evaluations that usually began, "Lisa presents as . . ." and then went on to detail her precise deficiencies:

> The results of the Boehm Test of Basic Concepts reveal that Lisa is lacking the following basic concepts: Through, between, next to, above/below, at the side of, center, separated, forward, most, second, third, whole/half, zero, equal numbers of, medium, pair, not first or last, left/right, always, skip, other and alike.

On the other hand, one test found that:

> Lisa can correctly and expressively identify apple, orange and banana with 100% accuracy, while pear is 100% receptively and 80% correct expressively. In the animal category, Lisa is able to identify horse, cow, sheep, and chicken with 100% accuracy, receptively, and pig with 50% accuracy. Expressively, she is able to identify all animals except cow and pig with 100% accuracy. Cow is at 40% accuracy and pig is at 60%.

Part of the mandated evaluation process is that on the basis of such test results, trained personnel are required to write out goals and objectives several times a year. Given the nature of the test results of the child I am calling Lisa, her official school records contain goals like the following: "Will demonstrate improved syntactical and morphological agreement for a) regular/irregular past tense b) regular/irregular plurals c) present progressive tense d) possessives and pronouns."

These and similar goals required that Lisa work with speech and language specialists both privately and in school. After only ten months in this country, Lisa was criticized for "improper pronoun usage, lack of subject-verb agreement," and using three- to five-word sentences. However, the specialist's conclusion was that "prognosis is good due to Lisa's motivation for earning stickers." In fact, one speech therapist even awarded Lisa stickers for "good sitting," "good listening," and "good walking."

The notion that children learn a language for the sake of stickers rather than basic communication has always puzzled me. Language is so basic to feeling and thought that to treat it as a set of tricks or "skills" to be learned in little segments with rewards for "positive reinforcement" (like a dog given biscuits for learning to beg) seems to me a travesty. It happens that Lisa had been adopted from an orphanage in another country and was making a valiant effort to adjust to a new home, a new family, a new language, a new country, a new culture, and a new school. Obviously, she was in need of special help with these formidable challenges, and was indeed under the care of a sympathetic and skilled therapist. But to evaluate her in terms of the percentage of correct identification of farm animals or of words she failed to recognize on a test is clearly a trivialization of her language learning, as well as a misunderstanding of the way young children learn language and the function of language for this child.

As a matter of fact, Lisa was passionately involved with language learning all the time. From the first day of school, she was extremely eager to make contact with other people, to join discussions, to make friends, and to be liked. Her domain was the house corner where she could be the mother, the boss of the family, taking care of numerous children and household chores. Lisa had survived a difficult early childhood of loss and deprivation by asserting as much control as she could, and her play was marked by stormy scenes when things didn't go her way. If there were disagreements with the other children, Lisa would stomp off, have a tantrum, refuse to listen, put her hands over her ears, and glower sullenly.

Gradually, Lisa realized that to keep the social play going and to sustain friendships, she would have to express her wishes and be able to argue and make compromises. ("I lose my temper and I lose my heart, I feel so bad," she dictated once after a fight with her friend.) As Lisa concentrated on speaking more clearly and making herself understood, her language improved rapidly in vocabulary, pronunciation, and precision of thought. Lisa, like most young children, was learning language in the *context* of a setting, situation, and relationship. It was vitally important for her to make relationships and to express her fantasies in story, drama, and conversation. She didn't need external motivation like stickers to pour energy into language learning. After less than two years in America, her fervent wish to communicate resulted in fluent English that was highly expressive, if not always strictly correct in verb tense or prepositions. Correspondingly, she made progress in all areas of learning.

However, at the same time that Lisa was getting daily practice in using language effectively at school and at home, she was also getting speech therapy at school, and there her performance was considered deficient. Her therapist complained that Lisa was "manipulative," that she "frequently misinterprets pictures and therefore misses the point," that she was "unwilling to work on the areas of greatest weakness for her as she is very afraid that others will find out that she does not have mastery of the target area." It seems what Lisa really wanted to do was act out scenes with puppets all the time, rather than do the real work of drawing lines on paper to illustrate

413

concepts like "under" and "over" (Is there really an under and over on a two-dimensional picture?). The therapist proudly explained how she solved that problem by telling Lisa that another teacher had borrowed the puppets and therefore Lisa couldn't use them. The whole thrust of the sessions seemed to be to push Lisa in areas where she felt at a disadvantage, and to suppress her areas of strength in language: drama, storytelling, fantasy, and dialogue. Yet one could easily argue that any language concept that can be learned with paper and pencil can undoubtedly be learned even more effectively with puppets and through literature. For a child who is aware that she has missed out on many experiences that other children her age take for granted, it would seem especially unwise to stress deficiencies rather than strengths. Moreover, those deficiencies in language were seen in terms of standard test format. It is no wonder that at the end of the year in speech therapy, the therapist wrote that Lisa "still becomes anxious to the point of refusing to continue if she misses several items in a row." So might we all, if we were continually confronted with "items in a row" to be done correctly under the watchful eye of a tester.

Not only is speech progress seen in terms of test items, but so are the "goals" that are mandated for each child who receives special services in the school. Here are some of the end-of-year goals written in the education plan of a child named Perrin, who had severe emotional and behavioral difficulties:

> Given visual-motor tracking patterns from the Frostig and DLM See-It, Do-It program, Perrin will complete them correctly in 8 of 10 trials. Given cutting activities involving straight turning corners, Perrin will maintain proper position of the scissors and paper and correctly turn the paper.

> Given simple pictures and shapes, Perrin will trace and color them with increased activity.

Considering that all year long, Perrin had been the focus of intense concern and help from his parents, his teacher, and several other members of the school staff to make it possible for him to function within the class community, such goals as using scissors "correctly" or coloring within lines are again both trivial and dubious in value. But it is mandated that goals be written by learning center staff, and it often happens that the person writing the goals barely knows the child. In one case, the person assigned to write out goals for an IEP (which becomes part of the child's official school record) had actually never worked with the child in question or observed her or spoken with her. In another case, an outside consultant who had seen a child only once for an evaluation expressed reluctance about writing out goals for a child she had just met, and was told by school personnel that under state law she had to do so.

Our local children's clinics sometimes use a form letter to get around the necessity of writing recommendations. A report on Perrin from a prestigious hospital clinic appended a list of twenty-one recommendations for "a child like Perrin." The trouble was that this was *Perrin,* a unique, complicated boy, and not a child "like" him, so that the recommendations had no relevance to his particular behavior or problems. They were premised on a standard school situation in which Perrin might be presented with "an entire page of twenty problems" or where he might have a "desk" to sit at all day. The clinicians evidently had made no attempt to see the actual school setting or speak with Perrin's teachers. That was too bad, because I would have welcomed some thoughtful and intelligent suggestions on how to deal with the challenges that Perrin posed. As it was, school guidance personnel suggested early on that Perrin was "Learning Disabled." When I said I thought he was very bright, they said they meant his psychological problems prevented Perrin from learning like other children. It is true that Perrin had his own ways of learning, but so does every child. The words "Learning Disabled" imply a kind of illness, or at least a serious deficiency. They don't imply to most people that a child is extremely capable but not using those abilities in a conventional manner. A parent who is told that his/her child is LD would either be terribly distressed and worried, or would angrily fight back on the basis of better knowledge of the child's capabilities, as Perrin's mother fortunately did.

One of the children termed an LD risk on the screening test results was David, whose quick and thoughtful responses had impressed me from the first day of school. When I asked for the basis of this judgment, I was told that he "perseverated." It was my first encounter with this word, one that I subsequently could not find in my unabridged dictionary, and I asked its meaning. It seems that David had difficulty in moving from one set of test items to the next. He got "stuck" on each one. He also started his drawings of figures from the legs upward, which was apparently an ominous sign. Intrigued by the word "perseverate" and the idea of it as a serious defect, I tried to fit it into my observations of David during activity periods. There was no doubt that he had staying power way beyond most children his age. When he got involved with a project, he pursued it for days, often weeks. He stuck with things until he mastered what he set out to do. Thus he got started on building complex inclined plane structures for marbles to roll through, and spent weeks perfecting ramps, curves, bridges, tunnels, and decorative touches for his marble rolls. When he started to construct domino block buildings where long series of blocks could be toppled by pushing the first one, he would spend all morning setting up complicated series of standing blocks. David showed sophisticated knowledge of the mechanics of how and why the domino effect would or would not work in each case. While David tended to be impatient with other people, he had infinite patience with materials and projects, trying out variations and fixing unsuccessful attempts with no sign of anger or frustration.

When David began to copy the text of books (usually factual science picture books which interested him) for hours on end, begging to borrow the classroom books to finish at home, I did become a little uneasy at this seemingly compulsive behavior. I would lead him into other activities or suggest he do something else, but eventually he would find his way back into copying texts. By the middle of the year, it turned out that the copy work was his way of teaching himself systematically to read and write. From knowing letter sounds and a few words, he jumped to fluent reading of quite difficult material and writing just about anything he wanted to. I encouraged him to use "invented spelling," but his spelling was amazingly accurate for a beginner. His excellent visual memory permitted him to spell correctly words like "money" or "trying" and to include in a list of written words "incorporated," which he said he had seen on TV.

David, who was seen to be at risk for LD, was clearly an unusually able child and an avid learner who independently taught himself to read and write and perform outstanding engineering feats, among other skills. His style was to fasten on one challenge at a time and run it into the ground before moving on to something new. It was this quality that had gotten in his way in a test situation that required switching quickly from one thing to another. It is true that David had a tendency to be rigid and sometimes intolerant or emotionally closed to others, but these qualities, which changed considerably during the year, had to be seen in the context of his whole personality and his activities and interests. The only way to know David was through extended contact with him and observation of him within the classroom. If I had taken his "LD risk" seriously, I might not have suggested difficult things for him to do or given him the benefit of the doubt when he went on his book-copying jags or building projects. But I had the advantage of many years of teaching experience, open skepticism about testing, and the freedom to do what I wanted in my classroom. For new teachers or teachers dominated by administrators and rigid kindergarten curricula, it might not be easy to ignore such predictions or labels. David might have been considered a "special ed" candidate to be coached in a resource room or given remedial workbook exercises. In this case, David's real abilities would have undoubtedly surfaced eventually, but perhaps at serious cost to his sense of purpose and independent learning. A school report mentioning LD could easily have undermined his and his family's confidence about his development.

In my criticism of special services, I am not advocating a do-nothing-and-wait attitude on the part of teachers and other school personnel. There is

416

no doubt that children do often have difficulties in early grades, that time does not solve all school problems, and that there are many special things schools can do to help children learn. I would like to suggest a practical alternative to the testing, labeling, and remediation that compose the usual approach to children having difficulties. When teachers have questions about children in their class, they need help in observing and understanding what is happening, re-thinking their classroom program, and making productive plans to help particular children. One approach that has proved particularly effective for teachers in many different schools across the country is a staff review process developed by Patricia Carini and others at the Prospect Center in North Bennington, Vermont.

The staff review group consists of a group of teachers and other school personnel who meet together (often at regular intervals) to help each other study the children in their care in order to make more effective educational responses in the classroom:

> The primary purpose of the Staff Review of a child is to bring varied perspectives to bear in order to describe a child's experience within the school setting. On the basis of this description and discussion of its implications, the staff comes to recommendations for supporting and deepening the child's school experiences and, according to need, offers ways to support the teacher bearing major responsibility for the child in implementing the recommendations.[4]

To illustrate the staff review process, I will describe one of the most dramatic staff reviews I have ever attended. It took place in a group of teachers who had met together about once a month for almost four years. Whereas most staff reviews focus on particular concerns about children's learning — for example, problems with reading, social skills, or over-dependence — this one was a desperate cry for help from an exceptionally dedicated and thoughtful teacher who had come to the end of her rope. Linda, who was trying to cope with a large and particularly difficult class, felt she could no longer deal with eleven-year-old Mario, who disrupted everything, got into constant trouble with his classmates, could not do his work, and constantly tested Linda to her limits. It so happened that on the same day as the teachers' group meeting, Linda had been to a special needs review of Mario at school, and she came to the meeting feeling depressed, discouraged, and hopeless, doubting whether there was any point in doing the staff review at all. But because this group of teachers had worked together a long time and trusted each other and cared about each other, Linda was urged to give the staff review a try.

As the "presenting teacher," Linda had conferred before this session with the chairperson (a rotating job), who had helped her prepare a full description of Mario, based on these categories:

The child's stance in the world, the child's emotional tenor and disposition, the child's mode of relationship to other children and to adults, the child's activities and interests, the child's involvement in formal learning, the child's greatest strengths and areas of greatest vulnerabilities.[5]

Now, at the beginning of the meeting, Linda posed her focusing question: "What manageable, consistent routines can I set up with Mario, so that negative communications will be minimized?" She then proceeded to describe Mario in as rich detail and as vividly as she could. For about fifteen minutes we listened carefully as Linda gave us a portrait of Mario that really evoked his presence in the room. We saw a short, handsome, energetic child who talked incessantly and bounced around the room, got into verbal battles continually, slammed himself up against lockers, and was wildly unpredictable. A streetwise kid, Mario talked the way an adolescent would about having a sports car with a girl in the front seat, and wanted desperately to be "cool" and make friends, but the other children were consistently turned off by his wild boasting and inability to come through in work or play. With adults, Mario was manipulative, playing one against another, constantly seeking attention and never satisfied, no matter how much he got. Yet occasionally Mario's streetwise bravado could melt into a hug, and he showed some care for classmates who were upset or hurt. Although he could be charming, Mario took swift advantage of any positive feelings toward him, pushing adults into the position of prison warden.

As Linda continued her portrayal of Mario, recounting incidents and describing him without using any labels, jargon, or clinical terminology, we learned about Mario's lack of academic skills, his expulsion from remedial math class, his passionate interest in fast cars and fireworks, his daily hour after school with Linda, and his inability to focus on anything in class. Linda ended with a summary of Mario's strengths: his toughness, self-reliance, honesty, and a certain softness that kept adults from giving up on him. He was easily upset and extremely impetuous. Mario was getting himself and other children into trouble, jeopardizing his own and other people's safety. Linda was finding herself increasingly distrustful of Mario and having negative communication with him more and more frequently, much to her distress.

When Linda finished, the chairperson summarized the presentation, related Mario's school history, and added some family and medical data that were part of the school record. Care was taken not to include speculation or neighborhood gossip, and thus not to violate Mario's or his family's privacy. We then asked Linda questions for further elucidation: Were there any books he liked? (Yes, short and humorous ones or books read aloud to him.) Was there any activity he could do without getting into trouble? (Yes, painting and other art work.) Did he like drama? (Too hard for him to handle

— he wrecks it every time.) Linda's last response to a question concerned Mario's lack of confidence in himself, and his questions to her: "Would you be upset if I die? If I die, will you care?"

After the chairperson's summary of the further information yielded by the questions and answers, it was time for group members to give recommendations based on Linda's whole presentation. Ordinarily, during staff reviews, people are quick to come up with suggestions and ideas, but Mario's story seemed so serious to us, and Linda's position so difficult, that there was a long silence. The first comment was that Mario should have professional help immediately, that the death talk is serious and needs professional attention for Mario's own protection, in view of his impetuous nature. Then, tentatively, one of us suggested that perhaps Mario could use basic materials like clay, water, and sand (something he had probably missed earlier in his life) to make scenery and build a model race track, which he knew a lot about and loved. It was as though we were suddenly released, and suggestions started flooding in: Try success in small doses, fifteen-minute tasks, and reward him immediately with something he enjoys, like painting. For homework, let him design an ideal car; write letters to car dealers, asking for information. Help him make math board games with a car-racing format. Have a stuffed-animal day in class for which Mario could be in charge. Perhaps it could be arranged to have Mario work with younger children in the kindergarten once in a while. Channel Mario's interest in fireworks through books about the history of fireworks, Japanese paintings, batteries and bulbs for a science project. Supply joke books and riddle books for Mario to read and share with others. Use cameras or ready-made photos for stimulating stories that he could compose with a group, under adult supervision. Let him dictate some stories, if possible, so that he could produce creditable products.

As the day's notekeeper, I was recording all the suggestions, along with the whole proceedings as summarized by the chairperson, to be typed and sent to all the participants, but Linda was also writing down the suggestions. As she responded to each one and realized that there were possibilities that had not been tried and might make life easier in the classroom and more productive for Mario, Linda's mood visibly changed. Instead of the pained, hopeless expression she had started with, there was now energy, enthusiasm, and liveliness. The whole atmosphere in the room was changed also. While people saw Mario realistically as a very troubled boy who needed help, they also saw him as a child with positive qualities that could allow him to respond to new approaches. Moreover, we had become aware of some of the hurt and deprivation that must underlie Mario's difficult behavior, and there was sympathy both for him and for Linda. The last comment, and perhaps the one that most impressed Linda, was that Linda should relax more and realize that she could not fix everything for Mario, that she was not the cause of his problems, nor solely responsible for his future. Linda could do her best with Mario, but a little relaxation and distance would do her good and allow her to cope better with him.

The meeting broke up in a mood of amazement that the staff review process could change a view so drastically from an entirely negative, closed position to one that held some possibilities for change. All of us were buoyed up by the realization that a combination of viewpoints could open up "impossible" situations, and that we were able to help each other. For the rest of the year, Linda obviously still struggled with Mario and her extremely difficult group, but she was able to get some perspective (including humor) on the problems, and to try new activities and classroom procedures that lightened the load and permitted her to work more productively.

The differences between such a staff review and the currently prescribed series of tests and remediation plans are evident both on an immediate day-to-day basis and on a deeper philosophical level. The staff review addresses a teacher's questions about a particular child in a particular classroom. The child is observed carefully within the fluid context of an actual classroom instead of in a static test situation, and the rich details that emerge are the basis for thinking about the child's life in school. What the teacher ends up with are recommendations based on the full portrait of a whole child instead of a disjointed collection of test scores, and they come from a group of engaged, thoughtful teachers pooling their resources and classroom experience.

The reliability of the description presented in a staff review is promoted by several factors, primarily by the simple but definite structure of the process. It is built into a staff review to have an experienced chairperson help the presenting teacher prepare a full descriptive account according to the inclusive categories cited above. The chairperson, through questions, suggestions, and perhaps even supplementary observations, can broaden and deepen the teacher's observations. Often the teacher also brings along the child's work (samples of writing, drawing, classwork, a journal, and so on) as part of the staff review. Sometimes, if the group wishes to pursue the child study even further, a separate session is devoted to a closer look at these samples. Also built in is the safeguarding of the child's and family's privacy, thus eliminating irrelevant or unverified information. The questions and comments of the participants bring out knowledge that the presenter may have left out or not previously noted. Sometimes there may be additions to the presentation by the child's previous or concurrent teachers, who can contribute supplementary observations. At the end of each staff review there is a critique of the session, during which participants can express any doubts they may feel about the review and its outcome. The formal structure of the process sometimes surprises newcomers, but it is absolutely necessary in order to maintain professional standards and full participation by all members of the group. It also protects the presenting teacher from being put on the spot or criticized. Another advantage of the structured format is that it can be applied to many situations and learned easily by any group. Naturally, longer experience with staff review brings greater skill, and a group that works together over a period of time builds up increasing trust and depth of understanding.

Learning to present in descriptive, not *pre*scriptive, language is an important aspect of using the staff review, and a skill that takes practice. The language of the recommendations in a staff review is that of teachers striving to find ways to gear everyday classroom activities toward the children's needs, whereas the language of test results is often abstract jargon.

In clinical reports it is common to find language that serves to obfuscate adults' understanding of children, or to alarm teachers and parents. Here are a couple of sentences from a report I was given about one of my children:

> Naming was mildly reduced, although within broad normal limits and commensurate with his fund of information. Praxis was intact for axial, buccofacial and limb commands.

> His delayed initiation of voluntary saccads was suggestive of ocular-motor apraxia.

I could find no useful meaning in such description, and nobody offered any interpretation. In staff reviews, complexity arises from the layering of detail, described vividly and with precision rather than with obscure words. While suggestions in clinical reports may turn out to be not only hard to understand but also impracticable within a particular classroom situation, the staff review results in suggestions that can be implemented by the presenting teacher immediately. At the same time, it reminds participating teachers of similar children and concerns in their own classrooms, and thus makes everyone in the group more aware of the possibilities in curriculum, materials, and attitudes.

The purpose of a staff review is to concentrate on a child's strengths and widen teachers' responses to the daily challenges in the classroom. Because it is a process that depends on every participant's best concentrated thinking and intense effort to work together, teachers tend to leave the staff review with a feeling of exhilaration and renewed courage to extend themselves further in their teaching. When teachers leave a mandated conference designed to produce an IEP, they are often discouraged by the sense of the overpowering problems of a child, angry that their own input was slighted in favor of test results, doubtful about the efficacy of plans made by people who don't know the child well. They also may feel burdened by extra tasks that seem irrelevant to the child's needs but are being demanded of an already hard-pressed teacher. The staff review is amenable to extremely fine tuning, whereas the mandated process consists of only the broadest, roughest outline of a child's needs, mostly in negative terms and concerning the areas in which the child performs most poorly.

Interestingly, the very process of preparing a staff review — observing the child closely and recording observations; studying the child's drawings, writing, and other work; presenting a vivid portrait of the child to a group of colleagues — affects the relationship between teacher and child. Even if the teacher does not follow up on suggestions proposed during the staff review, a change in the classroom happens just because of the careful, sympathetic attention given to the child and the multiplicity of perspectives through which the child has been viewed. Almost inevitably, the child can feel a difference, and so can the teacher, who now regards the child in a broader context, with more familiarity and sensitivity.

The most common result of an official IEP meeting is to have the child receive special services outside the classroom, perhaps in a resource room or with a reading or speech teacher or a learning-disability specialist. Most typically, the children are scheduled several times a week, and sometimes every day, to one or more specialist periods. That means that children are continually going out of the classroom and coming back, disrupting class proceedings, breaking off activities in the middle, and reentering at awkward times. Some classes have so many entrances and exits that the teacher hardly ever has the whole class together at one time. The resulting fragmentation of the day and the class program is harmful to all the children in the class, and especially to the children receiving special services, because they are more vulnerable to begin with.[6]

More and more often, I find teachers, principals, specialists themselves, and others concerned with children's learning questioning the wisdom of having children leave classrooms for special help, instead of having specialists work within each classroom, taking advantage of the ongoing program, the child's support group of friends, the familiarity of the everyday surroundings and materials, the ordinary context of learning.[7]

In an increasingly fragmented society, with children's lives often chaotic and unpredictable, schools should consider ways to provide stability and to cut down as much as possible on further disruptions. Instead, schools tend to exacerbate confusions by bouncing children back and forth between their classes and special services, so that the day is full of arbitrary starts and stops with no real sense of belonging or continuity for the children who need this most of all. Often teachers have little or no contact with specialists who are working with their children, so that there is no real coordination of the child's instruction or a central, informed person responsible for the child's learning.

Most harmful to children, however, are the restricted expectations and narrow criteria for learning embodied in the ritualized "early identification" testing and labeling process, in which children as young as pre-school age are declared "at risk" and regarded as having learning problems, even as the children are demonstrably learning and growing. In my long experience as a primary teacher, I have never met a young child who is not a learner, who does not have a drive to experience the world and to impose some order on that experience. Children may be temporarily overwhelmed by difficulties or blocked in their expression, but that does not mean that they can't be helped to develop their strengths and their innermost potential. Predicting failure can be a way to ensure it.

If we are to remain responsive to children in schools, flexible in our adaptations to changes in children's lives and in the outer world, we need to change our laws and guidelines to serve children and teachers in the way that was originally intended. We need to study children in the context of their particular school situations and give children time to develop their own resources in the most thoughtful and stimulating school environment that we can provide. We need to refrain from jumping to hasty prediction of learning problems and instead welcome the endless variety of learning styles that are enacted by human beings responding to the world around them. We need to educate teachers to observe children keenly and sympathetically and to educate specialists to work within classrooms to help children gain a sense of continuity in their own lives and their everyday learning at school.

Perhaps if schools were to drop their screening procedures, to stop sorting out children on the basis of test results, and to refrain from predicting success or failure for entering students, they would be free to accept all children as learners with unique and interesting abilities. Staffs and small groups of teachers could work together to support each other's strengths, and thus support children's strengths, instead of dwelling on problems. Public education can only succeed when all children are accepted equally as contributors in a classroom community and when teachers work together, trusting themselves and children to learn.

Notes

1. For a cogent discussion of terminology in education, see Brenda Engle, "Education: A Universe of Discourse," *Teaching and Learning, 1* (1986), 4–12.
2. *Washington Post,* National Weekly Edition, October 26, 1987, p. 6.
3. I have given all the children and teachers in this account fictitious names to protect their privacy.

4. Patricia Carini, *The Lives of Seven School Children* (Grand Forks: University of North Dakota Press, 1982), p. 112.
5. Carini, *The Lives,* p. 112.
6. For a discussion of the devastating effect of fragmentation through special services, see Cecelia Traugh et al., eds., *Speaking Out: Teachers on Teaching* (Grand Forks: University of North Dakota Press, 1986), pp. 74–76.
7. For an excellent discussion of the failure of the Chapter 1 remedial reading program and PL 94-142 for learning disabled students, see Richard L. Allington, "Shattered Hopes," *Learning, 16* (1987), 61–64.

CORRESPONDENCE

Special Education in the Early Grades —
How Best to Meet Children's Special Needs:
A Response to Martin

KARYN R. GITLIS

We, a group of speech-language pathologists, read Anne Martin's article, "Screening, Early Intervention, and Remediation: Obscuring Children's Potential" in the November 1988 issue of the *Harvard Educational Review.* We were distressed by Ms. Martin's selective perceptions of the potential role and the reality of provision of support services in the schools. It is most unfortunate that her experiences with psychologists and speech-language pathologists have led her to believe that they are jargon-spewing, sticker-dispensing, insensitive people. We were, furthermore, disappointed that the *Harvard Educational Review* chose to publish Ms. Martin's diatribe.

We are receptive to and appreciative of her sentiments on acknowledging developmental differences, teaching to strengths, and helping children learn and grow in a nurturing educational environment. Schools do not always, or for all children, provide these circumstances. Nor do educational teams, which are legally required to include teachers, always make optimal decisions. Painting "special educators" as the responsible bogeys, without providing the full details, for what may constitute educational malpractice does not, however, address the problem.

We believe that specialists working in the school setting, in hopefully the vast majority of instances, have much professional expertise to offer, are sensitive and caring individuals, and are capable of collaboration with their teacher colleagues.

We would suggest that Ms. Martin examine her motivations for submitting her thinly veiled laundry list of complaints about other professionals. Current federal regulations require collaborative efforts in discussing and reaching decisions about individualized educational programs for children. If this is not occurring in her work setting, perhaps she needs to bring the situation to the attention of the appropriate administrative authorities.

If, on the other hand, Ms. Martin has some difficulty with the very premises fundamental to and inherent in the public education of children in the United States (for example, that all six-year-olds are emotionally, cognitively, linguistically, and metalinguistically ready to learn sound-orthographic symbol relationships), then we say to her, "Back to your books!" Creative and constructive ideas and efforts will be enthusiastically entertained by all professionals in educational settings.

Martin Replies to Gitlis:

I am sorry that my article was interpreted as an idiosyncratic attack on individual specialists or professions. Throughout my years of teaching, I have met many therapists and specialists whom I admire, and with whom I have been able to work productively. Moreover, in my article I made several references to situations where children were in need of a therapist, and I expressed the hope that support personnel might work directly with teachers in order to help children within the context of classroom life.

My criticism is not aimed at particular practitioners but at the institutionalized system that propagates a deficit view of children, arrives at questionable diagnoses of children's problems, and makes damaging (often self-fulfilling) prophecies of failure. There is nothing "thinly veiled" in my accounts: I describe explicitly and in as much detail as a short piece permits what actually happened to children I have known, quoting from reports I was given. If I sound passionate, it is because I know that children's future lives are at stake, and that the children most vulnerable to mislabeling and miseducation are from poor and minority families. I am saddened and angered when I see children stigmatized by labels, when expectations and opportunities for children are reduced, and when children's school days and instruction are further fragmented in the name of an alarmingly narrowed conception of what learning means. If my experience were unique, you could write it off as an anomaly, but unfortunately it is all too familiar to other teachers from whom I've heard whose experiences mirror and extend my own. These teachers and I are not alone in our concerns.

Contrary to what the writers of the letter imply, I have never left my books. Lately, I have been struck by the number of books and articles by special education experts who are questioning present practices and trends in schools. Professional organizations such as the National Association for the Education of Young Children are scrutinizing current practice in the testing, labeling, and tracking of young children,[1] and the growing national debate on special education is the subject of the April 1989 issue of the *Harvard*

Education Letter.[2] In a thought-provoking article in *Insights,* Steve Harlow, Professor of Special Education at the University of North Dakota, examines the misuse of the medical model in education, which results in "diagnostic categories that essentially keep labeled children from participating in the same educational experiences as their non-labeled peers." He points out that eventually the "difference which the label denotes becomes equated with inferiority." Harlow deplores the suppression of differences in the classroom and the "piecemeal education" that is so often doled out to children in the guise of special services.[3]

A comprehensive view of these issues is provided by Gerald Coles's *The Learning Mystique,* a scholarly, thorough examination of the basis of our knowledge about the ubiquitous disorder termed "learning disabilities."[4] Step by step he pursues a careful and convincing critique of studies underlying the concept of a brain dysfunction that would account for these learning problems. Coles finds that the easily accepted medical explanation of learning disabled does not hold up under close scrutiny, and he suggests a different perspective on learning disabilities in terms of children's social context: "The alternative theory attempts to be the opposite of reductionism by interweaving the interactions of the individual within a variety of social relationships and explaining the development of the individual's learning problems and neurological makeup as part of the totality of these interactions."[5]

There is more literature that could be cited to show that many theorists and practitioners, both within and outside the field of special education, are uncomfortable with the medical model of diagnosing children's school problems (which in fact often leads to prescriptions of drugs such as Ritalin). In this connection, it is striking that my angry critics term themselves "speech-language *pathologists*" (my emphasis). Webster's Dictionary defines pathology as the study of diseases, and as deviations from normal that constitute disease. This is a good illustration of what I mean about hidden implications of professional language in education: the word "pathologist" lends a pseudomedical legitimacy to the enterprise, and also suggests that these specialists work with children who suffer from illness.

I find confusing the obscure, not to speak of "jargon-spewing," sentence that challenges me to agree that all "six-year-olds are emotionally, cognitively, linguistically, and metalinguistically ready to learn sound-orthographic symbol relationships." Is that supposed to mean that all first graders can learn to read through phonics? I would hate to think that this is a fundamental premise in U.S. education. It is not an immutable law that reading and writing must start with the breakdown of words and sounds into phonic symbols. The development of children's literacy is a wonderful, complex process that cannot be reduced to a matter of learning phonics and decoding words. A growing awareness of this has revolutionized language teaching in many schools across the country, supported by such developments as the Whole Language approach to reading and the Process Writing movement.

When absurdly high percentages of four-year-olds are screened out from admission to kindergarten, or five-year-olds from promotion to first grade, it indicates not that children are failing but that we are failing them. Expectations that have become too rigid are probably a major source of that failure. It is important to guard against dogmatic generalizations of what we want children to be or do at every stage of their development, and instead to leave room for the endless variations and differences that make teaching a surprise, a puzzle, and a source of renewal and challenge to us every day. I would say that the most fundamental premise in the field of education is (or should be) that we can never know all there is to be known about teaching. In our continual search for more effective ways to respond to the children we teach, our steady focus must remain on the children. When we learn to listen, observe, and reflect with our colleagues about what we see, without the interference of distracting labels and preconceptions, the children themselves can become our best teachers and sources of knowledge.

Notes

1. NAEYC Position Statement on Standardized Testing of Young Children 3 through 8 Years of Age, *Young Children* (March 1988), 42–47.
2. *Harvard Education Letter* (March/April 1989).
3. Steve Harlow, "The Constriction of the Classroom: The Submergence of Difference," *Insights, 21* (November 1988), 1–7.
4. Gerald Coles, *The Learning Mystique* (New York: Fawcett Columbine, 1989).
5. Coles, *The Learning Mystique,* p. xviii.

Notes on Contributors

DOUGLAS BIKLEN is Professor of Special Education at the School of Education, Syracuse University. His professional interests include social policy and disability, attitudes and disability, and facilitative communication for people who do not speak or whose speech is severely impaired. His publications include "The Culture of Policy: Disability Images and Their Analogues in Public Policy" in the *Policy Studies Journal* (1987) and *Schooling without Labels: Parents, Educators, and Inclusive Education* (1992). He was also Executive Producer of "Regular Lives" (PBS, 1988), a television documentary on school and community integration of people with disabilities.

MILTON BUDOFF is Director of the Research Institute for Educational Problems in Cambridge, Massachusetts. He is interested in adapting challenging instruction for low achievers in regular classes, and in developing school-based models for preventing school failure among poor children. His books include *Due Process in Special Education: On Going to a Hearing* (with A. Orenstein and C. Kervick, 1982), *Teaching Language Disabled Children: Communication Games Intervention* (with S. Conant and B. Hecht, 1983), and *Microcomputers in Special Education* (with J. Thormann and A. Gras, 1984).

JOHN A. BUTLER, who died in 1988, was Assistant Professor in the Department of Social Medicine and Health Policy, Harvard Medical School. His professional interests included education and health care policy for children. His publications include *National Health Insurance and Primary Medical Care for Children* (1976).

JOSEPH CAMBONE is an Instructor in the Faculty of Professional Studies at Wheelock College, Boston, Massachusetts, as well as an Instructor in the Adjunct Faculty of Education at Lesley College, Cambridge, Massachusetts. His teaching, research, and writing focus on bridging the knowledge gap existing between special education teachers and regular education teachers. He is particularly interested in fostering a conversation among those teachers regarding what constitutes effective curriculum and pedagogy for troubled and troubling children. He is author of "Trouble in Paradise: Teacher Conflicts in Shared Decision Making" in *Education Administration Quarterly* (with C. H. Weiss and A. Wyeth, forthcoming).

GERALD S. COLES is Associate Professor of Clinical Psychiatry at Robert Wood Johnson Medical School in Piscataway, New Jersey. The psychology of learning and literacy are his current professional interests. He is author of *The Learning Mystique: A Critical Look at "Learning Disabilities"* (1988) and *Reading Lessons: The Debate over Literacy* (forthcoming).

ALAN GARTNER is Director of the Office of Sponsored Research at the Graduate School and University Center of the City University of New York. His present professional interests center on developing high-quality, equitable schools for all students, and on achieving civil rights and full inclusion for all people regardless of race, religion, national origin, sexual preference, and impairment. His recent publications include *Caring for America's Children* (1989), *Beyond Separate Education: Quality Education for All* (with D. K. Lipsky, 1989), and *Supporting Families with a Child with a Disability* (D. K. Lipsky, 1991).

KARYN R. GITLIS is a Speech-Language Pathologist with the Tempe (Arizona) Elementary Schools. Adolescent language development and language disorders, and the identification and treatment of language disorders in multicultural populations, are her major professional interests.

PETER H. JOHNSTON is Associate Professor in the Department of Reading and the Department of Educational Psychology at the State University of New York at Albany. He is also a senior researcher in the Center for the Teaching and Learning of Literature. His current teaching and research interests include evaluating teaching and learning, and the psychology and politics of becoming, and failing to become, literate. He is author of *Constructive Evaluation of Literate Activity* (1991) and of more than thirty research articles.

DAVID L. KIRP is a Professor at the University of California, Berkeley, Graduate School of Public Policy. Education policy, AIDS policy, and gender policy are his current areas of interest. He is coauthor of *Managing Educational Excellence* (with T. Timar, 1988), *Educational Policy and the Law* (with M. Yudoff and T. van Geel, 1991), and coeditor of *AIDS in the Industrialized Democracies* (with R. Bayer, 1992).

MICHAEL LIPSKY, Professor of Political Science at the Massachusetts Institute of Technology, is currently on leave to work on governance and public policy issues at the Ford Foundation. His publications include *Protest in City Politics* (1970) and *Street-Level Bureaucracy* (1980); *The Age of Contracting* (with S. R. Smith) is forthcoming in 1993.

DOROTHY KERZNER LIPSKY is Superintendent of the Riverhead (New York) Central School District. Her professional concerns include refashioning schools to serve and succeed for all students, developing family support systems, and full inclusion of persons with disabilities in all aspects of society. She is coauthor of *Beyond Separate Education: Quality Education for All* (with A. Gartner, 1989) and *Supporting Families with a Child with a Disability* (with A. Gartner, 1991).

JAMES H. LYTLE is a Regional Superintendent in the School District of Philadelphia. His professional interests focus on helping schools become "Learning to Learn" organizations, and on special education integration and inclusion. He is author of "Reforming Urban Education: A Review of Recent Reports and Legislation" in *The Urban Review* (1990).

430

ANNE MARTIN teaches kindergarten at the Lawrence School in Brookline, Massachusetts. Her major professional concerns are classroom teaching, writing about children in the classroom, and working collaboratively with other teachers to deepen understanding of children's learaning and to improve teaching practice. Her publications include "Back to Kindergarten Basics" in *Harvard Educational Review* (1985).

CARL MILOFSKY is Professor and Chair of the Department of Sociology and Anthropology at Bucknell University, Lewisburg, Pennsylvania. His current work focuses primarily on the sociology of nonprofit organizations, and he continues to write about the sociology of special education. As part of his work as Editor-in-Chief of the *Nonprofit and Voluntary Sector Quarterly*, he is studying an alternative school. His publications include "Special Education and Social Control" in the *Handbook of Theory and Research for the Sociology of Education* (1986), *Community Organizations: Studies in Resource Mobilization and Exchange* (1988), and *Testers and Testing: The Sociology of School Psychology* (1989).

TIMOTHY REAGAN, Assistant Professor of Educational Studies at the University of Connecticut in Storrs, is interested in the education of cultural and linguistic minorities. His publications include "How Do You Sign 'Apartheid'? The Politics of South African Sign Language" in *Language Problems and Language Planning* (with C. Penn, 1990), "Cultural Considerations in the Education of the Deaf" in *Research in Educational and Developmental Aspects of Deafness* (1990), and " 'On That Day the Deaf Shall Hear': Deaf-Hearing Interchange in South Africa" in *Sign Language Studies* (with C. Penn and D. Ogilvy, 1991).

JUDITH D. SINGER is Associate Professor of Education at the Harvard Graduate School of Education. An applied statistician, her professional interests center on quantitative analysis, research design, and educational evaluation, with a particular focus on special education policies and practices. Her publications include "Should Special Education Merge with Regular Education?" in *Educational Policy* (1988), *Who Will Teach?: Policies That Matter* (with R. Murnane, J. Willett, J. Kemple, and R. Olsen, 1991), and "Are Special Educators' Careers Special?" in *Exceptional Children* (in press).

THOMAS M. SKRTIC is Professor of Special Education at the University of Kansas in Lawrence. Special education policy and administration, educational reform, and philosophical pragmatism are his major professional interests. His publications include *Exceptional Children and Youth: An Introduction* (with E. L. Meyen, 1988) and *Behind Special Education: A Critical Analysis of Professional Culture and School Organization* (1991).

RICHARD A. WEATHERLEY is Associate Professor in the School of Social Work at the University of Washington, Seattle. His areas of research include policy implementation, teen pregacy, and the politics of welfare reform. He is author of *Reforming Special Education* (1979).

Author Index

Subject Index